NINE FACES OF KENYA

NINE FACES
OF KENYA

Compiled by

ELSPETH HUXLEY

VIKING

VIKING
Published by the Penguin Group
Viking Penguin, a division of Penguin Books USA Inc.,
375 Hudson Street, New York, New York 10014, U.S.A.
Penguin Books Ltd, 27 Wrights Lane, London W8 5TZ, England
Penguin Books Australia Ltd, Ringwood, Victoria, Australia
Penguin Books Canada Ltd, 2801 John Street, Markham, Ontario, Canada L3R 1B4
Penguin Books (N.Z.) Ltd, 182–190 Wairau Road, Auckland 10, New Zealand

Penguin Books Ltd, Registered Offices:
Harmondsworth, Middlesex, England

First American Edition
Published in 1991 by Viking Penguin,
a division of Penguin Books USA Inc.

1   3   5   7   9   10   8   6   4   2

Pages 428–430 constitute an extension of this copyright page.

LIBRARY OF CONGRESS CATALOGING IN PUBLICATION DATA
Nine faces of Kenya / compiled by Elspeth Huxley.
p.   cm.
Includes bibliographical references (p.   ) and index.
1. Kenya. I. Huxley, Elspeth Jocelin Grant, 1907–
ISBN: 0–670–83872–1
DT433.522.N56   1991
967.62—dc20   90–50749

Printed in the United States of America

Contents

For Michael Blundell
Citizen of Kenya

I have done the state some service –
Othello

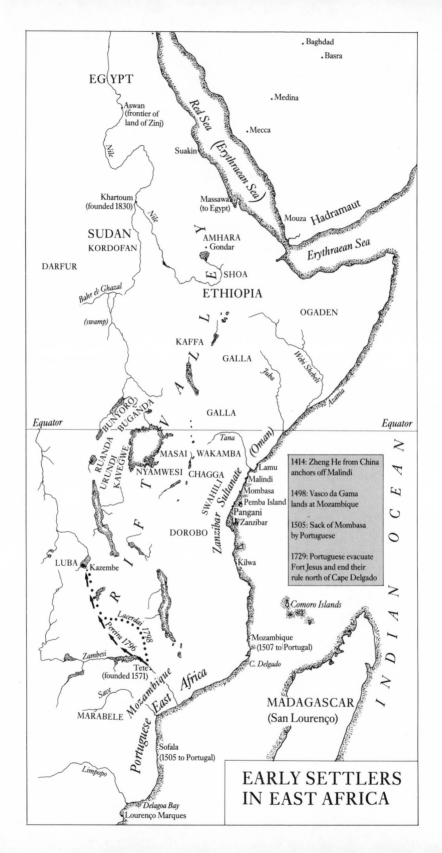

EGYPT

Baghdad
Basra

Aswan
(frontier of
land of Zinj)

Medina

Mecca

Suakin

Massawa
(to Egypt)

Khartoum
(founded 1830)

SUDAN
KORDOFAN

AMHARA
Gondar

SHOA

ETHIOPIA

OGADEN

DARFUR

Mouza Hadramaut

Erythraean Sea

Red Sea (Erythraean Sea)

Nile

Nile

Bahr el Ghazal

(swamp)

KAFFA

GALLA

Juba

Webi Shebeli

Azania

GALLA

Equator

BUNYORO
BUGANDA

RUANDA
URUNDI
KAVEGWE
NYAMWESI

Tana

MASAI WAKAMBA
CHAGGA

Lamu
Malindi
Mombasa
Pemba Island
Pangani
Zanzibar

DOROBO

Swahili Sultanate (Oman)

Kilwa

Equator

1414: Zheng He from China
anchors off Malindi

1498: Vasco da Gama
lands at Mozambique

1505: Sack of Mombasa
by Portuguese

1729: Portuguese evacuate
Fort Jesus and end their
rule north of Cape Delgado

LUBA
Kazembe

Lacerda 1798
Pereira 1796

Comoro Islands

Zambesi

Tete
(founded 1571)

Mozambique East Africa

Mozambique
(1507 to Portugal)

C. Delgado

Save

MARABELE

Portuguese

MADAGASCAR
(San Lourenço)

Limpopo

Sofala
(1505 to Portugal)

Delagoa Bay
Lourenço Marques

INDIAN OCEAN

R I F T   V A L L E Y

EARLY SETTLERS
IN EAST AFRICA

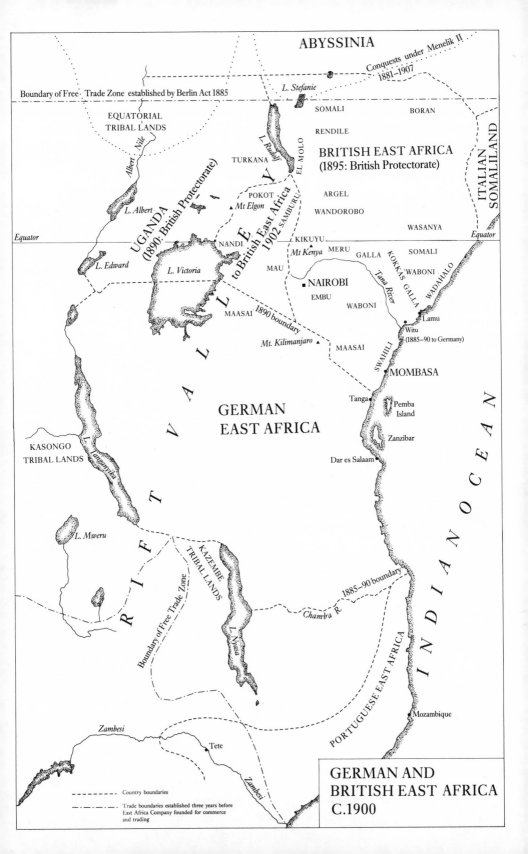

ABYSSINIA

Conquests under Menelik II
1881–1907

Boundary of Free Trade Zone established by Berlin Act 1885

EQUATORIAL
TRIBAL LANDS

L. Stefanie

SOMALI   BORAN

RENDILE

BRITISH EAST AFRICA
(1895: British Protectorate)

Albert Nile

L. Albert

L. Rudolf

TURKANA

EL MOLO

POKOT   ARGEL

Mt Elgon   WANDOROBO

UGANDA
(1890: British Protectorate)

to British East Africa
1902

SAMBURU

WASANYA

Equator   Equator

L. Edward

L. Victoria

NANDI

KIKUYU

Mt Kenya   MERU   GALLA

MAU

NAIROBI

EMBU   WABONI

SOMALI

'WABONI

Tana River

KOKKAS GALLA

WADAHALO

Lamu
Witu
(1885–90 to Germany)

MAASAI

1890 boundary

Mt Kilimanjaro

MAASAI

SWAHILI

MOMBASA

Tanga

Pemba
Island

GERMAN
EAST AFRICA

Zanzibar

KASONGO
TRIBAL LANDS

L. Tanganyika

Dar es Salaam

I N D I A N   O C E A N

R
I
F
T

V
A
L
L
E
Y

L. Mweru

KAZEMBE
TRIBAL LANDS

L. Nyasa

Boundary of Free Trade Zone

1885–90 boundary

Chambia R.

PORTUGUESE EAST AFRICA

Mozambique

Zambesi

Tete

Zambesi

GERMAN AND
BRITISH EAST AFRICA
C.1900

- - - - -   Country boundaries

-·-·-·- Trade boundaries established three years before
East Africa Company founded for commerce
and trading

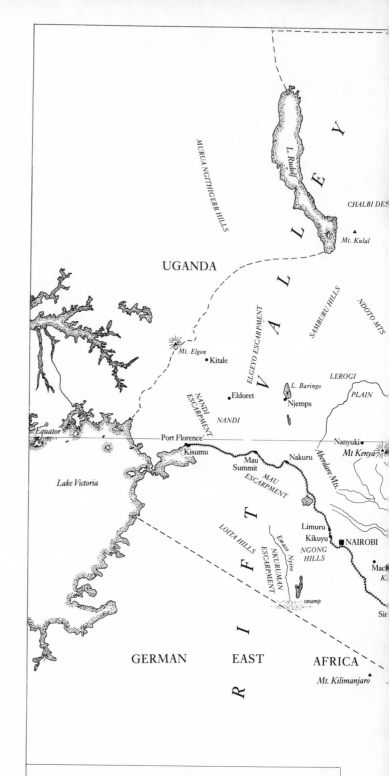

THE EAST AFRICAN PROTECTORATE c.1910
SHOWING THE NEW RAILWAY

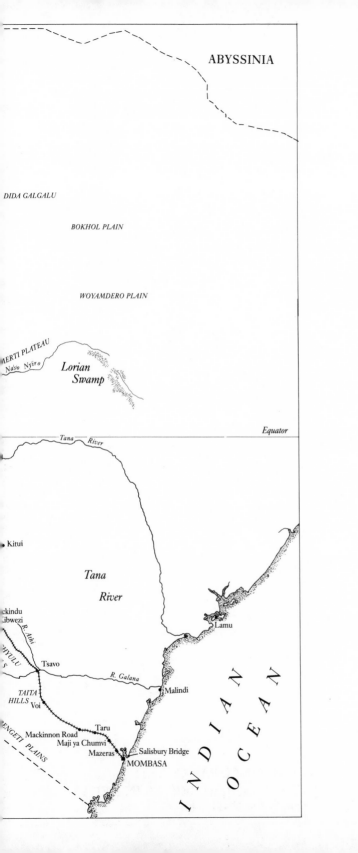

ABYSSINIA

DIDA GALGALU

BOKHOL PLAIN

WOYAMDERO PLAIN

MERTI PLATEAU

Na'so Nyiro

Lorian
Swamp

Equator

Tana River

Kitui

Tana

River

ckindu
Kibwezi

R. Athi

Lamu

HYULU
S

Tsavo

R. Galana

Malindi

TAITA
HILLS Voi

ENGETI PLAINS

Mackinnon Road
Maji ya Chumvi
Mazeras

Taru

Salisbury Bridge
MOMBASA

I N D I A N

O C E A N

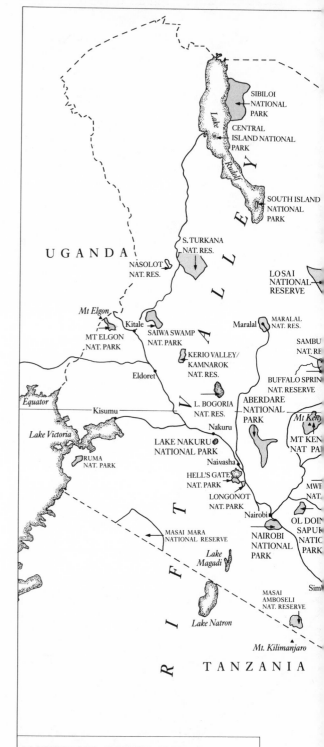

SIBILOI
NATIONAL
PARK

CENTRAL
ISLAND NATIONAL
PARK

SOUTH ISLAND
NATIONAL
PARK

U G A N D A

Lake Rudolf

S. TURKANA
NAT. RES.

NASOLOT
NAT. RES.

LOSAI
NATIONAL
RESERVE

MARALAL
NAT. RES.

Maralal

Mt Elgon

Kitale

SAIWA SWAMP
NAT. PARK

MT ELGON
NAT. PARK

SAMBU
NAT. RE

KERIO VALLEY/
KAMNAROK
NAT. RES.

Eldoret

BUFFALO SPRIN
NAT. RESERVE

Equator

Kisumu

L. BOGORIA
NAT. RES.

ABERDARE
NATIONAL
PARK

Mt Ken

MT KEN
NAT PA

Nakuru

Lake Victoria

RUMA
NAT. PARK

LAKE NAKURU
NATIONAL PARK

Naivasha

HELL'S GATE
NAT. PARK

MWI
NAT.

LONGONOT
NAT. PARK

Nairobi

OL DOIN
SAPUK
NATIO
PARK

MASAI MARA
NATIONAL RESERVE

NAIROBI
NATIONAL
PARK

Lake Magadi

Sim

MASAI
AMBOSELI
NAT. RESERVE

Lake Natron

Mt. Kilimanjaro

R

I

F

T

V

A

L

L

E

Y

T A N Z A N I A

NATIONAL PARKS AND
NATIONAL RESERVES IN KENYA

The earliest National Park was Nairobi (1948)

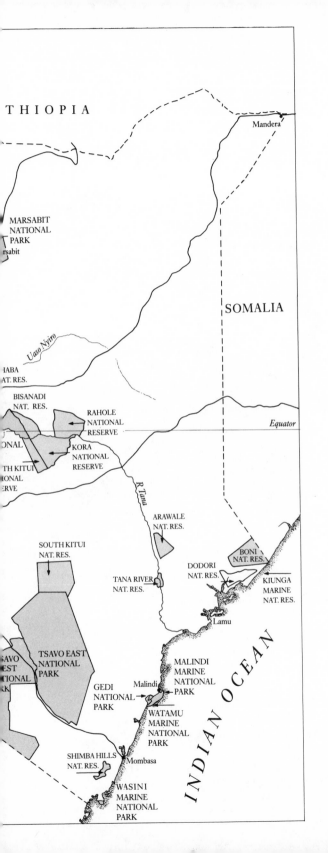

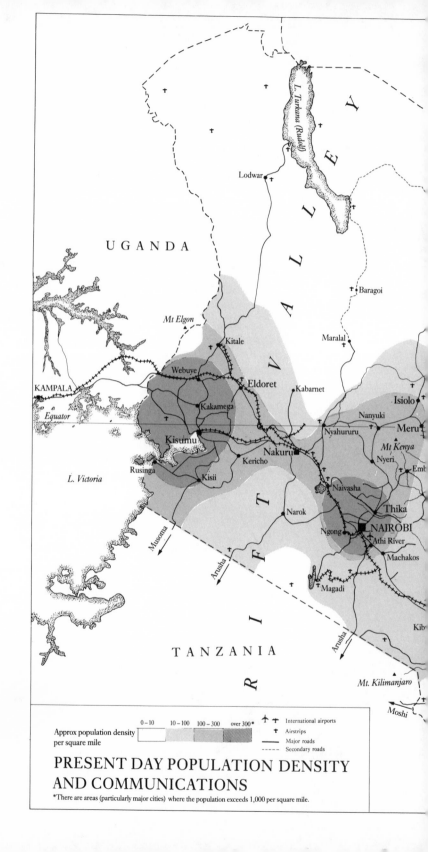

UGANDA

L. Turkana (Rudolf)

Lodwar

Baragoi

Mt Elgon

Kitale

Maralal

Webuye

Eldoret

Kabarnet

Isiolo

KAMPALA

Kakamega

Nanyuki

Equator

Nyahururu

Meru

Kisumu

Mt Kenya

Nakuru

Kericho

Nyeri

Emb

L. Victoria

Rusinga

Kisii

Naivasha

Narok

Thika

NAIROBI

Ngong

Athi River

Musoma

Machakos

Arusha

Magadi

TANZANIA

Kib

Arusha

Mt. Kilimanjaro

Moshi

Approx population density per square mile	0 – 10	10 – 100	100 – 300	over 300 *

✈ ✈ International airports
✈ Airstrips
── Major roads
- - - Secondary roads

PRESENT DAY POPULATION DENSITY
AND COMMUNICATIONS

*There are areas (particularly major cities) where the population exceeds 1,000 per square mile.

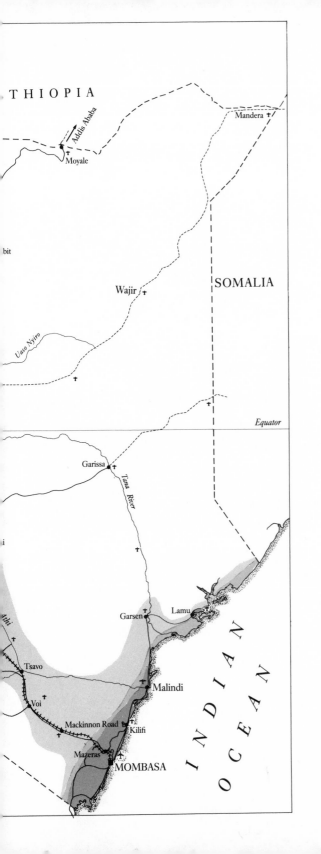

THIOPIA

Addis Ababa

Mandera ✝/

Moyale

bit

Wajir /✝

SOMALIA

Uaso Nyiro

✝

Equator

✝

Garissa ●✝

Tana River

✝

i

Garsen ●✝

Lamu ●

I N D I A N

thi

✝

Tsavo

Malindi ●

Voi ✝

Mackinnon Road ✝

O C E A N

Kilifi ●

Mazeras ●

✝ MOMBASA

Chronology

AD

95–110	*The Periplus of the Erythraean Sea* written by an anonymous Greek.
622	The Hegira: flight of Muhammad from Mecca to Medina and start of the Muslim era.
650–800 approx.	Arab and Persian settlers colonize East African coastal towns.
1414	Chinese fleet arrives off the coast of Zinj (East Africa).
1415	The K'i-lin (a giraffe), a celestial horse and a celestial stag presented by the King of Malindi to the Emperor of China.
7 April 1498	Vasco da Gama's fleet anchors in the roadsteads of Mombasa.
7 Jan 1499	Vasco da Gama's fleet reaches Malindi on its return from India.
1505	Sack of Mombasa and other East African settlements by Francisco d'Almeida, and start of Portuguese rule.
1587	Invasion of Mombasa by a tribe of cannibals, the Zimba, who devour its inhabitants.
1593–96	The Portuguese build Fort Jesus in Mombasa.
March 1696	Arrival of hostile Arab fleet at Mombasa, and start of the siege of Fort Jesus.
12 December 1698	Remnants of the garrison of Fort Jesus surrender to the Arabs of Oman.
26 November 1729	Final evacuation of Fort Jesus by the Portuguese and end of their rule in East Africa north of Cape Delgado.
1832–40	Sayyid Said ibn Sultan, ruler of Oman, moves his headquarters to Zanzibar, and confirms his sovereignty over the East African city states.
11 May 1848	Johann Rebmann, in the employ of the Church Missionary Society, sets eyes on the summit of Mount Kilimanjaro.
10 November 1848	His colleague Johann Ludwig Krapf sights the peaks of Mount Kenya.
28 July 1862	John Hanning Speke reaches the source of the White Nile at the Ripon Falls issuing from Lake Victoria.

1873	Sayyid Barghash ibn Said, Sultan of Zanzibar, signs a treaty with the British Government prohibiting the export of slaves from his dominions and closing all the slave markets.
11 December 1883	Joseph Thomson and James Martin reach Lake Victoria from Mombasa after passing safely through the highlands dominated by the Maasai.
5 March 1887	Count Samuel Teleki von Szek and Lieutenant Ludwig von Höhnel reach and name Lake Rudolf, later Turkana. First contact with the Kikuyu.
3 September 1888	The Imperial British East Africa Company, founded by Sir William Mackinnon, receives a Royal Charter to open up the British "sphere of influence" to "legitimate commerce".
1889	The IBEA Company opens its first inland station at Machakos.
1890	Captain Frederick Lugard builds Dagoretti station.
1893	First coffee planted at Kibwezi by John Patterson.
1894	Revd and Mrs Stuart Watt walk from Mombasa to Machakos with seeds of first apple, plum and quince trees.
15 June 1895	Her Majesty's Government proclaims the British East Africa Protectorate, taking over from the IBEA Company and leasing a ten-mile coastal strip from the Sultan of Zanzibar.
1895–1905	Five military expeditions against the Nandi tribe, following their raids on neighbouring tribes, attacks on trading caravans and thefts of railway lines, culminating in the death of their principal laibon (medicine-man) in October 1905.
1896	First British settlers walk from Mombasa to Fort Smith near Nairobi, bringing the first plough.
1897	Lord Delamere and Dr Atkinson reach the Protectorate's highlands from Berbera on the Red Sea.
July 1900	The East Africa Turf Club holds its first meeting in Nairobi; there was a race for mules.
1901	First hotel opened in Nairobi by Tommy Wood.
20 December 1901	The Uganda Railway, begun in 1896 and laid mainly by labour brought from India, reaches Lake Victoria at Mile 582.
1902	First tea planted at Limoru by G. W. L. Caine.
April 1902	Those parts of the Uganda Protectorate east of Lake Victoria and extending as far as Naivasha transferred to the British East Africa Protectorate.

1904	First Agricultural Show held in the Jeevanjee Gardens, Nairobi.
1905	Zionists offered the Uasin Gishu plateau as "an ante-chamber to the Holy Land"; after a visit, they decline.
1907	Legislative Council formed, with two members representing the settlers, all the other members being government officials.
1908	Forty-seven Afrikaner families led by Jansen van Rensburg trek by ox-wagon to the Uasin Gishu plateau to settle there.
1910	First European farmer arrives in the Nanyuki district with four dogs and thirteen chickens.
1911	Maasai moved from Laikipia to Narok, following the second Maasai treaty.
1912	The Trans Nzoia region opened to European settlement.
4 August 1914	Britain's entry into First World War, and formation of the East African Mounted Rifles.
March 1916	British forces under General Jan Smuts invade German East Africa (Tanzania) and force General von Lettow-Vorbeck's army into a long-drawn-out retreat.
25 November 1918	General von Lettow-Vorbeck surrenders to a battalion of the King's African Rifles at Abercorn in Northern Rhodesia (Zambia).
1919	Launch of the Soldier Settlement Scheme offering land in the highlands to ex-service men and women on easy terms.
1920	The British East Africa Protectorate becomes Kenya Colony.
1921–22	Indian currency, rupees and pice, replaced by British-based currency, at first florins, then shillings and cents.
1923	Following demands by the Indian community for the franchise on a common roll, the Secretary of State for the Colonies issues a White Paper stating that "the interests of the African natives must be paramount", and that if those interests should clash with those of the "immigrant races", the interests of the Africans must prevail.
1925	The railway extended to Eldoret on the Uasin Gishu plateau, and ultimately to Kampala in Uganda.
1926	Commercial tea plantations established at Kericho.
1928–34	Invasion by locust swarms which devastate crops and pastures throughout East Africa.
1930	Start of the World Depression, which leads to drastic falls in commodity prices and widespread poverty and distress in eastern Africa.

October 1935	Italy invades Abyssinia (Ethiopia).
10 June 1940	Mussolini declares war on the Allies: in August, Italians occupy British Somaliland.
25 February 1941	East African forces capture Mogadishu, capital of Italian Somaliland.
6 April 1941	Fall of Addis Ababa to the Allies.
27 November 1941	Capture of the fortress of Gondar, and end of the East African campaign. East African forces despatched to Burma.
10 August 1945	Surrender of Japan and end of the Second World War.
1946	First National Park – Nairobi's – established, followed by Tsavo in 1948.
1948	Amalgamation of railway systems of Kenya and Tanganyika, and linking of other services common to Uganda, Kenya, Tanganyika and Zanzibar, in the East African Community.
August 1950	Banning of the Mau Mau secret society among the Kikuyu.
6 February 1952	Princess Elizabeth becomes Queen of England, on the death of King George VI, while watching game at Treetops at Nyeri.
20 October 1952	State of Emergency declared, and arrest of Mau Mau leaders.
March 1953	Massacre of all the inhabitants of village of Lari in the Rift Valley by Mau Mau guerrillas.
April 1953	Jomo Kenyatta found guilty of managing a "proscribed society" and sentenced to seven years imprisonment.
1954	First elected ministers take office in the colonial government.
21st October 1956	Capture of "General" Dedan Kimathi, and *de facto* end of the Mau Mau revolt.
1960	Official end of the Mau Mau Emergency.
January 1960	First Lancaster House Conference in London at which the British Government's intention is made clear to liquidate European settlement, introduce immediately majority rule based on universal suffrage, and withdraw from the scene.
1960–61	Implementation of the "million acre scheme" whereby roughly one million acres of the "white highlands" was bought by the Government to be redistributed as smallholdings to African farmers.
12 December 1963	The Duke of Edinburgh hauls down the Union Jack in Nairobi and Kenya becomes an independent nation, with Jomo Kenyatta as its first Prime Minister.

12 December 1964	Kenya becomes a Republic; Jomo Kenyatta takes oath of office as its first President and swears in his Cabinet.
July 1967	Murder of Tom Mboya, Minister of Economic Planning and leader of the Luo people, by Kikuyu gunman.
1968	Asian exodus starts, following Africanization policy.
July 1974	Swahili declared to be the national language.
April 1977	Closing by Tanzania of Kenya/Tanzania border and dissolution of the East African Community.
May 1977	Kenya Government bans the hunting of wild animals.
22 August 1978	Death of President Jomo Kenyatta, and immediate succession of Vice-President Daniel arap Moi.
31 December 1980	Norfolk Hotel destroyed by bomb with many casualties.
August 1982	Attempted coup by members of the Kenya Air Force fails to topple the government of President Moi.
December 1983	Kenya's population passes the twenty million mark, all set to double in the next fifteen or sixteen years.
1987	Kenya declared a one-party state, with the Kenya African National Union as the one party.
1987–8	Secret ballot replaced by system of queuing openly behind the candidate of the voter's choice.
1989	Ivory poaching threatens the extinction of Kenya's elephants and Dr Richard Leakey appointed Director of Wildlife Services to combat it.

Introduction

All anthologies reflect a personal choice: I think one should also consider the reader. The editor casts his net: what sort of fish does he hope to hook? Perhaps historians? Armchair travellers? Academics? Students? Tourists? Would-be big game hunters? Wildlife enthusiasts? Or that mythical creature the Ordinary Reader, scanning the shelves of his, or more often her, local library for something to fill in the time between favourite television programmes?

At the back of my mind I have had a special pair of readers. One is the Curious Visitor, who either contemplates a trip to Kenya and wants to find out something about the country he is about to see, or who has just been there and wants to find out more about a country that has pricked his curiosity. In a national memorial to the dead of both world wars in Canberra there is a set of stained glass windows each of which depicts a separate virtue of the fighting man: Courage, Endurance, Loyalty, Fortitude, Valour and so on. Among them is a window depicting Curiosity. I had never before thought of this as a virtue: in fact, as children we were told that it killed the cat. Not so, it seems, in Australia; and it was refreshing to see this quality, the attribute of children and journalists, so enshrined.

My second hypothetical reader is the Young Kenyan with only a sketchy knowledge of his country's past, its peoples and its potentialities. Most of us share this ignorance of the land we live in; we stick to our patch. I am not thinking of facts learnt at school, but of the people who lived here before us, where they came from, what they did: not just the great and famous but also the humble and obscure. Kenya is a country of great diversity of peoples, cultures, races, customs and tongues, each with its own identity yet all linked together like the necklaces of beads that not so long ago provided the country's currency, and now adorn many supple necks. The Swahili living on the coast, heir to centuries of Muslim tradition and Arabic culture, may know little of the lives of nomads of the northern deserts; the sophisticated government minister or international banker of Nairobi has little in common with the peasant woman trudging to a roadside market with the produce of her shamba on her head or back. All are part of the mosaic which evokes the Kenya of today.

I have divided this anthology, as its title indicates, into nine sections, each devoted to one aspect of what was formerly, and for thousands of years, an anonymous part of a mysterious continent; then partially a Portuguese conquest; then a British colony; and finally a sovereign republic. The arrangement is by subject rather than chronology, which I hope is more convenient for the reader, who can pick and choose according to his interest, whether it lies in wildlife or exploration, in poetry or in war. Inevitably, the subjects sometimes overlap.

I must emphasize what this anthology is not. It is not a political history, or any other kind of history, as such. Aspects of history come into it of course, but I have tried to steer clear of politics. Politics, that is, in the narrow sense of polemics revolving round the issues of the day; in the wider sense, all the major events of history are, I suppose, rooted in political decisions made by conquerors and kings, by priests and parliaments, even by philosophers and scribes. But chronicles of dead and decided issues, however compelling in their day, are, save to professional historians, as stale as old cabbage leaves twenty, thirty, forty years on.

I have tried, so far as possible, to select extracts only from first-hand accounts – "I was there", either as actor or as eyewitness. This has not always been possible, but it has remained the aim. For this reason I originally ruled out the subject of pre-history on the grounds that fossils cannot write, and that a subject so complex and disputatious must lead the layman into dangerous waters. It was pointed out to me, however, that recent discoveries which support the theory that here, in East Africa, is the likely site of the origins of mankind and his immediate ancestors, are too important to be left out. I cannot attempt to set these discoveries in their pre-historical context, but fortunately members of the remarkable family who have made or inaugurated them – Dr Louis Leakey, his wife Dr Mary and their son Dr Richard – have described them in vivid and popular as well as in scientific terms. I have therefore included as a prologue extracts which describe three of their major finds at the moment of discovery.

When compiling an anthology about a country one ought to be able to define it, but until recent times this was impossible. Today's Kenya was formerly just part of eastern Africa, unpartitioned, boundless and, from a European point of view, unexplored. Not until 1895, when a British Protectorate was declared, did it receive a name, then British East Africa; not until 1920 did it become Kenya. Since the first records began, around AD 100, the story of today's Kenya was the story of the coast, colonized by Arabs and Persians probably in the seventh and eighth centuries, conquered by the Portuguese at the start of the sixteenth century, reconquered by the Arabs and ruled from Zanzibar, then taken over by the British when the "opening up" of the interior began. Following millennia when life went on more or less unchanged, and such changes as occurred went unrecorded, changes of revolutionary proportions were telescoped into roughly seventy years. As from the eggs of crocodiles buried in the sand, a modern state emerged complete with all its limbs and brains and senses, to hurry down to the dangerous and uncertain waters of today's capricious world.

The word anthology is derived from the Greek for flower, and flowers can be plucked only from plants that actually grow; the compiler cannot invent them. So gaps in the arrangement may be due to limits of space, but also to a lack of deserving material from which to quote.

A word about nomenclature and spelling. Explorers were in the habit of calling lakes, mountains and other natural features after European royalty, Lake Rudolf for example, and after patrons, such as Lord Aberdare, and sometimes after themselves, such as Fort Hall and Thomson's Falls. The correct African names have now replaced nearly all these alien terms, with the exception of Lake Victoria, whose waters are bordered by several different peoples and so has no common African name. Porters of the old Swahili caravans knew certain tribes by derogatory nicknames given them by the Maasai, such as Suk, meaning snot, and Lumbwa, from umbwa, meaning dog. These have been discarded and the correct names, respectively Pokot and Kipsigis, reinstated. The Maasai have acquired an extra "a", Masai having been the former spelling. In the past, the prefix "ki" was attached to the noun Swahili to indicate the language, Ki–Swahili. This was grammatically correct, but has fallen out of general use. Similarly, the Dorobo people were called Wandorobo, and the Kamba the Wakamba, "wa" being the prefix used to indicate the plural in many Bantu languages. African society was, and still mainly is, divided into tribes, each with its separate language, set of customs and tradition of a common ancestry. I have retained the spelling of place names and Swahili words used by the authors of the selected passages, although they vary considerably, sometimes in a rather wayward fashion. The word "tribe" is now somewhat frowned upon, and the euphemism "ethnic group" preferred. As tribe was the word in general use until quite recently, I have continued to use it.

I am afraid that the appearance of such colonial terms as "native" and "boy" will give offence to some, which I naturally regret. When, where and why adult males were first called "boys" I have no idea, but it was the general term and therefore cannot be avoided when quoting from writings of the time.

Colonialism is now a dirty word to many, arousing feelings of indignation in black breasts and guilt in white ones – emotions equally disruptive, in my opinion, to a calm assessment of past history and the profitable conduct of present affairs. The most cogent summing-up of colonialism I have seen was handed down by the quarterchief of Wum in Cameroon to the indefatigable traveller Dervla Murphy in the words: "Colonialism is like the zebra. Some say it is a black animal, some say it is a white animal, and those whose sight is good, they know it is a *striped* animal."

The Africa and its peoples encountered by the first agents of the West has vanished, and will never come again. The wild animals in their amazing abundance and variety have also gone forever, save for surviving pockets in parks and reserves. So perhaps this is a good moment to try to draw together some of the strands that have united to form the sovereign state of Kenya today. I hope that the visitor will find something in these pages to remind him of a land of great beauty, beguilement, harshness and infinite variety; the native in the wider sense something to interest, entertain and even amuse. As Henry James observed – though he was thinking of cats and monkeys – "all human life is there."

The Background

Fifteen million years ago there was no Great Rift Valley, no towering highlands, and a carpet of forest covered the land down to the Indian Ocean. Then came a collision of titanic proportions: the African continent rammed into that of Eurasia and two massive blisters, one in Kenya and one in Ethiopia, arose.

Swellings of molten lava from deep down in the earth's mantle heaved up the land by 3000 feet and more to form these two nations' highlands. The crust groaned under tremendous pressure as it was forced higher and higher: in the end the strain was just too much; the crust had to crack, and it did. Countless trillions of tons of rock crashed downwards as fault lines opened up, stretching from northeast to southwest: the blisters were lanced, creating the first visible signs of what was to become the Great Rift Valley.

Inevitably the boiling, swirling lava and gases found ways to escape, tearing explosion craters in the hillsides and building huge volcanoes that, in middle Miocene times (say 12 million years ago), soared up 20,000 feet. They would have been snow-covered then, just as Mounts Kenya and Kilimanjaro are today. Through the ages the ancient volcanoes were ground down by the elements, leaving mere stubs a tenth of the original size; their pulverized rocks contributed to the layer upon layer of deep sediments in the lava floor of the valley, a floor that is now more than 4000 feet thick. Through the ages too that floor sank lower and lower, partly because of the weight of the sediments and lava and partly because of the movement apart of the plates. These days, in the region of Lake Baringo, which was the highest point of the Kenyan blister, the walls of the valley rise 3000 feet from the lava floor, and they are virtually sheer. And the bottom of the valley, through Tanzania, Kenya, and Ethiopia, is littered with lakes and more or less extinct volcanic cones. It is littered too with fossil sites rich in the remains of our early ancestors and their australopithecine cousins. . . . As the blisters rose higher and higher they eventually reached a point at which they threw the land to their east into rain shadow, thus depriving the thirsty tropical forest there of its sustenance. The forests of East Africa shrank, producing a patch-work of embryonic savanna (open terrain) and woodland, and leaving a scattering of West African-like trees, birds, butterflies and animals in the Arabuko Soreke coastal forest just north of Mombasa and up to the Tana River as a reminder of times past.

The pruning of East Africa's forests by the birth of the highlands is ecological modification on a grand scale. But the cracking and blistering geological face of this area generated more subtle, local effects too: within a radius of just a few miles around any part of the rift, but particularly in the highest areas, there is a mosaic of dense tropical forest, semi-arid desert, alpine meadows, grasslands, open woodland, and every ecological shade in between. It is a remarkable piece of topography, and it has been that way since the middle Miocene right up to the present. The creation of this matrix of ecologies as the blisters swelled and cracked provided an unusual diversity of habitats for the animals there to exploit. And this may well have been an important factor in speeding along the pace of hominid evolution in East Africa. (Hominid is the name used for humans and their close evolutionary relatives such as the australopithecines.)

As the Rift Valley sweeps northwards out of Kenya and into Ethiopia in modern-day Africa it forms the spectacular Lake Turkana basin. Spectacular, not only for the stunning beauty of the lake itself and its powerfully stark surroundings, but also for its rich treasure trove of pre-human fossils buried in the layered deposits on the eastern shore of the lake. Beginning with a small tentative expedition in 1968, it is here that Richard Leakey leads the search for ancient human ancestors in Kenya.

People of the Lake Richard Leakey and Roger Lewin.

Finds made by the Leakey family in Olduvai Gorge in Tanzania – "the place of wild sisal" – have made archaeological history.

Since I first began to live most of the year at Olduvai a systematic search of the exposures for hominid and other fossils has been made at the end of each rainy season. At this time the fossils have been washed clean and can be seen much more clearly than when they are covered in dust during the dry season. Some important discovery has been made almost every year in the course of the annual search.

One of the most significant aspects of the work at Olduvai during the 1960s was the discovery that *Australopithecus boisei* lived side by side with an early species of *Homo*. This was later borne out by discoveries at East Turkana in Kenya. . . .

The discovery of the skull of *Australopithecus boisei* (*Zinjanthropus*)* was one of the occasions when both perseverance and luck played a part. Despite the fact that we had found very few hominid remains on our early visits to Olduvai, Louis and I had remained firmly convinced that they would one day come to light, and we kept on looking.

On 17 July 1959 I was out hunting for fossils by myself, with my two Dalmatian dogs for company, while Louis rested in camp after a slight attack of flu. As I was working over the slopes of Bed I, I suddenly saw the skull. I was doubtful, at first,

---

Australopithecus boisei was named after Mr Charles Boise, who for many years aided our work financially and also set up the Boise Fund in Oxford to assist in the study of early man.

whether it was hominid, since the mastoid region that was exposed was quite different from any I had seen in human skulls. Instead of being solid bone it was permeated with air cells, such as are found in skulls of particularly heavy animals, to compensate for excessive weight. However, after brushing away a little of the covering soil I saw two teeth that were unquestionably hominid. I was tremendously excited by my discovery and quickly went back to camp to fetch Louis. When he saw the teeth he was disappointed, since he had hoped the skull would be *Homo* and not *Australopithecus.*

When the skull had been partially exposed we found that it had been broken into a great many fragments, although all the pieces lay close together within an area approximately forty-five centimetres in diameter. . . . The task of reassembling the fragments took many months, and it was not until three years after the discovery that the final reconstruction was carried out. . . .

We resumed work at Olduvai in February the following year, 1960.

The discovery of *Homo habilis* was made by my eldest son, Jonathan, who was working with me at Olduvai after leaving school. While excavations were in progress at the *"Zinjanthropus"* site, Jonathan often wandered off to search for fossils elsewhere. One day he returned with a very strange mandible which he had found on the slopes of Bed I. The mandible was later identified in the Nairobi Museum as the lower jaw of a sabre-toothed feline or machairodont, which is one of the rarest animals in the fauna of Olduvai. We immediately began a search for other parts. None came to light, but a single well-preserved hominid molar turned up most unexpectedly in the sieves. The discovery of the tooth led to extensive excavations, which proved to be among the most rewarding and exciting ever carried out at Olduvai. Jonathan directed the excavations and himself found the mandible and parietals which became the type of *Homo habilis.* . . .

Louis discovered a skull of *Homo erectus* on 2 December 1960. He had been visiting various sites with a geologist, and while they were walking through the side gorge Louis noticed a small, insignificant gully that he believed had not been examined previously. He walked across to it the following morning and immediately noticed a little rounded mass of bones lying in the bottom of the gully, where Bed II was exposed. At first glance these seemed very similar to the bony carapace of a fossil tortoise. Since this resemblance had deceived us both on many occasions, Louis was wholly astonished to discover that on this occasion what appeared to be a tortoise was in fact a human skull. . . .

In all, three types of early hominids have been found at Olduvai: *Australopithecus boisei* (first called *"Zinjanthropus"*); *Homo habilis*, a small, lightly-built creature; and *Homo erectus*, a hominid whose brain capacity was considerably larger than the other two. . . .

East Africa has been claimed by some to be the "cradle of mankind"; others postulate an Asiatic origin for the early hominids. The question has not been resolved, but it is certain that the conditions for preservation of early fossils in East Africa are unparalleled elsewhere. Active volcanoes depositing ash at relatively frequent intervals combined with fluctuating lakes in closed basins have preserved the remains of early man, his tools and the contemporary fauna in an unprecedented fashion. Such a wealth of evidence leads to the assumption that man originated in East Africa.

Olduvai Gorge: My Search for Early Man Mary Leakey.

Other important finds came to light at Koobi Fora on Lake Turkana's eastern shore. Richard Leakey describes one made in 1978.

Kamoya and I were out on foot relocating a fossil site his men had discovered a week or so earlier at Ileret, some 70 kilometres (45 miles) north of the main camp. While we walked I was talking to Maundu, one of Kamoya's assistants, and he was reporting the news of the previous two weeks' work. As usual, we were all keeping a sharp look-out for signs of any interesting fossils as we went. Suddenly my eye was drawn to a small scatter of bone fragments protruding less than two centimetres through the grey sand. Maundu had also noticed the fragments and we both stopped and carefully knelt to inspect them more closely. We quickly agreed that they appeared to be some of the smaller bones from the underside of a hominid skull. Such finds are tremendously exciting and we immediately began to speculate about the chances of there being a whole intact cranium buried just beneath the surface. The answer had to wait until we could make a proper excavation the following day.

We returned the next day at dawn and soon revealed a problem I had feared: the bone was extremely fragile and as Meave and I gradually exposed more and more of the skull we had to apply a hardening solution of plastic to strengthen it. . . . By 5.00 p.m. I was able to lift from the ground the delicate but intact cranium of a hominid who had lived and died close to the lakeshore almost one-and-a-half million years ago. Registered in the museum as KNM-ER 3883, the fossil is a fine example of *Homo erectus*, the hominid that immediately preceded *Homo sapiens*.

From other fossil material that has been unearthed, it is clear that the skeleton of *Homo erectus* was essentially modern. A little stockier than the average human today, perhaps, but not all that different. The head and face, however, were still "primitive": the forehead sloped backwards and was mounted with prominent brow-ridges, while the brain, though larger than that of *Homo habilis*, was only seventy per cent of the size of a *Homo sapiens* brain. The face protruded less than in *Homo habilis*, but it was not as flat or "tucked in" as in *Homo sapiens*. The chin that is so characteristic of modern humans was present but poorly developed.

Palaeoanthropologists view the anatomical characteristics of *Homo erectus* as being distinctive enough to deserve recognition as a new stage in human evolution, an advance on *Homo habilis*. What is most striking about *Homo erectus*, however, is not the development of new anatomical features but the changes in behaviour. Through the development of the food-sharing, hunter-gatherer way of life and a sharpened intelligence, *Homo erectus* expanded into territories where no advanced hominid had lived before. Around a million or more years ago, some groups of this hominid moved into Europe and Asia. With this move, our ancestors changed from being exclusively tropical creatures, and learned to cope with the fluctuations in food availability that go with the changing seasons of temperate regions.

Homo erectus is first recognized in the fossil record from about one-and-a-half million years ago, and continued until about 300,000 years ago when *Homo sapiens* began to emerge. *Homo erectus* spread across the continents of Africa, Asia and Europe, though not to the colder northern extremes of Eurasia and not into America or Australia. It was the time when hunting-and-gathering became firmly established, with active hunting as opposed to opportunistic scavenging becoming more and more important. Large-scale hunting first developed in this period, we see the first signs of the systematic and controlled use of fire, and there are indications of ritual in the lives of these hominids. Stone-tool manufacture became controlled and patterned. New challenges were being faced and overcome, and new lifestyles developed. The age of *Homo erectus* was clearly an important phase in human evolution.

The Making of Mankind Richard Leakey.

The chance find of some fossil zebra and antelope teeth in a load of sand used for building led, several years later, to the discovery of the "Laetoli footsteps" by a team led by Dr Mary Leakey.

By an astonishing combination of circumstances, a very ordinary event which happened some three-and-three-quarter million years ago led to what is probably the most dramatic archaeological discovery of this century. Three hominids left a trail of footprints that have been clearly preserved, presenting us with an amazing picture of a few moments in the lives of some of our ancestors.

The place where it happened is now called Laetoli, a wooded area near a volcanic mountain, Sadiman, some 40 kilometres (25 miles) south of the present-day Olduvai Gorge in Tanzania. The dry season was probably nearing its end and the sight of gathering rain clouds promised welcome relief from months of drought. For a week or two the volcano had rumbled restlessly, occasionally belching out clouds of grey ash that settled over the surrounding countryside. Nothing violent or startling, just a steady background of subterranean stirrings such as is still experienced today from the Oldoinyo Lengai, 70 kilometres (45 miles) southeast of Olduvai. Like the ash from Lengai, the ash that Sadiman produced had a chemical composition that made it set like cement when dampened slightly and then dried by the sun.

As luck would have it, the end of that dry season was signalled by a scattering of brief showers. Large raindrops splashed onto the newly fallen ash, leaving tiny craters as on a miniature moonscape. The clouds passed; the promised downpour was yet to come. The carpet of ash was now in perfect condition for taking clear impressions: less rain and the ash would have blown about in the breeze, more rain and any impressions would have been washed away.

Following the rain, various animals left their tracks in the damp volcanic ash as they went their ways. Spring hares, guinea fowl, elephants, pigs, rhinoceroses, buffaloes, hyaenas, antelopes, a sabre-tooth tiger and dozens of baboon all made their marks. And so did three hominids. A large individual, probably a male, walked slowly towards the north. Following behind, then or a little later, was a smaller individual who for some reason placed his or her feet in the prints of the first individual. A youngster skipped along by their side, turning at one point to look to its left. The sun soon baked the prints into rock-hard impressions. More ash, rain and windblown sand covered and preserved the prints until they were discovered by a lucky chance in 1976.

"They are the most remarkable find I have made in my entire career," says my mother, who is directing the excavations. "When we first came across the hominid prints I must admit I was sceptical, but then it became clear that they could be nothing else. They are the earliest prints of man's ancestors, and they show us that hominids three-and-three-quarter million years ago walked upright with a free-striding gait, just as we do today.'

The Making of Mankind Richard Leakey.

When the first men were fashioned in the Good Lord's forge
He sent them, it seems, to Olduvai Gorge.

Punch

PART I

Exploration

The history of that part of East Africa now known as Kenya has been, since time immemorial, the history of the East African coast. The people of its seaboard settlements may have been trading with Arabia, Egypt and the Persian Gulf before the Roman Empire arose; the ivory and apes, if not peacocks, brought by his navy to King Solomon could have been shipped from their harbours. Settlers from the Arabian mainland gradually established Arab culture and control, together with the Islamic faith, along the coast and on its offshore islands. From inter-breeding between Arab and Persian settlers and indigenous African women arose the Swahili race. Then came the Portuguese, who for over two hundred stormy years ruled the coastal cities from their headquarters in Goa. They left the hinterland alone, but Arab and Swahili caravans marched far inland to gain slaves and ivory. In the eighteenth century the Arabs exercised political control under the ruler of Oman, who in the 1840s moved his seat of government to Zanzibar. The British arrived on the scene first as Christian missionaries, then as explorers bent on verifying rumours of great lakes, mountains and rivers far inland. In the last half of the nineteenth century, the geography of Eastern Africa was laid bare. Thoughts then turned to trade and exploitation, and in 1888 the Imperial British East Africa Company was formed to this end. The task proved beyond its means, and in 1895 a British Protectorate was proclaimed over the present Kenya, the Germans taking what was to become Tanganyika, the main part of today's Tanzania.

> *The earliest known document describing parts of the East African coast is the* Periplus of the Erythraean Sea, *attributed to an unknown Greek or Greek-speaking Egyptian writing sometime between AD 95 and AD 130. The Erythraean Sea was the Greek phrase for the Red Sea, Persian Gulf and Indian Ocean. Already there was a lively trade between the Arabian mainland and settlements along the East African coast, then known as Azania, mainly in ivory, tortoiseshell, rhinoceros horn and slaves, exchanged for iron weapons, wine and glassware. The "sewn boats" in which this trade was carried probably differed little, if at all, from the dhows which continued to ply between Arabia, the Persian Gulf and East Africa almost for another two thousand years. The anonymous author of the* Periplus *described the island of Menouthias, probably Pemba, as*

low and covered with trees, in which are rivers and many kinds of birds, and mountain tortoise. Of wild animals there are none except crocodiles; but they hurt no man. There are in it small boats sewn and made from one piece of wood, which are used for fishing and catching marine tortoises. In this island they catch them [i.e. fish] with a local form of basket trap instead of nets stretched across the mouths of the openings along the foreshore.

CHAPTER 16

From here after two courses off the mainland lies the last mart of Azania, called Rhapta, which has its name from the aforementioned sewn boats, where there is a great deal of ivory and tortoiseshell. The natives of this country have very large bodies and piratical habits; and each place likewise has its own chief. The Mopharitic chief rules it according to an ancient agreement by which it falls under the kingdom which has become first in Arabia. Under the king the people of Mouza hold it by payment of tribute, and send ships with captains and agents who are mostly Arabs, and are familiar through residence and intermarriage with the nature of the places and their language.

CHAPTER 17

There are brought to these marts things made specially in Mouza:
Spears λόγχη.
Axes πελύκια.
Small swords μαχαίρια.
Awls ὀπήτια.
Several kinds of glassware λιθίας ὑαλης.
And to some places wine, οἶνος and corn, σῖτος not much, nor for trade, but for expenses in making friends with the Barbaroi. There are exported from these places a great deal of ivory, though it is inferior to that of Adouli, and rhinoceros horn, and tortoiseshell, next in demand to that from India, and a little coconut.

CHAPTER 18

And these are almost the last marts of Azania on the right hand (coming) from the land of Bernikē. For after these places the unexplored ocean curves round to the west, and extending southwards in the opposite direction from Aithiopia and Libya and Africa, mingles with the western sea.

The harmless crocodiles were probably giant water-lizards, known to the Swahili as kenge. *The site of Rhapta has not been identified; the town has disappeared. Mouza was probably situated about twenty-five miles north of present-day Mocha in South Yemen, and Bernikē was a port on the western shore of the Red Sea.*

Azanian fishermen were adept at catching tortoises; their method was described by Pliny (AD 23–79) in his massive natural history of the Roman world published in 37 books. (The only time he stopped working, his nephew wrote, was when he was in his bath.)

PLINY, *Book IX*

The Indian Ocean produces tortoises (*testudines*) of such a size that a single shell is enough to form a hut to live in, and the inhabitants of the islands in the Red Sea use them as boats. They are caught in many ways, but chiefly when carried out to sea in the warm hours before midday. They float on the surface with their backs out of water, and the pleasure of breathing freely so lulls them into forgetfulness that their shells are dried by the sun's heat and thus they cannot sink, but float aimlessly, an easy prey to the hunter. They feed at night; when they have eaten enough they return in the morning and sleep on the surface of the water. The noise of their snoring betrays them to the fishermen who swim up quietly and capture them, three men taking one tortoise between them: two men turn the creature on to its back, and the third puts a noose round it, and thus it is pulled to the shore.

Tortoises have no teeth, but instead jaws with sharp edges, the upper shutting on the lower like the lid of a box. They feed on shell-fish, for their jaws are so strong that they can break stones with them. They come out on land and lay eggs like birds' eggs, up to a hundred in number; they bury them in the ground out of the reach of water, cover them with sand, and smooth it with their breasts; they sit on them at night. The eggs are hatched after a year. The female flees from the male till he puts some sort of herb on his unwilling partner. In the Troglodyte country there are tortoises with horns like lyres, but moveable, which they use as oars when swimming. This kind is called *chelyon*; it has a valuable shell, but is rare, because the Tortoise-eaters are afraid of the sharp rocks among which they live; and the Troglodytes whose coast they visit account them sacred.

The Periplus of the Erythraean Sea, ed. G. W. B. Huntingford.

Arabs were great travellers, and several accounts survive of visits to what they called the coast of Zinj, or Zanj, meaning black. The following report was written by Abdul Hassan ibn al Mas'udi, who was born in Baghdad at the end of the ninth century and died in Old Cairo in AD 956 or 957. With a flair for arresting titles that might be envied by a modern publisher, he called his East African volume Meadows of Gold and Mines of Gems. *His voyage took place in AD 916.*

The sea of the Zanj reaches down to the country of Sofala and of the Wak-Wak which produces gold in abundance and other marvels; its climaté is warm and its soil fertile. It is there that the Zanj built their capital; then they elected a king whom they called *Waklimi*. This name . . . has always been that of their sovereigns. The *Waklimi* has under him all the other Zanj kings, and commands three hundred thousand men. The Zanj use the ox as a beast of burden, for their country has no horses or mules or camels and they do not even know these animals. Snow and hail are unknown to them as to all the Abyssinians. Some of their tribes have sharpened teeth and are cannibals. The territory of the Zanj begins at the canal which flows from the Upper Nile and goes down as far as the country of Sofala and the Wak-Wak. Their settlements extend over an area of about seven hundred parasangs in length and in breadth; this country is divided by valleys, mountains and stony deserts; it abounds in wild elephants but there is not so much as a single tame elephant. . . .

Although constantly employed in hunting elephants and gathering ivory, the Zanj make no use of ivory for their own domestic purposes. They wear iron instead of gold and silver. . . .

To come back to the Zanj and their kings, the name of the kings of the country is *Waklimi* which means supreme lord; they give this title to their sovereign because he has been chosen to govern them with equity. But once he becomes tyrannical and departs from the rules of justice, they cause him to die and exclude his posterity from succession to the throne, for they claim that in thus conducting himself he ceases to be the son of the Master, that is to say of the king of heaven and earth. They call God by the name of Maklandjalu, which means supreme Master. . . .

The Zanj speak elegantly, and they have orators in their own language. Often a devout man of the country, pausing in the midst of a numerous crowd, addresses to his listeners an exhortation in which he invites them to serve God and submit to His orders. He points out the punishments which disobedience must entail, and recalls the example of their ancestors and their ancient kings. These peoples have no code of religion; their kings follow custom, and conform in their government to a few political rules. The Zanj eat bananas, which are as abundant with them as in India, but the basis of their food is *dorrah*, a plant called *kalari* which they take from the ground like a truffle, and the *elecampane* root. . . . They also have honey and meat. Each worships what he pleases, a plant, an animal, a mineral. They possess a great number of islands where the coconut grows, a fruit that is eaten by all the peoples of the Zanj. One of these islands, placed one or two days' journey from the coast, has a Muslim population who provide the royal family; it is the island of Kanbalu. . . .

Abdul Hassan ibn al Mas'udi, *Les Prairies d'Or*, Vol. III, Paris 1884.
From *The African Past* Basil Davidson.

Slaves were the principal export from the coast of Zinj in the Middle Ages. The trade was in the hands of the Arabs, one of whom told this story.

Ismailawaih told me, and several sailors who were with him, that in the year AH 310 [=AD 922] he left Oman in his ship to go to Kanbalu. A storm drove him towards Sofala on the Zanj coast. "Seeing the coast where we were, the captain said, and realizing that we were falling among cannibal negroes and were certain to perish, we made the ritual ablutions and turned our hearts towards God, saying for each other the prayers for the dead. The canoes of the negroes surrounded us and brought us into the harbour; we cast anchor and disembarked on the land. They led us to their king. He was a young negro, handsome and well made. He asked us who we were, and where we were going. We answered that the object of our voyage was his own land.

"You lie, he said. It was not in our land that you intended to disembark. It is only that the winds have driven you thither in spite of yourselves.

"When we had admitted that he spoke the truth, he said: Disembark your goods. Sell and buy, you have nothing to fear.

"We brought all our packages to the land and began to trade, a trade which was excellent for us, without any obstacles or customs dues. We made the king a number of presents to which he replied with gifts of equal worth or ones even more valuable. When the time to depart came, we asked his permission to go, and he agreed immediately. The goods we had bought were loaded and business was wound up. When everything was in order, and the king knew of our intention to set sail, he accompanied us to the shore with several of his people, got into one of the boats and came out to the ship with us. He even came on board with seven of his companions.

"When I saw them there, I said to myself: In the Oman market this young king would certainly fetch thirty dinars, and his seven companions sixty dinars. Their clothes alone are not worth less than twenty dinars. One way and another this would give us a profit of at least 3,000 dirhams, and without any trouble. Reflecting thus, I gave the crew their orders. They raised the sails and weighed anchor.

"In the meantime the king was most agreeable to us, making us promise to come back again and promising us a good welcome when we did. When he saw the sails fill with the wind and the ship begin to move, his face changed. You are off, he said. Well, I must say good-bye. And he wished to embark in the canoes which were tied up to the side. But we cut the ropes, and said to him: You will remain with us, we shall take you to our own land. There we shall reward you for all the kindnesses you have shown us.

"Strangers, he said, when you fell upon our beaches, my people wished to eat you and pillage your goods, as they have already done to others like you. But I protected you, and asked nothing from you. As a token of my goodwill I even came down to bid you farewell in your own ship. Treat me then as justice demands, and let me return to my own land.

"But no one paid any heed to his words; no notice was taken of them. As the wind got up, the coast was not slow to disappear from sight. Then night enfolded us in its shrouds and we reached the open sea.

"When the day came, the king and his companions were put with the other slaves whose number reached about 200 head. He was not treated differently from his companions in captivity. The king said not a word and did not even open his mouth. He behaved as if we were unknown to him and as if we did not know him. When we got to Oman, the slaves were sold, and the king with them.

"Now, several years after, sailing from Oman towards Kanbalu, the wind again drove us towards the coasts of Sofala on the Zanj coast, and we arrived at precisely the same place. The negroes saw us, and their canoes surrounded us, and we recognized each other. Fully certain we should perish this time, terror struck us dumb. We made the ritual ablutions in silence, repeated the prayer of death, and said farewell to each other. The negroes seized us, and took us to the king's dwelling and made us go in. Imagine our surprise; it was the same king that we had known, seated on his throne, just as if we had left him there. We prostrated ourselves before him, overcome, and had not the strength to raise ourselves up.

"Ah! said he, here are my old friends! Not one of us was capable of replying. He went on: Come, raise your heads, I give you safe conduct for yourselves and for your goods. Some raised their heads, others had not the strength, and were overcome with shame. But he showed himself gentle and gracious until we had all raised our heads, but without daring to look him in the face, so much were we moved to remorse and fear. But when we had been reassured by his safe conduct, we finally came to our senses, and he said: Ah! Traitors! How you have treated me after all I did for you! And each one of us called out: Mercy, oh King! Be merciful to us!

"I will be merciful to you, he said. Go on, as you did last time, with your business of selling and buying. You may trade in full liberty. We could not believe our ears; we feared it was nothing but a trick to make us bring our goods on shore. None the less we disembarked them, and came and brought him a present of enormous value. But he refused it and said: You are not worthy for me to accept a present from you. I will not sully my property with anything that comes from you.

"After that we did our business in peace. When the time to go came, we asked permission to embark. He gave it. At the moment of departure, I went to tell him so. Go, he said, and may God protect you! Oh King, I replied, you have showered your bounty upon us, and we have been ungrateful and traitorous to you. But how did you escape and return to your country?

"He answered: After you had sold me in Oman, my purchaser took me to a town called Basrah, – and he described it. There I learnt to pray and to fast, and certain parts of the Koran. My master sold me to another man who took me to the country of the king of the Arabs, called Baghdad – and he described Baghdad. In this town I learnt to speak correctly. I completed my knowledge of the Koran and prayed with the men in the mosques. I saw the Caliph, who is called al-Muqtadir [908–32]. I was in Baghdad for a year and more, when there came a party of men from Khorasan mounted on camels. Seeing a large crowd, I asked where all these people were going. I was told: To Mecca. What is Mecca? I asked. There, I was answered, is the House of God to which Muslims make the Pilgrimage. And I was . told the history of the temple. I said to myself that I should do well to follow the caravan. My master, to whom I told all this, did not wish to go with them or to let me go. But I found a way to escape his watchfulness and to mix in the crowd of pilgrims. On the road I became a servant to them. They gave me food to eat and got for me the two cloths needed for the *ihram* [the ritual garments used for the pilgrimage]. Finally, they instructing me, I performed all the ceremonies of the pilgrimage.

"Not daring to go back to Baghdad, for fear that my master would take away my life, I joined up with another caravan which was going to Cairo. I offered my services to the travellers, who carried me on their camels and shared their provisions with me. When I got to Cairo I saw the great river which is called the Nile. I asked: Where does it come from? They answered: Its source is in the land of the Zanj. On which side? On the side of a large town called Aswan, which is on the frontier of the land of the blacks.

"With this information, I followed the banks of the Nile, going from one town to another, asking alms, which was not refused me. I fell, however, among a company of blacks who gave me a bad welcome. They seized on me, and put me among the servants with a load which was too heavy for me to carry. I fled and fell into the hands of another company which seized me and sold me. I escaped again, and went on in this manner, until, after a series of similar adventures, I found myself in the country which adjoins the land of the Zanj. There I put on a disguise. Of all the terrors I had experienced since I left Cairo, there was none equal to that which I felt as I approached my own land. For, I said to myself, a new king has no doubt taken my place on the throne and commands the army. To regain power is not an easy thing. If I make myself known or if anyone recognizes me, I shall be seized upon, taken to the new king and killed at once. Or perhaps one of his favourites will cut off my head to gain his favour.

"So, in prey to mortal terror, I went on my way by night, and stayed hidden during the day. When I reached the sea, I embarked on a ship; and, after stopping at various places, I disembarked one night on the shore of my country. I asked an old woman: Is the king who rules here a just king? She answered: My son, we have no king but God. And the good woman told me how the king had been carried off. I pretended the greatest astonishment at her story, as if it had not concerned me and events which I knew very well. The people of the kingdom, she said, have agreed not to have another king until they have certain news of the former one. For the diviners have told them that he is alive and in health, and safe in the land of the Arabs.

"When the day came, I went into the town and walked towards my palace. I found my family just as I had left them, but plunged into grief. My people listened to the account of my story, and it surprised them and filled them with joy. Like myself, they embraced the religion of Islam. Thus I returned into possession of my sovereignty, a month before you came. And here I am, happy and satisfied with the grace God has given me and mine, of knowing the precepts of Islam, the true faith, prayers, fasting, the pilgrimage, and what is permitted and what is forbidden: for no man else in the land of the Zanj has obtained a similar favour.

And if I have forgiven you, it is because you were the first cause of the purity of my religion. But there is still one sin on my conscience which I pray God to take away from me.

"What is this thing, oh King? I asked. It is, he said, that I left my master, when I left Baghdad, without asking him his permission, and that I did not return to him. If I were to meet an honest man, I would ask him to take the price of my purchase to my master. If there were among you a really good man, if you were truly upright men, I would give you a sum of money to give him, a sum ten times what he paid as damages for the delay. But you are nothing but traitors and tricksters.

"We said farewell to him. Go, he said, and if you return, I shall not treat you otherwise than I have done. You will receive the best welcome. And the Muslims may know that they may come here to us, as to brothers, Muslims like themselves. As for accompanying you to your ship, I have reasons for not doing so. And on that we parted".

Buzurg ibn Shahriyar of Ramhormutz, *Kitab al-Ajaib al-Hind.*
From *The East African Coast: Select Documents* G. S. P. Freeman-Grenville.

In 1414 a great fleet from China sailed into the Indian Ocean.

It was commanded by Zheng He, Grand Eunuch of the Three Treasures. Three times already since 1405 Zheng He and his ships had descended on the ports of Indochina, Indonesia, south-west India and Ceylon. Now they were advancing into more distant regions, covering in the process a larger total quantity of water than any seafaring people had before.

Zheng He was the Chinese Columbus. He has become for China, as Columbus has for the West, the personification of maritime endeavour. Yet he differed from his Western counterpart in a number of major ways. Three-quarters of a century before Columbus crossed the Atlantic, this Ming dynasty admiral had at his disposal resources which make the Genoese explorer look like an amateur. Columbus had three ships. They had one deck apiece, and together weighed a total of 415 tons. Zheng He had sixty-two galleons, and more than a hundred auxiliary vessels. The largest galleons had three decks on the poop alone, and each of them weighed about 1,500 tons. They had nine masts and twelve sails, and are said to have measured 440 feet long by 180 feet wide. With a force of perhaps a hundred men, Columbus might have been grateful for the company of

868 civil officers, 26,800 soldiers, 93 commanders, two senior commanders, 140 "millerions" (captains of a thousand men), 403 centurions, a Senior Secretary of the Board of Revenue, a geomancer, a military instructor, two military judges, 180 medical officers and assistants, two orderlies, seven senior eunuch ambassadors, ten junior eunuchs and 53 eunuch chamberlains

who travelled in Zheng He's retinue, along with an unspecified number of signallers, interpreters, scribes, professional negotiators, purveyors, Chinese and foreign navigators, helmsmen, military and civil mechanics, naval captains, common sailors and cooks. Columbus's crew, whose diet included dirty drinking water and flour baked with sea water, might also have appreciated the abundance of grain, fresh water, salt, soya sauce, tea, liquor, oil, candles, firewood and charcoal which Zheng He brought with him in his attendant supply ships and water tankers.

The Star Raft Philip Snow.

In the following year a present from the king of Malindi arrived at the court of the Emperor of China and created a great stir. It was a K'i-lin, a giraffe, together with a "celestial stag", an oryx, and a "celestial horse", a zebra. The giraffe was equated with a mythical creature believed to appear only at the courts of rulers of exceptional virtue and wisdom. It received a warm welcome from the Emperor.

Now in the twelfth year of which the cyclical position is *chia-wu*,
In a corner of the western seas, in the stagnant waters of a great morass,
Truly was produced at K'i-lin whose shape was high 15 feet,
With the body of a deer and the tail of an ox, and a fleshy boneless horn,
With luminous spots like a red cloud or a purple mist.
Its hoofs do not tread on (living) beings and in its wanderings it carefully selects its ground,
It walks in stately fashion and in its every motion it observes a rhythm,
Its harmonious voice sounds like a bell or a musical tube.
Gentle (仁) is this animal that in all antiquity has been seen but once,
The manifestation of its divine spirit rises up to Heaven's abode.
Ministers and people gathering to behold it vie in being the first to see the joyful spectacle,
As when the Phœnix of Ch'i sang in Chou or the Chart from the River was presented to (the Emperor) Yü.
The hundred myriads this year are united and observe the same rules of conduct.
Your servant on duty in the Forest of Letters, cherishing the presumptuous ambition to record this,
Has intoned this poem in order to present a hymn of praise to the Sacred Ruler.

Composed by Your servant, Shên Tu, *Shih-chiang-hsüeh-shih, Feng-hsün-ta-fu* of the Han-lin-yüan.

Thus it happened that the giraffe from the African wilderness, as it strode into the Emperor's Court, became the emblem of Perfect Virtue, Perfect Government, and Perfect Harmony in the Empire and in the Universe. Rarely have such extravagant cosmic claims been made in such refined language for any living animal.

China's Discovery of Africa J. J. L. Duyvendak.

On 8 July 1497 a fleet of four Portuguese vessels under the command of Vasco da Gama put to sea from the mouth of the Tagus river. Each of the largest pair had a displacement of only 250 to 300 tonnes. The total crew comprised 148 seamen plus twelve convicts to be used for missions of the greatest danger. Da Gama's small fleet sailed without mishap across the south Atlantic, rounded the Cape of Good Hope and made their first contact with the Moors (Arabs) at Mozambique, where they were provided with pilots. Arrived at the outer roadsteads of Mombasa, the inhabitants at first appeared to be friendly.

On Palm Sunday [8 April 1498] the King of Mombaça sent the captain-major a sheep and large quantities of oranges, lemons and sugar-cane, together with a ring, as a pledge of safety, letting him know that in case of his entering the port he would be supplied with all he stood in need of. This present was conveyed to us by two men, almost white, who said they were Christians, which appeared to be the fact. The captain-major sent the king a string of coral-beads as a return present, and let him know that he purposed entering the port on the following day. On the same day the captain-major's vessel was visited by four Moors of distinction.

Two men were sent by the captain-major to the king, still further to confirm these peaceful assurances. When these landed they were followed by a crowd as far as the gates of the palace. Before reaching the king they passed through four doors, each guarded by a doorkeeper with a drawn cutlass. The king received them hospitably, and ordered that they should be shown over the city. They stopped on their way at the house of two Christian merchants, who showed them a paper (carta), an object of their adoration, on which was a sketch of the Holy Ghost.* When they had seen all, the king sent them back with samples of cloves, pepper and corn,† with which articles he would allow us to load our ships.

On Tuesday [10 April], when weighing anchor to enter the port, the captain-major's vessel would not pay off, and struck the vessel which followed astern. We therefore again cast anchor. When the Moors who were in our ship saw that we did not go on, they scrambled into a *zavra* attached to our stern; whilst the two pilots whom we had brought from Moçambique jumped into the water, and were picked up by the men in the *zavra*. At night the captain-major "questioned" two Moors (from Moçambique) whom we had on board, by dropping boiling oil upon their skin, so that they might confess any treachery intended against us. They said that orders had been given to capture us as soon as we entered the port, and thus to avenge what we had done at Moçambique. And when this torture was being applied a second time, one of the Moors, although his hands were tied, threw himself into the sea, whilst the other did so during the morning watch.

About midnight two *almadias*, with many men in them, approached. The

---

*Burton (*Camoens*, iv, p. 241) suggests that this picture of the Holy Ghost may have been a figure of Kapot-eshwar, the Hindu pigeon-god and goddess, an incarnation of Shiva and his wife, the third person of the Hindu Triad.

†Trigo tremez, corn that ripens in three months. This, according to a note furnished by Sir John Kirk, would be sorghum.

almadias stood off whilst the men entered the water, some swimming in the direction of the *Berrio*, others in that of the *Raphael*. Those who swam to the *Berrio* began to cut the cable. The men on watch thought at first that they were tunny fish, but when they perceived their mistake they shouted to the other vessels. The other swimmers had already got hold of the rigging of the mizzen-mast. Seeing themselves discovered, they silently slipped down and fled. These and other wicked tricks were practised upon us by these dogs, but our Lord did not allow them to succeed, because they were unbelievers.

A Journal of the First Voyage of Vasco da Gama trans. E. G. Ravenstein.

The Portuguese poet Camoens (1524–1580), who was born in Lisbon in the year of da Gama's death, took a more romantic view of these confused events. Luckily the goddess Dione, daughter of Oceanus and mother of Aphrodite, had taken the bold navigators under her wing; she flew like an arrow to their assistance and summoned reinforcements from the deep.

> She calls together Nereus' snowy daughters,
> With all the azure Flock that haunts the deeps;
> (For, being born from the salt-sea, the Waters
> In her obedience as their Queen she keeps)
> And, telling them the Cause that hither brought her,
> With all in squadrons to that part she sweeps
>   Where the ships are, to warn them come no nigh,
>   Or they shall perish fundamentally.

> Now through the ocean in great haste they flunder,
> Raising the white foam with their silver Tayles.
> Cloto with bosom breaks the waves in sunder,
> And, with more fury than of custom, sayles;
> Nise runs up an end, Nerine (the younger)
> Leaps o'er them; frizled with her touching Scales,
>   The crooked Billows (yielding) make a lane
>   For the fear'd nymphs to post it through the Maine.

> Upon a Triton's back, with kindled Face,
> The beautious Ericyna furious rode.
> He, to whose fortune fell so great a grace,
> Feels not the rider, proud of his fair load.
> Now they were almost come upon the place
> Where a stiff gale the warlike Navy blow'd.
>   Here they divide, and in an instant cast
>   Themselves upon the Ships advancing fast.

The Goddess, with a party of the rest,
Lays herself plum against the Admiral's Prow,
Stopping her progress with such main contest
That the swol'n sail the wind in vain doth blow.
To the hard Oak she rivets her soft Breast,
Forcing the strong Ship back again to go.
    Others (beleaguring) lift it from the Wave,
    It from the bar of enemies to save.

As to their store-house when the Housewife Ants,
Carrying the unequal Burthens plac't with flight
To their small shoulders (lest cold Winter's wants
Surprise them helpless) exercise their might;
This tugs, that shoves, one runs, another pants;
Strength far above their size, they all unite;
    So toil the Nymphs, to snatch and to defend
    The men of Lusus from a dismal end.

Confused and alarmed by these supernatural events, the Muslims who had clambered on board da Gama's vessels panicked, flung themselves overboard and swam ashore. So da Gama's fleet was saved.

O great, undreampt of, strange deliverance!
O miracle most clear and evident!
O fraud discovered by blind Ignorance!
O faithless Foes, and Men devilishly bent!
What care, what Wisdom, is of sufficience
The stroke of Secret mischief to prevent,
    Unless the Sov'raign Guardian from on high
    Supply the strength of frail Humanity?
        From *Lusiads* Luis de Camoens (trans. Richard Fanshawe).

At Malindi, Mombasa's rival, da Gama received a much more amicable welcome.

The king wore a robe (royal cloak) of damask trimmed with green satin, and a rich *touca* (turban). He was seated on two cushioned chairs of bronze, beneath a round sunshade of crimson satin attached to a pole. An old man, who attended him as a page, carried a short sword in a silver sheath. There were many players on *anafils*, and two trumpets of ivory, richly carved, and of the size of a man, which were blown from a hole in the side, and made sweet harmony with the *anafils*.

On Thursday (19 April) the captain-major and Nicolau Coelho rowed along the front of the town, bombards having been placed in the poops of their long-boats. Many people were along the shore, and among them two horsemen, who appeared to take much delight in a sham fight. The king was carried in a palanquin from the stone steps of his palace to the side of the captain-major's boats. He again begged the captain to come ashore, as he had a helpless father who wanted to see him, and that he and his sons would go on board the ships as hostages. The captain, however, excused himself. . . .

On the following Sunday, 22 April, the king's *zavra* brought on board one of his confidential servants, and as two days had passed without any visitors, the captain-major had this man seized, and sent word to the king that he required the pilots whom he had promised. The king, when he received this message, sent a Christian pilot, and the captain-major allowed the gentleman, whom he had retained in his vessel, to go away.

We were much pleased with the Christian pilot whom the king had sent us. We learnt from him that the island of which we heard at Moçambique as being inhabited by Christians was in reality an island subject to this same King of Moçambique; that half of it belonged to the Moors and the other half to the Christians; that many pearls were to be found there, and that it was called Quylee [Kilwa]. This is the island the Moorish pilots wanted to take us to, and we also wished to go there, for we believed that what they said was true.

The town of Malindi lies in a bay and extends along the shore. It may be likened to Alcouchette [a town on the Tagus above Lisbon]. Its houses are lofty and well whitewashed, and have many windows; on the land side are palm-groves, and all around it maize and vegetables are being cultivated.

A Journal of the First Voyage of Vasco da Gama trans. E. G. Ravenstein.

Da Gama's fleet sailed on to Calicut in India but had to leave precipitately, pursued by many small boats. On the return voyage the crew were so afflicted by scurvy that "their gums grew over their teeth so that they could not eat", and thirty men died. "We had come to such a pass that all bonds of discipline had gone".

On 7 January 1499 the ships once more anchored off Malindi and were hospitably received with the customary gifts of goats and fruit. Assurances of friendship were once more exchanged between the King and Vasco da Gama. The crews had the opportunity of recuperating on a diet of fruit, fowls and eggs, which were brought to the ships in large quantities for barter. Seven of them were unable to make up in time the privations they had suffered in the last few months and they died in Malindi. In accordance with Vasco da Gama's wish, the King consented to the erection of a heraldic pillar, the usual memorial put up on the Portuguese voyages of discovery. It was dedicated to the Holy Ghost. Today there still stands, on a small promontory near the sea close to and southwards of Malindi, an old grey conical pillar, built of coral rock and surmounted by a cross bearing the Portuguese coat of arms. This can scarcely be that erected on the original voyage, but will be one put up by the Portuguese of a later century on the same spot as a replacement of the original, for the position corresponds to that of the earliest descriptions. The pillar is therefore rightly marked on modern charts as the "Vasco da Gama Pillar" – a visible reminder of the original voyage of discovery.

The Portuguese Period in East Africa Justus Strandes.

The homeward voyage was beset by troubles but, on 20 August 1499, da Gama saw his native land again. Of the 160 men who had set out, only 55 returned. The Portuguese continued to rule the coastal cities, uneasily, for the next two hundred years. After their expulsion by the Arabs in 1729, the powerful el-Mazrui clan governed Mombasa island, nominally on behalf of their overlord in Oman, the Imam of Muscat. In 1815 the current el-Mazrui governor sent a defiant message to the Imam, and appealed to the British governor in Bombay for protection against anticipated reprisals. His appeal was twice rejected. Thereupon the Mazrui stitched up a British flag of their own. Two British warships, HMS Barracouta and HMS Leven, were cruising along the coast on survey duties. Captain William Owen of HMS Leven was imbued with a crusading passion to extirpate the "hell-born traffic in slaves". When, on 8 February 1824, HMS Leven put into Mombasa harbour, the Mazrui's homemade Union Jack was flying over Fort Jesus.

Lieutenant Reitz immediately went on shore with the interpreter, and was saluted on landing with five guns; but shortly returned with a son of the sheikh's, who informed us of the Imam's endeavours to subjugate them, and their exertions to defend their liberty and rights which they had so long been fighting for. He stated that they had now collected twenty-five thousand men, but, having no ships, they feared that they could not succeed without the assistance of the English. In fact, he recapitulated all the arguments before used to Captain Vidal, and concluded by requesting Captain Owen's permission to place themselves under the British Government and hoist the English colours. . . .

The following morning, Captain Owen went on shore, when he was met by the chiefs who conducted him to a room in the castle, where the members of the council were assembled to receive him. They acknowledged having hoisted the English colours without any authority, but unanimously craved permission to place the whole country under the protection of the British nation. Captain Owen informed them that, provided they would consent to the abolition of the slave trade, he would transmit their proposal to his government for their decision, and that he would have no objections to hold the place in the meantime. To these conditions they readily assented, and made a formal cession of their island, that of Pemba, and the country from Malindi to Pangani. Our third lieutenant, Mr John James Reitz, was made commandant, and Mr George Phillips (midshipman) a corporal of marines, and three seamen were appointed to remain with him until further instructions should be received.

Narrative of Voyages to Explore the Shores of Africa, Arabia and Madagascar performed in HM ships Leven and Barracouta under the direction of Captain W. F. W. Owen, RN, London 1833. From The British in Mombasa 1824–1826 Sir John Gray.

Lieutenant John James Reitz was twenty-three when the governorship of Mombasa, Pemba and the coast from Malindi to Pangani devolved upon him. Four months later he died "in a most awful state of delirium". His replacement, Acting Lieutenant James Emery, governed Mombasa for nearly two years and survived. Meanwhile, "a voluminous and prolonged discussion" between London, Muscat and Bombay ended in the arrival at Mombasa of HMS Helicon; on 26 July 1826 the British flag was hauled down over Fort Jesus and Lieutenant Emery with his small garrison and some liberated slaves sailed away, leaving the people of Mombasa to their fate. For the Mazrui clan, it was a grim one; its leaders were either thrown overboard to drown or starved to death in prison in Oman. The export of slaves from the interior continued for another seventy years until the declaration of the second, this time official, British Protectorate in 1895.

In spite of edicts of the Sultan of Zanzibar, legal orders promulgated by the Chartered Co., and also of every effort made by the Naval squadron to crush slavery, it died slowly, and if the mango trees sheltering the little Arab settlements hidden away up the tidal creeks on the East Coast could speak, they would have some curious tales to tell of dhows creeping out to sea in the dead of night, laden with human freight and bound for Arabia . . .

Kenya: From Chartered Company to Crown Colony C. W. Hobley.

It has been estimated that twenty thousand to thirty thousand slaves were exported annually from the Sultan of Oman's East African dominions. They were the survivors of the many more who had started on their via dolorosa from the interior.

Johann Ludwig Krapf, a German pastor in the employ of Britain's Church Missionary Society, arrived in Mombasa in March 1844 hoping to start a mission to the Galla people inland. Within three months he was prostrated by fever which carried off his wife and new-born daughter. He was joined by Johann Rebmann and the two missionaries established a base at Rabai near Mombasa. In 1848 both men set out to explore inland with a view to opening mission stations, Krapf to the country of the Wakamba, and Rebmann to that of the Chagga. Rebmann took only nine porters, and on 11 May

In the midst of a great wilderness, full of wild beasts, such as rhinoceroses, buffaloes, and elephants, we slept beneath thorn-bushes, quietly and securely under God's gracious protection! This morning we discerned the mountains of Jagga more distinctly than ever; and about ten o'clock, I fancied I saw the summit of one of them covered with a dazzlingly white cloud. My guide called the white which I saw, merely "Beredi", cold; it was perfectly clear to me, however, that it could be nothing else but snow. Resting for a while soon afterwards under a tree, I read in the English Bible the 111th Psalm, to which I came in the order of my reading. The promise made a lasting impression upon me, in sight of the magnificent snow-mountain; for the sixth verse expresses so majestically and clearly that of which I had only noted down the presentiment in my journal on Saturday last.* . . .

The wounds on my feet prevented me from leaving my hut until the 20th of May. The king's vizier and other chief men of the land visited me several times almost every day. On the 14th I was asked by some of them, with the aid of what weapons I had come thither? To which my guide at once replied, that I had nothing with me but my umbrella; but I added, pointing to Heaven, that "I had come, trusting in God, the Christians' 'Eruwa', alone!"† They rejoined: "In Eruwa alone!" "Yes," I said, "for He alone is all and everything, and wild beasts, as well as wicked men, are in His hand." They could scarcely believe, much less understand, how I could have made so long a journey without spear and shield, or without the use of powerful enchantments.

Travels, Researches and Missionary Labours Johann Ludwig Krapf.

On 11 July 1849 Krapf left Rabai with a few Wanika porters and his trusty umbrella intending to start a mission to the Wakamba. He camped near the village of a friendly chief called Kivoi, where he heard news of another snow-capped mountain unknown to the rest of the world. The missionaries' reports of snow on the equator was greeted with scepticism in London.

With respect to those eternal snows on the discovery of which Messrs Krapf and Rebmann have set their hearts, they have so little of shape or substance, and appear so severed from realities, that they take quite a spectral character. No one has yet witnessed their eternity; dogmatic assertion proves nothing; of reasonable evidence of perpetual snow there is not a tittle offered.

W. D. Cooley, *Inner Africa Laid Open*, (1852). From *East Africa Through Contemporary Records* Zoë Marsh.

Krapf's entry in his diary for 10 November 1849 disposed of Mr Cooley's arguments.

This morning we had a beautiful distant view of the snow-mountain, Kiliman-

---

* "He hath shewed his people the power of his works, that he may give them the heritage of the heathen."

† All the time of my residence in Jagga it rained in torrents almost every night, on which account the sun is welcome to the inhabitants, and is their god; − Eruwa = sun, heaven, god.

jaro, in Jagga. It was high above Endara and Bura, yet even at this distance I could discern that its white crown must be snow. All the arguments which Mr Cooley has adduced against the existence of such a snow-mountain, and against the accuracy of Rebmann's report, dwindle into nothing when one has the evidence of one's own eyes of the fact before one; so that they are scarcely worth refuting.

Krapf confirmed his sighting of Mount Kenya less than a month later.

However, it happened that on leaving Kitui on the 3rd of December, 1849 I could see the Kegnia most distinctly, and observed two large horns or pillars, as it were, rising over an enormous mountain to the north-west of the Kilimanjaro, covered with a white substance.

Travels, Researches and Missionary Labours Johann Ludwig Krapf.

Kivoi invited Krapf to accompany him, together with a party of Kivoi's wives, attendants and slaves, to the upper reaches of the Tana River to recover some ivory he had stored there. After irritating delays caused by Kivoi's search first for the missing handle of Krapf's umbrella and then for some ostrich feathers,

Kivoi's slaves on a sudden pointed towards the forest towards which we were marching from the grassy and treeless plain. I ran to Kivoi's side, and saw a party of about ten men emerging from the forest, and soon afterwards came other and larger parties from another side, evidently with the object of surrounding us. Our whole caravan was panic-stricken, and the cry, "Meida", they are robbers, ran through our ranks, upon which Kivoi fired off his gun, and bade me do the same. After we had fired thrice the robbers began to relax their pace, probably because they had heard the whistling of our bullets through the air. In the confusion and the hurry of loading I had left my ramrod in the barrel of my gun and fired it off, so that I could not load again. Whilst we were firing and our caravan was preparing for a conflict, Kivoi ordered one of his wives to open my umbrella, when the robbers immediately slackened their speed. They were also obstructed by the grass, which Kivoi had set on fire that the wind might blow the flames in their faces. . . . A great confusion arose; our people threw away their burdens, and discharged their arrows at the enemy, begging me imploringly to fire as quickly as I could. I fired twice, but in the air; for I could not bring myself to shed the blood of man. Whilst I was reloading a Mkamba rushed past me wounded in the hip, a stream of blood flowing from him. Right and left fell the arrows at my feet, but without touching me. When our people saw that they could not cope with an enemy 120 strong they took to flight. Rumu wa Kikandi and his people ran away and left me quite alone.

I deemed it now time to think of flight . . .

Krapf, now quite alone, without sustenance or means of defence – he had stopped the barrels of his gun with strips of torn trouser-leg and filled them with water – had to make his way through unknown and dangerous country to Kivoi's, knowing that the chief was almost certainly dead.

I wended on my way through thick and thin, often tumbling into little pits, or over stones and trunks of trees; but the thorns and the tall grass impeded me most of all, and I was troubled, too, by thoughts of the many wild beasts known to be in the neighbourhood of the Dana (Tana). I was so impeded and wearied by the tall grass that I determined to lie down and sleep, even if I were to die here in the wilderness; for it seemed as if I never should reach the coast again; but then I thought, straightway, that in no situation should man despair, but do the utmost for self-preservation and put his trust in God as to the issue. I called to mind Mungo Park who had been in a similar strait in Western Africa. So, taking courage I marched forward again as swiftly as I could, and in due course emerged from the jungle and reached the great plain in which Kivoi had set fire to the grass. I now felt in better spirits, as I could proceed more quickly and with fewer obstructions. About midnight I came to a mountain which we had noticed in the course of our journey hither. As it had no name, I called it Mount William, in memory of the audience granted me in 1850, by his Majesty Frederick William IV of Prussia. This mountain commands a view of the whole region of the Dana, and serves as a landmark for the caravans which journey towards Ukambani, or towards Kikuyu and Mberre. Believing myself on the right track, I lay down behind a bush; for I was so wearied out that I could scarcely keep my feet, and for protection against the keen wind which blew over the plain, I cut some dry grass and spread it over and under my body. . . . After I had started again, I felt the pangs of hunger and thirst; the water in my telescope-case had run out, and that in the barrels of my gun which I had not drunk, had been lost on my way to Mount William, as the bushes had torn out the grass stoppers, and so I lost a portion of the invaluable fluid which, in spite of the gunpowder-flavour imparted to it by the barrels, thirst had rendered delicious. My hunger was so great that I tried to chew leaves, roots, and elephant's excrement to stay it, and when day broke to break my fast on ants. The roar of a lion would have been music in my ears, trusting he would provide me with a meal. A little before daybreak I did hear a lion roar, and immediately afterwards the cry of an animal which, however, soon ceased; for no doubt, the lion had seized his prey; but the direction from which the cry came was too distant for me to risk leaving my route and to descend into the plain.

Travels, Researches and Missionary Labours Johann Ludwig Krapf.

Krapf reached Kivoi's territory more dead than alive, only to be accused of failing to protect the chief who had, indeed, been killed. Escaping from his captors, he struggled on by night, hiding by day and sustained by sugar cane taken from the shambas, to reach the remnants of his caravan and his half-starved Wanika porters. Another three hundred painful miles separated them from Rabai, which they reached on 28 September 1851. Broken in health, Krapf left Mombasa in 1853 but returned to Abyssinia, to be finally forced by sickness and exhaustion to retire to Stuttgart, where he died in 1881.

It fell to Joseph Thomson, fifth son of a Scottish stonemason, to open a route across the highlands of the future Kenya, hitherto barred to travellers by Maasai warriors. In March 1883, aged twenty-five, he left Mombasa with a caravan of 140 porters accompanied by James Martin, born Antonio Martini, a Maltese sail-maker, and sponsored by the Royal Geographical Society. Their first encounter with the Maasai soon followed.

The news of our arrival soon spread. The Masai men and women began to crowd into camp, and we mutually surveyed each other with equal interest. The women had all the style of the men. With slender, well-shaped figures, they had brilliant dark eyes, Mongolian in type, narrow, and with an upward slant. Their expression was distinctly lady-like (for natives), and betrayed their ideas in more ways than one. Obviously they felt that they were a superior race, and that all others were but as slaves before them. . . .

Tents having been pitched, and goods stacked, properly covered from peering eyes, and surrounded with a strong guard, the more serious business of the day commenced. Wire, beads, and cloth were taken into the tent, so that we might prepare to dole out the black mail – the "chango" of this district, the "hongo" of the region further south. We had not long to wait. A war-chant was heard in the distance, and soon a party of El-moran, in all the unctuous glory of a new plastering of grease and red clay, appeared, marching in single file, and keeping step to their song, their murderous spears gleaming in the sun as they gave them now and then a rotatory movement. They carried their heavy shields by their side, on which was seen the newly-painted heraldic device of their particular clan. As they neared our camp they halted, and proceeded to go through a variety of evolutions distinctly military. This finished, Muhinna advanced, and held a consultation with them in the decorous manner already described.

This conversation settled the amount we were required to pay. For each party (and there were six of them) we had to make up six senengè (a senengè is a coil of twenty rings of iron wire about fifteen inches in diameter, which forms one leg ornament when coiled round from ankle to knee), five cloths (naiberès), thirty iron chains, and one hundred strings of beads. The scene that ensued on the division of the spoil was more after my preconceived notion of their ways, but was not encouraging. The El-moran, having laid aside their spears and shields, stand ready in a hollow group. My men, advancing with the hongo, suddenly throw it into the midst, and run for their lives out of the way. With a grand yell the warriors precipitate themselves upon the articles, on the principle of "every one for himself and the devil take the hindmost". A few of the boldest get the lion's share. In some cases two have seized the same article. It may be a bunch of beads, and the matter is settled by the strings being torn in twain, each one carrying off a handful, leaving a large number strewed on the ground. If, however, the disputants have seized a senengè, then the matter becomes more serious. They rave and tear like a couple of dogs over a bone, and if somewhat equally matched the blood gets heated and simès are drawn, or knobkerries wielded. Two men thus received some very ugly flesh-wounds, which, however, did not draw forth any comment from the on-lookers. A pack of half-starved wolves suddenly let loose on small animals could not have made a more ferocious and repulsive exhibition.

Party after party, each from its own district, arrived and received this tribute, and my spirits sank as I saw load after load disappear. How could we ever hope to travel many days further, if such was to be our fate? Then the El-morūū (or married men) had to receive their share, which was much smaller and more peacefully divided. Finally the important Lybons (medicine-men), Lengobè, Mbaratien, and Lambarsacout, had also to be attended to individually.

Towards evening the camp was crowded, and in response to repeated cries for the white Lybon, backed up by insolent attempts to tear open the door of my tent, I had to step out and bow my acknowledgments, though inwardly muttering maledictions upon them, as I was still weak, ill, and irritable from the repeated attacks of fever, the effects of which still hung about me. Submitting to the inevitable, I sat down on a box, the cynosure of every eye. They had now lost their calm and dignified bearing, and had become rude and obtrusive; the Ditto (young unmarried women) being the most insolent, and not showing the slightest trace of fear.

For some time I endured with patience their annoying attentions, let them touch me on the face, feel my hair, push up the sleeve of my coat, and examine with intense curiosity my boots. At last, however, growing bilious and irritable, especially at the repeated attempts of one ferocious-looking warrior to turn up my trousers to see the natural integument below, I gave him a push with my foot. With fury blazing in his face, and presenting the most diabolical aspect, he sprang back a few steps, drew his simè, and was about to launch himself upon me. I slipped aside, however, and was speedily surrounded by the guard, while some of the El-morūū laid hold of him, and, as he would not be pacified, led him away.

Matters were further enlivened by a Masai picking up an axe in the centre of the camp, and clearing off with it. This caused a dangerous rush, which, being misunderstood, made my men seize their guns. A very slight accident would have caused bloodshed and a general fight at this moment, but I contrived to yell out to them in time not to fire; and so ended the events of the day, the summing up of which did not increase my cheerfulness, though I was of too sanguine a temperament to despair.

Through Masai Land Joseph Thomson.

On the last day of 1883 Thomson was severely gored by a wounded buffalo. He was carried on a stretcher to a bleak camp at an altitude of nearly 9,000 feet above Kijabe, where he nearly succumbed to dysentery and bouts of delirium lasting six weeks. He was rescued by a friendly Swahili trader, gradually recovered in Ukambani, and on 25 May 1884, less than fifteen months after he set out, reached his starting point after a journey of nearly 3,000 miles during which, in the words of the Dictionary of National Biography, he had "passed through the midst of the most ferocious of African tribes when their hostility to the white man was at fever heat without firing a shot in self-defence or leaving anywhere a needless grave". Thomson led three more African expeditions before he died, aged thirty-seven, in 1895.

In 1884 a well-to-do young Yorkshireman, Frederick Jackson, arrived in Lamu on a shooting and collecting expedition. Five years later he joined the service of the newly formed Imperial British East Africa Company and, proceeding inland with a large caravan, saw for himself the devastation caused by slavers in the Lake Victoria basin.

We had traversed the habitable part of Ketosh (in West Kenya) on the third day. Numerous ruined, burned and abandoned villages bore testimony to the handiwork and treachery of the Mombasa slaver, Abdulla bin Hamid, and that prince of rogues, fat Sudi of Pangani. The gateways of every inhabited village we passed were strongly barricaded, and the heads of the few natives, as they peeped out at us over the walls, and small columns of smoke were the only evidence of their being occupied; inside them all was silence. . . .

It would appear that for many years past Ketosh had been the happy hunting-ground of the Swahili and Arab traders, particularly on those occasions when they arrived from Karamojo, via Baringo, after an unsuccessful quest for ivory and with plenty of trade goods on hand; or when the easy acquisition of a batch of slaves was too tempting to forego on their leaving Mumia's on their way coastwards. In either case their tactics were the same. Knowing full well that the various sections or clans were at loggerheads with one another, and it being their policy to widen any breach between them and prevent any form of cohesion, it was easy enough for experts in unctuous flattery and pretended friendship to hoodwink and lull such simple, naturally confiding and friendly savages into a sense of security and readiness to believe anything.

Having arrived at a village, and after accepting the proffered hospitality of a portion of it, the black-hearted ruffians would in due course announce that they required a large stock of food for their coastward journey, and that they were prepared to pay double the market price in order to obtain it quickly. That ruse, of course, attracted women and children from far and wide.

In the meantime, as a further blind, it was necessary for them to move camp outside the village and make a *boma* in order to collect the porters and prevent them from stowing themselves away on the day of their departure. When that tragic day arrived, the women and children were seized and any man who offered resistance was shot.

Early Days in East Africa Frederick Jackson.

Old Kitale.

On reaching Quitale [Kitale] I was delighted to find the remains of the double stockade which encircled the slave market, an area of about 4 acres on a slight rise, with open ground for about 200 yards on all sides and a glorious view of Mount Elgon to the west and of the Cherangani hills to the east. Old Mbarak became quite excited when he found himself back in his old haunts and took me round the stockade, explaining what went on in every corner of the camp. The main gate was on the south of the stockade, the latter being made of solid wooden uprights woven together with thorn and smaller branches. Much of it had decayed or had been burned, but several reaches were in almost perfect condition. Mbarak showed me where the Arabs slept, near the entrance, where the girls were kept, where the boys were kept and where they were castrated, and where the men were kept constantly shackled in eights to a heavy log by iron chains. I shuddered to think of the cruelty which must have gone on here; young children raped, boys castrated and left to recover without antiseptics, and the men bundled down to the coast under cruel conditions and simply shot if exhausted. . . . (I again visited this place, now Kitale, in 1956; so far as I can recollect, the present club is on the site of the old slave mart, but all traces of it have disappeared). . . .

Old Mbarak came round to my house this evening after supper. I gave him a sheep, for which he was most grateful. I tried to get more information from him about the Quitale slave market. I tried to find out how the slaves were taken to the coast, their casualties and the route taken, but he remembered very little. The only definite statements he made were that the castrated boys were the best looked after as they were the most valuable, but that over fifty per cent died before reaching the coast; the girls were not shackled but went free and were raped at night and all through the day whenever the caravan halted. About ten per cent of the men died from fatigue and under-nourishment; if a man showed fatigue he was shot and left. . . .

I asked him if he enjoyed it all. He said: "Plenty food, plenty women; very lovely!"

Kenya Diary 1902–1906 Richard Meinertzhagen.

At the end of 1886 a wealthy Hungarian nobleman, Count Samuel Teleki von Szek, together with Lieutenant Ludwig von Höhnel, fitted out a large caravan to explore a distant region where a large lake was rumoured to exist. They took an iron boat to launch upon its waters, 285 porters, 9 askaris, 9 guides and a monkey called Hamis. Setting forth from Pangani in January 1887, they passed with little trouble through Maasailand, but when they reached Kikuyu country were attacked by an estimated 2,000 warriors armed with bows and arrows. The Kikuyu refused to sell them any food, and when they reached Njemps (on Lake Baringo) they found that crops had failed and the people were starving. After "terrible privations" and deaths among the porters they reached their goal.

All of a sudden, as we were climbing a gentle slope, such a grand, beautiful, and far-stretching scene was spread out before us, that at first we felt we must be under some delusion and were disposed to think the whole thing a mere phantasmagoria. As we got higher up, a single peak gradually rose before us, the gentle contours rising symmetrically from every side, resolving themselves into one broad pyramidal mountain, which we knew at once to be a volcano. A moment before we had been gazing into empty space, and now here was a mighty mountain mass looming up before us, on the summit of which we almost involuntarily looked for snow. This was, however, only the result of an optical delusion caused by the suddenness with which the mountain had come in sight, and from the fact that the land sank rapidly on either side of it whilst we were gazing up at it from a considerable height. On the east of the mountain the land was uniformly flat, a golden plain lit up by sunshine, whilst on the east the base of the volcano seemed to rise up out of a bottomless depth, a void which was altogether a mystery to us. We hurried as fast as we could to the top of our ridge, the scene gradually developing itself as we advanced, until an entirely new world was spread out before our astonished eyes. The void down in the depths beneath became filled as if by magic with picturesque mountains and rugged slopes, with a medley of ravines and valleys, which appeared to be closing up from every side to form a fitting frame for the dark-blue gleaming surface of the lake stretching away beyond as far as the eye could reach.

For a long time we gazed in speechless delight, spell-bound by the beauty of the scene before us, whilst our men, equally silent, stared into the distance for a few minutes, to break presently into shouts of astonishment at the sight of the glittering expanse of the great lake which melted on the horizon into the blue of the sky. At that moment all our dangers, all our fatigues were forgotten in the joy of finding our exploring expedition crowned with success at last. Full of enthusiasm and gratefully remembering the gracious interest taken in our plans from the first by his Royal and Imperial Highness, Prince Rudolf of Austria, Count Teleki named the sheet of water, set like a pearl of great price in the wonderful landscape beneath us, Lake Rudolf. . . .

"Into what a desert had we been betrayed!"

The next day we resumed our march to the lake. Leader and men were alike in capital spirits, as was fitting on a fête day, for a fête day 6 March 1888 must certainly be for us. With a cheery "Haya puani!" ("Off to the beach") Count Teleki had chased his staff that morning: and with the eager shout from a hundred voices, "Haya puani", we should all certainly have rushed to the lake then and there, if the character of the country through which we had to pass had not been so bad. The mountain district between us and the lake was, in fact, a veritable hell, consisting of a series of parallel heights, running from north to south, which we had to cut across in a north-westerly direction. The slopes of these mountains were steep precipices, most of them quite insurmountable, and those that were not were strewn with blackish-brown blocks of rock or of loose sharp-edged scoriae. The narrow valleys were encumbered with stones or debris, or with deep loose sand in which our feet sunk, making progress difficult. And when the sun rose higher, its rays were reflected from the smooth brownish-black surface of the rock, causing an almost intolerable glare, whilst a burning wind from the south whirled the sand in our faces, and almost blew the loads off the heads of the men.

Almost at our last gasp, we hastened on towards the slightly rippled sheet of water – the one bit of brightness in a gloomy scene. Another hour of tramping through sand or over stony flats, and we were at the shore of the lake. Although utterly exhausted, after the seven hours' march in the intense and parching heat, we felt our spirits rise once more as we stood upon the beach at last, and saw the beautiful water, clear as crystal, stretching away before us. The men rushed down shouting, to plunge into the lake: but soon returned in bitter disappointment: the water was brackish!

This fresh defeat of all our expectations was like a revelation to us: and like some threatening spectre rose up before our minds the full significance of the utterly barren, dreary nature of the lake district. Into what a desert had we been betrayed! A few scattered tufts of fine stiff grass rising up in melancholy fashion near the shore, from the wide stretches of sand, were the only bits of green, the only signs of life of any kind. Here and there, some partly in the water, some on the beach, rose up isolated skeleton trees, stretching up their bare sun-bleached branches to the pitiless sky. No living creature shared the gloomy solitude with us: and far as our glass could reach there was nothing to be seen but desert – desert everywhere. To all this was added the scorching heat, and the ceaseless buffeting of the sand-laden wind, against which we were powerless to protect ourselves upon the beach, which offered not a scrap of shelter, whilst the pitching of the tents in the loose sand was quite impossible.

We now realized to the full that the lake districts were uninhabited, and terrible forebodings assailed us of days of hunger and thirst, when we remembered that the same conditions were pretty sure to prevail till we reached Reshiat. We had provisions for ten days only: and when we subjected Lembasso [the guide] to a searching cross-examination as to how we could improve our position, and how long it would take us to get to this Reshiat, his unchanging reply was fifteen days. He also said that Mount Kulall was inhabited, but that the people there were themselves suffering from famine, and that the wretched Elmolo, living by the lake, supported themselves entirely by fishing.

Fishing! We had never thought of that: and immediately lines and rods of every size and variety were got out and distributed to the men. But hour after hour passed by, and nothing was caught.

Throughout this terrible day one trouble, one disappointment succeeded another, until at last the sun went down, when our position became a little more tolerable. The parching heat was replaced by a tepid coolness: the wind blew less strongly, and finally sunk altogether, whilst the sand-storms ceased. A bath in the clear lake refreshed us, and later we actually managed to quench our burning thirst with its water. From the first it had struck us that this water had a quite peculiar lye-like taste. We concluded that it contained soda, which proved correct, for when we poured tartaric acid into some of it, it effervesced strongly. This improved the taste considerably, and it quenched our thirst more quickly than fresh water would have done.

Sunset was succeeded by a beautiful night: the canopy of heaven was spread out clear and bright above our heads, gleaming with twinkling stars, and the veil of night hid the dreary surroundings from our sight. Our men began to pick up heart again, and sat chatting or cooking round their fires, whilst we discussed the chances of the future with Jumbe Kimemeta and Lembasso.

The Discovery of Lakes Rudolf and Stefanie (Vol. II) Ludwig von Höhnel.

The expedition's privations on the outward journey were as nothing compared with those on the way back. Many of the porters perished, and everyone was starving half-way to death until Teleki authorized a raid to seize livestock which the Pokot had refused to sell. The corpulent Teleki shed ninety-seven pounds. Frederick Jackson, who camped next to him at Taveta, gave this unflattering picture of the Count.

He had lost much weight on the march up, something between four and five stone, and had shrunk visibly. He always wore his shirt open to its fullest extent, and he thereby exposed a large fold of loose skin across his chest. Amongst other little fads, he always kept his head shaved, and wore a white *kofia* (hat). He never wore a coat, even at dinner, only a shirt with sleeves folded well above the elbow, and he always smoked a long-stemmed, long-bowled German pipe. From what I saw of him, and subsequently heard of him, he was always calm and collected.

He was certainly very amusing and outspoken, and good company generally. Some of his ideas were quaint, if not actually jarring, others were quite brutal; two examples of the former occur to me. During his stay at Taveta, he rarely went out shooting, as he knew that most of the game near by was fairly wild, and a long crawl was not at all to his liking; furthermore, he was assured of as much as he wanted later on. One day, on his return with two or three heads, I congratulated him, whereupon he remarked, "Ah, I do not consider it good. I shall not be satisfied until I get my *ten pieces* a day"! On another occasion we were dining together and discussing the well-known African travellers, when the subject of some of their misleading statements and exaggerations cropped up, and I ventured to remark, "Well, Count, I hope when you write your book, you will stick to facts," to which he replied, "My dear Mr Jackson, all African travellers are liars; my old friend Burton was a liar, Speke and Grant were liars, Stanley is a liar, we know our friends Thomson and Johnston are liars, and" (with a slight bow, and patting his bare, brick-red chest) "I am going to be a liar. If I do not discover a lake, I shall say I did; if I do not discover a mountain I shall say I did; and who will disprove it, until long after I have received the credit?"

One example of his brutal ideas will suffice, as it would appear to account for many of his actions. On his return after he had discovered both a lake and a mountain, we met at Mombasa on board ship, he on his way to Zanzibar, I on arrival, on appointment to the IBEA Company; and he gave me a short but graphic account of his journey, including the shooting of 35 elephants and 300 'niggers.' When he came to the end of that part where he lost so many of his men from starvation, he said: "It was very bad. You know I do not like the black man, I regard him as one big monkey, but when I did see my men dying on the road, sometimes three or four, sometimes six in a day, then I did begin to pity them"!

Early Days in East Africa Frederick Jackson.

Despite his appalling experiences of African travel, von Höhnel volunteered to accompany a headstrong, twenty-three-year old American, William Astor Chanler, on an expedition to explore unknown territory east of Lake Rudolf (now Turkana). At Hameye on the Tana river their porters rebelled, and Chanler was forced to limit his ambition to finding a lake into which the Guaso Nyiro (now Ewaso Ng'iro) river was said to flow, and to making contact with the Rendile, a people known to Europeans only by repute.

We crossed the Guaso Nyiro the following morning, and marched four miles along the foot of the plateau. Upon reaching its end we made camp, and Lieutenant von Höhnel and I at once ascended it, this time climbing its northern face. We were rewarded by getting a view of the boundless desert, stretched on all sides to the horizon. Across this desert flowed the Guaso Nyiro, enshrouded in dhum palms and acacias.

In the northeast our eyes were greeted by the sight of what appeared to be an enormous sheet of water, distant about thirty miles. Lieutenant von Höhnel and I turned silently to one another, and with deep feeling clasped hands, delighted to think that the stories of the size of the lake had not been exaggerated. I at once set about guessing the number of days required to reach it, and Lieutenant von Höhnel, taking its bearings with his compass, decided and announced that it must be nearly sixty miles in length. . . .

Following the course of the Guaso Nyiro river, they came upon a waterfall which Chanler named after himself.

On this day the members of my caravan presented a most doleful appearance. Lieutenant von Höhnel and I were both stricken with fever; Sururu groaned from the back of my horse; one porter, borne in a hammock by two of his comrades, was dying of dysentery, and one of the Soudanese staggered along with the aid of a stick, his eyes wildly staring, and his lips muttering senseless phrases: he was unconscious from fever. Onward we silently and doggedly pressed. About noon we passed close to a herd of seven elephants, but looked at them with absolute indifference. Our minds were bent upon the single purpose of getting out of this dreadful country, and resting from our labours upon the shores of the lake. The soil was becoming moist under foot, and the grass wore a greener appearance. Where can the lake be? was our thought.

At one o'clock, seeing a tall sycamore tree across the river (at this point not ten yards wide), we stopped the caravan, crossed the stream, and climbed as high as possible up the tree. From this vantage point we took one long look, and then with half-suppressed curses descended to the ground. There is no *Lake* Lorian! It is but a vast swamp, overgrown with papyrus and water-grass. The narrowness and shallowness of the river at this point (it was but a foot deep) proved to us that it could not continue beyond the swamp – at least, in the dry season. Here, then, was the end of high hopes and incessant effort – no lake, no Rendile. The vast sheet of water we had seen from the top of the plateau had been a mirage. We felt that we had been tricked and duped by Nature at every turn. Our feelings of dejection were shared by every member of the caravan. They, too, had lived in glad hopes of reaching the lake. Time and again I had promised them that upon reaching it they should have their fill of camels' milk and goats' flesh. The burden of their muttered and incessant refrain was: "Wapi?" ("Where?") "Wapi bahari? Wapi ngamia? Wapi mbuzi? Wapi maziwa? Hapana kitu hapa! Gehennam tu!" ("Where is the lake? Where are the camels? Where are the goats? Where is the milk? There is not a thing here! It is simply hell!")

Our sympathies were with them, but it was unwise to allow them to remain long in this state; so they were at once set to work getting grass to strew upon the damp ground, while some were sent off in parties to collect what few dried sticks they could find. This work was soon accomplished. Each group of porters had a tiny fire, over which they were able to warm slightly their strips of meat. Lieutenant von Höhnel and I retired to bed, ill with fever. Our spirits were still further depressed by the night's experience; mosquitoes in myriads swarmed about us. Even the thick skins of the negroes were not proof against the attacks of the tiny denizens of the swamp. No one was able to sleep. Curses and impotent yells echoed throughout the camp. Lieutenant von Höhnel and I each had mosquito curtains; which, however, proved of no service as barriers from the pests. Throughout the long night we turned over in our minds but one project – how to get out as quickly as possible from this abode of pestilence and death.

Through Jungle and Desert W. A. Chanler.

Get out they did, and subsequently made contact with the Rendile, nomads owning camels and horses whom Chanler thought might be descended from the Shepherd Kings of Egypt (some had blue eyes). On their return journey von Höhnel was crushed almost to death by a charging rhino. After an agonizing nine weeks carried on a jolting stretcher with suppurating wounds and no drugs, he was operated on by a missionary doctor at Kibwezi and miraculously recovered.

In June 1892 Dr Walter Gregory, a professor of geology, with twelve porters, made a resolute attempt to reach the summit of Mount Kenya.

Through this dark and dismal forest we had to force a way. Occasionally an elephant path would run in our direction, and we could then make comparatively rapid progress. . . . The elephants, however, did not obey the rules of mountaineering, and their tracks soon ran down into valleys, so that most of the way we had to cut a path step by step. Every blow of the matlocks upon the bamboos shook the sodden canopy overhead, and continual shower-baths of water kept us wet and miserable. My clothes were soon soaked through, while the raw, damp cold chilled the porters to the marrow. We had to stop every hour to light fires to warm them, and even then they found the climate almost unbearable, and one or two cried like children. . . .

On the evening of the second day we had to pitch the camp on a slope, where the bamboos were so dense that we had to clear every foot of ground we wanted, while it was so swampy that we had to spread out the bamboos as a platform on which to support the tents. Determined not to lose a moment's time next morning, Omari, Funi and I went ahead at daybreak to cut the path, leaving the porters to follow as soon as it had become less cold. We made a desperate effort to get out of the forests, but when night fell we were still within them, and the bamboos as thick as ever. We were so exhausted that, when the order to camp was given, we all lay down where we stood; and it was not till some time afterwards that we could rouse ourselves to light fires and prepare food. So far the work had been simply miserable. We had not once seen or felt the sun since we left the meadows of Laikipia. We had never once seen more than 20 yards ahead, and it was only rarely that we could see up to the tree tops. The natural history had also been disappointing.

On the fourth day they emerged from the bamboos.

With a cheer we hurried forward. The bamboos became smaller and scarcer, and were soon left behind. The forests gave place to scattered clumps of trees, and the rank undergrowth to a firm rich turf; the long monotonous slope broke up into a belt of undulating ground, which, with its numerous swampy, mossy hollows, its irregularly scattered boulders, and its stiff, greasy clay, reminded me of a glacial moraine. The men threw down their loads and basked in the sunshine, while I examined the sections in the stream banks, and collected the flowers in the meadows.

A hailstorm assailed them on the next stage of their climb, and one of the porters named Wadi Sadi was found to be missing.

I rushed back at once; but as the snow had hidden our trail, I missed it, and had to search for an hour before I found him. He was lying on his load about three hundred feet below the level of the camp; he was covered with snow and nearly frozen to death. A little brandy revived him, but he was too weak to stand. As it was still snowing it would have been useless to have returned for help, for the porters were so cowed that they would have refused to move. I recollected that Wadi weighed less than the burdens some of my men had to bear all day long, so I resolved to carry him. He was able to cling to my back, and slowly, and with many halts, I struggled with him up the slope. If the porter had left his load when he first became too weak to carry it, he could no doubt have walked on with the others. I thought his action in staying out in the snow with it simply Quixotic, and, annoyed at the trouble it had given me, I rather brutally told him next morning that he was a fool. It is a point of honour among Zanzibari never to leave their loads, and I shall not forget the man's reproachful look as he asked, "How could I leave my load without my master's orders to do so?"

Another trait in the Zanzibari character was shown at the same camp. In the morning the men came to tell me that the water they had left in their cooking-pots was all bewitched. They said it was white, and would not shake; the adventurous Fundi had even hit it with a stick, which would not go in. They begged me to look at it, and I told them to bring it to me. They declined, however, to touch it, and implored me to go to it. The water of course had frozen solid. I handled the ice and told the men they were silly to be afraid of it, for this change always came over water on the tops of high mountains. I put one of the pots on the fire, and predicted it would soon turn again into water. The men sat round and anxiously watched it; when it had melted they joyfully told me that the demon was expelled.

Leaving everyone else in camp, Gregory continued upwards with Fundi, who had been on Teleki's expedition, and one of the porters. They bivouacked at the foot of a glacier and Gregory and Fundi continued the climb.

That morning he [Fundi] was weak and ill, but he plodded steadily, though painfully, upward. He had often asked me about the great white fields he had seen with Dachi-tumbo [Teleki] and how bitterly disappointed he had been at not reaching them. He had taken a keen personal interest in this expedition, and his influence with the men had been most useful. I therefore waited for him to pass me, that he might be the first man to set foot on the glaciers of Kenya. He came up, laid his load upon the ground, kicked off his zebra-hide sandals, and mounted upon a boulder. Then, with his hands together before him, he began to pray. I could not understand all he said, but sufficient to know that he thanked Allah for having enabled him to come where neither native nor white man had ever been before, and to stand on the edge of the great white fields he had seen with Dachi-tumbo from afar. He assured Allah that he was now more anxious to return in safety to the coast than he had ever been before, so that he might tell his friends of the wonders he had seen.

After the prayer was over, I told Fundi to go on to the glacier. He went a few steps farther, and then, with a pleading look, said, "No farther, master; it is too white."

There we lighted a fire, and boiled the thermometers, obtaining data which placed the altitude at 15,580 feet. As soon as the instruments had cooled, I prepared to continue the ascent. But Fundi, whose curiosity was now satisfied, begged to be allowed to return. He complained that his head was aching, that his stomach was very bad, that he felt very sick, and that his legs *would* not do what he told them. It was obvious he was suffering from mountain sickness, and it was not fair to take him farther. I therefore added his share of the load of instruments, firewood, and "pitons" (or pegs on which to fasten the rope) to my own, and let him go back. Before doing so, I fear I completely ruined any reputation for sanity I might have had left, by executing a Masai war-dance on the snout of the glacier, and then pelting Fundi with snowballs.

The Great Rift Valley J. W. Gregory.

Eight years later the summit was scaled by Mr (later Sir) Halford Mackinder and his Swiss guides César Ollier and Joseph Brocherel.

At last, on 12 September 1899, César, Joseph, and I left our top camp at noon to make the final attempt to reach the summit. The journey round the peak, made by Hausburg, had clearly shown that no way was practicable up the northern precipice, and we had already failed twice on the southern side, once on rock and once on ice. We now planned a route partly over rock and partly over ice. We followed our first track up and across the Lewis glacier, and up the face of the southern *arête*, near the top of which we spent the night under a Mummery tent. We were up at earliest dawn, and away as soon as the sun rose out of the cloud roof to eastward, thawing our hands so that we could grasp the rocks. A traverse, with steps across the head of the Darwin glacier, brought us to a rocky rib descending from the western corner of Nelion, and up this we crept for a short way. We then decided to cross the glacier which hangs from the Gate of the Mist between the two points, and drains by a couloir into the Darwin glacier below. It proved very steep and intensely hard, so that three hours were consumed in cutting steps on a traverse which we had hoped to make in twenty minutes. A final rock scramble enabled us to set foot on the summit of Batian precisely at noon on 13 September. The view from the Gate of the Mist had been magnificent. At the summit we were a few moments too late, for the mist, driving up, gave only momentary glimpses into the valleys beneath.

The mountain-top is like a stunted tower rising from among ruins and crowned by three or four low turrets, upon which we sat, feet inward. There was no snow there, and the thermometer slung in the air gave a temperature of 40°F, while several kinds of lichen grew on the rocks. We dared, however, stay only forty minutes – time enough to make observations and to photograph – and then had to descend, not from any physical inconvenience due to the elevation, but for fear of the afternoon storm. We made our way downward from step to step cautiously in the mist, and reached our sleeping-place of the previous night at sunset; but we continued down the rocks by the moonlight, and arrived in camp after 10 pm, exhausted, but victorious. We supped by the fire at midnight, with the sound of the Nairobi torrent ringing on the rocks and swelling and falling in the breeze, and from time to time with the hoot of an owl or bark of a leopard, yet none of them seeming to break the silence of the great peak which rose among the stars, sternly graceful, in the cold light of the sinking moon.

"A Journey to the Summit of Mount Kenya, British East Africa",
The Geographical Journal, Halford Mackinder.

Fifty years were to elapse before the peaks were scaled again, by Eric Shipley and P. Wyn Harris in 1929.

Captain Frederick Lugard, ordered in 1899 to impose the Pax Britannica *on the war-torn kingdom of Buganda, describes his preparations for the long march from Mombasa to Kampala.*

There is a charm in the feeling of independence which a farewell to civilization brings with it, and in the knowledge that henceforward one has to rely solely on one's own resources, and that success or failure depend on one's self. At rare intervals opportunities may occur of sending mails and reports to the coast, but between these times – few and far between – the tyranny of the pen is overpast, saving only for the daily diary and the mapping work.

Daybreak brings a stir among the sleeping forms; in later expeditions the Sudanese reveille roused the camp generally before the earliest sign of dawn. You tumble out of your last unfinished dream and your camp-cot, and substitute the realities of a heavy pair of boots, leggings, knee-breeches, and karki jacket, with a pith "solar" hat, shaped like the substantiation of the ethereal halo round the head of a saint in a stained-glass cathedral window. You buckle around you the belt, which contains your hunting-knife and rounds of Winchester ammunition: you fill your haversack with the paraphernalia which only long experience has taught you to select – a tobacco-pouch and pipe, matches, a small file, a spare foresight, a bit of bee's-wax, a measuring-tape, the road-book for surveying, a couple of dry biscuits, and a cloth cap (in case accident or design should keep you late), two or three small straps, a bit of whip-cord, a tiny bit of chalk, a small screw-driver, and I know not what queer knick-knacks besides, understandable only "by the trade."

The man you call your gun-bearer presents himself, and you proceed to dress him up like an (African) Christmas tree. The costume would delight our gilded youth at a fancy ball. In front of his loin-cloth he ties an untanned goat-skin to save him somewhat from the thorns and spear-grass, and the creepers he will have to brush through in the narrow path or in the jungle, should you diverge from the march to follow game. As he leads the way in the early dawn through the high matted grass this skin will be soaked with the dew, and become as it was the moment it left its parent goat, plus a smell. Later in the day it will become a petrified board in the scorching sun. But to return to our Christmas tree. Over his shoulders we sling the haversack, the aneroid, and the prismatic compass, each with its separate strap; round his waist he fastens his own belt and hunting-knife;

over this comes the belt and cartridge-pouches, containing the ammunition of the gun he carries; fixed somehow among these appurtenances is a huge calabash for water – his inevitable companion. In it he probably carries the balance of his day's ration of dry grain. If your caravan is heavily loaded, and his own gear has to be carried as well, he will have a bundle on his head or strapped across his shoulders, consisting of his mat, his little tent, and a bone or two of the last beast shot (probably "high"). Nailed on, so to speak, wherever he can find a few inches of space about his person, you will see a native pipe, a flageolet made from a hollow reed, a chunk of meat, possibly a cooking-pot, and other ornaments. Above all he shoulders your rifle, and "stands confessed," "a thing of shreds and patches" and whatnots innumerable.

The dawn has hardly broken when we emerge from our tents to give the order to the caravan headman "to take up loads". These, during the night, have been stacked under the guard in front of the tents, and while you and I were rapidly dressing, the caravan *askari*, according to custom, have laid them out one by one in long rows on the ground. At the word there is a rush from all parts of camp; every porter seizes his own load, and he seems to have a dread lest it should be appropriated by another, however heavy and unwieldy it be, and carries it off to lash on to it his mat and his cooking-pot and his little all, and that done, to sit upon it and discuss the delicacy of a few roasted grains of *mahindi* (maize), or to gnaw the white bones of last night's *nyama* (game). Still in the grey dawn, while the *askari* are striking the tents, and the servants and the porters who are to carry them are tying up your bed and bedding, etc., and the other men adjusting their loads, we sit down to discuss a chunk of meat and a cup of tea – generally in my own case the meal which is to last me till evening.

Just as the sun appears above the horizon I lead the way, followed by a few *askari*. Every porter shoulders his load, the Wanyamwezi strike up their strange but musical chant, and in two minutes the camp, but now a scene of animated life, is deserted, the smouldering fires die out with the rising sun, and the infinite but silent life of the forest replaces the chatter of the camp.

The Rise of our East African Empire F. D. Lugard.

Until the advent of the railway no expedition, great or small, could have left the coast for the perilous interior without the porters carrying loads on head or shoulders. Porters had their own code of conduct, techniques of porterage and pride in their achievements.

Though you might not ask a man to carry more than his sixty-five lb., there was nothing to prevent him from carrying more if he liked; and the stronger men did like, for a good reason. Three classes of porter were recognized; one-load, two-load and four-load men. The first was the ordinary porter; he carried his burden on his head all day, and when the safari halted to camp for the night upon him fell the task of cutting grass for the pack animals, collecting wood for the fires and bringing water; often troublesome and tedious jobs after six hours or more of marching under a load. The two-load man did none of this camp work, drew double pay and a double ration of food; the four-load man was free of all rules and ate as much as he liked; which was a good deal. I should perhaps explain that he did not carry all 240 lb. at once; he made two journeys: thus the camping places on the old safari route to Uganda were on the average twelve or thirteen miles apart; the four-load man shouldered his two loads at any hour in the morning, probably at four, carried them to the first camping place, and strolled back for two more. It will be admitted that a day's journey of from thirty-six to forty miles, two-thirds of it under a weight of 120 or 130 lb., proves fine physique and staying power. The four-load man would thus do the 400-mile journey to Naivasha.

On the old ration of 1½ lb. of rice per day, forty men ate one load per diem, and the four-load man's burden was eaten first; thus his load was reduced, first to three loads, then to two loads, then to one. To shepherd and protect every ten porters was an *askari* with a rifle; none might become an *askari* unless he had graduated as a two-load man, because it was his duty to see the loads safely into camp, and if accident disabled a man the *askari* had to make over his rifle to somebody else and take up the load or loads himself. Disabling accidents of the temporary sort were, and are, common; and it often happened that the *askari* had to turn porter for the nonce. Men, lamed by thorns, stones, or otherwise injured, were left to be brought in by the *neapara*, an official who *funga safari* – "closed the safari" – and brought the last man into camp. The *neapara* sometimes had hard work.

The Kavirondo are good porters; I have had them march for five hours with a single halt to rest, keeping up with mules which travel a good three miles an hour, often more; the going, I need hardly say, was good, neither deep sand, nor hills nor detaining bush to hinder; but even so, five hours going with a load of from sixty to seventy lb. was fine work. The trouble with Kavirondo is their clumsiness; when cutting grass they are sure to damage themselves somehow with the knives; I have had to doctor three men the same evening for the same mishap – each had cut his little finger nearly off. By way of compensation, be it said, these men are patients to delight a doctor, so easily do they heal. I used to dress the wounds with Stockholm tar and grease, bind them up and dismiss the man, safe in the knowledge that the worst cut would heal "by first intention" on these healthy fellows. Never go on safari without Stockholm tar; messy and disagreeable as it is to use, there is nothing like it for treating cuts and sores, whether on man or beast.

There are bad and indifferent porters: dawdlers who can't or won't keep up with the rest, stupid fellows who lose themselves on small provocation, poor-spirited fellows who give in when tired. I once had a man give in so completely that he asked me to shoot him; he was persuaded to struggle on till we camped, and was unmercifully chaffed by the others who had no sympathy with one who confessed his job too much for him.

It is a hard life the porter leads on safari. Up at daylight, five or six hours' march under a sixty lb. load; reaching camp, down with the load, only to seek out wood, grass and water; dinner, 1½ lb. of rice – meat, only if the gods are good; sleep, in the open, with, it may be, thought of lions; up again at daylight to go through the same routine; and so for days together. Small wonder that the men become safari-stale; the marvel is that they continue for so long at a time the cheery, light-hearted fellows they are.

A Game Ranger on Safari A. B. Percival.

The ivory caravan.

The *kilangozi* (head porter) generally carried the largest tusk, and was also leader in the singing. Immediately behind him came all those carrying large single tusks, then those carrying large bundles of cow-tusks, or two small bundles attached to each end of a strong five-foot long shoulder stick, known as an *abdalla*. Anything extra heavy was slung on a pole, and was carried by two men; it was known as a *zega-zega*. Owing to their carrying everything on their shoulders, the Wanyamwezi are (or were) remarkable for the conspicuously large and highly developed muscle on the top of each shoulder.

It was, however, the transfer of the load from one shoulder to the other that was the most spectacular "stunt" – personally, I have seen sixty to eighty men do it – as every load, at a given verbal signal at the end of a chorus of a song (of triumph, self-glorification, or flattery of their *Bwana*), was simultaneously changed from left to right, or *vice versa*, by simply ducking the head downwards, and then with a sideways swoop, upwards.

One of the self-imposed duties of the *kilangozi* was to encourage his tired comrades. I have seen one who was carrying a tusk of 115 lb. at the end of a twenty-two miles' march, return on his tracks, and *dance* back over a mile, in order to put heart into the men, and to pass the word along that camp was near.

When we returned from Uganda, our *kilangozi*, a splendid fellow named Mganga, danced up and down the main street of Mombasa while the caravan was closing up, and according to custom he collected quite a considerable sum from the onlookers. It was also a recognized custom to issue all the leading porters who carried big tusks, an extra allowance of *posho* (food).

Early Days in East Africa Frederick Jackson.

PART II

Travel

After the departure of the Portuguese, various Arab factions ruled the coastal settlements theoretically in the name of the Sultan of Oman who, between 1832 and 1840, transferred his capital from Muscat to Zanzibar. His successor, Barghash ibn Said, after long negotiations centred on the abolition of the slave trade, leased to the British Government for £11,000 a year a coastal strip about ten miles wide. Meanwhile an energetic Glaswegian ship-owner, William Mackinnon, in 1888 formed the Imperial British East Africa Company to open up to "legitimate commerce" the country between the coast and the kingdom of Buganda, raising for the purpose £250,000. The task proved beyond the Company's means and in 1895 it was taken over by the British Government. The first duty of a government saddled with a chunk of Africa larger than France, thinly populated by tribes constantly at war with each other and dominated by the dreaded Maasai, was to establish the *Pax Britannica* and a framework of administration. The decision was made to build a railway. The railway opened the doors of eastern Africa to the rest of the world, and changed forever the country's destiny and way of life of its peoples.

THE UGANDA RAILWAY

What it will cost no words can express;
    What is its object no brain can suppose;
Where it will start from no one can guess;
    Where it is going to nobody knows.
What is the use of it none can conjecture;
    What it will carry there's none can define;
And in spite of George Curzon's superior lecture
    It clearly is naught but a lunatic line.
                Quoted in *The Lunatic Express* Charles Miller.

Even the Commissioner of the newly-created British East Africa Protectorate appeared to agree.

It is a curious confession, but I do not know why the Uganda Railway was built, and I think many people in East Africa share my ignorance. It is a little hard to believe that the only motive was purely philanthropic – namely, the suppression of the slave trade – nor are the strategic advantages of the line very obvious, for though it certainly might be used as an alternative route for sending troops to the Sudan, no attempt has been made to open up communication on the higher waters of the Nile, and the journey would in any case be long. It is most remarkable that at the time when the construction was decided on, there appears to have been no idea of the value, or even of the existence, of the high temperate region to the east of Lake Victoria. On the other hand, there was probably an exaggerated idea of the riches and fertility of Uganda, a country of great interest, with a large and exceptionally intelligent native population, but in most parts at any rate not suited for European settlement, and not as yet proved to yield any produce which would approximately repay the cost of the line. Yet, looking at the completed railway today, I think even hostile critics will admit that it justifies its existence. The slave trade has disappeared so entirely that one is apt to forget that only a few years ago it was a real horror and scandal which called for energetic suppression. The line is found to pass through a healthy and fertile district which ought to soon become a considerable European colony with good commercial prospects. Above all, the completion of this route has had the most remarkable effects in opening up the countries of Central Equatorial Africa, and dissipating the cloud of ignorance by which they were concealed. What may be the whole consequences in the future of this sudden illumination of the Dark Continent, no one can predict, but one remarkable result is our control of the sources of the Nile, and the grandiose plans now set forth for regulating the water supply of Upper Egypt.

It is perhaps not superfluous to repeat that the Uganda Railway is not in Uganda at all, but entirely in the East Africa Protectorate, the whole breadth of which from the sea to Lake Victoria it traverses. It is as if the line from Charing Cross to Dover were called the French Railway. In some of the earlier reports it was described as the Mombasa-Victoria Railway, a far more correct name, which has, however, been entirely dropped in favour of the shorter title. . . .

The most serious criticism passed on the Uganda Railway is that it was unduly costly. Elaborate defences have been made to prove the contrary, but I think that every one who has an adequate knowledge both of the country and of the history of the construction is agreed that the line ought really to have cost about four millions sterling, whereas "the total expenditure out of Parliamentary grants up to the date the Committee ceased to control the outlay" (which is not quite the whole expenditure) "was £5,317,000." The expenditure on accessories was, no doubt, very ample; on housing the officials and the subordinate staff, on building whole towns, on the medical and police departments. I do not find fault with the expenditure, but Africa would be a very different place from what it is if everything were done on this scale, and I think it would have been more natural and more advantageous to have enlarged the corresponding departments of the Protectorate administration instead of creating duplicate departments. . . .

But, no doubt, the chief assignable cause of the excess in expenditure was the enormous amount of temporary work on the line. A German official, who travelled over the railway shortly before its completion, said, on returning, "I am ashamed of my country. We have not built one railway to the Lake yet, and the English have built two." For a large part of the line this was hardly an exaggeration. Even now the traveller sees everywhere traces of temporary bridges and temporary lines, and sometimes two of the latter, making three lines in all, before the final route was laid.

The East Africa Protectorate Sir Charles Eliot.

Labour to build the railway was brought from India; the men were called coolies. As the line approached Tsavo at Mile 121 its notorious man-eating lions emerged to halt construction altogether for three weeks in December 1898. Lt.-Col. J. H. Patterson of the Indian Army tells the story.

At first they [the lions] were not always successful in their efforts to carry off a victim, but as time went on they stopped at nothing and indeed braved any danger in order to obtain their favourite food. Their methods then became so uncanny, and their man-stalking so well-timed and so certain of success, that the workmen firmly believed that they were not real animals at all, but devils in lions' shape. Many a time the coolies solemnly assured me that it was absolutely useless to attempt to shoot them. They were quite convinced that the angry spirits of two departed native chiefs had taken this form in order to protest against a railway being made through their country, and by stopping its progress to avenge the insult thus shown to them.

I had only been a few days at Tsavo when I first heard that these brutes had been seen in the neighbourhood. Shortly afterwards one or two coolies mysteriously disappeared, and I was told that they had been carried off by night from their tents and devoured by lions. At the time I did not credit this story, and was more inclined to believe that the unfortunate men had been the victims of foul play at the hands of some of their comrades. . . . This suspicion, however, was very soon dispelled. About three weeks after my arrival, I was roused one morning about daybreak and told that one of my *jemadars*, a fine powerful Sikh named Ungan Singh, had been seized in his tent during the night, and dragged off and eaten.

Naturally I lost no time in making an examination of the place, and was soon convinced that the man had indeed been carried off by a lion, as its "pug" marks were plainly visible in the sand, while the furrows made by the heels of the victim showed the direction in which he had been dragged away. Moreover, the *jemadar* shared his tent with half a dozen other workmen, and one of his bedfellows had actually witnessed the occurrence. He graphically described how, at about midnight, the lion suddenly put its head in at the open tent door and seized Ungan Singh – who happened to be nearest the opening – by the throat. The unfortunate fellow cried out "*Choro*" ("Let go"), and threw his arms up round the lion's neck. The next moment he was gone, and his panic-stricken companions lay helpless, forced to listen to the terrible struggle which took place outside. Poor Ungan Singh must have died hard; but what chance had he? As a coolie gravely remarked, "Was he not fighting with a lion?" . . .

We found it an easy matter to follow the route taken by the lion, as he appeared to have stopped several times before beginning his meal. Pools of blood marked these halting-places, where he doubtless indulged in the man-eater's habit of licking the skin off so as to get at the fresh blood. (I have been led to believe that this is their custom from the appearance of two half-eaten bodies which I subsequently rescued: the skin was gone in places, and the flesh looked dry, as if it had been sucked.) On reaching the spot where the body had been devoured, a dreadful spectacle presented itself. The ground all round was covered with blood and morsels of flesh and bones, but the unfortunate *jemadar*'s head had been left intact, save for the holes made by the lion's tusks on seizing him, and lay a short distance away from the other remains, the eyes staring wide open with a startled, horrified look in them. The place was considerably cut up, and on closer examination we found that two lions had been there and had probably struggled for possession of the body. It was the most gruesome sight I had ever seen.

There followed a long duel between the man-eaters and the Colonel. Night after night, Patterson sat up in a tree to which a goat or donkey had been tethered as bait, only to hear screams from a distant camp which told him that his enemies had again eluded him. The lions grew bolder and bolder, forcing their way through the thickest thorn fences erected round the camps; the men more and more demoralized, demanding to be sent back to India and retreating at night into holes dug in the floors of their huts.

Hitherto, as a rule, only one of the man-eaters had made the attack and had done the foraging, while the other waited outside in the bush; but now they began to change their tactics, entering the *bomas* together and each seizing a victim. In this way two Swahili porters were killed during the last week of November 1898, one being immediately carried off and devoured. The other was heard moaning for a long time, and when his terrified companions at last summoned up sufficient courage to go to his assistance, they found him stuck fast in the bushes of the *boma*, through which for once the lion had apparently been unable to drag him.

Within a few days of this the two brutes made a most ferocious attack on the largest camp in the section, which for safety's sake was situated within a stone's throw of Tsavo Station and close to a Permanent Way Inspector's iron hut. Suddenly in the dead of night the two man-eaters burst in among the terrified workmen, and even from my *boma*, some distance away, I could plainly hear the panic-stricken shrieking of the coolies. Then followed cries of "They've taken him; they've taken him," as the brutes carried off their unfortunate victim and began their horrible feast close beside the camp.

At last the climax came. Ensconced in his tree, Patterson heard "the rustling of a large body forcing its way through the bush".

"The man-eater," I thought to myself; "surely to-night my luck will change and I shall bag one of the brutes." Profound silence again succeeded; I sat on my eyrie like a statue, every nerve tense with excitement. Very soon, however, all doubt as to the presence of the lion was dispelled. A deep long-drawn sigh – sure sign of hunger – came up from the bushes, and the rustling commenced again as he cautiously advanced. In a moment or two a sudden stop, followed by an angry growl, told me that my presence had been noticed; and I began to fear that disappointment awaited me once more.

But no; matters quickly took an unexpected turn. The hunter became the hunted; and instead of either making off or coming for the bait prepared for him, the lion began stealthily to stalk *me*! For about two hours he horrified me by slowly creeping round and round my crazy structure, gradually edging his way nearer and nearer. Every moment I expected him to rush it; and the staging had not been constructed with an eye to such a possibility. If one of the rather flimsy poles should break, or if the lion could spring the twelve feet which separated me from the ground . . . the thought was scarcely a pleasant one. . . .

In a short while I heard the lion begin to creep stealthily towards me. I could barely make out his form as he crouched among the whitish undergrowth; but I saw enough for my purpose, and before he could come any nearer, I took careful aim and pulled the trigger. The sound of the shot was at once followed by a most terrific roar, and then I could hear him leaping about in all directions. I was no longer able to see him, however, as his first bound had taken him into the thick bush; but to make assurance doubly sure, I kept blazing away in the direction in which I heard him plunging about. At length came a series of mighty groans, gradually subsiding into deep sighs, and finally ceasing altogether; and I felt convinced that one of the "devils" who had so long harried us would trouble us no more.

The Man-Eaters of Tsavo J. H. Patterson.

Patterson shot the second man-eater a few weeks later. Both were big lions in good condition.

From the edge of the escarpment at mile 362 the line was manoeuvred down an almost sheer drop of over 1,500 feet into the Rift Valley; then up the other side through dense forests and over deep ravines to Mau Summit at mile 489 and an altitude of 8,700 feet. Down the other side the line was taken through the hilly country of the Nandi tribe, whose warriors found steel rails and telegraph wires an irresistible temptation.

It must not be supposed that the Nandi had any idea of cutting our communications, or even of committing acts of political hostility. Their operations were simply burglarious. A railway line appeals in the strangest way to both sexes of African natives. Telegraph wires are regarded as a most ornamental and desirable article of female attire, and the male sex find, in various bolts and rivets used to secure the rails, perfect weapons obviously intended for braining their enemies. One can imagine what thefts would be committed on a European railway if the telegraph wires were pearl necklaces and the rails first-rate sporting guns, and it is not surprising that the Nandi yielded to the temptation, but rather that within a comparatively short time they were broken of the habit.

The East Africa Protectorate Sir Charles Eliot.

Breaking the Nandi of the habit took ten years and five military expeditions. Despite these disruptions and beset by many troubles, the railway continued on its way.

First, a wave of dysentery swept the party. On its heels came widespread recurrences of malaria. Half the railhead work force, including Preston, was laid low. Then the skies reopened with a fury that rapidly turned the already spongy terrain of western Kavirondo into a jellied consommé. The newly laid embankments became so soft that materials trains had to be unloaded while moving; if a locomotive stopped, it would simply topple over on its side and sink into the morass. Jackson described one such train near Kibigori, "coming slowly and cautiously along, rocking from side to side, heaving gently up and down like a ship in a choppy sea-way, and squirting liquid mud for ten feet on each side of it, from under the sleepers, after the manner of a water-cart". And what little platelaying could be done in these conditions was further curtailed by new outbreaks of tribal banditry. Making little effort at concealment, Nandi warriors treated the camp as if it were a hardware store as they carried off rails, sleepers, keys and tools, while the fever-broken workers, virtually defenceless even at the best of times, could only look on dully.

Nandi buccaneering had a more telling effect than simply to delay the advance of the tracks. The tribe had already stolen so much wire that the Telegraph Department found itself unable to overtake the rails, and the result was almost to cripple delivery of materials. Without telegraphic communications,the two trains serving railhead from the forward supply base at Muhoroni had to operate on a rigidly constricted schedule if collisions were to be avoided. Neither train was allowed to leave either station until the other had completed its run. . . .

By mid-December, the rains had ended, the Nandi had vanished into the hills, the telegraph line had finally reached railhead, and nearly all the workers had recovered from their fevers. Once again the tracks moved forward, and on Friday, 20 December 1901, Preston was able to write that the men had put down "the record length of 10,400 feet of line which brought us to Port Florence Station". At four o'clock in the afternoon of the following day, there was a brief ceremony. As Preston and a few other officials of the line looked on, Florence Preston put aside her parasol, took up a keying hammer and clumsily drove home the last key in the last rail of Britain's newest imperial highway. Only a few minutes later, one of the supply trains clanked wearily to the end of the line at the very edge of the

lake. One almost imagines the locomotive puffing: "I *knew* I could . . . I *knew* I could. . . ."
The Lunatic Express Charles Miller.

The statistics, perhaps, need grouping. The line was 582 miles long. It was begun on 5 August 1896 on the Mombasa mainland and it reached Port Florence on Lake Victoria on 19 December 1901. The capital cost was £5,502,592. The cost in lives was 2,493 Asians and 5 whites. 31,983 coolies were imported from India. Of these 6,454 were invalided back to India and 16,312 were repatriated or dismissed. 6,724 Indians remained in East Africa to become the main progenitors of the present Asian population. 43 stations were built and 22 construction locomotives worn out. The bridging included the Salisbury Bridge (joining the island of Mombasa to the mainland) of 21 spans of 60-foot girders, 35 viaducts on the Kikuyu and the Mau Escarpments; and 1,280 smaller bridges and culverts.
The Iron Snake Ronald Hardy.

The construction of the railway created a demand for victuals on which to feed the men who were laying it. There was plenty of food in Kikuyu country, but fear of ambushes and poisoned arrows kept traders out. In 1898 John Boyes, a twenty-four-year-old Yorkshireman who had gone to sea as a cabin-boy, arrived in Mombasa in an Arab dhow. Two years later he set out from Naivasha with seven porters, a Maasai guide and a rifle, to reach the shunned Kikuyu country across the Aberdare (Nyandarua) range of mountains.

Continuing our march, we arrived, on the third day, in sight of the first native village. I had heard some one cutting wood in the forest off our road, and the news of our coming had spread. At the first sight of us the natives had started running away, but we soon heard the native war-cry being taken up from hill to hill round about, and could catch occasional glimpses of the natives themselves as they gathered in force towards the village. They were certainly a wild-looking lot, with their bodies smeared all over with grease and red clay, or, in some cases, a kind of whitewash, in which patterns were drawn according to the fancy of each individual, while fastened to the leg was a rattle, with an iron ball inside, which, as they moved about, made a noise very much like a railway train. Many of them wore wonderful head-dresses, made of the skin of the colobus monkey, and all were armed with spears and shields. . . .

In a short time quite five hundred warriors, fully armed, were drawn up outside the village, and, getting within speaking distance, I told my Masai interpreter to tell them that I had come to see the chief of the district. . . .

Instead of attacking Boyes and his small party, the chief, Karuri, sought his help in defending his village from an onslaught by warriors of a rival clan.

My duty was clear. These people had brought the trouble on themselves by befriending me, and the least I could do was to give them such help as I could. . . .

Seizing my rifle, I made for the scene of the fight, accompanied by a crowd of yelling savages, delighted at my decision. When I arrived the row was at its height and the sight of the hand-to-hand conflict among the warriors, surrounded by the burning huts, was a stirring one. Seeing the reinforcements, headed by myself, coming up, the attackers began to waver, and when I had fired a few shots with effect, finally turned tail and bolted. After pursuing them for some distance, to make sure that they were completely scattered, the triumphant warriors returned to the village, and made quite a hero of me, being convinced that their victory was entirely due to my help. This incident was of the greatest value to me, as it fully established my reputation as a useful member of the community, and they became very friendly. I learned that they had had a lot of trouble with this particular clan, who had frequently raided them, killing many of their men, and carrying off their cattle, and sometimes their women.

After this Karuri came to ask me if I would stop in his country, and I told him I would think about it. I said that I had other work to do, but that if he would sell me flour and other foodstuffs I would come back to him. I told him that the flour was for friends of mine, who were coming along the caravan road. He said that he did not want any more white people in the country. I could stop as long as I liked myself, and his people would be my friends, but they did not mean to have any strangers. I explained that though my friends were coming along the caravan road they had no intention or desire to enter the country. This explanation seemed to satisfy them, and I told them that I would not decide at once about staying in the country, but that when I had taken the flour to my friends I would come back and talk matters over with them. They then asked what I had to give in exchange for the flour, and I produced a bottle of iodoform, some of which I had used on their wounds after the fight with good effect. They thought it was a great medicine, and all wanted some, and in exchange for a small quantity, wrapped in paper, would give from ten to twenty pounds of flour.

They looked upon me as a great medicine man, and members of the tribe came to me daily to be cured of various complaints during the fortnight I stayed with them while the food I wanted was being collected and brought in. When it was all in I found that I had about two hundred loads, and the trouble then was to find porters to carry it out of the country; but by dint of persuasion I finally succeeded in impressing a number of the people into my service, and started off with my loads.

On account of my little difference with Captain Gorges, I decided not to go to Naivasha, but to carry my loads down towards the Kedong. As the route to the Kedong Valley led through the Masai country, my men would not go right through with it, so I set them to build a hut on the caravan road, where I established a store for the flour, and within a few days I sold the lot to the railway surveyors and caravans for about thirty rupees a load, which made me highly satisfied with the result of my first venture among the Kikuyu.

Returning to Karuri's, Boyes entrenched himself as a de facto *super-chief, training and arming a force of warriors who subdued other sections of the tribe who were at odds with his ally. He dispensed justice, made roads, built stores and introduced English vegetables, fruit trees and black wattle. About once a month a caravan of 500 to 1,000 men went down to Naivasha carrying food for the railway workers. Such happy days could not last. When rumours reached the Protectorate's officials that a freebooting trader was exercising sovereign rights and flying the Union Jack over his encampment, they despatched two of their officers to bring to book the presumptuous trader. Boyes' askaris were stripped of their insignia and he himself placed under arrest and charged with the serious crime of dacoity.*

My greatest crime of all in the eyes of these officials, however, was the fact that I was flying the Union Jack, which my men carried with them, as they were accustomed to do on all their expeditions. I mildly put the question to the officer as to whether he expected me to fly the Russian flag, or any other except that of my own country, but it seemed that, to the official mind, it was a most serious offence for an Englishman to display the flag under which he had been born and for which he had fought, unless he held some position in the official oligarchy which ruled, or was in the habit of thinking it ruled, the country. . . .

The next four days were spent in collecting evidence against me, and as nobody could be persuaded to go to my headquarters to collect evidence against me on the spot, Captain Longfield himself finally went, taking with him the whole of his troops, while during his absence Mr Hall gathered all the information he could from the chiefs and other natives at Mberri. . . .

When they had, as they thought, satisfactorily arranged for sufficient evidence to secure my conviction, the Kikuyu who had come in with me had their arms restored to them, and I and my personal bodyguard, together with about two hundred native witnesses, were sent down to Nairobi under charge of an escort of about ten native soldiers, commanded by a black sergeant! The situation was ludicrously Gilbertian. Here was I, a (so-called) dangerous outlaw, being sent down to be tried for my life on a series of awful indictments, through a country in which I had only to lift a finger to call an army of savage warriors to my assistance. I was accompanied by a personal following twenty times as numerous as the guard of ten natives who kept me prisoner, and who trembled every time they passed a native village lest the inhabitants should rush out and wipe them out of existence; while on the first day out the humour of the situation was considerably increased by the sergeant in charge of the escort handing me the large blue envelope containing the statement of the evidence against me, with a request that I would take charge of it for him, as he was afraid he might lose it! I must say that I thoroughly appreciated the humour of the whole affair. I was the only mounted man in the whole outfit, still having my mule, and it struck me as distinctly amusing that I should be practically taking myself down to Nairobi, to be tried for my life, with the whole of the evidence under my arm!

John Boyes, King of the Wa-kikuyu, ed. C. W. L. Bulpett.

John Boyes was brought to trial, acquitted on all charges, and resumed his trading activities among the Kikuyu, though without his private army. Later he took to farming. He died in Nairobi, a respected family man, in 1951.

To cement his friendship with the chief, John Boyes had made blood-brotherhood with Karuri. This was a widely practised ceremony with many local variations. The missionary Stuart Watt described his exchange of pledges with the Kikuyu chief Watiti.

Soon the chief made his appearance, with about fifty of his elderly advisers, and a passage was opened up for them through the multitude until they reached my tent. Once more I had to submit to the usual spitting process, and was amazed at the secretive power of the chief's salivary glands. We heartily exchanged salutations and grasped each other's hand; and, after some little time, the ceremony of making blood-brotherhood was commenced.

Another large sheep was presented to me for the occasion. This was killed by one of my men, and a small portion of meat from the loin and a piece of the liver and the heart were put on the camp fire to roast. While this was being done the elders placed the chief and myself face to face, in close proximity. My head-man and interpreter stood by my chair, while around the chief, who was seated on his stool, were several elders.

The man who had been set apart to officiate in the ceremony of the day then brought from the fire the three roasted pieces of flesh and cut each in two. With a piece of sharpened iron, used for shaving the head, this adept of the blade made a small gash on my breast, from which the blood oozed freely. He then made a similar incision on the chest of the chief, and as the red blood flowed down over his ebony skin he took three small pieces of the different kinds of meat, and dipping them in the blood of the chief he gave them to me to eat, while the other three pieces, which he besmeared with my blood, were handed to the chief.

As we partook of the meat, for which I had little relish, the announcement was made that the great Mzungu, who had come to their country with a good Message, and the chief Watiti were now brothers. If the one ever approached the other with murderous intent he was to fall in his own blood; and that if the people of the one attempted to kill those of the other they themselves would not live to see another sunrise.

In the Heart of Savagedom Rachel Stuart Watt.

Divine intervention.

Upon reaching the station of Machakos, we found John Ainsworth pluckily struggling to establish his influence over the Kamba tribe, with little outside support. During our halt here, we were visited by a curious character named S—— W——, who posed as a missionary and a settler, and came with a tale of woe, begging for provisions to stave off starvation from a wife and children, an appeal which it was impossible to resist. I never heard that he did much missionary work, but he founded a valuable fruit farm which in time proved lucrative. His was a type which appealed to few, for he claimed to be the special charge of the Deity, and told with great gusto the story of how one day when out on the plains he suddenly found himself charged by an infuriated rhinoceros. He ran; the rhino gained on him, and he thought all was lost, but No! Suddenly a voice came out of Heaven, and the Lord said to him, "Throw down your hat." He obeyed the mandate, and lo! and behold the rhino stopped, then charged the hat and went off with it impaled on its horn.

Kenya: From Chartered Company to Crown Colony C. W. Hobley.

The Uganda Railway killed off, metaphorically speaking, the foot porter, and reduced the journey from the coast to Nairobi from six weeks or more to less than twenty-four hours. The rail trip became a social event. Captain C. H. Stigand conducts his readers up-country, circa *1908.*

The train vibrates a good deal, and if you look at the lines you will see that they are wavy, a condition, I believe, caused by the great expansion of the metal under the tropical sun. Therefore reading is tiring, so if you are a card player, take a pack of cards with you with which to beguile the time.

Take also a few bottles of soda and a little whisky; even if you do not need them yourself you will find yourself popular with fellow travellers who have not been equally provident. Failing this, take a corkscrew, as someone is sure to have a bottle and no corkscrew; lending yours will establish a claim on his hospitality. Also take some light provisions, as if you play bridge that night you may feel hungry after a rather early dinner.

If you elect to make your own tea or cocoa in the morning, hot water may be obtained in two ways. In both cases the preliminaries are the same, that is, you take a teapot or kettle, and when the train stops, proceed to the engine and stand near the waste pipe or whatever the end of a pipe projecting on the near side is called. From this point onwards the two methods differ: The first is to make yourself very agreeable to the driver, and then inadvertently show him the teapot. The second method is, concealing the pot from his view, to make remarks calculated to raise his anger. If you do either of these things sufficiently well, the driver will probably find that he can dispense with a little steam and water, and turn on some handle inside the machine.

If you intend to crane your head much out of the window to look at the game, a pair of goggles are useful to keep the dust and also the sparks from the wood fuel out of your eyes. Do not forget to take a pillow or bolster to use at night, and if you are a man of luxury, a few cushions and bolsters or bundles of rugs to rest the elbows and back against are comfortable during the day.

If you intend making up a bridge four, two camp stools and a camp table or drawing-board should be taken, and then people can sit in normal positions.

Otherwise two players must sit side by side, leaning away from each other, saying in duet, "Hold up your hand, please."

But I have given away enough lucrative tips for one chapter, and the train is just starting, so we say goodbye to Mombasa and steam off, pass Kilindini, and then wind slowly on to the magnificent bridge connecting Mombasa Island with the mainland. From here there is a splendid view of the harbour and creeks running up into the mainland.

A few miles out of Mombasa the observant traveller will notice some of the abominable tall elephant grass which makes travelling so hideous in most central parts of this continent.

So on past Mazeras, and the country becomes more open and less populated till Maji ya Chumvi is reached, and now we begin to enter the waterless tract. Presently we will come into the red earth and thorn of the Taru, the thorn scattered at first, but growing thicker and thicker as Voi is reached.

At this place we adjourn to the Dak bungalow for dinner.

If the complaint book of this place is referred to, it will be found that the quality of this dinner is one of the burning questions of the moment in the Protectorate, and one on which people are fanatically divided. It would appear as if many a true friendship must be broken at Voi, husband and wife parted, or father must disown son over this controversy.

Read the ecstatic remarks written in the book by this one. "Never has he eaten such a dinner out of Europe, and but once has he been better served, whilst dining in the city. The chef is a true artist, etc., etc."

And now this one, a member of the same party. "Excepting of course the food served on German liners, never has he tasted such filth, etc., etc." . . .

The railway is divided into sections, at each of which there is a change of guards, drivers, etc. Voi was the first landmark in the journey; Makindu, the next, will be reached in the early hours of the morning. It is just after this station that lions are constantly met with, and even run down by the train, just before dawn, as they use this part of the line as a road to and from their hunting grounds and lying-up places.

When dawn breaks we should be at about Simba station, already the highlands, but here clothed with sparse and stunted acacia, which will presently give place to open plain.

From here on to Nairobi, the distance of 100 miles, the line will traverse the great Kapiti and Athi plains. During practically the whole of this distance, game is never out of sight, and large herds may generally be seen in all directions, paying little heed to the train, being too busy grazing.

Some even allow it to pass within 150 yards of them, merely looking up curiously and then resuming grazing. Were the train, however, to stop, they would at once take the precaution to move a little further off.

The Land of Zinj C. H. Stigand.

In those days there was a certain casual atmosphere about the railway which disappeared for ever after the war. The railway was a social institution as well as a method of transport. A train would nearly always stop to allow a passenger to get out and photograph giraffe or to watch a herd of elephant striding across the plain. Sometimes an English but Mohammedan settler who lived down the line from Nairobi would spread a little feast of fruit, cakes, honey and milk on the bare veld by the side of the line where it ran past his farm. Any train which came past used to stop while the passengers alighted and were served with this strange gratuitous meal by the settler in his fez.

It was not surprising that a more carefree attitude towards tickets than is usually displayed by railways prevailed. Passengers often bought their tickets at the other end of the journey. (One man reached England on a second-class ticket from Nakuru to Elmenteita, but this was an unusual and something of a classic achievement.)

On one occasion Delamere arrived at Elmenteita station with his bull-terrier bitch and a litter of four puppies which he was taking to Nairobi. In the preoccupation of getting them comfortably settled he forgot to take tickets either for himself or for the dogs. When the train had gone the station-master telegraphed a warning to Nairobi in these terms: "The Lord is on the train with one bitch and four sons of bitches. No tickets. Please collect."

White Man's Country (Vol. I) Elspeth Huxley.

The log-burning puffers of the old Uganda Railway gave way to powerful diesel-burning locomotives; basic meals in wayside dak bungalows to succulent dinners in the restaurant cars of the East African Railways and Harbours, which came into being in 1948 with the amalgamation of the Kenyan and Tanganyikan systems.

I drove down to Nairobi and caught the overnight train to Mombasa, jostling with the crowds that thronged the single platform of the Nairobi railway station in vibrant confusion. Turbaned and bearded Sikhs; elegant, sari-clad Indian women; African families carrying bulging cloth-wrapped bundles on their heads; bright-eyed, jet-black children struggling with gaping, string-tied cardboard suitcases; back-packing overlanders and the laughing, effervescent groups of teenage Settler children.

There was something of a carnival atmosphere about all these departures, everyone leaning out of the carriage windows – each with the names of the occupants neatly typed on a rectangle of card – and shaking the upraised hands of those who had come to see them off. Then, with a triumphant, if asthmatic, toot on the steam whistle and a bumper-joggling lurch, we chugged out from the station amidst much clapping and shouted farewells, the deep chuff-chuff cadenza of the engine running away before settling down to a steady beat, the clackety-clack of the carriages echoing over the track. I was already beginning to relax.

As we pulled through the shanties on Nairobi's outskirts, groups of children waved excitedly from the banks as we passed by . . . This was the sad, flip-side face of Africa. A jungle of cardboard igloos and beaten petrol-can huts, home to those drawn to the city in the hope of work.

They were unlovely and unloved wastelands, looked over by a few dusty, barren trees – bare like gallows – and garlanded with the garbage of the twentieth century; discarded milk cartons, bits of string, plastic bags, and ragged strips of faded cotton cloth. Then, as we chugged away into the Athi plains, we left behind the sour, pig-slop smells of the Shanties' open drains, and exchanged them for the fresh cowpat, hay and pollen smells of summer meadows; the unmistakable, all pervasive musk of the African savannas.

Later, as darkness fell, a porter lugged a bulky, canvas-covered bedroll into my cabin and took orders for early morning tea and coffee. Shortly afterwards, the first of the dinner relays was heralded by a one-man glockenspiel band. Dressed in an immaculate white uniform, the beaming waiter swayed down the rocking corridor hammering out a catchy jungle beat. I made my way to the dining car and was shown to an elegantly side-lit table draped with a crisp linen cloth and neatly laid with a full set of gleaming and monogrammed silver; EAR & H – East African Railways and Harbours. The logo was even embroidered on the linen napkins. My order was taken and in no time at all the multi-course feast was being served by smiling waiters wearing white tunics and red fez hats who seemed to take genuine pride and pleasure in serving me, removing the lids of the great silver tureens with a magician's flourish, decanting fine vintage wine and generally pandering to my every whim.

Afterwards, I climbed into my snug bunk and fell asleep to the lulling, four-beat clatter of the carriage wheels; the steam and the smoke and the dull-red sparks streaming past the window. Every so often throughout the night, I was woken by the jerky clanging of bumpers as the carriages concertinaed to a halt at one or other of the small, *en route* stations and our engine driver took additional water on board.

Come the dawn, I was roused by the "tap-tap" and cheery "Jambo, Bwana!" which signalled the arrival of a tray of piping hot coffee and then, after a full English breakfast, I gazed out of the window at the coconut palms, heavily-laden mango trees and clustered banana groves, drinking in the warm, sultry air as the long train snaked down the hills towards Mombasa and the coast.

Shortly before nine o'clock, we pulled into Mombasa station and I hailed a highly individual, bougainvillaea-festooned taxi to take me to my hotel.

Black Moon, Jade Sea Ian Meredith Hughes.

Following the break-up of the East African Community in 1977, the logo of the East African Railways & Harbours was painted out on the rolling stock, and the logo of Kenya Railways painted in.

"Transportation is civilization" Kipling wrote; civilization, it was generally believed, would follow the twin steel rails that superseded Africa's own system of

winding footpaths and plodding feet. The railway was a spine: from it spread
out dust-shrouded or mud-boggled tracks traversed by ox-drawn wagons
making ten or twelve miles a day. The wagon had its own mystique.

They were delicious, those mornings, once the agony of dressing in the icy dark
was past. There is a freshness about dawn in Africa that is very invigorating.
Everything is clear and sparkling and joyous; the fragrant, downy, white leaves of
leleshwa shrubs shining against a deep blue sky. Our oxen swish slowly through
the dew-laden grass, their supple hides glossy in the sunlight. Cries and laughter
from the camp, the clinking of trek-chains, and pleasant pungence of wood
smoke combine to put new life into one's soul.

We met with minor vicissitudes, naturally. Once the wagon upset, and we were
eight hours without food. Once we sat up for a lion, only to find next morning that
it had quietly visited a Dutchman's team of oxen – outspanned defenceless – half
a mile farther along the road. On another occasion we ran out of bread, and riding
to a farm close by to beg for a loaf, had the discomfiture of seeing our loose mule
fly at one of the settler's large black pigs and gallop – with her teeth fixed firmly in
the squealing victim's tail – half-way up to the house. Again, when near our
destination, the mules got away during the night and went home ahead of us, on
their own account.

But it was all great fun. The journey took six or seven days, for we were able to
follow the shorter route by Thomson's Falls and the Pesi, which saved twenty
miles. The falls themselves were a delight and wonder to the newcomers; so close
to the highroad and so totally unexpected, as if the river disappeared into space
twenty yards below the bridge. But the *safari* itself was what they appreciated
most. I enjoyed sitting on the wagon among the bulky bundles and baggage as
much as any of it. There is something so solemn and fateful about a wagon's
progress, when one is merely a passenger, and the hoarse shouts and ceaseless
activity of the drivers only seem to accentuate this sense of detachment. Seen
from one's lazy perch above, rocking and heaving, the long team of oxen
undulates onward like some monstrous centipede.

"*Ouch!* Sh-Sh-Sh – Sh-Sh-Sh!" the drivers cry, swinging their whips with
a report like a pistol-shot. They spring from side to side of the dissel-boom
at awkward places, and admonish each ox in turn. One learns to know the
characters of them all – lazy, willing, nervous, or placid – as one watches from
aloft.

Perhaps a stream has to be crossed, and then, for a perilous moment, one
seems to topple on the very verge, when, with a downward plunge, the wagon
lurches safely into the water.

Most enthralling by far, however, is night, when, gathered round the camp-
fires, one sees the near trees and tent-flies lit up like frosted silver against the
purple mystery beyond. Can anything be lovelier than dancing firelight, with its
ruddy glow and flickering shadows? Within earshot of one's deep-breathing
oxen, tied in line to their yokes, and in sight of the phantom outlines of mules and

ponies, stamping uneasily at their pickets, a glamour lies over *safari* life not easily to be forgotten.

A Kenyan Farm Diary V. M. Carnegie.

After the wagon came the motor car, at first the "box body" loaded up with spades, axes and chains, with spare springs and gaskets, with cans of petrol and water, with iron rations, first aid kits, dogs and guns and other equipment needed to cope with anything from a flooded river to a charging rhino. Lorries lurched across lava deserts, along rutted forest tracks and up and down precipitous hills. Sometimes distressing incidents occurred.

In 1925 there was very heavy rain, and one day no less than seven cars were stuck on an extremely bad patch of mud. Admiral Blunt volunteered to try and find a diversion and so took off into the *bundu* [bush]. After waiting for some time we thought we had better go and find out what had happened, but no trace of the Admiral, his wife or his car was to be seen. It eventually transpired that they had all disappeared into a newly formed *donga* [gully] and the bush had closed over the car, leaving no sign.

On another occasion the Admiral, travelling with his wife from Solai to Nakuru in his box-body Model T Ford, hit a pothole with such impact that not only did his good lady hit the roof, but her head went straight through it. The plywood then, as plywood will, closed round her neck and nothing that the Admiral could do would release her. As the vehicle was also stuck in the mud, there was nothing for it but to walk to Nakuru for help. As the Admiral trudged on it began to rain. The road surface became muddier and muddier. By the time he reached Nakuru he was exhausted, soaked, and covered in mud. His friends rallied round him. A little drink would do him a power of good. Two little drinks . . . Several hours later someone asked the Admiral how his missus was. It was the first time he had given the poor woman a thought.

Pioneers' Scrapbook, eds. Elspeth Huxley and Arnold Curtis.

This journey from Marsabit to Isiolo took place in 1935.

The lorry had only one light, which kept flickering on and off. An abundance of old rope kept the mudguards more or less in the right position. All the springs in the cab seat reared nakedly out of the rents in the leather cloth covering and I was thankful for the cushions Racha put in for me at the last moment. . . .

Mr Fernandes climbed into the driving seat. He was perhaps the leading trader in Marsabit, and was something of a local landmark. I had travelled with him before and enjoyed it; he was an interesting companion because he knew so much of the local history and was full of unexpected bits of information. He knew every inch of the road by heart. . . .

Mr Fernandes was flogging his old lorry for all it was worth. It roared and squeaked and groaned and grated as we crashed over the rough road at a disconcerting speed. Every time we went over a bump both sides of the bonnet flew open and flapped helplessly, like an overweight bird struggling to get airborne, and at each bad jolt the one and only headlamp flickered. I could faintly make out the do-or-die expression on Mr Fernandes's face as he gripped the wheel and swung the lorry violently off course to avoid a rock or an antbear hole. It was almost more than I could stand.

A vast elephant scampered out of our way with startled indignation. Hyena crouched near the edge of the road, blinking green eyes at us before slouching off into the bush. Nightjars fluttered up from the road, with a hint of ruby eyes and white wing tips. Hares ran in front of us, transparent ears flopping foolishly, until it occurred to them to dive into the undergrowth at the side. A large porcupine bustled, bristling, across our path.

Much to my surprise we got off the mountain without mishap. All the guardian angels must have been working overtime that night. Now that we were bowling along on more or less level ground, on a wider, smoother road, I told myself there was no need to go on feeling tied up in knots and to die unnecessary half-deaths in cowardly anticipation. But I had forgotten the drifts of loose sand at the side of the road. Twice we skidded and mounted the bank between the road and the drain, and in the end, nearly voiceless and trembling, I asked Mr Fernandes to go a little more moderately.

He took his eyes off the road to stare at me in reproach.

"But Bwana Reece very ill," he protested, and I felt as craven as could be as I muttered something about an hour or two not making all that much difference. Instantly he slowed down to such a painfully snail-like pace that I wished I had held my peace.

About half-way through the night Mr Fernandes stopped the lorry to brew tea.

The crew and the one or two passengers on the back jumped down and hacked at the palm trees, piling the cut fronds on an open space. Mr Fernandes, with a nice mixture of ritual and reluctance, threw on half a gallon of precious petrol. The flames leapt skywards, curling the ends of the green palm fronds overhead, and were reflected redly on the unsmiling faces of the tired party standing round. When the first fierce flames subsided, the turney-boy brewed a strong mixture of sugar and tea leaves in a big saucepan, the traditional "strongui" drunk without milk. . . .

The break over, the fire was stamped out and a shovel of sand put on the last glowing cinders, and we climbed back on the lorry. Mr Fernandes retired to the back of the lorry, undid his bed and went to sleep. The Oliver Hardy driver took his place. He was immensely full of chat and rather querulous, but he was so near sleep it seemed better to let him talk his heart out in case it helped him to stay awake.

We reached a tricky part of the road, which had sudden washaways, and broken approaches to narrow bridges barely wide enough to take the lorry and often without parapets. Our poor driver kept flopping over the wheel, but he got angry with me every time I jogged his arm or jabbed him frantically in the ribs. He swore he knew every pothole and rock and washaway, could drive the lorry with his eyes shut, and he was certainly doing his best to prove it.

At the foot of Lololokwe, we saw another elephant and a rhinoceros in the first light. It was just dawn when we reached the Guaso Nyiro. The water was low and its usual muddy red, but both the water and mudflats reflected the tawny orange which heralded the sun's appearance. The pale dust and rocks were touched with pink, and even the black lava rocks glowed. The palm trees were silhouetted against the vivid sunrise. Just beyond the bridge a huge lion was asleep across the road. He turned and blinked at us as the driver sounded his horn; taking his time he rose and stretched himself voluptuously before ambling off into the bush. The sun was over the horizon by this time and the numerous small herds of buck were streaking to more private places than the main road by daylight.

To My Wife – Fifty Camels Alys Reece.

Mary Nicol, the future wife of Dr Louis Leakey, fared no better on the Kenya/Tanganyika border.

We got to the Kenya border at Pussumuru without much difficulty, but there we found the Indian trading community terrified by the news that Masai at Narok had murdered District Commissioner Grant in retaliation for his making some of their warriors work on the roads, which they saw as something worse than an insult. The Indians were clearly in fear of a Masai revolt. Not much farther on, Louis accidentally drove the car off the road and into a deep gully, where it stuck fast, in the middle of nowhere, with nightfall near. There was nothing to do but sleep beside the car overnight. We then spent all next day trying to dig a shallow ramp through the side of the ditch, up which we could try and push the car onto the road. The only really odd thing about this operation was that our digging equipment consisted of table knives and two enamel dinner plates. The inevitable crowd of young Masai warriors gathered to watch, with great amusement, and one can see that our efforts did indeed have considerable entertainment value. It was beneath the warriors' dignity to help, of course, and with the news that we had gathered at Pussumuru Louis did not seek to persuade them, though in fact they showed no signs of hostility. By dusk we had actually successfully completed the digging, though daylight would be needed before we attempted to move the car itself, and so we prepared for a second night. But at that point our own lorry turned up, loaded with useful items like shovels and tow ropes, and in no time the car was safely back on the road and we were hearing the history of mechanical troubles that had caused the lorry's delay.

Disclosing the Past Mary Leakey.

Foot porters, mules, ox-wagons, cars and lorries: then the aeroplane.

CAPTAIN TONY GLADSTONE, AFC

by J. K. Twist

On 28 November 1924 Captain Tony Gladstone, AFC, set out from London with Captain T. K. Twist on a safari from Cairo to Kisumu, arriving in March 1925. They followed the Nile, as far as it was possible to do so, with the object of surveying and planning a route for a flying boat service from Khartoum to Lake Victoria. The proposal was to carry air mail to Cairo from East Africa and the Sudan, and gold from the Congo, and eventually to extend the service to the Cape.

They had an eventful journey, partly by river steamer and partly by bicycle. From Rejaf to Nimule (100 miles) they rode second-hand bicycles bought in Khartoum; these were always breaking down and were eventually abandoned, and they reached Nimule on foot. They received no encouragement for their scheme at first; in fact Sir Geoffrey Archer, Governor of the Sudan, told them to pack their kit and return to England. But in Kenya Lord Delamere gave strong support to the scheme, as did Kenneth Archer and the Chamber of Commerce. As a result, in October 1925 £2,000 was voted by the Kenya Legislative Council to test the possibilities of air communication between Khartoum and Kisumu.

In November 1926 Captain Gladstone brought out a seaplane with a Jupiter engine, which he named the "Pelican". Unfortunately it was so badly damaged by hitting a submerged object in the Nile at Khartoum that it had to be written off. The British Air Ministry then lent him a Fairey seaplane in which he made several flights between Kisumu and Khartoum. But again there was a stroke of bad luck. When taking off at Kisumu in March 1927 the pilot, not Captain Gladstone, crashed, and the seaplane was another write-off.

By this time Tony Gladstone had proved his scheme's feasibility. Fresh proposals were made in February 1928 by the Blackburn Aeroplane Company and Sir Alan Cobham's Aviation Company to the three East African Governments, and to the Sudan Government. Subsequently the interests of the new Cobham-Blackburn Company were acquired by Imperial Airways. This company started a flying boat service between Cairo and Kisumu. Later on the flying boats were discarded in favour of land planes, and thus began the air services between Europe and East Africa which have grown to what they are today, Imperial Airways having changed to British Airways.

Tony Gladstone was the real pioneer of civil aviation in East Africa. When he arrived in March 1925 there were no aircraft or landing grounds whatsoever. It was a tragedy he was killed in a flying accident in South Africa, together with Lt. Cdr. Glen Kidston, in May 1931, and so never saw the results of his pioneering efforts.

Pioneers' Scrapbook, eds. Elspeth Huxley and Arnold Curtis.

Imperial Airways began the first scheduled flights between London and Cape Town in 1932. Passengers slept the night in rest-houses, rose at three or four am to endure bumpy hours in unpressurized cabins flying unhurriedly at five or six thousand feet, and proceeded between Brindisi and Paris by train. The Nairobi to Croydon stage took six days.

Passengers in the early days of flying could expect adventure rather than comfort. The final stages of this London to Nairobi flight took place in 1935.

At Alexandria we were called at 3.30 am and took off in the Hengist, but had to change into the Horsa at Cairo. In the front part were Proctor, Megson, self and two of the most lousy, affected, giggly, selfish English girls you've ever seen, going on a visit to Entebbe. . . . Away we went from Cairo, destination Khartoum, coming down at Assiut, Luxor, Wadi Halfa (lunch) and a new place, Kariema. Took off at 6.30 pm from there and on came several *haboubs* [sand whirlwinds]. The machine was chucked about anyhow, the pilot could only just control it; he couldn't get through to Khartoum on the wireless, so at 7.45 pm they turned round to make back to Kariema. This is a tiny place with only one European, the wireless man. . . .

Along came the old Horsa, the pilot tried to do a downwind landing in terribly bad visibility with very sketchy flares, took the hell of a bump, then another, when our wings hit some hillocks or something. Off he fluttered to have another go, had to do a terrific bank to miss a tent, which actually did remove our starboard wingtip light, and caught our left wing in the sand. So when we finally came to rest, it was to find the fabric badly torn on both wings. It was rather alarming because of the extreme dark, and howling wind, and lots of lightning. However, the only casualty was a broken leg to my specs, which got trodden on. We bundled out into the desert. About half a mile away was the wireless man's hut, where he produced three beds, so the lousy ones and I slept in his garden, and the rest on the airstrip, in the tent or outside – most wisely the latter, as there were scorpions in the tent.

There was a marvellous steward on board, a perfect man, he produced enough food and drink that night from the plane (emergency rations). We were called at 5 am and foregathered to embark, the staff having worked all night to mend the wings with the wireless man's shirt and the windsock. But as the pilot was stepping in, he noticed that a strut had snapped off, and examination revealed quite serious wing damage, so we all bundled out again into the sand, and they wirelessed to Cairo for engineers and parts. The steward commandeered a donkey and galloped off to the native village to get eggs etc. We passed the day as best we might. . . . The poor relief plane – an Avro monoplane – met frightful weather, couldn't find us at all, got knocked all over the place, and finally arrived at Khartoum at midnight with four minutes of petrol left. It got to us next day about 10 am. Meanwhile we'd really had quite a good party. . . . The lousy girls got worse and worse, wilting and grousing. No one could bear speaking to them, they were so nasty. Finally I had to speak to them sharply. . . . It turned out that the Horsa was really badly damaged, so the Avro took us three females, the Italians, the German and the Indian to Khartoum and went back to fetch the others with the minimum of luggage – I personally have only what I stand up in. The next thing is, how to get us away. . . . The Italians had two grand planes waiting for them, and fluttered away quickly to Eritrea. It came through on the wireless that war had begun, though the League of Nations said it hadn't. [It had] . . .

That Saturday morning at Khartoum the rest of our passengers were brought in by the Avro. The Hanno, the next service after ours from Croydon, arrived on time on Saturday evening but they wouldn't let anyone on board, it was full to the brim; they took our mail and departed. We gnashed our teeth and settled down to another day at Khartoum. . . . At 5 pm on Sunday in came the mended Horsa. At 1 am we were called and proceeded to the aerodrome, sat in the plane waiting to go, when the wind suddenly changed, necessitating a completely new set of flares. Then up came a couple of heavy thunderstorms and our cautious, slightly-shattered captain had us bundled back to the hotel at 3 am. At 7 am we really did get off; gave Kosti a miss so had to fly mostly at about fifty feet to save petrol, it was definitely bumpy. Got to Juba about 6 pm, to be greeted with the news that the Hanno, hurrying on ahead with our mail, had crashed at Entebbe. A tyre had burst in the air, in the dark. The pilot evacuated everyone to the very back of the plane and did his best, but it was a crash all right. The pilot went through the windscreen, but was only shaken. We saw the poor Hanno yesterday, its nose buried in the ground, both paws missing, one wing hanging by a thread and the two propellers firmly established in the front cabin. They'd had a nasty moment, as one engine wouldn't stop until the petrol was switched off and the exhaust kept billowing flames. It was a marvellous escape. . . . They sent two Atalantas for us to Juba which we left at 5 am Tuesday and proceeded uneventfully by the usual methods to Nairobi which we reached at 2.30 pm.

Nellie: Letters From Africa, ed. Elspeth Huxley.

PART III

Settlers

Once the railway had been built, some method had to be found to enable it to pay its way. For miles and miles it ran through country either unpeopled altogether, or sparsely and intermittently peopled by nomadic cattlemen. There was nothing for it to carry out, and no cash to pay for anything it might carry in.

The only answer the British Government could see to this conundrum was to invite in settlers who would cultivate unused land, introduce crops and livestock marketable in other countries, and so provide a basis for a viable economy and bring in revenue for the railway. This was the rationale behind "white settlement", a policy that Sir Charles Eliot, the Commissioner, proceeded to implement in the early 1900s. Instructions were issued that only land not in occupation by Africans was to be leased to the incoming settlers. Generally speaking these instructions were carried out, but there were unforseen factors that, as time went on, were to call in question the policy's morality and the justice of its execution.

Epidemics of smallpox in humans, and of rinderpest in cattle, had, in the early 1890s, so reduced the Kikuyu population that some areas of formerly cultivated land had fallen into disuse, therefore appearing to surveyors as unoccupied, and so available for European settlement. These areas were mainly in and around the region of Nairobi and small in extent – amounting, it was subsequently estimated, to less than seven per cent of the total area in Kikuyu occupation – but they were to become seeds of impassioned grievances which were to germinate into a powerful political cause.

The concept of the outright sale of land was unknown among the Kikuyu. Land that had been lent to others could always be reclaimed. Thus Europeans who had secured from the Government legal titles to their land had, in Kikuyu eyes, merely made a temporary arrangement that could be ended at any time. Ignorance of Kikuyu law and custom was widespread among Europeans, and led to misunderstandings that were to be used in future in support of the nationalist cause.

Can pastures intermittently grazed by nomads' flocks and herds be said to be "occupied"? The settlers thought not. The Protectorate Government compromised. Some of the Maasai's vast grazing grounds, which spread over most of the East African highlands, were set aside as their reserve, while land in the Rift Valley traversed by the railway was divided into farms and ranches for Europeans. So the Maasai lost out. Nowhere can the way of the nomad ultimately resist the way of the settler of whatever colour, with his villages and towns and the web of civilization that he spins.

No one foresaw the enormous increase in population that followed the introduction of colonial rule. The abolition of the slave trade, of inter-tribal wars, of famines, of epidemics such as smallpox, bubonic plague and sleeping sickness, above all a drastic reduction in infant mortality – these and other factors led to a fourfold rise in population in the colonial period, a rise that has escalated ever since. Kenya now has the highest birthrate in the world. While people have multiplied, the land that supports them has not. Pressure on land has therefore intensified, and continues to do so.

Finally, in the first half of this century public opinion worldwide on the subject of colonies underwent a *volte face*. What was formerly believed to confer enormous benefits on "backward" peoples through the introduction of law and order, better health, higher standards of living and so on is now seen, as it were, through the other end of the telescope, to be an intolerable exercise in racial arrogance, oppression and colonialist exploitation. His Excellency the Emperor is seen to have no clothes. The cause of African nationalism swept the continent from end to end. These factors, and no doubt others, in sixty years brought white settlement to an end.

Early Days

Strangely enough, one of the first two "white settlers" to seek their fortunes in British East Africa was dark brown. He was Dr Henry Albert Boedeker, Eurasian by birth, Parsee by religion, small in stature and almost black. He and his newly married bride sailed from Tilbury docks on 6 June 1896, bound for Mombasa.

Dr Boedeker was planning to farm as far as possible from the stigma of being coloured. He had studied, trained and qualified as a doctor at Glasgow University and it was here that he fell in love with his wife, the daughter of Sir Henry Wardlaw of Tillicoultry. Their relationship was considered scandalous and the question of a permanent union even more outrageous. He spoke English impeccably but neither the fact that this was one of his most attractive qualities or his medical expertise had had any palliative effect on the disapproval.

Just as they were searching for a chance to start a new life, an article describing Kikuyu country as a land flowing with milk and honey appeared in a British newspaper and this convinced them that they should emigrate to the British East African highlands. They set about ordering large quantities of "candles, matches, soap and tinned goods", and a "great deal of clothing" for Mrs Boedeker who was almost painfully aware of her clothes and appearance. . . . Her boxes contained a large variety of hats, not of the protective sort, but wide-brimmed and small, trimmed with osprey and veiling to match a selection of gowns in the high fashion of the day. None was suited to travelling in the bush but she was one of those women who kept up standards despite everything. Into her cabin trunks in 1896 went piles of exquisite laces, velvets, silks and muslins; the high-necked dresses with leg-of mutton sleeves were without doubt quite unbearable for marching along in the dust and the heat.

Dr Boedeker had been more perceptive as to their needs than his frivolous bride. His luggage included a mould-board plough, so called because of the curved plate which turned the furrow and the first, as far as is known, to arrive in British East Africa. They sailed on the SS *Góorka*, a slow boat which called at every port for food and water. Sheep and cattle were bought in Mediterranean markets, taken aboard and slaughtered when required. At Aden, the Boedekers transhipped to the SS *Goa* when, after the excitement of seeing flying fish for the first time, "a frightful passage' ensued. They were relieved to come ashore at Mombasa.

To reach the highlands, the Boedekers joined forces with a blacksmith from Dumfriesshire and his wife Mary, and another couple called Wallace. They set forth across the Taru desert.

Years later when Mary McQueen's children begged her to describe this safari she usually recalled the joy of reaching Kibwezi where a small river ran cold from the mountains, the relief of dangling her stockingless feet in the water and of how she carried their father part of the way after he had sprained his ankle. Fortunately she was strong and, being six feet in height, taller than her husband. She explained how she cooked their meals on a piece of flat iron perched on three stones. Tinned meats and pigeons varied their diet from freshly-killed goat, which Mrs Boedeker described as "tough enough in all conscience". Mary McQueen never talked much about the problems of the walk. Yet, as if crossing almost fifty miles of the vicious bush thorn was not enough, the party was harassed by petty thieving in the Taru as well. Food and blankets were stolen and, to her husband's outrage, his cut-throat razor disappeared with them. He was a quick-tempered man and swore in his fit of anger, that he would never shave again. Nor did he for his remaining forty years and in Nairobi where men were more often bearded men than not in the early days, McQueen was easily distinguishable from the rest by his waist-length black beard.

Dysentery next afflicted the small cavalcade. The Europeans recovered but many of their porters died from it. The loss meant that the two Muscat donkeys which had been purchased for the women to ride now had to be used to carry loads instead. Other porters defected after they had been paid in advance.

For Mary Wallace and Mary McQueen in particular, the historic journey across those blistering miles of heat in 1896 was an exercise of great fortitude because they were both expecting babies. Mrs Wallace was seven months pregnant when she arrived at Machakos.

Not surprisingly, the baby Mary McQueen had carried from Mombasa, for a time together with her injured husband, was born dead. But subsequently four daughters and two sons were born at Mbagathi, twelve miles from Nairobi, on the forest land they made into a farm.

They called it Rhino Farm – later Rhino Park – because there were so many. Morning and evening the tank-like creatures came to drink from the Mbagathi River or wallow in the mud near the slope from which the McQueens drew their water supplies. McQueen built the house. He made all the hinges, nails, shutters and doors himself and encircled it with a thorn *boma* to keep the leopards and bothersome rhinos away. Water was taken up in old paraffin tins slung over their donkeys' withers. Three stones and an improvised Dutch oven made from the baked clay of Kikuyu formed Mary McQueen's kitchen. The same flat griddle she had brought from Scotland was used for frying for as long as she lived. Food was cheap. McQueen shot birds and game for the pot. Before long a Somali butcher opened from whom they bought local mutton. Occasionally they killed a steer and pickled it in brine and the salt beef kept them going for months. Bananas could be exchanged for the foul-smelling iodoform, which, ever since John Boyes had introduced the ointment to the Kikuyu, was much valued by them in the prevention of septicaemia from wounds. A large bunch of bananas could be traded with them for as much iodoform as could be placed on a pice piece the size of a silver sixpence. The McQueens lived at Rhino Farm until the blacksmith died in 1944. Mary McQueen educated her children by reading to them from her family Bible or *Pilgrim's Progress* before losing her eyesight prematurely. . . .

John, Jean, Madge, Minnie and Jim McQueen kept tame gazelles and saw nothing unusual in rhino drinking from their stream. Other children reared cheetahs, monkeys, lion cubs, mongooses or hyraxes which were accepted no less than white mice as pets. The McQueen children conversed with one another in Kikuyu and played tribal games learned from their helpers. The most favourite and bizarre of these was to steal beads which they would commandeer from the dying women as playthings before the hyenas did their undertaking. Neither they nor their parents thought anything of it; it never crossed their minds that they could be causing offence.

Possibly as often as every six months the McQueens walked to Nairobi on a shopping expedition. Newcomers were surprised by the strange cavalcade headed by the blacksmith whose wife dwarfed him, and each child walking one pace behind the last. They never wore shoes and had travelled so many native tracks barefoot through the bush that, as with the Africans themselves, it had become second nature to walk single-file in order to avoid the wait-a-bit thorns, even when in town. Unlike other Europeans then, the McQueens never wore spine-pads or pith helmets though shoes were introduced when they went to "proper'" school at the age of ten.

The Kenya Pioneers Errol Trzebinski.

Hugh Cholmondely, third Baron Delamere, reached the future Kenya in 1897 after a two-year trek from Berbera in Somalia. Six years later he returned for good to take up a grant of land from the Protectorate Government and to become the country's boldest and most influential pioneer and rancher, and the political leader of the white settlers.

Delamere reached his new estate on a stretcher. This was in January 1904, just a year after his accident. He could only walk a little. The train stopped at a level crossing between Njoro and Elburgon stations. He was carried to a couple of rough grass huts which Dr Atkinson's brother had built for him on a little rise below the forest's edge. He named the farm Equator ranch: the line of the equator ran through one corner of it.

His huts stood on the lower slopes of the Mau escarpment, the Rift Valley's south-western mountain wall, looking over a wide sweep of game-dotted plain beneath to a range of blue tumbled hills beyond. To the east ran the mighty cleft of the Rift Valley and on its far side rose the peaks of the Aberdare mountains, their crest a dark blue line against a changing background of banked or fleecy cloud. At the back of the huts lay the deep forests of the Mau. Most of the trees were junipers, known as cedars. Their trunks were straight and tall, and a sort of lichen hung like drooping grey-green whiskers from their crown of dark foliage. They were magnificent trees, dwarfing the paler olives which shared the mountains with them. The forest rose and fell in ridges. From the summit of one ridge you could look down on to the tree-tops from above and see two shades of colour, sea-deep of cedars and spring green of olives, splashed with the racing shadows of clouds, merging into a restless pattern like a leafy ocean. . . .

Delamere's huts were planted down in the open with no more disturbance to the natural panorama than the shaving of a little patch of grass. The windows (they were holes in the sides of the hut) looked out on to a long grass-covered slope merging into the flat plains below. You could see from these apertures slow-moving and compact herds of zebras, gazelles and hartebeests, mingling with awkward, striding ostriches and, occasionally, a placid rhino ruminating beneath a thorn-tree. . . .

Everywhere colours were vivid and deep and always changing, distant escarpments sharply defined, the sky rich with moving clouds, the atmosphere clear with the rarity of mountain air and charged with a sense of space and freedom blown on cool, crisp breezes from the hills.

There was no luxury about Equator ranch. The grass huts were surrounded by a corrugated iron *boma* into which cattle were driven every night. In the rains the ground was churned into a bog and the buggy often stuck up to its axles in mud. There were no proper doors or windows to the grass huts, so that at night the cows were liable to poke their heads through the apertures and breathe heavily into the sleeper's face. After a year or so a little wooden hut was built for Lady Delamere.

The inside of the huts presented a strange contrast. The floors were made of earth. They were uncovered and largely unlevelled as well, full of hills and valleys. Some good furniture had been imported from England and fine mahogany sideboards and valuable oak tallboys stood at drunken angles on the uneven floor round the walls of the huts. Good china and silver plate seemed incongruous in these crude surroundings.

Lady Delamere started a garden, but her days were so filled with looking after pigs, poultry and, later, ostriches that she had little time to give to it. . . .

Delamere dressed to suit his surroundings. Ever since he had suffered from sunstroke in Somaliland he had dreaded the sun and even in the highlands, where a felt hat generally gives ample protection, he was never without an enormous sun helmet (the biggest ever seen in East Africa) which practically obscured his face and dwarfed his slight figure. Since his third accident he had adopted a special precaution against the impact of the sun's rays on the back of his neck. This was to wear his ginger hair unusually long. He allowed it to hang down almost to his shoulders. He generally dressed in an old pair of khaki breeches and a woolly cardigan. . . .

When sheep and cattle failed at Njoro Delamere turned to agriculture. He evolved a theory that ploughing should be done in the cold of the early morning before sunrise. He used to get up at four o'clock and breakfast, muffled up against the sharp night air, off Thomson's gazelle chops by the light of a hurricane lamp and to the accompaniment of his favourite tune played, several times over, on the gramophone – "All Aboard for Margate".

White Man's Country Elspeth Huxley.

In 1902 Abraham Block, a penniless Lithuanian Jewish refugee from Russian pogroms, reached the embryonic Nairobi from South Africa. The Stanley Hotel, called after the explorer, had recently been opened by Mayence Tate, née Bent, Nairobi's first successful milliner and dress-maker.

The newness of the corrugated iron was all that separated its appearance from the other scores of buildings on stilts with wooden steps but apart from the fact that she had no mattresses she was ready to receive guests. Block heard of her dilemma and seized the opportunity to earn some money out of it. While he was riding about looking for work earlier that September he had noticed a great many bundles of dried grass which had been cut from either side of the railway. Believing that this would make suitable mattress filling he obtained permission from the Railway Superintendent to collect enough; he found ticking in the Indian Bazaar and, with the help of Mr R. M. da Souza, a Goanese merchant who provided Block with a tailor, worked out the dimensions. And then Block discovered that there were no mattress needles with which to assemble them. Ingenuity worthy of any pioneer overcame the problem; he sharpened and punctured two old bicycle spokes and stitched them with these instead. Mayence Bent approved the sample and ordered twenty-three more. He delivered them three weeks later and was paid 10 rupees each (the equivalent of about 14/6 in 1903).

With his mattress profits Block decided to buy a farm on the "pay-as-you-earn" system. Dotting the Kiambu landscape were a number of new homesteads belonging to Europeans; mostly *rondavels*, round thatched huts built in the Kikuyu tradition; the walls were made of red mud and cow dung and cost little to construct. The roof was thatched and the floors were of beaten earth. Some were already surrounded with patches of experimental crops, others barely developed at all.

Two German farmers, Dr Ufferman and Mr Lauterbach, alerted Block to the fact that a man called Corran had put the disposal of his 640-acre farm "Njuna" seventeen miles from Nairobi in their hands and left the country. They offered it to Block for 1,500 rupees and were willing to accept payment at his convenience. "Njuna" was in the Upper Kiambu district; the ground was cleared but not broken. Though it was not like Block to buy without seeing anything first, perhaps he feared that, by riding out to inspect the land first, he might lose the favourable deal to someone quicker off the mark. He paid Ufferman a deposit of one hundred rupees and sought legal advice to clinch the verbal arrangements. . . .

When Block got to Njuna he discovered that it had more to its name than he thought. There was a hut in which was a crude home-made bed and some cooking pots and there were even a few chickens scratching about outside and some pigeons but a local mongoose took these before he had the chance of a meal from them himself. The frames of the door and windows were covered by sacking and there were also a number of paraffin boxes, the inevitable alternative for furniture. . . .

The need for a plough posed a new financial crisis. His ponies were precious to him but they were also his only saleable asset. Reluctant as he was to give up his only form of transport, he concluded that something to ride was less vital for survival than machinery to break the soil. Imported ponies were scarce and commanded a high price at the time and so there was no difficulty in finding a buyer. . . .

Block had to walk a total of eighty-five miles just to get his plough and six oxen to Njuna. He had been lucky to find a plough to buy because until 1904 none were imported on a regular basis and the demand had been so erratic that the shortage was acute. Wealthier settlers were able to import them but farmers like Binks and McQueen had resorted to making their own. . . .

Block's Rudsak plough was borne home on the backs of Kikuyu women traditionally by means of a strap which went up round the forehead; it was adjustable so that each load sat snugly in the small of the back. To take the weight off the brow, the women stooped forward constantly so that by middle-age most of them bore a deep depression round the forehead and were pigeon-toed from having already spent half their lives in toil.

Hearing of a building plot for sale in the centre of Nairobi, Block pawned his watch and chain, made a down-payment with the proceeds and then sold half the plot to meet the rest of the purchase price. Twenty-three years later he exchanged the plot plus £500 for the Norfolk Hotel, thus laying the foundations of an empire which, carried on by his sons, was to embrace several of Kenya's leading hotels and game park lodges, and set a standard of catering respected throughout the world.

In 1947, ten years after Fred Tate died, Block's eldest son purchased the New Stanley from Mayence Tate on his father's behalf. People remember Block standing on the steps of the New Stanley, after he became its owner, a familiar figure wearing a suit and a worn Trilby, his hands clasped behind his back. Alternatively he could he found sitting in his favourite chair at the Norfolk in the foyer, puffing away at an expensive cigar (he bought only the best once he could afford them; they were his one concession to luxury). As the receptionist dealt with guests' accounts on the day of their departure, Block would lift his hand towards her, so that she could pass him the bill for scrutiny. It was then handed back. Unless it was at fault not a word passed between them. . . .

Block's sons acquired more land on the hotel's frontage and by the time they had finished developing it in 1974, though it had long been the centre of Nairobi, the New Stanley with its world famous "Thorntree" meeting point, was valued at almost half a million pounds.
The Kenya Pioneers Errol Trzebinski.

In 1902 Joseph Chamberlain, then Secretary of State for the Colonies, visited East Africa and, impressed by the land's apparent fertility, its emptiness of people and the healthiness of the climate, offered a free grant of 5,000 square miles to the Zionists who, following an especially ghastly pogrom in Russia, were pressing for a home for the Jews in Palestine. Despite a hostile reaction by many Zionists and an even sharper one by the Protectorate's few but vociferous European settlers, the Zionist leader Dr Theodor Herzl agreed to consider the offer. In 1904 three Jewish commissioners arrived to inspect the promised land on the Uasin Gishu plateau. A deputation of British settlers waited on Sir Charles Eliot to reiterate their opposition to the proposal.

They also asked if one or two settlers could accompany the Jewish commission on their tour of the country in search of a new Zion. The settlers' knowledge of the country might, they suggested, be of some value to the visitors.

"I am sure, gentlemen," Sir Charles Eliot replied courteously, "that you will be able to show members of the commission many things that they would not otherwise see."

The three commissioners were escorted to the Uasin Gishu by an officer sent out with them by the Foreign Office and by a couple of settlers. From Londiani on the railway they had to walk. It was a stiff climb over the escarpment, and the commissioners were not used to walking. They learnt that blisters could be a painful affliction.

They camped at the edge of the forest on the top. That night there were trumpetings and crashings in the forest and a herd of elephants passed within a hundred yards or so of the tents. There was a great turmoil in the camp and little rest.

The next day they marched on to a part of the new Zion. Here they encountered a column of Masai, some way from their usual beat. They were dressed in full war kit, with tall ostrich feather plumes waving in the wind above their curiously painted faces, barbaric anklets of black and white Colobus monkey fur, bare limbs glistening with castor oil and red ochre, and naked spear-blades glittering in the sun. The *moran* surrounded the party with every demonstration of ferocity, brandishing their spears and long narrow shields painted with heathenish emblems, and shouting hideous war-cries.

The settlers reasoned with them and they drew off, but only to perform a war-dance. As the rhythm quickened their gestures grew fiercer and their faces became distorted with apparent rage. The commissioners gazed with distaste on this savage medley of red, fat-smeared whirling limbs, demented ostrich plumes and flashing spears. Finally the Masai retreated, but a double guard was placed round the camp that evening and the settlers took it in turn to sit up all night with a rifle over their knees. There was little sleep in the camp that night either.

No native attacks occurred, but lions were grunting outside the ring of fires round the tents, and next morning the commissioners were shown pug-marks approaching uncomfortably close to the tent in which they had slept. The Jews were told the story, famous by now, of the man-eaters of Tsavo.

The commission only stayed about three days on the plateau. They returned to England and reported the district to be, on the whole, unsuitable for the settlement of fugitives from Russia.

Opposition to the scheme from the true Zionists had, in any case, won the day among the Jews themselves. They preferred "to continue to risk massacre and mutilation rather than to endanger the attainment of their ideal by permitting the movement to be shunted into a siding. Zion, and Zion alone, was their goal."

In August 1905 the East African commission reported to the Zionist congress at Basle and the offer of the British Government was, with sincere thanks, rejected.

White Man's Country (Vol. II) Elspeth Huxley.

Sea Captain Ernest Fey, his wife Mary, his son Jim and two daughters set out from Naivasha station in 1906 to climb to the forest's edge on the Kinangop saddle of the Aberdare mountains. His grandson Venn recalls the occasion.

To reach their chosen destination they used a bullock cart which they brought with them from India, and engaged one hundred porters under the leadership of a young Kikuyu warrior called N'jiri Karanja, who was later to become famous as the Senior Chief of the Fort Hall Kikuyu people. His own village at Kinyona contained the huts of over fifty of his wives and offspring.

My grandmother travelled in a sedan chair, a wicker work contraption with roof and side curtains, mounted on four stout bamboo poles which they also brought from India. . . . The bullock cart and team of oxen were laden with the heavy travelling trunks of the times, which contained personal effects and breakable possessions, the allotment of headloads to the assembled army of porters. Swahili and Indian domestic servants possibly stood aloof, away from the sweating gang of crude humanity. My grandfather and my father would be in the vanguard with firearms shouldered; my two aunts, in their early twenties, dressed in ankle-length khaki skirts and blouses with mutton-chop sleeves, double terai wide-brimmed felt hats, and spine-pads to ward off the treacherous tropical sun that was reputed to cause insanity to anyone who ignored adequate precautions. I see the raising onto stalwart shoulders of the sedan chair in which my diminutive grandmother sat imperiously!

There is the dust and clatter and shouts, the crowd of interested spectators. Just ahead, beyond the few tin-roofed Indian shops and the offices of the British Administration, was the grey-leafed Ol-leleshwa bush, and beyond that the dark line of the forest edge, through which there wound the rough and dusty track made by the Maasai and their herds of cattle and sheep when they moved from the Rift Valley floor to the grass plateau above, and where now there is a tarred road, and all memory of that epic setting forth into the wilderness has long since been forgotten.

The name of this locality in which my grandparents settled was called by the Wa Kikuyu "eN'Chappini". This name was derived from the sound made by feet walking across grassland during the rains when much of the plains were inundated. "Chappi, chappi, chappi, chappi" described the splashing, squelching sound of feet treading wet ground. Hence the name eN'Chappini, translated literally, "In the place of chappi, chappi."

And so my grandfather named his farm, "N'Jabini," a misspelling that remained to the end, as did so many other original Kenyan place names. . . .

They travelled first through forests of cedar and wild olive that were full of buffalo and rhino, lions, and leopards besides other animals of the forest, which terminated on the eastern escarpment of the Rift Valley. After a climb of about two thousand feet the country opened out into a wide and mainly flat plateau, the habitat of literally thousands of zebra, hartebeeste, eland, and gazelle. It was an area dominated by the Maasai people, who carried on a sporadic warfare with the forest-dwelling Wa Kikuyu who also cultivated the eastern slopes of the Aberdare range. . . .

My grandfather became friendly with both Kikuyu and Maasai alike, and although he and his young family lived at N'Jabini for three years before other white settlers arrived on the scene, they were never molested. Their house was built from the timbers of giant cedars pit-sawn on the lower slopes of the mountain. I still have two "monk's benches," red-brown with age, that were made from timber extracted from the first cedar to be felled on the farm. They were placed one on either side of an ingle-nook containing a huge fireplace in the drawing room. As a child I sat on a stool by the fire using a monk's bench as a table and ate my supper whilst a bedtime story was read to me.

Behind the house was the heavily forested mountain. South and westwards stretched the great plateau. In the morning the sunlight first fell on the far rim of the plateau, quickly advancing toward the mountain. Once a week, as the first rays and golden disc of the sun rose over the eastern shoulder of the mountain, my grandmother wound and reset all the time pieces at 7 am precisely.

Since we were on the Equator, the variation in the time of sunrise throughout the year was a mere half-hour.

If you stood on the big lawn in front of the house on a clear sunny morning you could see the great sweep of the mountains and the vast expanse of the plateau bathed in golden sunshine, truly, in every direction, a wide horizon.

Wide Horizons Venn Fey.

Hopes unrealized, 1907.

As one rides or marches through the valleys and across the wide plateaux of these uplands, braced by their delicious air, listening to the music of their streams, and feasting the eye upon their natural wealth and beauty, a sense of bewilderment overcomes the mind. How is it they have never become the home of some superior race, prosperous, healthy, and free? Why is it that, now a railway has opened the door and so much has been published about them, there has not been one furious river of immigration from the cramped and insanitary jungle-slums of Europe? Why, most of all, are those who have come – the pioneers, the men of energy and adventure, of large ambitions and strong hands – why are they in so many cases only just keeping their heads above water? Why should complaint and discontent and positive discouragement be so general among this limited class?

I have always experienced a feeling of devout thankfulness never to have possessed a square yard of that perverse commodity called "land". But I will confess that, travelling in the East African Highlands for the first time in my life, I have learned what the sensation of land-hunger is like. We may repress, but we cannot escape, the desire to peg out one of these fair and wide estates, with all the rewards they offer to industry and inventiveness in the open air. Yet all around are men possessing thousands of fertile acres, with mountains and rivers and shady trees, acquired for little or nothing, all struggling, all fretful, nervous, high-strung, many disappointed, some despairing, some smashed.

What are the true lineaments concealed behind the veil of boundless promise in which this land is shrouded? Are they not stamped with mockery? Is not the eye that regards you fierce as well as bright? "When I first saw this country," said a colonist to me, "I fell in love with it. I had seen all the best of Australia. I had prospered in New Zealand. I knew South Africa. I thought at last I had struck 'God's own country.' I wrote letters to all my friends urging them to come. I wrote a series of articles in the newspapers praising the splendours of its scenery and the excellence of its climate. Before the last of the articles appeared my capital was nearly expended, my fences had been trampled down by troops of zebra, my imported stock had perished, my title-deeds were still blocked in the Land Office, and I myself had nearly died of a malignant fever. Since then I have left others to extol the glories of East Africa."

My African Journey Winston Churchill.

God had sifted three kingdoms to find the wheat for this planting.

Wordsworth

"I started to grow wheat in East Africa," Delamere wrote, "to prove that though I lived on the equator I was not in any equatorial country."

In 1909 over 1,200 acres of wheat were sown in a single field. Delamere pinned all his hopes to this crop. It was to wipe off his overdraft, pay for the thresher which he had bought on credit, and prove wheat to be a sound foundation for farming in East Africa. From week to week he calculated the yield it would give when the reapers and binders went in to bend the hollow stems over the knife with their flails and leave the severed plants in rows of yellow bundles on the stubble. He was counting on well over 2,000 bushels.

But a new disaster, perhaps the most disheartening of all, descended upon Equator ranch. Another rust fungus – yellow rust, which destroys the ears it infects – attacked the wheat. It swept through the 1,200 acres like a flame and left it withered, not worth the harvesting. Over half the wheat had to be ploughed in. . . .

In England and in Canada the rust menace had been met by the scientific breeding of rust-resistant wheats. Delamere decided to adopt the same tactics.

An obvious difficulty was that there were two distinct kinds of rust which attacked wheat at Njoro. It was subsequently discovered that black stem-rust, a warmth-loving species, was usually found at altitudes of 7,000 feet and below, whereas yellow rust, the European kind, could only flourish in the colder districts at 7,000 feet and above. It was unfortunate for Delamere that at Njoro, at an altitude of almost exactly 7,000 feet, the two rusts overlapped.

There was also a third variety, known as orange leaf-rust, which was found all over the country. This one was less severe.

There was another serious difficulty.

Wheat which was resistant to one rust was usually particularly susceptible to another. Thus, while Rietti (the Italian wheat) stood up well against black stem-rust, it succumbed very easily to the yellow species. Gluyas (the Australian wheat) was fairly resistant to yellow rust but an easy prey to black stem-rust. The scientist was faced with the complicated problem of breeding a wheat resistant to all three species at once – or, if that was impossible, at least to the two more important kinds.

The eventual solution of this problem and of the complications which later arose out of it is considered to be an exceptionally fine piece of plant-breeding work.

Delamere started it by importing twelve different varieties of wheat from New South Wales. These were grown in plots at Njoro. His idea was to cross them with Rietti in the hope of combining in the progeny a certain amount of resistance to both black and yellow rust and, at the same time, of obtaining a wheat with a shorter growing season than Rietti.

He engaged a young man, Mr G. W. Evans, who had been a pupil of the famous plant-breeder Professor Rowland Biffen of Cambridge, to do the hybridizing. A rough laboratory was erected at Njoro. By a piece of good fortune Rietti flowered at the same time as the Australian wheats, and it was possible to cross-fertilize them. Had one type of wheat flowered a month later than the other, hybridization would have been impossible.

Rietti was crossed with the different Australian wheats and the progeny were grown and carefully studied. More wheats were obtained from all over the world – India, Egypt, South Africa and Canada. The Canadian wheat Red Fife, an ancestor of nearly all the famous prairie varieties grown to-day, was crossed with Rietti and promising offspring resulted.

At one time there were over 2,000 samples of different hybridized wheats growing in little cages made of amerikani cloth at Njoro. Most of these were abandoned, but about thirty-two varieties were grown in bulk.

All this applied scientific work was done at Delamere's own expense and the Government at first took no part.

White Man's Country Elspeth Huxley.

Nyasore, the thin man.

Sometimes, as thoughts about the future churned through my mind, I would go to Ndabibi and wander round the fifty-thousand-acre neighbouring ranch that had belonged to my father's old friend Gilbert Colvile. He had become a legendary figure because of his relationship with the Maasai, and his spirit seemed to linger everywhere.

His solitary grave lies on a small hillock rising about the plain, beside that of his stillborn child and his faithful dog. Before he died, he told the Maasai that he would never leave them and would watch over them and his herd, even after he was gone. The small fever tree planted on the site never rose more than six or seven feet. It never grew, but neither did it die.

One day, when Dorian and I were buying bulls at Ndabibi, we met Raua, the Colviles' old cook, and three other old retainers, on the road. They had been sitting up near Colvile's grave.

"What were you doing at Nyasore's grave?" Raua asked us inquisitively.

"We just went to visit him," we answered.

The four Maasai veterans piled into the car and we drove with them back to Colvile's wooden house, now empty and silent, but not abandoned. The doors and windows were closed and the wooden slats on the walls had turned a dark brown colour with age. The red paint had peeled off the faded corrugated iron roof. A gnarled acacia tree spread its leafy branches like an umbrella over the sparse, well-tended space that had once been a garden. Bushes and creepers with great leaves grew in disarray around the house. We peered through the glass panes in the windows. The room was cool and dim. The interior was swept clean, two old armchairs and a faded sofa were still neatly set out around the empty fireplace as they had been on the day he died. A threadbare carpet lay in the same place on the floor in front of the hearth.

"Nyasore was a Maasai like us. There has never been another white man like him," Raua began telling me. "When he first came here his land was covered with many wild animals. There were thousands of Tommy gazelles and impala everywhere. They ate much of the grazing for the cattle and we had to shoot them so that they would move away. Nyasore hunted them on horseback. There were also many lions lying in the bushes during the day and at night they prowled around among the cattle killing the calves and young steers. Nyasore would get very mad because he loved his cattle, just like we do. He hunted the lions with his dogs and guns, accompanied by our warriors with spears. There were all kinds of skins piled up in heaps in his house and many of his clothes were made from lion and Tommy skins. When Nyasore was hunting he could walk all day with only a cup of tea and an egg in his stomach. You would never think he was so strong when you looked at him. We called him 'Nyasore' – the thin man – because he was so lean."

He started with eight Boran cows, two of which were sterile. He added to these with cattle bought from Somalis, or seized in raids, and twenty years later ended up with ten thousand head.

African Saga Mirella Ricciardi.

How sweet is the shepherd's sweet lot!
William Blake

This business of looking after fourteen thousand sheep was no joke. I came to hate these animals, with their round woolly backs and obstinate selfish mouths. To prevent scab I was always having to dip them. At certain intervals they would be put through a long bath filled with a solution of Cooper's dip which, when first mixed, was a bright yellow colour, but later would become a foul brown. I and two natives stood at the edge of the channel and with our plungers pressed the head of each animal under water as it passed.

The sun would beat down upon us, the dust from the yard would rise in clouds over the fences, and the procession of sheep as they clambered up to the dipping pens would seem endless. Once in the pens the animals would shake themselves, and as I counted them out with the round yellow sodom-apples, which I used as tallies in my hands, my nostrils would be filled with the fumes of the arsenic, sickly warm fumes mixed with the ammonia which rose from the steaming brown backs. On such occasions it would seem to me that I was under the influence of some strange hypnotic trance, and I would bitterly curse my fate, the miserable monotonous fate of a scurvy shepherd superintending the washing of his flocks.

It was better in the lambing season. This always took place in October, so that the ewes might have the advantage of the fresh grass springing up with the falling of the light autumn rains. I would arrange the lambing camps in different parts of the farm, and pleasant enough it was to come upon these centres of ovine life, with the anxious mothers fitfully nibbling at the creeping grass and the lambs snow-white, long-legged, long-tailed, frisking about on the open veldt. As soon as the lambs were six weeks old I could go from camp to camp ear-marking, castrating, and tailing them. I made a point of doing this in the very early morning, so that the coldness of the air would lessen the bleeding. I became completely hardened to this occupation and would sear off the long appendages of these little symbols of salvation with expert deftness, and as I handled the red-hot copper implement a long thin ray of light would suddenly come slanting across the blood-stained, scorched board at which I worked, and immediately the nervous barking of the impala would cease and the first birds begin to call. When the affair was over I would kneel down and count the lambs by the number of severed tails which lay in a heap at my side, recording the total in my notebook with bloody, sacrificial hands. A dozen or so of the fattest tails I would take back with me, and Kamoha would fry them and serve them up for breakfast like a dish of eels.

In January shearing would begin, and the long rough shed which for the rest of the year remained closed and empty, like a deserted church, would now suddenly become the centre of the farm work. Sheep would baa, natives would chatter, shears would click, the old wool-press would creak, and all would be stir and bustle. It was my business to class the wool, and as fleece after fleece was carried to me I would allocate them to the various bins according to the quality of the staple. There were bins for fleeces, for bellies, for first pieces, for second pieces, and for locks. And the contents of each bin in turn would be baled up and the bales, when they had been stencilled, would be placed on a bullock wagon and hauled to the Uganda railway, to be eventually transported to the London market, there to be ripped open by indifferent merchants, unmindful of the far-distant thickets from which the burs had been caught up, those burs which they so casually noticed deep embedded in the soft crinkled wool.

I would have my breakfast and lunch brought over to the shearing shed and would work there from sunrise to sunset; and often as I stood sharpening the shining knives against the framework of a pen, polished to a rich mahogany brown by countless black fingers greasy from handling sheep, I would look out through the open door and see the wide African country stretching away, mile upon mile, outlandish, unkempt, to where the high mountains rose, upon whose terraces the heavy-limbed marauders slept, their gibbous, gently heaving, obscurely spotted bellies warm in the sun.

And so the long years passed slowly by. I saw little of the neighbouring settlers. My life became reduced to one unending struggle with the material world. To deal with it at all required enormous concentration of energy. My mind alone remained free. That, at any rate, could not become completely subject to an alien domination. Riding along great valleys with a hundred eland before me, riding across open clover-grown plains with ostriches zigzagging out of my way, my mind still retained its accustomed detachment.

Black Laughter Llewelyn Powys.

Five beautiful lions and a fig tree.

We decided to form a little company which we christened by the somewhat grandiloquent name of Sisal Ltd. The original members were, besides myself: Alan Tompson and his cousin Ronald Tompson, who both fell in France, my brother-in-law Mervyn Ridley, and Donald Seth-Smith who had just left Oxford where he had been a distinguished athlete. Mervyn and Seth-Smith were to be joint managers, and rare good ones they were to prove. The former had already had six months of most valuable pupilage at the hands of our early friends Swift and Rutherfoord, and Seth-Smith was well acquainted with local conditions, and was a born farmer and sportsman. . . . The first thing was to select a site for our house. We owned between us some 25,000 acres, and that's nearly 40 square miles and takes quite a lot of exploring. A considerable proportion of the area was plain, but there were thousands of acres among the foothills and it was cut up by a number of wooded gullies. Permanent water was, and is, none too abundant, though we did not at first realize how much is required to run a sisal factory. We made a standing camp with grass huts in a central position, and from it explored our territory on horseback and on foot in every direction. In the evening we would meet and weigh with the fiercest argument the merits of various house and factory sites. The latter was the easier problem. We knew enough to appreciate that the sisal leaves must, as far as possible, come downhill to the decorticator, that there should be available as much water as possible in the vicinity of the latter, and we rightly conjectured that the rich red loam rather than the black clay soil would give the better results in cultivation.

There was, in fact, only one site which really fulfilled these conditions; but for the homestead it was different. We all of us wanted a view, we mostly wanted shade, good drinking water was essential, and my wife was insistent on the best of soil for the garden. All these desiderata could be obtained in a greater or lesser degree in various places, and it appeared unlikely that we should ever make our decision. However, one day two of our party saw a nice eminence with a large fig tree standing imposingly thereon. They rode up to investigate, passing a nice little spring on the way up. On the top they found seated under the tree five beautiful lions who rose and trotted off into the long grass in dignified fashion. That settled it. It was unanimously felt that what was good enough for five lions should be good enough for us five. The next day we started erecting a grass hut, and my wife laid her first plans for the garden. Rightly eschewing the obvious name of Simba (lion), we christened our new home Makuyu, the native name for fig tree. The site faced a long undulating vista over the Kikuyu Reserve to Mount Kenya, its peak usually wreathed in clouds save at dawn or nightfall during the rainy season. Behind us rolled plains on which herds of game fed, the zebras barked and the lions grunted, till in the distance rose the square mass of El Donya Sabok. On our right sloped the bush-clad Ithanga Hills. It was a pleasing spot in 1907. Today the house is surrounded by tens of thousands of acres of blue-green sisal and dark-green coffee, not a buck or zebra is left upon the remnant of the plain, and from the verandah of the house the electric lights of some forty bungalows can be seen twinkling in the night. Magnificent progress indeed, but it contains, as always, its elements of sadness. We, who are in part responsible, cannot fail to appreciate the latter.

Kenya Chronicles Lord Cranworth.

The Van Rensburg trek to the Uasin Gishu plateau.

The trek started in June, 1908, from three stations on the Pretoria-Delagoa Bay line. There were forty-seven families in all, and three single men, making a total of between two and three hundred souls. All the families but two brought their own wagons, and more than half of them brought a horse, or several horses: but no oxen, as these could be procured in East Africa.

Mr van Rensburg, the Kommandant, had chartered a German boat, the *Windhoek*, for £1,750. She sailed from Delagoa Bay and reached Mombasa in seven days. The railway provided five special trains. The passenger accommodation consisted of trucks with wooden benches on which mothers bestowed their childen as best they could. . . .

A few families got off at Athi River to settle there. The rest continued to Nakuru, and arrived on 18 July, with 72 horses, 42 wagons and 2 predikants. They established their camp about five miles outside the town, near the site of the present airfield.

A meeting of the men decided to send ahead immediately a party of horsemen, with a light cart and oxen, to reconnoitre the ground and choose a path for the heavier wagons to follow. Those who stayed in camp were to train the raw oxen, none of which had ever seen a yoke before, bought at a sale of cattle arranged by the District Commissioner.

The party rode out to Eldama Ravine and followed a native track, probably first made by elephants, up the steep escarpment through cedar forest to Timboroa. Here, from a hill on what became known as Farm One, they could see across the Plateau to the landmark of Sergoit Rock. There lay the promised land – flat, treeless, swarming with game, empty of humans: like the high-veld near to Bethel, but without settlements; and their hearts were glad.

They trekked on for three days and looked across the Elgeyo border where the van Breda brothers and John de Waal were settled, and there they spied out the land. They saw no Africans, but all the rifle-fodder they could want, and they returned well pleased. After their account, four families turned back. The rest started their trek on 4 August, 1908.

Such a sight had never before been seen in the Protectorate – upwards of fifty wagons, (the newcomers had bought more locally), each with a span of sixteen oxen, jolting along a barely marked track that wormed among trees and bush, the bearded men with long whips cracking like rifle-shots beside them, horsemen riding ahead and at the flanks with rifles in their hands. The wagons were of the old Dutch type, half-covered, with a tented portion at the back which the women and children shared. At night the wagons were drawn up in a defensive ring around the cooking fires, and a *boma* of thorn bushes built for the oxen, and the men slept beside their wagons under the stars.

The trekkers travelled in two columns. Ten wagons went ahead in the first column, which crossed the Rongai river on the second day. On the third day they crossed the Molo river and on the fourth they reached Eldama Ravine. Here they camped for three days to rest the oxen and give the women a chance to wash clothes, and to bake bread. To make an oven, they scooped a hole in the side of an ant-heap or a river-bank, lit a fire and placed in the hot ashes big cast-iron pans, brought with them for the purpose, containing dough.

One more day's trek brought them to the forest's edge on the steep escarpment rising above Ravine. Here they halted for five days while the men widened a track through seven miles of forest. This track was wet. The first column managed the seven miles in one day but the wagons in the second and larger column came to grief in the mud and took four days to get clear. Meanwhile, the men of the first column cut a track through the bamboos and made a causeway over the swampy patches with the canes.

After struggling through the first belt of bamboos, both columns rested for two days; but there was a second belt to tackle, harder than the first. To get heavily-loaded wagons up this steep escarpment along the rough, narrow, treacherous track, with inexperienced oxen and in a wet year, was a truly remarkable feat, and only Afrikaners could have performed it. At last, after prodigious effort, they reached the top and pitched camp at a place they called Brugspruit, near Timboroa. Here they could at last look out over the promised land.

Next day, all the men went out shooting for the pot and brought back kongoni. Not a scrap was wasted; the fat was melted down for lard, the hides tanned for shoes, the offal fed to dogs. That night, they had their first tragedy. A two-year-old girl died, probably from pneumonia, and was buried next morning under a big cedar tree.

Both columns started off again together through the area now known as Burnt Forest, and reached Sugar Vlei. Here they encountered a swamp, infamous in years to come, and fifteen of the wagons stuck so badly that each one needed three teams – forty-eight oxen – to pull it out.

On the following day the going was so heavy and the climb so steep that they covered only five miles. Once again they halted while the men built causeways with brushwood and sods over two more swampy places. Another day of sticking and straining, heaving and hauling, brought them to better ground where the road to Kipkabus now leaves the main road, just south of Plateau station. The going was easier now, and one further day's trek brought them to the Sosiani river. They crossed the Sosiani and camped the next night at John de Waal's.

From Sergoit, all the Afrikaners fanned out and each man picked the piece of land that pleased his eye. A simple survey had meanwhile been made, mainly by Piet van Breda, and angle-irons planted in the long grass to mark the corners of blocks demarcated in units of 900, 1,400, 2,600 and 5,000 acres, at an annual rental of 18, 12, 6 and 3 cents (of a rupee) respectively. It was a condition of the lease that a sum equal to forty times the rent must be spent on development within five years, and no leases were to be granted until this had been done. In all 104 farms were demarcated on the Uasin Gishu and offered on these terms.

Most of the trekkers had brought with them small ploughs and they began in earnest to break the veld, and then to work it down with harrows made from triangles of thorn-tree logs spiked with pegs cut from the tough olive. As they had no nails, they did without. Theirs was an economy of self-sufficiency and barter that seldom called for money. But ammunition they needed, and a few clothes: to get the necessary cash they sold buffalo or kongoni hides, and sometimes the young men went off to work as ox-drivers for English settlers. Perhaps they would return with enough to buy not only a shirt and trousers (which could be had for Rs. 3/50 the two) and some cartridges but a Nandi cow (for Rs. 15/-) to lay the foundations of a herd.

Londiani was rail-head. The distance was sixty-four miles from the Sosiani river at the point which subsequently became Eldoret, and the return journey took thirty days if you were lucky, and up to twice as long if your wagons stuck, as they so often did, in the appalling mud. The longest time recorded for the single journey was twenty-eight days. The swamps became infamous, particularly one known as Campi Nyasa or the Red Sea, at Mile 32 from Londiani, where oxen in their traces were known to drown. "Where the mud moves, there are oxen" was a saying of those days. Six span – ninety-six oxen – were sometimes hitched to a single wagon to haul it through. It was a common hazard for wagons to sink into mud up to their rails. Dissel-booms and wagon-chains constantly snapped and had to be repaired then and there by the trackside, while the oxen waited up to their bellies in mud.

No Easy Way Elspeth Huxley.

Their first crops failed: the Afrikaners persisted. A sample exhibited at the agricultural show at Nakuru in 1909 was the first wheat grown on the Uasin Gishu plateau. Thirty years later, the plateau was known as the bread-basket of Kenya.

Throughout March and April a dozen or more puffs of dust could be seen curling up from the plain below the homestead, where ox-teams dragged heavy ploughs through the grass-encrusted loam. For the veld it was a christening of steel. The discs cut keenly through matted grass roots, leaving a brown gash on the pale surface of the plain. Native ploughmen hung tightly to the handles to prevent the plough from bucking out of its furrow as it encountered some hidden stone or stump. The air was thick with sharp raucous cries imitated from Dutchmen and with the cracking of the long hide whips.

Never before, through the immeasurable ages of geology or the shorter centuries of man, had this particular piece of soil been carved into by the discs, thrown on its back to expose its accumulated plant food and its microscopic life to the glare of the sun, beaten into clods and pulverized into a soft, even seed-bed. To the mind of the pioneer there was something peculiarly satisfying in the surrender of virgin country. It gave him a satisfaction born of the consciousness of a job well done and of the reflection that here, where zebras had roamed over wasted pastures, a million ears of wheat would slowly fill into golden pips of gluten worth so many shillings the bushel in the world's markets.

Possibly, also, it filled some aesthetic need in a nature left unsatisfied by the pioneer's crudity of surroundings – mud huts, furniture knocked together out of packing-cases, cattle *bomas*, corrugated iron, a cracked gramophone and a few tattered copies of illustrated papers from London.

Pioneers like Delamere often seem to have a dead side to their natures. They seldom appear to take any interest in music or art, or to look for beauty in existence. They cannot afford to do so. They must not admit the need for such spiritual stimulants in the midst of the raw, prosaic realities which surround them; they must force themselves to be content to live out of contact with art and intellect.

Some may have few finer wants, a low standard of intellectual living. Others, perhaps, may find some aesthetic satisfaction in this arduous business of taming new land and imposing the order of man's design on nature's apparent chaos. These men exercise their imagination by creating waving wheat-fields out of veld and bush; see beauty in the lines of a ram or a bull perfect of its kind; hear music in the swish of the reaper.

Pioneering itself may be a sort of art, in its own way as creative as the painting of a picture. Has not the artist a landscape for his canvas, ploughs for brushes and axes for a scalpel? Daubs of brown go in with broad sweeps of the brush, to be changed again, here to green and there to yellow; buildings appear to give the composition balance; forests are erased in one corner and added in another; sheep bring contrast to the pastures; roads add proportion to the design. And at the end, when the macrocosmic artist surveys his canvas, he may see a grace in the homesteads with their gardens and their solidarity that his mind has conjured out of scrub, just as the painter knows that he has created beauty out of the pigments in which he has clothed his inspiration.

White Man's Country (Vol. I) Elspeth Huxley.

First aid.

In 1910 anyone living in the Kiambu district was twenty miles from the nearest hospital. Dorcas Aubrey, the niece of Isabella Beaton and married to an early coffee planter at Ruiru, like everyone relied on ox-transport which was unbearably slow. When she received word that a Kikuyu was dying on the path below her house she found that he had had a fight with another African and his intestines were spilling from a gaping hole in his abdomen. He could not be moved until his guts had been replaced. Unless she could think of some means of saving him herself he would certainly die. She removed a string from her violin and threaded it through a sacking needle to sew the man up where he lay on the path. A litter was made from branches of trees to carry him up to her house, where she nursed him back to health. Innovation such as this went on in every homestead.

The Kenya Pioneers Errol Trzebinski.

Nairobi's best-known, best-loved and at times most-dreaded doctor was Roland Burkitt, an Irishman who started a general practice there in 1911. At a time when few Europeans escaped attacks of malaria, he was famous for his cold water cure.

A story, which illustrates the determination of the man, is told of a mother who was convinced that if the slightest cold reached her baby while its temperature was high, it would assuredly die of pneumonia. Dr Burkitt placed it naked in an open-work basket, which he hung in a doorway for the sake of the extra draught and sprayed it with a watering can. The determined efforts of the mother to rescue her child were met only with quiet restraint and confidence. Unable to stand it any longer she rushed from the scene of what she was convinced was murder and locked herself in a bedroom from where she showered threats on Dr Burkitt's head of what she would do to him if anything happened to her child. All this he took with quiet calm, and, when the child's temperature had reached normal, he knocked on the door and invited the mother to come and see what cold water could do.

Another tale, illustrating his belief in increasing heat loss, is told of a very big woman whom he went a distance into the country to see, and found her with a very high temperature. He decided to bring her into hospital in Nairobi. Her relatives wanted to wrap her up in blankets, afraid she would get cold, but Burkitt refused. Instead he insisted that she should travel naked in the back of his open Ford car. On the way in he stopped and took her temperature. He found it was dropping, so he took off his coat and wrapped it round her. As the story goes, the patient eventually reached the hospital dressed in all Burkitt's clothes, while he arrived naked.

During the influenza epidemics and in the malarial seasons, which in those days were common but now are happily things of the past, Dr Burkitt had patients all over the town in cold baths, under wet sheets, being sprayed with watering cans or merely being sponged, while he hurried from one case to another checking temperatures. Woe betide the relative or nurse who abandoned treatment before the desired result was obtained, but some people were not above setting an African servant on watch to give warning of the doctor's approach so that a comfortable bed could be abandoned for the bathroom. Prominent and worthy citizens, men holding high executive posts and large employers, in response to a warning from the watcher, could be seen rushing in their pelts along passages to the bathroom and plunging into a cold bath, while the doctor's Ford car chugged up to the house. When he found the temperature still up Dr Burkitt would shake his head and exclaim, "This is a terrible bad case." He was utterly guileless that his treatment was not being rigorously followed. . . .

He was an early riser, and every morning he was up at or before dawn reading in his study wrapped in a warm Jaegar dressing-gown over his pyjamas. In cold weather he put on socks and sometimes a muffler. For two hours he divided his time into bible study and reading scientific medical journals or books. If an urgent call came during those hours or in the night he would set off to see the patient in this unconventional garb, surmounted by a sun-helmet.

At 6 o'clock his African servant brought him a large pot of tea and he drank several cups well sweetened. The tea was intended to wake him up, and the sugar to give him energy. If he had guests staying in the house it gave him great pleasure, if they would join him at this hour and listen to his discourse on some abstruse theosophical problem. The study of the scriptures and the origin and history of words used in the Bible was a constant source of interest to him. . . .

At 7.30 o'clock he shaved and every morning of his life in Kenya he took a cold bath, with the exception of one week after I had shot a wild pig and he and Colonel Guinness decided to pickle it in the bath. None of us had a bath for a week.

Once he killed a puff-adder on the lawn of Mr Claud Watson's house where we were all having tea. He brought it home and skinned it carefully, saving the meat to make a savoury. Next day he told the cook to chop the meat up and serve it for luncheon in scrambled egg. That day he invited Mrs Philip Percival, Miss Percival, Miss Hughes his nurse, and other friends. When we had finished the savoury, he enquired how his guests had enjoyed it. The mischievous look on his face immediately aroused Miss Hughes' suspicions, and she demanded to know what was in it. When he told her it was puff-adder she immediately went outside and was sick. This amused him immensely as the amount of snake flesh among the egg was infinitesimal. . . .

He never entered a cinema except once and that was only to please Miss Hughes, who insisted that he should go to see the Martin Johnson film of big game life in East Africa. Miss Hughes was his surgery nurse, of whom he was very fond, and I do not believe anyone else could have prevailed on him to go. She had a job keeping him in his seat while the supporting programme was run through. He refused to admit he enjoyed the film, and I think he did not, because he was so firmly convinced that all cinemas were of the devil.

Under the Sun J. W. Gregory.

Dr Burkitt was not the only eccentric doctor about. One of them, Dr John Gilks, kept a tame leopard which he took with him when he went visiting his patients. It was called "Starpit". The Africans thought that was its name as they had heard Dr Gilks saying "Stop it, stop it," to it. One of Dr Gilks' patients who was ill in bed with a liver complaint claims that she was cured by sheer fright when the leopard came in behind the doctor and leapt straight on top of her in bed.

We Lived on the Verandah Suzanne Fisher.

In February 1900, Dr Rosendo Ayres Ribeiro, Nairobi's first private medical practitioner, made his appearance. His tubby, Goanese figure became familiar as he rode his tame zebra about the Bazaar or along Station Street. He pitched his tent where the bakery later stood in Whitehouse Road. Wearing a stetson, his black beard trimmed neatly, his buttons looking as if they would pop off his waistcoat at any moment, Dr Ribeiro visited the sick among all communities. He became famous in Nairobi for his special malarial cure, which he patented and which was sold to an international pharmaceutical company eventually. For six months he and his assistant, Mr C. Pinto, shared a tent as home and practice. In the evenings, by the light of a candle and a kerosene lamp they made up prescriptions of the young Goanese doctor's invention. He cured many grateful settlers of fever with his nameless, grey powders; the first dose induced vomiting which produced a lot of green bile but that was the extent of discomfort. After completing the course his patients were assured of freedom from fever for many months.

As the Indian Bazaar expanded Dr Ribeiro moved into more luxurious quarters and their next surgery was built from the packing cases in which his drug supplies had been shipped from England. A tarpaulin, borrowed from the railway, provided temporary cover and when it was reclaimed he practised with no roof, like Aesculapius in the Sacred Groves, receiving many a tough native chicken in lieu of payment for his cures. It was Dr Ribeiro who, in 1902, had diagnosed bubonic plague in two Somali patients and reported it. The Medical Officer of Health, with no experience of tropical diseases, panicked at the news, ordered the Indian Bazaar to be evacuated and burned it to the ground. Dr Ribeiro's surgery went up in flames with the rest. This drastic measure cost the Government £50,000 but Dr Ribeiro fared rather well out of the disaster. He was compensated for the loss with the gift of a domestic plot near the station. There he built the usual '*Dak*' bungalow on stilts, from which he carried on with his work and, in 1903, was given a concession of sixteen acres behind Victoria Street by the Government in recognition for services rendered over his report on the plague.

The Kenya Pioneers Errol Trzebinski.

I will take some savage woman, she shall rear my dusky race
Tennyson

I had one adventure with a Kikuyu maiden who could not have been more than sixteen years old. I had ridden far into the forest when suddenly here she was before me, a young native, bending over a water-hole filling a gourd. I reined in my pony. She started with a cry as soon as she saw me. I was the first white man she had seen at such close quarters. I began talking to her in Swahili, but she did not understand a word of that language. However, she soon lost her nervousness, and with the confidence of her sex when they know they are beautiful, stood laughing there before me.

She wore a thin strip of leather across her loins. Except for this she was naked. Her brown skin, the colour of an oak-apple, was smeared over with the oil they extract from a eucalyptus-smelling berry. I rode by her side until she reached her hut, a round kraal hidden in a forest glade. I found her father there, busy with his mealie plot. He knew a few words of Swahili and I had some talk with him. After that I rode away. But try as I might I could not get the memory of this forest-child out of my mind. The long, lonely years I had passed in Africa had made my whole being cry out for something to love, for some romance, for it is exactly this that is lacking in the great dark continent.

For several months after this event, whenever I was free in the late afternoon, I would ride up to the forest and stand waiting by the water-hole till Wamboy came. We used to sit side by side under a great forest tree, and I would try to teach her to pronounce certain English words and tease her when her curved lips found difficulty in stammering out the unfamiliar syllables. She was proud and evasive and in every way inaccessible. The sound of her laughter was the prettiest thing I have ever heard in my life. It was clear as the cry of a widgeon on a frosty January morning, clear as the sound of wind in a tall unpollarded poplar-tree. The more I saw of her the more impossible it seemed that I should ever be able to rid myself of the spell she had cast over me. I began to contemplate marrying her. Why not? After all, we have only one life, and surely, I thought, I could spend mine in many worse ways than living in the forest with this lovely creature. I also, like her father, could occupy my time in cultivating a mealie plot, letting all the vulgar importunity of the modern world go to the devil. Other white men had deliberately abandoned civilized life and taken to living with black people; why should not I? I made overtures to the father. He seemed more than agreeable, and told me that if I gave him fifteen goats, ten sheep and one heifer, I could take the girl away whenever I wished. As soon as our plan reached Wamboy's ears she grew frightened. She had been willing to laugh and play, but when she understood that I was really serious a new scared look came into her eyes. It would hardly be true to say that this was altogether unpleasing to me; however, on the whole, it seemed best to avoid meeting her any more. For more than a month therefore I refrained from riding up to our trysting place.

At the end of this time the old man came to see me. His avarice had evidently been roused. "Take her," he said. "I myself will bring her to you by force any evening you name. When she has lived with you she will come to love you and be no longer frightened." It was, indeed, a most tantalizing proposal, but the pathos of the girl's alarm and the whole inarticulate grace of her personality made it impossible for me to carry negotiations further. I told the old man to go back to his mealies, and never again looked into the provocative eyes of this rare hamadryad of the African forest.

Black Laughter Llewelyn Powys.

William Northrup McMillan, who hailed from St Louis, Missouri, bought land near the mountain Ol Donyo Sapuk north-east of Nairobi and settled down with his wife Lucie to develop a self-contained estate. He was knighted for his services to Britain during the First World War.

The estate was called after two West African images brought to Kenya by Northrup McMillan and known as Ju and Ja. Numerous superstitions surrounded them, and eventually Lady McMillan buried them somewhere in the Ndarugu Valley, but she never disclosed where. One of the superstitions was that the images would bring bad luck to the idols' owners, some of whom would die at sea. Sir Northrup McMillan died at sea off Mombasa on a return journey from England.

In 1905 the pre-fabricated sections of Juja House arrived from England, ending their journey by mule-cart from Nairobi. Juja was soon a thriving community with an area of one square mile enclosed in a ten-foot fence on three sides, with the river as the fourth protection to keep out wild animals. Within the compound was a post office and a telegraph office, and housing for a European staff consisting of a manager, a chauffeur, two gardeners, a groom, a storeman and Lady McMillan's maid. There was stabling for twenty-six horses, which were carefully netted in at night against the dreaded tsetse fly. Each horse had its own syce who slept and ate with it and ran alongside when it was ridden out, ready to take the reins at any time.

Juja House was surrounded by formal gardens and approached by an avenue of trees, plants and flowers. Below the house were large fruit and vegetable gardens, also grain and maize. Attempts were made to farm ostriches, pigs, cattle and sheep, but all were more or less defeated by disease. However, a slaughterhouse, bacon factory, dairy and cheese factory were built, also an elaborate block of stone pig houses. From this ran a light railway to facilitate cleaning out the pig houses. Juja was famed for its hospitality and there was a camping site set aside for any passing safaris. Colonel Theodore Roosevelt was on one of these safaris, and stayed at Juja for some time.

From 1914 to 1918 Juja House was a hospital and convalescent home for British officers. Having attempted all kinds of farming without success, Sir Northrup sold the estate in 1919 to Mr F. N. Nettlefold, a wealthy Englishman, and went to live at Donyo Sabuk House, which he had recently built. He became enormous, weighing, it was said, over twenty stone. When sitting in an ordinary motor car, one leg and almost half the rest of him overflowed. The National Bank of India had a seat made specially to hold him.

He was buried on Ol Donyo Sabuk. The hearse was made with skis on the bottom and a tractor pulled it up the hill, followed by the mourners. Many cars burned out their clutch-plates, and when the tractor eventually reached the shoulder of the hill it also stopped, so the burial took place there instead of at the top, which had been the original plan. Oak trees were planted by the grave.

Pioneers' Scrapbook, eds. Elspeth Huxley and Arnold Curtis.

Odd men out.

The next morning, having out-distanced the wagon, I sat down under a tree to enjoy the scene, when the silence was broken by a tinkle of bells, and I saw a neat little wagon drawn by sixteen donkeys trotting down the track towards me. The good-looking, bearded Englishman sitting in front, seeing me, jumped down and came forward to meet me. He was a highly-cultured gentleman, who had served in the British Army, but eventually, weary of the complications of civilized society, had cleared right off the map and lived a pleasant nomad existence in this delightful country, with his well-equipped little wagon as his home. He out-spanned and told me his history while his boy prepared a meal native fashion, for he despised European stores. Later, when my wagon came up, he dined with me, and we sat talking far into the night as men will who meet by chance and will probably never see each other again.

At dawn we went our different ways with mutually pleasant recollections. Afterwards I heard that he had been in trouble with the authorities over some question of trading ivory with the natives, and believe that he packed up and trekked off farther afield again, away from the inevitable restrictions of man-made laws.

At the very farthest point on the edge of the forest we came across an old Scotchman quite alone. He lived in a dilapidated grass hut without even a native boy to fetch wood and water for him. Near his hut lay the body of a zebra which had been half devoured by lions. He had only a very old-fashioned rifle and four rounds of ammunition. He said that he was not afraid of the natives, they never interfered with "Old Sam," or of the lions that had killed so near his hut. His only trouble apparently was "Those blamed hogs" which came and rooted up his mealie patch. He told me that he had pioneered in every new country as it opened, and generally sold out after sitting on his claim for a few months. Surely he was the most lonely old man in Africa, and seemed to want nothing so much as to be left in peace.

Havash! W. Lloyd-Jones.

The unimportance of time

In early 1914 the spirit of the white highlands in the East Africa Protectorate was one of unbounded optimism, of faith and a great love. The pioneers were out of the ruck, all set for the making of a new heaven on a new earth. In the Native

Reserves, by which white settlement was immediately surrounded, peace, trust and goodwill prevailed. Tribal entities were absolute; there was no semblance of a dream of nationhood. Perhaps the greatest blessing, which was shared by all, was the supreme unimportance of time. The sun set and the sun rose. It was just a matter of night and day.

Nakuru, at this time, was regarded as being the capital centre of the European farming community – the hub of the inviolable sanctuary of the white highlands. Every settler was the lord of a manor, no matter whether his holding were great or small – his homesteads built of stone or mud. His rights were sacred and inalienable for all time and his dominion within the boundaries of his farm was feudal. His loyalty to the Crown was absolute, but his attitude towards Government was a mixture of resentment and contempt. He came in quest of freedom and independence, determined that the land of his adoption should yield him a livelihood. Every one of them considered himself a pioneer regardless of his length of residence and, in a sense, he was justified, as there was no great amount of experience behind anyone. They also believed they could govern the country in a proper manner and bitterly resented the meagre representation allowed them. Perhaps they were right in their belief; there were certainly very able men among them. . . .

Government regime was despotic. Tribal resistance had been quelled. There was a tremendous sense of security. Except in the remote north, law and order prevailed in a remarkable degree. Benevolent despotism was the order of the day, but the white highlands had no use for despotism in any shape or form.

Lion in the Morning Henry Seaton.

Between the Wars

In 1919 the British Government launched the Soldier Settlement scheme. It was a lottery; each successful applicant drew a number which entitled him, or her in a few cases, to a block of unpopulated and undeveloped bush or veld, of varying size, in the Protectorate's highlands. The Soldier Settlers and their families, if any, made their way to Nairobi and then set out to find their prizes.

Within a few days the new arrivals had mostly left Nairobi and were scattered in all directions, either to stay with friends or to look for their farms. There were hardly any roads and no particular landmarks, and quite a number of people started operations on someone else's land – it was all guesswork. The new settlers were nearly all amateur farmers besides being new to the country, and some of them expected their farms to be like English ones, with hedges, fields, buildings and cultivation; and one or two even gave up in despair when shown by a neighbour a mere tract of country as their "farm".

We left Nairobi at 4 pm, and until dark enjoyed the views of the new country; but it became very cold as we climbed to the higher altitudes, and when we got out at a station for dinner, it was raining hard and blowing a gale.

Few things are more depressing than arriving at a strange place in pouring rain. When the place is a little wayside station and the hour five-thirty in the grey dawn of a morning in the rainy season, wet and cold, a certain amount of courage is needed to face life! . . .

We had seventy miles to go (by ox-cart) and hoped to do it in a day and a half, and, considering the road was a quagmire most of the way, we got on fairly well. But at 4 pm we had only done twenty miles, and when darkness fell, were in dense forest and a violent storm of rain began.

Oxen cannot work in the rain, the yokes gall their necks; so we stopped and they were outspanned and left to wander about and graze, and we prepared to camp for the night in the cart. There was a hut near by for the boys, to which they thoughtfully carried off our only lantern, and we were left with the candle without which no thoughtful person travels in the blue; but we had no candlestick, and the candle promptly fell over the side of the cart into the mud, and in the darkness took some time to retrieve.

The altitude was in the neighbourhood of 9,000 feet and it was bitterly cold, so we decided that the situation demanded a hot dinner; and had one, with the help of the tea-basket – a handsome three-course dinner of hot tinned soup, fried sausages, bread and jam and tea. Then we turned the dining-room into a wagon-lit, spread the valises and blankets out on the floor, and slept soundly until 4.30 am, when Charles went out and roused the boys. . . .

The rain had stopped before dawn, and though it was very cold before the sun rose, the early morning start was delicious; and in spite of the hardness of the floorboards of the cart, in that wonderful air we had rested well. The road improved as we got nearer Eldoret, and at each halting place we got down and walked a little way or had a meal if one was due; and there was only a distance of thirty miles left to go when a wheel came off our cart, and it fell over with a crash against a bank – the only place for miles where there *was* a bank and it saved a bad mishap. The pin of the hub had gone and was lost in the mud, but by the greatest luck a six-inch nail was discovered on the floor of the cart; the wheel was replaced with the nail to act as pin and away we went, praying that the nail might prove a strong one, and that there might be a friendly bank to break the fall next time we went over.

The journey seemed interminable, but at about four o'clock we came in sight of Eldoret – then a little *dorp* of tin-roofed bungalows and grass huts, with one unpretentious Bank building and a butcher's shop – we crossed the Sosiani river and rattled up the only street, and turned at the top into the open country, but still on the rutty track that did duty as a main road. . . .

It was wonderful to descend from that abominable cart and realize I need not get into it again! To go into a comfortable stone house and rest in an armchair, and presently have a bath and a good dinner! – I registered a vow that night that nothing should induce me to leave the Plateau until I could go by train, if the only alternative to that was a post-cart.

Perhaps the most essential tool on every farm was the debbi, *sometimes spelt* debbe.

It is an oblong tin, fourteen inches high by nine inches square, and comes packed in a deal box holding two. It holds four Imperial gallons of petrol or paraffin, and has become the standard measure for the sale of linseed oil, plough oil, lard, ghee and honey. . . .

In East Africa many a settler's house is furnished throughout with kerosene tins and their complementary adjuncts. The tin can be made to serve countless purposes; painted green and filled with earth it is an ornamental flower-pot for the verandah; cut in half longways it is a pan for growing seeds. For every domestic purpose it is invaluable, from an oven to a boiler. Two tins hung over a donkey's back bring water up from the river, the bath-water is heated in them – hams or bacon are boiled in them when too big for the saucepans. Coffee pickers are paid by the tin-full; tins are used for cleaning and winnowing maize, for carting away rubbish, bringing earth or manure for the garden, beaten as drums to scare off locusts (or the devil). The native name for the tin, and the name we all call it by, is *debbi*.

If the *debbi* is invaluable in its original form, it has almost limitless scope in other shapes. With top and bottom cut off and the sides laid out as a flat sheet, it makes a good weather-proof roofing; and the sides, bent upwards, can be used as guttering, or bent downwards, as ridging for the roof. Huts in the native and Indian quarters of many African towns dazzle the eyes with their kerosene-tin roofs, which, when painted red, present quite a distinguished appearance.

But while enumerating the myriad uses of the tin, the box it comes in must not be forgotten. It may be used singly as a hen-coop or in numbers as a box-body for the car: built up in geometrical patterns for wardrobes, writing-tables, dressing-tables, book-cases, pews, and even as reading-desks in bush churches. The floor of many a bungalow is made entirely of the wood from these boxes, and in ironmongers' stores the cupboards are phalanxes of oil-boxes lining the walls. They may be put up in trees to allure wild bees that would otherwise sojourn under the floor or in the roof; mounted on wheels to produce a perambulator or a wheelbarrow; while out of two cases, cut in an artful manner, a comfortable armchair may be contrived.

The Youngest Lion Eva Bache.

From the dark woods that breathe of fallen showers,
Harnessed with level rays in golden reins,
The zebras draw the dawn across the plains
Wading knee-deep among the scarlet flowers.

Roy Campbell

The biggest obstacle to wheat growing at this time and place was not rust or weather but game, especially zebras. Enormous herds still roamed these open plains and ignored the sturdiest of fences. Fields of ripening wheat vanished before them like a dew before the sun. So much damage was done that in 1922 a deputation headed by Mr T. J. O'Shea laid before the Governor of the day, Sir Robert Coryndon, a scheme for exterminating these handsome animals that had become an economic plague. Many of the farmers had emerged from the war in possession of a .256 Mauser rifle of a type taken over from the Portuguese, and the Government held large stocks of ammunition which was due to be dumped into the sea. The proposal was that the Government should issue this ammunition in exchange for zebra tails.

The scheme was adopted and ten rounds issued free; after that, each zebra tail earned two further rounds. At about this time, a process was discovered in the United States for tanning zebra hides, which then became saleable instead of worthless, as had been the case before. These factors together spelt the doom of the zebra. Tens of thousands were slaughtered, and, in the next few years, kongoni, eland, giraffe, wildebeeste and gazelle also paid the price for inconveniencing mankind. The Uasin Gishu was stripped of what had been its greatest glory; but fences stood, and wheat grew.

No Easy Way Elspeth Huxley.

Lord Delamere on the pioneer spirit.

22 April, 1930

. . . Lunched at the Avenue with the Cobbs and the Harpers. I am so sorry for the Cobbs. They have been hoping against hope that the rain would stop and let them harvest their crop, but now with the heavy rain of the last week or two the last 700 acres of beautiful barley has simply rotted on the ground. They harvested the rest, a good many thousand bags, and it is hardly worth taking to the station at the price. Mrs Cobb finally deserted her post the day before yesterday and came down to Nairobi to join him. I have never before seen her disheartened, but she says this has really been the last straw after working herself on the harvesters ever since you and I and the Neville Chamberlains went there together.

I'm afraid it means their selling the developed part of their farm and starting again on another bit. Rather hard at Cobb's age to start all over again, and for her after making their house so nice. But it has happened to all the pioneers in all the countries they have made. Their joy is in the creation of something out of nothing. Cobb has already left one beautiful place, Keringet, into which he put years of his life, and now he is probably going to do it again, leaving a home made out of the bare veld for someone else. And he will probably do it again.

New capital comes in and takes over in a different spirit, investing in proved things.

Cobb has made large profits out of farming, but it has always gone back into increased acreages or something he is trying. The result is the first two or three bad years on end leave him stranded and he starts again. The pioneer mind only sees forward. If it didn't it would never do what it does. But it seldom consolidates for the same reason.

White Man's Country (Vol. II) Elspeth Huxley.

In 1925 Michael Blundell, aged eighteen, abandoned the aim of an Oxford scholarship and sailed in the SS Matiana, bound for a then remote farm-to-be in western Kenya.

I had two tin trunks, one shot-gun and £100 to my name. After I had paid my railway fare and met the Customs dues, I left for up-country with £73 only. The terms and conditions of my job were that I worked for my keep for a year, so I had to count on this £73 for the next twelve months. It took more than forty-eight hours from Mombasa to reach my destination, which was Eldoret, at that time the railhead on the new line being constructed to Uganda. . . . My fellow passengers were all settlers like myself, excited and enthusiastic over the prospect of making a new country. Showers of advice were poured upon me; to do nothing for a year and see what the country was like, to enter the motor trade which must thrive as the country expanded, to take 1,000 acres of land in the Burnt Forest and to grow wheat which was then the newest industry in the agricultural world. To all this I listened, with excitement too, and I looked out of the windows at the tall greeny grey cedar trees festooned with their beards of grey lichen and wondered what the farm of my employer was going to be like. At Eldoret the train could go no farther as the line from there was still under construction, and my future boss met me in his motor-car. He was a slight spare man of medium height, desperately weak from seven years of colitis; his blue eyes showed up in his sallow, suntanned face, and a tuft of hair on his cheek bones was always left unshaved on either side of his face. The car was a ramshackle black Overland tourer which had a clearance of something like ten inches from the ground, a godsend in the rainy season when the roads largely became mud and quagmire.

I have often wondered about the theory of reincarnation because from that moment onwards everything that happened to me and all that I saw seemed so natural and did not surprise me in the slightest as if indeed I had already been there and had accepted it all in the past. The red dirt roads, the narrow farm tracks branching off from them, with the sections of long grass down the middle between the tracks; the stems of the grass arching themselves across the tracks, with their copper-coloured seeds hanging from the stems like drops of frozen rain, all fascinated me and yet seemed to be part of a pattern to which I was already accustomed. We arrived in darkness, and in the dim lantern light the Africans carried in my luggage – my two trunks and my shot-gun – into the hut which was to be my home for fifteen months. The hut was hexagonal in shape, about fifteen feet across, constructed of mud and wattle, with a grass roof, badly thatched, with a hole in the centre at the top of the apex. Lizards ran across the grass in the roof, and the floor, which was made of murram, rough and uneven, harboured innumerable jiggers and fleas, which attacked my feet if I was foolish enough to get out of bed and walk across the floor without shoes. The furniture was simple and made from white deal petrol boxes, and my bath was a round galvanized iron tub into which the water was poured by hand from a blackened four-gallon tin, while a strong smoky smell filled the air.

My farming day was a simple one. I rose at 6.15 am and went out at 6.30 to set the labour to work, detailing tasks, and seeing them started. This generally took until 8 o'clock, when I returned for breakfast. After breakfast we would ride round the farm looking at the growing crops, superintending the work in progress and exploring the remoter sections to see what was going on. We had two steeds on the estate – one Joe Cobb, a slow lethargic Somali pony whose main object in life was to get through it with the minimum effort to himself, and the other, Rosinante, a highly intelligent self-opinionated mule who was quite determined that she knew the best way to go everywhere and the best manner in which to do it. . . .

Owing to our distance from the nearest township we had largely to live off the farm, and every evening we would go out shooting for the pot. My boss would take his rifle, I would take my shot-gun, and we would bring back antelope, partridge, guinea-fowl, snipe, duck or lesser bustard, as the case might be. Often we would see forty to a hundred waterbuck in one herd, together with hartebeeste, duiker, reedbuck and oribi. In the evenings sometimes I climbed the steep granite hills and sat on the top watching the habits of the animals as they grazed below me in the long grass. The explosive snort of the waterbuck, the sudden stamp of the hartebeeste as they sensed danger, the whistling of the reedbuck and the clicking of their heels as they leapt through the grass when they tried to escape from any sudden and unexpected contact, delighted me. . . .

In March as there was a shortage of labour, especially of drivers trained to handle a team of oxen, my employer bought a John Deere tractor. It was a powerful but unpredictable machine, and as he did not trust the Africans to handle it properly, he ordained that I should drive it. Hour after hour I bumped through the hot dusty African fields, ploughing and harrowing the light greyish-brown soil. I got up in the early morning before dawn, primed the monster's inside with petrol through a small priming cup and swung the great heavy fly-wheel. Sometimes I would swing it for an hour or more until I could hardly turn the fly-wheel over before it would come to life with a few hesitant coughs and snorts. Nevertheless, I had the satisfaction of ploughing, of seeing the long furrows curling out behind me; or, if we were using the large single furrow mould board plough, of holding it steady and feeling it carving through the warm dusty soil so that a long never ending wave of earth constantly turned and fell before me like the waves under the bow of a ship in a placid sea. One day, as I ploughed out my first furrow over a hundred acre field, I saw the sun rise over the edge of the field and tip the grass and clods of earth with gold; the same evening, on my last furrow, I drove the tractor into the full moon, as she in her turn rose above the edge of the field while the hot African evening gave way to the cool of the upland night and the grass and furrows were translated into half seen mysterious silver. The teams of oxen were already passing away, like many other beautiful things. It was a grand sight to see the crops loaded on to six or seven wagons, each eighteen feet long and pulled by sixteen sweating bullocks, all matched for colour; blacks, reds, blues or brindles. The sacks of maize would be neatly stacked along the wagon boards, and to the cries of the drivers and the crack of the whips, creaking and groaning, the wagons would get under way one after the other as the drivers cried out the names of the leaders – "Captain", "Sportsman", "Delamere", as the case might be.   *So Rough a Wind* Michael Blundell.

Coffee became Kenya's most important crop; Karen Blixen (Izak Dinesen) its most famous writer.

There are times of great beauty on a coffee-farm. When the plantation flowered in the beginning of the rains, it was a radiant sight, like a cloud of chalk, in the mist and the drizzling rain, over six hundred acres of land. The coffee-blossom has a delicate slightly bitter scent, like the black-thorn blossom. When the field reddened with the ripe berries, all the women and the children, whom they call the Totos, were called out to pick the coffee off the trees, together with the men; then the wagons and carts brought it down to the factory near the river. Our machinery was never quite what it should have been, but we had planned and built the factory ourselves and thought highly of it. Once the whole factory burned down and had to be built up again. The big coffee-dryer turned and turned, rumbling the coffee in its iron belly with a sound like pebbles that are washed about on the sea-shore. Sometimes the coffee would be dry, and ready to take out of the dryer, in the middle of the night. That was a picturesque moment, with many hurricane lamps in the huge dark room of the factory, that was hung everywhere with cobwebs and coffee-husks, and with eager glowing dark faces, in the light of the lamps, round the dryer; the factory, you felt, hung in the great African night like a bright jewel in an Ethiope's ear. Later on the coffee was hulled, graded, and sorted by hand, and packed in sacks sewn up with a saddler's needle.

Then in the end in the early morning, while it was still dark, and I was lying in bed, I heard the wagons, loaded high up with coffee-sacks, twelve to a ton, with sixteen oxen to each wagon, starting on their way in to Nairobi railway station up the long factory hill, with much shouting and rattling, the drivers running beside the wagons. I was pleased to think that this was the only hill up, on their way, for the farm was a thousand feet higher than the town of Nairobi. In the evening I walked out to meet the procession that came back, the tired oxen hanging their heads in front of the empty wagons, with a tired little Toto leading them, and the weary drivers trailing their whips in the dust of the road. Now we had done what we could do. The coffee would be on the sea in a day or two, and we could only hope for good luck at the big auction-sales in London.

                                Out of Africa Karen Blixen.

Not all settlers were white. Indians had been settled on the coast for generations, and moved up-country in the wake of the railway. Relatives joined them, and a network of Hindu, Sikh and Muslim communities spread from Nairobi's humming bazaar to the remotest outposts. Everywhere you came upon dukas *where everything from blankets to tea in ten-cent packets, paraffin lamps to cigarettes, hoes and pangas to pulses and spices, were bargained for in crowded little wood-and-iron bungalows, often with a tailor treading at a peddle sewing machine on the narrow veranda. Asians – called Indians before the sub-continent's partition – manned post offices, railway stations and dispensaries, owned lorries and butcheries, made shoes and clothing, succeeded as merchants and money-lenders. Many worked as* fundis *(artisans) on whose skills, until Africans had been trained in sufficient numbers to replace them, the country's superstructure mainly depended. One such* fundi *worked on Karen Blixen's farm at Ngong.*

Pooran Singh's little blacksmith's shop down by the mill was a miniature Hell on the farm, with all the orthodox attributes of that place. It was built of corrugated iron, and when the sun shone down upon the roof of it, and the flames of the furnace rose inside it, the air itself, in and around the hut, was white-hot. All day long, the place resounded with the deafening noise of the forge – iron on iron, on iron once more – and the hut was filled with axes, and broken wheels, that made it look like some ancient gruesome picture of a place of execution.

All the same the blacksmith's shop had a great power of attraction, and when I went down to watch Pooran Singh at work I always found people in it and round it. Pooran Singh worked at a superhuman pace, as if his life depended upon getting the particular job of work finished within the next five minutes, he jumped straight up in the air over the forge, he shrieked out his orders to his two young Kikuyu assistants in a high bird's voice and behaved altogether like a man who is himself being burnt at the stake, or like some chafed over-devil at work. But Pooran Singh was no devil, but a person of the meekest disposition; out of working hours he had a little maidenly affectation of manner. He was our Fundee of the farm, which means an artisan of all work, carpenter, saddler and cabinet-maker, as well as blacksmith; he constructed and built more than one wagon for the farm, all on his own. But he liked the work of the forge best, and it was a very fine, proud sight, to watch him tiring a wheel.

Pooran Singh, in his appearance, was something of a fraud. When fully dressed, in his coat and large folded white turban, he managed, with his big black beard, to look a portly, ponderous man. But by the forge, bared to the waist, he was incredibly slight and nimble, with the Indian hour-glass torso. . . .

The Native world was drawn to the forge by its song. The treble, sprightly, monotonous, and surprising rhythm of the blacksmith's work has a mythical force. It is so virile that it appals and melts the women's hearts, it is straight and unaffected and tells the truth and nothing but the truth. Sometimes it is very outspoken. It has an excess of strength and is gay as well as strong, it is obliging to you and does great things for you, willingly, as in play. The Natives, who love rhythm, collected by Pooran Singh's hut and felt at their ease. According to an ancient Nordic law a man was not held responsible for what he had said in a forge. The tongues were loosened in Africa as well, in the blacksmith's shop, and the talk flowed freely; audacious fancies were set forth to the inspiring hammer-song.

Pooran Singh was with me for many years and was a well-paid functionary of the farm. There was no proportion between his wages and his needs, for he was an ascetic of the first water. He did not eat meat, he did not drink, or smoke, or gamble, his old clothes were worn to the thread. He sent his money over to India for the education of his children. A small silent son of his, Delip Singh, once came over from Bombay on a visit to his father. He had lost touch with the iron, the only metal that I saw about him was a fountain pen in his pocket. The mythical qualities were not carried on in the second generation.

Out of Africa Karen Blixen.

Errant earls and dashing barons.

The Sherbroke-Walkers opened the Outspan Hotel (at Nyeri) on 1 January 1928, and soon afterwards Lady Bettie's sister, Lady Victoria Feilding, arrived on a visit. The sisters came of a family of ten born to the 9th Earl of Denbigh and his wife. The earl had been Lord-in-Waiting to Queen Victoria, who had consented to stand as godmother to the Denbighs' newest offspring, but had died before she could fulfil her promise. The child was nevertheless christened Victoria. The Denbighs owned five thousand acres and their residence had one hundred rooms – or so it was thought; no one had actually counted them. In the garden was an elm tree in whose branches the children had built a house from which to watch rabbits. Eric Sherbroke-Walker, when a guest and prospective son-in-law, had observed this tree-house and said to himself: "If rabbits, why not elephants?" That, so the story goes, was the origin of Treetops.

The resources of the family did not run to supporting their brood, and after she came to Kenya Taffy, who had decided to stay on, rubbed along in a number of jobs, such as delivering milk and helping on a poultry farm, before marrying Miles Fletcher, a brawny and impecunious Tasmanian. Instead of an engagement ring, he gave her a second-hand tyre for her lorry which was so dilapidated, she wrote, that "it wouldn't pull the skin off a rice pudding". . . .

Taffy could turn her hand to anything – decarbonizing engines, plucking fowls, repairing tractors, dosing sheep, icing cakes, rearing lambs – though not so artlessly as a Turkana woman she saw suckling her baby from one breast and a lamb from the other – and she was generous, witty, good fun and rather stout. Eventually her marriage foundered, Miles took another wife (and then another), their two sons sought their fortunes in Australia, and thither, in the evening of her days, Taffy followed them to come to roost in a caravan. . . .

But it would be wrong to assume that most of the white farmers discarded the standards of their race and class to live like tinkers. It was only a few who did so, and they only did so sometimes. The apparent prevalence of earls and Old Etonians in Kenya's white society has created an impression that the settler population was drawn mainly from Britain's aristocracy. This was far from the case. Afrikaner transport riders, Scottish cattle traders, Italian mechanics, Irish garage owners, Jewish hoteliers, and farmers drawn from the despised and mediocre middle classes, were all there too, in much greater numbers. They did not make news, whereas errant earls and dashing barons did. These were in a small minority. We hear a lot about small minorities these days, always making headlines by blowing up, gunning down and outrageously offending the great, virtuous, law-abiding majority. It is naive to dismiss such activists because they are few. The yeast moves the dough. It was, after all, a very small minority of Jews – eleven, to be precise – who started the spread throughout the world of the Christian religion. The errant earls and dashing barons did set a certain stamp on the colonial society they adorned, and sometimes scandalized.

They came in quest of adventure, stayed to make a colony, and, in the process, destroyed what they had come to seek. They brought wives, and wives make homes. An inexorable process began. Patterned chintz replaced the sacking and amerikani spread over packing-cases to be used as tables; curtains went up over unglazed windows; china cups bought at local sales replaced tin mugs. Soon prints of the Midnight Steeplechase hung on mud-block walls, followed by the Laughing Cavalier and Van Gogh's sunflowers on roughly chiselled stone ones; creepers half-concealed corrugated-iron roofs; then came dressed stone bungalows with wide verandas, and tennis courts and stables, herbaceous borders, tea on the lawn. By stealth, civilization had arrived.

Out in the Midday Sun Elspeth Huxley.

Evelyn Waugh enjoyed the hospitality of several up-country farmers, mainly of the up-market kind, during his visit to the colony in 1930.

The houses of Kenya are mainly in that style of architecture which derives from intermittent prosperity. In many of them the living-rooms are in separate buildings from the bedrooms; their plan is usually complicated by a system of additions and annexes which have sprung up in past years as the result of a good crop, a sudden burst of optimism, the influx of guests from England, the birth of children, the arrival of pupil farmers, or any of the many chances of domestic life. In many houses there is sadder evidence of building begun and abandoned when the bad times came on. Inside they are, as a rule, surprisingly comfortable. Up an unfenced cart-track, one approaches a shed made of concrete, match-boarding, and corrugated iron, and, on entering, finds oneself among old furniture, books, and framed miniatures.

There are very few gardens; we went to one a few miles outside Njoro where an exquisite hostess in golden slippers led us down grass paths bordered with clipped box, over Japanese bridges, pools of water-lilies, and towering tropical plants. But few settlers have time for these luxuries.

Boy and Genessie, with whom I spent a week-end, have one of the "stately homes" of Kenya; three massive stone buildings on the crest of a hill at Elmentaita overlooking Lake Nakuru, in the centre of an estate which includes almost every topographical feature – grass, bush forest, rock, river, waterfall, and a volcanic cleft down which we scrambled on the end of a rope.

On the borders a bush fire is raging, a low-lying cloud by day, at night a red glow along the horizon. The fire dominates the week-end. We watch anxiously for any change in the wind; cars are continually going out to report progress; extra labour is mustered and despatched to "burn a brake"; will the flames "jump" the railroad? The pasture of hundreds of head of cattle is threatened.

In the evening we go down to the lakeside to shoot duck; thousands of flamingo lie on the water; at the first shot they rise in a cloud, like dust from a beaten carpet; they are the colour of pink alabaster; they wheel round and settle further out. The head of a hippopotamus emerges a hundred yards from shore and yawns at us. When it is dark the hippo comes out for his evening walk. . . .

Again the enchanting contradictions of Kenya life; a baronial hall straight from Queen Victoria's Scottish Highlands – an open fire of logs and peat with carved-stone chimney-piece, heads of game, the portraits of prize cattle, guns, golf-clubs, fishing-tackle, and folded newspapers – sherry is brought in, but, instead of a waistcoated British footman, a bare-footed Kikuyu boy in white gown and red jacket. A typical English meadow of deep grass; model cowsheds in the background; a pedigree Ayrshire bull scratching his back on the gatepost; but, instead of rabbits, a company of monkeys scutter away at our approach; and, instead of a smocked yokel, a Masai herdsman draped in a blanket, his hair plaited into a dozen dyed pigtails. . . .

"I will lift up mine eyes unto the hills, from whence cometh my help."
Sometimes it doesn't come.

One year the long rains failed.

That is a terrible, tremendous experience, and the farmer, who has lived through it, will never forget it. Years afterwards, away from Africa, in the wet climate of a Northern country, he will start up at night, at the sound of a sudden shower of rain, and cry, "At last, at last."

In normal years the long rains began in the last week of March and went on into the middle of June. Up to the time of the rains, the world grew hotter and drier every day, feverish, as in Europe before a great thunderstorm, only more so.

The Masai, who were my neighbours on the other side of the river, at that time set fire to the bast-dry plains to get new green grass for their cattle with the first rain, and the air over the plains danced with the mighty conflagration; the long grey and rainbow-tinted layers of smoke rolled along over the grass, and the heat and the smell of burning were drifted in over the cultivated land as from a furnace.

Gigantic clouds gathered, and dissolved again, over the landscape; a light distant shower of rain painted a blue slanting streak across the horizon. All the world had only one thought.

On an evening just before sunset, the scenery drew close round you, the hills came near and were vigorous, meaningful, in their clear, deep blue and green colouring. A couple of hours later you went out and saw that the stars had gone, and you felt the night-air soft and deep and pregnant with benefaction.

When the quickly growing rushing sound wandered over your head it was the wind in the tall forest-trees – and not the rain. When it ran along the ground it was the wind in the shrubs and the long grass – and not the rain. When it rustled and rattled just above the ground it was the wind in the maize-fields, – where it sounded so much like rain that you were taken in, time after time, and even got a certain content from it, as if you were at least shown the thing you longed for acted on a stage, – and not the rain.

But when the earth answered like a sounding-board in a deep fertile roar, and the world sang round you in all dimensions, all above and below, – that was the rain. It was like coming back to the Sea, when you have been a long time away from it, like a lover's embrace.

But one year the long rains failed. It was, then, as if the Universe were turning away from you. It grew cooler, on some days it would be cold, but there was no sign of moisture in the atmosphere. Everything became drier and harder, and it was as if all force and gracefulness had withdrawn from the world. It was not bad weather or good weather, but a negation of all weather, as if it had been deferred *sine die.* A bleak wind, like a draught, ran over your head, all colour faded from all things; the smells went away from the fields and forests. The feeling of being in disgrace with the Great Powers pressed on you. To the South, the burnt plains lay black and waste, striped with grey and white ashes.

With every day, in which we now waited for the rain in vain, prospects and hopes of the farm grew dim, and disappeared. The ploughing, pruning and planting of the last months turned out to be a labour of fools. The farm work slowed off, and stood still.

On the plains and in the hills, the waterholes dried up, and many new kinds of ducks and geese came to my pond. To the pond on the boundary of the farm, the Zebra came wandering in the early mornings and at sunset to drink, in long rows, two or three hundred of them, the foals walking with the mares, and they were not afraid of me when I rode out amongst them. But we tried to keep them off the land for the sake of our cattle, for the water was sinking in the ponds. Still it was a pleasure to go down there, where the rushes growing in the mud made a green patch in the brown landscape.

The Natives became silent under the drought, I could not get a word on the prospects out of them, although you would have thought that they should have known more about the signs of the weather than we did. It was their existence which was at stake, it was not an unheard of thing to them, – and had not been to their fathers, – to lose nine-tenths of their stock in the great years of drought.

Their shambas were dry, with a few drooping and withering sweet-potato and maize plants.

After a time I learned their manner from them, and gave up talking of the hard times or complaining about them, like a person in disgrace. But I was a European, and I had not lived long enough in the country to acquire the absolute passivity of the Native, as some Europeans will do, who live for many decennaries in Africa. I was young, and by instinct of self-preservation, I had to collect my energy on something, if I were not to be whirled away with the dust on the farm-roads, or the smoke on the plain. I began in the evenings to write stories, fairy-tales and romances, that would take my mind a long way off, to other countries and times.

Out of Africa Karen Blixen.

The Rocco family lived on the shores of Lake Naivasha and their vegetable crops thrived on its fertile margins.

A passing horticultural expert from England told us he had never imagined such bountiful yields possible. The blue-grey cabbages, fat and round, weighed up to ten pounds each. Only a few lucky farmers with abundant water could produce such crops in the dry season. Lorries came from everywhere to buy and take them away. . . .

Then one day the weather changed. The blue sky was spattered with fleecy clouds like snowflakes hanging in the air. The sun rose in an orange haze and tinged the wispy clouds with pink and gold. Longonot was suspended in a misty curtain. For the first time in many months I did not feel the bite of the sun on my back. That night I lay and listened to the sound of distant thunder. My heart began to sink.

Every day the sky began to fill, the fleecy clouds turned grey and pregnant with rain. We were well past the rainy season. But the rhythm had somehow been upset. The wind rose and hurtled through the trees. They bent and sighed and shed their leaves. The dust-devils spiralled once again high into the sky. At noon, heavy silence hung over the farm – the hush before the thunderclap.

Two inches of rain fell that night. The thirsty ground drank its fill and the surplus ran in rivulets along the roads and lay in puddles everywhere. The scent of rain and damp earth filled the air. The flowers smiled with rain drops on their petals, fish eagles screamed as they glided on the wind, cavorting in the sky, giant ibis left the ground with raucous cries and rain birds ululated from every tree. Everything that lived and breathed rejoiced.

It rained every day for a week. The lake began to swell and rise. The joyous feeling of a few days before turned to anxiety. The weather forecast announced heavy rain and storms across the country. Dorian arrived and rushed upstairs to my room.

"We'll lose the crop if it goes on like this," he bellowed with disappointment and rage. "Bloody rain," he muttered, as he moved out onto the terrace and looked down at the sodden world around us. We had been caught again. I tried to find some words with which to console him but I knew it was hopeless. It rained for two months. The lake rose seven feet and our new acres went under. We called in men and women and children from all around. Knee deep in mud and water, they once again pulled up the crops from the gooey ground and fought off the fat black leeches that clung to their legs with engine oil and grease. I had to use my horse for transport, as no vehicle could approach our flooded fields.

Each new day began clear and crisp. In the early mornings, before the work began, I visited the silent fields and momentarily forgot the battle we were fighting. I wondered whether it was not better to let nature take her course, and bow our heads to Africa and gracefully retreat. Pelicans drifted across the fields, catching fish among the cabbages and turnips. Saddle-bill storks, herons, crested cranes and egrets picked their way on delicate legs among the lacy carrot tops and rose, on graceful wings, in front of my chestnut mare, Malaika. Taka-Taka, my Doberman, yapped as he chased after them in a spray of water.

But by midday the fat, white clouds had fused and become dark and menacing. Thunder rolled in the hills and echoed across the lake. At night I listened to the raindrops fall, and in my room the ceiling leaked. Three weeks later, we lost the crop.

African Saga Mirella Ricciardi.

And the grasshopper shall be a burden, and desire shall fail.
Ecclesiastes xii.1.

5 Nov, 1928. "Drove through swarms of locusts. . . ."
It was on our way through Gilgil that we first met the fateful "hoppers" – precursors of those vast swarms of locusts that winged their way later, like a red shadow, over the devastated land.

The whole road was alive with them – a teeming, moving mass, as if tea-leaves had been scattered two or three inches deep on the dusty road by some diabolical housemaid. And as the black heaps and drifts struggled across, more and ever more came forward from beneath the leleshwa bushes to take the place of those that had gone.

Each insect resembled a tiny grasshopper, and was no more than three-quarters of an inch long, if so much – yet their countless billions gave an impression of horror out of all proportion to their size.

I think part of the loathing inspired by locusts is due to the effect they have upon one's mind. It is like being suddenly forced to look through the wrong end of a telescope – one finds oneself wondering what it must feel like to *be* a "hopper" down there in the suffocating dust, without individuality, without room to move freely – in that involved, tangled, overwhelming heap possessing but one instinct in common to its atoms – an appetite.

And after weeks of hopping over hot arid ground, razed as bare as a board by the advancing hosts, the locust swarms become winged, and then their horror still continues in a different shape. For now they are like brown snow-storms whirling over the plain day after day, settling at night in huge, grotesque, pinkish or, as maturity approaches, yellow swathes. Every bush and shrub is deformed by them, and will raise stripped imploring branches to the morning sun when the swarm takes to its wings once more. At mid-day one may come upon it feeding on the plain, and then the ground seems to move in hideous tremors underfoot, while with a dry rustling of countless wings the spindrift of locusts flies up under one's feet, only to settle again a few yards farther.

One insect is exactly like another with its blank, glassy stare, and suggests a Robot transmigrated to a lower sphere.

A Kenyan Farm Diary V. M. Carnegie.

Locust swarms invaded the country for the next five years, devastating crops and pastures and bringing famine and ruin in their wake. First came the desert locust (Schistocerca gregaria) *followed by the migratory species* (Locusta migratoria).

All that Sunday – all day Monday – all day Tuesday, from nine in the morning till five in the evening, that swarm was going over; sometimes they would get caught in a pocket of wind and come rattling down on the roof like hail. All those three days we lived in a kind of twilight, always conscious of the muffled roar of their going overhead. When one lot got up, another came down, warming themselves at the smudge fires they were by way of detesting, and at night the country for miles round was literally carpeted with locusts.

Amakobe and I gave up the useless fight. I had been rushing about among the brutes, ringing the dinner-bell in their faces, but they only cocked an eye at me and went on eating. The bell, bought years before in the Cairo Mousky, was of fine Damascene work and had once been the helmet of a Crusader; and as I sat with it in my hand, I found myself wondering how many swarms of *greg.* and *mig.* its wearer had ridden through on the march in Palestine; and whether his batman, after a long day's fighting, went out and collected the helmet full of them as a dainty for the gallant knight's supper.

By twelve o'clock all the boys were back from the maize fields. All the maize was eaten and there was nothing to wait for. Amakobe sat down under a tree and told me stories while we watched the locusts bustling about, searching for provender on the former lawn.

"Truly, I have seen bigger swarms," he said. "Swarms that would break that great tree yonder into firewood."

"How many years ago was that?"

"That was when I was a boy, in the year of the Great Sickness." (Rinderpest, in 1892.) "It killed all the cattle of the Kavirondo and the Masai; only the Maragoli had any cattle left. There was nothing to eat; the locusts had eaten all the grass and the grain. For five years, men ate locusts only; the women ate them before their babies came, and the babies as soon as they were born ate locusts. This year the locusts are thin and have no meat on them. In the old times they were very fat and good to eat." . . .

On Monday, at 9 am, they were getting up and more coming over, thicker than ever, and washing-day had to be postponed, for locusts will settle on garments unwarily left outside and eat large holes in them. Everywhere in sight, instead of being green with young grass as it was early the day before, the country was brown, as it is at the end of a long dry weather.

They laid over our farm and all the surrounding farms, including a big sisal plantation, and we knew that we had only a month or five weeks' respite before the young hoppers would begin to hatch out. The locust digs a little hole in more or less open ground and deposits from seventy to a hundred eggs in it, and the young are at first small, black grasshoppers, increasing in size and voracity with every moult.

The farmers of the districts met, and called upon the Government to open a station for mixing poison bait, the method being to mix arsenic powder with bran; but needless to say, the entire supply of bran throughout the country was finished in a few days. After that, everything was used – maize refuse, coffee pulp, cow-dung, and as soon as it was mixed, it was bagged and sent out by rail and lorry to the districts and the Reserves day after day for months. . . .

By the time they had completed their first moult and were ravenous, the bait was ready. Every morning we set out in different directions, starting early and carrying on till the sun was hot. When we had gained a little experience, we found it better policy to wait until they had climbed down from their roosting places in high grass and low shrubs, and put the bait down *damp*, in front of and through the ranks of the army on the march. They marched along roads, paths and especially along the railway, and as soon as the sun became really hot they took the bait greedily. By baiting a swarm in this way, every other day, we destroyed countless millions, for the survivors eat their dead friends and not a spot of arsenic is wasted. . . .

The worst time was when we found, after tea, that a swarm about four miles long by half a mile deep was settling for the night within fifty yards of the house and *boma* – we were not keen on putting down quantities of arsenic round the cattle *boma*. . . . All I remember of the next day is walking round for hours in masses of those loathsome insects, grown to two inches long, and sowing bait among them. . . .

The whole country smelt of bad fish, for the rain washed the carcasses together in heaps and they smelt to Heaven. The locust-birds disappeared altogether – killed, it was feared, by the poisoned hoppers. Hens did not seem to be affected by the arsenic, but they all laid eggs with red yolks!

The Youngest Lion Eva Bache.

Most European farms were starved of capital between the wars. Kapsiliat was lucky.

On reaching the hills, we motored through a lovely green valley forested with every variety of acacias. We were now on Mervyn's estate, and climbing through the undulating wooded country it reminded me of England, a mixture of Sussex Wolds and smooth green hills like the Cumberland Fells. To our right flowed the Moiben River, which Mervyn (Ridley) has stocked with trout. Always ascending higher through woods, which here and there opened to show us glimpses of green hill and blue mountain afar, we passed through some gates which led us by green lawns, past groves of flaming shrubs, to the red-brick house, which, with its gables, brick pavements and wide loggias, gave the impression of an Old English cottage; a cottage within which were beautiful rooms, surprisingly big, and rare furniture; bedrooms a marvel of comfort, several bathrooms and electric light. The shingled roof and rose-pink bricks had all been made on this estate, while the fine panelling in the dining-room was cut by the saw-mill from the forest cedars.

Here, nearly 8,000 feet above sea-level, perched on the slope of Kapsiliat, was this charming home, created by the genius of my host and hostess on what had been a bare hillside. Great podo and cedar trees, the last remains of the old virgin forest, threw shade on the acres of grass lawn, while wide herbaceous borders filled with every variety of English flower, petunias purple and pink, phloxes, iris, delphiniums, led to further gardens enclosed in clipped hedges. A fountain played in a basin, round which ran a pavement of red bricks, carpeted with many-coloured verbenas, while roses, lilies and heliotrope made a tangle of loveliness and cannas bore immense trusses of flower that would raise the envy and astonishment of a gardener at home.

In the shade of the podo trees were clumps of yellow daffodils, grape hyacinths, and blue cinerarias. Beyond this enchanted garden was a park-like country, stretching down to a valley through which flowed the river Moiben, and farther on rose the forested hills of the Elgeyo Reserve.

The cattle on this estate of 10,000 acres, which is mainly agricultural land, number roughly a thousand head. There is a large herd of graded cows, the result of pure-bred Red Poll bulls, imported from Suffolk, and the native cows, and after one crossing the cows have already lost their horns and humps. Masai herdsmen look after the animals; they are the best cattle-men in the colony, and take a great pride in the welfare of the herds.

This estate, which is most perfectly run and has absorbed an immense capital, is self-supporting in everything except sugar and flour, and next year Mervyn hopes to be able to grow enough wheat to keep the house going in the latter. The capital sunk had yielded no return as yet, and while the prices of dairy produce remain beneath the cost of production there is no promise of better times. Let us trust that all the labour, hope and capital that helped to make this land fruitful will one day reap its reward.

Kenya: The Land of Illusion Lady Evelyn Cobbold.

Mervyn and Sybil Ridley are buried at Kapsiliat, now the property of many families of the Elgeyo tribe.

The Last Lap

After the Second World War the colonial government set up a second settlement scheme, better planned than the first, to help new settlers develop new farms. The land was excised from undeveloped parts of existing European-owned farms and ranches, and in some cases from forest reserves. A former RAF pilot, disenchanted with the prospect of a career in the family firm of stocking manufacturers in the Midlands, chose a stretch of former forest on the borders of the Uasin Gishu plateau.

Once or twice before I'd had that terrible alone, on-your-own feeling – like the time I did my first solo in an aircraft. But just as the child who has been lost on a crowded beach forgets its panic at the sight of its mother, they too were temporary experiences that left no scar on my memory. It was a different and more helpless feeling of loneliness that came over me when I found myself on that large tract of Africa, surrounded by dark high forest, without a real access road, thirty-five miles from the nearest town, and with the knowledge that I had to make it our home. The finality of the step I'd taken was an awful thought. I even had nostalgia for the smell of the dye-works and all the industrial horror from which I'd escaped; I would have given anything at that moment for the warmth and friendliness of Uncle George's pub. The picture of it in my mind's eye was embellished until it became a sort of paradise lost.

Thirteen hundred acres is a lot of land. I knew the boundaries to the south and west. The thick, black, impenetrable forest would always keep me on my own pitch in that direction. The other boundaries had been vaguely pointed out to me as "about there", "and there" and "over there". "About there" and "over there" were a long, long way from the hill in the middle.

The farm I had known in England, the one on the edge of the Charnwood Forest, had small orderly fields bordered with neat, well-cut hedges and white low-roofed buildings. If you stood on the north side boundary of the farm, you could shout and be heard on the south side. But it would need a wireless set to carry my voice from the hill in the centre of my African farm to "over there". And there were no hedges or buildings in between.

The first thing to do, obviously, was to plant some sort of cash crop. But before you plant you have to plough. No doubt ploughing is easy in England on land that has been farmed since 1066. It might even be easy on the virgin soils of Africa if the ploughman had ten generations of farmers in his family tree; but to a new farmer on new land with a new, insufficiently powered, tractor and a decrepit plough, the situation was a little difficult. It wasn't as if I could start at one end of the farm and just plough till I reached the other. There were patches of rocks and tree stumps, parts were too steep and other parts too damp and swampy. So the ploughed lands were irregular in shape and varying in size. The biggest plot was fifty acres and the smallest seven.

From January until May the tractor chugged round every minute I could keep it working. But breakages and stoppages were frequent, and often it meant a journey of thirty-five miles for a spare part.

What I would have done without Piet, my neighbour, is hard to imagine. . . .

He took me under his wing when he saw how hopeless I was. A note would bring him over at the double. I tried setting the ploughs with string as we were taught at the school and they bounced out of the furrow. Piet set them by eye and they stayed in. The spot of sunlight to the left of his nose and both those on his neck appeared the day he cut washers for my tractor from the brim of his felt bush hat, after the paper ones I had made proved useless. The brim of Piet's hat looked like a crocheted table mat so many gaskets and washers had been taken from it. It gave his face a mottled effect, as though he had ringworm or was plagued with leprosy. Yes, if a thing could be patched up or any improvisation made, Piet was the boy. He lent me nuts and bolts and bits of iron, he even stripped threads from the tail of his shirt to seal a petrol union in my truck: I can't imagine what I should have done without Piet. . . .

Good rains came in late March. The massive, rough-turned sods were soaked through and through. The plough was pulled aside and a decrepit disc harrow, that I had bought at an auction sale for more than its price new, worked overtime cutting the large turfs to a reasonable tilth. Then the ploughs were put back and the furrows worked in the cross direction. Once again the harrow, more decrepit than ever and braced with angle iron and tied with wire, was hurried over and over, until by the middle of May I had 200 acres that could be planted in wheat.

From 18 May I spent my life on the running board of that planter – watching, fascinated, the seed and fertilizer pour into the earth. And I felt good. There is no time like planting time. All the hopes of life are there. It is like saying, "I commit this seed to the good earth for Your blessing, Oh Lord!"

And then, one morning, the first bright green rows appeared in the brown soil, glistening in their virginity.

By 15 June planting was over. One by one, patched out in brilliant green, the contours of the wheat-fields appeared against the backcloth of the coarse brown veldt. Here indeed was magic. I knew that rain and sun and good rich earth would make the seed grow. But the mystery of the embryo is beyond my ken. The quietness and the quickness of the miracle is a wonderful thing. . . .

Harvest time.

Ever since it arrived on the farm the combine harvester had been standing on blocks, oiled and greased and in absolute readiness for the "off". It was new, shining, and a complete mystery to me. By borrowing up to the hilt on the planted wheat, and promising immediate payment of the balance as soon as the crop was in the store, I had induced the trusting agent to allow it to come out and take pride of place among the farm implements.

The next morning Piet and Dris came over on horses to see the fun; and I was glad of their company for the operating manual of the harvester had so many "be sure" instructions that I had become utterly confused. I managed to start the engine just as they arrived. . . . I let the wheat trickle through my fingers like dry sand as it fell from the hopper to the sacks and felt the glow of satisfaction that comes to those who see the fruition of their labours. It had been a long wait from that January day when I first chose the land to plough.

The expression on my face as I got down from the harvester must have been loaded with self-satisfaction, for Dris said in a voice calculated to take the smugness from anyone, "You got rust. You didn't say you got rust."

I didn't say because I hadn't known.

"Have I?" I asked.

He showed me the straw he had pulled. "Them little black spots on the stem. Them's black stem rust, they cut the sap and make the heads so light you could blow them away. It ain't so bad on this shamba. If she had come two weeks earlier she would have cut your crop by half." . . .

Every day, as the fifty or sixty bags of wheat were taken into the incomplete store, I stepped out the acreage cut in an effort to estimate the eventual total. It did not get me very far, my forecast varied from day to day.

"You can never tell till them's all weighed and in the store", said Dris when I asked him what he thought he was going to get.

What I did notice in those over-anxious reckonings of my wealth-to-be was that as we went from shamba to shamba, larger and larger patches were cut for the same number of bags. This puzzled me for the stand of wheat, all over the farm, was so even. Then I remembered Dris and black stem rust. Sure enough I found, on closer examination, that the ears were getting lighter and lighter. The earliest planted was the least affected, because when the disease struck the ears were practically full. As the rust took hold of all the wheat at the same time, it followed that the more immature it was the more it suffered. And so the yield got less and less as the harvest progressed, from the promised eight bags per acre to five or six and then finally to four; until my hopes of wealth, in this my first year, vanished.

The Gate Hangs Well James Stapleton.

On his farm on the slopes of Mount Elgon, the Earl of Portsmouth devised a Christian-pagan celebration of harvest home.

Even in the early 1950s I had understood something of the dullness we had injected into indigenous African life. The missionaries imposed boredom because they condemned the outward manifestations of sin and paganism. The Administration discouraged dances and orgiastic occasions because it meant fewer broken heads and blunted emotional outlets. The settler followed suit partly from lack of imagination and partly to keep within the framework of the law. Yet the promise of the golden age of good citizenship, perhaps to rise to be chairman of a committee on drains, was a sorry substitute for the lion head-dress and the lion dance. I felt this to be true of a farm-worker's life in spite of its freedom to come and go between African land units.

The school and the football ground was not enough, especially as police were always raiding beer-drinking parties in huts in the bush. Sometimes, when a circumcision party was raided for beer over and above the legal amount allowed, I almost wept with frustrated rage. As I have said earlier it is a great moment in a boy or girl's life, it is also a great family, clan and tribal moment, and demands the ancient convivial hospitality. To break this occasion up, often for no better reason than that a few gallons of home-made beer are outside the law's permission, seemed a crass interference in normal private occasions. . . .

I was determined to make an effort to relieve the tedium of day-to-day farm life. So some eleven years ago I decreed a three days' holiday at the end of coffee harvest in February. Christmas occurs in the full flush of coffee and corn harvest and so is a truncated affair as far as merrymaking goes, but in normal years the end of February or early March is the moment of pause on the farm and of preparing for the new year crops. On the Equator there is no winter solstice, or there is no feeling of it. The Equinoxes, when one casts no noonday shadow, are far more marked, for in March one sows and towards Michaelmas comes the slackening of growth and the first filling of the ears for harvest.

I think in all true festivals there should be solemnity followed by its reverse in merrymaking. Bank holidays are the contrivance of uprooted city minds. The idea of Easter preceded by Good Friday and committal to the earth and the joyous rising on Easter Day is as old as pagan Europe. The dedication of the King or Queen at Coronation followed by fireworks and dancing in the street is the true pattern for making merry England. Hence, we planned on the first day to have a service of dedication to the new season and thanks for the rhythmic ending of the old.

At nine o'clock on a bright cool morning all the workers assembled on the football ground. The school children arrived singing in procession, and took their place on one side of a square formed on the other three sides by the farm-workers and ourselves. In the centre were tractors, ox-teams and ploughs, bags of coffee, a few green leaves of tea, also bags of wheat, maize, oats and barley from last season's harvest ready for new sowing. I had managed to secure a Roman Catholic Father, a Church of England Chaplain and a Church of Scotland African Reverendi. I wrote a hymn; as near-pagan as I dared, and two or three very simple prayers specially for translation into Swahili. Meanwhile, the tractors and oxen and wagons for the grain had appeared and been decorated with green branches, sprays of bougainvillea and flowers mostly taken from our garden secretly at dawn. It was a heart-warming touch of African spontaneity and I gladly turned a blind eye on the ravaged garden. Each minister took his allotted part in the impromptu service, and the Catholic Father blessed the people and the workers' uplifted hands were sprinkled with holy water; also he blessed the tractors and oxen, and the new seed for sowing. Below us Africa was spread before us almost to infinity, cloud-stippled in the sunlight. The shaded coffee shambas climbed up the mountain above us. The solemn service ended in this clear serenity of vision.

Then small ox-teams moved into the coffee to do a cultivation competition between the rows of coffee trees. I had asked my friend Chief Jonathan Baraza from Elgon Nyanza, a few miles farther round the mountain, to judge the ploughing and cultivation matches, and stay with us for the festival. At that time he told me he was on the Mau Mau black list. If his life was in danger he showed a cheerful God-trusting indifference to the threat. All that morning we had the ploughing match followed by a prize-giving, and rested in the afternoon. The next day we had sports and a football match. Saturday was given to lighter things. We had an African play (home-made and home-produced) and much comic miming. Our West Kenya people are born impromptu actors with a glorious sense of the ridiculous. We saw ourselves and themselves and the DC taken off until we almost broke our ribs with laughing. At the farm committee's request the Lloyd family, father, mother and children, gave a horse-jumping display, which caused more happy cheering as one fell off and the odd horse refused at some home-made obstacle.

Eight hundred pounds of maize had been brewed into beer and two oxen had been killed so that feasting, merriment and dancing in the firelight continued until moonset close to dawn. Sunday followed for recuperation, and when work resumed on Monday two just discernible black eyes were all the damage noted. For the next two or three months afterwards the whole round of work on the farm went with marked smoothness and far more laughter even than usual. Man not only needs to create by work but to have recreation of himself in the rhythm of the year. This is especially true where man is far closer to the elements than he is in the west, in suburb and factory, where eye and ear are tuned to ready-made diversion in which the body and spirit can have little or no awareness and spontaneity. This numbing dullness should have no part in the new Africa, impatient as she may be for technical education and material standards of living to approximate older industrial countries.

A Knot of Roots Earl of Portsmouth.

The glory of the garden.

I loved going to this quiet place. Even before clearing, it was delightful to sit there in the green gloom, and to feel the prickly dead leaves – so unlike their brethren in the old country – small and hard and greyish, rustling under my hand. Twisted scabrous stems of creepers writhed upwards, like antediluvian reptiles, into a dense canopy overhead, but one could still catch the crimson flash of a crested plantain-eater's wings, as it flitted among the tree-tops high above.

Sometimes, if one sat very still, there would be a quick thudding of tiny feet, and a little brown mouse-deer (dik-dik) would scamper by with lowered head, so close that one could have touched it. Before our dogs had become numerous enough to hunt these pretty creatures, they were strangely fearless, and one of the most charming glimpses of jungle life I have ever stumbled upon was a fight between two diminutive bucks.

With shrill squeaks of fury they flew at each other, their two-inch long prick horns bent with murderous intent, and it was only after repeated charges that one of them turned tail and fled, hotly pursued, out of sight. . . .

We cut down all the tangling parasites and weedy saplings, leaving only the gnarled trunks of some large olives and a few grey-stemmed, thick-foliaged, smaller trees. A withy fence was put up round the irregular garden patch, and the main part was roughly levelled and planted with fast-spreading, bright-green, Kikuyu grass. Borders were mapped out, and paths, but I felt that some central feature was lacking, until I noticed a natural hollow in the bank, and decided at once to make a round rose-bed there, encircled by a sunk stone wall. . . .

Grass swept to the edge of my horse-shoe-shaped wall. Along the top, and among its very stones, blazed the pinks, reds, and yellows of dwarf snap-dragons; below ran a narrow path of crazy paving, and then came the low mound of the round rose-bed. It is true that my roses obstinately refused to flourish there, but pansies, asters, petunias, and carnations did, and provided me with a riot of colour after the rains.

There was a cultivated annexe beyond, in which I tried to grow vegetables, rambler roses, and honeysuckle, but, alas! lack of regular rain, and insufficient watering, prevented its ever being a great success, except in the wet season.

For a few precious months in the year, however, the garden bloomed delightfully, and then was the time to retreat there, alone and at peace, the burden of farm worries for a brief hour forgotten. There is surely something primitive in the deep content that fills one's soul, while fine warm earth runs through outspread fingers, giving soothing promise of sheaves to come. It is a happy solitude, an ecstatic if silent communion with nature, and it rests the mind as few other recreations can.

The fascination of my garden was so strong upon me that often I would visit it by moonlight also. Then the bizarre beauty of those slanting olives, the tremulous silver lights and inky shadows, the pale sweet ghostliness of white blossoms and dark mysterious depths of the jungle beyond, all lent it an enchantment not easily conveyed in words.

A Kenyan Farm Diary V. M. Carnegie.

I too will something make
And joy in the making:
Although tomorrow it seem
Like the empty words of a dream
Remembered on waking.
                    Robert Bridges

From the second week in September to Christmas, Kenya is usually at its glorious best. For eleven months of the year the Highlands boast the finest climate in the world; and of these eleven months, those following September are the real jewels. February, March and April are always dry and sometimes dusty, though never unbearably hot.

All the world over the farmer is, traditionally, a grumbler; a grouser with whom things are never just right. True to form, we in Kenya rave and curse in the dry weather and sag dispiritedly in our one depressing wet month. No farmer anywhere has a better climate than ours, but like all the others of our trade we magnify our ills and talk a lot about the bad weather. But in the middle of September everything usually *is* all right; wet, mud, and dust are forgotten, and it is hard to fault a single thing.

Flowers, from the garish bougainvilleas to the bursting blimpish hydrangeas, from the sky-high hollyhocks to the earth-bound pansies, face up and thumb their noses at depression. We watch the strong pipes push up from the leafy wheat fields; while, regimented in even squares like guards at a tattoo parade, the giant twelve-feet tall maize plants throw out their tasselled plumes and wave boisterously at the pageant.

The bounty of the kitchen garden is at its sweet-tasting best. New potatoes are really new; corn on the cob is milk-full and tender; peas are sugar steeped and beans are fleshy and crisp and still without string. The lettuces and cabbage are big and succulent. It is a time when soil, moisture and sun are all mixed in the right proportions and the resultant dish is fit for a King.

And then the pipes of wheat unwind to expose the thickening ears. Powdered with pollen, they put a nap on the bright green carpet of the grain fields. Broken ploughs, unserviceable tractors, hot wearying days of preparing the land, the long hours on the planting machine, are now nothing but a bad dream.

Cattle grow fat and sleek and browse contentedly in the lush pastures, and the natives, hypnotized by the colour, the warmth, the verve of the world, leave their blankets behind and work with an enthusiasm that is foreign to their nature.

And Elizabeth and I forget our overdraft and worries; for this year will surely be a bumper, and trouble and debts will be no more.

New Kenyans.

Susan was in high school in Nairobi. Towards the end of term she would write, "Only three more weeks and then I'll be home."

Patricia's school was just outside our town. Copied from the blackboard in irregular, joined capitals she would write "Term ends on 28 July. Then we come home."

Home. I still looked upon that small corner of the English Midlands as home; the place that was so full of sisters and brothers and aunts and uncles and relatives; the place that was steeped in warmth and love; the place hewn out of generations of traditions and stability – that was home as I knew it.

And here were our children calling an unkempt bit of Africa home. A place cut out of the bush, with insecure foundations temerariously laid by me. A place without tradition and very little stability – to our children this had become home.

Born of a chance seed sown in a war-scarred mind, fertilized by a restlessness, nurtured in the struggle to bring order where there had been only wildness and disorder before, something we had not dreamed of had sprung up: something our children, and their children, and perhaps their children's children, would call home.

The Gate Hangs Well James Stapleton.

Early in 1960 the "wind of change" struck Kenya with gale force. Britain's Tory government had decided to pull out of Africa without reservation and, in Kenya, to liquidate the policy of white settlement begun less than sixty years before. In January 1960 delegates representing all political factions in the colony, black and white, were summoned to a conference at Lancaster House in London to hear the British Government's intentions for the colony's future. These were to introduce immediately majority rule based on universal suffrage, followed by withdrawal of the British authority. To the European settlers, this came as a bolt from the blue. To satisfy the pressing African demand for land, a scheme was introduced to buy immediately about one million acres of the "white highlands" and subdivide it into plots on which to settle African small-holders with individual title to their parcels of land.

Happy Valley, 1963.

We were looking down over the Wanjohi, the once notorious Happy Valley, haunted perhaps by the raffish ghosts of people like Lady Idina, six times husbanded, and Joss Erroll, one of the husbands, destined to be the victim, in middle age, of a *crime passionel*; and Boy Long, whose handsome looks and gaudy shirts and broad-brimmed hats dazzled eyes and broke numerous hearts. And many others. All this took place a long time ago, in the twenties; the great depression of the early thirties obscured and eventually dispersed those Happy Valley dwellers who had survived *delirium tremens*, Muthaiga Club parties, needle pricks, and being shot at by jealous lovers on railway stations.*

Gin-soaked as they were, they enhanced rather than damaged the natural charms of their valley by leaving the native trees alone and creating gardens of outstanding beauty, by paddocking green pastures for butter-yellow Guernseys, stocking streams with trout and building attractive, rambling, creeper-festooned bungalows of local timbers with shingle roofs.

After they faded out, a different lot of settlers – white still – replaced them; they changed the valley, still without abusing it. They planted pyrethrum, an attractive crop with sheets of white flowers and sage-grey foliage; they bred good sheep, some of the finest in Kenya, from imported rams and ewes; and sold butterfat off

---

*Alice de Janzé, one of the dwellers, shot Raymond de Trafford in the stomach at the Gard du Nord. He recovered.

pastures they improved by modern methods of grassland management. The Wanjohi became a productive valley: still happy, on the whole, but on more *bourgeois* lines than in the days of its notoriety.

Now it has passed to a third lot of settlers. The plan is to settle fifteen hundred Kikuyu families here and on the slopes of Kipipiri, between forest and plateau. Many of the small-holdings extend to only seven acres – not much at an altitude too high for maize, the Kikuyu staple, and best suited to livestock, for which most of the plots are too small. On poorer land, plots are larger: but poorer land produces less.

The industry of these Kikuyu women is phenomenal. When they are on their own land, working for their own families, they never pause. In their different sphere the men, no doubt, are just as busy, but it is a sphere more of tongue and wit and less of muscle: buying and selling, bargaining, seeking out new opportunities in old lorries.

The last of the forest is going up in smoke from dozens of small fires, scenting the air so sweetly that we drew in deep breaths for the sheer pleasure of it. Perhaps I was sentimental to regret the trees. But our guide said: "In a few years' time what will have happened to the streams? They're bound to dwindle, in a drought they'll dry up altogether. This is a catchment area. It's sheer lunacy to let the forest go."

Forks and Hope Elspeth Huxley.

At midnight on 12 December 1963, in the presence of the Duke of Edinburgh, the Union Jack was hauled down and Mzee Jomo Kenyatta became Prime Minister of an independent Kenya. Harry Thuku, for many years a champion of African freedom, with Tabitha his wife celebrated uhuru *in their own way.*

Let me say how my wife and I spent our independence day in 1963. There was one very flat piece of land in our farm, and Mr Mirie with the other agricultural people had said that I must not plant coffee there – only beans. Well, when independence came round, I was sent a ticket as a director of KPCU (Kenya Planters' Coffee Union). It was very heavy rain at the time, and I could see that many people would be losing their shoes in the mud of the stadium. So I told my wife, "Now is the time; everybody – government, agriculturalists, and all people – have their eyes fixed on the independence stadium. But as there is very good rain, we shall have our independence here. We have in fact received our political independence whether we actually go to the stadium or not. We shall therefore celebrate our independence by planting our coffee where it is forbidden by the agricultural people." We had our own nursery for seedlings, and we reckoned it would be at least four months, with the change-over of administration, before officers came round, and by then there would be more than six inches of growth. So we celebrated our political and economic independence by planting something like 15,000 little trees! Eventually when they came round, they were astonished, and I told them it was a fitting celebration of independence because I had been fighting for Africans to grow coffee ever since 1921.

An Autobiography Harry Thuku.

Farewell happy fields
Where joy forever dwells.
John Milton

And so my farming life ended as it had begun, with me sitting and eating my sandwiches under the big cedar tree. . . . Gitau, Kimani, and Kamiri, who had been helping to get the furniture out of the house, went off to their own huts; and I sat down under the tree to eat my lunch as I had done when I had first come there and dreamed – a generation earlier.

I had sat under this same tree which then was the outpost tree at the edge of the forest, and I had looked at the open grassland before me, and at the mountains – green, grey, and purple – rising clear-cut into the sunlit sky as a backcloth to the scene that I saw and the scenes that I foresaw.

More than thirty years had passed since I had first sat there, and almost all that I had foreseen and planned had come to pass. I had dreamed of a house and a garden like to the country houses and gardens I had known as a boy, and now around me were the sweeping lawns under shady trees and the flowerbeds bright with the flowers of Africa and Europe; there were the trim clipped hedges, and beyond the hedges was the orchard with the rich fruit hanging on the branches. In front of me was the sprawling house of grey stone with flowering creepers growing up the walls and "home" written all over it; and the ghosts of the dogs that had shared it with us were lying on the door-steps and in front of the french windows. Beyond it was the old wooden house where we had lived when our children were small and where, in later years, had lived the farm manager and his wife and their children.

There was the tennis court where there had been tennis from the days when it was all that the players could do to hit the ball over the net to the days when the tennis was worth watching for its own sake. There were the farm buildings, now empty and deserted and with weeds beginning to grow in the yards, which had always been noisy and warm with well-tended livestock. There were the paddocks on the ridge beyond the buildings. . . .

There were the water tanks and the drinking troughs, and I remembered how we had saved and skimped to get the money to lay the pipelines, and had rejoiced to see the life-giving water extend from place to place. In those earliest days, that did not in retrospect really seem so far away, I had pictured, as a dream that might come true, the days when pedigree stock might perhaps be shown off to visitors in fit surroundings, and when the trophies they had won might also be shown. That was a dream that had also come true, and that had brought a lot of satisfaction in its realization.

But the farm and what had gone into it and what had come out of it – satisfying though it all had been – had only been the means to bigger things, and those dreams also had come true. Now they walked the earth in the reality of young men and women who had grown to maturity in the surroundings that we had made for them – our children and the children of others who had spent their holidays with us. They had played in the garden and had ridden their ponies round the farm; they had fished the river for the speckled trout that lay below the waterfalls, and they had gone shooting along the edge of the forest glades; they had climbed the mountains and had camped on the moors; they had grown up strong and self-reliant; and filled with that humanity that comes from close contact with nature.

What we had done was good in concept and in the carrying out of it, and – whatever may come to Kenya – no one can take that certainty from us, and no one can take that background from those young people who grew up with it, and who have it to sustain them through their lives.

I doubt if anyone who did not know the spirit of the old Kenya of the early farms, and the enthusiasm and the spirit of endeavour that pervaded it, and the hard work and the sacrifice of easy things that accompanied it, can ever comprehend our feeling of utter certainty that what we were doing was good and constructive and would last, and then our bitter disillusion when the evil in others broke out and swamped our efforts, and when those who know not Africa blamed us for the evil. Many of those who started their time in Kenya later than we did, and who, maybe, were not quite so steeped in that early atmosphere, have not taken the knock so hard. Perhaps those who merely grew up in the old Kenya will be, by virtue of their youth, more adaptable than those of my generation; let us hope so.

But certain it is that those of us who began at the beginning, or near the beginning, have lost something in our lives that had meant much in our lives, and I doubt if we can ever be the same again. It is not that we doubt whether what we did was good; we still know with complete certainty that it was good. It was the sense of this something that we have lost that softened the wrench of leaving the results of thirty years' work, and of seeing those results beginning to revert. If I could have handed the farm over to someone else who would have carried it on as I had started it I would not have minded so much: but if, on the other hand, I had had to abandon it when the old spirit still lived I should have minded much more.

All this, and more besides, I thought to myself as I ate my sandwiches in the garden under the cedar. But even so I realized that if what had happened had to happen I could count myself lucky that it had happened when it did. At least the time allowed to me had seen my family through. The picture left to us, and the picture left to them, is a complete picture and a picture to which we can always look back in the knowledge that it is a picture that would take a lot of beating anywhere in the world. I doubt if it could be beaten. By that measure we have been fortunate.

We Built a Country J. F. Lipscomb.

Tailpiece.

By now it was dark. Through the portholes of the plane I saw the red glow from the exhaust of the engine and beyond it the faint shadows of cumulus clouds bobbing in the high thin air. The woman sitting next to me lit a cigarette. When I had first taken my seat I had noticed her, like a fading figurehead from the prow of a tall ship. Her hands, covered with calluses, resembled old taproots, and her sunburned face seemed to be lost in a sea of white hair.

She was a pioneer of Kenya, she explained to me. She leaned back into the seat and puffed on her cigarette. With her parents, she continued, she had trekked onto the highlands in an ox wagon. She remembered the thatched hut which was their first home in Kenya, the struggle the family had made to discover what crops grew best, the mornings when they found that elephants had trampled the *shamba* and the nights when lions slept on the veranda. She paused for a second to look out into the night through the porthole. She lit another cigarette and told me about her old servants, of those who had broken the trust to take the Mau Mau oath and of the others who even to this day remain loyal.

The plane began to lose altitude and out of the starboard window I saw the lights of Machakos and Athi. Somewhere to the right of the wing tip was her old farm. "It was sold last week," she explained. "I'd always been able to run it by myself ever since my parents died, but these days everything has begun to change. This country no longer belongs to white people like you and me." She paused to look out the window. "I'm not bitter that the black man has finally come into his own but I know that there is no place left for me out here." The airplane was making its final approach and soon I saw the lights of the runway flashing under the wings and felt a soft nudge as the tires met the runway. "Tomorrow I'm booked on a flight to Australia. I've already bought a farm out there and I plan to start all over again."

The Imminent Rains John Heminway.

PART IV

Wars

Wars have been endemic in East Africa, as in the rest of the world, since records began and no doubt before that. The Arab/Swahili city states were often at odds; Mombasa and Malindi were old rivals. Warriors from the interior such as the Galla were a constant threat to the safety of the civilized inhabitants of the coastal settlements. The first wars to be recorded by Europeans were those fought during the intermittent Portuguese occupation, 1505–1729. In the interior the tribes, or ethnic groups, fought each other to capture livestock, sometimes women, and slaves, the latter mainly at the instigation of Arab and Swahili traders. In the early days of the twentieth century both Britain and Germany engaged in minor wars, then called punitive expeditions, to enforce a major peace. They did away with inter-tribal wars but soon involved their respective colonies in international wars, the tribes of which those colonizing powers were originally composed having coalesced into nations. Three major wars have left their mark on Kenya during its short period of colonial history.

The Portuguese Wars

Vasco da Gama's visit to Mombasa and Malindi in 1498 ushered in more than two centuries of intermittent conflict between the "Moors" and the Portuguese. In 1505 Dom Francisco d'Almeida attacked and burned Mombasa.

The Grand-Captain ordered that the town should be sacked and that each man should carry off to his ship whatever he found: so that at the end there would be a division of the spoil, each man to receive a twentieth of what he found. The same rule was made for gold, silver, and pearls. Then everyone started to plunder the town and to search the houses, forcing open the doors with axes and iron bars. There was a large quantity of cotton cloth for Sofala in the town, for the whole coast gets its cotton cloth from here. So the Grand-Captain got a good share of the trade of Sofala for himself. A large quantity of rich silk and gold embroidered clothes was seized, and carpets also; one of these, which was without equal for beauty, was sent to the King of Portugal together with many other valuables.

When night came the Grand-Captain ordered all the men to a field which lay between the town and the sea. A section of it was allotted to each captain and a watch was set for the night. They were at a distance of a gun shot from the palm grove where the Moors were with their king. On the morning of the 16th they again plundered the town, but because the men were tired from fighting and from lack of sleep, much wealth was left behind apart from what each man took for himself. They also carried away provisions, rice, honey, butter, maize, countless camels and a large number of cattle, and even two elephants. They paraded these elephants in front of the people of the town before they took it, in order to frighten them. There were many prisoners, and white women among them and children, and also some merchants from Cambay.

On Saturday evening the Grand-Captain ordered that all should return to the ships in a disciplined manner, keeping a watch for the Moors as they went on their way. And as the Christians left by one way, so the Moors entered by the other to see what destruction had been done. For the streets and houses were full of dead, who were estimated to be about 1,500.

The distress of Mombasa's ruler prompted him to write to the king of Malindi as follows.

May God's blessing be upon you, Sayyid Ali! This is to inform you that a great lord has passed through the town, burning it and laying it waste. He came to the town in such strength and was of such cruelty, that he spared neither man nor woman, old nor young, nay, not even the smallest child. Not even those who fled escaped from his fury. He not only killed and burnt men but even the birds of the heavens were shot down. The stench of the corpses is so great in the town that I dare not go there; nor can I ascertain nor estimate what wealth they have taken from the town. I give you these sad news for your own safety.

There were more than 10,000 people in Mombasa, of whom 3,700 were men of military age.

The East African Coast: Select Documents G. S. P. Freeman-Grenville.

In 1587 a Turkish brigand named Amir Ali Bey captured Mombasa Island. A Portuguese fleet sent from Goa to dislodge him found unexpected allies in a tribe of cannibals, the Zimba, who had eaten their way up the coast from the mouth of the Zambesi river. A Dominican friar, Father Joao dos Santos, gave his version of these events.

At Tete, on the other side of the River within Land to the East and North-East, are two kinds of Man-eating Cafres, the Mumbos and Zimbas or Muzimbas, who eate those they take in warre, and their slaves also when they are past labour, and sell it as Beefe or Mutton. The Captayne of Tete with his eleven Encosses, and their Companies slue six hundred of the Mumbos in a Battell, not leaving one alive, and carried away their Wives and Children Captives. This was at Chico-ronga a Mumbos Towne, in which was a slaughter-house, where every day they butchered their Captives; neere which the Portugals found many Negroes, men and women, bound hand and foot, destined to the slaughter for the next dayes food, whom with many others they freed. . . .

These Zimbas worship no God, nor Idol, but their King, who (they say) is God of the Earth: and if it rains when hee would not, they shoot their Arrowes at the Skie for not obeying him; and he only eates not mans flesh. These are talle, bigge, strong; and have for Armes, small Hatchets, Arrowes, Azagaies, great Bucklers, with which they cover their whole bodies of light wood, lined with wild beasts skinnes. They eate those which they kill in warre and drink, in their skuls. If any of their own Cafres be sicke or wounded, to save labour of cure they kill and eate them. . . .

One of these Zimbas ambitious of that honour, which they place in killing and eating of men, to get himselfe a name, adjoyned others of his Nation to him, and went Eastward, killing and eating every living thing, Men, Women, Children, Dogs, Cats, Rats, Snakes, Lizards, sparing nothing but such Cafres as adjoyned themselves to their companie in that designe. And thus five thousand of them were assembled, and went before the Ile of Quiloa; where the Sea prohibiting their passage, a traiterous Moore came and offered his service to guide them over at the low ebbes of spring tides, upon condition to spare his kindred, and to divide the spoyles with him. The Zimba accepted it, and effected his cruell purpose, slaying and taking (for future dainties to eate at leasure) three thousand Moores, and tooke the Citie Quiloa, with great riches, the people escaping by hiding themselves in the wildernesse till the Zimbas were gone; then returning to their Citie (antiently the royall Seat of the Kings of that Coast) and to this day are seene the ruines of their sumptuous Mezquites and Houses. Now, for the reward of the Traytor, he sentenced him with all his kindred to be cast into the Sea, bound hand and foot, to bee food for the fishes; saying, it was not meet that one should remayne of so wicked a generation, nor would he eate their flesh, which could not but be venomous.

After this he passed along the Coast, till he came against the Ile of Mombaza; which foure Turkish Galleyes of the Red Sea defended, and slue many of them with their Artillery: but Thome de Sousa arriving with a fleet from India tooke the Turkes, and withall destroyed Mombaza in the sight of the Muzimbas. The Captaine said that the Portugals were the Gods of the Sea, and hee of the Land; and sent an Ambassadour to Sousa, professing friendship to them, and requesting that seeing they had honourably ended their enterprise, he might beginne his, namely, to kill and eate every living thing in the Iland, which by their consent he did accordingly, burning the Palme-trees and Woods where many men were hidden, whom hee tooke and eate with all hee could get.

Thence he returned to the Coast, and went to Melinde, where Mathew Mendez with thirty Portugals ayded the King, and three thousand warlike Cafres, called Mossegueios, came also to his succour, which came suddenly on their backes when they had gotten up the wall, and were almost possessed of the Bulwarke, and chased them with such a furie, that only the Captaine with above one hundred others escaped; having found none in three hundred leagues march, which durst encounter them. And thus much of the Zimbas. . . .

The East African Coast: Select Documents G. S. P. Freeman-Grenville.

The Siege of Mombasa

In 1632 the Portuguese reoccupied Mombasa to find it a wilderness: buildings razed, palm trees felled and only one survivor. They rebuilt the city and held it uneasily until 15 March 1696 when an Arab fleet sailed into Kilindini harbour and the entire population, Christian and Muslim, numbering over 2,500 souls, fled into Fort Jesus. So began a siege which was to last for thirty-three months. At the end of 1696 a relief fleet from Goa managed to land supplies and a few reinforcements, but with them came "the swelling sickness", probably bubonic plague, which swept through the garrison.

As early as 28 January 1697 the Captain was reporting that three or four men were dying every day. It was mostly the pure-bred Portuguese, and especially the men, who succumbed; the immunity of the women they sought to explain by the fact that they were not exposed to the hardships of the watch. No drug or medicament appeared to be of any use. . . .

Things went from bad to worse. At the end of January there were only 20 men, that is, no doubt, reckoning only the Portuguese, under arms in the Fort. The ships had left without taking any letters and without, as had been promised, freeing the garrison of its useless members. . . .

Matters then became even worse. At the end of June the only Portuguese survivors were the Captain, the Augustinian Prior, who was a useful man-at-arms as well as a priest, two soldiers and two young children. Yet these, together with a few surviving native troops, managed to repulse an assault made with ladders by the enemy one night. Even African women were armed and had to help and they did what was required of them courageously. A few days later three more Portuguese died, leaving alive only the Captain António Mogo de Mello. His hour too was at hand, and anticipating his end, he had his grave dug in the chapel of the Fort on 24 August. On 28 August he too died.

Upon his death the command passed, in name at least, to a sick Goan called Pascoal Diniz. In fact he was nothing more than the keeper of the keys of the Fort for the few days which he still survived. The seventeen-year old Bwana Daud bin Sheikh, the Prince of Faza, was actually in command of the Fort. . . .

The authorities in Goa roused themselves to make one more effort to save the threatened Fort. At the end of 1698 a third relief fleet was hastily fitted out, this time with money lent personally by the Viceroy. This fleet, which consisted of four frigates and a galliot with about 500 landing troops and 700 crew on board . . . reached Mombasa on 13 or 14 December, 1698. The effort had been in vain, for the red Arab flag was already flying over the Fort. It had fallen only a few days previously, possibly only one day before the arrival of the fleet. The fleet sailed on to Zanzibar without attacking the Arabs, and without even approaching land. Nothing was known in Zanzibar of the fall of Mombasa. . . .

An Arab ballad gives the date of the fall of Mombasa as 9 Jamada Alkhir of the year 1110, i.e. 12 December 1698. There is no confirmation of this date in official Portuguese reports of the period. No Portuguese survived who might have given information about events at the end of the siege. . . . A year later an enquiry was ordered from Lisbon, but it was not for another two years that some light was shed on the darkness of the last days. On 29 September 1701, an Indian called Braz Fialho arrived in Goa, who had been employed on board Luis de Mello Sampaio's frigate. He arrived after escaping from Muscat and claimed to have participated in the last days of Mombasa.

His story was briefly as follows. On the eve of St Lucia's Day, 12 December 1698, the sick Captain, Leandro Barbosa, sent an African youth out of the Fort to fetch fresh leaves to use as wound dressings. This youth was captured and betrayed to the Arabs the weakness of the defenders, whose total number was only eight Portuguese, three Indians and two women. That same night the Arabs attacked at two points, namely on the flag bastion (on the town side) and on the bastion where the emergency door was situated. The few defenders withdrew into the cavalier bastion, called Santo Antonio, and here turned the guns inwards on to the attackers. They defended themselves until midday on the following day. When however, the Captain, who had stepped forward a few paces, received two fatal wounds, the rest of the defenders laid down their arms. They were led away in chains but their lives were spared, for the Arabs hoped to obtain from them information as to where certain treasure, which was supposed to be hidden away, was concealed. In the end only two Portuguese remained alive, and these became servants of the Arabs in the Fort. On the pretext of revealing the whereabouts of the treasure, one went into the church and the other into the storeroom and they there managed to fire off the stocks of gunpowder, thus blowing up themselves and two hundred Arabs.

In 1728 a fleet from Goa reached Mombasa and, overcoming a feeble resistance, reoccupied Fort Jesus. But not for long. Thirteen months later, the townsmen fell upon the Portuguese outside the fort and murdered them all. Those inside the fort held out for eight months before hunger forced them to surrender.

The story ended when on 26 November 1729, they sailed off to Mozambique, in two dhows given to them by the Mombasans. Each man was allowed to take with him only what he could carry. This was the final farewell and the collapse of Portuguese rule in northern East Africa. The exiles did not reach Mozambique until 3 February 1730, and the only survivors were the Governor, the factor, three captains, five warrant officers and twenty men.

The Portuguese Period in East Africa Justus Strandes.

Cities and Thrones and Towers
    Stand in Time's eye
Almost as long as Flowers
    Which daily die.
But, as new buds put forth
    To glad new men,
Out of the spent and unconsidered earth
    The Cities rise again.

                    Rudyard Kipling

Colonial Conflicts

The establishment of British rule over the peoples of the interior, roughly between 1890 and 1905, though on the whole peaceful was not without resistance, first by the Kikuyu and then by the Nandi. A party led by a Swahili headman named Maktub sent out in 1891 from Fort Smith, near Dagoretti, to buy food, was ambushed and wiped out to a man. An expedition commanded by Captain Macdonald sent to impose a fine of goats and cattle repulsed an attack by eight hundred to a thousand Kikuyu warriors.

Next day we continued our advance. Village after village was occupied and searched, and in some we found tokens, such as portions of the dead men's accoutrements, which clearly showed that the inhabitants had participated in the attack on Maktub. All this time the enemy hovered round at a distance, but did not venture near; only once, when their position was a very good one on the far side of a particularly difficult ravine, did they make a stand. They drew up and taunted us, inviting us to come on and share the fate of Maktub and his men, as they wanted more clothes and arms; but when our two leading companies accepted the challenge and advanced up the slope, their hearts failed them, and they retired rather hastily into some villages.

On gaining the high ground, we found ourselves on a great open clearing, surrounded by seven large villages, and, as soon as the main body came up, these were attacked. Pringle advanced on three strong kraals on the left, Austin took two in the centre, and Purkiss cleared the right flank. In no case did the enemy make more than a shadow of resistance, and soon seven pillars of smoke rising skyward announced to the countryside that the enemy's main stronghold had shared the fate of the other hostile encampments we had already destroyed.

Back at Fort Smith one of the officers, Purkiss, was in his room when the local chief, Wyaki, suddenly appeared.

He looked in at the messroom window and passed on to Purkiss' room. In a few minutes we heard a tremendous row, and rushed out to see Purkiss and Wyaki emerge from the former's room, locked in a deadly struggle. Before we could reach the combatants, Purkiss snatched away Wyaki's sword, and gave him a violent blow on the head. We now dashed forwards and separated them, and in less time than it takes to tell the story Wyaki was bound and helpless. It was with great difficulty that we prevented Purkiss' infuriated followers from spearing his treacherous assailant on the spot. The news had by this time spread outside the fort, and we heard the alarm-cry echoing far and wide across the countryside, and the cattle being hastily driven off to the woods. However, the two friendly Kikuyu chiefs were still with us, and these we sent with the message that Wyaki should be tried for his offence next day, and that we did not intend to make a *casus belli* of his unsupported action. For several hours we heard nothing, and meanwhile all the sentries were doubled, and everything made ready to repulse an attack. About 11 pm our envoys returned to say that Wyaki's relatives had decided not to take up his quarrel, and that the country was settling down.

It appeared that Wyaki, who was rather drunk, went into Purkiss' room to taunt him with his failure to secure the cattle of Guruguru. Purkiss, seeing the state he was in, ordered him out of the house, and on Wyaki becoming still more insolent, pushed him towards the door. Wyaki at once drew his sword and attacked Purkiss, who was unarmed, and could not get to the weapons he had laid aside on entering his room. An unequal struggle now commenced, and Purkiss grappled with the Kikuyu chief, in an endeavour to deprive him of his sword. The rest of the struggle we had ourselves witnessed.

Wyaki was tried next day in the presence of seventeen of his brother chiefs, to whom all the evidence was translated. Of the verdict there could be no doubt, nor had Wyaki any defence to make, except that he was drunk. So we decided to take him away with us to the coast, and deport him permanently from the country, where he had proved such a treacherous enemy, and the cause of so much bloodshed. This decision was far more lenient than the Kikuyu chiefs had expected, and they then and there made a treaty of friendship with Purkiss.

Wyaki, apparently none the worse for his wound, was marched down to the coast with Macdonald's party, but died on the way at Kibwezi from complications following a fractured skull.

Strange to say, poor Purkiss died at the same station a few years afterwards, on his way down from Uganda, and the graves of the two combatants lie close together.
Soldiering and Surveying in British East Africa J. R. L. Macdonald.

Some sixty years later Wyaki was re-born as a folk hero, and his story retold.

Because the Kikuyu from early times have attached great importance to their land and to their property, the people of Waiyaki's time were very pleased with his actions and words, because he was the most important leader then. . . . Thus when the white people came they tried very hard to bribe people so that, through cunning, they might steal the rich earth.

But Waiyaki himself did not like what the white people were trying to do because he was aware of the importance of the rich earth. Also his destiny had been foretold by the prophet Mugo son of Kibero, who had prophesied what would happen. So with his army of many people he endeavoured to prevent them. But because the Europeans came with guns it was not possible to drive them away completely, although the warriors were very strong and brave.

During those days when he was working against the white people they had cunning plans to arrest him. When the white people had completed their plans they sent for the respected leader, Waiyaki, telling him to go to the place where he had given the white people a plot of land to build on [Fort Smith] so that they would negotiate a settlement. When he arrived one of the servants who had come with the white people said to him: "Do not go in for the white man is very angry". But because Waiyaki had no fear, and because he was a leader, and also because he knew that he was in his own country, he was very stubborn when he heard that he should not enter, especially as it was he who had given them the land.

So, being a brave man he was not afraid; so he entered. When he had entered he saw that the white man was really very angry. He pulled out his sword, but the Europeans combined to hold him and disarmed him. Indeed he was wounded on the face. When the young people saw that their leader was arrested they shed tears of rage. But as you know, Waiyaki was a fighter for justice and peace and a lover of his people. He knew that if the young people fought the Europeans they would be wiped out by the guns.

When he saw that fighting might break out he spoke with a loud voice, saying: "I beseech you, my people, beware of fighting, for it is not good that you should lose your lives because of me. Let me be taken where I shall be taken. If I die, I die, so be it".

And the people present were astounded and offered much property, goats and cows, so that Waiyaki might be released. But the Europeans were adamant in their refusal. When the Europeans refused to release Waiyaki the people went home, hearing his words of wisdom, for without doubt he was highly respected. . . .

When Waiyaki died he prayed earnestly to God to resurrect him because he saw that he had left his country in a state of much hardship. Let us say that Waiyaki, when he died, went to the right hand of God, and because God loved His people He heard Waiyaki's prayers that it should be made possible for him to reach the white man's country to learn his customs so that he might return again to his own country to lead his people from slavery.

So Waiyaki was born again as a young child with another name and he was brought up and became a man with his own home. It came to pass, as God wished, whose wisdom never fails, that he followed the very route he had followed to Kibwezi, and he went to Europe, where, through the kindness of God and the diligence of our hero, he worked with all his heart to overcome many hardships until he finally obtained what had caused him to go to the land of the strangers for some eighteen years. . . .

Now the Waiyaki of whom I am speaking, the one who was born again, is, of course, Jomo Kenyatta. Therefore because I believe that there is no one who does not wish that Waiyaki had lived, know ye all that he has been resurrected.

Mahoya ma Waiyaki Mbugua Njama, trans. James Ngugi.
From *The Scottish Mission in Kenya 1891–1923* Brian Mackintosh.

One of the first tasks of the British administrators was to put a stop to inter-tribal warfare.

The Wakamba make up for lack of warlike discipline by craft and cunning. At all times, day and night, they have scouts located in the outlying hills north of Machako's; anxiously looking out for Masai war-parties on the Kapote plains. These scouts are also greatly assisted by their hunters, who follow the antelope even into the plains beyond the Athi River. Should any of these discover that the Masai kraals are greatly weakened in Elmoran [warriors] by the departure of strong war-parties to distant raiding-grounds, word is at once passed to the Wakamba, who assemble a force of fighting men and elect their war-leaders. This force is then divided into two or more battalions, and moves north, under cover of the hills, to the edge of the great grass plains on which are dotted the low black kraals of the enemy.

The Wakamba then wait till dark, when, by a rapid and noiseless march, they approach the hostile kraal. But they know better than to dream of surprising the ever-vigilant Masai, and it is now their craft comes in. With much uproar, one battalion advances on the kraal, and the alarm is hardly sounded before the Masai Elmoran spring out to confront the foe. The battle is soon being hotly waged, but the Wakamba battalion, avoiding too close a combat, retires slowly, covered by flights of poisoned arrows, which whistle through the darkness. The impetuous Masai warriors, eager to flesh their spears, press forward in triumph, and are led farther and farther from the kraal by the cunning foe.

Meanwhile, the other division of the Wakamba creeps round and falls on the now undefended village camp. Short work is made of the few feeble old men who attempt to defend it, and women and children, cattle, sheep, goats, and donkeys are hastily driven off. After having allowed sufficient time for this manœuvre, the first Wakamba battalion makes some show of resistance, and thus prevents the Elmoran from detailing any large number to recover the cattle, and under shelter of the darkness and confusion a good deal of the booty is often triumphantly carried off. They are not, however, always so successful, for the Masai, having learnt caution from previous raids, sometimes divide their force, and the Wakamba find great spears flashing up to oppose both their parties, and are forced to retire discomfited.

On the other hand, the Masai freely raid the Wakamba, and cause great loss in cattle, if not in life. The Wakamba scouts are sometimes caught napping, or more frequently the raiders make such a rapid advance that no preparations can be made to offer a combined resistance. In such a case each little Wakamba village thinks only of its own safety. The women and children flee to the mountains, and the men, instead of assembling to resist the invaders, endeavour to drive off their flocks and herds to the same haven of refuge. When each village is thus playing for its own hand, the disciplined Masai find it an easy matter to cut off some of these isolated parties, and retreat with their spoil, with hardly the loss of a single man. These raids are often carried out successfully by parties of only a couple of hundred; but they are mostly confined to the other Wakamba districts, for the Masai, after an experience they had some years ago, are chary of becoming entangled in the mountain gorges.

On that occasion they raided deep into the mountains, and reached Kilungu. They had been successful, and had collected a large number of cattle, for the Wakamba, as usual, had offered only a feeble resistance. The Masai, however, had proceeded too leisurely, and those of the Wakamba who had got their property to the safety of the rocks and caves now joined those who had been caught *en route*; and as the Masai, encumbered with herds of cattle, began to retire, the Wakamba bowmen made good practice from every bush and clump of jungle that commanded the road. Again and again the Masai charged to the flank and rear, and as often the Wakamba fled, but only to return and ply afresh the death-dealing bow.

So far the invaders' road had not been blocked in front, but as they toiled up the rugged gorge that opens on to the grasslands of Kapote, near the great rock pools of Bondani, they found the Wakamba warriors of Maka perched on the rocks which commanded the outlet, and drawn up across the gorge itself. To contend against the Parthian tactics of those behind, fight this fresh foe in front, and at the same time control the great herd of cattle, was manifestly impossible. For some time the Masai Lagonani attempted to save his spoil; but his wearied followers were now falling fast, for the great war-shield could protect only one side of the body, and the arrows were raining down from every direction. At last he gave the order to abandon the spoil, formed up the remainder of his party, and charged the men of Maka like a whirlwind. The great spears flashed and fell, and the Wakamba line was at once broken before that mighty rush. Only about one-third of the Masai war-party emerged on the grass plains, but these at once reformed and faced about. The Lagonani, however, saw they were too exhausted to renew the fight, and the remnant of his party retired in good order and unmolested, for the Wakamba considered them, wearied and disheartened although they were, too formidable to attack in the open. The Wakamba loss had not been small; but they had absolutely beaten the Masai, and since that day the inland districts have suffered but little from raids.

Soldiering and Surveying in British East Africa J. R. L. Macdonald

A rough-and-ready cart road from Mombasa to Uganda made under the direction of Captain B. L. Slater, RE, in 1895–6, passed through the margins of the Nandi's country. Nandi warriors attacked caravans passing along it, and fell upon the rails and telegraph wires of the advancing railway. The first of five military expeditions designed to stop the raids and secure the subjugation of the Nandi elders took place in 1895.

Only a few natives could be seen on the ridge and it was with astonishment we suddenly saw a crowd of about 500 coming over the top of the hill at great speed, apparently excellently organized, and formed in three sides of a square, above which a dense thicket of long-bladed spears flashed in the sunlight. Wheeling to the left as if by some common impulse, on they came in spite of the Maxim gun posted behind the river, and charged down with tremendous dash on to the force which was some way up the slope on the east bank, and which closed up as well as it could to face the impending attack. It was a critical moment, but luckily the Sudanese stood firm, and as the great mass of natives approached closer the heavy fire began to tell. Nearer and nearer they came, and it almost seemed that they would overwhelm No. IV Company, which had to bear the brunt of the attack; but at last, wavering before this leaden hail, which they had never before experienced, their ranks broke and they scattered in all directions, leaving many of their number on the ground. Half a company left at the bridge had, on the first alarm, advanced to the support of their comrades, and the flying natives had now to run the gauntlet of the fire from these men as they retired over the hill, leaving the ground strewn with their big shields and spears. It was a splendid charge and if continued for 30 yards or more would have been a successful one. . . . Over a hundred Nandi were left dead on the field, but the warriors had killed fourteen soldiers and irregulars, including Sgt Chongo, whose scarlet tunic was rent with many spear holes, and two porters. IV Company had stood firm and saved the day, but the disciplined bravery of the Nandi warriors had made a lasting impression on the Sudanese troops and their British officers.

Lt. C. Vandeleur *Campaigning on the Upper Nile*,
from *Nandi Resistance to British Rule* A. T. Matson.

The Nandi, like the Maasai, deferred in all important matters, and especially in matters of warfare, to their laibons, or medicine-men. The Nandi's chief laibon was believed to be behind the raids, but three more military expeditions failed to make contact with him or with the elders. Not until 1905, four years after the railway reached its goal, did the fifth and final expedition win the day. Captain Richard Meinertzhagen of the 3rd King's African Rifles describes the end of the affair.

28.IX.1905. *Nandi Fort,*
My intelligence service is working well, most of my men being Masai from the local Manyatta or young Nandi living near my house whom I feel I can trust.

There is no doubt now that I have become the focus of the Laibon's hatred and that he is anxious to meet me, lay an ambush and kill me. His name is Koitalel and he is a man of about 40 or so. He has told his warriors that the white man's bullets will be quite harmless if only he can get bits of my anatomy for his medicine, especially my brains, heart, liver, palms of the hands and eyes. He would mix all these with certain plants, bring the whole to a boil, and sprinkle his warriors with the broth; then nothing would harm them. He is going to pose as a peace-maker, entice me out to an ambush and secure the necessary parts of my anatomy. As he shakes hands with me, he will pull me over towards him and a man near him will spear me. He will have many warriors in the bush nearby and these will fall on my party and annihilate them. Koitalel's father had apparently, many years ago, brewed a broth which he claimed would turn bullets, but it proved useless and his fighting men killed him. Koitalel has promised that this will not happen again. He is, according to my agents, fearful of assassination by his own people and always has, day and night, an armed guard near him.

Koitalel is a wicked old man and at the root of all our trouble. He is a dictator, and as such must show successes in order to retain power. He is therefore in favour of fighting the British. Many of his hot-heads support him, but the bulk of the Nandi I have met are a peaceful and lovable lot, enjoying jokes. I have many friends among them; they trust me and I trust them. I can, or could until quite recently, walk about their country unarmed; they would not touch me but might not think twice about killing my men, just for fun.

My main reason for trying to kill or capture the Laibon is that, if I remove him this expedition will not be necessary and the Nandi will be spared all the horrors of military operations.

Meinertzhagen laid plans to confront the laibon during a meeting arranged at Koitalel's request.

Only half an hour ago I returned from the scene of my meeting with the Laibon, and both he and his retinue lie dead where we met. We left Nandi Fort at 5 am and have covered 24 miles. The risk and excitement of the whole business have tired me considerably, so I shall only record the main facts, leaving the detail for an official report. I took with me Sammy Butler and 80 men with a machine gun. Leaving Sammy with 75 men and the machine gun, I advanced to meet the Laibon with 5 men. As I suspected, he ambushed me as soon as I shook hands with him; but we were ready, and he, the interpreter and several others, some 23 in all, were left dead. I had my clothes torn by both spear and arrow and one of my men was slightly scratched by a spear. Before going down to meet the Laibon I had warned Butler to open fire at once if he saw us being overwhelmed. He mounted the machine gun and covered the place of meeting. As soon as the affair was over, we trekked for home as fast as our legs would carry us. The swiftness and suddenness of the blow momentarily stunned the Nandi, who had been gathered about in large numbers to see our discomfiture, but when the tables were turned they did nothing. But they soon recovered and were hard at our heels for the last 8 miles of our homeward journey. I was really glad to get back again to my little fort, as our ammunition was almost exhausted when we met a welcome patrol which had been sent out on my instructions to cover our retreat.

So may all the King's enemies perish. The Nandi Laibon deserves some obituary notice, as he was a man of some consequence. He was both spiritual and temporal chief of all the Nandi, his office being hereditary. As both he and all his successors male were gathered today, I much regret that the dynasty must stop from today. The only people I am sorry for are his wives, for they most certainly will be buried with him as is the custom. It is their own choice to be interred dead or alive.

I have sent a brief wire to Headquarters announcing my success. The long-expected Nandi Expedition has now commenced, and I am entirely satisfied with the first day of operations.

(I revisited Nandi in 1956 and on returning to my old quarters found them occupied by a local chief called Elijah, a Christian, decked out in immaculate shirt, bow tie and flannel suit. I had known him as a small boy. A few days later I was asked to be present at a parish council at Kapsabet, my friend Elijah being chairman. There were some 25 Africans present, all immaculately dressed in European clothes. I was introduced to each in turn with some appropriate remark:

"This is the gentleman whose house I now live in."
"This is the gentleman who lived in Nandi before you were born."
"This is the gentleman who knew Bwana Mayes."
"This is the gentleman known as Kipkororor."

When we arrived at the final chief, a young and extremely good-looking young man, Elijah to my horror said: "This is the gentleman who shot your grandfather."

This was greeted with much clapping. Not knowing what to say, I muttered, "I hope you will forgive an act of war," at which there was renewed applause.)

The laibon's death, as Meinertzhagen had foreseen, took the heart out of the Nandi; their resistance crumbled, and the campaign was brought to a successful end. Meinertzhagen was recommended for a Victoria Cross, but a sour note intruded into the chorus of praise.

I heard today for the first time that somebody is spreading rumours that the methods employed by me which culminated in the death of the Nandi Laibon were of a disgraceful nature. They say that I invited the Laibon to a friendly conference and shot him as he was shaking hands with me, and that afterwards I shot the Government interpreter to keep his mouth shut. Headquarters and my many friends naturally do not believe it. But among the heterogeneous crowd on the expedition there are many who are only too willing to listen to scandal when framed against the "brutal" soldiery. I have asked Headquarters to find out who originated these rumours and to give me an opportunity to challenge them. I suspect my old enemy Mayes,* who feels he has a good deal to get back on me. If the rumours persist I shall ask for a military court of enquiry to enable me to clear myself.

1.XII.1905. *Nandi Fort*
The court of enquiry which I had demanded took place today under the presidency of Col. Gorges. The opinion of the court is as follows and speaks for itself: "The court is of the opinion that the Laibon Koitelel was killed by a native officer of the 3rd King's African Rifles during a fight, which was the result of treacherous conduct on the Laibon's part, at a meeting which had previously been arranged between him and Capt. Meinertzhagen."

Kenya Diary 1902–1906 Richard Meinertzhagen.

> *Nevertheless the rumours persisted and two more courts of enquiry were held, both of which exonerated Meinertzhagen. This did not satisfy the Commissioner, Sir James Hayes-Sadler, who reported unfavourably to the Colonial Office. Meinertzhagen was informed that his action had "resulted in the reputation of the British Government for fair dealing and honesty being called in question, and the Colonial Office consider it undesirable that I should continue to serve in East Africa". So he left with an implied reprimand instead of a medal. There is little doubt that both he and the laibon intended to kill each other. Meinertzhagen succeeded. The exact circumstances surrounding the affair will never be known.*

The First World War

> *4 August 1914 found the East Africa Protectorate altogether unprepared for war, whereas the Germans in their neighbouring colony (now Tanzania) had anticipated the event. Lieut.-Col. Paul von Lettow-Vorbeck, an officer of outstanding ability, had recently arrived in Dar es Salaam to take command of the Schutztruppe, the colony's defence force.*

When war broke out the Germans possessed an overwhelming military superiority. They had probably at least 3,000 white men trained to arms, 8,000 high-class native troops, 70 machine-guns and 40 guns. Against these British East Africa could muster about 700 native troops (admittedly of the highest quality) and two machine-guns, one of which was out of action. We had perhaps available an equal force in Nyassaland.

*Walter Mayes was a political officer whom Meinertzhagen had accused of fraud and brutality. He was transferred and demoted, and became Meinertzhagen's implacable enemy.

There were an immeasurably greater number of potential native troops in German East Africa than in either Kenya, Uganda or Nyassaland, where indeed the vast bulk of the native population are of a peaceable, which is not to say of a cowardly, nature. A large army of first-rate fighting men could be raised and trained in what is now Tanganyika. Probably at one time Von Lettow, even with his limited resources, had 30,000 rifles in the field.

Kenya Chronicles Lord Cranworth.

On the outbreak of war British settlers of all ages and nationalities converged on Nairobi bringing their own weapons and mounts, from mules to polo-ponies. Spontaneously formed units called after their leaders – Cole's Scouts, Wessel's Scouts, Bowker's Horse – coalesced into the East African Mounted Rifles. Six companies of the 3rd King's African Rifles with 125 rifles each, summoned from places as distant as the Juba river, the Abyssinian frontier and Zanzibar, comprised the rest of the military establishment. Patrols sent out towards the German frontier bivouacked in the bush and sometimes found the local fauna more threatening than the Germans.

It was towards the end of the dry season, the grass where it was not burnt was yellow, and all but the permanent waters were dry, and on such waters the game was concentrating. Of course we heard lions every night, but this night at dinner they seemed especially numerous and to be gradually closing on our camp. As they approached the noise became most awe-inspiring and actually shook the glasses on the table. Denys Finch-Hatton insisted on taking me out and I insisted on taking a loaded rifle. He, of course, took nothing but a torch. Steadily the roars approached till they seemed all around us and I broke into a cold sweat. There came a minute's pause and then the awe-inspiring sound boomed off right against us and the hair rose on my head. Denys switched on his torch and focussed it full on a great tawny brute, certainly not ten yards away. "You can stay and be eaten if you like. I'm off to the mess," I said. Denys only laughed and came with me only with the utmost reluctance. Gradually the sounds receded. We reckoned that there were at least twenty separate animals roaring, and three walked through the small perimeter of the camp. We shot during these months about half a dozen lions and only such buck as were necessary for food. Our larder, however, was kept continuously supplied with birds, since quail, sand-grouse, guinea-fowl and francolin were innumerable.

Kenya Chronicles Lord Cranworth.

Defence of the Uganda Railway, which ran in places within fifty miles of the German border, was the first and overriding task of the Protectorate's tiny force. Von Lettow-Vorbeck outlined the German strategy.

The guiding principle of constantly operating against the Uganda Railway could, however, be resumed, as here it was in any case impossible to act with larger forces. For it was necessary to make marches of several days' duration through the great, waterless and thinly-populated desert, which provided little sustenance beyond occasional game. Not only food, but water had to be carried. This alone limited the size of the force to be employed. Such expeditions through districts providing neither water nor food require a degree of experience on the part of the troops which could not possibly exist at that stage of the war. A company even was too large a force to send across this desert, and if, after several days of marching, it really had reached some point on the railway, it would have had to come back again, because it could not be supplied. However, these conditions improved as the troops became better trained, and as our knowledge of the country, which was at first mainly *terra incognita*, increased.

So there was nothing for it but to seek to attain our object by means of small detachments, or patrols. To these patrols we afterwards attached the greatest importance. Starting from the Engare-Nairobi, small detachments of eight to ten men, Europeans and Askaris [African soldiers], rode round the rear of the enemy's camps, which had been pushed up as far as the Longido, and attacked their communications. They made use of telephones we had captured at Tanga, tapping in on the English telephone-lines; then they waited for large or small hostile detachments or columns of ox-wagons to pass. From their ambush they opened fire on the enemy at thirty yards' range, captured prisoners and booty, and then disappeared again in the boundless desert. Thus, at that time, we captured rifles, ammunition, and war material of all kinds. . . .

The patrols that went out from the Kilima Njaro in a more easterly direction were of a different character. They had to work on foot through the dense bush for days on end. The patrols sent out to destroy the railway were mostly weak: one or two Europeans, two to four Askari, and five to seven carriers. They had to worm their way through the enemy's pickets and were often betrayed by native scouts. In spite of this they mostly reached their objective and were sometimes away for more than a fortnight. For such a small party a bit of game or a small quantity of booty afforded a considerable reserve of rations. But the fatigue and thirst in the burning sun were so great that several men died of thirst, and even Europeans drank urine. It was a bad business when anyone fell ill or was wounded, with the best will in the world it was often impossible to bring him along. To carry a severely wounded man from the Uganda Railway right across the desert to the German camps, as was occasionally done, is a tremendous performance. Even the blacks understood that, and cases did occur in which a wounded Askari, well knowing that he was lost without hope, and a prey to the numerous lions, did not complain when he had to be left in the bush, but of his own accord gave his comrades his rifle and ammunition, so that they at least might be saved.

The working of these patrols became more and more perfect. Knowledge of the desert improved, and in addition to patrols for destruction and intelligence work, we developed a system of fighting patrols. The latter, consisting of twenty to thirty Askari, or even more, and sometimes equipped with one or two machine-guns, went out to look for the enemy and inflict losses upon him. In the thick bush the combatants came upon each other at such close quarters and so unexpectedly, that our Askari sometimes literally jumped over their prone adversaries and so got behind them again. The influence of these expeditions on the self-reliance and enterprise of both Europeans and natives was so great that it would be difficult to find a force imbued with a better spirit.

My Reminiscences of East Africa General von Lettow-Vorbeck.

The first serious engagement of the war took place at sea when, on 20 September 1914, the German cruiser Königsberg entered Zanzibar harbour, sank HMS Pegasus, which had put in for repairs, made off at speed, and disappeared into the delta of the Rufiji river.

The delta of the four-hundred-mile Rufiji river, German East Africa's mightiest waterway, encompasses an area roughly the size of metropolitan New York. Lying in the sodden embrace of mud and mangrove trees, it is a morass of serpentine creeks and brackish tidal channels, clogged with sandbars, writhing with crocodiles, snarling with mosquitoes, trembling with the crash of elephant herds in the matted rain forest around its banks. The delta does not welcome man; one almost expects to find rubbery prehistoric animals wallowing about in its miasma. It breathes isolation and spawns disease. Even a fugitive would hesitate before seeking asylum here.

But (Captain) Looff had not hesitated on the day he sank *Pegasus*. If he were to make desperately needed repairs on his ship – or at least try to make them – he must have temporary refuge from the Royal Navy. The Rufiji offered the nearest haven. And if its delta was a forbidding cesspool, so much the better: few if any other spots on the coast could have been more ideally suited as a hideout. The seaward side of the river mouth was guarded by a line of reefs and islands. The delta itself had six main arms to the ocean, at least four of which – the Kikunja, Simba Uranga, Suninga and Kiomboni channels – were not only navigable for a light cruiser of *Königsberg*'s relatively shallow draft but were also joined to each other by a network of narrow creeks. Several of these, barely navigable at high tide, would enable *Königsberg* to confound her pursuers by dodging about far inland, well beyond range of British guns. Further protection was offered by the tall and dense vegetation on the banks: with topmasts housed or camouflaged, *Königsberg* might well remain invisible for months.

Ships of the Royal Navy mounted guard at the entrance to the delta's main channels ready to pounce upon Königsberg when she emerged. She never did. Nor could British warships reach her up the shallow tidal fingers of the delta. Two monitors, small ships of very shallow draught designed to operate in coastal waters, were towed out from Britain. They crept up one of the delta's channels and opened fire on the heavily armed and camouflaged battleship concealed among the vegetation. Badly battered, the monitors retreated for repairs. Their second attempt succeeded.

Königsberg had now become a waterborne abbatoir. Her centre funnel missing, the cruiser was ablaze from stem to stern. All gun crews and ammunition parties in the forward part of the ship were dead. "Blood flowed all over the deck," wrote Lieutenant Wenig; "only shovelfuls of sand made it passable. . . . Corpses lay in heaps near the forecastle. Two torn-off heads rested side by side beneath a locker." On the unprotected bridge, officers had been begging Looff to take cover. He had refused. Even when a shell fragment punctured him for the second time and turned his naval whites scarlet with his own blood, he had insisted that his presence on the bridge would buck up the crew. A few minutes later, however, he was forced to step down: another explosion studded him with shrapnel in a dozen places, one splinter slicing his stomach wide open. First Officer Georg Koch immediately took command of the cruiser from its dying captain.

Even without guns to fire back, *Königsberg* stayed alive for a while under *Severn*'s merciless hammering. It no longer seemed to matter that the monitor had been deprived of its spotter: the gunners now had the range and an oily obelisk of smoke, nearly a mile high, clearly marked the cruiser's position. Between 1.00 and 2.30 that afternoon, *Severn*'s decks jumped continually to the recoil of forty-two more salvoes, the shells gradually crawling aft along *Königsberg*'s entire length. *Mersey* soon joined the bombardment with twenty-eight broadsides, and after 1.40, with the arrival of the relief spotter plane, hardly a salvo failed to bring the signal "H.T." – hit target.

At 2.20, just as *Severn*'s Fullerton decided that he had begun to waste shells, the spotter confirmed this was the message: "Target destroyed."

Looff had now resumed command of his floating heap of scrap metal. By rights he should have been dead, but the steel in his stomach had been stopped short of the abdominal wall by his heavy watch and a gold cigarette case. At 1.30, while bulkheads and deck plates screamed under the relentless blows of the falling six-inch shells, Looff – lying prone on a mattress which someone had brought to the bridge – gasped out four orders to First Officer Koch. They were swiftly obeyed. First, the breechblocks of all the guns were removed and thrown over the side, while a party felt its way below decks to flood the magazines. Then the wounded were placed aboard the ship's boats and rowed ashore, through continually exploding water, by the rest of the crew. Koch was the last man to leave the cruiser; Looff, too weak even to sit up, had been taken off with the other wounded. Koch joined him on the beach after carrying out the fourth order: to arm a torpedo and break *Königsberg*'s back.

At two o'clock, Looff watched the torpedo do its work: "A muffled noise, weaker than we expected, hardly noticeable in the thunder of the enemy shells. . . . With a short jerk, the ship turns slightly on its side, and sinks slowly to its upper deck in the mud-coloured water of the Rufiji. . . ."

That was as far down as she would ever go. Her battle flags still flew. At sunset, an officer went aboard and lowered them as a bugle sounded and the crew gave three cheers for the Emperor. Then the Imperial Eagle was carefully folded. Later, it would be presented to Looff.

Königsberg *had a sting in her tail.*

Divers recovered the breechblocks. Work parties removed the guns from their mountings and poled them on rafts to the shore. They were then lifted on to wagons and dragged through the bush, by four hundred sweating, chanting Africans, to Dar es Salaam. Here, the machinists at the naval shipyard and railway workshops improvised mobile gun carriages. It was not long before the German land forces boasted ten new field pieces – the heaviest artillery in East Africa. *Königsberg* might have been a gutted skeleton of buckled steel, but her guns had not been silenced.
The Battle for the Bundu Charles Miller.

These powerful long-range guns were to prove invaluable to von Lettow-Vorbeck in the long-drawn-out campaign to come.

Following the disastrous failure, in November 1914, of a large force sent from India to capture the German port of Tanga, 1915 was a year of stagnation while men and matériel *were assembled in the British Protectorate for the invasion of German East Africa. Both sides sent patrols over the border to gain intelligence and boost morale. Captain Richard Meinertzhagen, now serving with the Royal Fusiliers, took part in one of these.*

28.XII.1915. *Karungu, Victoria Nyanza*

On the 23rd I left Karungu with Drought and fifteen Intelligence scouts. We carried nothing except what we could take in our ruck-sacks and we each had 150 rounds of .303 ammunition. We crossed the border on the 25th and soon got news from natives of an enemy patrol at Kitambi Hill, so we continued our march and at 5 pm we located four tents, fires burning and by the mercy of God, no precautions, no sentries and men lounging about. We could count fourteen askaris. The country was good for stalking and we were well in position for a rush at dusk. In fact, the men having left their rifles in their tents and there being no sentry, we rushed them silently from not more than a few paces. We used bayonets only and I think we each got our man. Drought got three, a great effort. I rushed into the officer's tent where I found a stout German on a camp bed. On a table was a most excellent Xmas dinner. I covered him with my rifle and shouted to him to hold his hands up. He at once groped under his pillow and I had to shoot, killing him at once. My shot was the only one fired. We now found we had seven unwounded prisoners, two wounded and fifteen killed, a great haul. I at once tied up the prisoners whilst Drought did what he could for the wounded. We covered the dead with bushes and I placed sentries round the camp and sent out a patrol of three men. Drought said he was hungry, so was I, and why waste that good dinner? So we set to and had one of the best though most gruesome dinners I have ever had, including an excellent Xmas pudding. The fat German dead in bed did not disturb us in the least nor restrain our appetites, but looking back on it now I wonder we could manage it. After that excellent meal, I searched the German's kit. He was a reserve officer and apparently by name _____, a letter on his person being addressed to Graf_____. So I must have shot a Duke. The first Duke I have killed. His luncheon-basket was a most elaborate arrangement, with plated dishes and cutlery, all marked with a coronet. These Drought and I purloined, thinking it a pity to leave them to be looted. We cleared out after dark, but were unable to bury the bodies, having no tools with which to dig. With our prisoners we marched till midnight and then slept with sentries out and we were off again on the 26th and reached here without incident yesterday afternoon.

Army Diary 1899–1926 Richard Meinertzhagen.

With the arrival at Mombasa on 19 February 1916 of General Jan Smuts as Commander-in-Chief, the go-ahead was given for the long-awaited invasion of German East Africa. Reinforcements from India and South Africa had already arrived. A two-pronged advance was planned, one on each side of Mount Kilimanjaro, starting from Longido. Captain Angus Buchanan was with the 1st Division.

It was on a Sunday morning, the 5th of March, 1916, that the advance began. . . .

We were an infantry column, a column made up of variously dressed soldiers of different races, a column of various kind and equipment, eloquent of the brotherhood of colonies. We streamed out in column of route, after scouts had preceded us by half an hour or so. The 129th Baluchis, olive-hued Indian soldiers in turbans and loose-kneed trousers, were in advance; then their maxim battery of gunners and side-burdened, bridle-led mules. Then came the 29th Punjabis, another regiment of similar kind, followed closely by some battalions of South African artillery – a bold array of gun-carriages and ammunition wagons, each drawn by eight span of sturdy South-American-bred mules, and driven by reckless Cape boys mounted on the line of near mules. Then followed more infantry, the 25th Royal Fusiliers, of familiar face and colour, of our own kind, but soiled and sunburnt with long exposure; the 1st King's African Rifles, well-trained natives of stalwart appearance, khaki-clad as the rest, but with distinctive dark-blue puttees and light close-fitting headgear. And so on, and so on, down the line, except that one might mention the ammunition column in the rear, a long line of two-wheeled carts, drawn by two span of patient, slow-gaited oxen. In the rear, trailing far behind, came the miscellaneous transport – some motors, large four-wheeled mule-wagons, Scotch carts, and water carts, an assortment of varied, somewhat gipsy-like kind. The wagons, which were most in evidence, and which carry from three thousand to four thousand pounds, were drawn by ten span of mules, or by sixteen to twenty span of oxen, and all were ordered and driven by capable management of men from South Africa, who had long experience in trekking in their own country. In all it was probably a column of a fighting strength of from 4,000 to 5,000 men, with its necessary large following of accoutrements.

When the column reached far out into the grass-grown, sandy plain – for it was open highland here – one could look back, almost as far as the eye could distinguish, and see the course of the column, as the fine line of a sinuous thread drawn across the blank space of an incomplete map! To-day, the map was marked; to-morrow, the thin dust-line would be gone onward, and the desert veld would again lie reposed in vagueness.

Thus did we leave our harbour of safety to venture far into the enemy's country on "the long trek"; to travel amidst dust, and dryness, and heat, for many days.

Three Years of War in East Africa Angus Buchanan.

Riding through the featureless and fever-ridden bush of the Pangani valley Francis Brett Young, medical officer attached to the 2nd Rhodesia Regiment, came to an immense swamp.

When the sun began to beat through the moist air myriads of dragon-flies, which had laid all night with folded wings and slender bodies stretched along the reeds, launched themselves into the air with brittle wings aquiver. Never in my life had I seen so many, nor such a show of bright ephemeral beauty. They hung over our path more like aeroplanes in their hesitant flight than any hovering birds. Again I was riding the mule Simba, and as I rode I cut at one of them with my switch of hippo hide, cut at it and hit it. It lay broken in the path, and in a moment, as it seemed, the bright dyes faded. I was riding by myself, quite alone; and as I dismounted I felt sick with shame at this flicker of the smouldering *bête humaine*; and though I told myself that this creature was only one of so many that would flash in the sun and perish; that all life in these savage wildernesses laboured beneath cruelties perpetual and without number: of beasts that prey with tooth and claw, of tendrils that stifle, stealing the sap of life, or by minute insistence splitting the seasoned wood, I could not be reconciled to my own ruthless cruelty. For here, where all things were cruel, from the crocodiles of the Pangani to our own armed invasion, it should have been my privilege to love things for their beauty and rejoice in their joy of life, rather than become an accomplice in the universal ill. I cursed the instinct of the collector which, I suppose, far more than that of the hunter, was at the root of my crime; and from this I turned back to the educative natural history of my schooldays, in which it was thought instructive to steal a bright butterfly from the live air to a bottle of cyanide, and to press a fragrant orchid between drab sheets of blotting-paper. And I thought, perhaps, when this war is over, and half the world has been sated with cruelty, we may learn how sweet a thing is life, and how beautiful mercy.

Marching on Tanga Francis Brett Young.

The East African Mounted Rifles started its brief career with six squadrons plus a maxim gun and signallers. The regiment took part in several battles during Smuts' advance into German East Africa in 1916. Its Medical Officer reports an incident.

Our casualties in the EAMR included Trooper C. A. Sherwood killed, and Lance-Corporal L. H. le May, wounded and captured when the advance guard was surprised. Later in the action Lieut R. C. Hill, commanding our Maxim Gun Section, as he galloped his guns out of action, was shot through the foot during the last intensive burst of fire from the enemy. There are various ways in which one may report oneself as a casualty, but this officer's method was certainly peculiar. He was galloping at the time side by side with the Medical Officer and suddenly made the surprising remark: "Can I see you some time when you are not busy?" Since the Medical Officer was at the moment particularly busy in getting out of the way of a most unpleasant number of bullets, this apparently fatuous question caused a certain amount of irritation and profanity, until it was followed by the intimation: "I think I've been hit." Sure enough, subsequent examination that evening by the inadequate light of a surreptitiously struck match revealed a bullet hole drilled clean through the ankle joint.

The Story of the East African Mounted Rifles C. J. Wilson.

The EAMR, the settlers' regiment, never died but simply faded away. Transfers to the King's African Rifles, the East African Transport Corps, Intelligence and other units reduced it to a single squadron. By May 1917 it had dwindled to the commanding officer, Major Clifford Hill, sergeant W. E. Powys and trooper L. M. Joubert. They, too, were transferred and that was the end.

When the horses, mules and oxen on which the army's transport depended in the early days of the campaign had perished almost to the last animal from horse-sickness, trypanosomiasis and exhaustion, the human porter became, in Kipling's words, "the feet and hands of the army". By the end of the campaign nearly 180,000 carriers had been recruited, registered, paid, fed and deployed, and of these some 40,000 had died, mainly from dysentery, malaria, pneumonia, hookworm and sheer fatigue.

The plight of the porter, with his load of over fifty lbs, passes imagination. Cold, wet, hungry, sick with dysentery, pneumonia or both, their only food half-cooked porridge made of mealie-meal which was fermenting from being soaked, many staggered off the road to die in the reeking mud.

The Carrier Corps Geoffrey Hodges.

Never was road like that Handeni road. I remember it as one of the show roads of the colony: broad, hard, and clean. We found about two feet of dust on its surface. . . . dust that made of one colour all races of men, and gave us all one common cough "to the pits of all our stomachs" as Kipling has it. . . . And to the dust was added a stench that passes words: a stench now subtle and suggestive, now throttling and entirely disgusting; a stench that attracted one's gaze only that it might be repelled by visions of a sated jackal's half-eaten meal. For horses, oxen and mules have died by thousands. . . . Truly, war is hideous even at its base. . . .

Another glory of the road was its lack of water. I knew Zigualand from painful experience. . . . But on my arrival I was given an official list of wells and watering places (made during the rains) . . . twice did we resolve to halt where the army said good water was. . . . And twice did we repent ourselves of our trusting and confiding spirit. On the first occasion it was midday . . . and there was no water at all: only a vast camping place where water had once been. . . . The second day we had marched nearly fifteen miles and wanted food. The so-called well was . . . a museum of dead frogs. . . . It remained to do another six miles onward. And the man who has not had to do extra miles beyond his promised halting place, under tropical sun, has yet much to learn of what a broken spirit really means.

Bishop Frank Weston quoted in *The Carrier Corps* Geoffrey Hodges.

Von Lettow-Vorbeck's strategy was to avoid encirclement, fight rearguard actions and continually retreat, thus drawing his enemy farther and farther south and stretching to the limit and beyond the British lines of communication. By mid-1917 the cruelly depleted but constantly reinforced British army was approaching the border with Portuguese East Africa, over six hundred miles from Moshi as the crow flies. Here some of the bitterest fighting of the campaign took place.

12 August 1917

About 11 am, when drawing in to the hillcrest overlooking Narunyu, which is situated in a valley bottom, the first-second King's African Rifles, in the lead, encountered large forces of the enemy, and entered into action. On their establishing a firing line, the rear of the column was drawn in, and a perimeter was formed, for, in the thick bush we were then in, attack might threaten from any direction. This was a wonderfully wise and fortunate precaution, for no sooner were our lines on all sides established than the enemy opened a determined attack on our right flank; and, as the fight continued, fierce and sustained attacks developed later, even in our rear and on our left. In other words, the enemy were all around us and trying to break through our "square" in the bush. It was a day of tremendous battle. There were, within the circle, the first-second King's African Rifles, 25th Royal Fusiliers, and Stoke's Guns, and back to back they fought, without one minute's cease in the deafening fusillade, until long after dark. It was here that one saw, and realized, the full fighting courage to which well-trained African troops can rise. The first-second King's African Rifles was one of the original pre-war regular battalions, and magnificently they fought here; and we, who were an Imperial unit, felt that we could not have wished for a stouter, nor a more faithful, regiment to fight alongside of. About 8 pm the firing ceased and we had at last a breathing space and could hear each other speak in normal voice. But all was not yet over. At 9.30 pm an enemy whistle blew sharply – and instantaneously a great burst of enemy fire swept the square from the right flank, and from closer quarters than before. An enemy force had crept in in the darkness and silence, and tried to take us by surprise. But they reckoned wrongly, and in the end, after a fierce encounter, they were driven off and silenced: though movement and groans, from beyond our front, continued long into the night while the enemy collected their dead and wounded. . . .

At last our anxieties ceased. Weary, powder-blackened, mud-filthy, thirsty beyond the telling, the line slept fitfully through the remainder of the night. . . .

It was decided that we were to hold on here, and arrangements were made to bring water to camp, while bully and biscuit would be our ration – no tea, no cooked food, for no fire could be allowed on account of the smoke, which would have marked our position to enemy artillery. The enemy were shelling the square and shooting dangerously close, but were unable to locate us exactly, or tell where their shells were landing, in the dense bush. To-day all ranks were very exhausted after the past week of blanketless, half-sleepless nights and the extreme strain of yesterday.

For five days we lay in the confined square in our shallow trenches, drinking sparingly of foul water, and holding impatiently on, while smaller engagements went on with the enemy, who continued to invest our front closely and our right flank. Our porters had a bad time here. In time cooked food was sent up for them from the rear, but on the first two days it was common to see the poor creatures hungrily munching their uncooked ration of hard rice-grains. At the end of the five days, many of them were almost unable to walk, and could not be burdened with an ammunition load.

On 22 August our battalion received orders to withdraw under cover of night to the reserve column at the main camp back some miles on the trolley line and west of Tandamuti – a camp which was designated c23.

The withdrawal was quietly accomplished, and at 9.30 pm we camped at c23. And then we had, what in the past few days we had come to dream of – tea, tea, tea. Camp-fires were started everywhere, and we sat there and feasted our fill of tea that tasted threefold more fragrant and delicious than ever before, and on cooked food, warm and palatable, and long we sat into the hours when weary heads should have been asleep.

We remained at c23 until 4 September, and at intervals each day were shelled by the enemy's long-range guns, at aggravating intervals.

A large camp had sprung up at c23, and additional forces and additional stores were daily arriving. But we were in terribly unhealthy country; the air was close and oppressive, and the sun merciless; and men went about their duties with listless bearing. The hospitals were full of sick, and troops and porters were being evacuated in hundreds every few days. The native African was suffering as much as if not more than the European. The 25th suffered no less than other units, and our forces were sadly growing smaller and smaller.

On 4 September the battalion left C23 and advanced to the centre and left camps before Narunyu, to occupy the front line there; relieving the 8th South African Infantry, who were tottering with sickness and unfit for further service in active fields.

Here utter physical exhaustion, and fever, which had gripped me for some time, began slowly to master endurance.

On 9 September I had not strength to walk, and later in the morning I was taken to hospital. I was beaten, hopelessly overcome, though no man likes to give in.

The war was over for Captain Buchanan, MC, and was soon to be so for his famous regiment, the Legion of Frontiersmen, the 25th Royal Fusiliers.

In the final action which my unit undertook – the only one after my departure – the remnants of the band, steel-true men who had come through everything till then were pitted against overwhelming odds when covering a retirement, and fought till they were cut to pieces. It was a tragic ending.

Three Years of War in East Africa Angus Buchanan.

The 25th Royal Fusiliers was the regiment which the famous hunter, Frederick Selous, had joined at the age of over sixty. He was killed in action during the campaign.

Von Lettow-Vorbeck's army survived on self-sufficiency.

More dangerous than the enemy seemed to me the material position of our men. The cargo of wheat from the relief ship was coming to an end, and I thought it questionable whether bread could be baked from Mtama [sorghum] flour alone, without the addition of wheat flour. At that time I still regarded bread as an indispensable necessity for the nourishment of Europeans, and therefore I made experiments personally in baking bread without wheat flour. Unfortunately the results were unsatisfactory. Afterwards, under the stress of necessity, we all produced excellent bread without wheat. The methods differed widely. Later we made bread not only with mtama, but also with muhogo, sweet potatoes, maize, in short, with nearly every kind of meal, and with mixtures of all sorts of combinations, and later still improved the quality by the addition of boiled rice.

The necessary kit also required attention. A shortage of boots was in sight. My experiments showed me that a European can go barefoot where there are tolerable paths, but never through the bush. Sandals, which anyone can make, given an odd bit of leather, proved helpful, but did not take the place of boots. To be ready for any emergency, I had some lessons in boot-making, and succeeded, with supervision, in producing an object that at a push could be taken for a left boot, though it was intended to be a right. It is very convenient for a European who knows the simplest rudiments of this craft to be able to kill an antelope and make a boot, or at any rate repair one, from his skin a few days later, without the help of any of the tools of civilization. A nail must serve as an awl, a tent-pole as a last, and the thread he can cut from the tough leather of a small antelope. As a matter of fact, however, we were never driven to these extremities, as we were always able to obtain the necessary kit and equipment from captured stores, and many captured saddles were cut up to make soles and heels for boots.

Every European was becoming more and more like a South African "Trekker" and was his own workman. Naturally, not always in person, but within the small independent household, consisting of his black cook and his black servant, which followed him about. Many had even provided themselves with a few hens which they took about with them, and the noise of these betrayed the position of German camps even as far as the native settlements. An order issued in one force that the crowing of cocks before 9 am was forbidden brought no relief.

The important question of salt was very simply solved by the troops at Kilwa, by the evaporation of sea-water. In order to secure the supply, which was beginning to run short, against the loss of the coast, salt-yielding plants were collected and the salt obtained from their ashes by lixiviation. We got this idea from the natives of the district, who supplied themselves with salt in this way. The salt thus obtained was not bad, but was never required to any extent, as we were always able to meet our requirements from the captured stores. The large numbers of elephants in this district furnished us with fat; sugar was replaced by the excellent wild honey which was found in large quantities. The troops had made an important step forward as regards supplies of grain. They found out how to ripen it artificially, and in this way provided against want.

After retreating across the Portuguese border, von Lettow-Vorbeck captured a sufficient quantity of arms, ammunition and medicines to stave off surrender. For almost a year he led his troops, with a rabble of camp followers, through bush, swamp and mountain until, some 1,500 miles later, on 12 November 1918, he was 150 miles into the British Protectorate of Northern Rhodesia (Zambia). A motor-cyclist brought him the unsuspected news that on 11 November Germany had surrendered. On 25 November, at Abercorn, the remnants of his army surrendered to a battalion of the King's African Rifles. His force numbered 155 officers, 1,156 African askaris and a cavalcade of porters, women and children, some of the latter having been born on the march. The officers were permitted to retain their arms. In Dar es Salaam the general was all but fêted; a house and car were put at his disposal and that of his senior officers, and their movements were unrestricted until they boarded a ship to take them home.

In cold truth our small band, which at the most comprised some 300 Europeans and about 11,000 Askari, had occupied a very superior enemy force for the whole war. According to what English officers told me, 137 generals had been in the field, and in all about 300,000 men had been employed against us. The enemy's losses in dead would not be put too high at 60,000, for an English press notice stated that about 20,000 Europeans and Indians alone had died or been killed, and to that must be added the large number of black soldiers who fell. The enemy had left 140,000 horses and mules behind in the battle area. Yet in spite of the enormously superior numbers at the disposal of the enemy, our small force, the rifle strength of which was only about 1,400 at the time of the armistice, had remained in the field always ready for action and possessed of the highest determination.

I believe it was the transparency of our aims, the love of our Fatherland, the strong sense of duty and the spirit of self-sacrifice which animated each of our few Europeans and communicated themselves, consciously or unconsciously, to our brave black soldiers, that gave our operations that impetus which they possessed to the end. In addition there was a soldierly pride, a feeling of firm mutual co-operation and a spirit of enterprise without which military success is impossible in the long run.

My Reminiscences of East Africa General von Lettow-Vorbeck.

The Second World War

When Mussolini declared war on the Allies on 10 June 1940, his Abyssinian armies numbered about 300,000 well equipped men with powerful artillery and air support. Facing them in Kenya were six battalions of the King's African Rifles and one mounted Indian battery, numbering approximately 7,000 men. The Italians made the opening move by capturing the outposts of Moyale and El Wak, but in December 1940 the British launched their offensive with a lightning and successful raid on El Wak. Reinforcements came from South Africa, the Rhodesias, Nigeria and the Gold Coast (Ghana), including units of the South African Air Force which patrolled the parched and barren Italian Somaliland/Kenya border. An aircraft was obliged to make a forced landing.

Fortunately it was a full moon and we walked all that night through the eerie and silent bush, making westward with the aid of the plane's compass, carrying as much kit as we could; a Very pistol in case we needed to signal, and the rear machine gun, which we had removed from the aircraft. We had two drums of ammunition and we were prepared to argue with any enemy troops or wandering banda [bandits] who came along.

By nine o'clock the next morning the sun was blazing. The altitude was only about 400 feet above sea level and the sun struck back with terrible effect from the limitless sand and sparse thorn bush. Walking was impossible except at the price of rapid exhaustion. We had seen nobody during the night and in the morning the land seemed empty of life. But it was enemy territory and we carefully avoided game and camel tracks. All that day we rested in the bush and set out again at night.

On the second day our water supply ran out in the afternoon. The two-gallon tin had been damaged in the crash and was leaking. Again we travelled by night, moving with increasing difficulty, and on the third day, unable to find water, we rested and plodded on again. Four days after the crash we came upon a dried up water hole, a mere pool of mud, baked nearly hard. Rigging up a Heath Robinson contraption made chiefly from film spools, we contrived a long pipe and managed to distil some water. It worked very well and the water, caught in shaving tins, was a precious thing.

That night it was very difficult. Parts of the bush were fairly open and we could march with some ease, but sometimes it was so thick that we had to force our way through. Wild life was stirring in the undergrowth and among the thorn trees. Once we found ourselves within 200 yards of a lion's kill and frequently we came upon elephant tracks. In the darkness these tracks were a trap for tired men when a bad stumble might cause a broken leg. Fortunately we all knew something about bushcraft and hunting. In South Africa in the shooting season we knew the Low Veld and were not afraid of it. The same afternoon we had come across quite a good water hole not very far from the mud pool. We renewed our supplies, filled water bottles and even tried to carry water in a kit bag. After that we devoured our emergency rations and felt better. Since leaving the machine we had not eaten a bite of food. Our little store had been resolutely husbanded against the time when we must eat. Having no water we did not wish to eat, and thirst and starvation had made us all very weak. . . .

The long halts during the day were beginning to tell. All we could do in the terrible heat was to lie absolutely still in such shade as we could find. We were in a constant condition of profuse perspiration and any water we drank evaporated through our bodies before it could give us any benefit. All the next day, nearly a week since we began our trek, we went without water. One of us, who had had an operation only a few months previously, was in a serious condition. We had no food and even if we had, our mouths were so swollen with thirst that we could not have eaten it. The machine gun and ammunition had been discarded in the bush because we could not carry them any longer. Both were useless to us and the added weight was telling on us. We kept the Very pistol and the magazine of photographs we had taken on the flight. The compass, too, we retained, but days before in desperation we had drained off the alcohol in it to wet our lips.

At eleven o'clock on the morning of the seventh day we found another water hole. We had abandoned caution and were following a camel track in the hope that it would lead to water. Our lips were burst and bleeding, our tongues swollen and we knew we could not survive unless we found water soon. The moon did not rise that night until about eleven o'clock, and the bush was very thick with thorn trees that tore at our clothes and bodies. We could not travel for more than twenty minutes without rest. Our feet were badly blistered and our progress was slow and painful. That morning we heard British aircraft on frontier patrol.

At this water hole we had to take a decision. I was still feeling fairly fit but my companions were in a state of exhaustion, so I decided to carry on to the border and try to get help. It was arranged that, whatever happened, the other two would stay by the water hole for three days and try to recuperate their strength, though all they had to recover with was water. In that scorched, forsaken bit of Africa there was not even a berry they could eat. It was agreed that, if they had sufficiently recovered at the end of three days, they were to set out again due west. If they did not, they had to remain at the water hole until such time as help was sent out, or . . .

I struck the frontier in the forenoon about a day and a half later. I judged I was only a few miles south of a British post. So I struck north along the well-defined track that marks the border. While resting I was overtaken by two Somalis, who had seen my tracks some hours before, and had trailed me. They were friendly and helpful, though neither I nor they understood the other, and they took me to their village a few miles on the Kenya side of the frontier. The Somalis apparently knew me to be a British soldier. That village felt like an oasis. The Somalis gave me plenty of goat's milk, which revived me completely. They were intelligent and knowledgeable about place names, and I soon gathered that the post for which I was seeking lay to the south, and that I had, in fact, been walking away from it. Finally I persuaded three of them to escort me. More refreshing goat's milk was drunk with appropriate Somali ceremony and, in that strange place and strange company, I lay down in a hut and rested, while the kindly Somali passed round a bowl of milk mixed with fat from which each of them, including their unheralded guest, drank in turn. It was a strange experience. And after it was over I thought I had better leave some mementos of my visit – odds and ends from my shaving kit, bits of soap, a comb, a mirror. The Somalis were greatly intrigued. Then they washed my hands and feet, which were raw and blistered and swollen.

Then we set off walking again, four of us this time, heading south. We walked all through the night and in the morning two of the Somalis volunteered to go ahead with a note asking for help. The third Somali stayed behind. I could scarcely walk, and on this the eleventh day, progress was even slower than before, but I knew now that help would come.

The officer, in the last stages of thirst and exhaustion, fell asleep under a small tree, and woke to find that his Somali companion had disappeared. Thinking himself deserted, he staggered on until he could go no farther.

I collapsed under a tree near the road and there I was found about midday by the Somali whom I thought had deserted me. But, in fact, the Somali had walked nearly twenty-five miles to find water and the same distance back again. He had walked steadily for twenty-four hours, day and night, fifty miles to rescue the white man he had befriended in his village. Goat's milk had also been brought, and with that I revived again and we set out for the Somali village twenty-five miles away where the Somali, by gestures, conveyed the welcome news that there was water and plenty of food. It was a painful journey, but with the help of the Somali I made it that night. My socks had long ago given out and I had wrapped my feet in cotton wool to ease the pain. Once there I was among friends. There, too, I found the other Somalis, who had set out with us. They had searched for miles for a KAR post and failed to find it. They gave me a hut to sleep in and fed me royally on milk and boiled goat's flesh.

The next day a British aircraft flew over the village, but they failed to recognize me among the tribesmen. So I decided to continue my journey, mindful of my two companions left behind by the water hole in enemy territory. After a night's rest the last stage began. The village headman set me on a camel, and with a small party we started along the road which led to an important frontier post. Ali Mohamed, the friend in need, who had walked fifty miles to find water to save my life, made his salaams and went back to his own village. And so it was that, late in the afternoon of the thirteenth day, an aircraft found us on the road, recognized the man who had been given up as dead, and dropped a message of good cheer. That night a lorry arrived and a few hours later I was shaking hands with a Kenya District Commissioner. At once a reconnaissance party was sent out back to the water hole, and a day later the two men were rescued in the last stages of exhaustion.

Nobody can realize what thirst is like unless one has experienced it. I shall always remember those foul vultures. They came from nowhere, circled overhead and then sat on the trees under which we were lying. We tried to ignore them. But they just sat silent and still.

Abyssinian Patchwork Kenneth Gandar Dower.

> Somali – Somali – we're here for your sake
> But what the hell difference does the NDF* make?
>   Mussolini can have it with a great rousing cheer –
> Moyale, Mandera, El Wak and Wajir.
>
>   They say that the Itis are ready for war –
> They want Abyssinia – but God knows what for.
>   But if they want somewhere, why not NDF?
> They can have every acre – it's OK by me.

Song written by three British officers of the KAR stationed at Wajir 1935–36.

By August 1940 the Italians had invaded and occupied British Somaliland. The overall British commander, General Wavell, planned a three-pronged invasion of Abyssinia (Ethiopia): from the east through British Somaliland which had first to be retaken; from the south from Kenya; and from the north

*Northern Frontier District.

through the Sudan. An East African, a South African and a Nigerian brigade advanced at whirlwind speed into British Somaliland and in February 1941 captured the capital, Kismayu, without a fight. They continued into Italian Somaliland and occupied the capital, Mogadishu. The pace quickened as they sped inland through mountainous country towards the Abyssinian capital, Addis Ababa. With the 22nd East African Brigade, commanded by Brigadier Fowkes, was Captain W. E. Crosskill, who describes the end of what has been said to be the fastest pursuit in military history.

Brigadier Fowkes had always said that he would reach Addis Ababa first with the 22nd Brigade. He was then well to the fore, leading the field and determined to win the race by hook or by crook. Some of the stories told of the measures he took to ensure this may be apocryphal but those who knew him will be certain that there was some substance in them. One thing I do know; his Brigade transport and his alone had sufficient petrol to get there. Whilst in the Mogadishu area he had told his transport officer, Budge Gethin, to acquire, "liberate" or seize enough of the petrol abandoned by the Italians to take his Brigade Group a thousand miles. That efficient officer went into the petrol-running business enthusiastically and, during the "rest" period at Merca, had dumped hundreds of drums at various hideouts along the Strada Imperiale.

All went well and according to plan. He was first over the Awash River and well placed with only one hundred and forty miles to go. But at this point the Divisional Commander intervened. He had orders from Force Headquarters that the South Africans should have the honour of being first into the capital, so he sent a personal signal to our Brigadier saying "Halt and allow 1 SA Bde to pass through" – or words to that effect. Undaunted the Brigadier dealt swiftly with this. Following the Nelson tradition he turned a blind eye and replied that the signal had been mutilated in transmission and was not understood. All his vehicles had plenty of petrol so on they sped.

He had already envisaged the possibility of the General then sending another message to him by despatch rider so, in order to avoid any such catastrophe, he had instructed his rear party not to allow anyone to pass up the column – in, of course, the interests of security. But, as he bowled along, his blue pennant flying in the breeze and Addis Ababa almost in sight, the Divisional Commander played a trump card – he sent a plane to stop him. The pilot spotted the column without difficulty and then, flying so low that the drivers instinctively ducked their heads, dropped his message bag with ribbons fluttering almost on to the bonnet of the Brigadier's car. This was *force majeure* with a vengeance and he halted – ten miles from the capital.

In the event the honours were divided fairly. General Wetherall was accompanied by Brigadier Fowkes, Brigadier Pienaar of the 1st South African Brigade and Brigadier Smallwood of the Nigerian Brigade when they went to the Duke of Aosta's residence for the signing of the armistice.

The Two Thousand Mile War W. E. Crosskill.

On 6 April 1941 Addis Ababa capitulated, forty days after the start of the advance from Kismayu. A war correspondent, George Kinnear of the East African Standard, *reported on the entry of the British troops.*

On we trundled through the tall blue gum trees, which we were soon to grow to hate, through the endless suburbs, which always seemed about to emerge into the central plazas of a magnificent city, and never did, through the jumbled confusion of the slums of two civilizations that had been piled on top of each other and interspersed with an occasional magnificent building, well-designed, well-finished, and then dumped down illogically in the middle of a mess. The saluting got more and more terrific – British salutes from Fascist soldiers, Fascist salutes from the Abyssinian civilians – everyone was most punctilious according to his lights, except me, that is, I couldn't salute or I would have fallen off.

And so at last we came to the Duke of Aosta's palace. This was a heavy, but rather imposing, building, with plenty of pillars and steps. To one side of the steps was drawn up a Fascist guard of honour, and between the pillars, swathed in green and gold, a collection of somewhat tubby-looking Fascist dignitaries stood, determined, if not to die for their regime, at least to see that it collapsed with pomp and circumstance. . . .

Suddenly, from beyond the palace gates, came a most impressive roar of engines. This din marked the arrival of the British, but it was actually created by a troop of Italian police on motor bicycles, who were heading our procession. They were wearing crash helmets and suits of shiny black, and as they swept up the drive they really made a most alarming spectacle. The British, however, did not seem to be co-operating with any real sympathy for these theatricals. The cars contained only one or two leading officers and their staffs. There were no troops whatever, and the only display of force that I can recall was one apologetic-looking armoured car which crept away as soon as it could and hid itself under the shade of a stupendous tree that stood beside the palace, as though it were most embarrassed at having to be there at all. This car was decorated with a little Union Jack, made by Katharine Biggs, the daughter of Mr Walter Harragin, Kenya's Attorney-General.

The proceedings were short and sharp and lamentably business-like. There were no flowery speeches. General Wetherall got out of his car, met General Mambrini, was saluted by the Italian guard of honour, and dived straight into the palace to get on with the signing.

The Italian flag had been hauled down as soon as the British arrived, well before anyone was ready for it, and General Wetherall had it reflown in order that it could be given full military honours. Once this had been done, down it came again and up went the Union Jack, to be saluted in return by the Fascist guard. That was the end of one of the most business-like ceremonies I have ever seen. As I walked out of the palace gardens to take my first proper look at this strange new city, which now was ours, I found my mind running over the details of the morning. Surely, I kept on thinking, no people in the world could have surrendered their capital so friendly as had the Italians; surely no people in the world could have occupied a conquered city, the goal of their ambitions, so altogether unostentatiously as had the British.

Despite the fall of the capital, Italian resistance continued in the towering mountains and savage bush. At the battle of Colito in May 1941 Sergeant Nigel Leakey of the Kenya Regiment stalked a tank.

The first thing I remember was Leakey shouting to his men, "Come on! I can hear some lorries trying to get away. Let's stop them". He was just going forward with three or four men. I thought they sounded most unlike lorries – more like tractors, and I said, "Hell, look out! I think it's a tank".

Just about that time we heard several start up. They were in front of us in the thick bush. Then the noise stopped and for a bit we couldn't hear a thing. And Leakey was just going forward in front of my men when we heard a noise behind us.

This time it was obviously a tank, and we could hear the noise coming nearer to us. Suddenly we saw it, about fifty yards away from us, not going very fast – keeping to the thick bush. Eventually it stopped behind the bush and Leakey did a sort of stalk, as if he were stalking a buck or something, only it was a pretty quick one. He did a certain amount of crawling, but most of the time he was doubling from one bush to another. And then he got to the bush behind which the tank was hiding. He crawled right through the middle of the bush, up underneath the tank, and then leaped on to the front of it. I can remember seeing, as he leaped up, the chap pulled down the vizor in front.

The tank went mad. It came out into the open, then on to the road, and went off like blazes, firing all that it had got. It had a cannon and two machine-guns on it, with an all-round traverse in the turret. Leakey was straddling the machine-gun, one leg on either side, and there he was, quite happy on top of the tank, struggling with the lid of the turret.

After the tank had gone, I suppose, a hundred yards, I saw the lid of the turret come up. I then saw Leakey poke his revolver inside and fire four or five shots rapid. The tank immediately stopped. Then Leakey jumped off and opened the side door of the tank, and pulled out two dead bodies. One was the colonel commanding this lot of tanks. Inside the driver's seat was a miserable specimen, who hadn't been shot, so Leakey jumped in beside him, poked a revolver in his face, and made him drive the tank on to the side of the road. He then hauled the driver out, put an askari to guard him, and then he said, "By God, we'll get the others – with this tank we've got 'em absolutely cold. We'll get the cannon to work".

And he struggled with the cannon for, I should think, three or four minutes, but couldn't find out how to get it to work. It was no good asking the driver. He was so frightened that he was hardly a human being.

So Leakey said, "Oh well, I'll get 'em on foot", and off he went with two askaris. I never saw him again.

Although I have had no opportunity to contact the eye-witnesses, there is a second half to this story. Sergeant Leakey was as good as his word; he set out to catch the remaining Italian tanks, and these were last seen in full retreat, with Leakey climbing on to the back of one of them. Sergeant Leakey never returned and his body was never found, but the enemy tanks took no further part in the battle of Colito.

Sergeant Nigel Leakey was awarded a posthumous Victoria Cross.

While Leakey charged Italian tanks, Italian tanks charged a captain in the KAR at the battle of Bubissa. His company ran into a concealed tank position and had to scatter into the bush.

The company just disappeared like that. I started running off at my best speed, which is 3 mph in thick mud. I was about 175 yards in front of the tank, which was coming after me with its pom-poms going past me like "phut". As I ran, I found Lance-Corporal Caprono, crouching down in a furrow where the ravine ran – he was crawling with his legs smashed, so I stopped beside him (purely because I was out of breath – no courtesy about it) and he said, "Don't leave me, bwana". I said, "All right, I'll wait for you down in those huts".

The tanks were coming in line ahead. They couldn't go much faster than I could at first, but then we reached a downhill bit and they started to gain. Suddenly, to my delight, I saw David still firing his mortar. I said, "For Christ's sake pack up that thing", and he bumped off with the bipod. David was there with two askaris – both of whom got the MM – firing their guns to the last. I managed to pass David, because he was weighted down with the bipod. The tanks were about eighty yards behind us. There were three native huts. I nipped round the right and went to the left one. I tried to get inside, and at that moment I heard the tank coming so I flung myself into a thorn bush and pretended to be dead – pretty good imitation it was too.

Luckily my hat fell over my face and they couldn't see if I was white or black because I was so covered with mud.

The tank passed about five yards off – from here to the door. I thought there was a rear gunner and I expected a bullet at any moment, or the tank to swing into me. I was just going to move when another blighter came. Then I saw a door and I took a header through it and I thought I'd dash about in and out of the huts.

I then saw David and was delighted when I had another human being somewhere near me. He came crawling in – he had been lying on his face shamming dead and they had each had a shot at him as they passed.

After a few seconds – it seemed ages – poor old Caprono came crawling in and another fellow who was coughing blood and had been hit just above the heart. We did what we could for him – though I thought it was far better to put a pistol to his head. He was trying to give some message to his toto. David gave him his water bottle.

By this time the tanks had spread out a bit and our own guns were registering on the huts we were in. One shell hit within nine yards. David was lying on the ground in sheep dung.

We discussed what we should do – stay till dark or beat it? You see we were only 400 yards from the Italian main positions. We decided to clear out, if we could, as we had a wounded fellow with us. We asked him if he could crawl with us – and he was jolly good about it. He said, "Yes, I will".

So off we slipped. We crawled for about a mile and a quarter, and David kept plaintively complaining that my bottom was sticking up in the air and kept on showing above the young maize. David couldn't help laughing. He said I was purple in the face and covered in mud with a great bottom sticking up.

There were machine-guns going off all the time.

The tanks were still scouting for people, but luckily Caprono put up a marvellous show. We decided to carry him after a mile and a quarter, and he kept on saying, "I can see you are getting tired, bwana, and it's getting open country. Put me down and I'll crawl the next 200 yards. You go to the next tuft". So we'd go there and wait for him and hide. We did that at odd times, but we carried him for three miles. Just as we were about done, I stopped three Abyssinians with spears, who seemed fairly friendly. I took their spears and made them carry Caprono.

We got back to the post at last – the big tree – I have never been so delighted to see the Intelligence Officer and some askaris.

We hid Caprono at the bole of the tree and made him a stretcher out of twigs and branches. We kept on having to stop, when we heard the tanks moving.

Then we carried him about another two miles, but we had more people to do it now. The shock had set in by now. Old Caprono was shivering and saying "Mazuri tu" [I'm all right]. We gave him a coat and a cigarette, and told someone to fetch a lorry. I remember there was a calf. The calf came trotting behind us and we stuck him in the back of the lorry.

We got back, and I was never so glad to get back. We took Caprono to the Doctor. We went off for a cup of tea and a bath. Then we came back to see how he was getting on. And it was the sweetest thing I have ever seen. He solemnly produced a five bob note and apologized very profusely and said, "There you are, bwana, it's all I have got. Will you accept it as it's all I've got? I have always said that bwanas would never leave us behind on the battlefield, but now I know". He said, "Whereabouts is your shamba?" I said, "Well it's in England". He said, "Oh well, you must come and visit me at mine".

Abyssinian Patchwork Kenneth Gandar Dower.

The Italian supremo, the Duke of Aosta, was still entrenched in the mountain stronghold of Amba Alagi. In May 1941 a mixed force commanded by General Mayne, whose lines of communication stretched 500 miles to the Sudan and

700 miles to Kenya, had the task of storming this apparently impregnable fortress. By dint of sustained bombardment and scaling cliffs by men hauled up by ropes, they succeeded. On 16 May 1941 the Duke indicated that he wished to discuss terms of surrender.

So, after total capitulation and the evacuation of the fort was demanded and agreed, the garrison was granted the honours of war. Some five thousand Italians, with their arms, filed out past a Guard of Honour while the pipes played "The Flowers of the Forest". The Duke came out last and was given a Royal Salute. He then thanked the South Africans for bringing his forty-four uniform trunks from Dessie and was driven off to meet General Platt. It was all over.

The Two Thousand Mile War W. E. Crosskill.

Not quite. There remained the fortress of Gondar in the north, which was stormed and taken by a mixed force of British troops and Abyssinian patriots on 27 November 1941, in the last battle of the campaign. Their victory accomplished, the East and West African troops were re-grouped and transported to South-East Asia, where they fought in the jungles of Burma against the Japanese. With them was a Maasai askari.

The last time I had spoken to a Masai was on a high ridge in Burma which stank of high explosive. The Masai was an NCO, lying on a bloody stretcher with several holes punched through his body by a Japanese machine gunner, dead now over his Nambu machine-gun, while not far off were a couple more Japanese slain by this Masai, one of them an officer whose long Samurai sword was now clutched in the Masai's hand.

The Japanese officer had come for him in the hand to hand fighting, swinging his sword, and the Masai – they love to fight even as much as the Japanese do – killed him and, taking his sword, went in and fought with it until he was shot down. The Brigadier, knowing how generous the Masai could be, had written a little note and attached it to the wound tag round the Masai's neck. "Please do not take this sword from this soldier. He is a Masai". The Masai reached East Africa with his sword, and he has it now where he lives, far down in Masai-land.

Warriors and Strangers Gerald Hanley.

One of the war's strangest episodes was the escape from their camp at Nanyuki of three Italian prisoners of war, with the unlikely intention of climbing to the summit of Mount Kenya. One of them describes a highlight of their brief taste of freedom.

At a place where the sun was shining on a smooth rock near the water we stopped for a short lunch of biscuit and toffee, spreading out our soaked boots and socks beside us to dry in the meantime. It had already become our habit to keep watch in every direction, so I sat one side of the narrow stream near our drying footwear and my companions on the far side, some six or seven yards from me.

I was just dipping a piece of dry biscuit into the river to allow it to swell and give me a real mouthful when the bamboo-thicket, some thirty yards behind my companions, parted.

Walking in our direction towards the stream was a wonderful, solitary bull-elephant.

I say "wonderful" on purpose because my first impression was not of fear, either for my friends or for myself, but one of genuine, deep admiration. No other creature, I thought, could represent in such a perfect way the strength, the dignity, the gravity and majesty of creation.

At last I roused myself and shouted to my companions: "Look!"

They turned their heads towards the huge brute and leapt to their feet. Never in my life shall I forget the spectacle of my two bare-footed friends gazing amazed at the amazed-looking elephant, scarcely twenty yards from them.

He was the first to take the initiative.

Renouncing his drink when only a few yards from the water he stopped and gave each one of us a short, almost contemptuous glance from his little vivacious eyes. Then he lifted his trunk almost vertically, together with his age-worn reddish-brown tusks, and dropped it gently and slowly in a disdainful half-circle. Immediately after that he wheeled in a right-about-turn, surprisingly swift for such a huge body, and, nonchalantly waggling his ridiculous-looking short tail and flapping his umbrella-like ears, ascended the path by which he had approached. A moment later his black shining back, surrounded by a halo of midges, was hidden by the leaves which bowed to his passage and then closed fan-like as though to mark the end of the show.

For a long time we stood where we were, gazing spellbound at the closed curtain as if blinded by an unnatural vision.

Had we not met at close quarters the king of the forests of Mount Kenya?

"Was he not worth the twenty-eight days' cells?"

"He was worth everything, all our past and future toils".

No Picnic on Mount Kenya Felice Benuzzi.

The three prisoners of war failed to scale the highest peak of Bation, but planted their homemade Italian flag on the summit of Lenana. Within three weeks they reported back to the astonished Camp Commandant, who reduced the statutory twenty-eight days in cells to seven quite convivial ones.

Michael Blundell who, in his subsequent career as a politician, was to support the transfer of power from white to black Kenyans, assesses the effects of their wartime experiences on the askaris who returned.

During the war, and especially after we had gone over to South-East Asia and seen an immense concourse of troops from other countries, the askaris became increasingly conscious of any differences in treatment between themselves and the troops of other countries. They asked why only Europeans were officers in the East African Army and why the food scales were different as between white and black soldiers. They learnt that courage, fear, hunger and physical exhaustion were common to men of all races. I noticed afterwards in my political life that there was a marked difference in outlook between many of the European electorate who had served with the African in the field and those who had not been so privileged. To the former the barrier of race was much less formidable and the eventual right of the African to achieve man's estate in his own country much more acceptable.

The first real seeds of African nationalism were sown in the later years of the war, when the African thus began to question the traditional differences between himself and the white man. As I have written, he suddenly wished to be accepted as a man amongst the other races of the world. He was no longer in contact with a few white men, often specially selected for or drawn to Africa, but came in contact with them in the mass. He formed his own opinions and came to the conclusion that they were much the same as his fellow tribesmen, with the same physical fears and courage, the same vices, and possibly the same virtues.

So Rough a Wind Michael Blundell.

Mau Mau

An underground movement aimed at the recovery of land they deemed rightly to be theirs, and at the expulsion of the Europeans, had for some time been spreading among the Kikuyu, both within their reserve (tribal territory), and among Kikuyu living as "squatters" on European farms. In August 1950 this movement, or society, was banned, but it continued to spread and on 20 October 1952 a State of Emergency was declared. At the core of the movement lay a series of oaths that every member had to take. Karari Njama, a Kikuyu schoolmaster, gives an account of his initiation.

After Sunday service I met Mr Samuel Ndiritu Njagi, a clerk in the Ministry of Works, a true friend and a schoolmate at Kagumo who had recently married my relative. He kindly invited me to his home. When we arrived, I learnt that he had brewed beer in his mother's hut. We spent the whole of the afternoon drinking and talking on one's job and the country's politics. A few persons came and shared the drink with us. In the evening we left toward home. On the way, Ndiritu told me that he had been invited to a feast by my neighbour, Charles Ngatia Gathitu, a pitsawyer and licence holder on timber trades, situated about 400 yards east of my home. We passed many people on the way and arrived at the house at twilight. There were some people standing outside, including Charles, the owner of the feast. He led us into one of his big huts. Inside, were many people sitting and a hurricane lamp was burning. We were told to wait there while some preparations went on in the other hut. Groups of men and women continued to come until there was very little room for anyone to sit. A few persons would be called by names and moved in the next hut. When I was called to go to the next hut, I was very pleased, but arriving outside in a clear moonshine, I could see hundreds of people standing some armed with *pangas, simis* (swords) and clubs. They formed a path on both sides leading to the door of the next hut. I became certain that the day had arrived for me to take the oath, and I had to face it manly, I thought.

As I led my group marching in the cordoned path, they waved their *pangas* and swords over our heads and I heard one of them asking whether there was an informer to be "eaten". With a reply that we were all good people from another person, we entered the next hut.

By the light of a hurricane lamp, I could see the furious guards who stood armed with *pangas* and *simis*. Right in front of us stood an arch of banana and maize stalks and sugar cane stems tied by a forest creeping and climbing plant. We were harassed to take out our coats, money, watches, shoes and any other European metal we had in our possession. Then the oath administrator, Githinji Mwarari – who had painted his fat face with white chalk – put a band of raw goat's skin on the right hand wrist of each one of the seven persons who were to be initiated. We were then surrounded (bound together) by goats' small intestines on our shoulders and feet. Another person then sprayed us with some beer from his mouth as a blessing at the same time throwing a mixture of the finger millet with other cereals on us. Then Githinji pricked our right hand middle finger with a needle until it bled. He then brought the chest of a billy goat and its heart still attached to the lungs and smeared them with our blood. He then took a Kikuyu gourd containing blood and with it made a cross on our foreheads and on all important joints saying, "May this blood mark the faithful and brave members of the Gikuyu and Mumbi* Unity; may this same blood warn you that if you betray our secrets or violate the oath, our members will come and cut you into pieces at the joints marked by this blood".

We were then asked to lick each others' blood from our middle fingers and vowed after the administrator: "If I reveal this secret of Gikuyu and Mumbi to a person not a member, may this blood kill me. If I violate any of the rules of the oath may this blood kill me. If I lie, may this blood kill me".

We were then ordered to hold each others' right hand and in that position, making a line, passed through the arch seven times. Each time the oath administrator cut off a piece of the goat's small intestine, breaking it into pieces, while all the rest in the hut repeated a curse on us: *"Tathu! Ugotuika uguo ungiaria maheni! Muma uroria muria ma!"* ("Slash! May you be cut like this! Let the oath kill he who lies!").

---

* Gikuyu and Mumbi are the legendary Adam and Eve of the Kikuyu, whose daughters gave rise to the nine clans.

We were then made to stand facing Mount Kenya, encircled by intestines, and given two dampened soil balls and ordered to hold the left hand soil ball against our navels. We then swore: "I, (Karari Njama), swear before God and before all the people present here that . . ."

We repeated the oath while pricking the eye of a goat with a kei-apple thorn seven times and then ended the vows by pricking seven times some seven sodom apples. To end the ceremony, blood mixed with some good smelling oil was used to make a cross on our foreheads indicating our reception as members of Gikuyu and Mumbi (while) warning us: "Forward ever and backward never!"

We were then allowed to take our belongings, put on our coats and shoes and were welcomed to stay. We paid 2/50s. each for registration. During the course of our initiation, one person refused to take the oath and was mercilessly beaten. Two guards were crying (out) seeking permission from their chief leader to kill the man. The man learnt that death had approached him and he quickly changed his mind and took the oath.

Mau Mau From Within Donald Barnett and Karari Njama.

Mugo Gatheru comments on the psychological effect of the oaths on his people.

First of all, the taking of oaths was not new to the Kikuyu. It was an integral and powerful part of our society, as in most societies at one time or another in their development. The variety of oaths was large to suit the many serious occasions of life, a binding force providing an important moral sanction of society. They were an essential part of tribal law, like the ordeals of fire and water of early English society. Basically, the oaths fell into two categories, major and minor.

If a man denied responsibility for the pregnancy of a girl, the Council of Elders would administer a minor oath to test his innocence. If the man lied, the punishment which he himself had invoked would fall on him between seven days and seven months from the oath. His body might erupt with boils, his animals (his wealth) or even he himself might die; whatever its form, the punishment was inevitable.

The major oath was used to settle land disputes, allegations of larceny and other criminal offences and to test witch doctors suspected of using black magic to poison others, on their own account or hired to do so. Again, the Council of Elders, having failed to solve the problem by arbitration, would administer the oath. However, the major oath had such terrible consequences, involving the man's family and even his entire clan, that he had to obtain their permission before submitting to it. The punishment to follow a major oath dishonestly sworn would fall three and a half years after the oath, 'imera mogwanja', and would be incalculable in its effects.

The psychological effect of the oath was literally terrifying to the Kikuyu. If a man lied, he lied not only to society but also to the ancestors' spirits, whom we have seen could cause great suffering if displeased, and still more he lied to the Creator, Ngai himself. Once taken, it followed that an oath was irrevocable.

PART IV WARS 167

There was no possibility of mental reservation or de-oathing; during the
Emergency, the colonial administration held "de-oathing" ceremonies, the only
effect of which was to confuse the people with one further variety of fear.
Certainly, few felt that the ceremonies absolved them and their families from the
evils to follow the renunciation of their original oath.

Child of Two Worlds Mugo Gatheru.

*A British Intelligence officer outlines the movement's development after the
State of Emergency was declared, and the principal known or suspected leaders
arrested and detained.*

Gradually Mau Mau became organized for war and its members divided
themselves into two groups known as the Militant Wing and the Passive Wing.
The Militant Wing lived mostly in the forest and consisted of gang members. The
Passive Wing comprised those people who provided money, supplies, shelter,
recruits or intelligence for the gangs. They lived in the towns, on the farms, or in
the Reserve. While carrying on their normal work they formed a network of
committees all over the area to fulfil their obligations to the movement. They
were just as brutal as the gangsters and organized oathing ceremonies and killings
to achieve their ends. The term "Passive Wing" was one of the most staggering
misnomers of Emergency terminology.

By the middle of 1953 it was evident that there was no central Mau Mau
authority. It seemed instead as though three separate spheres of influence
existed; one in Mount Kenya, one in the Aberdares, and one around Nairobi.
Such information as was available showed that the Mau Mau was an amazing
compound of craziness, efficiency, superstition, courage, detailed planning and
boastfulness. As an example of boastfulness it is interesting to recall that one of
the leaders described himself as Prime Minister of the Kenya Parliament,
Commander in Chief of the Gikuyu and Mumbi Trinity Armies and Towns-
watch Battalions, President of the Kenya Young Stars Association, President of
the Gikuyu and Mumbi Itungati Association, President of the Kenya African
Women's League and Chairman of the Kinyarikalo Memorial Club!

Another limiting factor was the supply of arms and ammunition. Most of the
ammunition came from the Passive Wing who collected it, if necessary, one
round at a time. They also supplied arms though the gangs collected a lot by
raiding. Furthermore, a large number of guns were made by the terrorists
themselves from old pipes, door bolts, wood, nails and elastic bands. Such
weapons were not very reliable but they made a bang which was good for morale.
They also looked like real weapons, especially at night, and this was good for
terrorizing the population. Occasionally they exploded in the faces of their
owners, which was good for a laugh according to the Kikuyu mentality. They
therefore had their uses.

Altogether the Mau Mau seemed to be a fairly formidable force. In spite of the
comic names and crazy weapons there was not much to laugh about. Few people

realized that the ragged terrorists whose antics were occasionally reported in the newspapers belonged to such an intricate and well ordered system as existed in August 1953.

As time went on, attacks by Mau Mau activists on Europeans and their families intensified. Some were hacked to death by pangas (long slashing knives). All those living in threatened areas went armed, and fortified their houses.

On this occasion there was a large cocktail party in the Settlers' Club just outside Kiambu. These events were not common and people from all over the local Settled Area had flocked in to attend. Most of those present were coffee farmers who were living with their families on isolated estates round the edge of the Native Reserve. It was easy enough to tell that they were living under a shadow from the uproarious way in which they were enjoying their evening out. A few were a bit drunk perhaps but the majority were just relaxing from the tension. I did not stay late because I wanted to make up for lost sleep, so I went back to Kamiti soon after eight o'clock.

As I was driving the last few yards up to my house I heard a burst of firing from another house about half a mile away, which belonged to an elderly couple. As it happened, I knew that the man was away in Nairobi for the evening. Eric Holyoak had also heard the shots and had come running out of his room. Together we drove round as fast as possible.

We arrived at about the same moment as some other neighbours. The sight that greeted us was appalling. The windows were broken, the door knocked down and bits of clothing and other oddments littered the yard. After a moment we summoned enough courage to go inside. The lights were all out but the beam of Eric's torch revealed a more frightful shambles even than had appeared outside. We all knew what it would be like to find the old woman. Often enough we had seen pictures of similar scenes taken by daylight next morning. As a result I hoped that it would not be I who came across the corpse. I was horrified to think that I might at any moment put my hand on it when turning up a chair or be the first to see some bleeding remnant picked out by the torchlight moving from side to side of one room after another.

In this way we passed through the dining room and the living room and had just started our search of a bedroom when we heard a faintly apologetic little voice calling out from the room through which we had just come. We went back and made our identity known but still we could see nothing. After a moment or two there was more of the little voice and then the gallant old lady appeared from under the floor. She had apparently taken the precaution of loosening some of the boards and as the gangsters hacked down the door she had disappeared under the floor. She turned out to be quite unharmed and hardly troubled by the affair. In fact her friends had difficulty in persuading her to go home with them for the night.

Gangs and Counter-Gangs Frank Kitson.

The Kikuyu people were split in two by the Emergency which became, in effect, a civil war.

Those who resisted Mau Mau did not necessarily do so out of loyalty to the Government but because they just could not tolerate degradation and depravity and they also foresaw that the Mau Mau would bring nothing but sorrow and ruin to the tribe. The elders of the Kikuyu tribe, personified in and led by Senior Chief Njiri, resisted because they saw that Mau Mau violated all their traditions and background. Those who had embraced Christianity resisted because they saw that there could be no compromise between their faith and the teachings of Mau Mau.

On 26 March 1953 the Lari massacre shocked much Kikuyu and other African opinion as well as that of Europeans. A Mau Mau gang wiped out the entire village of Lari, killing ninety-seven men, women and children in ghastly ways. The chief was tortured to death and many houses burnt down with their occupants inside. A Kikuyu Guard was set up to resist the gangs and protect, so far as possible, those "loyalists" who had refused to take the oath.

The Home Guard, or Kikuyu Guard, had been built up slowly and carefully over a period of months by the administration in the Central Province, from loyal members of the Kikuyu, Embu and Meru tribes. A very large percentage of the Kikuyu had taken the first oath and in so doing they swore not to give away Mau Mau secrets; if they did they were told they would die and this the vast majority believed implicitly. One or two came into a chief or an officer and confessed what they had done or been made to do. Gradually people realized that those who confessed did not come to harm from supernatural causes as they had expected. Others who wished to resist the Mau Mau came forward to confess. The Kikuyu called it *Kahungwa muhori* or "to have the lungs cleaned". Before any Kikuyu could be a member of the Guard he had to confess fully in this manner; only then was he eligible to be taken on probation into the Guard as a junior recruit.

Initially the movement was based on volunteer effort and self-help. There was no pay for them; activity and interest were maintained by the Guards' own desire to fight against the forces of Mau Mau. Special funds were available, however, to cover incidental expenses and for the payment of occasional reward money for such special items as arms and ammunition recovered. Officers in charge of Kikuyu Guard units were encouraged to learn Kikuyu and gain the trust of the men.

The Charging Buffalo Guy Campbell.

As the raids grew better organized, so did the defence.

The gang had evidently gone into the assault with great determination and they had done a lot of damage. The reason why they were not entirely successful was that they had chosen the wrong settler to attack. Mr and Mrs Grimwood had hit back hard.

Mr Grimwood met me when I arrived and showed me what had happened. The gang had come out of the forest and split into two parties. One party had destroyed the African labour lines and the other had attacked the house. This group had advanced shouting and blowing whistles. I saw innumerable bullet marks on the house and a scar on the floor of one of the rooms where a hand grenade had exploded. Mr Grimwood, aided by his wife, had moved from window to window firing at the gang until a very brave police inspector came tearing up the drive in his Land-Rover. The gang, not knowing that he was by himself, made off.

After seeing the house I went to the charred remains of the labour lines. There had been no great loss of life because the Grimwoods had organized a safety drill to be carried out by their Africans in case of emergency. Even so, one or two had died, and I noticed a woman who had been hit by a small calibre bullet just above the breast. The gang had later hacked her around in the usual way but there was no hiding the bullet hole.

Having seen all I could, I looked at the bodies of the four terrorists killed by Mr Grimwood during the action and had a talk with one of the Rift Valley Special Branch officers who had come along to investigate. He reckoned that the gang must have been about seventy strong; it had been armed with rifles, stens, a small calibre weapon of some sort, shotguns and grenades.

Gangs and Counter-Gangs Frank Kitson.

An elderly retired couple offered less resistance.

21 March 1954
Just after my last letter we had the Bruxnor Randall murder which really was the most horrible thing. Poor old harmless things; do you remember them at Thika? She had a lovely collection of Waterford glass, very unusual in the early colonial period: I wonder whether that got slashed to death with *pangas* too . . .

Nellie: Letters From Africa ed. Elspeth Huxley.

The heartland of Kikuyu country lies between the forests of Mount Kenya on one side and those of the Aberdares (Nyandarua) on the other. In these dense forests, mostly pathless save for tracks made by wild animals, the Mau Mau gangs set up their camps.

In addition to large rivers such as Chania, Gura and Marewa, the forests of Nyandarua are filled with many smaller rivers and streams. It is not surprising to find twenty or more such streams in an area of one mile. Usually we set up our camps near one of these cold, clear, silent flowing streams, which provided us with cooking water as well as fish from the big streams. High in the mountain these rivers and streams are extremely cold and freezing to death or drowning was a danger of which we were all aware – particularly when one of the larger rivers had to be crossed during the flooding season.

All the various types of wild animals in the forest became our friends with the exception of the rhinos, which we called "Home Guards" because of their brutality and willingness to destroy human life. They became accustomed to our presence and smell and, after a few months in the forest, they treated us as simply another form of animal life and we in turn learnt all their habits and calls. This proved extremely useful to us in detecting the presence or approach of strangers. Security forces entering the home of the animals smelling of soap, cigarettes and laundered clothing were greeted with many danger and warning signals or calls from the animals. In many cases they were charged by rhinos, elephants and buffaloes.

The deer, monkeys and *ndete* birds, with their acute sense of smell and sight (respectively), were our best guards against the encroachment of strangers or enemies. Whenever we observed these animal warnings we sent out our scouts to investigate. Almost without exception, we found the warnings of our "allies" to be accurate and because of this assistance they rendered us, we passed a strict rule prohibiting the killing of friendly animals who had kindly welcomed us into their home.

These forests then, while cold and damp and with thunder storms and heavy rains during most of the year, became the home of over 20,000 men and women revolters fighting for the Kenya African Freedom. Many, like myself, lived and fought in Nyandarua for two, three or even four years. For us, these forests became a home and a fortress as well as the provider for our most basic needs.

Mau Mau From Within Donald Barnett and Karari Njama.

British soldiers in boots and smelling of soap and cigarettes had little chance of success against forest gangs in league with the local fauna. Increasingly the security forces came to rely on locally born young men of the Kenya Regiment and Police Reserve who operated in patrols in the forest.

Every man going into the forest had to be able to kill silently, by knife, rope or hands, and all carried a length of blind cord for securing prisoners. It was important that each man should know exactly where all his equipment was; for instance that his torch was on his left, handkerchief in his right trouser pocket etc., because any movement had to be swift and silent. The sound of a voice, or a sneeze, could carry far in the forest. Hand signals were used for communication and sometimes, when moving in the dark, a patch of luminous paint on the back helped one man to follow the next along the track. Frequently the patrol would halt and move off the track since there was always a danger of being followed and surprised from the rear. Constant vigilance was needed, however weary one felt, in order to be able to cope with a burst of rifle fire from an unseen source, or a sudden charge by startled game. Patrols were often obliged to follow game tracks through the dense bush, which was the home of buffalo, elephant and rhino, to name but a few animals which could also be a serious hazard.

Breath becomes short at heights of eight to ten thousand feet and each man had to carry a sleeping bag, water, ammunition and rations. Sometimes torrential rain could drench both load and clothes, so adding to the weight. At the same time the severe heat combined with the altitude was very inducive to sleep during the day, while nights were often tense and sleepless, but to have given in to the temptation to doze on patrol could have meant not only that the chances of contacting a gang would be lost, but the patrol itself would be rendered vulnerable.

Patrols could last from three to fourteen days at a stretch: hot days of climbing up and down deep gulleys, and freezing cold nights. The entire operation was mentally and physically tense, to such a degree that some men suffered hallucinations and most became jumpy and short-tempered. Because it was vital for teams to act in harmony, friends were posted to the same patrols whenever possible. Certain men would be detailed off for safeguarding prisoners or assisting the wounded. Leaders had to develop understanding and the power to command instant obedience in moments of crisis.

Edwin Bristow recalls that patrols were "*tough* – we weren't allowed to wash, weren't allowed to clean our teeth, we had to grow beards, and smelt terrible at the end of three weeks but it was the only way to combat the chaps we were trying to catch, who smelt even worse".

This was an important point: smoking, washing, shaving, talking – all the daily habits one takes for granted in normal life had to be abandoned in the forest. Iain Morrison, who was attached to Special Branch in Nyeri, quotes the following Mau Mau reply he received to his standard question, "Which of the Security Forces did you fear most?": "The *Wa Johnny* (British Troops) washed in perfume, their tin cans rattled, they could be heard and smelled two or three miles away, but the *Kenya Gombis* (Kenya Regiment) never washed. They left all their equipment in one place and patrolled quietly and were good trackers. They walked through the forest like us; that wasn't fair. . . ."

Forest patrols worked virtually blind, as map coordination in the Aberdares was at best mere guesswork. If there was information from a prisoner, or if a gang were suspected of being in the vicinity, small patrols would scour the area, starting from a firm base. The Mau Mau gangs used false hideouts and laid imitation tracks, walking backwards, breaking off branches or foliage and leaving scraps of food, clothing and even blood to suggest that they were moving in a particular direction. At the same time they camouflaged their real trails brilliantly, and could hide underwater, breathing through reed pipes for hours on end without any betrayal of their presence. Such methods are said to have been used by the American Indians with equal skill, and by the Royal American Regiment (later to become the 60th Rifles), in the days of Braddock and Amherst. . . .

Probably the most important development of all this was that the Regiment evolved what was later to be called the "pseudo-gang". "Pseudo-gangs" were originally known in Kenya as "impersonators". Early in 1953 Captain Francis

Erskine wrote a paper requesting official permission to carry out an operation with loyal Kikuyu disguised as Mau Mau. This did not receive the attention it merited, but was supported by the Kenya Regiment and Erskine went on to develop the method. He was subsequently awarded a well-deserved Military Cross. From this early start the regiment developed its own methods of defeating Mau Mau terrorists. The first regimental pseudo-gang consisted of Bill Woodley, Steve Bothma and Gibson Wanbugu from Squairs Farm, where I Force was stationed under Major Neville Cooper. Gibson was decorated for gallantry.

The Charging Buffalo Guy Campbell.

By the end of 1955 the 12,000 to 15,000 guerrilla fighters in the forests had been whittled down to about 1,500, but the most influential of the leaders, "General" Dedan Kimathi, was still at large. Karari Njama had joined him while at the zenith of his power, and describes him thus:

Kimathi, aged 33, stood almost six feet, strong and healthy; his long self-woven hair hanging over a fair brown oval face; his big grey-white and brown eyes protruding below black eyebrows separated by a wide short flat nose. A very little moustache grew above the thick lips; his large teeth with a wide natural gap on the center of the upper jaw and a wider gap on the lower jaw in which two middle incisors had been customarily removed; his oval round chin covered with little beards; his long neck shooting out of his wide shoulders, dressed in a suit of whitish-grey corduroy jumper coat, on which three army stars were fixed on both shoulders, and long trousers. Three writing pens were clipped on his top right hand jumper coat pocket, a heap of exercise books in his left hand, in which the ring finger had been cut off at the second joint, an automatic pistol hoisted at his leather waist belt, a metal bracelet on his right hand wrist – which he told me had been given him by Paul Njeru Gicuki, a close friend and Thomson's Falls KAU official who had been captured and detained several months earlier. His L-shaped curved brown walking-stick, touching the ground, stood vertically and parallel to his trousers. His black shoes prevented him from feeling the damp frozen soil.

Mau Mau From Within Donald Barnett and Karari Njama.

Early in 1955 Dedan Kimathi summoned his followers to witness his installation as Prime Minister of the "legitimate interim government of Kenya", with Karari Njama as its Chief Secretary.

We entered in my hut and dressed. Abdullah and I dressed like elders. We took off our clothes, remaining with undershorts only, and smeared all over our body with castor oil. I then put on a sheep cloak, tied a sword around my waist with its bright red sheath, put *munyeni* on my head – a feather- or fibre-made beret, rattles on my legs, rubber sandals, an elderly leather satchel under my left shoulder, a black honorary walking staff – *muthegi*, made of *mungirima* tree – in my right hand, together with *mataathi* leaves – elders' handkerchief – a flywhisk and a traditional three-legged stool in my left hand.

Being fully dressed, we walked out of the hut pretending to be really old men. We had so greatly changed that our comrades could not recognize us. Amid cheers and laughters and doubts, we went to Kimathi's hut and found that he and Ndururi had dressed like ourselves, but didn't have *muthegi, mataathi*, flywhisk or satchel, for they were juniors. We exchanged greetings: "*Wanyua*," "*Wanyua*" – father, *Mwangi*, to son, *Irungu*. "*Wanyua wakine*," was exchanged between persons of the same [generation] age.

While sitting down, Kimathi took his *ndahi* – a little gourd half the size of a glass – and filled it with the pure honey beer which he had brewed. After each of us had drunk one *ndahi*, we filled two *itete* with beer to be used in the ceremony and the rest we put in *nyanja*, gourds for storing beer. Wang'ombe Ruga took one *gitete*, a little gourd with sheep's fat, blood and abdominal dung, and went to the main entrance where he stood cleansing all the fighters as they entered the ceremonial hall.

When Wang'ombe sent a report that he had cleansed all the fighters, Kimathi and his wife to be, followed by Ndururi Vindo and Macaria Kimemia, entered the hall. When they were all seated, Abdullah and I, Wandere my advisor and two other elders who carried the paraphernalia required, entered the hall. All the warriors stood up as we slowly walked the 120 feet along the narrow path between the standing columns. On our arrival at the platform, I filled a horn with beer from the *gitete*, purposely letting it flow over to the ground. I held the horn in my right hand and the little fat gourd in my left. Facing Kirinyaga (Mount Kenya), I asked the audience to attend prayers:

> Our Heavenly Father, I beseech you; draw nearer and hear our prayers. (*Thaai*! audience). Our merciful Father, forgive us all our sins and wash our hearts, hands and minds as it satisfies thy will, so that we may be clean in your eyes. (*Thaai*!). Oh God! defend and guide us for we are your children, your own creation. We believe that you are our leader, general and King of Kings, and we humbly pray you to lead and supervise our ceremony. (*Thaai*!) I now present to you fat and honey (pouring a little to the sides and front), our best produce, your own choice, and which you have instructed our forefathers to present to you in all ceremonies.
>
> Now God, I pray you power and wisdom to enable me to accomplish this ceremony in your name, Father, I present Dedan Kimathi to you, the man you chose to lead us in this forest. We have gathered here today to pray you to glorify Kimathi, fill him with power and wisdom, defend and keep him, and let him lead us to victory in your home. (*Thaai thathaiya Ngai thaai* – three times).

All sitting down, Kimathi and his party standing, I turned to Kimathi and, pouring fat and honey on his head, I said: "May this be the sign that we all here accept and witness Dedan Kimathi as the Head Leader of all our armies. May

God bless this head, fat and sweet honey help it to grow and rise above all heads in the name of our god. *Thaai.*"

I sipped the beer and made a spitting gesture on my both shoulders and sipped again, spraying Kimathi and his girl with it from my mouth. I said: "May you have power to defeat the enemy, long life, many children and popularity."

Karari Njama then made a long speech of praise which ended:

"Kimathi, my son, for your good service to your country, your willingness to sacrifice your life for your people, your bravery, your industriousness, your good conduct and leadership has made the Kenya Parliament, which is the people's eyes, to promote you today, 6 March 1955, to become the first Prime Minister of the Kenya African Government (amid cheers) and knight you Sir Dedan Kimathi, Knight Commander of the East African Empire. Here (handing him the envelope containing a letter and 500s.), in the name of Gikuyu and Mumbi and the Kenya Parliament's authority. You will now be leader of the leaders, an elder of the first order who only advises and settles down quarrels. Let another warrior rise as much as you have done in the army. This is the elder's honour (handing over the *muthegi, mataathi* and flywhisk) which marks that you have passed the warriors stage (shaking hands and exchanging greetings – '*Wanyua,*' '*Wanyua wakini*')."

But, for the Knight Commander of the East African Empire, the bell had already tolled.

News from the reserves was not pleasing, for Government had greatly increased its forces and arms, forced all people in the Central Province into villages which were strongly supervised as prison camps. We had been cut off from Nairobi supplies and communication and worse still from our supporters in the reserves. For the last two months I had noted and notified our Nairobi base that the (little) ammunition we had could only be used for defending or fighting for food. We couldn't make any more offensive attacks. Over 30,000 Kikuyu, Embu and Meru had become loyal Home Guards to the Government, most of whom were previously our strong supporters. After their surrender they accused other supporters whom they beat and tortured badly until they confessed and became converted in their faith. In addition, our *itungati* (warriors) who had either surrendered or were captured had given the enemy sufficient information about the forest fighters and, worst of all, (some) had joined the enemy's pseudo-platoons and had become their guides to our *mbuci* (forest camps). In fact the wind had changed, this time against us.

Mau Mau From Within Donald Barnett and Karari Njama.

The final meeting of the "Kenya Parliament" was held in July 1955, after which the gangs dispersed and operated without central authority. Hope of victory gave way to a personal struggle for survival. The hunt was on for Dedan Kimathi.

From information supplied by former gangsters, a picture was pieced together of Kimathi's daily habits. Every morning he prayed to his God while resting his head against a mugumo *tree, the wild fig sacred to the Kikuyu God. The police officer in charge of the hunt reports.*

By the evening of 8 August 1956, all the large mugumo trees in the "Kimathi Area" had been plotted on our map. These trees are not common in the forest of the Aberdares, and they are quite rare in our hunting ground. Jeriko had said that there were at least forty, but we only found eighteen and ten of these were in spots which Kimathi would certainly not visit because the approaches were unsafe. We turned to the remaining eight.

That same night, eight well-armed teams made their way to the trees. The march was a taxing exercise in bushcraft. Our teams had to avoid open spaces where an alert sentry could see them; they had to avoid the likely resting places of bushbuck and duiker, for if Kimathi found the hoof-marks of a running antelope, he might suspect that his enemies were at hand; our men also had to avoid those birds or animals which raise an alarm as soon as they see human beings, such as the Sykes monkeys, whose loud warning calls can be heard for miles through the forest. Then there is the tiny little brown *ndete* or call bird. Whenever they see something move they fly over and perch themselves on a nearby bush where they jump frantically from branch to branch and make as much noise as they can to tell the forest of their discovery. He is a most difficult creature to get rid of. Fortunately he chatters whenever he sees anything move so he is a far less reliable "alarm bell" than the less excitable Sykes monkey and it can often be a pure waste of time to check up on his warnings. But nothing was ever too tiring or troublesome for the timid Kimathi. Whenever he heard the *ndete*, he would study the situation from afar for some time in the hope of identifying the cause of the bird's alarm, then, if he could not see anything, he would dart away.

Some of the wild fig trees were several miles up the slopes of the mountain and it was not until the afternoon of 9 August that all our teams were finally in position. . . .

Our men took up the best positions they could find and after covering their legs with their animal-skin coats to shield them from the hard-biting horse flies, which can sting a man to the border of frenzy, the long wait began. Here they were to lie for four days and nights unless Kimathi favoured them with a visit. Rain, heat, cold, wind, ants, caterpillars, wild animals, snakes, and all the other dangers and discomforts of the forest would have to be endured as they lay there. In those same positions the calls of nature would be answered by turning slowly onto their backs and scraping a small hole in the soft, forest soil with their fingers. They would lie there as still as death, but all the time they would be alert and sensitive for the faintest rustle in the bushes, a suspicious sound or a movement in the trees. . . .

I had often watched our teams on operations in the forest. They would lie absolutely motionless for so long that I wondered whether they would ever be able to move their cramped limbs again. All the time their chins would be resting on their clenched fists and they would be staring at some particular spot where they believed they would first see something coming. They were, curiously enough, seldom wrong. Their stare would be so intense you would think they had seen something and you would try to see for yourself, but without looking at you they would sense your curiosity and slowly shake a finger to show there was nothing there. Sometimes you would hear a rustle in the forest and look at them inquiringly, but they would still be staring at the spot they had been watching for hours. Perhaps they had not heard it, you would think, but before you could move, they would quietly whisper "*Ngima*" ("Sykes") or "*Thwara*" ("Buck") or "*Kanyoni*" ("Bird") and you would lie back feeling ignorant and a bit embarrassed. In the forest they knew the answers to everything, outside to nothing. In the forest it was always safest to leave everything to them. After operating with them a few times you would very quickly realize when something unusual was in the vicinity. Instinctively they would pull their fists away from their chins and their heads would drop an inch or two. This was a reflex action developed in the days when they were often under fire. Then their heads would turn very slowly in the direction from which they suspected the intruder was coming and by tapping a little twig on the ground or on a dry leaf, they would signal messages to one another. Their bodies would curl up. And then one man would give the signal to attack. A low in-drawn whistle meant "Fire"; two sharp clicks with a finger meant "Rush"; and when they fired, or when they rose to their feet and rushed, they would react with surprising speed, darting through the tangled, forbidding undergrowth with a grace and ease that were fascinating.

Four days and nights passed in this tormented fashion but God had warned Kimathi in a dream and he escaped the trap. Nevertheless the pseudo-gangs were closing in and Kimathi's followers were reduced to thirteen. Every day they moved on.

At the first glimmer of dawn, Kimathi rose and set off alone to study the behaviour of the partridges. He believed, as did most other Mau Mau, that if partridges took to wing and scattered as soon as human beings came upon them, the day would end in tragedy. On the other hand, if they scurried along the ground for a few yards before flying away, they would be showing the *muirigo* or the way and this was an omen of good fortune. When he returned to the hide-out, he was in a better frame of mind and his followers knew that the partridges must have scurried. . . .

Some time that night – nobody had any idea what time it was – Kimathi ordered his gang to break camp and move on. They crossed the Kinaini river, and then the Muringato river, on their way to a cave once used by Juma Abdalla as a food store. But when they reached it they found it was empty. All the food had been cleared out by our teams some time before. So on Kimathi and his followers went until they reached that part of the jungle which they called Mathakwa-ini.

During the next few days when new game traps were being laid, the gang grew more and more hungry. The few fruit-yielding trees were bare. Most of the bees had eaten their honey during the misty period and had not replenished their hives. Meat was, as yet, unobtainable as their traps were only now going up. What little food they did find was given to Kimathi and Wanjiru (his female companion). Three hyrax were caught in an ingenious but cruel way. When their holes in the trees were discovered, a long, pliant stick, spliced at the tip, was thrust up the hole until the hyrax felt the tip boring into their bodies and screeched. Then the terrorists turned the stick so that the soft woolly hair of the animals was wound round the tip. They were then pulled down, clubbed to death and given to Kimathi and Wanjiru. For the other members of the gang, lack of food soon became a desperate problem. Old buckskin garments were boiled and eaten after the hair had been scraped off, rats were welcome morsels, while some roots were dug up and boiled for their juices. The gangsters took it in turn to sit near their game traps to make sure that, when a buck was caught, it would not be eaten by hyenas or leopards. Spurred on by hunger, Kimathi's men were sitting in pairs by their widely-scattered traps. They were still sitting there when our operations began again after the abortive operation of Rurimeria hill and in the first week of September we caught four more of Kimathi's men. All four were sitting beside game traps when the teams found them and none had eaten any food for several days.

Soon afterwards, Kimathi's last remaining followers were captured and then he was alone. He fled without direction until he collapsed near the forest's edge after covering nearly 80 miles in just under 28 hours. A little after sunrise on 21 October 1956 he was spotted by several Kikuyu tribal policemen, challenged, and wounded in the thigh as he fled. He was taken to hospital, recovered, tried for murder, sentenced and hanged. Ian Henderson concludes the story.

After visiting Kimathi in the hospital at Nyeri, I went straight back into the forest to unwind our operation and stand down the oddest army that ever fought for Queen and country in the history of the British Empire. Runners were sent out to bring all our teams back to Kinaini Camp. During the next forty-eight hours they trickled into camp tired out and weary. Gati was almost the last to arrive, lagging far behind the rest of his men, walking slowly, picking at his teeth with a piece of stick. He was deep in thought.

When I saw him coming, I went over and took him aside. We sat beneath the shade of a big tree to talk. "Well, it's all finished, Gati," I said. "Yes, Kinyanjui," he replied, "it finished as Kingori prophesied – in the tenth month before the rains for millet planting began." Then I remembered Kingori's words in prison some six months before. The prophecy had been fulfilled.

The last ambush team from the prayer trees was now coming into our camp. Of all Kimathi's prayer trees, those *mugumo* trees to which he had made his pilgrimages in search of his god Ngai, there was one which had attracted him more than the rest. Perhaps its shape or its surroundings fitted more accurately with the *mugumo* tree he had seen in his dream when "god had taken him by the right hand and led him to it".

This tree stood in the part of the forest which the Mau Mau called Kahiga-ini. It was an enormous tree with a huge trunk and heavy, hanging branches which reached almost to the ground. It had stood there for many years, probably since the turn of the century. Now our team came over to make their last report – the *mugumo* tree had fallen. *The Hunt for Kimathi* Ian Henderson and Philip Goodhart.

There are always two points of view. A patrol led by Major Owen Jeoffreys had surprised a forest gang and captured a number of weapons. In retaliation, "Brigadier" Karari Njama had raided Jeoffreys' farm, burnt the buildings, sacked the house and abducted three servants.

The following day, I wrote a letter to Major Owen Jeoffreys:

Dear Jeoffreys,

I visited your home on the previous night and found that you were absent. I had come for the nineteen guns, clothing and utensils you took away from our fighters at Ruthaithi last week. Though I did not get the guns, I managed to get a radio, sewing machine, camera, utensils, clothings, food and medicine.

Your servants are now our active fighters. What I have done is just to make you feel what I and my colleagues felt last week for your actions. Your unfriendly action resulted in a revenge. I wonder how much you expect to live in Kenya while you spend most of your time and energy in destroying the Kenya Africans and creating enmity with us.

If I had revenged as I had been ordered by Kimathi, I would have put your living house on fire, but I spared it in order to prove to you that we are not so destructive as you might think. In fact, you must have seen that I stopped one warrior from tearing your books. All we want is freedom to form an African Government which will ban all discriminatory bars and extend individual freedom in movement, press and speech, give better pay and conditions to the workmen and most important eliminate European's selfishness and pride. We do not hate the white man's colour, but we cannot tolerate seeing a foreign settler with 50,000 acres of land, most of which only the wild game enjoy, while thousands of Africans are starving of hunger in their own country. Nor can we accept the white man to remain as a master and the African as a servant.

Your only alternative is either cooperate with the Africans as equal human beings by creating friendship and good relationship which your bombs and guns will never achieve – for they only increase enmity; or quit Kenya and leave the African to manage his own affairs. I intend to make it clear to you through this letter that the more you fight the Africans, the more you endanger your future in Kenya. You cannot kill ideas by killing people. Since the declaration of emergency almost two years ago you have killed thousands of people, but you have neither killed the idea nor won the battle. Our battle is really between right and might. The six million Africans standing for right will definitely beat sixty thousand Europeans standing for the might, irrespective of your army strength. I am afraid that your Government had so many clever and wise men that are all blind to see the simple facts I have written you.

Your New Kenyan
Brig. Gen. Karari Njama
Chief Secretary, Kenya Parliament
September 1954

>   *Mau Mau From Within* Donald Barnett and Karari Njama.

The State of Emergency ended officially in January 1960, although after the capture of Dedan Kimathi in 1956 the fighting virtually came to an end. Jomo Kenyatta was still restricted in his movements, although his seven-year prison sentence for "managing a proscribed society" had ended. In 1961 he was finally released to lead his country into Independence.

Kenyatta's period in prison gave him time for reflection away from the turmoil of politics. He could read, rest on his oars and think. Instead of being warped by prison, he seemed to find a new stability. At a press conference just before his final release he said, half jokingly, "We have been in a university. We learned more about politics there than we learnt outside."

After Kenyatta became "First Minister" as a prelude to his presidency, he made two important speeches – more than two, of course, but these were crucial. Most European farmers were frightened, depressed, and could see no hope for the future. For four years many of them had lived under siege, locked in at night with their revolvers for fear of gangs bursting in to hack them to pieces; the personal friends of some had died in this gruesome fashion, and many more had seen their cattle hamstrung or poisoned. The price of land had slumped to next to nothing, and a million acres had already been compulsorily bought to be split up into African shambas. Now the arch-enemy whom they believed to be responsible for all this was to become the ruler of their country.

A meeting of white farmers was called at Nakuru and the arch-enemy invited to address them. By a coincidence of history the son of that Lord Delamere who had virtually started off white settlement was in the chair. It was a glum and hostile audience. This is part of what Kenyatta had to say:

> I am a politician, but I am a farmer like you . . . I think the soil joins us all and

therefore we have a kind of mutual understanding. If you want to understand each other, then the best thing is to talk together . . . I believe that the most disturbing point among us is suspicion, fear. These are created by not knowing what the other side is thinking. If we must live together, if we must work together, we must talk together, exchange views. This is my belief. And one thing which I want to make clear is this. It is, that we must also learn to forgive one another. There is no perfect society anywhere. Whether we are white, brown or black, we are not angels. We are human beings, and as such are bound to make mistakes. But there is a great gift that we can exercise, that is to forgive one another. If you have done harm to me, it is for me to forgive you. If I have done harm to you, it is for you to forgive me. All of us, white, brown and black, can work together to make this country great . . . Let us join together and join hands and work together for the benefit of Kenya. This is what I beg you to believe, that this is the policy of your government.

I was not at this meeting, held in mid-1963, but those who were told me that tension and hostility almost tangibly eased, and that Kenyatta's next few sentences drew laughter

Many of you, I think, are just as good Kenyans as myself. I think some of you may be older than myself a little bit. I am 73 myself and I have my age-group among you. Therefore you are just as good Kenyans as myself. I think some of you may be worried – what will happen if Kenyatta comes to be the head of the government? He has been in prison, maybe he has given trouble. What is he going to do? Let me set you at rest. That Kenyatta has no intention whatever to look backwards. Not at all. I want you to believe what I am saying now, that we are not going to look backwards. We are going to forgive the past and look forward to the future. Because if we start thinking about the past, what time shall we have to build the future?

The M'zee, as he had become, sat down to an enthusiastic clapping of white hands. His words did much to persuade some, at least, of those white farmers who had contemplated leaving to stay on and give the future a chance.

This message of "forgive and forget" was not addressed to Europeans only. Kenyatta's own people were deeply divided. Those who had taken an active part in Mau Mau were in a minority; many had joined a Home Guard recruited by the administration, and the chiefs, as well as the numerous Christians, had stayed loyal to the Government. Civil war had left its inevitable bitterness, and many feared that a night of the long knives would follow for those Kikuyu who had fought the freedom-fighters. Kenyatta knew that, unless he could overcome these festering enmities, he could have little hope of leading his nation to a peaceful future. In a speech he made a few months later he told his people that ignorance, sickness and poverty – not, by implication, Europeans – were Kenya's true enemies, and that only hard work and unity could overcome them. Only the burial of hatchets and the dismantling of tribal barriers could create a contented country. We must work together, strive together, join together – harambee! That cry so familiar to drivers stuck in the mud became the rallying call of the nation.

The night of the long knives – or the sharpened *pangas* – never happened. Wild-eyed "generals" with matted hair emerged from the forests, and "rehabili-tated" oath-administrators with "Jomo beards" from the detention camps, to mingle with "loyalist" home guards and stalwart Christians and turn back together into ordinary citizens. Harambee worked. How much, so quickly, was really forgotten none but a Kikuyu could say, but forgiveness was apparent, thanks to the wisdom of Jomo Kenyatta, the M'zee.

Out in the Midday Sun Elspeth Huxley.

On 12 December 1963 the Union Jack was hauled down and the flag of the independent Republic of Kenya raised in Nairobi, thus ending sixty-eight years of colonial rule. The M'zee died in Mombasa on 22 August 1978, and on the same day the vice-president, Daniel arap Moi, was sworn in as President, an office that the incumbent can enjoy for life.

PART V

Environment

The landscape of Kenya has infinite variety, great beauty, and runs to extremes. Africa's second highest mountain and the tropical verges of the Indian Ocean lie within its bounds. From the coast the land rises slowly to the highlands, roughly between 4,000 and 8,000 feet above sea-level, and is bisected by the Great Rift Valley, whose wide-spreading floor is broken by extinct volcanoes and adorned by a chain of lakes stretching from the soda-impregnated Natron on the Tanzanian border to Turkana, whose tip thrusts into Ethiopia. Beyond the Rift's western wall the land falls again to the fertile basin of Lake Victoria and the border with Uganda; to the north lies a region of dusty deserts, lava rock and thirst that occupies about one half of Kenya's total area. Here nomads trek from well to distant well, and elephants once dug for water in the sand. The Republic's rainfall varies from an inch or two, and sometimes none, to a hundred inches and more in a year, and is the key to man's existence in Kenya: where rain falls plentifully but not excessively he prospers, where it is scant and unreliable he endures. The human population, formerly sparse, scattered and more or less static, now rockets upwards at a rate that threatens to exhaust the country's natural resources. Nearly two centuries ago Jonathan Swift observed that geographers in Afric maps "O'er unhabitable downs / Place elephants for want of towns." Technological man has hammered the elephants and supplied the towns.

The Bush

The bush embodies the intrinsicality of Africa. It can be vicious, deadly, dangerous and cruel; also verdant, lovely, seductive and kind.

Put your foot down and more often than not you tread on rough volcanic rubble; where there is not volcanic rubble there is fine dust that rises in clouds when herds of cattle or game move over it. Touch a tree and it is thorny; camp near water and you are eaten alive by mosquitoes, although you need not fear the lions that will still roar around you in the wilder parts. Sit in the shade and you will sit on a thorn, if not something worse. Such country is not for those who like an easy life, but it has its attractions for lovers of wild landscape and the freedom of the bush.

The Mystery of the Flamingos Leslie Brown

"The vegetable image of democracy."

I have so often used the word "scrub," and it is so important an element in East African geography and scenery, that I must describe exactly what it is. The chief constituents are thorny acacias, generally with flat tops and white stems. In dry weather they look gaunt, bare, and bony; in wet weather they are connected and partly covered with a network of creepers, and may even acquire a certain grace when draped with masses of convolvulus. Occasionally, too, one finds in the scrub flowering shrubs of marvellous beauty. But this is rare: what strikes one most about it is its formlessness, its utter want of distinction, and its terrible strength. It is the vegetable image of democracy. It grows no great trees and makes no fine views, but it has taken entire possession of the country, and you cannot turn it out. At present one merely regrets that so much land should be wasted, but before the construction of the railway the journey across the Nyika was the most formidable part of the march to Uganda, especially the forty miles between Samburu and Maungu, where there was no water. The horrors of the scrub are increased by the number of thorns, "the tyrants of the forest," as Krapf called them. The vegetation is spiny, spiky, and forbidding. Almost all the plants bear thorns: some bear nothing else, and exist solely in order to be disagreeable and obstructive. The "Wait-a-bit" thorn tells its own tale. Had it been desired to erect an artificial barrier for preventing the entry of civilization into the interior, it would have been very hard to invent one more effective than that which Nature has provided.

The East Africa Protectorate Sir Charles Eliot.

The spirit of the bush.

Whether you are observing the bigger and more dangerous varieties of game, or the lovely profusion of gazelles in their infinite variety, you should always – if your spirit is akin to the spirit of the bush – act with consideration, and should not inflict human presence too closely or inconsiderately on those to whom it is not welcome. Then, if you act in proper manner, you reap your reward because you will see the elephants talking together as they drowse away the heat of the day under the cool shade of the trees along the river banks; you can watch the lion cubs playing hide and seek among grass tussocks in the sinking rays of the westering sun while their mothers stretch, and stand up, and sniff the evening air, and the black-maned lions lift their heavy heads and yawn.

And, while you wait and watch, the tall and elegant giraffes will approach almost within touching distance while they nibble the young leaves from the flat tops of thorn trees and look around them with soft and wondering eyes.

The bush is alive in the early morning, around dawn and sunrise, before the comfortable heat of the day drives all living things – including man when man is in the bush – to laze and drowse in the shade, and it is alive also in the coolth of the evening when those who live by grazing come out into the open to graze, and those who live by hunting come out to hunt. But the animals which may be hunted do not live in terror of the hunters; it is only the individual which is hunted that is terrified and his terror is only momentarily communicated to those around him. Just for a moment terror is there; in a few moments terror has gone; and a lion will walk through a herd of game which will be no more than wary of him and do no more than give him his distance. Nature, by allowing only the fittest to survive, makes wariness and alertness an integral part of her creatures, but fear is not a persistent part of them; it comes and is gone again, and that is all. That is why man can find beauty and peace among the denizens of the bush, and in the bush itself, and a satisfaction that is beyond the comprehension of those who only dwell in cities.

We Built a Country J. F. Lipscomb.

The pyramid of life.

Most typical of the trees in the *nyika* [bush] are the thorny acacias – above all the flat-topped *tortilis*. By the river some of the *elatior* acacias are eight hundred years old. Out in the bush the baobabs, whose bulbous trunks hold water like sponges, can live to a thousand. My friend Malcolm Coe, the zoologist, discovered that baobabs depend on fruitbats or bushbabies, brushing through their branches, for fertilization. Indeed most of our plants and trees can reproduce only if their seeds are dispersed by animals or birds.

Ninety per cent of the energy harnessed by these myriads of leaves is burned up in the process of growth, flowering, fruiting and seeding but the rest is available for other forms of life to exploit. There is little enough grass along the banks of the river to satisfy the impala, zebra, buffalo and hippos; there is still less further inland. Yet there is plenty of nourishment on the shrubs and the trees for the specialist browsers. The lowest shoots are nipped off by the dik dik. Higher up Joy's favourites, the lesser kudu, with their lovely spiralling horns and crescents of cream on their pale grey flanks, and the lumbering rhinos, make their mark. But the elegant gerenuk, with its long curving neck, will rise up on its hind legs to reach even higher.

The trees are beyond the reach of the gazelles and the antelopes, but not of the giraffes. The whole of this animal is a miracle of adaptation. Its neck, its mouth, its long twisting tongue and even its viscous saliva are all designed to make the most of the furthest tips of the branches, rich in their protein, if sometimes uncomfortably thorny. A giraffe makes do with exactly the same number of vertebrae as we have, but it has a special lightweight skull, valves in its arteries to stop it blacking out when it bends to drink and neck muscles of extraordinary strength. I have seen a photograph of a drinking giraffe whose head had been seized by a crocodile: in a second frame the giraffe has managed to straighten up and the crocodile is hanging vertically by its jaws. Only the elephant can compete with the giraffe in getting at the tree canopy. It will stand on its hind legs to extend the range of its trunk and, if it is still frustrated, will use its forehead and tusks to knock the tree over. It will also tear open the baobabs with its tusks to get at their moisture.

Ten per cent of the energy trapped by the plants, at the base of the food chain, has now gone up one level as it has been consumed by this vast and diversified army of herbivores. They, too, use up ninety per cent of this energy in movement, digestion, fighting, fleeing, courtship and breeding: only ten per cent remains for the flesh-eating hunters at the top of the chain. Because the reservoir of energy shrinks each time it goes up a step, the structure of life has been seen by some scientists as a pyramid. The carnivores prowl at the top.

My Pride and Joy George Adamson.

In Tsavo East National Park: drought, death and deliverance.

Day after day the merciless sun beat down from a brassy sky with a fierce, dry, intensity. It was pitiful to see the decline of such large numbers of elephant as they wearily hung around waiting for the end with mute resignation and silent apathy It was not uncommon to see entire herds fast asleep beneath the scant shade afforded by a few gnarled trees, lying flat on their sides, or standing dejectedly in a huddle patiently waiting for an old, emaciated leader to make the move she plainly never would. It was pitiful also to see the attempts made to raise a dying comrade, or lift a far gone calf to its feet, but what was most tragic, day after day, was the great grief of a mother who had lost her calf, or a calf standing pathetically beside an inert mother. On one occasion a cow, whose small calf had collapsed, spent several hours painstakingly trying to urge it to its feet again.

Alas to no avail, and when the calf had breathed its last, she felt every inch of the lifeless little body as though to imprint it on her mind forever, before turning deliberately away and slowly ambling off. One could sense the intense emotional suffering of this cow, which was far worse, I am sure, than the physical pain connected with the drought. Post-mortem examinations carried out on several carcases revealed that the stomachs were in fact full, but that the protein value of the contents was as low as two per cent. . . .

The first half of November came and went, and although the clouds banked up promisingly each afternoon and the humidity was oppressive, still the rain held off – and more elephant died. This pattern was repeated day after day until the end of November, when the heavens suddenly opened one afternoon and those elephant in the eastern belt that had had the tenacity to cling to life until this day were spared.

Joyfully everyone hurried outside to savour the first life-giving drops; to watch them fall in a puff of dust on the powdery soil, and to see them come with ever increasing intensity until the ground began to glisten and the water creep along in little rivulets. One could almost sense the quickening of the earth; the hidden excitement of the birds, the insects, the frogs and the animals and the revival of the poor old elephants, as that soothing liquid straight from heaven poured over their emaciated bodies and brought with it the promise of renewed life. . . .

And, before the week was out, not a single elephant remained in the stricken eastern belt. Somehow the survivors managed to trek again, and they deserted that area of so much misery to congregate where the heaviest falls of rain had made the *nyika* burst again to life. For although elephant may be very conservative in the dry season, as soon as heavy rain falls, even many miles away, they somehow seem to know and overnight they migrate *en masse*. How they know where to go will remain a secret of Nature, probably forever, but the fact that they do is demonstrated every single year in Tsavo. Water in the inland pans means that fresh feeding grounds are now accessible, and the elephant are able to fill their stomachs again.

The Tsavo Story Daphne Sheldrick.

The Plains

The Athi plains.

After a cup of tea we drove along a rough track towards the Athi in search of a pride of lions seen the day before at a place called the Camp of Stones. This, one would say, is the perfect hunting-ground: neither open plain where a man finds no cover, nor thick bush where thorns obstruct him. The twisted *combretum* bush, its thin trunks nobbly as apple trees and mellowed by a westering sun, rise from a sward now succulent and springy, and the tall graceful acacias quietly spread their branches against the sunset. A flash of brilliant blue and cinnamon brought the car to a standstill while my companions debated whether a bird eyeing us from the branches was the European or the lilac-breasted roller; the point settled, we clambered up a clump of high granite boulders.

No sign of human life intruded, no smoke of fires, no homing goatherd. This was Africa as it used to be and soon will be no longer, lonely, magnificent and alive with secrets. Away stretches the world for ever, as it seems, into the sunset; empty, as you think, of all life, fresh from the hand of God; yet some movement catches your eye – a herd of impala grazing on a patch of green; across to your left hurries a white-tusked warthog, her four piglets trotting behind in single file; over there something tawny slips into a grove of thorn-trees – an oryx, a waterbuck, a lion? You think you are alone, but eyes are watching every movement; you think you are hidden, but nostrils quiver on the alert; you think all is silent, but a baboon barks from the rocks, a francolin calls, a reedbuck gives his shrill long whistle.

The Sorcerer's Apprentice Elspeth Huxley.

Typical of the open plains is the whistling thorn, whose black galls emit a weird sibilance.

The whistling thorn belongs to the acacia family, as do eighty per cent of the trees in the arid plains country of the Rift. But this variety has its peculiarities. On one I noted a large clear globule of sap, the first I had seen on any acacia. More distinctive of this type, however, are its dark round galls. Ants burrow into the galls and through the holes they make, the wind whistles sharply; hence the name for the tree.

But the ants also do the thornbush a service: the formic acid they secrete acts as an irritant to the muzzles of browsing animals. Thus there is a mutually beneficial relationship between these two incongruous parties, the ants getting nourishment from the galls and, in exchange, protecting the thornbush from rhino, giraffe and antelope.

Africa's Rift Valley Colin Willock.

Laikipia.

It is given to others to yearn for the great grass plains of whistling thorn which stretch for miles down the Great Rift and northwards across Laikipia to the deserts of the Turkana. These are the ranching lands of Kenya with their swamps and their rivers which have their sources in the mountain ranges, with the homesteads clustering beneath the flat-topped thorns beside the watercourses. For much of the year these grazing lands are scorched by the sun and the high north-easterly gales from off the frontier, and they turn to an even brown, scarred only by the trees which follow the winding, dry river-beds. Spouts of dust move slowly across the scene like leeches reaching to the sky, and as the drought holds for month after month, one can marvel at the sleek cattle which live on the sparse but rich stargrass, which, with the passing of the rains, dries into a hay of unsurpassed quality and richness, but which is nonetheless often deficient in trace elements. When the rains at last break, the dry, grey pasture turns to green in a few days, starred with bulbous flowers and of a hue not seen in the higher sourveld. In these lands a man can only see the thorn trees and the clouds, and far away, the snow peaks of Mount Kenya or the towering cliffs of the Rift which light to gold in the evening when the sun sinks into a cauldron of smoke and haze. This is the weft and weave of life for those who love the plains.

Dimbilil: The Story of an African Farm Errol Whittall.

Fire on the plain.

As the dry season advances, fires begin to sweep through the park. Over two thirds of the woodlands and large portions of the long-grass plains are burned annually. Some of these fires are set by pastoralists outside of the park, for burning stimulates green grass to grow on the burn, a nutritious source of food for livestock at a time when otherwise only dry forage remains. Frequent heavy grazing of such green shoots may be detrimental to the grasses. By growing at a time when they should lie dormant, they use up the stored nutrients they need to survive the dry season, and the heavy grazing prevents them from depositing more food in their roots. On the other hand, dry stems may be grazed to the ground by hoofed animals with little effect on the grasses because they have their energy already stored. Other fires start through carelessness – a discarded cigarette, an untended campfire – or from a mere pyromaniacal impulse. As the fires burn, distant hills disappear in the smoke haze and at midday the sun is a pale disk that changes to a fiery, coppery orb as toward evening the earth leans slowly away from it. Fires that in daytime creep inconspicuously up some hill become visible at night as disembodied flames dancing in glowing lines inexorably into the sky. Yellowish smoke and ash permeate the air. On the plains, dust devils spin over the ground now bleak and bare except for a few scorched tufts of grass. In the woodlands flames have swept away the grass, assaulted thickets, and devoured dead trees. With the rocky bones of the hills exposed, the earth dry and cracked, the Serengeti now presents a bleak appearance, its bright colours leached away.

The large mammals almost ignore the advancing fires, casually detouring around flames or moving onto burned ground that is still warm. One male lion fed on a warthog, seemingly oblivious to the line of flames that crackled toward him through the grass. At last, with the fire only three feet from his paws, so close that I was afraid his mane might ignite, he reluctantly dragged his meal to a safer spot. Some birds benefit directly from fires. Marabou storks pace gravely around the edge, their preoccupied mien interrupted by occasional rapid thrusts of their bills, which may net them a mouse, snake, or other small vertebrate fleeing from the flames. Lilac-breasted rollers, spectacular in their iridescent blue plumage, plunge into the smoke to snag grasshoppers. Small animals may be harmed by the flames, and I particularly remember a leopard tortoise dragging its house along on scorched legs, moving even more slowly than usual.

Golden Shadows, Flying Hooves George Schaller.

Divine protection.

Looking up from my book, I would see the herds of cattle being driven up from the water and browsing through the glade on their way inland to pasture. They were small and humped, mostly black and white or tawny, and some carried magnificently sweeping horns. But I watched them anxiously as they pushed and jostled and bellowed, and the dust rose under their stamping feet, while the herdsmen whistled through their teeth, and the dogs yapped in and out; for a little partridge had her nest somewhere in the grass they trampled. Every evening on my way home from hunting, I used to pass by that way to see how she was getting on, till she became so tame that she would eat the crumbs I brought her while sitting on the nest. One evening I could not help exclaiming in wonder to find that the nest had still escaped, though the cattle had trampled there all day; but Mohamed answered, with naive simplicity: "For every creature, God is there" (*killa kitu, Mungo iko*).

Speak to the Earth Vivienne de Watteville.

Forests

And here were forests ancient as the hills,
Enfolding sunny spots of greenery.

Samuel Taylor Coleridge

It is one of the noblest forests in the world. It is not like the Ituri forest of the Congo, a sky occluding vegetable growth. Always there are openings with glimpses of the heathland peaks or vistas of long blue distance. It has many kinds of trees, perhaps a score of the olive family, one of which, the Elgon olive, soars with straight pale-stem branching to a heavy crown anything up to a hundred and fifty feet above the ground. I, who love woodland, could write page after page in its description. Sometimes the trees are burdened almost to extinction by thorny lianas, some with yellow flowers or red wait-a-bit thorn in due season. But the forest king on Elgon is *Podocarpus gracilior,* called for short a Podo tree. No other mountain has Podos to equal Elgon's. The odd one is found in wooded spruits at 6,000 feet, but the great Podo belt on Elgon begins about 8,000 feet. It is evergreen, has a narrow foliage looking like pine needles in the distance. It has green ball-shaped seeds, not cones. At lower altitudes it looks like a mighty oak in shape, rising about ninety feet, with a huge rough bole and a many-branching crown. In its perfect habitat on Elgon it dwarfs all else in majesty. It can grow over fifteen feet in diameter at shoulder height and rises clear in one huge stem for over a hundred feet and then branches to a great oaklike crown another fifty feet and more above. The foresters reckon their life at over fifteen hundred years. I have seen a grove of Californian Redwood trees. They are older, larger and taller, but I think for sheer majesty the Podo claims equality. Medium-sized Podo makes a timber of fine larchlike quality. Every night we dine off a wide table made of one Podo plank. Thanks be to God no Kenya saw-miller has yet been able to tackle some of the great forest monarchs.

There are great twenty-foot bamboo brakes in the forest, mostly between 8,000 and 9,000 feet, eerie stretches with only elephant trails among them, silent places and hard with their fallen stems to traverse. In the distance they look like downs of pale grass. At about 11,000 feet the forest thins to scrubby lichen-bearded trees and ends in heath with giant senecios and everlasting plants to mark your path to one of Elgon's many summits surrounding its seven-mile-wide crater. It is broken by volcanic cliffs and at least one giant gorge. Yet from the crater's lip the whole crater really looks like a downland subsidence a million years away from our own time. Once I climbed to its flat-topped summit, the most prominent feature on the Kenya side of the crater. It was walking-climbing only except for a few yards on hands and knees in a narrow fissure. Although there was a slight haze, distance from this summit was beyond comprehension, because it is the lonely mountain. We camped for two nights on the forest's upper edge at about 11,000 feet. It was a safari with donkeys for porters. Three miles away, and perhaps five hundred feet below us, were two Elgon Masai flat-roofed long huts made of peat and heath. It was all the life we saw except for the odd bird and one red forest duiker racing head low to escape us. All night there were seven great fires kept blazing to keep the heathland lion from eating our donkeys. On the wetter trails were buffalo and elephants' tracks. The district commissioner and the forest officer were my companions. I shared a tent with the elderly forest officer. I remember that as the tent-flaps flickered in the counter-lion fires and the southern cross showed through the opening, the forest officer lulled me to sleep with observations on Aristotle, Epictetus and Apollonius of Tyana. He was a great classical scholar, utterly charming, but vague and woolly as a forest officer. He was glad to find an understanding audience. Next morning we broke the ice on our water-pitchers, and no donkeys had been eaten. . . .

The forest is always unexpected. Once, sitting quiet in a gentle dream, I suddenly caught a flutter in the bush and turned my eyes but not my head. Only a few yards away was a green and gold and carmine smallish turaco with his crested head. He shifted suddenly from branch to branch about me as turacos do. Then I lost sight of him in thicker foliage. I waited but he did not return, and I have never seen his sort again. He was one of the forest species with a small territory of his own; it is only by rarest luck that he appears, and only when one is still for a long time.

A Knot of Roots Earl of Portsmouth.

In the forests of the night
William Blake

Somehow or other these bamboo forests seem mysterious and uncanny. The noise of the *panga* as it cuts through the stout stems; the noise of the fallen bamboos being hauled out of the way or stamped underfoot; the noise of the wind among the bamboo tops – somehow they all disturb and irritate the mind. Even the noise of the porters, the cheerful laughter and the chaffing and the squabbling, sounds hollow and unnatural. You move along with an undefined sense of insecurity. You feel as though you were walking through a tunnel. The stout stems of the bamboos rattle together, swayed by a wind you cannot feel; above you in the thickest parts, their grass-like leaves interlace with beard-moss and climbing plants, until the canopy almost keeps out the sun, whose light breaks fitfully on to your path. A steady drizzle sets in, the thick mist comes down and hangs like a pall over the forest. The mossy turf underfoot becomes sodden as a sponge and the column advances with muffled tread, almost without sound. And still you carry with you the vague sense of discomfort, almost of danger. . . .

Perhaps at the end of an hour's march you may sit down with your back to a friendly tree trunk, a rarer find now, and watch the resting porters and listen to their chatter. Even then, you are still oppressed by the surrounding silence. You feel that you are in a small circle of sound and that all around is utter silence, a silence before some indefinite catastrophe. Yet there is no feeling that you and your men are alone, for as you idly sit against your trunk you feel that somewhere watching eyes are observing you through the impenetrable growth, watching until you all pass on, until you hand back the forest to immemorial silence. You stare through the close columns of bamboos, but you see no movement; you only feel that something is there. You contemplate the fretwork of the bamboos against the sky, but your mind is disturbed by the gentle swaying of their canopy. You watch the porters cutting young bamboo shoots. Suddenly your eye is caught by a long frond on one of the bamboo stems near by; without warning it has become unaccountably agitated. You look again. You see that all the other fronds from the same stem preserve the pervading stillness of their surroundings, and only this one is waved this way and that, up and down and round and round, like a signaller's flag. You watch more closely. You can see no reason for this behaviour. At first you think there must be a lizard, or perhaps a rat, among the leaves that lie heaped up around the roots. But there is nothing at all. And even while you are vaguely puzzling at this mystery, the movement stops as suddenly as it had begun. It stops, but its impress is left with you; and even this small happening, mysterious and incomprehensible, troubles your mind. But in sober reality it is not the waving frond, not the chance of becoming lost, not the tremendous presence of unseen elephants and buffaloes and leopards, but a feeling of littleness among vast, silent, incalculable surroundings that steals from you confidence and even peace of mind. You become as one in a dream, who traverses a nightmare forest, waking and falling asleep by turns, a prey to unimaginable fears.

Kenya Mountain E. A. T. Dutton.

Mountains

The silence of Mount Kenya's peaks.

Their ethereal beauty holds you breathless. The great silence, the subtle stillness that broods over all, the dazzling serenity, sets you gasping. The peaks struck us then as something incomparably beautiful, something dazzling and hard, unmoved and invincible, waiting for us to come and go, and leave them again to their unending solitude. Prometheus might have been chained here. . . . And then, look down at your feet, and there you will see those glorious ones reflected in the green and brown waters of the tarn. A moment passes, and that dream view will fade and pass away. A glance upwards will show you that it has been obscured by clouds drifting high above. You look back once again, over the way you have come, and you will see hurrying, flying mists setting out for the snows from the valley below. They stream through the Nithi Gorge like banners of the pagan gods. What are these flying phantasies? Their speed, their strange shapes, their unending evolutions make them unlike anything you have witnessed below. Surely, you say, surely they must be evil exhalations prepared in the dark caverns far below the earth, and sent forth through the grey abyss of the nether world, to obscure the clear air and cloudless skies above.

And, at the end of the day, when the sun drops behind the peaks, the sky becomes a miracle of colour. . . . When it is all over, I have felt as though I have listened to the beautiful voice of a fine singer. There is a point in the sun's setting which is the highest, most poignant note before the voice dies away into an enchanted silence. Everything for one moment is still; it is a stillness made the deeper by the desolate and void surroundings. For some reason, sunset in Africa always brings a momentary silence, a pause – a silence "when you may hear the shadows of the leaves as they fall on the ground" – and then, in less empty surroundings, there is a happy chorus from frogs, and grasshoppers and night birds and the hyrax, and the many prowlers of the night. Sometimes you may hear the deep note of the lion, or the bark of the leopard, or the inhuman cackle of the hyena. But here on the mountain the silence is complete. When that still moment has passed, when the sun's reflection no longer lights up the sky, perfect silence begins her reign and the peaks stand out, strongly silhouetted against the cold blue of the western sky.

Kenya Mountain E. A. T. Dutton.

The flowers of the forest.

Towards evening we were within sight of Marsabit Mountain, and near enough to get some idea of the vast extent of the forest. At dusk we reached the "kudu board", which forbade the shooting of greater kudu within thirty miles of the government station. Here the road began slowly to rise. There had been enough rain showers on the mountain to cause some boggy patches which accounted for our taking nearly five hours to cover the last thirty miles. After the dust and heat of the day the forest-scented air was cool and delicious, and the moon was beautiful. I think Gerald had stage-managed my arrival to coincide with the full moon. The lichen-festooned forest looked magnificent, and it was bright enough to see many many miles when a break in the cosy little grass-covered hills on the other side of the road gave one an uninterrupted view over the desert country below.

In spite of the short night and the exhaustion and excitement of the long preceding day, the dawn chorus woke me early next morning. As the first fingers of light steal across the sky, spontaneously every bird on the mountain bursts out singing, and sings its heart out to greet the coming day. Then abruptly it stops, as though too much emotion were bad for birds, and a short deep silence follows. But, like the call to prayer from the mosque, it is the sign for the day to begin, and the early morning noises bring the small township vividly to life.

The anvil bird in the forest starts up for the day with its single pleasing note that never tires. From the village comes the peaceful tutter-tutter of the little "posho" mill where the maize is ground down for rations. The donkeys bray on their way to the well. The crows caw as they wheel hopefully above the plantations. Occasionally there is the wild disturbing cry of a kite high above the forest. The cattle are lowing in the milking enclosures the other side of the little town. From the police lines comes a bugle call, and the sound of the police askaris drilling on the square. Someone in the forest picking up firewood sings to keep the animals away. The breeze stirs the huge papery banana leaves. . . .

There is no high ground between Marsabit and the Indian Ocean, and the low-flying clouds meet nothing before they reach the forest-covered mountain; this keeps the place wonderfully green and full of flowers. . . .

There were little pearl or pale pink gladioli by the thousand and blue butterfly bushes ablaze with flowers and buzzing with contented bees. The hills were carpeted with a small creeping shrub whose pinky-mauve flowers from a distance look like early heather; and jasmine bushes covered with sweetly scented flowers. There was also a waste-paper flower that looks like a piece of crushed white tissue paper but has the spicy scent of clove carnations.

There were flowers even in the forest; some slopes were carpeted with red fuzzy lilies and along the watercourses the yellow bauhinia grew, all the more beautiful for the vast numbers of butterflies and dragonflies which flickered and hovered over it. There were ferns everywhere, and sometimes one had the good fortune to find a cascade of perfect little orchids with an exquisite scent. There was also a very common tree in the forest that had flowers like lilies-of-the-valley, and had the same perfume. When the flowers began to fall they formed a thick creamy carpet and every step one took released more perfume. And besides all these flowers there were ridges which were white with mushrooms.

To My Wife – Fifty Camels Alys Reece.

Lakes

Africa's largest lake, Victoria Nyanza, is trisected by the boundaries of Kenya, Uganda and Tanzania. Sighted by John Hanning Speke in 1858, twenty-five years later Joseph Thomson reached its shores.

Half an hour sufficed to bring us to the top of a low range of hills, and there lay the end of our pilgrimage – a glistening bay of the great Lake surrounded by low shores and shut in to the south by several islands, the whole softly veiled and rendered weirdly indistinct by a dense haze. The view, with arid-looking euphorbia-clad slopes shading gently down to the muddy beach, could not be called picturesque, though it was certainly pleasing. This scene was in striking contrast of all the views of African lakes it had yet been my privilege to see. In all previous cases I had looked down from heights of not less than 7,000 feet into yawning abysses some thousands of feet below; but here I stood on an insignificant hill and saw it gradually subsiding to the level of the great sheet of water.

We had no patience, however, to stand and take in all the details of the scene, we were too eager to be on the actual shores. An hour's feverish tramp, almost breaking into a run, served to bring us to the edge of Lake Victoria Nyanza, and soon we were joyously drinking deep draughts of its waters, while the men ran in knee-deep, firing their guns and splashing about like madmen, apparently more delighted at the sight of the Lake than I was – though doubtless the adage held good here, as in so many cases, that still waters run deep.

When my escort had thus effervesced to some extent they gathered round, and the good fellows, knowing that my dearest wish had been attained, shook hands with me with such genuine heartiness and good-will that they brought tears to my eyes. . . .

Next day I rested from my labours with the delicious consciousness that a great feat had been accomplished and that I had home as the new beacon-star ahead to direct my wandering footsteps. Next day, finding ourselves among a very pleasant people, we laid aside our natural reserve, and, pocketing our high dignity, we set all the young people of the village to trip it. In the cool of the evening Martin and I illustrated the "poetry of motion" as practised in Malta and Scotland; that is to say, Martin tried to initiate the damsels into the mysterious charm of the waltz, while I showed them how to do the "fantastic" in the spirited movements of a Scotch dance. Need I say that Martin was simply nowhere, while they became enthusiastic over my performance.

Through Masai Land Joseph Thomson.

Birds of calm sit brooding on the wave.
John Milton

The open waters of the lagoons were covered with water-lilies, bearing purple or sometimes pink flowers. Across the broad lily-pads ran the curious "lily trotters," or jacanas – richly-coloured birds, with toes so long and slender that the lily-pads support them without sinking. They were not shy, and their varied colouring – a bright chestnut being the most conspicuous hue – and singular habits made them very conspicuous. There was a wealth of bird life in the lagoons. Small gulls, somewhat like our black-headed gull, but with their hoods grey, flew screaming around us. Black and white kingfishers, tiny red-billed kingfishers, with colours so brilliant that they flashed like jewels in the sun, and brilliant green bee-eaters, with chestnut breasts, perched among the reeds. Spur-winged plover clamoured as they circled overhead, near the edges of the water. Little rails and red-legged water-hens threaded the edges of the papyrus, and grebes dived in the open water. A giant heron, the Goliath, flew up at our approach; and there were many smaller herons and egrets, white or parti-coloured. There were small, dark cormorants, and larger ones with white throats; and African ruddy ducks, and teal and big yellow-billed ducks, somewhat like mallards. Among the many kinds of ducks was one which made a whistling noise with its wings as it flew. Most plentiful of all were the coots, much resembling our common bald-pate coot, but with a pair of horns or *papillæ* at the hinder end of the bare frontal space.

African Game Trails Theodore Roosevelt.

Lake Turkana is notorious for sudden, savage storms which make sailing on its waters extremely dangerous. In the 1930s George Adamson, future game warden and lover of lions but then a penniless prospector for gold, made an unorthodox crossing with two companions.

I was dozing off when Nevil suddenly remarked: "Instead of walking two hundred miles around the end of the lake, what about going across it?" I thought, "Poor Nevil, at last the hardships have proved too much for him, he has gone off his head"; indeed, I felt quite alarmed. Go across the lake – in what? But after Nevil had explained his idea in detail and knowing that he had been an amateur boat builder, I became infected by his enthusiasm. We talked far into the night, discussing ways and means of building a boat. Two days later we reached the narrowest point of the lake where we judged the distance across to be only about twelve miles. Indeed the opposite shore looked absurdly close and through our glasses we could even see small bushes growing on sandbanks.

The camp we chose for building the boat was at the mouth of a large sandy river-bed called the Serr el Tommia. This means the River of the Elephants. Here there was a certain amount of acacia timber but it was impossible to find a straight piece of wood, so we had to take small pieces and bind them together with a thong; fortunately there was shade under which to work. Meanwhile, after patching them up, I sewed a couple of canvas ground sheets together with the stout thread we used for repairing pack saddles – I was the sewing expert and Nevil the designer of the hull of the boat. Then came the most difficult task: binding the sticks together into the semblance of a boat frame. We used strips of raw hide for this purpose.

At last, on the 9th of June, the hull was ready. We made oars from acacia poles bound to boards taken from donkey boxes. A mast was stepped and a sail fashioned from our canvas bed-rolls. Nevil even contrived a most ingenious rudder and lee-board out of pieces of donkey boxes. All we now had to do was to wait for a favourable wind, launch the boat, set the sail and loll back in comfort while being wafted gently across the lake. How we pitied our staff and donkeys having to trudge through the heat and across the lava. . . .

That evening we foolishly left the boat on the beach, loaded down with stones to prevent it from blowing away, and retired to our camp under the acacias. Next morning we found it a wreck; jackals had eaten all the thongs binding the frame. At first we were very depressed; the outlook was bleak indeed, since we now had no transport, and also no food. But the way the thing had happened was so funny that in the end we roared with laughter. We set-to and rebuilt the boat, using the inner bark of acacia trees for binding. This entailed considerable labour as all the suitable bark trees were over a mile inland and, besides this, since we had sent off our remaining provisions of dried meat with the foot party, we had to look for food which was not easy to find, for at this point of the lake game was scarce and fish almost non-existent. Fortunately, along the river bed there were thickets of *mswaki* or toothbrush scrub (*Salvadora persica*), which carried bunches of fruit, not unlike the English blackcurrant in appearance and flavour, but with a tang of nasturtium. However, *mswaki* berries alone were not sufficient to keep us going, and we had to spend a great deal of time foraging for more solid fare.

On one occasion I came on a goose sitting on its nest up in a thorny acacia tree. If I fired from below, undoubtedly I should hit it, but at the same time smash any eggs it might be sitting on; painfully and cautiously I climbed another thorny tree a few yards away until I was on the same level as the goose. Very carefully I took aim and blew its head off. That night we had three lovely fresh eggs and a tender goose. Next day Nevil returned to camp beaming – he had collected a dozen goose eggs. We told Yusuf to boil the lot and sat down in happy anticipation at having four eggs apiece. Unfortunately they were in a rather advanced state of development, but beggars can't be choosers, so we ate the lot.

When at last we once again had a boat, violent gales were blowing from the south and there could be no question of our sailing across. We built our hopes on the fact that at noon the wind usually dropped and a few hours later there was flat calm which lasted until about nine or ten pm. We decided therefore to row across during the period of calm, hoping we could make the opposite shore before the gale got up again. As the sun set about six thirty pm we should have to make part of the crossing in the dark. We had no option.

At three pm, ten days after the donkeys had left, we launched the boat and set off. Nevil and I rowed like mad and Yusuf bailed with an old cooking pot. As we progressed he was kept increasingly busy. By dark we judged ourselves to be half-way across. As there was no moon it was not possible to see the western shore but we could faintly discern the outline of the Loriu Hills which gave us a guide. Rowing doggedly, our hands raw and bleeding from the chafing of the rough wood of the oars, we had lost count of time when, suddenly, I heard a distant sound. We stopped rowing and listened, thinking it was the wind and meant the end of our chances. Then I recognized the noise as the croaking of multitudes of frogs. This meant that we must be near land. We redoubled our efforts and half an hour later hit the western shore. In the darkness it was impossible to tell where we had landed; all we knew was that it was on a pebbly beach.

My thoughtful mother had again provided a half-bottle of brandy with her usual instruction as to conditions in which we might open it. Nevil agreed with me that the appropriate emergency had arisen, so we shared it between us, pitying poor Yusuf who, being a devout follower of the Prophet, could not join in. Half an hour after we had landed the gale started, and blew like fury for the remainder of the night and till late into the morning. Had it caught us out at sea the boat could not have lived for more than a few minutes.

Bwana Game George Adamson.

Beside Lake Turkana.

My father-in-law spent many years walking in the country around Lake Turkana. One day he was visited in his tent by an old man. His face was grand with age and wrinkles, and he wore nothing but his leather apron and beads. His eyes were wise with the years and intensely human. Alfred and he talked many hours into the late evening in a halting version of his language which Alfred had picked up. The sun began to drop like a golden ball into the surface of the green water. The night wind began to blow, taking with it gusts of sand across the desert. The two men grew silent. Then the old Turkana summed up their thoughts. "You and I" he said, "are like two cows, one black and one white, but we belong to the same herd." The truth of this statement rings down the years and is precious in its expression of human meeting and response.

Different Drums Michael Wood.

The tragedy of Africa.

Africa has been described as "miles and miles of bloody Africa," and the emptiness of great tracts of land is oppressive. Great plains of scorched grass and thorn, a grey emptiness during the day, turning to a burnt sienna in the evening. The great hills and volcanoes lie athwart the plains like monsters in profound sleep, their flanks scarred by the erosion of countless centuries, and in contrast, the high forested hills have withstood the weathering but are now threatened by another enemy – the growing population who now survive famine, disease, and premature death as a result of modern medicine. It is a triumph of Western civilization, but it will be the tragedy of Africa. The hypodermic syringe is man's worst enemy, more deadly than bombs, for a man can live without the former, but civilizations will pass by reason of famine. The African worships the "sindano," or needle, as more potent than any medicine or charms, and such is the power of mind over matter that an injection of distilled water is preferred to no injection, because the cure lies in the charm of the needle and not in the contents of the syringe.

Dimbilil: The Story of an African Farm Errol Whittall.

The Capital

1899

A sergeant once set up a tent
And pitched a capital.
John Roberts

Nairobi in the month of May 1899, the month and year in which we moved camp to this place, may be described thus: A bleak, swampy stretch of soggy landscape, wind-swept, devoid of human habitation of any sort, the resort of thousands of wild animals of every species. The only evidence of the occasional presence of human kind was the old caravan track skirting the bog-like plain.

The Genesis of Kenya Colony R. O. Preston.

The first man to camp on the site was said to be Sergeant Ellis of the Royal Engineers.

1902

But Nairobi was changing. The administrations of both Whitehouse (chief railway engineer) and Ainsworth (assistant commissioner) had converged upon it, bringing some five or six thousand men. Buildings, tents and shanties were rising on the soft lands around the swamp. The Masai kraals had been shifted from north of the river down to the Ngong. . . . The station was finished, and a road west of it to the Nairobi River. The road was named (predictably) Victoria Street and was the main Nairobi thoroughfare. Near to the station Wood's Hotel was rising. There were many familiar names. Boustead and Ridley had come from Mombasa to build a European Club (always a priority); George Stewart & Co. had a circle of warehouses; and a German named Huebner was building a trade-post for Lansing & Co. Below the bridge Alidina Visram had formed the nucleus of a bazaar. There was a half-built soda-water factory under the name of Jeevanjee (that astute Indian who had already made a fortune from railroad contracts). The place was unstill. It vibrated with noise and a febrile air of urgency.

Across the river John and Ina Ainsworth had built their house. It was a low white bungalow and the ground around it was fenced and planned for the flowers and vegetables they would grow. It was named Daraja. Below them Nairobi was naked of trees. But they planned to clothe it. This was to be a capital. It needed the dignity of avenues, the shade of leaves. The important roads were already dug for the planting of eucalyptus trees, the holes which would take the roots spaced so that a bullock-team might turn. Even the swamp would be drained, the papyrus cut and the soil turned for the seeds of vegetables.

The town was vividly described by a missionary from the Sagala Mission Station: ". . . The shacks, or landies as they are called, lean into each other to join and shut out the light. It is a labyrinthine place in which people and rats live together in a common squalor. The ground squelches under the feet like the crust over a morass and one treads with care around great piles of garbage and open gutters transporting night-soil to one or other of the big open cesspools. Here, they say, one can cut one's finger and it will fester within an hour.

"The town has already divided into sections. The Indian commercial district and the bazaar sprawls over several acres and adjacent to it is the market for produce, vegetables and meat. The filth is incredible. Garbage rots in uncleared heaps. Rats abound. Meat and other edibles hang within inches of human ordure and all of it stinks in the tropical sun. The market area gives way to the Dhobi Quarter, a gloomy alley of brown men and women all scrubbing feverishly at a variety of clothes and fabrics and where the stenches of pollution are joined by the smells of sour steam and yellow soap. One crosses the stepping-stones of the Nairobi River to official residences and newly-cut roads leading to the Military Barracks. Here, all is good order and cleanliness but, again, it is evidently thought proper that sewage should run along open cement channels and into a river from which most of the population draws its water."

The Iron Snake Ronald Hardy.

1909

Nairobi has one charm that should not be denied it. That is the fine broad, well-metalled main street that runs for more than a mile straight from the railroad depot to the Norfolk Hotel.

I cannot fancy any other mile of roadway in semi-civilized Africa so interesting. Farmers, Boers, civil officers, and soldiers very smartly dressed, in well-fitting canvas or khaki, and last, but by no means least, the rare Englishwoman, far more admired and petted here than she ever is at home, in every sort of dress and undress and on every sort of "mount" – pony, mule, donkey, bicycle, in rickshaw or wagon, motor-car or camel cart – passes ceaselessly up and down.

There is movement and colour everywhere. Smart black women, often with very fine figures, in their most picturesque cotton togas, stand in groups at many a corner, laughing and chaffing the idle native porter as he saunters by, while hundreds of their more virtuous (let us hope), and much more naked sisters, stand in companies or squat on the ground outside some Indian's store or contractor's office, a black baby in an unspeakably oily bag at their breast, and sixty pounds of mealy meal, tightly bagged, slung by a headstrap, and carried low down behind their shoulders. Yes, I never can get tired of sauntering in Nairobi main street.

The Europeans, whose bungalows dot the wooded hills that on two sides surround the town, have a fine view over the Athi plains. With Zeiss glass it is still possible to see immense herds of game – harte beste, zebra, gnu, Grant's and Thompson's gazelles – feeding. Thirty miles away stands Donyea Sabuk – a partly wooded precipitous hill; rising some three thousand feet, and round its base – within a circle of a few miles, I suppose it is no exaggeration to say, that twenty white men have been killed or mauled by lions.

The flowers in Nairobi are a delightful surprise and wonder. Even in the dusty streets of the town they are plentiful. In poky little ill-kept gardens, or on unsightly corrugated iron roofs they climb and twine. When some pains are taken with them, and they are tended and watered in drought, they bloom and flourish as Italian roses do, only instead of blooming as these, for a few weeks only, at Nairobi roses bloom nine months in the year. Roses, passion flowers, pomegranates, orange trees, Bougainvillea, and many more, make scores of cheap little houses seem bowers of delight.

The Land of the Lion W. S. Rainsford.

Government House, 1920–2

One solemn duty of loyal subjects out on a spree is the writing of their names in the book at Government House. It is no longer the adventure it was when Sir Edward Northey's Zoo were for the most part at large in the grounds, and the startled visitor might meet a wart-hog or hyena in the porch.

Meals at Government House were most exciting for the same reason. I have often longed to propound it as a social conundrum to the lady dealing with such matters in *Home Chat*: "What should one do at a big dinner-party, when something with claws seizes one's leg, tearing one's stockings – and in the case of a gentleman, his trousers – and the host noticing a disturbance, calls down the table, 'It is only the cheetah'?" My love of wild nature failed me for a moment on another occasion when we were staying there, and a half-grown lioness bounded into the room. She was only looking for tit-bits, some fat ham or curried beef, but I followed her with a nervous eye as she frisked hoydenishly round the room. The Governor was absolutely without fear, and had a wonderful gift for handling wild animals: he would stroke the leopards growling uneasily on their chains near the flagstaff in the dusk, and go into the lion's house, a solid structure of cement and iron bars, to make friends.

Race Week, 1926

The thrill of my first polo tournament dwarfed for me every other event of that week. The groups of ponies belonging to the different clubs, some first-class imported animals, some country-breds, a very few carefully picked Somalis, were all wonderfully well turned out, the muscles under their shining coats rippling as they moved in the sunlight. The KAR band were wrestling, wonderfully successfully, with a new foxtrot near the tea pavilion; the little buglers, supremely conscious of immaculate smartness, sold programmes up and down the long line of cars. On the ground itself a breathless struggle was taking place in the finals of the Connaught Cup, the blue shirts of Njoro and the yellow-coated, yellow-martingaled Nyeri men striving hotly to score a goal in the last minutes of the last chukker. When the excitement over Nyeri's win had died down a little, there was a rush for tea, a sumptuous affair in the transformed pavilion, – usually a dreary shed, open on one side, the dusty repository of a few broken chairs. Then the Governor's wife gave away the cups before she and HE and some of their house-party stepped into the big Government-House car flying a tiny Union Jack from the bonnet, and were whisked down the dusty road, followed a moment later by a stream of cars of every make and age, from a baby Austin and a rattling old Ford to a Hudson super-six and a Rolls-Royce. . . .

Every night in Race Week is a gala night at Muthaiga, the low stone-built club (low architecturally, of course) four miles from the centre of Nairobi. Usually deserted except at lunch time and in the evenings, the club is thronged all that week, every bedroom and annexe is booked months ahead, the drives are blocked with cars. We had a large party one year for the New Year's Ball, several friends from home all deliciously apprehensive of what the night would bring forth. With all its respectability, Muthaiga has managed to acquire among the uninitiated a darkly-intriguing reputation for bacchanalian revelry. Dinner was an invigorating preliminary, in the long, crowded dining-room and its annexes beyond, specially built for the occasion, of interwoven papyrus stems, and lit with Chinese lanterns. We were still sitting over coffee and cigarettes when the band struck up. We adjourned hastily to dance while there was still room to move in the ball-room. There was a thrill in the air born of the feeling that every one was determined to enjoy themselves to the full, making the most of every moment until beer and bacon and eggs should take the place of morning tea. In the olden days in Kenya every one knew every one else; now that our white population has risen to over 12,000, that is scarcely possible any longer, yet at a Muthaiga New Year's Ball you feel instinctively that your neighbour is your oldest and dearest friend. Denser and denser grew the crowd till the crowning moments just before midnight when all the lights were put out. There was a breathless pause in the babel of voices, and then as the light flashed on again, showing the hands of the clock at twelve, we all linked hands in swaying ecstatic circles while we sang the old year out and the new year in. Then a rush for the wide gravel space outside. Chinese lanterns and fairy lights swaying in the tall clumps of feathery papyrus, where the towering bonfire, twenty feet of paraffin-soaked logs, was being lit. . . . A week of Muthaiga nights, sandwiched between the strenuous days, make most people thankful for a breathing space if they are going on to any of the polo tournaments that follow the one in Nairobi, and they are only too glad to settle down again on their farms if they are not polo players, and are dependent on the farm earnings for bread and butter and their passages home.

Kenya Days Aline Buxton.

1929

The train stopped for us to eat a very unpalatable dinner at a station. We got to Nairobi about 8 am next morning and, on Mr Dobbs's advice, I went to the New Stanley Hotel. It was dirty and inefficient and full of white tykes. For almost the first time in my travels I was "annoyed", in the legal sense, by men on the stairs and in sitting-rooms. Rowdy groups were always drinking and hanging about the entrance-hall. Indeed, my expectation that all the people of Kenya, if politically wrong-headed, were socially impeccable, got a rude shock. As far as I could see

Nairobi was largely peopled with young men wearing corduroy plus-fours or shorts, lurid green, orange, blue and purple shirts, and Stetson hats. Some had revolvers in their belts. They imparted a certain reckless Wild West atmosphere to the town but some of them, to judge by their looks, would have to be very careful if they were not to become "poor whites" in the almost technical South African sense.

Nairobi itself is a most disappointing town. I had expected something rather smart and well-built. It is one of the shabbiest and shoddiest towns I have seen in my travels, which is saying a great deal. There are hardly any pavements and the roadway itself is most primitive. You either stumble through mud or are blinded by gritty dust. The only decent public building is the railway office. (Government House is outside the town). Most government offices are tumbledown tin shacks: the Supreme Court is like an abandoned warehouse.

East African Journey Margery Perham.

1930

The Nairobi my wife and I first looked upon had not given any thought to style or permanence, though the ambitions of those for whom it served as capital were already high-ranging. Far from matching such ambitions, its prevailing characteristics were shoddiness, paltriness in building, and for ways of movement either adhesive mud or choking dust. For a British Colony with a decisive rôle to play in Africa this Buffalo Bill frontier-post setting seemed to me bad; instead of teaching the young to value themselves and the heritage they were born to improve and enrich, it encouraged hand-to-mouth, poor-white sloppiness and sloth which spelt degradation for the unfolding promise of youth. I made up my mind within a week of my arrival to revolutionize all this. There was a loan fund available, a minor part of which had been allocated to a new Government House in Nairobi, before we came out. A splendid Government House in a sordid capital and unschooled Colony would not, however, do what seemed imperative for Kenya or Kenya's youth. So I got leave to build schools, law courts, hospitals and offices, as fast as local facilities would permit. But not on Public Works Department lines; Kenya deserved and needed beauty and dignity in what man raised upon her soil equal to her own spacious loveliness. Lord Delamere was always sympathetic in this, and in this direction I also had the strong support of my Secretary of State.

As Governor accordingly I spent more on building than any Governor before or after me, and I regret only that my successors did not follow my example while building was cheap as we reckon costs to-day. . . .

So far as I know, Kenya soon lost the feeling that I had built too much. There is now a second large Boys' School in Nairobi. . . . There is the MacMillan Library, the new building for Legislative Council, the Highlands Cathedral approaching completion, the Aga Khan's Mosque, large bank buildings, blocks of flats, imposing hotels, arcades and shops, wide, well-kept streets, and a statue of Lord Delamere. Nairobi has now received the charter of a City.

Kenya's Opportunity Lord Altrincham.

1931

We arrived in Nairobi a little before lunch time. I took a taxi out to Muthaiga Club. There was no room for me there, but the secretary had been told of my coming and I found I was already a temporary member. In the bar were several people I had met in the *Explorateur Grandidier*, and some I knew in London. They were drinking pink gin in impressive quantities. Someone said, "You mustn't think Kenya is always like this." I found myself involved in a luncheon party. We went on together to the Races. Someone gave me a cardboard disc to wear in my button-hole; someone else, called Raymond, introduced me to a bookie and told me what horses to back. None of them won. When I offered the bookie some money he said in rather a sinister way, "Any friend of Mr de Trafford's is a friend of mine. We'll settle up at the end of the meeting."

Someone took me to a marquee where we drank champagne. When I wanted to pay for my round the barman gave me a little piece of paper to sign and a cigar.

We went back to Muthaiga and drank champagne out of a silver cup which someone had just won.

Someone said, "You mustn't think Kenya is always like this."

There was a young man in a sombrero hat, trimmed with snake skin. He stopped playing dice, at which he had just dropped twenty-five pounds, and asked me to come to a dinner party at Torrs. Raymond and I went back there to change.

On the way up we stopped in the bar to have a cocktail. A man in an orange shirt asked if we either of us wanted a fight. We both said we did. He said, "Have a drink instead."

That evening it was a very large dinner party, taking up all one side of the ballroom at Torrs. The young lady next to me said, "You mustn't think that Kenya is always like this."

After some time we went on to Muthaiga.

There was a lovely American called Kiki, whom I had met before. She had just got up. She said, "You'll like Kenya. It's always like this."

Next morning I woke up in a very comfortable bedroom; the native boy who brought my orange juice said I was at Torrs. . . .

Another Nairobi scene; an evening picnic in the game reserve from Government House. We consist of the Acting-Governor and his wife; the ADCs, an agricultural expert from England, and the race-week house-party; the latter includes a whiskered cattle rancher, very tall and swarthy, in the clothes of a Mexican bandit; oddly enough he is called "Boy"; his wife is slight and smart, with enormous eyes and an adventurous past; she once rode alone from Addis Ababa to Berbera; she too has a queer name – Genessie.

We drive to a place called Lone Tree, disturbing herds of zebra and wildebeeste; their eyes flash bright green, dazzled by our spotlight. We make a detour and see some hyenas – but not as close as the one at Harar – and little jumping creatures called diks-diks. Meanwhile, the servants have lit a great bonfire and put motor cushions round it. We sit down and eat supper, the ADCs doing all the polite drudgery that makes most picnics hideous; presently most of the party fall asleep. . . .

Already, in the few days I had spent at Nairobi, I found myself falling in love with Kenya. There is a quality about it which I have found nowhere else but in Ireland, of warm loveliness and breadth and generosity. It was not a matter of mere liking, as one likes any place where people are amusing and friendly and the climate is agreeable, but a feeling of personal tenderness. I think almost everyone in the highlands of Kenya has very much this feeling, more or less articulately. One hears them grumbling about trade conditions, about the local government and the home government, but one very rarely hears them abuse the country itself as one hears Englishmen abroad in any other part of the world. . . . People were insistent that I should not regard Race Week as typical of the life of the country, because "the Happy Valley" has come in for too much notoriety in the past. No one reading a book about smart people in London or Paris takes them as representing the general life of the country; but it is exactly this inference which is drawn when a book is written about smart people in Kenya. Even in the set I met at Muthaiga, only a small number are quite so jolly all the year round. "Boy," for instance, owns the largest cattle farm in the country and, incredible as it sounds, knows almost every beast individually by sight. Of the settler community in general, the great majority are far too busy on their farms to come to Nairobi, except on an occasional predatory expedition to the bank or the Board of Agriculture.

Remote People Evelyn Waugh.

1963

Nairobi used to be one of the nastiest capitals in the world: dirty, dusty, squalid and at the same time pretentious, a frontier town whose sprinkling of flashily over-dressed safari visitors, minor film stars and local glamour-types, imitating celluloid white hunters, gave it an air of bogus Hollywood or failed St Tropez. Now it has become one of the most attractive and certainly the most flowery of capitals. Those banks of cherry-red and flaming orange bougainvillaeas, of ramping golden shower and other flowering shrubs and trees, which you pass through as you drive along the Princess Elizabeth Way (now Uhuru Avenue) must present one of the finest approaches to any city in the world, or at any rate on this continent.

Nairobi teems with bluebell-flowering jacarandas; hibiscuses and beds of succulents lurk in every spare corner. Most of the former stuffy little wooden rabbit-hutch-like buildings with rusty corrugated iron roofs have been replaced by glittering modern concrete towers of dubious merit but a good deal of dash, inventiveness and often colour, which goes well in this bright and brittle montane atmosphere.

The streets are lined with sun-reflecting, eye-assaulting parked cars and, at rush-hours, choked with opulent-looking traffic; every empty lot is a car-park crammed with vehicles and the scene of savage encounters around eight in the morning, when offices open, among converging commuters in search of parking space. In places, segments of empty lot have been fenced off, for some reason; and here, overshadowed by off-white, or light grey, or speckled concrete towers, little plots of maize have sprung up, tended by bare-footed Kikuyu women in their shapeless cotton dresses, bent industriously over their hoes among the modern buildings.

There's still, of course, plenty of squalor. Just off-centre, those grubby narrow streets lined with Asian shops smelling of spices, second-hand clothing and sweating humanity, and the narrow alleys, designed as sanitary lanes for night-soil collecting and smelling of urine, haven't changed; and, on the perimeter, there's still a vast, ever-growing, subsistence-level African population packed into accommodation that remains, for the most part, depressingly sordid – ugly little bare boxes dumped down on a hot, flat, treeless kind of wasteland, spattered with sentry-box latrines.

The City Council keeps re-housing people as fast as its rate-payers can manage, and all sorts of benefactors are weighing in with aid; but Nairobi is a magnet drawing Africans from the Ethiopian border to the shores of Lake Nyasa, from Zanzibar to the Mountains of the Moon, and the Council keeps pounding along behind the population statistics like a Kafka-type figure trying to catch a train that's perpetually just pulling out of the station. . . .

In 1947 Mr Peter Greensmith, equipped with no more horticultural training than war-time service in the Royal Navy could afford, walked with mounting gloom from the station along Government Road. Dusty, shadeless, unkempt and filthy – he remembers human excreta and a dead dog – the place stank.

Mr Greensmith's disgusted inclination was to take the next train back to Mombasa and never set foot in the place again. But he had the promise of a job with a firm of nurserymen. Some years later, he answered an advertisement, secured a junior municipal post and, remembering his dreadful first impression, resolved to do his utmost to brighten up the city.

Before long, he found himself in charge of its all but non-existent parks. I don't know when he started on the bougainvillaeas, which today give Nairobi half its character, these and the jacarandas and hibiscuses: horticulturally it's a bougain-villaea town. And now he revealed not only the greenest of fingers, but a talent for making plants play tricks. Bougainvillaeas and bignonias are creepers and before that had always crept, or climbed rather, clinging to veranda-posts, trees, roofs, walls, anything. Mr Greensmith obliged bougainvillaeas to stand on their own feet, like standard roses, and bignonias to creep about on the ground like a vetch;

hence the glories of Princess Elizabeth Way. The idea of turning bougainvillaeas into standards came to him, he says, in a flash one day when he noticed a creeper that had been snapped off in a storm.

Besides the major city park, umbrageous and set with flowering trees, little parks have sprung up in odd corners; every roundabout bulges with creepers and succulents, every verge with trained, obedient shrubs. No wonder the mayor, Alderman Charles Rubia, and his councillors are proud of what has been done.

Forks and Hope Elspeth Huxley.

1978

It was mid-morning and the open-air pavement terrace attached to the New Stanley Hotel was crowded with tourists dressed for Africa. Bush-shirts and sun hats banded with leopard skin of synthetic garishness were everywhere in evidence. Cameras and binoculars dangled from sun-tanned necks. German, French and American voices rang in the air. Out on the street was parked a convoy of zebra-striped Volkswagen vans. The smell of safari – of tented bush, of elephant, of hippopotamus, of lion – suffused the bright morning. Noisy traffic choked the broad expanse of Kenyatta Avenue. Fashionably dressed blacks streamed along the pavements, the men carrying briefcases, the women swinging handbags. Nairobi vibrated with cosmopolitan splendour. A crippled beggar, his knees padded with foam rubber, his hands encased in sandals, crawled nimbly on the periphery of the terrace. "Jambo . . . jambo . . ." The waiters, smartly dressed in white and green tunics, kept him at bay. A thorn tree, rising centrally from the terrace, threw a dappled green shade across the metal tables.

Without asking if they could, two Americans came over and sat down at my table. They were an oddly contrasting pair. One was well over six foot tall, slope-shouldered and concave-stomached. His hair, frizzed and teased out in "Afro" style, formed a dark, woolly halo; his skin, bronzed and toughened by exposure to the sun, was leathery in appearance. The other was at least six inches shorter and anaemically white. He had lank, shoulder-length hair. His pale blue eyes, unfocussed and restless, hinted at a kind of semi-idiocy. The tall one produced a roll of cigarette paper and a packet of loose tobacco.

"Got any stuff on you, Stan?" The idiot boy drummed his ivory-coloured fingers on the table.

"No," Stan said, carefully sprinkling tobacco down the length of the paper. "And even if I had I wouldn't let you score off me. You smoke too damned much, Andy."

"I feel awful, Stan." Andy's parted lips drooled as he watched Stan manipulate the tobacco.

"I'm not surprised," Stan said. "What sort of crap were you on last night?"

"They were only mandies, Stan."

"You'll kill yourself one of these days," Stan said. "But I'm not going to pay your funeral expenses." He ran his tongue down the edges of the paper and sealed the tube. "Why do you do it? Why do you feed yourself all that shit?"

"I get bored easily, Stan. I need a lift. . . ." He waved at two black girls. They came over. They sat down.

Stan lit the cigarette. He put his arm round the neck of the girl sitting next to him. "Why aren't you out and about looking for work, sweetie?"

"I want a beer," she said, pouting petulantly. "I'm tired." She was a strange-looking creature. The lobe of her right ear was missing – it looked as if it had been bitten off; her knees were patterned with blotched pink patches; a scar crossed one of her cheeks diagonally.

"Beer makes you fat, sweetie. It's bad for business. I don't get turned on by fat chicks. Not even by fat black chicks." He pulled her truncated ear. She scowled, shaking off his embrace, and snapped her fingers at a passing waiter. She ordered two beers.

"I'm not paying for two beers," Stan said.

"I'll pay for my own," the other girl said. Disdainfully, she flung a handful of coins on the table. She muttered something. Both girls laughed.

"What did she say?" Stan asked.

"Nothing."

Stan grabbed her wrist. "I want to know."

"She said that *mzungus* (white people) are all the same."

"Where'd you pick them up?" Stan asked Andy.

"She's a friend," Andy said. "I got lots of friends."

"Yeah . . ."

"I got lots of friends," Andy said. "Lots and lots of friends." His eyes roamed the terrace. "Everywhere I go I make friends . . ."

But Stan was not listening. He was looking speculatively at me.

"From distant parts?"

I nodded.

"What kind of currency are you carrying?"

I told him.

He clucked his tongue. "Sterling . . . that's not so good. Still, I could give you eighteen shillings to the pound."

I said I preferred to change my money legally.

He laughed. "Hear that, Andy? The guy says he prefers to change his money *legally*."

"The guy's a sucker," Andy said.

Stan leaned towards me. "How about a woman?"

"Not now, thanks."

"A boy?"

"You deal in those too?"

"I deal in most things – currency, dope, women, boys. I'll fix you up with anything you want. You could say I'm one of the pillars of the tourist trade in these parts."

"They allow you a work permit for that?"

Stan's laughter echoed across the terrace. "Hear that, Andy? The guy wants to know if we have work permits."

Even the girls were amused.

"We've got friends," Andy said. "We've got lots and lots of friends. When you got lots of friends like we have you don't need a work permit."

"In a place like this," Stan said, "you can get away with murder if you know the right people. Money *talks* in this country."

"Lots of friends," Andy said. "We've got lots and lots of friends."

"Business must be good."

"Booming," Stan said. "The only comparison is Jo'burg. Nairobi is the finest city north of South."

North of South Shiva Naipaul.

Circa *1980*

The sky was a hot clear blue. Not a promise of a drop of rain that August.

The drought had taken a heavy toll in the park. The ground was a deep dusty brown, bare and parched. Dried bits of grass stuck forlornly out of the numerous cracks like pleading tongues out of hell screaming for a drop of water. Dry leaves shed by the thirsty trees ran rustling in front of the light breeze. This city, in a desperate effort to keep itself beautiful, had watered the more delicate flowers planted like oasis islands at various points over the dirty brown park.

The vast park quietly shimmered in the oppressive sun. The boat-house sat sadly hunched over the shoulder of the lake, the dirty muddy water lapping softly at its withdrawn feet. Up the hill to the west the red-tiled roof of the cathedral was visible half-hidden among the tall dark blue gums, the gaunt walls giving it an appearance as ominous as the castle of Count Dracula. Among the trees higher up the hill, there were more modern fortresses, the ministerial offices, towering over the aged blue gums with youthful impunity, hundreds of glass windows winking at the park below. Across the park from the ministerial offices was the city itself, lying low, a dormant dragon growling with clogged-up traffic. The huge highway stretched taut between them restrained the city from intruding on the park.

From the park grounds, if one lay facing east, one looked up straight into the frowning faces of the parliament and city hall clocks. Every hour on the dot the two struck suddenly together, regulating the tired city's pulse and reminding the park loungers just how many hours they had wasted lying idle, pleading with them to get up and be useful. Mostly the pleas went unheeded. But every now and then a misplaced person rose with a start, squinted up at the clocks' accusing fingers and, brushing grass and dust from his bottom, slunk defeatedly across the highway into the city maze. Others shook their heads defiantly at the insistent clocks, cursed them loudly and, facing the other way, went back to sleep. These were the insolent few. If they had anywhere to go at all, they did not want to go there.

Cars brayed on the highway. Brakes shrieked. Ambulances wailed away, racing against death. Half a kilometre away trains whistled urgently. Time to go. Go where? The park people were there to stay. They had arrived. The sounds were sounds from another world.

On the stroke of one the dam burst. A flood of hungry office workers gushed out of the ministerial offices, and in a furiously ravenous torrent swept down the hill. They came in armies.

Time had once again thrown the floodgates open. They swarmed down the hill into the park, past the first icecream man, round the lakes to the eastern exit. The second icecream man blocked the only way on to the highway, determined to make a sale today. The swarm swirled round him and over him and away. Today, like yesterday and the day before, not one bar of icecream was bought by the hungry ones. Once across the highway, the waves disintegrated into individuals and dispersed. Some rushed for the meat-roasting places down River Road, others joined the queues at the numerous fish-and-chip joints where they dutifully swallowed soggy fried chips with watered-down ketchup. In a few seconds the thousand-or-so-strong swarm had been swallowed up by the yawning concrete jungle. With its usual idle curiosity the sleepy park witnessed this spectacle. The park waited. In an hour the tide would return.

The parched park was almost dead, alive only with a few idlers and the dust-raising wind, the dry fallen leaves scampering to hide from the hot breeze which, like the hungry humans, blew down the narrow path, across the highway and into the humming city. The icecream man's bell still rang lonely and unwelcome like a lost leper's warning bell.

Under the gnarled bare trees, in fact anywhere there was the slightest shade, a few men lay half awake hiding from the tormenting sun. A shaggy, thin man sat under a shrub, scratching numbers and letters on his black dry skin with a used match. By his side were the two oversize fruit baskets he had been selling from all morning and which he would resume hawking after the lunch break. Now he scratched his head with the matchstick and tried to balance the morning's sales. He mumbled to himself, cursed and, rolling up his trouser legs, continued writing on his thigh. Finally he flung the stick away and, wetting his palm with saliva, violently erased what he had scribbled. Then he fell unceremoniously on his back and covered his rough bearded face with two bony hands.

On the lake a couple of men paddled vigorously in two small hired boats. A few others sat on the cement bank, unshod feet swinging only a few inches above the dirty grey water and, ignoring the icecream man's cries, watched the boaters. With undivided interest they witnessed every move, every paddle stroke. Some sat alone muttering to themselves. Those who sat in twos or threes communicated only in monosyllables. Every day the same watchers watched the same rowers move their boats over the lake and under the bridges; every day unconsciously reacting to the maxim that spectating is the next best thing to participating.

Meja Mwangi *Incident in the Park.* From *An Anthology of East African Short Stories,* ed. Valerie Kibera.

1987

Foreigners who know Kenya tend to like it. Compared to most of its neighbours, they say, Kenya is paradise. It is pragmatic, generally efficient, and a pleasant place to visit. I arrived at Jomo Kenyatta Airport in Nairobi after leaving the Organization of African Unity summit in Addis Ababa. A policeman tried to hustle a handout, but he was polite and his uniform was clean. He scurried away when I suggested that importuning the public was bad form.

At the summit, Kenya had joined the chorus in demanding total isolation of South Africa. But I was back to reality. A lilting voice on the public-address system announced, "Olympic Airways for Johannesburg is boarding at gate number four."

In the comfortable hotels, lavish restaurants, and immaculate game parks, life can approach the idyllic. I visited a friend in the Ngong Hills, and hiked around the neighbourhood. Gardens were lush and the unmistakable African air was soft and peaceful. Night fell, and I flicked on what I thought was the light. A bloodcurdling howl arose, sending every neighbour within earshot leaping for his elephant gun. I had turned on the burglar-bandit-Mau Mau alarm.

Kenya grapples with its identity with a blend of pain and panache that only Africa can manage. It is a modern state, with the trappings of high technology. But in 1987 the cold chamber at Nairobi's morgue held a man locked in an ancient tribal conflict. Silvano Melea Otieno, a highly respected Kenyan lawyer, died of a heart attack in Nairobi. He was a Luo. His wife is an aristocratic descendant of Kikuyu chiefs. When she ordered the body buried in family ground in the Ngong Hills, Otieno's family objected bitterly. The body had to be buried in Luo territory, where survivors could make sacrifices. Luos did not leave their dead to wander alone in the bush.

The case went to the high court. Each day, Luos in traditional dress sobbed and danced outside the courtroom. Each evening, an anchorman in coat and tie reported the news on national television.

Squandering Eden Mort Rosenblum and Doug Williamson.

Mombasa

A Picture of Paradise.

Mombasa has all the look of a picture of Paradise, painted by a small child. The deep Sea-arm round the island forms an ideal harbour; the land is made out of whitish coral-cliff grown with broad green mango trees and fantastic bald grey Baobab trees. The Sea at Mombasa is as blue as a cornflower, and, outside the inlet to the harbour, the long breakers of the Indian Ocean draw a thin crooked white line, and give out a low thunder even in the calmest weather. The narrow-streeted town of Mombasa is all built from coral-rock, in pretty shades of buff, rose and ochre, and above the town rises the massive old Fortress, with walls and embrasure, where three hundred years ago the Portuguese and the Arabs held out against one another; it displays stronger colours than the town, as if it had, in the course of the ages, from its high site drunk in more than one stormy sunset.

The flamboyant red Acacia flowers in the gardens of Mombasa, unbelievably intense of colour and delicate of leaf. The sun burns and scorches Mombasa; the air is salt here, the breeze brings in every day fresh supplies of brine from the East, and the soil itself is salted so that very little grass grows, and the ground is bare like a dancing-floor. But the ancient mango trees have a dense dark-green foliage and give benignant shade; they create a circular pool of black coolness under-neath them. More than any other tree that I know of, they suggest a place to meet in, a centre for human intercourse; they are as sociable as the village-wells. Big markets are held under the mango trees, and the ground round their trunks is covered with hen-coops, and piled up water-melons. . . .

Out of Africa Karen Blixen.

Life with a Hindu family.

When I was there, the National Museums of Kenya were conducting a salvage operation on a Portuguese ship lying at the bottom of the sea just off the fort. People from several nationalities took part in this endeavour; divers went down from a special vessel anchored in the bay and at the fort rooms were set aside to catalogue and preserve the artefacts.

I came to know a Welsh girl attached to this operation and she introduced me to the Hindu family with whom she was staying, which led to my being invited to share their vegetarian meals at midday and in the evening and they also arranged for me to sleep at the temple of the Hindu Union. This family lived in the old town of Mombasa, in a house off an alley off a sidestreet off the main thoroughfare. As one pulled the bell cord outside their secretive yard gate they operated a system of pulleys from upstairs to unlatch the door. Passing through the courtyard and up the open-air stairs, one found oneself in a higgledy-piggledy but airy first-floor flat with rooms leading off in every direction, a kitchen, a scullery, various sitting rooms and bedrooms. The father, a prosperous business-man, was often away in Nairobi or Kisumu or abroad, but mother was the calm centre of the family, cooking mouthwatering meals and bringing up three teenage children. In one of their rooms they had an ashram, a little corner with figures of divinities in front of which they lovingly placed small offerings of food and flowers. This was not done from a sense of duty or to placate fate, but more out of gratitude for the blessings of life.

At the temple where I slept there was also an altar with various deities which was just as lovingly looked after by the priest. Every morning at ten past five and every evening at dusk he was joined by other residents of the temple and members of the Hindu community outside for a service of bell ringing. This was an energetic affair accompanied by the blowing of a conch horn into all four compass directions and on the first morning, when it started in the courtyard just outside my bedroom, I nearly fell out of bed. The evening service was a more sociable gathering; families arrived well before time and the women sat on the floor for a chat while their children played around the goddesses and in the courtyard. My abiding memory of these services is that they were happy celebrations of the end of the day.

The temple was a peaceful abode to which I always returned gladly. Within the bare walls of my room there was nothing except the iron bedstead and mattress, my bags and a huge rotary electric three-speed ceiling fan. A number of similar rooms were set aside for other needy travellers. We all shared tiled shower and wash facilities. My door gave on to the courtyard which was the haunt of thousands of pigeons cooing contentedly all day except when they inexplicably panicked and the whole flock took off in a tornado of flutterings to settle on the gutters and the temple spire. There were concrete benches around the courtyard, warmed during the day by the hot equatorial sun, and when at night I returned from my evening meal I would find them still warm and would sit and talk with temple residents or with fellow travellers until the air was cool enough for sleeping. Sometimes in the morning I woke up before the temple service started, for outside my room on the street side was the depot where newsboys collected the early editions of the papers, and on such occasions I could hear the haunting cry of the muezzin at the Baluchi Mosque not far away calling the faithful to prayer, and I might reflect for a few minutes on the undisturbed peace between the faiths which especially distinguishes life in Kenya.

The Kenya Magic John Schmid.

Dhows –

> It was so old a ship – who knows? who knows?
> – And yet so beautiful, I watched in vain
> To see the mast burst open with a rose,
> And the whole deck put on its leaves again.

James Elroy Flecker

Once the *kaskazi*, the north-east monsoon, is established, the Old Harbour prepares to receive the dhows. These sturdy, adventurous little craft have been coming to Mombasa since time immemorial across the Indian Ocean from Arabia, India and Somalia, transforming the Old Harbour from a sleepy backwater into a hive of activity.

There are several different kinds of dhow. Many are the large double-enders, with stem heads thrusting upwards and forwards. The rounded end of the projection is painted black with a white band, and often, near the tip, on the jackstaff, is a model aeroplane. These are the Booms which, in the main, come from Iran. Their raised poops narrow to a strong rudder post from which the rudder hangs. A tall painted flagstaff dominates the stern, and two pointed "toilet" boxes hang from the ship's side flanking the rudder.

The Sambuks are the next most numerous. These square-sterned vessels vary according to their port of origin, but all show the stem head curving upwards from the water-line to end just above the hull, with the forward edge reaching higher than the after edge. It resembles a scimitar cleaving the waters ahead. . . .

The most delicately carved and decorated ships are the Ghanjabs from Sur and the Kotias from India. The transom arches are usually much broader than those of the Sambuks, and looking out from the stern are five windows with curved pillars between them. Many parts of these ships are blessed with attractive carving. It is said that these are the females of the dhow fleet and therefore much care and attention is lavished upon their decoration. The Booms are their masculine counterpart.

There are several other varieties to be seen at the height of the season, including the quaint Badan or Bedeni with their tall rudders and rudder posts, the small Babnus with their masts raked far forwards, the Zarooks, and a small Baghla that is a constant visitor. Dhangis and a variety of ships that go under the general name Barig (a corruption of brig) come from India.

The dhows bring wares of many kinds for sale. Brass-studded chests are piled one on top of the other around the walls of the Customs House main hall, whilst the floor is covered with a great variety of carpets. Coffee pots and small money boxes fill up the unoccupied corners. Milling around are merchants and visitors eager to strike a bargain, while the dhow men sit and survey the scene. There are cargoes also of salt, fish, dates and, until recently, tiles.

In the Old Harbour the dhows lie four or five abreast alongside the jetty. Stevedores carry sacks of coffee and other foods on their backs to be tipped into the holds while the ships await the change of the monsoon which will speed them on their homeward journey. Very few rely on sail these days, and the sight of a dhow moving out of the harbour in full sail with the large lateen billowed out by the wind is comparatively rare. The small coastal dhows from Lamu are an exception.

The harbour empties rapidly once the *kusi* is established, the bustle in the godowns and on the jetties dies away, and the Old Port settles down to a period of

comparative lethargy until the next season comes round. Ocean-going dhows are now almost extinct.
Pioneers' Scrapbook, eds. Elspeth Huxley and Arnold Curtis.

– and the men who sailed in them.

It was one of those motionless afternoons in April when everything is veiled in a shroud of heat, the time of the year when the east coast of Africa holds its breath, a period of silence between the monsoons. The white and purple bougainvillaea bushes and the great baobab trees around my house stood out against the pale, hot sky, looking withered and exhausted as they waited for a breath of air to ripple through their leaves. Sibillo, my cat, lay panting on the straw mat beneath the rustic Arab bed on the veranda where I was reading. It was too hot to concentrate. The effort to hold up the book was too much and I let it fall to the floor. I looked out at the sea through the wide arches that frame the outer reef and the *mlango* – the passage into Kilifi Creek.

I heard a faint rustle in the bushes that flanked the tiny path leading to the beach. Three men moved slowly up the path; they did not see me. When I greeted them they looked at me in startled surprise; their haggard faces dripped with perspiration. They managed a tired smile when I asked them in Swahili what they wanted. "We are in trouble, Bwana," they said. One of them came forward and clutched my hand with both of his, bowing slightly as though he were going to kiss it.

The men wore faded *kikois* knotted round their waists and held in place with a leather belt. They carried *khanjars*, those magnificent curved silver daggers, fastened to their buckles. Limp cotton turbans were wound around their heads. Their weather-beaten faces, the distant look in their eyes, and their gnarled hands made me recognize them as sailors. They needed water: they came from a dhow, they said, and had been drifting at sea for ten days with a broken rudder. A passing *jahazi*, a small Lamu dhow, had brought them ashore and they needed help.

Lorenzo Ricciardi loaded up his motor-boat with water containers and, with the three sailors, sped out to the distressed dhow. She was carrying at least fifty passengers.

Bare to the waist, they wore dirty grey pieces of cloth and faded turbans; they were mostly tall and thin, with long sinewy muscles and sharp features, their glittering black eyes set in gaunt faces. I guessed the passengers were Somalis, and the crew were Arabs or Omani from the Arabian Gulf. The dhow was a *sambuk*, with one huge mast.

Their captain, the *nakhoda*, was one of the three men I had brought back with water and some timber to repair the rudder. It was only when we saw him among his people that we realized his rank. He gave orders in a soft yet firm voice; and the glances that he threw at his men and at the passengers as they moved the water-containers on to the dhow were enough to make everyone know he was in command.

A cargo of dried dates was piled high in the stern, with large cans of fat and dried fish. These were squashed under a faded green tarpaulin through which brown stains of sticky juice seeped on to the deck. Mysterious bundles wrapped in straw matting were strewn around, together with smaller packages of long rectangular shape – perhaps skins. Worn manilla ropes were heaped in brown hairy piles, and makeshift bedding had been arranged against them. Above all this mess towered the great mast. The tattered sail provided some shade. Sliced kingfish, their flesh orange and gold, hung from the spars and sent an evil stench downwind.

I tried to talk to the *nakhoda* using my sailor, Said, as interpreter. Said was a Bajun from Lamu Island and spoke some Arabic. Through him I learned that the dhow was out of Salalah in Oman, bound for Mombasa with a cargo of dried fish, dates and other merchandise. In a month or two it would load up with *boriti* (mangrove) poles in Lamu and sail home. I suspected that the passengers were mercenaries joining the Tanzanian Army – Somalis make good warriors.

When he bid them farewell they thanked us profusely, bending themselves in half and praising *Allah akbar*. He had heard their prayers, but I was the instrument He had chosen to save their lives. It was very moving.

The Voyage of the Mir-el-Lal Lorenzo Ricciardi.

Lamu

After the siesta.

My favourite time of day in Lamu is the late afternoon. Around 4.00 pm the town slowly begins to reawaken. Almost everyone has retired after the midday meal for a siesta, and upon re-emerging from their houses, the shopkeepers unlock the bolts on their doors and begin the best part of the day's business. This is the time when the fishermen and dhow crews come to buy their goods, having been too busy in the morning to do so. The shops are friendly places and news flickers from one to another. A crier goes past all the shops through the main streets, bellowing out advertisements for the film that will be shown in the evening which will very probably be an Indian musical. Many of the men make their way to the mosques to say their prayers and to chat with friends, for mosques in Lamu serve as social meeting places. Here the talk may well centre on religious topics interspersed with titbits of news from the Hadhramaut or elsewhere in the Indian Ocean where Lamu people may have friends or relatives. Strangers to Lamu usually gather at the mosques in the afternoon and, upon telling their news, they receive a hospitable welcome from the residents. The strangers have been led to the mosques by the sound of the *muezzin* calling the faithful to prayer, (now on cassettes).

By sunset, the town is a hub of activity. It is a traditional and particularly enjoyable pastime to walk along the seafront just as the sun begins to go down. There is a tendency for the various groups of people to walk together. The Swahili and Arab ladies, covered from top to toe in their black *buibuis*, but with their eyes carefully made-up with kohl, dart back and forth, visiting friends' houses and gossiping about who is with whom. The Ithnaashariya women gather in little groups together, their *buibuis* usually being a dark royal blue. The Arab men look the most aristocratic of Lamu's populace, and though they now lack the money to buy the colourful silks that they wore way back in Vasco da Gama's time, their waistcoats are still beautifully embroidered in front, sometimes in matching white thread, sometimes in pale beige. Often whole families gather together on the benches looking out to the sea towards Manda and the mangrove swamps.

In the early part of the evening, the aroma of charcoal-roasted meat pervades the streets throughout the southern part of town. Tiny kiosks sell roasted beef on skewers to the passers-by, and there are also small restaurants which offer Swahili cakes and other sticky sweets along with tea. Inside these places are long benches and trestle tables where mainly the Bajuns gather to spend the evening together. They take their tea in the old-fashioned manner, pouring it from their cup into the saucer and sucking it up.

Later on, the coffee vendors appear on the streets. They have lovely old brass pots which they set up on charcoal braziers on any street corner. They also have with them little buckets (sometimes old paint tins), filled with water in which they rinse the china cup that is used by everyone who buys a cup of coffee. Lamu coffee is not as thick as the Turkish variety, but it is heavily sugared and has a superb aroma. After supper, you find many men sitting on the benches outside their houses or outside the restaurants playing dominoes, the favourite game in Lamu. There are also games of *bao* and draughts. The boards vary considerably; at one time an enterprising soap company in Kenya printed the checkered squares on the back of their boxes of soap powder which must have boosted their sales in Lamu tremendously! Lots of these are seen around Lamu, but there are also many home-made boards. Quite a few of the Arab, Swahili, Bajun and African residents play rummy with dog-eared cards that have been cherished for years. It is said that the Portuguese introduced playing cards to East Africa.

Meanwhile, the ladies are up to other activities. Women's Lib takes a peculiar turn in Lamu. When a little girl reaches puberty she is usually strictly guarded inside the women's quarters of her home until a suitable husband is agreed upon by the family members. Before she is married, the older aunts explain to her the art of love, and both the Swahili and Arab women of Lamu are notorious for their skills in making love. The prospective bride is almost always a virgin, but she already knows how to give pleasure to a man. Quite often she is still under sixteen when married. Once she has a husband, she is freer than she has been since reaching puberty. She may not remain faithful to her husband, but keeps up appearances. If her husband loses his temper with her he may divorce her; indeed divorce is common in Lamu.

The wife's girl friends are very helpful in arranging rendezvous with lovers. Since men are not allowed at the parties women give for one another, it is very easy for a woman to borrow a friend's pair of shoes at such a time and if she wraps herself modestly up in her *buibui*, no one will recognize her when she goes out on the street. With the borrowed shoes (she usually borrows them from someone with an entirely different shape, so that woman won't be thought to be the one "out on the loose" either), she slips out of a back entrance of the house where the party is being held to go to wherever it is that she has agreed to meet her lover. If her husband happens to come to the house to pick her up from the party and take her home, the one who opens the door will of course not allow him entry to the women's quarters and will instead offer to go and fetch his wife for him. She finds out who knows where the wife has gone and sends a friend to get her while the husband waits. Back to the house via another entrance, the wife changes into her own shoes and demurely meets her husband. He accepts having had to wait for her, for everyone knows how difficult it is for a woman to break off a gossipy conversation with another woman! Besides, he may have come just at the time when tea and cakes were served and it would have been rude for the wife to leave without sampling the delicacies provided for guests.

Lamu rats.

At high tide, when the seawater level is almost as high as that of the drains, rats are forced up through the drains. Little boys enjoy catching them and showing them to little old ladies from Chicago. After such a display of doubtful goodwill, it is highly unlikely that the ladies will want to make another visit to Lamu. Attempts have been made to eliminate the rats, many of which are much larger than the Lamu cats. The last really major effort was made in the late 1950s. In 1959 the District Commissioner proudly reported that 949 rats were caught, but a little later he lamented, "Again the courage and stamina of the Lamu cats failed them and it is believed that the rats actually eat the cats here."

Cargoes of the East Esmond and Chryssee Bradley Martin.

Malindi beach, 1947

Gaiety here is indigenous, speed exotic. The sun sparkles on a blue ocean and pours with intensity on to dense dry bush and dusty road, forcing men to seek shade and hammering the very vigour from their blood. From the road you can see little but bush and forest. Here and there your eye is caught by a flower whose creamy, wax-like petals are fringed with deep flamingo-pink, and whose soft fragility seems strangely at variance with its harsh surroundings, even with the fleshy spikes on which it is borne. This is the *adenia*, a desert plant whose water-storing bulb is so heavy that two men are needed to lift it.

Small palm-thatched houses stand in a wide arc above Malindi bay within sound of breaking chocolate-coloured rollers – brown with the topsoil of the highlands washed hundreds of miles down the Sabaki river. The mouth of this river lies four miles north, yet the whole bay is red with particles of soil, millions of tons of it held in suspension.

A wind off the sea blows all day long, keeping the air fresh; and when it drops at night the breakers subside into wavelets which spill on to the sand gently, their moonlit crests the colour of Ovaltine. In front dance the little crabs, in such multitudes that the whole beach seems agog with them; where the waves spread out in a fine film they dart in, gliding sideways like ballet-dancers in crinolines.

These little monsters wear their eyes on the end of long springy stalks. Sometimes, as if in contemplation, a crab will put up its front claws, pull down the stalks and then rub its hands together, while the eyes spring back into place. At night in the quiet moonlight on this deserted beach they dance in and out of the waves as swiftly as dragon-flies, until the tremor of one's foot on the wet sand sends them scuttling into a thousand invisible burrows. They are queer and exquisite, and the purpose of their nightly ballet is to snatch morsels of offal from the waves.

Dawn over Malindi bay is monochromatic, in all shades of steel-blue and indigo. The sea is like grey silk, the sky dark, but pale blue above a marine horizon, and light puffy clouds of heliotrope hang over the water. To-day the moon was a silver thread, the old moon in its arms; over it shone a bright morning star; to the right, the lighthouse winked with steadfast tranquillity, all was gentle and still. Then salmon-pink intruded and the monochrome quality of an early water-colour faded; in a few minutes the sun burst forth and the first bathers ran down the beach to meet the waves before they lost their bite.

This was the day for goggling. We drove first down an avenue of flamboyants whose brilliant scarlet flowers burnt like fires in the green branches, overtaking as we went the morning procession of Giriama women marching in with baskets of frothy white cotton on their heads. These women, naked to the waist, wear short skirts apparently made of palm-leaves, but actually of cloth cunningly pleated to resemble the older and traditional material. They look sleek and sturdy, but their figures are clumsy.

My Swedish companion, a sort of Viking burnt mahogany-colour by this equatorial sun (by trade a coffee planter near Nairobi), keeps a small canoe which he fashioned from a seaplane's float. We pushed this little vessel through shallow water as warm as a bath and chugged out to the reef.

A Swahili proverb says: "Where there are breakers, there is also a door through the reef."

The question is always to find the door; many wrecks along these coral barriers are the gravestones of vessels who failed; but the Viking did not hesitate and we passed safely over, leaving behind us the long creamy line of foam that, at low tide, marks the reef.

It was low tide now. The boat was anchored. Wearing heavy goggles, we swam over the rock-pools on our tummies, our faces thrust into the sea.

A fantastic, unimagined world lay under water: a Walt Disney world of corals, some waving like plumes, some fixed like calcified brains, all in pink and beige and carmine; a world of fishes of brilliant colourings and bizarre shapes. In and out of the mountain ranges and deep caverns of coral swam these little fishes: one plum-brown with two broad bands of light blue and orange feathery fins, another with blue peacock's-feather eyes on fins and tail. Some were slim, some square, some waved long graceful bristles; butterfly fish, angel fish, box fish, zebra fish – scores of different kinds. Tiny powder-blue creatures hovered in shoals over clumps of coral and melted away into crevices before our shadows.

Bigger shapes darted by twenty or thirty feet under water, and after these the Viking vanished, clasping a harpoon. He pursued them into a great cave, disappearing completely into the bowels of the sea for so long that I felt sure he had stuck in the caverns and drowned; as I began to look anxiously for bubbles, his feet appeared and he swam out backwards, two plaice-like fishes wriggling on his spear. They were a vivid orange covered with electric-blue spots. He threw them into the canoe, and their colour died with them; in a few minutes all the brilliance had gone, they had become a drab and ordinary brown.

Off Casuarina Point the sea is so warm that you can spend all day in it, climbing out to rest now and again on a nobbly rock of coral or to suck an orange in the boat. Sun, not cold, is the enemy. Those with white unhardened skins must go warily until they have baked themselves, little by little, to the Viking's mahogany.

The water round the horn of the bay is so limpid that you can see every waving branch of coral fathoms deep, and the spots, bars and whiskers of every fish. You enter an Aladdin's cave of brilliance and romance seen from a hot sea-bath under a blue sky with the sun and the air all round you. If the world can offer greater pleasures, they must be far to seek.

The Sorcerer's Apprentice Elspeth Huxley.

Gedi

Sixty-five miles north of Mombasa and ten miles south of Malindi lie the ruins of an old Arab city. In 1948 Gedi was declared a National Park and an archaelogist, James Kirkman, appointed to investigate it. The tangled forest was peeled away to reveal the lineaments of a walled city covering forty-five acres and containing a palace, a Great Mosque, lesser mosques, pillar tombs, wells, baths, courts, and all the appurtenances of a civilized Arab city.

The main block of the Palace is in itself a typical Gedi house, but in this case it serves as the anteroom for the two wings, one possibly for staff and storage, the other for women, since it leads down to another reception court. This is one of the most interesting rooms in the Palace. It is entered at one end over a *fingo* or spell, which consisted of a pot containing a piece of paper with words written on it which was buried in the floor with appropriate incantations and by which it was believed that a djinn had been induced to take up residence in the pot. If anybody came in with evil intentions he would be driven out of his mind. The pot was buried near the door so that the miscreant would not have an opportunity to do very much before the djinn got him. Once a week incense was burnt over the pot, just to remind the djinn that he was there for a purpose. . . .

The story of the Palace would appear to be as follows. A building consisting of the earlier audience court, the main block and the west wing or women's quarters was constructed in the early fifteenth century. In the second half of the century it was extended and the Annexe was built. At the beginning of the sixteenth century it was abandoned, but at the end of the century a large programme of renovation and tenementization was undertaken which was never completed.

Fourteen large houses in recognizable condition have been cleared, ten of them in the main excavated areas. They have been named after an architectural feature or the most interesting find in them. The majority are semi-detached, but unlike a semi-detached house of today the front doors are not side by side, so you do not have to know what your neighbour is doing. Of course you did, or your wife did, but it was not forced on your notice. The oldest surviving house in its original state is the House of the Cowries, built at the end of the fourteenth century. Some of the others are probably not much later but have been modified in the course of the fifteenth or at the end of the sixteenth century. . . .

The people who lived at Gedi were neither wealthy, luxurious nor artistic, but had most of what contributed in their day to good living. "Colonial and comfortable" would be an apt expression for their way of life. Outside the Palace were two large houses: the House of the Chinese Cash and the House of the Porcelain Bowl. The House of the Chinese Cash had been destroyed in the early sixteenth century. In the court a Chinese cash of the Emperor Ning Tsung (AD 1195–1224) was found. Copper cash were exported from China, but they have only occurred sporadically in Kenya, always in context much later than the date of the coin. The House of the Porcelain Bowl was small, with only two rooms and a lavatory, built in the ruins of a larger house which had been destroyed by fire. . . .

Sometime in the second quarter of the seventeenth century this thriving Arab city was abandoned forever. No one knows for certain why. The most likely theory seems to be an imminent threat of invasion from the warlike Galla people of the hinterland. The citizens departed, the forest closed in, only ghosts remained.

When I first started to work at Gedi I had the feeling that something or somebody was looking out from behind the walls, neither hostile nor friendly, but waiting for what he knew was going to happen. Some of the houses have a thick as opposed to a thin, empty or meaningless atmosphere. The something or somebody behind the walls has gone, but some houses still retain for me their peculiar aura.

The coastal African does not only conceive of ghosts as we see them, but he also believes in spirits as creatures in their own right. One of the most unpleasant is a monstrous sheep that follows you wherever you go. One can sympathize with the unpleasantness of having always as a companion the symbol of the essential oneness of the human race.

The ghost stories of the Europeans are mainly associated with inexplicable misfortunes and inconveniences associated with a visit to Gedi. One of the best is of a camping party whose hurricane lamps would not burn and whose torches would not go on, finally the car lamps failed, so they felt they were up against more than they could take and went back to the main road. When they reached the road the lights came on again. This haunting is now a thing of the past. People have camped at Gedi with permission of the authorities and nothing particularly unpleasant or interesting seems to have happened to them which could not have occurred anywhere else. The hand of man, even an archaeologist, has restored Gedi to normality. The local inhabitants say that it is still bad, but not as bad as it used to be in the past. This grudging admission concedes more than it reserves. The ghosts of Gedi have gone, yet if you walk round the walls between half past five and six in the evening you may well have all the authentic feelings that precede or accompany an apparition. The things that were not in Horatio's philosophy are still there, though we are living in the best of all materialist eras.

Men and Monuments of the East African Coast James Kirkman.

Wajir

Wajir lies in the remote north-eastern district of Kenya, a dusty little town in the middle of a desert. Bristling thorn bushes grow out of the grey sand for miles in every direction. Anyone so ill-advised as to leave the road can get lost within minutes, so flat and monotonous, so spotted with thorn bush, is the landscape. Wajir is famous for its wells. Legend has it that some three thousand years ago the Queen of Sheba watered her camels here. Today the scene could easily be the same, as thousands of camels stand in orderly groups round the wells, waiting their turn to drink.

The wells are only about twenty feet deep and are undoubtedly of great antiquity. Old skin buckets are let down and raised in a rhythmic motion, the water splashing amid cries, singing, the grunts of camels and the bleating of goats. The buckets are emptied in a circular trough surrounding the well head and the camels drink soberly, patiently, after their long weeks of browsing through the barren country.

The white buildings of the town with little minarets rising above tessellated houses have the atmosphere of a Foreign Legion fort. On the wall behind the

DC's desk are recorded the illustrious names of former DCs of the colonial era, now passed into history. On the outskirts of the town a strange-shaped building, named by some humourist in the colonial service "The Wajir Yacht Club", used to be a meeting-place for officers of all services. The streets of soft dust have few vehicles to scatter the small children playing on the ground and a few whitewashed stones, arranged in a circle, act as a traffic roundabout at one end of the main thoroughfare. There are two or three grocers' shops, a butcher's, a maker of sweet cakes, a cemetery hidden behind a low stone wall overgrown by weeds, and then the desert, containing and dominating everything. A timeless quality seems to pervade the whole atmosphere. On this particular morning, as David (Coulson) and I flew in on our medical missions, the flat arid land looked, from the air, like the floor of an ancient lake, an old sea-bed from the far-off geological past.

This oasis in the north east of Kenya is inhabited largely by Somalis. These lean Moslem nomads live with their camels in symbiotic fashion. The camel walks to its grazing, accompanied by its owner and his family, and only needs to return to the wells after three weeks' absence. The family survives on the camel's milk, while the camels carry the few possessions of the family, who walk alongside them. They are the only domesticated animals designed to survive without water in these pitiless wastelands. Their huge spongy feet are adapted to walking on the soft sand, but it is their ability to survive without water and still give milk that makes them not only indispensible but the basis of human life in the desert.

The freedom of this life lies deep in the hearts of these nomads. They defend it fanatically and are only happy in their natural environment. They are fierce and cruel, and indulge in fighting among their clans and with their neighbours, particularly the Ethiopians. In the past, as their grazing areas became exhausted they would raid southwards, extending their territory. The colonial era put a stop to this, but since Kenya's independence they have tried politically, and through poaching and banditry, to annexe the north-eastern part of Kenya. These days they are often armed with modern automatic weapons captured from raids over the border. Life is cheap and the will of Allah is inexorable, accepted with the fatalism that is part of their strength.

Different Drums Michael Wood.

Michael Wood, a surgeon, came to East Africa after the Second World War to combine a practice in Nairobi with wheat growing on Mount Kilimanjaro. Piloting his light aircraft between farm and surgery, he observed the lack of roads and towns, the isolation of scattered huts and villages. So was born the Flying Doctor service, whose trained personnel fly to the remotest places, hold clinics under thorn trees, inoculate children and treat patients who trudge for many miles to seek aid. The service grew, by degrees, into the African Medical Research Foundation, whose many projects work towards the betterment of life among African peoples. Michael Wood was knighted in 1985, and died of cancer three years later.

PART VI

Wildlife

The variety and abundance of East Africa's wildlife was formerly one of the wonders of the world. Then came the opening up of large parts of the highlands to European farmers and ranchers, most of whom shot most of the animals on their land or drove them out, and the escalation of the African population which led to the same result. "Human islands in a sea of elephants changed to increasingly small islands of elephants in a sea of people", Dr Richard Laws remarked. For elephants, read almost every other kind of mammal. First the colonial government, then its African successor, endeavoured to preserve as much wildlife as possible by setting aside National Parks and game reserves, mainly in areas too barren for cultivation to thrive, where animals have right of way and resident humans are, so far as possible but not always, excluded. In recent years poaching of the animals, formerly mainly for meat but now for money, has all but exterminated the black rhino in the wild, cut the elephant population to a fraction of its former size, and threatened several other species as well. Whether the parks and reserves can themselves resist the mounting pressure exerted by humans for more land and timber remains to be seen. While the animals have dwindled in numbers, understanding of their behaviour has grown through studies made *in situ*, and the use of modern techniques such as electronic radio collars. The passages that follow range from descriptions of sights no longer to be seen recorded nearly a century ago, to present-day accounts of animal behaviour observed in parks and reserves.

At the turn of the century the Uasin Gishu plateau, now altogether conquered by hoe, plough and fence, still belonged to the first-comers.

Here may be seen large herds of giraffes as one might see cattle peacefully standing about in an English park. . . . Elephants may be seen in great herds close by, but they affect more the scattered forest than the open plains. Where you see the giraffes you also see numerous rhinos in couples, male and female, or a female alone with her snub-nosed calf. . . .

It is a glorious sight, say an hour after the sun has risen and the shadows have begun to shorten, to traverse this grass country and see this zoological gardens turned loose. Herds of zebras and Jackson's hartebeest mingle together, and in face of the sunlight become a changing procession of silver and gold, and the sleek coats of the zebras in the level sunlight mingle their black stripes and snowy intervals into a uniform silver-grey, whilst the coats of the hartebeests are simply red-gold. Dotted about on the outskirts of this throng are jet-black ostriches with white wings, a white bob-tail and long pink necks. Red and silver jackals slink and snap; grotesque warthogs of a dirty grey, with whitish bristles and erect tails terminating in a drooping tassel, scurry before the traveller till they can bolt into some burrow of the ant-bear. Males of the noble waterbuck, strangely like the English red deer, appear at a distance, browsing with their hornless, doe-like females, or gazing at the approaching traveller with head erect on the maned neck and splendid carriage of Landseer's stags. Grey-yellow reed-buck bend their lissom bodies into such a bounding gallop that the spine seems to become concave as the animal's rear is flung high into the air. The dainty *Damaliscus*, or sable antelope, with a coat of red, mauve, black and yellow satin bordered with cream colour, stands at gaze, his coat like watered silk as the sunlight follows the wavy growth of glistening hair.

Once black buffalo would have borne a part in this assembly, but now, alas! they have all been destroyed by the rinderpest. The eland still lingers in this region, but seems to prefer the scattered woodland to the open plains. Lions and leopards may both be seen frequently in broad daylight, hanging about these herds of game, though apparently causing no dismay to the browsing antelopes.

The Uganda Protectorate Sir Harry Johnston.

Before they were constrained by wire fences, the antelopes, zebra and other plain-dwellers migrated in vast numbers along the Rift Valley. Such migrating herds were to be seen as late as circa *1910.*

It is a wonderful sight to see the game on trek when the rains have begun. The kongoni move, as soon as the first shower falls, in search of the new grass of which it brings promise, but the great treks are those of the smaller antelope, which shun the long grass where enemies may hide. In East Africa we do not see the vast herds of "trek-bok" known in the Kalahari, but nevertheless, the migrating herds are of enormous size at times. I have seen these movements in the Southern Reserve when, growth of the herbage prompting, the smaller game travels south to the dry country near the border; but there is a spot between Mount Menengai and the forest where the trek is to be seen at its best, the animals being on their way past Nakuru towards Elmenteita. The roads used on these occasions are well marked, and on these the animals may be seen. They do not, of course, come trooping past with the purposeful air of people in a London street. They drift along in seemingly aimless fashion, feeding, playing, or love-making as they go, but always on the move towards their Promised Land of short grass and change of food.

Of recent years the big trek of the zebra down the Rift Valley, from the Baringo region to Lakes Elmenteita and Nakuru has to a large extent been checked by the number of wire fences. Only a little time ago one might see thousands upon thousands of zebra as far as the eye could reach, for the most part feeding, but at the same time moving steadily *en masse* down the valley. I shall never forget marching at night from Nakuru to Elmenteita to surprise a party of Wandorobo hunters who were "wanted". We started at about 2 am, and, as we followed the road, the stampede after stampede of huge droves of zebra fairly shook the ground. One lot, getting our wind, would dash off, and others taking the alarm, but knowing nothing of the cause, would rush almost over us in their blind terror. When daylight dawned the sight was extraordinary; the whole plains were alive with animals, which, now they could see us, exhibited far less alarm than they had done in the dark. The contrast between their behaviour by night and that by day was very curious. The sun risen, we travelled between the herds, which would open out to leave a passage of about 200 yards, and close up behind almost immediately after we had passed. Like all other game on trek in large numbers, they were extremely fearless.

A Game Ranger's Note Book A. B. Percival.

Nature's great master-peece,
An elephant,
the onely harmlesse great thing:
The giant of beestes.

John Donne

9.x.1903. *Nyeri*

I witnessed a marvellous migration of elephant this morning travelling from Mount Kenya to the Aberdares. When it was barely light and the sun not yet risen, one of my men hammered at the door of my hut shouting "*Tembo, bwana, tembo nyingi sana!* – Elephant, sir, many elephant!" I tumbled out of bed, and there was the black mass of Mount Kenya in sharp outline with the sun scarce risen behind it; the light was poor, but my man soon pointed out a long black streak of moving animals not a quarter of a mile off and on the north of the river, all slowly moving west from Kenya to the Aberdares. I quickly put on a pair of long boots and dashed out in pyjamas, ran down to the river and got swamped crossing it – a good cold bath; I had no gun with me. Creeping up a small gully, I found myself but 60–80 yards off this huge stream of moving elephant, going very slowly, sometimes in small groups of eight or ten, sometimes two or three together and an occasional solitary beast; lots of calves; and to right and left I could see no end to the moving mass, each following in the other's trail. I tried in vain to count them, for the head of the column was in the far distance and the tail was approaching me, but I should say there must have been about 700 animals. They were moving at a steady walk, not feeding; the last beasts to pass me were a cow and a very small calf, and the rear of the column was level with Nyeri Hill as the sun rose behind Mount Kenya. I shall never again see anything like that.

Kenya Diary 1902–1906 Richard Meinertzhagen.

The spectacular migrations of former times followed the rain, and were Nature's
way of resting pastures in rotation; the Maasai with their cattle did the same.

One such large-scale migration can still be seen, that of the wildebeest which move in armies across the Serengeti and the Maasai-Mara plains.

We came to the wildebeest migration soon after seven o'clock and were driving slowly through the glistening armies for about four hours. These pewter-coloured, white-bearded creatures move in long, close-packed columns at a steady pace and in a constant direction and, when the time comes to graze, spread out as far as the eye can see in every direction – and probably the eye can see for about twenty miles – like great hordes of ants speckling the plain. All the time, when on the move, they emit harsh grunts, something like the sound of frogs, something like that of old men clearing their throats. People have called them ungainly because of their high shoulders and sloping hindquarters, and also clowns because of their long pale faces and white beards, but in fact they move with grace and sometimes playfulness, leaping and cavorting with apparent *joie de vivre.* Their heads go down, their tails go up, they bounce like balls, kicking up eddies of dust. When disturbed they gallop off together and make curious jinking swerves, at the same time lashing their tails.

There are said to be about two million wildebeests or gnu (*Connochaetes taurinus albojubatus*) on the Serengeti. It seemed as if we saw them all that day. Of course, we saw only a fraction of their numbers; other armies, perhaps bigger still, were on the march across a front of maybe a hundred miles. Their numbers are increasing year by year. Hyenas, lions, cheetahs, wild dogs and leopards do their bit to keep them down, but prey has outstripped predator. Wildebeests are much like smaller, lighter bison, and this is what the plains of North America must have looked like a century and a half ago – minus the Red Indians.

Every year, the wildebeests migrate in search of fresh grazing within an area of perhaps fifteen thousand square miles. When rain falls on the open plains, they come in from the bush lying to the north, west and south to enjoy the short, palatable grasses which spring up immediately after a downpour or two, and which are rich in calcium. If the rains come according to plan (quite often they don't) they start in December and continue, on and off, until May or June.

The wildebeests' term on the short-grass plains is timed to coincide with their calving, so that the calcium will enrich their milk and give a good start in life to the calves. This calving is astonishing: it all takes place within a month. A positive deluge of calves overwhelms the predators. A great many are, of course, taken; hyenas in particular gang up and chew them to bits as soon as they are born; but a great many more survive. . . .

The first wildebeest calves arrived on the Serengeti at about the same time as I did, in mid February. That first day, we saw scarcely any; a week later, a lot; by the end of the following week thousands of them were galloping beside their mothers or resting beside them on the grass. Although adults are silvery-grey, the offspring are light brown with black faces, and save for their sloping quarters look rather like Guernsey calves. The speed with which they recover from birth is amazing. One minute a calf, wrapped in a membrane and trailing an umbilical cord, is deposited on the ground. Within five minutes, quite often, and seldom more than six or seven, it is up and away, galloping with its mother on long spindly legs and shaking its head.

The process is fascinating to watch. The mother, who gives birth lying down, immediately gets up, thus rupturing the cord. She may gently nose the infant, but the first one I watched did nothing to help it to its feet. Within a few minutes it was struggling to rise. At first it fell over every time, but each try was better than the last until it managed to stagger a few paces before collapsing again. The mother just looked on. It got up again, still tottering; the mother walked away; unsteadily, the calf followed; within the regulation six or seven minutes it was galloping after her to join the herd. Wildebeest calves, scientists have said, gain co-ordination quicker than any other ungulate. This is a necessary condition of survival. Five minutes of helplessness are plenty for any hyena. The mothers try to fight off attackers, but seldom succeed.

With all these thousands on the move, it is not surprising that many calves get separated from their mothers. It is distressing to see these small creatures with their soft brown hair and long black faces stand alone on the vast plain and bleat, or run, towards every adult they see in the hope, only too often a vain one, of finding their dams. Meanwhile, there are mothers distractedly galloping about looking for their lost children with equal lack of success. Cows have been observed searching for a lost calf for as long as three days.

No cow will accept a calf not her own. How do mother and child recognize each other? By the sound of her voice, I was told, in the case of the calf; but the mother knows her child by her sense of smell. Two million wildebeests, each with a different grunt! It seems incredible. But then, one thinks of people. We can distinguish each of our acquaintances, if we shut our eyes, by the sound of his or her voice. In a hall full of Chinese, I should not be able to tell one voice from another, but each of the Chinese could do so. Nevertheless I still find it extraordinary that each of those frog-like, wheezing grunts should sound a different note, undetectable to a human ear but recognizable by a day-old wildebeest.

Last Days in Eden Elspeth Huxley and Hugo van Lawick.

The Brotherhood of Elephants and Man

My brother Terence has always believed in the brotherhood of elephants and man, and when we were once discussing their virtues he told me about one he had found trapped in a well. His road building gang begged him to shoot it for meat but Terence told them to bring him barrows of stones which he dropped, one by one, into the pit. The elephant understood exactly what was happening and carefully lifted its feet as the stones raised the floor of its prison. The labourers fled as it reared up and finally heaved itself out but Terence had kept murmuring reassurance to the elephant throughout its ordeal and occasionally patted its anxious and questioning trunk. Once free, the elephant moved slowly towards him as if in thanks; it was some time before Terence could persuade it to return to its herd. . . .

In moments of sickness, danger or death elephants show a loyalty to each other which moves me very much. I was once summoned to Marsabit where four marauding bulls had been robbing maize-storage cribs. It was not only costly but dangerous as the cribs were in the heart of the police lines. On the night I arrived I sat for two chilly hours, down wind of the maize, waiting for the elephants to appear in the moonlight. When they emerged into view I aimed at the shoulder of the leader and fired. He fell immediately. But then his comrades gathered round him and, supporting him, made off with him into the forest. It would have been futile, not to say suicidal, to have pursued them that night so I waited until dawn.

Lembirdan and I followed the spoor and splashes of blood till we came on the elephant lying dead in the forest. It must have taken enormous strength and determination to get him so far.

I was even more impressed to discover that elephants seem to attach special significance to death. An old Boran told me that he was familiar with a small group of bulls who always stayed together on the Tana. When the oldest died his companions kept watch over his body for more than a week. They then drew out the tusks and carried them off into the bush. Many years later I read Iain Douglas-Hamilton's description of an elephant family taking away the bones of a relative in much the same way.

I found it more difficult to explain the sense an elephant has of human death. At Barsoloi a Samburu had been killed as he returned to his hut from the river. Halfway along the path he came across a fallen tree and as he picked his way over it he realized, too late, that it had been knocked over by an elephant which was hidden in the foliage. When the elephant went for him he tried to escape by burrowing under the branches but the elephant pulled him out with its trunk. Then it literally pounded him into the ground with its tusks and feet. The headman showed me where the elephant had repeatedly gored its victim and an area of about thirty square feet that looked as if it had been dug with a spade. He said that every afternoon since the tragedy the elephant had returned to the spot, and stood there until evening.

My Pride and Joy George Adamson.

The first road engineers.

Reference to the "elephant-path" over the heights of Kenya invites mention of one of the animals' most interesting habits. In districts where they are numerous, elephants use the same route regularly, and in course of time form the most perfect roads. In the dry season on the plains these roads are generally good enough for a bicycle; all grass and vegetation trodden down, all thorns destroyed, they are as smooth and pleasant tracks as man can desire. But it is in hilly country that the elephant displays his real skill as road engineer; he possesses an instinctive knowledge of the easiest gradients, and invariably adopts them. If an elephant path lie before you, take it, and rest assured you cannot improve upon it. I don't know how they get their information on this point, but they have it! If a tree should lie or fall across the chosen route they step over, or when too high for that, go round one end and resume the original direction; the smoothed bark shows where their hind legs rub in the act of stepping over.

The finest roads I know are those on Mount Kenya. Some of these are really marvels: ground beaten flat and smooth, all branches and overgrowth cleared away – eaten by the passing beasts, I apprehend, for the elephant is always feeding. Now and again you may have to cut away a branch which is too stiff to tempt elephant appetite and not stiff enough to hinder his passage, or cut through a fallen tree-trunk, over which elephants, but not mules, can step, but that is all. On an elephant road you may travel in the comfortable certainty that where it leads, pack animals and porters with loads on their heads can go with perfect ease. Other wild animals use these roads regularly, one reason for their patronage being that sooner or later they lead to water. . . .

On my first visit to Meru, in 1904, we followed elephant roads almost the whole way; there was no recognized track thither in those days. Twice we met the makers, but they gave us a wide berth, much to the relief of the men, for the district had a bad reputation at the time; people had been attacked by elephants on their roads – so the report ran. My own belief is that the scare was established by a single rogue, and his offences were set down to the whole species.

A Game Ranger's Note Book A. B. Percival.

The first well diggers.

The families drifted slowly upstream until they reached the clear water. There were young bulls who dared not come too close to the females and who stood at the water-holes where the river stopped flowing. Since at this season the water was only inches deep and not all the elephants could use the top pool, I noticed for the first time how they began digging holes along the river's edge. The well diggers were usually bulls or old cows. Using their feet as shovels to loosen the earth, they kicked the sand backwards and forwards, until a wide hole was formed. At times they would dig down three feet or more with their trunks and feet, their toenails acting like a spade. They would push the sand with the side of a foot on to the curved end of the trunk, which they used like a cupped hand to throw the sand to one side. When the sand got damp and the water began to seep into the hole, they used the tips of their trunks, like fingers, to dig a deep, narrow, clean hole. The muddy water was rapidly sucked up and spewed around in circles or blown out like a suction pump and with the same noise. It was amazing how professional they were at the job. Within about a quarter of an hour little wells had been dug all over the place, some only a few feet away from each other. . . .

Elephant families walking up and down occasionally stopped to greet each other with their trunk to mouth gesture, while young babies walked up to a big bull and one by one greeted him. In return the bull put his trunk to each little mouth, or touched the babies on their heads in the way in which Maasai elders greet their children. A small cluster of elephants stood a little way from Boadicea waiting patiently for her to leave the water-holes, their trunks slung over their tusks, or just hanging like a length of hose from a fire engine. None showed any sign of aggression, except when the young bulls ventured too near. The only ones who never seemed to be able to get any water out of the holes were the smallest calves, who spent most of their time pushing, pulling or walking around their mothers. The older calves either drank elsewhere, or started digging holes themselves.

When Boadicea and her family had had their fill, they quietly ambled off to the flat piece of sand, where they threw trunkfuls of dust over themselves.

Covered in a rough loose-skinned armour the colour of stones, rich in ivory, Boadicea's polished tusks stood out like weapons, and I could imagine this great pachyderm preparing for battle. At one end hung a whiskered tail, sought after by man for its few hairs to twist into a bracelet. At the other end hung that masterpiece of the elephant – the trunk. It must be great to have a body of that size and also to be endowed with so rare an organ as a trunk, to do all the work the body needs to keep it always full and clean. Partly lip and partly nose, with two fingers on the tip, it is used as a worker's arm and hand. It has double hoses for sucking in and spraying out water or dust, and can test the wind. It can push down trees or pick off the smallest leaf. It can be as gentle and as loving as the most tender arms, to greet and tickle, to scratch and rub, to smell and caress, always twisting, moving, rolling in an infinite variety of postures. At the same time, it can change into an efficient weapon to kill, and when it detects the smell of man, rears back above the head like a serpent preparing to strike.

Among the Elephants Iain and Oria Douglas-Hamilton.

Elephants, although unmatched for strength, are never arrogant, and will extend great tolerance and consideration to other species, even preferring to stand aside rather than risk a confrontation with a cantankerous rhino or an old bull buffalo. David once witnessed a ridiculous scene from the air, when five elephants were grouped around a tree in a semicircle with only their heads in the shade and their bodies exposed to the burning midday sun. A closer look revealed the reason for this rather strange sight. A sounder of warthog were stretched out luxuriously enjoying the deep shade at the base of the tree, and the elephant were prepared to accept this situation, although it must have caused them a good deal of discomfort. . . .

The Tsavo Story Daphne Sheldrick.

Books about elephants often refer to "tummy rumbles", but these distinctive noises may emanate from the throat and be a means of communication between elephants.

Sound below the range of human hearing is called infrasound, that above ultrasound. While considerable work has been done on high-frequency sounds made by such mammals as bats, shrews, and porpoises, the elephant was the first terrestrial mammal reported to use infrasound. . . .

The discovery of the use of infrasound by elephants was fascinating in itself, but it also opened up a vast array of new interpretations of their behaviour. Joyce [Poole] has gone on to work with her own equipment and is primarily interested in the content of the vocalizations – that is, the messages that are being sent. It is known that low-frequency sounds travel over far greater distances and are less affected by trees and bushes than higher sounds. Theoretically some of the sounds that have been recorded in Amboseli (at up to 115 decibels) can carry for six miles, which could explain the coordination of movement and behaviour of separated elephant groups. Contact calls and answers no doubt help elephants within families and bond groups find each other.

Another important function of long-distance communication may be in finding mating partners. Almost inevitably after a female has been mated she gives a long, loud series of post-copulatory rumbles. These vocalizations contain infrasonic components. Joyce speculates that they carry over long distances and thereby attract males to the estrous female, who would then have a greater choice as to whom she mates with during the remainder of her estrous period. Males in musth make a characteristic rumble which is both very low and very loud. Joyce thinks that this rumble communicates different messages to different animals. It may attract estrous females and warn subordinate males to give a wide berth to the musth male. Often several males are in musth at the same time, and Joyce has noted that they manage to crisscross the park in search of females and yet usually avoid direct confrontations with each other. Infrasonic communication may very well be the key element in this spatial arrangement.

Elephant Memories Cynthia Moss.

Iain and Oria Douglas-Hamilton lived for five years among the elephants in the Lake Manyara National Park.

I was not afraid of elephants any more. I could stand up to a charging elephant and call his bluff with a wave of my arm, then walk away. It was not bravado. I just knew what I was doing. It was up to me to recognize danger and to get out of the way, or else I would fall to a really hostile elephant's tusks, in the same way that they would fall to a hunter's bullets. I could not help feeling a great admiration for them. I was drawn to them. Was it their size, their power, or their gentleness that attracted me? I could not tell. I just knew that I loved being surrounded by elephants and that this experience brought me great joy.

On moonlit nights when the elephants came up the river to drink, we would often lie on a rock close by and hear the trickle of water as it slipped over the sand and into their trunks. Huge dark shapes, making sipping-squirting-spilling noises, stood motionless and then wandered on past us. On these special nights, I could absorb the long hours of nothingness in the half-light of the moon, where there was no sadness or boredom, and where I was nourished by silence, and felt rich in my simple way of life.

By photographing elephants day in and day out, I soon discovered that they showed many of the old-fashioned virtues; loyalty, protection and affection toward each other. As we lived far away from our own species and became so deeply involved with the elephants, we both consciously and unconsciously drew parallels between their society and ours. The bond with my child, the tactile care of each other, the trust in leadership, the group defence if one of us were in trouble, all these increased.

For elephants, the unity of a family is one of the most important things in their lives. I was deeply moved by the constant affection and care which they showed every day within the families; mothers, daughters, sisters, babies all touching and communicating with each other in a very loving way. Stability seemed to be the key to their security. Unlike us they do not have male parents or companions living with them; but perhaps for elephants this is an advantage because they have to deal solely with female problems. They frequent the males only when they need them for mating, which is after all the purpose of survival: to reproduce the genes, and when the bulls arrived, the same greeting and touching ceremony took place. The matriarchs not only perform the usual maternal tasks, but also the roles which we tend to think of as male – leading and defending the family units extremely efficiently. Whatever the reason, these female-led families remain united and extremely stable.

I was no elephant expert, but at least during all the months that I lived with these animals, I was able to get a glimpse into the incredible complexity and sophistication that elephants show in their everyday activities. I not only learnt to understand and especially to respect them, I also longed to protect them. I could not bear to watch someone lift a gun to an elephant's head and blow its brains out, for sport or for man's greed. What a waste of life.

Months of living with and observing these animals taught me something that no text book could ever do. As a result I now felt a great deal more civilized.

When meeting elephants face to face, we found one of the secrets was always to keep still, to make no noise, and then to move very slowly towards or away from them. Elephants like Virgo and Right Hook, and well over a hundred others, accepted us as harmless. But even after five years of living with them, only Virgo actually came into friendly body contact with us. The others always stood a few feet away. When Saba (Oria and Iain's daughter) was three months old, and before our departure from Manyara, we met Virgo and her closest relatives one evening. I walked up to her and gave her a gardenia fruit, in a gesture of greeting. She was a trunk's length from me, took the fruit, put it in her mouth, and then moved the tip of her trunk over Saba in a figure of eight, smelling her. I wondered if she knew that Saba was my child. We both stood still for a long while, facing each other with our babies by our sides. It was a very touching moment. I feel sure that Virgo will remain a life-long friend of ours, even if we do not see each other for years. . . .

I knew that once I left our life with these animals and returned to live in a city, it would be hard to find the intensity of these relationships again. Like millions of other human beings, Iain and I would have to face an overcrowded and over-complicated environment and be ill-adapted for the complete change of living. Yet like those millions we also would survive.

Among the Elephants Iain and Oria Douglas-Hamilton.

Lions

Very softly down the glade runs a waiting, watching shade,
And the whisper spreads and widens far and near;
And the sweat is on thy brow, for he passes even now –
It is Fear, O little hunter, it is Fear!

Rudyard Kipling

A broad valley stretched to the west. Gathering at its rim, the lions surveyed the scattered herds of wildebeest and zebra and then waited while the plains changed slowly to a shadowy purple and finally grew dark. As if on signal, the lionesses fanned out and dissolved in the grass, each moving toward prey on her own, yet each taking part in a cooperative effort whose strategy was predetermined by many hunts. I waited beside Black Mane and Brown Mane, who stood there staring into the night with inviolable dignity. Suddenly hooves drummed and the wild scream of a zebra shattered the darkness. The males and I hurried in the direction from which the sound came. Driving rapidly cross-country without lights, never knowing when the car would drop into a hyena warren or straddle a termit hill, was a minor adventure in itself. When I reached the kill site, the air was already heavy with the odour of blood and rumen contents. The tawny mass of lions filling the night with menacing growls, as each animal fought for a share of the meat, was a drama of such naked emotion that the hair on my nape and back raised itself in subconscious apprehension for my safety. I was witnessing a pitch of passion that was almost foreign to human experience. Thirty minutes later the zebra was dismembered and each animal was cleaning meat off some bone; Brown Mane with a lunge and growl had taken possession of the whole ribcage, neck, and head. I felt myself relax suddenly and realized for the first time the silent and ancient fear this primitive scene had evoked for me. It is not so much what we see but what it suggests that arouses us. Almost palpably my racial memories rose of a past when man crouched vulnerably in the dark, listening to the growls of his enemies, and of a time when the smell and sight of red meat meant survival. Here under a pale rising moon the past met the present.

Golden Shadows, Flying Hooves George Schaller.

Royal Mail.

There was an occasion when one of my Turkana mail runners came all the way from Loyangallani to Barsaloi on his feet, travelling the whole of two nights and lying up for one day in between; we called the distance 124 miles or thereabouts. He was a wonderful athlete, a man of utter integrity, and with all the courage of the best men in his tribe. Why had he come at such a mighty speed, was what I wanted to know when I noticed the time and date-stamp of his departure. He explained that he would like to spend a day with his wife before going on. "But I am not a driver of slaves! You have only to ask and you can have a day off, or two or three whenever you want it!" "I have a duty, and if I want time off, I do my duty in less time, so as not to take pay for work that I do not do!"

I sent him off to stay with his wife, and then the interpreter said he thought I would be interested to hear of his encounter with a lion during one night of his journey. This intrepid runner had come across a lion on a kill; the kill was a buck, and the runner thought he would like some of it to eat himself, so he drove the lion off and sat down and had a meal. At the end of the meal he put the remaining haunch over his shoulder and set off down the trail. The lion followed at a respectful distance, making a few spits of annoyance from time to time, but keeping his distance until the moon went down. Then he came snuffing along the trail much nearer; the runner then paused to fill his metal cooking pot with stones, and having done so ran towards the lion rattling the stones in the pot – that was the last of the lion. "Then how is it that only last month when you met a lion one night, you spent the whole night in a tree with the lion waiting down below?" "The heart is not the same in every lion you may meet. The heart of one lion is such that you may chase him away; the heart of another is such that it is necessary to get into a tree until daylight!" This man had given up travelling with his spears, as he said any extra thing to carry in addition to the mail bags was very awkward, and he preferred to do without – this in a country where lions were everywhere and as cheeky as you please, and where at least two reliable white men had seen as many as fourteen together.

The Desert and the Green The Earl of Lytton.

The intelligence of lions is acknowledged and was demonstrated by a most extraordinary happening which took place when George was asked to kill two man-eaters. For the killing of man-eaters no methods are barred, so he put a small dose of strychnine into pieces of raw meat and placed these in the lions' latest pugmarks. They were soon taken. Observing this, George followed the lions' spoor; it led him to a bush covered with small red berries – *Cordia quarensis*. They are a violent emetic and Africans eat them when they wish to be sick. The lions had apparently laid up behind the bush, eaten the berries and vomited the whole contents of their stomachs, including the strychnine. Then they had walked off across rocks where it was impossible for George to track them.

Though hardly credible, it appeared that when the lions felt ill they deliberately ate the berries, presumably knowing that they would make them vomit.

The Searching Spirit Joy Adamson.

> *Love begets love, then never be*
> *Unsoft to him who's smooth to thee.*
> *Tigers and bears, I've heard say*
> *For proffered love will love repay.*

Robert Herrick

I asked Joy (Adamson) if she could explain not only the taming of Elsa, which in itself was not extraordinary, but the special link of mutual understanding and trust that she described. Lack of fear on both sides, total faith in each other, and the unusual intelligence of Elsa were, she thought, the main basis for this success. Possibly, she admitted, the fact that she actually held in her hands the meat with which she fed Elsa helped to create a link, and to seal the compact of what one can truly call "love"; for animals, unlike human beings, rarely bite the hand that feeds them. The gift was a sort of ritual, part of the bond which established their relationship.

On the occasion of our visit a goat was also brought, and was killed before arrival. After reaching the usual camping place and rendezvous, George stood in the clearing and fired his rifle in the air. We all waited. There was no sign of Elsa; so we were allowed to walk down towards the river to the enchanting place of great trees spreading over rocks with sandy beach and murmur of water, where Joy used to do her writing and sketching, while Elsa played with her cubs. A second shot, and soon we heard a chatter of baboons. "Elsa is coming," said Joy, "the baboons always give warning." We piled back in the Land-Rovers.

At last, bounding out of the bush in great easy strides, there was Elsa, leaping towards Joy whose outstretched arms moved forward to defend herself from too powerful an embrace; even then she was nearly knocked over. The two of them, Elsa's paws on Joy's shoulders, stood there like old friends meeting again. The cubs were close behind, led by Jespath, the favourite son. He was a gallant little lion, with ears cocked and eyes alert, ready to protect his mother. Joy did not touch him, but kept stroking Elsa's sleek head, calling her name and fondling her gently, while Elsa clearly returned all this affection in her own manner, her tail sweeping in wide curves as she nuzzled up to Joy.

Wild Lives of Africa Juliette Huxley.

George Adamson established at Kora on the Tana river a rehabilitation camp where lions, who would otherwise have been condemned to death or to imprisonment in zoos, were acclimatized to life in the wild.

By the time we get down to the river I am ready for a cool glass of gin from the thermos and, as the sun will be getting warm, the lions are quite happy to flop down on the sand or mess about in the shallows. Lions are among the laziest animals on earth and like to spend most of the day dozing, although if very hungry they will spring up at the chance of a kill whatever the heat.

It is extremely beautiful down by the Tana. The stretch we make for is more than a hundred yards wide if you take in the stream, the pools, the shallows, the rocks and the sand. There is shade from the palms and acacias, which are much taller here than those in the bush round the camp. Terence (George's brother) has identified all the plants and the shrubs – the deadly datura or moonflower with its lovely white trumpets, the sweet scented henna and the red-berried salvadora, so attractive to birds.

The game fades away at the approach of the lions but the baboons chatter and bark on the opposite bank, while the hippos wallow and snort out in the silted red water. Close in it is hard to tell if a dark ridged shape, gliding along with the current, is a log or a crocodile. The birds seem to have no fear of the lions and if I sit quietly a succession of waders will drop down to the river – silent white egrets and honking purple-black hadada ibis, mottled Egyptian geese and the formidable carnivorous sentries, goliath herons, tall yellow-billed storks and the large marabous, with their wicked beaks pressed against the scrotum-pink sacs on their chests.

Peaceful as it is, warmed by the sun and cooled by the contents of my thermos, I am always a little uneasy when I am here with the lions. After it has rained they make a frightful fuss when they have to walk through a puddle, but if something excites their interest on the other side of the river they plunge straight into the stream and swim directly across, despite the strength of the current. My worry is that crocodiles have drowned at least one of my lions and may easily account for others.

I usually walk the younger lions back to camp for lunch; in the first few weeks they are inclined to come to a call, like a dog. I leave the older ones by the river, or on Kora Rock, which we pass on the way. They are probably still there when I go down in the evening – or will come to me quickly if I call them with a megaphone.

I have had some tricky moments up on the rocks. Early one morning, in 1977, I let Suleiman and Sheba out of their enclosure to spend the day in the bush, while I drove to the hill to look for a lioness with cubs. I climbed to the foot of some cliffs where I thought her lair might be, but could see no sign of them.

As I started down Suleiman and Sheba appeared. They were in a playful mood and while I fended off Sheba, who butted me from the front, Suleiman jumped on my back, grabbing me by the neck and bringing me down on the steep hillside. I tried to beat him off, whacking him over my shoulder with a stick. This made him angry and he started to growl, sinking his teeth in the back of my neck. It was no longer play.

Luckily I was wearing my revolver because my search for the lioness and cubs might well have brought me face to face with a cobra or leopard while I was poking about in the rocks. I drew the gun now with the notion of firing a shot over Suleiman's head to scare him off. When I pulled the trigger there was just a dull click. It happened a second time and with a fearful chill I realized I had probably forgotten to load it. My hand was no longer steady as I broke the gun open to work out my chances. At least there was a round in each of the chambers and as Suleiman still had his teeth in my neck – I could feel the blood trickling down my shoulders and the sweat coming out on my forehead – I decided to try again. This time I managed to get two shots off into the air. They had not the slightest effect.

Suleiman bit harder. In sheer desperation I pointed the revolver backwards over my shoulder, and fired straight at him. Immediately he let go and, looking startled, went and sat twenty feet off with Sheba, who had leapt back at the sound of the first two shots. I could see blood on his muzzle and more on his neck. . . . Next morning, much to my relief, Suleiman turned up. The pistol bullet had run across the top of his shoulders and lodged under the skin. He looked little the worse for it and was as friendly as ever. My own damage might have been worse too. The Flying Doctor took me to hospital in Nairobi and as the wounds did not go septic I was out in a week. . . .

My Pride and Joy George Adamson.

Lions in the wild lead hazardous lives; a false move or ill-judgement in attack or defence may lead to serious injury or death from the horns or hooves of their prey, or tooth and claw of their own kind. But it is their life, unchanged for millions of years, since long before the ancestors of man learned to walk upright.

According to Korokoro the lion's roar translated into English goes: WHO IS THE LORD OF THIS LAND? . . . Who is the lord of this land? . . . I AM. . . . I AM. . . . I am. . . . I am. . . . I am!

Bwana Game George Adamson.

George Adamson was murdered at Kora by Somali bandits in August 1989.

The Leopard

Anthony Dyer decided that if he were to be reborn as an animal, a leopard inhabiting the northern slopes of Mount Kenya is the animal he would choose to be. He imagined that he was.

Last night the forest was cold and dark after the moon set, so I slept on a bed of dried leaves under shelter of a fallen tree. The forest was never silent; all night the hyraxes were merry with their echoing screams and creaks. With the approach of dawn the turacos challenged them with a racket of croaks, although it was still too dark for them to fly. I could imagine them running up and down their perches, looking wisely at nothing and all shouting together. I missed the soothing trill of the nightjars, but they had fluttered off on their soft wings to find breakfast.

Suddenly the colobus monkeys awoke, and set up a chorus of chattering calls that sounded like a battle of machine guns. The calls crackled from ridge to ridge, from treetop to treetop, a hundred and fifty miles around the mountain and back again. I was thoroughly annoyed, because I hate to get up in the morning before the sun is there to warm my old bones. I stretched and yawned, clawed the bark of a tree to shreds and then sang my own little morning song. *Ahhggrr, ahhggrr, ahhggrr, ahhggrr.*

The forest around me suddenly became silent.

The first answer came from a little doe bushbuck who raced off from quite close by, letting rip a sharp bark of fear every few bounds until she felt that her duty was done and all her kind had been advised of my awful presence.

Then the insults started, hyraxes and colobus monkeys vying with each other in their efforts to be rude to me. However, I am used to this and rather enjoy the screams of the mob. It adds a little spice when I eat them, and there is not one of them who does not risk being on the menu. The only time their abuse becomes a bore is when I am hunting, or stalking, or trespassing in another leopard's territory. Then I would rather be incognito, so to speak.

I slipped off down the elephant path to my kill of yesterday. Jammed high in a fork of an olive tree lay the remains of a fine male bushbuck I had killed last evening. It had been chasing a rival when they both ran directly under the branch I was lying on. Having pursued its rival as far as the next ridge, the bushbuck hurried back to its mate along the same track, so close to me. One jump and two bounds and I had it by the throat. It fought frantically in the last moments of its life, but I am very skilful at killing buck and in a moment its strong body was limp.

I lay there without moving and sucked the blood from its neck. Even a brief extreme effort, like a charge and a kill, is completely exhausting to us leopards. Killing requires a great explosion of energy, and then we must rest. The salty blood quickly became a part of me and I could feel the exhaustion leaving my limbs until I was a whole leopard again. What a wonderful sensation is the regaining of strength!

Leopards have a reputation of being disgusting eaters, but this is far from the truth. I can dissect an animal with skill and speed. I open a small hole inside the leg and eat the flesh through this hole so that no dirt gets in and the delicious meat does not dry up. Of course, it is true that I can eat meat that is high and even maggoty, for it makes an interesting change. If I am careful and can keep my wives away, I can make a bushbuck last for five ambrosial days.

With the sharp edge of my hunger satisfied, I opened the buck up along his brisket and quickly devoured his heart, liver, spleen and kidneys. Then I buried the offal in the soft forest loam in a neat, tidy way. Not only does offal stink, but it also attracts flies and my enemies, the hyenas.

I took the neck of the buck in my teeth and easily carried the seventy-five pounds that remained of him to the nearest convenient tree. A pull and a grunt or two, and my kill was securely wedged in a fork of the branches, twenty feet up. It was none too soon, for already a pair of hyenas were hurrying for their share. Their uncanny sense had told them of my luck and they ran fearlessly to where I had disembowelled my kill. Their filthy little tails flicked with excitement as they nosed around and dug up the guts, which they tore to pieces between them.

Then their ever-questing noses led them to my tree. They tried to climb up and anger seethed within me. I fear the hyena pack, just as I must fear the baboon pack. Any rashness with either pack can be fatal to a leopard, however bravely he may fight. In the end, the pack will always win.

I suppose I know instinctively that the hyenas will be my undertakers. They will not even let my old bones rest in peace, but will crush them to splinters with their strong jaws and digest them in their horrid stomachs until all that is left are snowy white hyena droppings, strewn along my old trails. Perish the thought.

I have often been treed by hyena packs. With a pack there is no alternative but to climb as high as possible, remain quiet and hidden, and refuse to be tempted into doing anything rash. But there is a world of difference between a pair and a pack. To be treed by a stinking pair of hyenas is too much. My fury burst and I roared down from the tree, springing from one to the other and catching each of them a ripping clout that nearly scalped them. They rushed off growling savagely, and I know it will be a long time before that pair comes near me again.

But even when you win a round against the hyena, you are left with an uneasy feeling. The very breath of death seems to be all around. Every sound in the forest becomes suspicious and you can almost hear the final rush of the pack with twenty pairs of ghastly snapping, tearing jaws. I slunk away to seek some escape from these sombre thoughts and soon forgot them in a chance encounter with my middle wife.

It was a wonderful sunny morning, for I live in the most perfect climate of the whole world. A favourite resting place of mine, after I have breakfasted, is the great sloping trunk of a jogoo jogoo tree that grows out of the side of a large valley. Most sunny mornings find me lying at ease on this vantage point, surveying my domain. . . .

As a cub new to the forest I had thought that an old sow forest hog was the worst enemy of leopards. A long scar still aches on my side to remind me of her tushes. But these great black pigs are like lambs, compared to man. A hog will chase you for a few yards and then ignore you if you leave her alone. Man will chase you remorselessly, forever. In spite of his clumsiness, his miserable teeth and his useless claws, man is dangerous! . . .

It also appears that man will soon pose a problem to us, even in this little paradise. So far he has not come here; he has always stopped below the bamboo thickets. But he is gradually creeping up the ridges and cutting down the great forest trees.

Classic African Animals: The Big Five Anthony Dyer.

Houdini

*In 1960 nine rhinos were trapped to make way for human settlement and taken
to the Tsavo East National Park. The largest and most savage bull was named
Houdini because of his determined efforts to escape from the stockade in which
the rhinos were confined before their release.*

It was his size and ferocity that impressed the Rangers and prompted them to
devote more of their time to him than to any of the others. Special delicacies were
singled out for him, and after only a few days, he would accept these gently from
an outstretched hand. Whenever he happened to be lying within easy reach of the
side of the pen, the Rangers would scratch his tummy with a stick, and while this
liberty was vigorously repelled at first, the time came when he would actually
invite it, by lying down on his side and lifting his legs to make as much expanse of
tummy "scratchable" as possible. Later on, he even allowed his face to be
rubbed, while a sloppy soft expression spread slowly over it, and his eyelids
drooped contentedly. We thought all this remarkable in an adult wild animal, and
especially a rhino, but what followed was even more so. The Rangers sat on the
stockade sides with their legs dangling over, touching Houdini's back. Noticing
that he didn't appear to object, but continued to chomp unconcernedly at his
food, they then went a step further, and one Ranger cautiously lowered himself
until he was actually sitting astride this enormous rhino. Even then, Houdini paid
not the slightest attention, and permitted all the Rangers to take it in turns to
perform this feat, allowing them to clamber on and off as they pleased. What
other animal would become so docile within a short space of time? Within
two weeks people could go into his enclosure with him, handle him, ride on
him, stand on him and pet him with complete impunity, and this must surely go
a long way towards dispelling the reputation with which all rhino seem to be
labelled. . . .

Eventually the time came when the rhinos were due for release. One by one the
doors were opened and they were allowed to wander off into the Park, while we
watched from the safety of the stockade sides as they hesitatingly explored their
new surroundings, ambling slowly off until they were swallowed up by the bush.
Some returned again at night, seemingly reluctant to leave the security of the
stockades, but eventually all the inmates had gone, with the exception of only one
– Houdini. Because of the strong attachment everyone felt for him, we had left
him until the last.

Everyone assembled round him to bid him God-speed, patting his rump and
rubbing his face, until the sun sank slowly below the horizon, and we left him
browsing peacefully around the stockades.

Poor old Houdini! By befriending him we had unwittingly sealed his death
warrant. He saw nothing amiss in wandering into the nearby thickly populated
Teita Reserve, for he had learnt to trust and like humans. He must have been very

puzzled when his innocent appearance put everyone to flight, and more puzzled yet when he lay down to rest in a small thicket near a village school and awoke to find himself surrounded by a screaming mob who proceeded to pelt him with rocks and stones.

Word travelled fast about the presence of this "vicious" animal, which was labelled as a threat to the people of the district. They demanded his immediate death, and no amount of persuading could convince the people that, left unmolested, this particular rhino had no desire to kill anyone, but simply wished to be friendly, and that if he were allowed to remain, he would probably move on and establish a home elsewhere. Finally, the allegations against Houdini reached such proportions that an order from high authority for his immediate despatch was received by the Game Department representative.

We did all in our power to try and save Houdini. David recced the area by air and on foot, hoping that it might be possible to immobilize him and transport him back into the Park, but several intervening deep ravines made the place inaccessible to vehicles. Anyway, by the time we got to him, we discovered that he was no longer the docile friendly rhino we had patted on the rump only a week ago, but instead an enraged and dangerous animal; the result of days of persecution and a betrayal of the trust in *homo sapiens* so foolishly taught to him by us. His predicament hung heavily on our consciences, for under normal circumstances, this rhino would automatically have shunned human habitation and would probably have survived. As it was, because he had lost his most valuable aid to survival – a fear of human beings – Houdini ended up by being shot.

The Tsavo Story Daphne Sheldrick.

An appointment at the end of the world.

Out on the Safaris, I had seen a herd of Buffalo, one hundred and twenty-nine of them, come out of the morning mist under a copper sky, one by one, as if the dark and massive, iron-like animals with the mighty horizontally swung horns were not approaching, but were being created before my eyes and sent out as they were finished. I had seen a herd of Elephant travelling through dense Native forest, where the sunlight is strewn down between the thick creepers in small spots and patches, pacing along as if they had an appointment at the end of the world. It was, in giant size, the border of a very old, infinitely precious Persian carpet, in the dyes of green, yellow and black-brown. I had time after time watched the progression across the plain of the Giraffe, in their queer, inimitable, vegetative gracefulness, as if it were not a herd of animals but a family of rare, long-stemmed, speckled gigantic flowers slowly advancing. I had followed two Rhinos on their morning promenade, when they were sniffing and snorting in the air of the dawn, – which is so cold that it hurts in the nose, – and looked like two very big angular stones rollicking in the long valley and enjoying life together. I had seen the royal lion, before sunrise, below a waning moon, crossing the grey plain on his way home from the kill, drawing a dark wake in the silvery grass, his face still red up to the ears, or during the midday-siesta, when he reposed contentedly in the midst of his family on the short grass and in the delicate, spring-like shade of the broad Acacia trees of his park of Africa.

Out of Africa Karen Blixen.

River-horses

Hippos with their huge piggy faces and terrier ears are the pyknic's dream of supreme sensual fulfilment. They look like prosperous African Churchmen, Harlem revivalists stepping into their limousines. Most of their activities take place under water but one can hear them eating at night, browsing and chopping with the monotonous efficiency of a motor mower; their call, usually represented as a repeated long and three or four short grunts, "hosh-haw-haw-haw-haw" is mysteriously comforting.

When the launch got too close to a large family the bull would retaliate by taking a vicious chop at the behind of a smaller rival who squealed with pain but could not get away fast enough. In spite of their jovial and benign appearance they fight savagely and as a herd submerges one glimpses bottoms covered with weals like clients pulled in from a house of flagellation.

The Evening Colonnade Cyril Connolly.

Giraffes

In the harbour of Mombasa lay a rusty German cargo-steamer, homeward bound. I passed her in Ali bin Salim's rowing boat with his Swaheli rowers, on my way to the island and back. Upon the deck there stood a tall wooden case, and above the edge of the case rose the heads of two Giraffes. They were, Farah, who had been on board the boat, told me, coming from Portuguese East Africa, and were going to Hamburg, to a travelling Menagerie.

The Giraffes turned their delicate heads from the one side to the other, as if they were surprised, which they might well be. They had not seen the Sea before. They could only just have room to stand in the narrow case. The world had suddenly shrunk, changed and closed round them.

They could not know or imagine the degradation to which they were sailing. For they were proud and innocent creatures, gentle amblers of the great plains; they had not the least knowledge of captivity, cold, stench, smoke, and mange, nor of the terrible boredom in a world in which nothing is ever happening.

Crowds, in dark smelly clothes, will be coming in from the wind and sleet of the streets to gaze on the Giraffes, and to realize man's superiority over the dumb world. They will point and laugh at the long slim necks when the graceful, patient, smoky-eyed heads are raised over the railings of the menagerie; they look much too long in there. The children will be frightened at the sight and cry, or they will fall in love with the Giraffes, and hand them bread. Then the fathers and mothers will think the Giraffes nice beasts, and believe that they are giving them a good time.

In the long years before them, will the Giraffes sometimes dream of their lost country? Where are they now, where have they gone to, the grass and the thorn-trees, the rivers and water-holes and the blue mountains? The high sweet air over the plains has lifted and withdrawn. Where have the other Giraffes gone to, that were side by side with them when they set going, and cantered over the undulating land? They have left them, they have all gone, and it seems that they are never coming back.

In the night where is the full moon?

The Giraffes stir, and wake up in the caravan of the Menagerie, in their narrow box that smells of rotten straw and beer.

Good-bye, good-bye, I wish for you that you may die on the journey, both of you, so that not one of the little noble heads, that are now raised, surprised, over the edge of the case, against the blue sky of Mombasa, shall be left to turn from one side to the other, all alone, in Hamburg, where no one knows of Africa.

As to us, we shall have to find someone badly transgressing against us, before we can in decency ask the Giraffes to forgive us our transgressions against them.

Out of Africa Karen Blixen.

Hyenas

"Come, brothers!
Together we are strong
And hunt tonight!"
Or each alone
Sniff out the dying.
Tomorrow, an odd bone
Will witness a passing
Of the spirit freed.
David Lockwood

Bloody Mary and Lady Astor, leading matriarchs of the Scratching Rocks Clan, began to run fast over the moonlit plain, their tails aggressively curled over their broad rumps. Behind them ran some eighteen other members of the clan. About sixty yards ahead two hyenas of the neighbouring Lakeside Clan were resting close to the boundary of their territory. It seems that they were fast asleep, for when they got up Bloody Mary and Lady Astor were only a few yards from them. One of the pair was lucky and escaped, running for its life, but the other was not quick enough. Bloody Mary and Lady Astor seized hold of it and a few moments later it was practically hidden from sight as more and more of its enemies rushed in to bite and rend at its body. The night was filled with the fearsome roars and low whooping calls and growls of the triumphant Scratching Rocks Clan and the horrible screams of their victim.

Suddenly, however, a group of ten hyenas of the Lakeside Clan materialized out of the night and came racing in tight formation towards the battle ground. This group was small, but it was within its territory and the hyenas, as they ran to defend their "rights", were confident and aggressive. The unruly mob of Scratching Rocksters retreated hastily, leaving behind their badly wounded victim. For a short distance the Lakeside Clan pursued them, but once they had crossed the boundary into Scratching Rocks territory they stopped, uneasy on foreign soil.

Meanwhile the Scratching Rocksters, once they were well within their own territory, also stopped, and the two rival clans faced each other, both sides keeping tight formation. Each individual held its tail curled stiffly over its rump, and the low growling whooping calls sounded louder and louder in the night air. And all the time both clans were swelling in numbers as more and more members, attracted by the calls of battle, hurried to the scene.

Suddenly I saw the shadowy forms of Bloody Mary and Lady Astor rush forward, side by side, and a moment later the rest of the clan was behind its leaders. For a short while the Lakesiders held their ground, and there were loud roars and shrill giggling, chuckling sounds as hyenas briefly attacked and chased each other in the skirmish. And then the Lakeside Clan retreated, running back into its own territory. After chasing for a short distance the Scratching Rocksters, who had once more crossed their boundary, began to feel uneasy and they stopped. Again the two clans faced each other, the whooping calls filling the air until the Lakesiders, reaching a peak of frenzy, rushed forward to renew hostilities. Another brief skirmish and then the Scratching Rocks Clan once more retreated into its own territory.

And so it went on, each clan surging forward in turn behind its leaders and then suddenly breaking and rushing back from the aggressive charge of the other. Eventually there were between thirty and forty hyenas on each side, and the cacophony of their weird calls, the rustling and pounding of their heavy feet, the menace of their dark shapes were everywhere around us in the moonlight.

Twenty minutes from the start of the affair the skirmishing suddenly ended and members of both clans moved farther and farther into their own territories, some occasionally glancing back over their shoulders as though to make certain there were no further infringements of the boundary.

Innocent Killers Hugo and Jane van Lawick-Goodall.

Hunting dogs.

We run because me must . . .
We run because we like it
Through the broad bright land.
                                    Charles Sorley

But that morning the pack simply looked for anything it could catch. Moving along in a ragged front, they now settled into that inexorable trot, which in its determination has an almost sinister force. Black clouds roiled ahead and the hounds bounded toward them as if their play in the Elysian fields was ended and they were now returning to a Stygian world. A herd of wildebeest appeared, a dark mass moving ponderously under the glowering sky. The dogs halted, scrutinizing the herd intently. I knew that they were looking for a small wildebeest calf. They spotted one, less than two months old and still in its light-brown natal coat. Blacky took the lead as the pack moved closer at a steady lope. Then, when the dogs were about four hundred feet from the herd, they bunched up and stealthily walked closer, their ears retracted, their heads lowered but with muzzles pointing forward, while the wildebeest stood looking at them. The dogs reminded me of a gang of toughs just before a fight. The formation has an important function. A slowly moving, bunched pack can approach prey more closely than a scattered one. Suddenly the tails of the dogs whipped up and the pack dashed at the herd, which wheeled and fled in a compact mass. The wildebeest ran slowly, at about twenty-five miles per hour, the calves crowding the flanks of their mothers toward the middle of the herd. Dogs must scatter the herd to reach a calf, and they now raced behind and beside it, yipping with excitement, each animal an integral part in this cooperative effort. When the herd circled, two dogs met it from the front. This was enough to split the herd and a fragment of it with a calf veered to one side. The pack immediately concentrated on that calf. At first its mother tried to place herself between the dogs and her offspring, but soon she just ran along, trailed by her doomed young. While two dogs nipped her legs, one of the others bit the calf in the thigh and pulled it to a standstill. Within seconds the others tore at its rump and abdomen. The chase had lasted only half a mile. The female wildebeest ran on. She stopped briefly to look back when her calf bleated, but then hurried after the departing herd. Ten minutes later, the first dog set off for home, his belly full, and five minutes after that the last dog abandoned the untidy remains to a hyena. And at the den the pups and their mother awaited their share. The morning's hunt had required only six miles of travel.
                                    Golden Shadows, Flying Hooves George Schaller.

Hugo van Lawick followed the fortunes of a pair of golden jackals, Jason and Jewel, and their pups Rufus, Amba, Cinda and Nugget.

The first disaster to strike the Jason family occurred when the cubs were about ten weeks old. Jason was curled up near the den and the cubs were spread out insect-hunting nearby. It was a cloudy day with no sun to throw a warning shadow, and none of us saw the black shape silhouetted against the grey sky until it had half folded its wings to dive. Then we heard the air whistle through its feathers as it plummeted to the ground. For a split second the jackals froze, but when they heard Cinda's terrible scream as the eagle's claws gripped her they ran – the other cubs towards the den and Jason towards the eagle.

Slowly the bird, a bateleur eagle, carried the screaming Cinda off the ground whilst Jason ran along underneath, his head pointed up as he watched the drama above, unable to help. The bateleur is one of the smaller eagles and it had difficulty in gaining height with its comparatively heavy burden. Suddenly it let go of its prey and Cinda hurtled to the ground. I felt certain that she would survive neither the wounds made by the eagle's talons nor the impact of landing – for she had fallen some twenty feet.

Jason at once ran to the place where Cinda had landed, in a patch of high grass. I drove over there too when Jason looked calmer, but I saw no sign of Cinda. For the remainder of the day I watched the rest of the family without enthusiasm. For the most part the cubs lay around the entrance of the den, and twice they darted down when birds flew overhead. Jason went off hunting and, eventually, the sun sank. As I lay waiting for sleep that night I could still hear the whistling of wind through folded wings and Cinda's terrible scream; and I could still see the small golden body crashing down from the sky.

At the den next day life continued as if nothing had happened. Jewel slept in a clump of grass, Rufus hunted insects and Nugget played with a stone, holding it with his front feet as he lay on his side and pawing it with his back feet like a cat that plays with a ball of wool. Then he played with Amba when she came over to try and groom him. Jason was not visible, and I presumed he was out hunting.

Two hours after arriving at the den I started as a small figure slowly appeared from the den. It was Cinda. She walked stiffly, and when I examined her closely through my binoculars I saw she had a deep cut under her chin. I could see no other visible injuries. She blinked in the sunlight and then lay close to the den entrance. After a while Amba groomed her.

Cinda's wound turned into a nasty abscess and for nearly a week she was lethargic. Jewel and Amba frequently licked the place, however, and Cinda's health gradually improved until, three weeks later, she was back to her normal self. . . .

When last I saw Cinda she was curled up a few feet from her mate, near the fifth den of her cubhood. Jane and I had seen her courtship consummated – she at least lived to propagate Jason's fighting blood in her offspring. The tropical dusk was giving place to darkness, and I was about to turn the car and drive back to camp. Suddenly, in the distance, I heard a jackal howling. It was joined by another and then another. When the trio quietened their neighbours took up the strange high-pitched call, and then I heard more jackals to the south, and two more to the west. Finally Cinda and her mate howled, sitting side by side. Their duet, to my ears at least, was the last.

How difficult for man, despite his efforts, to learn the secrets of the animals he studies. The howling of the jackals, back and forth across the plains, probably shouted the information I so badly needed. "Here am I, Jaaason. And Jewel toooo," might have been the message from the west. And perhaps Nugget and his mate had answered from the east. But I was a mere human and it would take me months of research to piece together the information which Cinda, in those few moments, had stored away in her golden head. I sighed a little as I turned the car and drove back towards camp.

Innocent Killers Hugo and Jane van Lawick-Goodall.

Colobus Monkeys

The worst foe of the colobus is the big monkey-eating eagle (*Nisætus bellicosus*), a grand bird, but one of which the monkeys live in terror; a single eagle will keep a whole district in an uproar, for when monkeys are frightened they let the world know it. I have not actually seen the bird in the act of killing, but the Wandorobo say it is a wonderful thing to watch: the eagle, having marked the presence of a family of colobus, floats down to a convenient tree, and perches to await his chance. Presently he sees it, and makes his stoop, to use the falconer's term; if he misses the quarry he returns to his chosen tree and waits while the monkeys storm at him with all the power of their lungs; and their lungs are distinctly strong. This goes on for a long time, the eagle trying to seize a young colobus. The males show courage in dealing with their enemy; an old monkey will jump at him if he chance to pass below, and I have little doubt that if he made a good shot and alighted on the bird he would quickly get the best of it; his weight on the back of the eagle in flight, and the use he would make of his teeth, must give him an easy victory.

The obvious way for the monkeys to find safety, one might suppose, is to seek cover among the undergrowth where the eagle could not get at them; but to do this would be to leave the frying pan for the fire. If the monkeys had the wit to hold their tongues they might take cover thus; but, as a friend – the best bushman I know – points out, to come to ground would simply mean falling into the jaws of that other foe of monkeys, the leopard. When the uproar begins on arrival of the eagle, the leopard well knows what it means, and is sure to be on the spot to take advantage of the occasion; the colobus, jumping at the eagle, may come to ground and the leopard is waiting for him.

A dweller in the lichen-clad trees of the high grounds, it will be supposed that the colobus is difficult to catch; so he is while he remains in the large timber, but, unfortunately for himself, he likes a change of diet at certain times of the year, coming down to the bamboo region which is about 9,000 to 11,000 feet, and once there he becomes the prey of the Wandorobo. These people mark down a troop feeding in the bamboos, and assembling with their dogs above the victims to prevent retreat to the big trees, drive them carefully down the mountain-side as far as seems necessary. Then, closing in, the men make a rush at some bamboo on which a monkey is feeding, and shake it till he jumps, either to another bamboo or to the ground. The latter seldom happens, for bamboos grow thickly and the colobus is as good a jumper as the rest of his kin; so the hunt goes on, the quarry shaken from one bamboo to another until at last he misses his grasp and falls to the earth, when the dogs seize him, or attack him; the male is no despicable antagonist, and will put up a good fight with a large dog before he is overpowered. I must add that he sometimes gets the best of it and escapes; but many are thus killed.

A Game Ranger on Safari A. B. Percival.

Birds

Bird watchers the world over are drawn to the alkaline lakes of the Rift Valley to see the flamingos which gather on their shores; over an estimated million have been observed at one time on Lake Nakuru. Another favourite haunt is Lake Bogoria, formerly Hannington.

In the full moon, at the mouth of the spring, there appeared a group of pale bodies, constantly moving about, while from the dim waters of the lake beyond others swam in and yet others swam out again. In the clear light they were faintly and exquisitely pink, and they had a strange aura of radiance. They were Lesser Flamingos come to drink fresh water at the mouth of the stream and as I crept towards them, fascinated, more and more came, and the murmur of their calling swelled. Crawling on hands and knees I was able to reach a point only thirty feet or so from them, and there I lay content, bitten to pieces by mosquitoes but forgetful of all but the strange scene before me. In the moonlight the colours of their bodies were largely lost but for the pale pink radiance. They swam in to the spring, calling excitedly, from the open lake, they drank, and then swam out again. From time to time some wader would start them all into panic and they would rush out in a body with wildly flapping wings, only to return in a minute or two. When at length the mosquitoes penetrated my fascination as well as my skin it was half past three in the morning and I had been lying beside the water for hours. I crept back to bed, profoundly thankful that I had come.

In the morning, when we woke, the flamingos were still drinking at the mouth of the stream, and there were other clusters of them at the outlets of all the small geysers along the bank and wherever any other source of fresh water ran into the lake. It was my first intimation of the drinking habits of the Lesser Flamingo, and I have since learned that they must have fresh water and that they chiefly drink at night, and will continue to water until quite late in the morning if supplies are short for the numbers of birds present. On this day drinking continued until about eight o'clock and, when the birds had finished, they stood about the shore in flocks of up to a thousand together.

If the scene in the moonlight had been strangely and secretively lovely, the early morning spectacle was well-nigh unbelievable. As the sun rose over the Ngendalel escarpment so it lit up first a bay filled with a broad band of drinking flamingos and then picked out, one by one, the countless birds that were still swimming and feeding on the open waters of the lake, until the whole expanse before us was covered with moving shimmering pink. We tried to count them, but gave up in despair; I should now say that there might have been fifty thousand birds in a bay two miles across and about as long, most swimming on the water like miniature pink swans, but many clustered on shore in a dense band like some enormous flower bed. I have seen greater numbers of flamingos elsewhere and a greater spectacle at the same spot, but I can remember nothing that produced quite the same unexpected impact of transcendent beauty as the rising sun that morning.

The Mystery of the Flamingos Leslie Brown.

The dance of the whydah birds.

But the most interesting birds we saw were the black whydah finches. The female is a dull-coloured, ordinary-looking bird, somewhat like a female bobolink. The male in his courtship dress is clad in a uniform dark glossy suit, and his tail-feathers are almost like some of those of a barnyard rooster, being over twice as long as the rest of the bird, with a downward curve at the tips. The females were generally found in flocks, in which there would often be a goodly number of males also, and when the flocks put on speed the males tended to drop behind. The long tail hampers the bird in its flight, and it is often held at rather an angle downward, giving the bird a peculiar and almost insect-like appearance. But the marked and extraordinary peculiarity was the custom the cocks had of dancing in artificially-made dancing-rings. For a mile and a half beyond our camp, down the course of the Kamiti, the grassland at the edge of the papyrus was thickly strewn with these dancing-rings. Each was about two feet in diameter, sometimes more, sometimes less. A tuft of growing grass, perhaps a foot high, was left in the centre. Over the rest of the ring the grass was cut off close by the roots, and the blades strewn evenly over the surface of the ring. The cock bird would alight in the ring and hop to a height of a couple of feet, wings spread and motionless, tail drooping, and the head usually thrown back. As he came down he might or might not give an extra couple of little hops. After a few seconds he would repeat the motion, sometimes remaining almost in the same place, at other times going forward during and between the hops so as finally to go completely round the ring. As there were many scores of these dancing-places within a comparatively limited territory, the effect was rather striking when a large number of birds were dancing at the same time. As one walked along, the impression conveyed by the birds continually popping above the grass and then immediately sinking back was somewhat as if a man was making peas jump in a tin tray by tapping on it. The favourite dancing times were in the early morning, and, to a less extent, in the evening. We saw dancing-places of every age, some with the cut grass which strewed the floor green and fresh, others with the grass dried into hay and the bare earth showing through.

African Game Trails Theodore Roosevelt.

Many writers have observed the strange behaviour of the Greater Honeyguide. Here is one account.

I have been asked in England if it be true that the honey-guide will lead up to game, and yield to the temptation to say a word about this curious little bird – the *indicator indicator* of science, the *ndegi ya myusi* (bird of honey) of the black man. The honey-guide is about the size of a skylark, dull greenish-grey all over, save for a touch of bright yellow on the neck, and the two outermost tail feathers, which are white, and show distinctly when the bird is on the wing. There are four or five species of *indicator*, but only one acts as guide. They are closely allied to the cuckoos, and, like them, have the toes set, two forward and two back; like them they place their eggs in the nests of other birds; also, like cuckoos, they are insectivorous.

The guide is an expected visitor to camp. If he has not come flying across the plain to join the safari, he arrives and hovers round, to keep up his chattering call as soon as the tents are pitched, or within half an hour. It always interests the new-comer to observe the behaviour of the boys towards the honey-guide. They take no notice of him till the necessary work is done, and then, in the most casual, matter-of-fact way, a few of them collect bucket, axe and firebrand to set off, whistling to the bird as you might to your dog. It is this for which the honey-guide has been waiting; forthwith he takes wing and with dipping flight speeds away to a tree perhaps 100 yards off, where he awaits the boys. I am afraid they try his patience, for they never hurry; they know the guide will wait. They reach the tree, and the honey-guide flies off to another, and thus he pilots them by easy stages to their destination. As he draws near it his flights are shorter, till at length he flits from bough to bough, when the boys know the bees' nest is at hand. The chattering never ceases from the moment of the bird's arrival till the nest is taken. As a rule it is soon discovered and robbed of its honey, the boys appearing quite unaffected by the stings.

A Game Ranger's Note Book A. B. Percival.

The flight of the quelia.

It is only in recent years that *Quelea quelea* has acquired its reputation as the most numerous and also the most destructive bird in the world – a kind of avian locust. . . .

My first introduction to this bird was in 1952 from a fisheries launch on Lake

Victoria. We were cruising close off-shore where a belt of forest came to the water's edge, when suddenly from out of the canopy appeared a cloud-like swarm of little birds, flying rapidly over the trees in a compact body. It was as though, once they had assembled in formation, an invisible elastic envelope encompassed them from without, to exert some intangible pressure on the whole flock so as to compress the birds into the smallest space compatible with flight. Meanwhile, each individual maintained the necessary flying room and in some miraculous way the several birds seemed to be evenly distributed within the flock. Thus, while each kept apart from its neighbours in a sort of aerial territory, the group as a whole moved like a compact animated ball.

A remarkable feature of this exhibition was the speed of flight and precision of movement. The congregation, which comprised some thousands of individuals, rose and swung and turned as a unit. There appeared to be no leader: there were no stragglers in this rolling, surging, plunging sphere. As we watched, the birds continued on a course parallel with the shore, and then it was that the astonishing thing happened, for from out of three trees – giants standing high above the rest – there rose three more bird-clouds, each in turn joining and being absorbed by the original group as it passed over their perching place, so that by successive increments the speeding ball of wings merely increased in size without changing shape. The whole flock then rose high and out over the lake, the specks within the mass turning and twisting as waterlogged particles might move in a glass globe. Sometimes the globe itself would be distorted as an oval, or would open and close like a concertina, but always to return to its proper spherical shape. On another occasion when we were perhaps half-a-mile off-shore the bird-cloud lifted from the trees like smoke such as might be caused by a heavy explosion. The mob of birds moved over the lake. As the individuals wheeled and turned in perfect unison, the appearance of the flock changed and changed again – at one instant darkening as the innumerable silhouettes banked over to be seen in broadside view, at the next the birds would wheel away and momentarily vanish as if vaporized, to reappear again in clear relief. The hurrying, pulsating globe then veered off towards the trees, and could no more be seen, except for an instant when in a final evolution all the wings simultaneously caught the sunlight.

The quelia, or Sudan dioch, became a menace to crops second only to the locust. In the 1950s, control measures included blowing up the roosts in bushes. A single explosion could kill over half a million birds.

Mutual aid.

According to Herodotus: "The crocodile is in the habit of lying with its mouth open, facing the western breeze: at such time the *Trochilos* goes into his mouth and devours the leeches. This benefits the crocodile, who is pleased, and takes care not to hurt the *Trochilos*." The identity of the *Trochilos* was much debated in the last century. Among modern ornithologists, and despite the observations of reliable witnesses, there has been a tendency to dismiss the story as a myth.

In Uganda the Spurwing Plover (*Hoplopterus spinosus*) is the reptile's constant companion on all the favoured basking grounds, and may be seen running on, flitting over or standing close beside the sprawled bodies. Crocodiles immediately respond to their shrill alarm call – "quick-quick-quick", which is sufficient to alert the whole congregation and to start a stampede to the water. Another commensal is the Common Sandpiper. These waders run up to a crocodile as soon as it has hauled-out on to the bank, and will systematically work round the body in quest of ectoparasites. . . .

On the lower reaches of the Nile the crocodile's companion was the Egyptian Plover (*Pluvianus aegyptius*). The German naturalist A. E. Brehm, who travelled in Egypt and the Sudan in the 1850s, says of this plover: "Without the slightest hesitation it runs around on a crocodile as if it were just a bit of green lawn, pecks at the leeches that are bleeding the reptile, and even has the courage to take parasites adhering to the gums of its gigantic friend. I have seen this on several occasions". Confirmation of this account is given by Colonel Meinertzhagen, who in the Sudan watched the plover perch on the jaw of a crocodile, inspecting and pecking at something in the mouth. On the Kafue River in Zambia, the same role is played by the Blacksmith Plover (*H. armatus*).

Looking at Animals Hugh B. Cott.

Bird watching beside the Suam river, north-west Kenya.

Although the days are too hot for any vigorous exercise, and lotus eating from about eleven in the morning until five o'clock is most desirable, it is never dull. At the first flush of saffron above the eastern peaks Egyptian geese call as they go by to some pool above. Then the doves start and the hammerheads' melancholy whistle. After that little Grant francolins fill every thicket with a strident chatter, shrikes start their cool bell-like notes, somewhere the gay little dancing barbet taps out his staccato song while he dances with his mate side by side upon a low thorn branch. Blue starlings flash in flocks with raucous voices – their assembly should be called anything but a "murmuration". Soon it is light enough to see the markings, even on the little red waxbills. Still, while sitting with a *kikoi* round one's waist, the moment comes to get the field-glasses out to watch the tiny sunbirds, or the carmine-breasted shrike in the bushes, or the monkeys across the river preparing to risk descent to drink, or the old baboon troupe-leader scoop out the sand until he finds sub-surface water closer to the trees than the river. Like the warriors in Canaan they watch as they drink from their hands. All day long the pageant of bird-life in incredible variety goes on. Rollers and bee-eaters, turacos and hornbills and weaver-birds of every colour. Close to the river the fishing-birds take over. Noblest of all is the fish eagle with his white chest and melancholy cry. He claims the best meat for himself, then the tawny eagle and the kites, and last the vultures are allowed if the corpse is big enough.

The speckled kingfisher is a pretty angler. First the kestrel hovers, then plummets into the water and then a tiny fish is in his beak as he rises nearly as vertically as he dived. Perhaps for sheer speed the brown-shirt crested hammer-head is the winner. Awkward, looking like an old brown dominie, he waits on a near-vertical wet rock beside a low cascade. As a fishlet flashes down the waterfall so his beak darts and the fingerling is gobbled almost before it knows what ate it. . . .

Just before night falls can be a magic moment. Sitting quiet with a glass in hand, a herd of waterbuck will go by like cautious ghosts to the river's edge. Egyptian geese will fly talking across the last sunset bars and the hammerhead goes mournfully to bed. Soon the sky is pricked with stars. Orion lies sideways on his sworded hip and the pointers of the Plough show where the Pole Star lies behind our Globe.

A Knot of Roots Earl of Portsmouth.

Fish

On the coral reef.

We swam through deep valleys, which often led into caverns, and we peeped into dimly lit tunnels, out of whose depths coral fish emerged, inquisitive and puzzled by our monstrous bulk; they had good reason for their surprise, since under water everything looks twice its natural size.

We saw fish resembling red striped porcupine when swimming, which changed their quills to feathery wings while hovering like butterflies close to a coral. Some, like golden boxes dotted with spots of blue, had cow-like horns above their eyes; some were of deepest blue, recalling seas, with yellow maps of Africa drawn upon their flattened sides; some looked like coloured chess-boards; some like zebras; some had masks and trailed their elongated fins like floating veils between them; some puffers bloated their balloons and threw up quills like hedgehogs in defence; some thrust up an inch-long knife behind the dorsal fin, in fear; some lay out flat upon the floor, like giant sole, well camouflaged amongst the shifting sand; there were the buried clams, their mouths a deadly trap, just showing above ground; the deadly poisonous stone fish, whose puff adder markings were concealed by bright red fringes and which kept so still against a coral rock, except for amber-coloured eyes, which followed every move and gave the fish away; then there were crayfish with their sharp hooked armour; however threatening they looked they were far the easiest to shoot. They waited stupidly, half hidden under rocks, for the harpoon to penetrate their shell, between the eyes. Their long thin antennae floated at alert, but rarely warned in time to let the fish escape. The sea anemones, which seemed to us a mass of lovely flowers, were fatal to small organisms, which swam between their ever-moving tentacles.

Luckily the poison rays were always quicker than we and shot off long before we could detect their blue-spotted shapes hidden in the sand.

Born Free Joy Adamson.

Insects

Inimical insects.

The great armies of soldier ants, locally known by the name of *siafu*, cannot fail at some time or other to obtrude themselves on the notice of the resident in Africa. They will suddenly invade a house, built of wood and iron, penetrate behind the lining boards and clear out white ants and every other insect. Any rats will temporarily evacuate their quarters; nothing can withstand them. Luckily they usually disappear after a stay of a day or two. Native hunters say that this ant is the only thing an elephant is really afraid of, for it is apprehensive of these pugnacious little creatures penetrating its trunk, and they allege that cases have been known where this has occurred, when the elephant went mad with pain and beat its head against a tree until it died. This may or may not be true, but anyone who has had experience of a mass attack from *siafu* will consider the story to be plausible.

They travel about the country in columns which are often as long as 200 yards. The workers march four or five abreast; and parallel with the column, but a short distance away, march a larger kind, having much bigger mandibles, these are, it is believed, the males. If a stick is inserted into the column it temporarily breaks up, and the ants rush around seeking to attack the cause of disturbance.

Much has to be learnt about their life history, but their pugnacity does not encourage research. Their nests are in the ground, generally near water and, just before the rains break, they appear to move to higher quarters, for they seem to sense an approaching change in weather. If one of their columns is observed at this season, it will be seen that many of the workers are carrying eggs. . . .

Luckily the bite of a *siafu* does not cause any appreciable irritation once the insect is removed, but it is not a thing which can be stoically endured, and the grip of the ant is so tenacious that he often allows himself to be torn in half rather than loose his hold.

Kenya: From Chartered Company to Crown Colony C. W. Hobley.

The drier grasslands sprout tall, chimney-like excrescences which impart a weird, surrealist appearance to the landscape. These are termite castles created by what are often, and wrongly, called white ants.

Termites are not, as we might think, related to other social insects such as bees, wasps and ants. This mis-named "white ant" is not an ant at all: it belongs in a group of its own, more closely related to cockroaches than to ants. They have no forms which develop from unfertilized eggs, as worker bees do. Instead of starting life as a larva, the young termite hatches directly from the egg into a nymph, an immature copy of the adult.

Some termites are actually able to eat wood with the help of minute single-celled organisms in their stomachs. The so-called "gut flora" produce chemicals which break down the tough plant fibres and render them digestible for the termites. Other termites like *Macrotermes bellicosus* (the "big warlike termite") have no such helpers. Their answer is to become agrarians and cultivate their own food.

Underground, in the heart of the lightless chambers, *Macrotermes* shapes the earth into convoluted hanging gardens seeded with the spores of a particular fungus species and fertilized with half-digested regurgitated wood pulp. The little mushroom-like growths which flourish in the dark are the real food of *Macrotermes*.

In the rains when the soil is soft and moist, a caste of males and females becomes sexually mature and sprouts wings. One evening, after a heavy shower, workers open tunnels to the surface and the winged emissaries fly up towards the failing light. In the darkness they drop to earth again and having shed their wings perfunctorily, males and females form pairs and run off in tandem to seek a suitable site for the beginnings of a new nest. Those two creatures are all that is necessary to form a new colony; the female even has in her gut a minute piece of fungus to be regurgitated and become the nucleus of their fungus gardens.

Of the untold thousands that flew from the one nest only a minute fraction will survive the depredations of numerous predators and live to establish another colony. And the thousands that die – are they wasted? The answer must be, no. Termites are extremely tasty fare to predators, and on their nuptial flight they are at considerable risk as they flutter in silhouette against the evening sky. But there are so many of them; probably more than enough to fill the local predator population who cannot cope with these seasonal excesses, since their numbers are controlled by the average amount of prey available all year round. The enormous sacrifice ensures that some termites survive; and in any event, all the material will be recycled via bird droppings or genet dung and will be used again one day by termites. Thus for the ecosystem the nuptial flight of the termite ends in a rain of nutrients.

Pyramids of Life John Reader and Harvey Croze.

Tricking the termites.

During the dry weather a mysterious rattling sound, explained as "beating for *dudus*" (insects), may be heard every evening and all day long on Sundays. When we investigated we came upon a little party of boys sitting round an ant-heap. The spot they had chosen could not properly be called an ant-*heap* at all, as it was a flat, very hard spot, a few feet across, with several holes like narrow shafts, three or four inches in diameter, going down deep into the ground. The boys were provided with a pitcher of water, some green leaves, and a quantity of puddled mud made of blue river clay.

They took handfuls of mud and shaped it into short tubes, which they stood on end over the holes. Each tube was then lined with a big leaf, water was trickled down inside, and a flat cake of the clay placed on each as a cover. Every shaft was moistened and covered in this way, and then a boy took up two short sticks and started beating them rhythmically on a third stick, and they explained that the white ants below saw the water coming down the chimneys and said one to the other, "It is raining! See the water!" Then they heard the sticks beating and said, "We can hear the rain beating on the ground!" So they all came up to see. And sure enough they did! Not at once, for the beating of the sticks went on without pause, and after about half an hour a boy raised one of the lids and peeped inside. Nothing! But a couple of minutes after, when he opened another, it was swarming with white ants, all with wings. Instantly the boys fell on them, cramming them by handfuls into their mouths and spitting out the wings; other tubes filled, and when they could eat no more they packed the ants into bits of *americani* (cloth) and corners of their blankets to take home. They say the ants are *marfuta* (fat), and very good for men, but they know no moderation and often become ill from a surfeit.

The Youngest Lion Eva Bache.

Flies by the cupful.

I once camped by water where Masai had made their manyatta during the rains – this is the only way I can account for the plague – and all the flies in the district seemed to assemble for my benefit. It was extraordinary: my tent was literally black as to the ceiling, the walls grading off to a sort of pepper and salt; I could not use the tent at all. Another time, when the swarms were rather worse than usual and interfered with my work on skins, I arose in wrath and declared war with the butterfly net; I swept up flies by the cupful, and went on sweeping till I had reduced their numbers to something endurable. I weighed the bag: two lbs. avoirdupois. Kill, if you can find enough, flies to the weight of, say, half an ounce, and see what two lbs. means! In cold weather the creatures fall, an intermittent shower of crawling, obnoxious helplessness on one's bed, table, clothes – everywhere.

Yet I prefer flies to the small red ticks which find one out at some camps. Against flies I can take active and drastic measures: those ticks are insidious foes, not only do they bite as venomously as the mosquito, they get under one's clothes which the mosquito does not, and bite you from head to foot. More, the bite of the red tick is likely to develop into what we call a veld sore. As for mosquitoes, I give the palm for these to the neighbourhood of the Lorian Swamp; I doubt if there be in the world a place to equal that for clouds of voracious mosquitoes.

A Game Ranger on Safari A. B. Percival.

Bee-lore in the forests of the Aberdare mountains, Nyandarua.

On our walks about the mountain Gichimu would often pause, and standing as in a trance he would listen to the voice of the bees in the tree tops. Then, with hand sheltering his eyes, he would gaze skywards between the leafy branches of the trees.

To an untrained observer nothing was visible, but Gichimu had seen the tiny dots as they sped away and noted their direction. As often as not he would motion me to be seated whilst he slipped away to examine some old dead tree he knew of across the valley. . . .

Kikuyu honey hunters recognize four distinct varieties of wild honey bees. Gichimu described these to me as we sat there with the sun climbing through a cloudless blue sky.

"First there is the Dambarari, a blackish bee whose distinguishing characteristic is that instead of packing its honeycombs across the inside of the barrel, it packs them lengthwise so that they are long and narrow instead of being round like a plate. These bees are not very fierce and quickly become docile as soon as smoke is blown into the hive.

"Then there is the Hiinga. This is a brown bee and the most vicious of all. The honeycombs are packed across the barrel and when smoke is blown in the voice of the bees becomes a high-pitched scream of anger. Many people who are unaccustomed to bee stings have fallen to their death from an attack of the Hiinga.

"The Hogi is a brown bee with black abdominal stripes. There are two types of Hogi, one smaller than the other, neither particularly fierce, just so-so.

"Lastly there is N'Jore. This is a small, black bee which only hives in the ground. They find cavities under trees and rocks in which to deposit combs of their very sweet watery honey, and are hard to find because their entrances are mere holes the size of a finger."

Gichimu went on to tell me more about the wild honeybees. To attract them to a new hive a substance called *githingu* is smeared inside the barrel and on the lid. This substance is prepared by the honey hunter from the following ingredient: fat from the stomach of a male goat. This forms a base and ensures cohesion. Dust is gathered from the roads and paths leading to the area, preferably from those which come from the different points of the compass and which are well used by hunters. This ensures that a travelling swarm will find its way safely to the new hive.

Bits of rubbish from some large market place are also gathered, such as particles of maize cob, banana skin and earth. This will ensure that a large and thriving swarm will come. Bee droppings from an old hive are gathered which contain a strong bee smell; sweet-smelling bark of the Muthaiti and the bulb of an onion-like plant called Kirago which has a very pungent smell are also used.

All these ingredients are pounded together until they are thoroughly mixed into a putty-like substance which smells pleasantly aromatic. . . .

On the way home we came down the valley in which Gichimu had his honey barrels. He led me along a little path which followed the contour of a hillside on which I had not previously been, which was Gichimu's own private honey-trail. As we went he pointed out his barrels high up in the forks of the trees.

"In the old days, *Bwana*, a man taught his sons how to collect honey and how to tend the hives, and when he became too old to climb the hills, his sons collected the honey, and brought it to him, each receiving their own share. Nowadays young men are no longer interested for it is hard work and the sting of bees is painful until a man is used to it. And anyway, the young people no longer drink the good honey mead of their forebears but choose to waste their money on the fizzy bottled beer at the markets."

Wide Horizons Venn Fey.

Postscript

The butterfly and the hereafter.

In contemplating the hereafter you should include in your deliberations the life cycle of the butterfly, which deposits its spherical egg the size of a pinhead on the leaf of a special plant utilized by its particular species as a food for its larvae. The embryo within the egg can have no possible inkling of its next stage or surroundings.

When the egg hatches, a tiny caterpillar or larva emerges, first devouring its shell before sallying forth to find a suitable leaf on which to browse. Every few weeks the larva moults, after which it is larger and takes on a brighter hue, until it is fat and rather sluggish and behaves as if it is on the threshold of death.

Then one day comes the amazing change that can only be likened to death. The larva writhes as if in torment, to such an extent that a novice would conclude that it had contracted some terrible convulsive illness. Shedding its last skin, it then changes its entire form as a caterpillar to that of a small green orb attached by a thread or a dab of glue to the underside of a leaf or a branch, where it remains in its pupa case, to all outward appearances, a corpse in its coffin.

Can this pupa in its coffin possibly know that on a certain day when weather conditions and its particular plant food are in their right condition the pupa case, the coffin, will split asunder and from its embalmment will emerge an entirely different insect to any of those previously described? This creature will have a head with large eyes and a pair of antennae, a thorax or chest, and an abdomen. It will also have stubby, fat embryo wings, and legs with which it will hang upside down to the rim of its old pupa case where it will commence the process of pumping its excess body fluids into its wings in order to expand them to their ultimate size.

When the wings have hardened, the butterfly begins to open and close them.

They are brand new and very beautiful, and ready for flight into a new world of sunshine and flowers, forests and wide skies.

We know not our hereafter, any more than did the little egg deposited on its plant, or the caterpillar munching its leaf, or the entombed pupa, that thereafter is to be reborn an entirely different being with the gift of flight in an environment such as it had never dreamed of.

Wide Horizons Venn Fey.

PART VII

Hunting

To Africa's indigenous peoples, with a few exceptions, hunting was a way of getting meat, as it remains where laws do not forbid it; where they do, you get poachers. East Africa's game drew from overseas first the ivory hunters, then sportsmen who hunted under licence from the government. This was the age of the white hunter and the lavish safari. As farmers, black and white, cleared land of bush and forest and drove away or shot the game, so the habitat of the wild animals contracted, and much of it disappeared. Game reserves were established at the start of the colonial period. In 1946 the first national park was gazetted, largely at the instigation of Colonel Mervyn Cowie: this was the tiny but game-rich Nairobi Park that can be reached in twenty minutes from the general post office. Others followed, notably the largest, Tsavo, two years later. Perhaps the best known, Maasai Mara, is not a national park but a game reserve, because the land belongs to the Maasai. In recent years public opinion has, in many countries, turned against killing animals for sport, and in 1977 all hunting, save for birds, was banned. Poachers, however, ignored the ban and almost eliminated the black rhino in the wild; only its presence in one or two closely protected reserves keeps hope alive for its survival. In the 1980s ivory poachers greatly intensified their activities and modernized their techniques, four-wheel-drive vehicles and automatic weapons replacing snare and bow and arrow. Elephant populations were decimated, but in 1989 the government declared an all-out war against the poachers. Tourists from the world over now pour into Kenya to observe the wild animals, and provide the major source of foreign currency. Even so, the animals are under threat from the pressure of an ever rising population, both of humans hungry for land and of their domestic livestock hungry for grazing.

Elephants and other animals have been hunted by man ever since mankind began and indeed before that, by early forms of hominid. These are among methods used in the second century BC.

Certain of them (the hunters) sit up in trees and watch the movements of the animals. As an animal passes, they descend swiftly, and pushing the left thigh with their feet they cut the tendons of the right knee with an axe made specially for this purpose; and thus with one hand they inflict such wounds and with the other they grasp the tail so firmly, that it is as if a life and death struggle is in progress, for they must either kill or be killed. As soon as the beast has fallen, from the force of the blow and from loss of blood, the hunter's companions appear on the scene, and while the animal is still alive they cut the flesh from its quarters and feast thereon with joy. The beast subdued in this way suffers a long and painful death.

The Elephantophagoi (Elephant-eaters) therefore live among great dangers. Others of them have a different method of capturing the animals. Three men equipped with one bow and plenty of arrows dipped in snake-poison station themselves in a glade where the elephants come out. When an elephant approaches, one of the men holds the bow and the other two draw the bowstring with all their force, releasing the arrow which is aimed at the middle of the animal's flank, so that on striking it will penetrate the inner parts, cutting and wounding as it goes in. Hence even so great a beast grows feeble and falls, convulsed with pain.

There is a third group of Elephant-hunters who hunt in this manner: When the elephants go to rest after eating their fill, they do not sleep lying on the ground, but lean against the largest and thickest trees so that the weight of the body is supported by the tree; so that you might call this a spurious rather than a true way of resting because the deepest sleep is troubled by the possibility of destruction through falling, for once these animals have fallen they cannot raise themselves. Therefore when the Elephant-hunters wandering in the forest see one of these resting-places they cut through one side of the tree with a saw in such a way that it will neither fall on its own nor support a weight, but will take only a very slight strain. The beast returning from pasture to its accustomed sleeping-place leans against the tree, which immediately gives way, and so a meal is provided for the hunters. The flesh from the quarters is cut away and the animal dies from loss of blood; the rest of the meat is then distributed among the hunters.

Ptolemy king of Egypt ordered these hunters by an edict to refrain from killing elephants, so that he himself might be able to have them alive; and he promised them great rewards for obedience. But not only could he not persuade them to obey, but they answered that they would not change their mode of subsistence for the whole kingdom of Egypt.

From *The Periplus of the Erythraean Sea*, ed. G. W. B. Huntingford.
On the Erythraean Sea Agatharkhides as epitomized by Photiōs.

Some two thousand years later, African hunters were still killing elephants with weapons of ingenious design.

The people with whom we are dealing at the moment were poor and therefore hunters. Africans differ from us entirely on the question of hunting; whereas among us it is the well-off who hunt, among them it is the poor. Having nothing but a few goats and sheep, these hunters inhabit the bush, shifting their village from site to site according to the movements of the game.

Their system of taking game is the snare; their only weapon a spear. The art of snaring has been brought to a unique development by these people, for they have snares varying in size for all animals from elephant down to dik-dik.

The snare for elephant is a great hawser, 4½ ins in diameter, of twisted antelope or giraffe hides. One may find in the same rope haartebeeste hide, eland, zebra, rhinoceros, buffalo and giraffe hide. If made of haartebeeste alone no less than eleven or twelve skins are required. The skins are scraped and pounded with huge wooden mallets for weeks by the women before being twisted or "laid" into the rope which is to form the snare. The running nooses at both ends are beautifully made. Besides the snare there is a thing like a cart wheel without any hub and with scores of thin spokes meeting in the centre where their points are sharp. The snare is laid in the following manner:

A well frequented elephant path is chosen and somewhere near the spot decided upon for the snare a large tree is cut. Judgment in the choosing of this must be exercised as if it is too heavy the snare will break, and if too light the snared elephant will travel too far. A tree trunk which ten or twelve men can just stagger along with seems to be the thing. This log is then brought to the scene of action and at its smaller end a deep groove is cut all round to take the noose at one end of the rope. After this noose has been fitted and pulled and hammered tight – no easy matter – the log is laid at right angles to the path with the smaller end pointing towards it. A hole a good bit larger than an elephant's foot is then dug in the path itself to a depth of two feet or so. Over this hole is fitted the cart wheel. Round the rim the large noose of the snare is laid and the whole covered carefully over with earth to resemble the path again. The snare is now laid, and if all goes well some solitary old bull comes wandering along at night, places his foot on the earth borne by the sharp spokes of the hubless wheel, goes through as the spokes open downwards, lifts his foot and with it the wheel bearing the noose well up the ankle, strides forward and tightens the noose. The more he pulls the tighter draws the noose until the log at the other end of the snare begins to move. Now alarmed and presently angry, he soon gets rid of the cart wheel, but as its work is already done, that does not matter. The dragging log is now securely attached to the elephant's leg, and it is seldom that he gets rid of it unless it should jamb in rocks or trees. Soon he becomes thoroughly alarmed and sets off at a great pace, the log ploughing along behind him. Should a strong, vigorous young bull become attached to a rather light log, he may go twenty or thirty miles.

As soon as it becomes known to the natives that an elephant has been caught, everyone within miles immediately seizes all his spears and rushes to the spot where the snare had been set and from there eagerly takes up the trail of the log. When they come up with the somewhat exhausted animal they spear it to death. Then every scrap of meat is shared among the village which owns the snare, the tusks becoming the property of the man who made and laid the snare.

The Wanderings of an Elephant Hunter W. D. M. Bell.

The Wandorobo sometimes employ a stalking-horse in hunting. I well remember the first time I saw a man thus equipped. I was out looking for Grevy's zebra when suddenly from behind a bush there appeared the strangest of figures leading – of all animals in the world – an oryx; at least, I took it for one at first. It proved to be a donkey disguised. His ingenious owner had fitted him out with a mask of zebra skin, the black stripe down the face, horns of stick fastened into it; and the flanks and legs of that donkey were embellished with marks like those of the antelope. He really looked wonderfully well! The sportsman himself was got up to suit the case, smeared all over with wood-ashes to the proper colour, matching both his donkey and oryx; he led the cuddy by a string to the nose and kept him going as required by an occasional touch on the rump. I watched him; he knew better than press his stalking-horse unduly; he kept him gently on the move, and when the donkey put down his nose to feed the man sat patiently on his heels till it seemed good to the sham oryx to move on again. I don't doubt that under cover of the metamorphosed donkey the man was able to approach within killing range of his game.

A Game Ranger's Note Book A. B. Percival.

Since time immemorial, the Waliangulu had hunted game. They were thought to have been the original inhabitants of the Tana River, and because they were only a small tribe, and not sufficiently strong to stand alone, they had formed an association with some families of the powerful, nomadic Galla people. In exchange for the protection afforded them by the Galla, the Waliangulu provided meat and ivory.

Over the years, as the threat of inter-tribal conflict gradually diminished, the Waliangulu drifted from the custody of their protectors, and formed their own small settlements, where they lived, and still live, entirely by hunting.

Bows and poisoned arrows are used for this purpose. The poison, which is placed on the head and steel shaft of the arrows, and then wrapped in a protective hide covering, contains an extremely toxic glycoside known as oubain, which is derived from boiling the bark and leaves of a certain species of *Akokanthera* tree in water for about seven hours until a sticky, tarlike substance is produced. Sometimes lizards, snakes and live shrews are thrown into the cauldron for good measure. The woody matter is then skimmed off the surface, and the mixture concentrated further by evaporation, until the required consistency is obtained. It is then packed in strips of maize husk, until ready for use, and this serves to shield the poison from the sun and rain which has a deleterious effect on its potency.

The poison is usually applied to the arrow shaft and head prior to an actual hunt. A great deal of secrecy and prestige is attached to the manufacture of the poison, and certain members of the Giriama tribe, who inhabit the coastal strip, are considered the foremost experts in this field. The potency of the poison deteriorates with age, but when fresh, it can kill an elephant within a couple of hours. It is active, however, only when introduced into the bloodstream, and causes death by upsetting the muscular contractions of the heart and arteries.

Although all *akokanthera* trees are poisonous to some extent, in most cases the berries are edible. For some extraordinary reason, however, certain trees growing in the coastal belt are particularly lethal and the poison-makers are careful to select their material from these trees, which can be easily detected by the presence beneath them of birds and rodents that have died as the result of having eaten the berries.

The potency of the poison is tested in rather a brutal way. A thorn, which has been dipped into the poison, is jabbed into an unfortunate frog or lizard, and the time it takes to die is carefully noted. If the poison is fresh, a frog or lizard should succumb within a few seconds. It is said, also, that if an egg is pricked, and a little poison inserted, it will burst within half an hour if the poison is of good quality.

The meat from animals killed by poison is edible, and in no way tainted. Whenever possible, the arrow head is extracted from the carcase, for not only can it be used again, but the head normally carries the identification mark of the owner; a very important factor when several hunters may be operating in the same area, and an elephant might wander for several days before it eventually dies. When the locality of the carcase is revealed by the presence of vultures, the markings on the arrow head establish positive proof of ownership of the animal. It is not considered "cricket" amongst the poaching fraternity to remove the tusks from an elephant killed by another man's arrow, and retribution for this offence can be extremely harsh.

The Tsavo Story Daphne Sheldrick.

The end of the nineteenth and early days of the twentieth centuries were the heyday of professional elephant hunters who led their caravans far inland to plunder the great herds that still possessed those unmapped lands. Perhaps the most famous of these hunters was Arthur Neumann, who at the end of 1893 set out from Mombasa with fifty Swahili porters to hunt in the mainly unexplored country north of Mount Kenya. It was near the shores of Lake Turkana that he had the narrowest of his many narrow escapes.

Advancing hastily thus, on the look-out for another shot, I came suddenly on two or three (elephants) round a corner of the path. Among them was the vicious cow, and she came for me at a rush. I say *the* vicious cow, because, from her short stature and small tusks, I believe she must have been the same that had made the short charge earlier in the day; I could also see that there was a large calf following her as she came. I stood to face her, and threw up my rifle to fire at her head as she came on, at a quick run, without raising her trunk or uttering a sound, realizing in a moment that this was the only thing to do, so short was the distance separating us. The click of the striker was the only result of pulling the trigger. No cartridge had entered the barrel on my working the bolt after the last shot, though the empty case had flown out! In this desperate situation I saw at once that my case was well-nigh hopeless. The enraged elephant was by this time within a few strides of me; the narrow path was walled in on each side with thick scrub. To turn and run down the path in an instinctive effort to escape was all I could do, the elephant overhauling me at every step. As I ran those few yards I made one spasmodic attempt to work the mechanism of the treacherous magazine, and, pointing the muzzle behind me without looking round, tried it again; but it was no go. She was now all but upon me. Dropping the gun, I sprang out of the path to the right and threw myself down among some brushwood in the vain hope that she might pass on. But she was too close; and, turning with me like a terrier after a rabbit, she was on the top of me as soon as I was down. In falling I had turned over on to my back, and lay with my feet towards the path, face upwards, my head being propped up by brushwood. Kneeling over me (but fortunately not touching me with her legs, which must, I suppose, have been on each side of mine), she made three distinct lunges at me, sending her left tusk through the biceps of my right arm and stabbing me between the right ribs, at the same time pounding my chest with her head (or rather, I suppose, the thick part of her trunk between the tusks) and crushing in my ribs on the same side. At the first butt some part of her head came in contact with my face, barking my nose and taking patches of skin off other spots, and I thought my head could be crushed, but it slipped back and was not touched again. I was wondering at the time how she would kill me; for of course I never thought anything but that the end of my hunting was come at last. What hurt me was the grinding my chest underwent. Whether she supposed she had killed me, or whether it was that she disliked the smell of my blood, or bethought her of her calf, I cannot tell; but she then left me and went her way.

My men, I need scarcely say, had run away from the first: they had already disappeared when I turned to run. Finding the elephant had left me, and feeling able to rise, I stood up and called, and my three gunbearers were soon beside me. I was covered with blood, my clothes were torn, and in addition to my wounds I was bruised all over; some of my minor injuries I did not notice till long afterwards. Squareface, on seeing the plight I was in, began to cry; but Juma rated him for his weakness and he desisted. I made them lead me to a shady tree, under which I sat supported from behind by one of them sitting back to back with me; was stripped as to my upper parts, and my wounds bound up. I then told Juma to run back to my camp as fast as he could for help to carry me in.

> *Neumann's journey lasted nearly three years. He mastered many tricks of survival. When suffering from thirst he shot a zebra, slit its stomach open and drank the water within. Clear, fresh water, he wrote, would result from a correctly made incision; otherwise it looked like weak tea and had a vegetable flavour; "after all, it is only grass." He dyed his clothes reddish-brown with a concoction of mimosa bark. "When standing motionless (the wind being favourable) I think an elephant takes one, so disguised, for a dry tree stump."*

At last, on 1 October 1896 we once more entered Mombasa; and the men – decked in showy clothes, and headed by drummers hammering out, in perfect time, the regular "safari" beat – enjoyed the long-looked-forward-to parade through the streets. And a picturesque sight it is to see a string of porters, with gleaming ivory arcs on their shoulders, threading slowly the narrow streets, thronged with dusky but cleanly-clad onlookers; the leading men jumping up and dancing about with their hundred-weight tusks, to show off before their admiring female friends. Indeed, it is often difficult to get them along at all, so proud and excited are they at entering their metropolis again after all the adventures of so long a journey; and custom allows the "kilangozi" (or leading porter) to refuse to move until backsheesh of rupees has been sent to entice him to proceed with the caravan to deposit their loads at the custom-house. That done, I give each man a rupee by way of "posho" for the day, and they disperse to make merry among their friends in the town. A weighty bag of silver has to be ready for them when they reassemble at my quarters the following morning to receive their pay. Careless, confiding fellows these porters; they make no attempt to calculate how much is due to them nor ever think of counting over what they receive. The one whose name is called holds out the corner of his cloth for the double handful of rupees, twists it up without a word, and off he goes – in most instances to squander recklessly the reward of a year or more's service. . . .

I fear the fact that my journey was attended with so few serious difficulties or privations detracts from its interest to others; but it is a source of considerable satisfaction to me to think that my men never suffered from either hunger, thirst, or disease; that they got their regular ration daily, without our having ever raided or taken anything from the natives by force; that they carried their loads willingly, cheerfully, and without suffering; and that, with the exception of the two whose tragic loss I had to mourn, I brought them all back, safe, sound, and happy, to Mombasa. (His personal servant, Shebane, was taken by a crocodile; his gunbearer, Squareface, by a man-eating lion). They on their part had been as good as gold to me while I was ill, and I feel the greatest gratitude to them for their kindly feeling towards me. I tried to treat them as well as I could, and they amply repaid me, and would, I know, follow me anywhere to-morrow.

Elephant Hunting in East Equatorial Africa Arthur Neumann.

At Elmentaita I met Neumann, whose name was given to the haartebeeste. He is a professional ivory hunter, conducting his work somewhere around Lake Rudolph. He is a quiet, unassuming little man, with a faraway and rather sad outlook on life. We had a long chat together about game and the glories of the simple wild life in Africa. Neumann's native name is Bwana Nyama, or the Lord of Meat. This was given to him on account of his fussiness in always insisting on his meat having a fly-proof cloth tied round it, a precaution the natives could not understand. Neumann is just off back to Rudolph.

Kenya Diary 1902–1906 Richard Meinertzhagen.

The true story of his African nickname, told to Mr Monty Brown by a 103-year-old Dorobo many years later, was as follows. A stew prepared for Neumann's enjoyment, left unattended for a few minutes, was gobbled up by one of the tribesmen in camp. Neumann, infuriated, shouted out 'wapi nyama yangu! Wapi nyama yangu!" – "Where's my meat! Where's my meat!"

Thereafter he became known as Nyama yangu *throughout his hunting grounds in the North. Neumann committed suicide in London in 1907.*

In the early 1900s W. D. M. Bell, a Scotsman barely turned twenty-one, reached Karamoja, then a no-mans'-land bordering on Kenya, Uganda and Sudan, unadministered, and with abundant elephants as yet little disturbed. Unlike most ivory hunters, he depended on a light rifle used with great precision, rather than on a double-barrelled blunderbuss. Pyjalé was a naked Karamajong warrior who attached himself to Bell as guide and counsellor.

Here we were face to face with such a gathering of elephant as I had never dared to dream of even. The whole country was black with them, and what lay beyond them one could not see as the country was dead flat. Some of them were up to their knees in water, and when we reached their tracks the going became very bad. The water was so opaque with mud as to quite hide the huge pot-holes made by the heavy animals. You were in and out the whole time. As we drew nearer I thought that we ought to go decently and quietly, at any rate make some pretence of stalking them, if only out of respect to them. But no, that awful Pyjalé rushed me, splashing and squelching right up to them. He was awfully good, and I began to learn a lot from him. He treated elephant with complete indifference. If he were moved at all, and that was seldom, he would smile.

I was for treating them as dangerous animals, especially when we trod on the heels of small bogged-down calves, and their mothers came rushing back at us in the most alarming fashion, but Pyjalé would have none of it. Up to the big bulls would he have me go, even if we had to go under infuriated cows. He made me kill seven before sundown stopped the bloodshed.

With great difficulty we found a spot a little higher than the surrounding country and fairly dry. As usual at these flood times the little island was crawling with ants of every description. How comes it that ants do not drown, although they cannot swim? They appear to be covered with something which repels water.

Scorpions and all kinds of other horrors were there also. One of the boys was bitten and made a fearful fuss all night about it.

I expected to do well on the morrow, but when it came, behold, not an elephant in sight. Such are the surprises of elephant hunting. Yesterday when light failed hundreds upon hundreds in sight and now an empty wilderness.

Karamoja Bell, as he was known, is said to have shot more than 1,000 elephants.

Elephant! *Atome!* (in Karamojo). Word the first to be learned and the last to be forgotten of any native language. A kind of excitement seizes us all; me most of all, the Karamojans least. Now the boys are told to stay behind and to make no noise. They are at liberty to climb trees if they like. I look to my .303, but, of course, it had been ready for hours. Noting that the wind – what there was of it – was favourable, the natives and I go forward, and soon we come upon the broken trees, mimosa and white thorn, the chewed fibrous balls of sansivera, the moist patches with froth still on them, the still steaming and unoxidised spoor, and the huge tracks with the heavily imprinted clear-cut corrugations of a very recently passing bunch of bull elephants. In numbers they were five as nearly as I could estimate. Tracking them was child's play, and I expected to see them at any moment. It was, however, much longer than I anticipated before we sighted their dull grey hides. For they were travelling as well as feeding. It is remarkable how much territory elephant cover when thus feeding along. At first sight they seem to be so leisurely, and it is not until one begins to keep in touch with them that their speed is realized. Although they appear to take so few steps, each step of their lowest gait is about 6 ft. . . .

I was now almost light-headed with excitement, and several times on the very verge of firing a stupid and hasty shot from my jumping and flickering rifle. So shaky was it when I once or twice put it to my shoulder that even in my then state of mind I saw that no good could come of it. After a minute or two, during which I was returning to a more normal state, the animal with the largest tusks left the line slightly, and slowly settled into a halt beside a mimosa bush. I got a clear glimpse at his broadside at what looked about twenty yards, but was really forty yards, and I fired for his heart. With a flinch, a squirm and a roar he was soon in rapid motion straight away, with his companions in full flight ahead of him. I was rather surprised at this headlong flight after one shot as I had expected the elephant here to be more unsophisticated, but hastily concluding that the Swahili traders must have been pumping lead into them more often than one imagined, I legged it for the cloud of dust where the fleeting animals had disappeared. Being clad in running shorts and light shoes, it was not long before I almost ran slap up against a huge and motionless grey stern. Recoiling very rapidly indeed from this awe-inspiring sight, I saw on one side of it an enormous head and tusk which appeared to stick out at right-angles. So drooping were the trunk and ears and so motionless the whole appearance of what had been a few seconds ago the very essence of power and activity that it was borne straight to even my inexperienced mind that here was death. And so it was, for as I stared goggle-eyed the mighty body began to sway from side to side more and more, until with a crash it fell sideways, bearing earthwards with it a fair sized tree. Straight past it I saw another elephant, turned almost broadside, at about 100 yards distance, evidently listening and obviously on the point of flight. Running a little forward so as to get a clear sight of the second beast, I sat quickly down and fired carefully at the shoulder, when much the same performance took place as in the first case, except that No. 2 came down to a slow walk after a burst of speed instead of to a standstill as with No. 1.

Ranging rapidly alongside I quickly put him out of misery and tore after the others which were, of course, by this time, thoroughly alarmed and in full flight. After a mile or two of fast going I found myself pretty well done, so I sat down and rolled myself a cigarette of the strong black shag so commonly smoked by the

Swahilis. Presently my native guides came with every appearance of satisfaction on their now beaming faces.

After a few minutes' rest we retracked the elephant back to where our two lay dead. The tusks of the first one we examined were not long but very thick, and the other had on one side a tusk broken some 2 feet outside the lip, while on the other was the magnificent tusk which had filled me with wonder earlier on. It was almost faultless and beautifully curved. What a shame that its companion was broken!

As we were cutting the tail off, which is always done to show anyone finding the carcase that it has been killed and claimed, my good fellows came up with the gear and the interpreter. Everyone, including myself, was in high good humour, and when the Karamojans said that their village was not far off we were more pleased than ever, especially as the sun was sinking rapidly. After what appeared to the natives no doubt as a short distance, but what seemed to my sore feet and tired legs a very long one, we saw the welcome fires of a camp. A kettle was soon on the fire for tea, while some strips of sun-cured haartebeeste biltong writhed and sizzled on the embers. Meanwhile my boys got the bed ready by first of all cutting the grass and smoothing down the knobs of the ground while another spread grass on it to form a mattress. Over this the canvas sheet and blankets and with a bag of cartridges wrapped in a coat for a pillow the bed was complete. Then two forked sticks stuck in the ground close alongside the bed to hold the rifle and all was ready for the night.

After a hearty supper of toasted biltong and native flour porridge, washed down with tea, I cleaned my rifle, loaded it and lay down utterly tired out and soon dropped off to the music of hyenas' howling.

Return with the spoils.

After consulting the donkey-headman it was decided that we had almost as much ivory as we could carry. Many of the tusks were too long for donkeys and should have been taken by porters. It was decided to return to our base through untouched country. The news was received with shouts of joy. It is wonderful how one comes to regard the base camp as home. Whereas, on our way up, the camps had been rather gloomy – disasters having been prophesied for this expedition – now all was joy. The safari chronicler became once more his joyous self and his impromptu verse became longer and longer each night. The chronicler's job is to render into readily chanted metre all the important doings of the safari and its members. It is a kind of diary and although not written down is almost as permanent, when committed to the tenacious memories of natives. Each night, in the hour between supper and bedtime, the chronicler gets up and blows a vibrating blast on his waterbuck horn. This is the signal for silence. All is still. Then begins the chant of the safari's doings, verse by verse, with chorus between. It is extraordinarily interesting but very difficult to understand. The arts of allusion and suggestion are used most cleverly. In fact, the whole thing is wonderful. Verse by verse the history rolls out on the night, no one forgetting a single word. When the well-known part is finished, bringing the narrative complete up to and including yesterday, there is a pause of expectation – the new verse is about to be launched. Out it comes without hesitation or fault, all to-day's events compressed into four lines of clever metric *précis*. If humorous its completion is greeted with a terrific outburst of laughter and then it is sung by the whole lot in chorus, followed by a flare-up of indescribable noises; drums, pipes, horns and human voices. And then to bed, while those keen-eyed camp askaris mount guard; although they cannot hit a mountain by daylight they fire *and kill* by night with a regularity that always leaves me dumb with astonishment. Remember they are using .450 bore bullets in .577 bore barrels, and explain it who can. They call it "medicine".

We traversed some queer country on our return to Dodose. All kinds were met with. We went thirty days on end without seeing an elephant, and in the succeeding four days I killed forty-four bulls. . . .

That safari was one of my most successful. We "shuka'd," or went down country, with over 14,000 lbs. of ivory – all excellent stuff.

The Wanderings of an Elephant Hunter W. D. M. Bell.

The long arm of government reaching out to the remotest regions put an end to the ivory hunters by restricting the number of elephants each man might shoot. Then came the white hunters, conductors of safaris paid for by rich men and women, most of whom killed for pleasure rather than profit. Some hunters collected specimens for museums, among them ex-President Theodore Roosevelt, who in 1909 embarked upon one of the most lavish expeditions of them all.

In the thirst the march goes on by day and night. The longest halt is made in the day, for men and animals both travel better at night than under the blazing noon. We were fortunate in that it was just after the full of the moon, so that our night treks were made in good light. . . .

The wagons broke camp about ten, to trek to the water, a mile and a half off, where the oxen would be outspanned to take the last drink for three days; stock will not drink early in the morning nearly as freely as if the march is begun later. We, riding our horses, followed by the long line of burdened porters, left at half-past twelve, and in a couple of hours overtook the wagons. The porters were in high spirits. In the morning, before the start, they twice held regular dances, the chief musician being one of their own number who carried an extraordinary kind of native harp; and after their loads were allotted they marched out of camp, singing and blowing their horns and whistles. Three askaris brought up the rear to look after laggards, and see that no weak or sick man fell out without our knowing or being able to give him help.

The trail led first through open brush, or low dry forest, and then out on the vast plains, where the withered grass was dotted here and there with low, scantily-leaved thorn-trees, from three to eight feet high. Hour after hour we drew slowly ahead under the shimmering sunlight. The horsemen walked first, with the gun-bearers, saises [grooms], and usually a few very energetic and powerful porters; then came the safari in single file; and then the lumbering white-topped wagons, the patient oxen walking easily, each team led by a half-naked tribesman with frizzed hair and a spear or throwing-stick in his hand, while at intervals the long whips of the drivers cracked like rifles. The dust rose in clouds from the dry earth, and soon covered all of us; in the distance herds of zebra and haartebeest gazed at us as we passed, and we saw the old spoor of rhino, beasts we hoped to avoid, as they often charge such a caravan.

Slowly the shadows lengthened, the light waned, the glare of the white, dusty plain was softened, and the bold outlines of the distant mountains grew dim. Just before nightfall we halted on the further side of a dry watercourse. The safari came up singing and whistling, and the men put down their loads, lit fires, and with chatter and laughter prepared their food. The crossing was not good, the sides of the watercourse being steep, and each wagon was brought through by a double span, the whips cracking lustily as an accompaniment to the shouts of the drivers, as the thirty oxen threw their weight into the yokes by which they were attached to the long trek tow. The horses were fed. We had tea, with bread and cold meat – and a most delicious meal it was – and then lay dozing or talking beside the bush-fires. At half-past eight, the moon having risen, we were off again. The safari was still in high spirits, and started with the usual chanting and drumming.

We pushed steadily onward across the plain, the dust rising in clouds under the spectral moonlight. Sometimes we rode, sometimes we walked to ease our horses. The Southern Cross was directly ahead, not far above the horizon. Higher and higher rose the moon, and brighter grew the flood of her light. At intervals the barking call of zebras was heard on either hand. It was after midnight when we again halted. The porters were tired, and did not sing as they came up; the air was cool, almost nipping, and they at once huddled down in their blankets, some of them building fires. We, the white men, after seeing our horses staked out, each lay down in his overcoat or jacket and slicker, with his head on his saddle, and his rifle beside him, and had a little over two hours' sleep. At three we were off again, the shivering porters making no sound as they started; but once under way, the more irrepressible spirits speedily began a kind of intermittent chant, and most of the rest by degrees joined in the occasional grunt or hum that served as chorus.

African Game Trails Theodore Roosevelt.

Comfort was the keynote of a safari conducted by Baron Bror von Blixen-Finecke, a popular white hunter between the wars, and consisting of Frederick Guest, his wife Amy, their two sons Winston and Raymond, and their daughter Diana. There were also two assistant white hunters, a transport manager, a flight mechanic in charge of a seven-seater aeroplane, and fifty Africans. Diana's ambition was to shoot an elephant.

We got onto the first spoor quite close to the big waterhole in the cliffs, twelve miles from camp. That was the one we examined yesterday and found that three bulls had been drinking there. I myself didn't think the tracks were particularly big, but Gondo (the tracker) was very enthusiastic. "One of them is the one that got away at the time when *Mtoto ya Kingi* was here," he said, very sure of himself. *Mtoto ya Kingi* (son of the king) was the Prince of Wales. We got out, left the car and driver, and started tracking. We were now walking due south and the wind was from the north, so conditions couldn't have been worse. However, Gondo was stubborn and wanted to continue. "They are not very close yet," he said. "They are on the other side of that hill. When we get as far as that the sun will be overhead and the afternoon breeze always comes from the northwest," so we ambled on.

You could only walk in the tracks, as the sansevieria was flattened and trampled down there and one would have been repeatedly pricked by its spikes. Nevertheless it was strenuous walking. One had to be on the alert all the time. If one happens to tread on one of the spikes, it can penetrate the sole of a shoe. The popular name "bayonet grass" is indicative of the damage it will cause when coming in contact with any part of the human body. It has been known to blind a man forever. You have probably seen them in other areas, a sporadic plant here and there, but around Kasigau they grow as densely as reeds. The natives also call them "the forts of the elephant," a very appropriate expression. So this is why we had to proceed so slowly.

The sun climbed higher, gradually it became hotter, and the contents of the water bottles warmer. I glanced at Diana's face, which had become pinker. "Go on, old boy, I'm okay!" Personally, I did not have much hope for today's hunt. Yesterday had been so lucky and successful that a repeat performance seemed impossible. Gondo, however, was still on his toes and optimistic. He held an old sock in his hands half filled with flour, which he shook periodically to determine the direction of the wind. Suddenly he stopped, sniffed, and shook his sock. "Now the wind has turned and it will blow from this direction for the rest of the afternoon." Behind the mountain the terrain is more open and nothing like as dense as where we were. "By the time it is four o'clock the bulls will graze there," he added with great conviction. Optimism always helps. The heat was now suffocating and every step was an effort. Admittedly, the gunbearers walked in front and with their razor-sharp bush knives cut the worst sansevieria leaves, but even so we couldn't avoid being pricked now and then.

Suddenly, without anybody having expected it, we heard the familiar sound of elephant ears flapping against a body and then some puffing, probably not more than a hundred yards away. All fatigue immediately vanished. Gondo carries my .505 and Juma Diana's .350. Gondo leads, then myself, Juma, and Diana. We produce our secateurs, the only instrument I know of that can silently cut off sansevieria and protruding branches. The wind remains steady and we creep slowly and carefully forward. Now we hear more flapping of the ears, and the occasional snorting seems to indicate he is half asleep. We are now so near that we can hear the protests from the swarms of insects as they are swept away by the enormous ears. A few steps more, extremely slowly and with bodies perfectly balanced. A gray shadow moves over there, slightly to our left. I shove Gondo to the side, push Diana in front of me, and take over her .350. Gondo is now behind me.

Any moment now the elephant should start coming in our direction. But he just stands there feeling safe within his fortress, to which there is no direct access. It is not yet four o'clock. Isn't he soon going to start grazing down in the glade? The terrain couldn't be worse; it is practically impossible to take a step to either side. Our way ahead looks like a description from the Middle Ages of a path of horror where the victim is forced to pass between rows of spears. Suddenly I realize that this is the worst possible place imaginable to take a young girl elephant hunting. How on earth could I have let myself get involved in a situation like this? I curse Gondo, silently but sincerely.

Now he moves again over there. He showers earth over neck and shoulders with his trunk and when he throws his head back he exposes a most magnificent pair of tusks high above the surrounding grass. All self-accusation immediately vanishes, life is beautiful and glorious, and Gondo is the most excellent man alive.

We are now only twenty-five yards from him, but the grass is very thick. In front of us and to the left there is a small tree exactly in the direction he is now taking. "High on the shoulder, when you see him," I whisper, and hand her the .350 with the safety catch off. At the same time I automatically receive my rifle from Juma.

Diana knows exactly where to aim. We have sketched this on paper every night. She has only once been nervous, and that was when she thought she might not be allowed to come on this safari.

Now the tusks emerge from the bushes, there comes the head, and then the forelegs. *Bang.* With a heavy sigh the giant sinks to the ground with a broken back and folding hindlegs. But a fallen elephant can get up again, and we wait with rifles at the ready. Then comes the drawn-out trumpet call signalling the end. "*Nakufa.*" He is dead.

Bror von Blixen: *The Africa Letters*, ed. G. F. V. Kleen.

Another well-known white hunter was Denys Finch Hatton, even better known as the lover of Karen Blixen, Bror Blixen's former wife.

A safari can be a misery if the organization is slapdash. Denys possessed a practical ability, the foresight to arrange expeditions that went off smoothly. Avoiding the unhappy results of haphazard packing he made it a rule to cover every eventuality without over-burdening the porters with loads of superfluous kit. He likened a safari to being marooned on a desert island: "Method maketh man". He said "remember that the real secret of ordering stores is to know how long each tin of sardines, so to say, will last you. You have to work it out by the law of averages. These mathematics will teach you that one pound of tea lasts one man a fortnight . . . a one pound tin of marmalade will last the same man a week and ten days to finish a tin . . . of plum jam . . . the whole art of buying stores lies in being able to estimate the 'life' of a tin of sardines."

No detail during Denys's preparation for safari was too small. Tents were inspected for rents, missing ropes or poles, and had to be at least eight feet high "so that a man of some inches may stand straight in it and be at ease". A tent bathroom he felt was "a most necessary annexe in which not only to bathe but to keep cameras, rifles and other dearer possessions". His efficiency was motivated by a natural desire to have things running smoothly so that he could relax and enjoy himself fully. Forgetfulness was dangerous for "it is no unusual thing to arrive late in camp . . . too tired but for an impromptu meal. . . . But where is the tin opener? The tin opener is in Nairobi . . . though your servants can . . . open a tin given time . . . it will not be before your temper is fairly frazzled. It is easy to forget things".

Silence Will Speak Errol Trzebinski.

Together with Bror von Blixen, Beryl Markham evolved the technique of spotting good tuskers from the air.

I think I am the first person ever to scout elephant by plane, and so it follows that the thousands of elephant I saw time and again from the air had never before been plagued by anything above their heads more ominous than tick-birds.

The reaction of a herd of elephant to my Avian was, in the initial instance, always the same – they left their feeding ground and tried to find cover, though often, before yielding, one or two of the bulls would prepare for battle and charge in the direction of the plane if it were low enough to be within their scope of vision. Once the futility of this was realized, the entire herd would be off into the deepest bush.

Checking again on the whereabouts of the same herd next day, I always found that a good deal of thinking had been going on amongst them during the night. On the basis of their reaction to my second intrusion, I judged that their thoughts had run somewhat like this: A: The thing that flew over us was no bird, since no bird would have to work so hard to stay in the air – and, anyway, we know all the birds. B: If it was no bird, it was very likely just another trick of those two-legged dwarfs against whom there ought to be a law. C: The two-legged dwarfs (both black and white) have, as long as our long memories go back, killed our bulls for their tusks. We know this because, in the case of the white dwarfs, at least, the tusks are the only part taken away.

The actions of the elephant, based upon this reasoning, were always sensible and practical. The second time they saw the Avian, they refused to hide; instead, the females, who bear only small, valueless tusks, simply grouped themselves around their treasure-burdened bulls in such a way that no ivory could be seen from the air or from any other approach.

This can be maddening strategy to an elephant scout. I have spent the better part of an hour circling, criss-crossing, and diving low over some of the most inhospitable country in Africa in an effort to break such a stubborn huddle, sometimes successfully, sometimes not.

But the tactics vary. More than once I have come upon a large and solitary elephant standing with enticing disregard for safety, its massive bulk in clear view, but its head buried in thicket. This was, on the part of the elephant, no effort to simulate the nonsensical habit attributed to the ostrich. It was, on the contrary, a cleverly devised trap into which I fell, every way except physically, at least a dozen times. The beast always proved to be a large cow rather than a bull, and I always found that by the time I had arrived at this brilliant if tardy deduction, the rest of the herd had got another ten miles away, and the decoy, leering up at me out of a small, triumphant eye, would amble into the open, wave her trunk with devastating nonchalance, and disappear. . . .

Sometimes I circle a herd for nearly an hour, trying to determine the size of its largest bull. If at last I decide that he carries enough ivory, my work begins. I must figure the course from the herd to the hunters' camp, reverse the course, jot it down on my pad, judge the distance, give details of terrain, warn of other animals in the vicinity, note water holes, and indicate safest approach.

I must find my smoke signal again, keeping an eye on the compass, a hand free for scribbling, and my course and distance calculator ready, should I need it. I feel triumphant when I can drop a note like this which Blix has returned to me and is still folded in my logbook:

Very big bull – tusks quite even – my guess over 180-pounder. In herd of about 500. Two other bulls and many babies in herd – grazing peacefully. Dense growth – high trees – two water holes – one about half-mile from herd NNE. Other about two miles WNW. Fairly open ground between you and herd, with open glade halfway. Many tracks. Large herd buffalo SW of elephant. No rhino sighted. Your course 220 degrees. Distance about ten miles. Will be back in one hour. Work hard, trust in God, and keep your bowels open – Oliver Cromwell.

Well Cromwell *did* say it, and it still makes sense.

All of it makes sense – the smoke, the hunt, the fun, the danger. What if I should fly away one morning and not come back? What if the Avian fails me? I fly much too low, of necessity, to pick a landing spot (assuming that there might be a landing spot) in such a case. No, if the engine fails me, if a quick storm drives me into the bush and sansivera – well that is the chance and that is the job. Anyway, Blixi has told Farah and Ruta what to do if I am ever gone for a longer time than my supply of petrol might be expected to last – get to a telegraph by foot or lorry, and wire Nairobi. Maybe somebody like Woody would begin the search.

Meanwhile, haven't I got two quarts of water, a pound of biltong – and the doctor's bottled sleep [a phial of morphine] (should I be *hors de combat* and the Siafu hungry that night?) I certainly have, and, moreover, I am not defenceless. I have a Lüger in my locker – a gun that Tom has insisted on my carrying, and which can be used as a short rifle simply by adjusting its emergency stock. What could be better? I am an expedition by myself, complete with rations, a weapon, and a book to read – *Air Navigation*, by Weems.

All this, and discontent too! Otherwise, why am I sitting here dreaming of England? Why am I gazing at this campfire like a lost soul seeking a hope when all that I love is at my wingtips? Because I am curious. Because I am incorrigibly, now, a wanderer.

West With the Night Beryl Markham

To shoot a lion was the primary aim of every visiting sportsman. The then Prince of Wales was no exception.

On 16 November, 1928, the Prince of Wales was to come to Arusha on his way from Nairobi to Dar-es-Salaam. It was an unofficial visit, but all the same the town was *en fête*; all the neighbouring farmers were to come; the hotel was giving a dance; the Masai had arranged a great ngoma. A battalion of the King's African Rifles was paraded for inspection; a football match had been fixed up; in short, there was as complete a festival atmosphere as the little town at the foot of Mount Meru could achieve.

My wife and I had driven our 115 miles into the town like the rest and pitched camp not far from the hotel. I was just shaking a cocktail when a little man came into the tent and said:

"I'm the Prince of Wales, and should like to make your acquaintance."

"You could not have chosen a more suitable moment," I replied with a smile, and put the ice-cold shaker on the table.

We drank to one another and sat down. The Prince asked if I could accompany him for a few days and help him to bag a lion. Of course I willingly placed myself at his disposal, and began my duties with him that very evening in the most pleasant way imaginable – my wife and I were invited to dinner at his hotel. . . .

I had put down the kills by night, after shooting several zebras, and when I visited them at dawn I found two lions on no less than four of the shot beasts – eight lions in all. I waited till they had finished their morning meal without disturbing them, but when they had withdrawn into the shade of the brushwood for their day's rest I sent for the royal party.

Unfortunately the boys I had sent for to take part in a drive had not turned up, so when I had placed the Prince and Finch Hatton at the most likely spot for the first lions, I had to constitute myself beater along with a few drivers and the Prince's suite. The lions broke out, but not till we had a few exciting moments when one of them rushed out, roaring savagely, only a few yards from the Prince's adjutant, who was armed only with a shot-gun.

At the next kill things went better, although the ground was not so favourable. I myself do not like hunting lion in long grass, and it was only after much hesitation that Finch Hatton and I decided to try it. But I proposed that the Prince should have more than one gun with him; and Finch Hatton, Captain Moore, and the

Prince's two equerries were placed on one side of the copse into which the lions had withdrawn to rest.

For a description of what followed I will take the liberty of quoting the Prince of Wales himself. His diary of experiences in Africa, which his secretary turned into a book, contains the following passage:

> Similar tactics were employed with this difference; that Blixen (whose attitude towards lions is that of the prophet Daniel) decided to be the sole beater. He had not gone far when a lion appeared at the edge of the covert. It turned rapidly and re-entered the bush. "Shoo," said Blixen, not to be denied, "Shoo," and he clapped his hands. Out bounded the lion.
>
> He really looked rather fine. Broadside on, he galloped across the front. HRH was shooting with a 350 double-barrel Express lent to him by Grigg. With the first barrel he missed cleanly and cleverly. A little rattled at that, he took more time to his second shot. The left-hand barrel was fired at the lion when he was 140 yards away. The grass was tallish, and the big, yellow beast went bounding through it in great leaps. It was a difficult shot because of the grass, and a long one. But it was a lucky one also, for it knocked the lion over and over. HRH reloaded and ran up to where it lay.
>
> The lion lay still after the shot, but on closer approach he got on to his legs and made off, but he was unable to get very far. He then stopped and wheeling round, obviously intended to charge. By this time HRH was close up to him and before he could get going gave him both barrels again, hitting him full in the chest each time. The last shot dropped him anew, but the grass was so long it was not until the rifle was right on top of him that he was seen to be dead.
>
> *African Hunter* Bror von Blixen.

Lions were a perpetual menace to the stockman. Lord Delamere hunted them sometimes on horseback, sometimes on foot.

The excitement of the sportsman may be imagined who has followed the mighty spoor for mile after mile over sand, through gullies and open bush till it disappears in a small dense clump of jungle, and the most careful search detects no mark of exit. It was by this method that Lord Delamere, the prince of lion-shooters, made the greater proportion of his bag. Single-handed, he has accounted for close on seventy lions, more than twice as many as stand to the credit of any other sportsman. He holds a far more wonderful record still. Of the first forty-nine lions at which he fired and wounded he did not lose a single one! Next to Lord Delamere, the most famous lion-hunters in East Africa are the brothers Hill, ostrich farmers on the verge of the Athi plains, and Mr A. B. Percival, the game-ranger.

A Colony in the Making Lord Cranworth.

I knew a Somali who without so much as a stick in his hand saved Lord Delamere's life with his bare hands. Lord Delamere was down under a wounded lion which had already broken one of Lord Delamere's legs and was crushing it in his jaws. The Somali seized the lion's head on both sides, and tugged at him till he dropped his victim and terribly mauled the deliverer. This lion was despatched by the Somalis the next day, and Lord Delamere set his own broken leg and nursed himself and his boy back to health, if not to soundness of limb. Lord Delamere goes slightly lame, and the Somali is maimed for life, but received a well-deserved pension from the man he saved.   *The Land of the Lion* Sir Alfred Pease.

This Nandi hunt was witnessed by ex-President Theodore Roosevelt on the Uasin Gishu plateau in 1909.

In an hour we overtook the Nandi warriors, who were advancing across the rolling, grassy plains in a long line, with intervals of six or eight yards between the men. They were splendid savages, stark naked, lithe as panthers, the muscles rippling under their smooth dark skins. All their lives they had lived on nothing but animal food – milk, blood, and flesh – and they were fit for any fatigue or danger. Their faces were proud, cruel, fearless; as they ran they moved with long springy strides. Their head-dresses were fantastic; they carried ox-hide shields painted with strange devices; and each bore in his right hand the formidable war-spear, used both for stabbing and for throwing at close quarters. The narrow spear-heads of soft iron were burnished till they shone like silver; they were four feet long, and the point and edges were razor sharp. The wooden haft appeared for but a few inches; the long butt was also of iron, ending in a spike, so that the spear looked almost solid metal. Yet each sinewy warrior carried his heavy weapon as if it were a toy, twirling it till it glinted in the sun-rays. Herds of game – red hartebeests and striped zebra and wild swine – fled right and left before the advance of the line.

It was noon before we reached a wide, shallow valley, with beds of rushes here and there in the middle, and on either side high grass and dwarfed and scattered thorn-trees. Down this we beat for a couple of miles. Then, suddenly, a maned lion rose a quarter of a mile ahead of the line and galloped off through the high grass to the right, and all of us on horseback tore after him.

He was a magnificent beast, with a black and tawny mane; in his prime, teeth and claws perfect, with mighty thews, and savage heart. He was lying near a hartebeest on which he had been feasting; his life had been one unbroken career of rapine and violence; and now the maned master of the wilderness, the terror that stalked by night, the grim lord of slaughter, was to meet his doom at the hands of the only foes who dared to molest him. . . .

It was a mile before we brought him to bay.

One by one the spearmen came up at a run, and gradually began to form a ring round him. Each, when he came near enough, crouched behind his shield, his spear in his right hand, his fierce, eager face peering over the shield rim. As man followed man, the lion rose to his feet. His mane bristled, his tail lashed, he held his head low, the upper lip now drooping over the jaws, now drawn up so as to show the gleam of the long fangs. He faced first one way and then another, and never ceased to utter his murderous grunting roars. It was a wild sight; the ring of spearmen, intent, silent, bent on blood, and in the centre the great man-killing beast, his thunderous wrath growing ever more dangerous.

At last the tense ring was complete, and the spearmen rose and closed in. The lion looked quickly from side to side, saw where the line was thinnest, and charged at his topmost speed. The crowded moment began. With shields held steady, and quivering spears poised, the men in front braced themselves for the rush and the shock; and from either hand the warriors sprang forward to take their foe in flank. Bounding ahead of his fellows, the leader reached throwing distance; the long spear flickered and plunged; as the lion felt the wound he half turned, and then flung himself on the man in front. The warrior threw his spear; it drove deep into the life, for, entering at one shoulder, it came out of the opposite flank, near the thigh, a yard of steel through the great body. Rearing, the lion struck the man, bearing down the shield, his back arched; and for a moment he slaked his fury with fang and talon. But on the instant I saw another spear driven clear through his body from side to side; and as the lion turned again the bright spear-blades darting toward him were flashes of white flame. The end had come. He seized another man, who stabbed him and wrenched loose. As he fell he gripped a spear-head in his jaws with such tremendous force that he bent it double. Then the warriors were round and over him, stabbing and shouting, wild with furious exultation.

From the moment when he charged until his death I doubt whether ten seconds had elapsed – perhaps less; but what a ten seconds! The first half-dozen spears had done the work. Three of the spear-blades had gone clean through the body, the points projecting several inches; and these and one or two others, including the one he had seized in his jaws, had been twisted out of shape in the terrible death-struggle.

We at once attended to the two wounded men. Treating their wounds with antiseptic was painful, and so, while the operation was in progress, I told them, through Kirke, that I would give each a heifer. A Nandi prizes his cattle rather more than his wives, and each sufferer smiled broadly at the news, and forgot all about the pain of his wounds.

Then the warriors, raising their shields above their heads, and chanting the deep-toned victory song, marched with a slow, dancing step around the dead body of the lion, and this savage dance of triumph ended a scene of as fierce interest and excitement as I ever hope to see.

African Game Trails Theodore Roosevelt.

Shooting a pair of lions in a coffee plantation after dinner was a more low-key affair.

At nine o'clock we went out.

It rained a little, but there was a moon, from time to time she put out her dim white face high up in the sky, behind layers and layers of thin clouds, and was then dimly mirrored in the white-flowering coffee-field. We passed the school at a distance; it was all lighted up.

At this sight a great wave of triumph and of pride in my people swept through me. I thought of King Solomon, who says: "The slothful man saith, There is a lion in the way; a lion is in the streets." Here were two lions just outside their door, but my school-children were not slothful and had not let the lions keep them from school.

We found our marked two rows of coffee-trees, paused a moment, and proceeded up between them, one in front of the other. We had moccasins on, and walked silently. I began to shake and tremble with excitement, I dared not come too near to Denys for fear that he might feel it and send me back, but I dared not keep too far away from him either, for he might need my torchlight any moment.

The lions, we found afterwards, had been on the kill. When they heard us, or smelt us, they had walked off it a little way into the coffee-field to let us pass. Probably because they thought that we were passing too slowly, the one of them gave a very low hoarse growl, in front and to the right of us. It was so low that we were not even sure that we had heard it. Denys stopped a second; without turning he asked me: "Did you hear?" "Yes," I said.

We walked a little again and the deep growling was repeated, this time straight to the right. "Put on the light," Denys said. It was not altogether an easy job, for he was much taller than I, and I had to get the light over his shoulder on to his rifle and further on. As I lighted the torch the whole world changed into a brilliantly lighted stage, the wet leaves of the coffee-trees shone, the clods of the ground showed up quite clearly.

First the circle of light struck a little wide-eyed jackal, like a small fox; I moved it on, and there was the lion. He stood facing us straight, and he looked very light, with all the black African night behind him. When the shot fell, close to me, I was unprepared for it, even without comprehension of what it meant, as if it had been thunder, as if I had been myself shifted into the place of the lion. He went down like a stone. "Move on, move on," Denys cried to me. I turned the torch further on, but my hand shook so badly that the circle of light, which held all the world, and which I commanded, danced a dance. I heard Denys laugh beside me in the dark. – "The torch-work on the second lion," he said to me later, "was a little shaky." – But in the centre of the dance was the second lion, going away from us and half hidden by a coffee-tree. As the light reached him he turned his head and Denys shot. He fell out of the circle, but got up and into it again, he swung round towards us, and just as the second shot fell, he gave one long irascible groan.

Africa, in a second, grew endlessly big, and Denys and I, standing upon it, infinitely small. Outside our torchlight there was nothing but darkness, in the darkness in two directions there were lions, and from the sky rain. But when the deep roar died out, there was no movement anywhere, and the lion lay still, his head turned away on to his side, as in a gesture of disgust. There were two big dead animals in the coffee-field, and the silence of night all around.

We walked up to the lions and paced out the distance. From where we had stood the first lion was thirty yards away and the other twenty-five. They were both full-grown, young, strong, fat lions. The two close friends, out in the hills or on the plains, yesterday had taken the same great adventure into their heads, and in it they had died together.

Out of Africa Karen Blixen.

Scruples.

I shot my lion. It was a fine lion – one of the best, Delacott said, that had been killed that year in Kenya. Nine feet five inches, measured unfairly after skinning, is not a remarkable length, but its crowning glory was an especially thick golden mane, just going black in places, which grew right back beneath the forelegs and far along the body. Lions are all that they have been made out to be, but they have been made out to be so much that when at last you meet them, even though they fulfil specifications, it is hard to avoid a feeling of anti-climax. Yet from the first moment I set eyes on this particular beast, I knew I was greatly privileged. And I murdered it. Or rather, I co-murdered it.

Hitherto I had always wondered at the reticence of certain men, not invariably reticent, when they described to me the climax of a hunt. They would tell of many a heart-breaking stalk, of arduous marches through the heat and the flies, of their feelings as at last the moment came. But the climax itself was often colourless.

I had thought to join the ranks of the strong and silent but I had not reckoned with the lion. More potent in death than in life, it hangs at the foot of my staircase and, as I go upstairs to bed, I meet its eye. It is not a real eye. It is a simple affair of glass. But for all that Messrs Gerrard and Sons could do, until I wrote this chapter, that eye had a wink in it.

"Exactly how proud are you," it seemed to say, "of having murdered me?"

Three sentences can tell the humiliating tale. As I fired the lion rolled over on its side. I turned to ask Delacott if I need shoot again. Just as I did so he fired himself and the lion lay dying on its back.

The boys came rushing up to me and shook me by the hand. Even our head boy, the usually unemotional Dunga, was wild with delight. Delacott's face was glowing. "I really do congratulate you," he cried. "This isn't an ordinary lion. It's about the finest specimen I've ever known shot in Kenya."

"Thanks," I said and was silent, hoping that he would take that silence for modesty or for the too-full-for-words condition. I was fighting desperately to keep control of myself so that as yet I should not spoil the pleasure of these people who had worked so hard for ten days to bring me this moment of triumph. Of triumph I felt nothing. All that was in my heart was a rising shame, a rising anger and a hope that I could get back to my tent before I burst into tears.

The Spotted Lion Kenneth Gandar Dower.

Game rangers and wardens were charged with the contradictory tasks of protecting both the wild animals and the crops these animals frequently destroyed. George Adamson queries the necessity.

Other elephants brought themselves into disrepute by indulging in mud baths in the Isiolo water supply and interfering with horticulture. Game Scouts shot five close to the scenes of their crimes, including a fine old bull which was well known to Isiolo residents and over the past ten years was often to be seen at all hours of the day peacefully feeding in the prison gardens oblivious of passing traffic and village urchins who came to throw stones at him.

I often wonder what future generations will think of us for destroying noble and rare living animals in order to preserve a few square yards of indifferent vegetables and flowers. But such is *progress*. Mankind, the least attractive and most expendable of nature's creatures, is ever the most destructive of life.

The current District Commissioner of Isiolo, reading my report, sent the following comment to the last paragraph: ". . . in order to restore the dignity of the species *homo sapiens* I should like to draw your attention to the last seven verses of the first chapter of the first book of Moses called Genesis."

As I am not a scholar of the Bible, I cannot think of an apt quotation in response but I believe the Koran says: "There is no kind of beast on earth, nor fowl which flieth with its wings, but the same is a people like unto you . . . unto their Lord shall they return. All God's creatures are His family and he is the most beloved of God who trieth to do the most good to God's creatures."

Bwana Game George Adamson.

The advance of photography and the shrinkage of prey led to the substitution of a telling picture for a dead animal as the sportsman's aim. Treetops in the Aberdare National Park became a favourite venue for watching and photographing game. In February 1952 Princess Elizabeth and the Duke of Edinburgh spent a memorable night in the house in the tree.

Next in the programme of the Royal Tour, Princess Elizabeth and the Duke of Edinburgh went to stay at the Royal Lodge on the slopes of Mount Kenya, the lodge which was Kenya's wedding present to our princess and her husband. One of the nights during their stay was allocated for a visit to Treetops in the Aberdare National Park, some thirty miles from the Lodge.

Many years ago David Sheldrick's father found a pool in the Aberdare forest much used by big game. Next to the pool was a very large fig tree which offered an excellent opportunity of watching elephants, rhinos, buffaloes, and other animals coming in at night to drink. Sheldrick built a platform in the tree and took his friends there to watch the pageant of forest dwellers when the moon was bright. Some of his first guests were Major Eric Sherbroke-Walker and Lady Bettie Walker, who, as pioneers and owners of the Outspan Hotel at Nyeri, saw at once the possibility of using this attractive forest pool and glade as a very exciting adjunct of the Outspan. A charming wendy-house was built in the branches of the big fig tree, and thousands of people from all parts of the world enjoyed the thrills of watching exciting events round the forest pool. It was therefore to be a highlight of the royal visit, but for me not without some trouble.

The trouble concerned protection of the royal couple alike from angry elephants and from Mau Mau gangs already forming in the surrounding forest. Mervyn Cowie and John Hayward, warden of the Aberdare National Park, reconnoitred the path leading to the tree.

Hayward took the first two hundred yards of the path, and I took the latter portion up to the tree-house. All was quiet as I stealthily moved along listening and watching until I reached the top of the rise. Then came a burst of squeals and trumpeting. Elephants were obviously in possession of the pool. I crept up to within range of the platform and spied Jim Corbett standing there watching. I caught his eye by flicking a white handkerchief, and he gave me a reassuring wave. Never had I known of so many elephants at Treetops at this early hour of the day. There seemed to be at least fifty. Some bulls were very cantankerous and kept lunging at each other and rushing off into the forest. It was superb, I thought, that the Princess would be greeted by so many elephants, but it was also very dangerous. The fighting bulls were in a bad mood.

Hearing a twig crack in the surrounding forest, Mervyn Cowie crawled through the undergrowth to see a bull elephant bleeding from a tusk-wound in the shoulder and standing within ten yards of the path. Somehow the angry elephant had to be moved away without stampeding the whole herd. Cowie formed a plan.

The plan was to give him my scent and trust that he would either charge upwind or downwind, but not sideways. Sideways would mean straight along the path. I searched for a pebble, not an easy thing to find in a forest, but where the pathway had been levelled, there were some small stones. I picked up a round one about the size of a small plum and rubbed it well into my armpit. Disgusting on a hot day, I thought, but I knew it to be the most effective way of obtaining some powerful human scent. It had been successful on other occasions. I took my unsavoury pebble and threw it just beyond the elephant and to windward of him. The noise of it falling through the branches alerted him, and out went his huge ears. The wind remained steady and the plan worked.

Suddenly his trunk went forward to sniff the air, and then down into a tight curl, and he took off as if he had been pricked in the backside, straight towards the scent and on through the forest. . . . All was well, and I retreated down the path to the first bend. After a few moments and before I really had time to get my breath I heard the party approaching. Very quietly I pushed into the undergrowth and watched the Princess and the Duke go past within a few feet. . . .

The next morning we went up to Treetops to meet and escort the Royal Party down. This time there was no anxiety. . . . No need to be secretive. The Princess was overjoyed and proclaimed the experience. She looked so youthful and happy. She had no idea that within a few hours of leaving Treetops she was to receive the sad news which cast a gloom across the world that her father, King George VI, had died. . . .

The Royal Lodge at Sagana was closed and has not been used since, and within eight months a state of emergency was declared in Kenya. Two years later Treetops was utterly destroyed by Mau Mau terrorists, leaving only a charred stump as a memorial to the famous house in the tree. It was not until 1957 that the security situation improved sufficiently to permit the building of a new and bigger Treetops overlooking the same forest pool.

Fly, Vulture Mervyn Cowie.

The death of Elsa's mother.

One dark night five men were asleep in their *boma* together with their flock of goats and sheep. One of the sleepers was wakened by a slight noise and discovered that the man next to him was missing. He roused the others and they soon realized that a lion had taken their comrade. At first light, the four remaining men and others from a neighbouring *boma* followed up the well-defined trail which led into the dense riverine jungle bounding the river's banks. A short way on, they came to the pitiful remains and heard the deep warning growl of the lion. The Boran are courageous hunters but the almost impenetrable vegetation, where visibility was reduced to a few feet, daunted them and they gave up.

Accompanied by three Boran and Game Scouts Godana Dima, and Kikango, we went by Land Rover to a range of low rocky hills reputed to be the favourite haunt of the man-eater. Lions in this hot arid region often lie up on hill tops for the sake of the coolness during the heat of the day. We walked along the foot of the hills hoping to come on fresh spoor leading up. After about an hour we came on fresh tracks of a lioness. We followed thinking she might lead us to the lion. The going was difficult, over and between great granite boulders. We had just crawled through a passage between two giant rocks when there was a furious growl and the lioness appeared on a rock above us, looking extremely truculent. We had no wish to shoot a lioness but she was much too close and looked as if she might charge at any moment. I signalled Ken to fire. At the shot, the lioness disappeared. We advanced cautiously and found a heavy blood trail, leading further up the hill. There is nothing more dangerous than a wounded lioness – a bundle of concentrated courage, strength and ferocity, armed with nature's most formidable array of weapons. We crept on step by step over the crest of the hill and came to a huge flat rock where the tracks were lost. I climbed on top to obtain a view. Ken skirted the rock below. Suddenly I saw him pause and peer under the rock, then he raised his rifle and fired both barrels. There was a savage growl and out came the lioness straight at him. I could not shoot as Ken was in the line of fire. Fortunately Kikango was standing alongside him and fired, causing the lioness to swerve and I was able to kill her. She was a big lioness in the prime of life with her teats swollen with milk. Now, I knew why she had been angry and faced us so courageously. There must be cubs nearby. We retraced our steps and found the place where she had been lying at the foot of a rock face. But there was no sign of the cubs. I told the scouts and the Boran to search over the hill carefully while Ken and I sat down and discussed the hunt over a Thermos of tea. Presently I heard faint sounds issuing from a crack in the rock. It was the cubs! Both of us put our arms in as far as we could reach. There were loud infantile growls and snarls just out of reach. We cut a long hooked stick and after a deal of probing dragged out three little lionesses, not more than ten days old. . . .

Back at camp Joy was waiting for us and the first question she asked was – "Did you get him?" I pointed into the back of the car and said: "Look what we have brought you!"

At once Joy took absolute possession of the cubs. Ibrahim was sent fifty miles in the Land Rover to Garbatula, the nearest trading centre, to purchase a case of evaporated milk and a feeding bottle. In the meantime, I devised a teat out of a piece of sparking plug lead with the wire core removed.

How little did Joy or I imagine that the story of the smallest of the three cubs, and the cubs she herself would have one day, would be translated into thirty-three languages, sell several million copies, be made into a film and, as we hope and believe, make a lasting impact on the way in which human beings regard and treat wild animals.

Bwana Game George Adamson.

So plentiful were black rhinos that, in 1902, Richard Meinertzhagen saw twenty-one in a single day.

I took a stroll round camp this evening after work and coming round a corner met a rhinoceros face to face walking in my direction. There was no cover, so I fired point blank at his chest at but twenty yards. He staggered and nearly fell, but recovering himself made off. I gave him another shot as he ran but failed to stop him. He bolted towards the camp, when all my men and about 100 Masai spearmen gave chase. I yelled to them to let him be, but it had no effect and the hunt continued. The rhino could neither go fast nor far with his wounds, and was soon brought to bay and charged the whole crowd of us. We scattered and he stood. I fired again and the Masai encircled him and tried to spear him, which prevented me firing again for fear of hitting a man. He soon charged again, and singling out a Masai hunted him as a terrier does a rat. Nobody could fire for fear of hitting a man, so we yelled and tried to divert his attention. But he stuck to his victim, caught him up and tossed him some ten feet into the air. The man fell clear of the rhino, who did not turn but went a short distance and stood. I quickly got the men out of the way and dropped the rhino dead with a shot in the neck. The Masai who had been tossed suffered a bad rip up the right thigh, but no artery or bone has been damaged. Dr Mann has him in hand and thinks he should be about again in a month or so.

On cutting up the rhino we found fifteen Martini bullets in him which had been fired by my men, three Mannlicher bullets of mine and two .303 bullets. These latter rather puzzled me, as none of us had been using such a rifle. There were also 37 Masai spears sticking in his hide when he fell dead. He looked like a Christmas tree.

Kenya Diary 1902–1906 Richard Meinertzhagen.

Winston Churchill gets his rhino in 1907.

Our oryx led us a mile or more over rocky slopes, always promising and never giving a good chance for a shot, until at last he drew us round the shoulder of a hill – and there, abruptly, was the rhinoceros. The impression was extraordinary. A wide plain of white, withered grass stretched away to low hills broken with rocks. The rhinoceros stood in the middle of this plain, about five hundred yards away, in jet-black silhouette; not a twentieth-century animal at all, but an odd, grim straggler from the Stone Age. He was grazing placidly, and above him the vast snow dome of Kilimanjaro towered up in the clear air of morning to complete a scene unaltered since the dawn of the world.

The manner of killing a rhinoceros in the open is crudely simple. It is thought well usually to select the neighbourhood of a good tree, *where one can be found*, as the centre of the encounter. If no tree is available, you walk up as near as possible to him from any side except the windward, and then shoot him in the head or the heart. If you hit a vital spot, as sometimes happens, he falls. If you hit him anywhere else, he charges blindly and furiously in your direction, and you shoot him again, or not, as the case may be.

Bearing all this carefully in mind, we started out to do battle with Behemoth. We had advanced perhaps two hundred yards towards him, when a cry from one of the natives arrested us. We looked sharply to the right. There, not a hundred and fifty paces distant, under the shade of a few small trees, stood two other monsters. In a few more steps we should have tainted their wind and brought them up with a rush; and suppose this had happened, when perhaps we were already compromised with our first friend, and had him wounded and furious on our hands! Luckily warned in time, to creep back to the shoulder of the hill, to skirt its crest, and to emerge a hundred and twenty yards from this new objective was the work of a few minutes. We hurriedly agree to kill one first before touching the other. At such a range it is easy to hit so great a target; but the bull's-eye is small. I fired. The thud of a bullet which strikes with an impact of a ton and a quarter, tearing through hide and muscle and bone with the hideous energy of cordite, came back distinctly. The large rhinoceros started, stumbled, turned directly towards the sound and the blow, and then bore straight down upon us in a peculiar trot, nearly as fast as a horse's gallop, with an activity surprising in so huge a beast, and instinct with unmistakable purpose.

Great is the moral effect of a foe who advances. Everybody fired. Still the ponderous brute came on, as if he were invulnerable; as if he were an engine, or some great steam barge impervious to bullets, insensible to pain or fear. Thirty seconds more, and he will close. An impalpable curtain seems to roll itself up in the mind, revealing a mental picture, strangely lighted, yet very still, where objects have new values, and where a patch of white grass in the foreground, four or five yards away, seems to possess astonishing significance. It is there that the last two shots that yet remain before the resources of civilization are exhausted must be fired. There is time to reflect with some detachment that, after all, we were the aggressors; we it is who have forced the conflict by an unprovoked assault with murderous intent upon a peaceful herbivore; that if there is such a thing as right and wrong between man and beast – and who shall say there is not? – right is plainly on his side; there is time for this before I perceive that, stunned and dazed by the frightful concussions of modern firearms, he has swerved sharp to the right, and is now moving across our front, broadside on, at the same swift trot. More firing, and as I reload some one says he is down, and I fire instead at his smaller companion, already some distance off upon the plain. But one rhinoceros hunt is like another, except in its details, and I will not occupy the reader with the account of this new pursuit and death. Suffice it to say that, in all the elements of neurotic experience, such an encounter seems to me fully equal to half an hour's brisk skirmish at six or seven hundred yards – and with an important addition. In war there is a cause, there is duty, there is the hope of glory, for who can tell what may not be won before night? But here at the end is only a hide, a horn, and a carcase, over which the vultures have already begun to wheel.

My African Journey Winston Churchill.

The distinguished Oxford academic Dame Margery Perham, lecturer and historian, nourished an uncharacteristic ambition: to shoot a buffalo. With Merikabor, an African tracker, and a young South African policeman, she set out along a track through tangled forest undergrowth.

Suddenly Merikabor stopped. With a gesture he threw us all noiselessly to our knees. There followed an interval which seemed endless: in the silence I seemed to hear as well as feel the beating of my heart. It banged against my ribs until I felt something must burst with the strain. I gazed into the green-black gloom searching for the darker, bluer shadows I might see. I marvelled that a few hours before I had left the security of a house and set out to bring myself into this forest and its inhuman company. I was afraid. Then Merikabor pointed and I saw the angle of a creature's quarters deep in the green, the flick of a tail, surely very small and thin with a tassel on top. I looked at Merikabor. He was laughing – but silently. A guttural Swahili word reached me in a whisper, *nguruwe*, "pig". True, there *were* wart-hogs. But not only wart-hogs. We had hardly resumed our silent struggle through the trees when we were upon them. The branches began to thresh about in the innermost cave of the green, and dark forms, half-seen, plunged and vanished. In a few minutes there was silence again. We had missed our first chance. The tension broke. We stood up straight and I grounded my gun. With the first contact, and especially with the beasts' escape, fear suddenly left me. I only wanted to be near them and the nearer the better.

We studied their tracks: two bulls, it seemed. The signs of their fear and flight were printed deep in the dark forest mould, the reckless slithering hoofmarks, the snapped branches; some spattered, steaming dung. They had turned upwards. So on again, single file, toes thrust into muddy incline, the free hand grasping at branches and trailing creepers. The trees grew more scant at the summit. Then down again into the massed green – how often up and down now, I do not know. I do not even look for the spoor: all faculties are absorbed in the effort to force my body onward in spite of a bar straining across my chest. Merikabor points to the earth. Where before there were two tracks, there are now fifty – a hundred – we cannot count. The forest deepens until movement is almost impossible. Creepers as thin as silk or as thick as hawsers have woven the forest into a net: each step is an achievement. Merikabor stops again. Nothing can be seen in this tangle: nothing heard. He powders a dead leaf and lets it drift down through the air. But we are in a pit where wind eddies and that is our undoing. We have not stirred; nor have "they". Yet, suddenly, a noise like a close, sudden clap of thunder! I cannot believe it is the herd. It must be a landslide. Surely only the elements could make a sound as if the whole forest, trees, boulders, tons of earth, were being flung at us. Then, as the first stunning effect of the noise passes, the sounds that make it up can be distinguished: the thudding of a hundred or more huge bodies rushing in all directions.

The main herd just missed us, but some rushed so close to me that the earth under my feet shuddered and the tree to which I was clinging seemed to sway. A few yards nearer and our three guns would have been useless, we should have been down. Almost more strange than the noise was the speed of its ceasing. Did heavy foliage stifle the thunder, or do the animals after the first plunging frenzy of alarm regain their cunning and move their bulky bodies like shadows through the trees? We stiffen again. They are coming back. I wrap myself round the nearest tree. This is no time for shooting. Half a dozen break past us. They are only a few yards away, yet so shrouded by the forest that I see little more than their broad, blue-grey flanks in the convulsion of their gallop. We relax. We *have* to relax. The South African lights a cigarette and as we see the almost circular drift of its smoke we see again what betrayed us. I dare to speak. "Surely it is hopeless. They must now be startled and alert beyond all catching." Merikabor does not agree. He is impatient to go on. Only a few yards away we find the marks of the main stampede: a ruin of trees, the forest moss and mould pounded into mud. On again – and up. We follow not a track but a road of hoofmarks. They divide, join, divide again. Merikabor never doubts which to follow.

At last the hunters come up with the herd: "green-black forest, blue-black

animals, dim under the first veil of twilight." Margery Perham, inching her
way forward, makes out the shape of a bull and fires.

"Did I hit him?" I asked in my pidgin-Swahili.
"Yes," he said. Of course I had! The picture that in some strange way had been driven out of my head by the rush re-formed itself in my mind: the bull falling and rising and going on again. I was so glad that I could have shouted and sung. The policeman came running back. Formality had gone. "Old thing, you got him!" he shouted and wrung both my hands.

We joined Merikabor, who was following the blood spoor. He showed me the light red blood of the external entry of the bullet in the thigh and, further on, the dark clotted blood from the internal wound. My bullet must have raked him through from back to front. They were quite sure he would die, if not tonight, tomorrow. They would get him. Meanwhile, it was madness to pursue. The dark was coming on. . . .

I do not think that I have ever been so exhausted in my life or ever shall be again as I was the night after the hunt. Yet I did not sleep. My heart seemed to continue its excessive beat. But it was not that which kept me awake. I hated myself for what I had done. Why had I killed that bull? Why had I ever wanted to do it? Was it a kind of vanity? To prove myself to other people? That was there, perhaps, but it was not the main motive. That was a desire to prove myself to myself. I knew then that never, never, as long as I lived would I again kill for "sport". Of course, for the time, I had to continue playing my part to the last act. After all, these others had done all they could to help me. . . .

Their lives were risked again, for next day they found my bull by its blood trail. It was dead. This time some of the herd charged them and they had to shoot three of them in self-defence. Even so, Merikabor would have been killed by a cow which charged from the side if she had not caught her horns in a branch. They sent after me to say that they had prepared the head so that it could be sent to England for mounting. I had to disappoint them by a grateful but definite and, to them, inexplicable, refusal.

East African Journey Margery Perham.

Ernest Hemingway, on safari in the 1930s, set out in pursuit of the last trophy,
a greater kudu. M'Cola "the Roman" was his gunbearer, an African so called
because he had a prominent nose.

It was after five when we struck off across the maize field and down to the stream, crossing where it narrowed in a high grass a hundred yards above the dam and then, walking slowly and carefully, went up the grassy bank on the far side, getting soaked to the waist as we stooped going through the wet grass and bracken. We had not been gone ten minutes and were moving carefully up the stream bank, when, without warning, the Roman grabbed my arm and pulled me bodily down to the ground as he crouched; me pulling back the bolt to cock the rifle as I dropped. Holding his breath he pointed and across the stream on the far bank at the edge of the trees was a large, grey animal, white stripes showing on his flanks and huge horns curling back from his head as he stood, broadside to us, head up, seeming to be listening. I raised the rifle, but there was a bush in the way of the shot. I could not shoot over the bush without standing.

"Piga," whispered M'Cola. I shook my finger and commenced to crawl forward to be clear of the bush, sick afraid the bull would jump while I was trying to make the shot certain, but remembering Pop's "Take your time". When I saw I was clear I got on one knee, saw the bull through the aperture, marvelling at how big he looked, and then, remembering not to have it matter, that it was the same as any other shot, I saw the bead centred exactly where it should be just below the top of the shoulder and squeezed off. At the roar he jumped and was going into the brush, but I knew I had hit him. I shot at a show of grey between the trees as he went in and M'Cola was shouting, "Piga! Piga!" meaning "He's hit! He's hit!" and the Roman was slapping me on the shoulder, then he had his toga up around his neck and was running naked, and the four of us were running now, full speed, like hounds, splashing across the stream, tearing up the bank, the Roman ahead, crashing naked through the brush, then stooping and holding up a leaf with bright blood, slamming me on the back, M'Cola saying, "Damu! Damu!" (blood, blood), then the deep cut tracks off to the right, me reloading, we all trailing in a dead run, it almost dark in the timber, the Roman, confused a moment by the trail, making a cast off to the right, then picking up blood once more, then pulling me down again with a jerk on my arm and none of us breathing as we saw him standing in a clearing a hundred yards ahead, looking to me hard-hit and looking back, wide ears spread, big, grey, white-striped, his horns a marvel, as he looked straight toward us over his shoulder. I thought I must make absolutely sure this time, now, with the dark coming and I held my breath and shot him a touch behind the fore-shoulder. We heard the bullet smack and saw him buck heavily with the shot. M'Cola shouted, "Piga! Piga! Piga!" as he went out of sight and as we ran again, like hounds, we almost fell over something. It was a huge, beautiful kudu bull, stone-dead, on his side, his horns in great dark spirals, wide-spread and unbelievable as he lay dead five yards from where we stood when I had just that instant shot. I looked at him, big, long-legged, a smooth grey with the white stripes and the great curling, sweeping horns, brown as walnut meats, and ivory pointed, at the big ears and the great, lovely heavy-maned neck, the white chevron between his eyes and the white of his muzzle and I stooped over and touched him to try to believe it. He was lying on the side where the bullet had gone in and there was not a mark on him and he smelled sweet and lovely like the breath of cattle and the odour of thyme after rain.

Then the Roman had his arms around my neck and M'Cola was shouting in a strange high sing-song voice and Wanderobo-Masai kept slapping me on the shoulder and jumping up and down and then one after the other they all shook hands in a strange way that I had never known in which they took your thumb in their fist and held it and shook it and pulled it and held it again, while they looked you in the eyes, fiercely.

We all looked at him and M'Cola knelt and traced the curve of his horns with his finger and measured the spread with his arms and kept crooning, "Oo-oo-eee-eee", making small high noises of ecstasy and stroking the kudu's muzzle and his mane.

I slapped the Roman on the back and we went through the thumb-pulling again; me pulling his thumb too. I embraced the Wanderobo-Masai and he, after a thumb-pulling of great intensity and feeling, slapped his chest and said very proudly, "Wanderobo-Masai" – "wonderful guide".

Green Hills of Africa Ernest Hemingway.

A bongo hunt in the forests of the Aberdares (Nyandarua).

It was the morning of the last day I ever had. My little bivouac tent was pitched at the edge of a small glade at an elevation of between nine and ten thousand feet. I had with me old Kiriboto, my gunbearer, a cook and the two Dorobos (they never came except in pairs). I rose at five o'clock, having listened for an hour to the hyrax calling in the trees, the intermittent "sawing" of a leopard, and other forest sounds, well knowing that though the Dorobo would surely be awake nothing would induce them to call me, and that nothing but the dawn would rouse Kiriboto. At 5.20 we were under way, the two little guides in front, a short spear in the hand of each, naked save for a goatskin over the shoulder.

The moon was still high and easily overpowered the first faint glow of the "false" dawn. We all felt the cold as we plunged into the long and soaking grass of the glade towards the farther bank of the encircling forest. Just as we got there we heard a bushbuck bark, while a big dark owl circling round uttered a querulous hoot. Arrived at the edge of the forest, our guides gave a glance round, hitched their goatskins tighter round their shoulders and then melted silently into the solid green wall. There was no melting about Kiriboto or myself. Brambles tore at us, malignant branches whipped our faces, twigs cracked, and streams of icy-cold water trickled down our necks. For twenty yards we struggled on and then the undergrowth cleared and we found the Dorobo reproachfully waiting, and once again off they stole up the hill. It was still dark, but the great boles of trees could by now be seen dimly rising from clumps of undergrowth somewhat like laurestinus.

There were game tracks about and now and again some animal plunged off through the thicket, but our guides paid no attention, and glided along the game tracks always upwards at a pace which had us panting. After a stiff ascent I was forced to rest for a minute. When I looked up the little figures had vanished into thin air. I remember that the first time this had happened Kiriboto and I were seriously alarmed, since we well knew that without their aid it might be a couple of days before we found our way out and back to our camp. This time I merely sat down with a sigh of relief. In five minutes, like Cheshire cats, they simply materialized, their mouths smeared with honey, and off we set upwards again and in a few minutes plunged through another thicket into another glade. . . .

On and up again, and now we came to a swiftly running stream through which we waded. It was waist-deep and icy cold, but I was already dripping with sweat and it was a pleasant interlude. The character of the forest now began to change. The trees were further apart and more lichen clung to the boughs. The laurestinus had disappeared and its place was taken by small clumps of low bamboo. Out of one such clump there burst as we passed a huge dark animal, looking as big as a young rhino. It was a giant forest boar weighing perhaps 700 lb. Their tracks were numerous hereabouts. But time was slipping on and we saw here and there patches of the low vegetation that the bongo loves. Tracks and droppings were, too, apparent, and every now and then a Dorobo would pick up a handful of the latter and sniff it with the air of a connoisseur. Next, by a gesture, they made us stop while they made a wide cast, moving with silent and effortless speed. In ten minutes they returned and the leader thrust into my reluctant hand a lump of dung still warm and they beckoned us forward, a finger to lips.

In a few minutes we came on the tracks quite fresh but not, as I had hoped to see, of a solitary bull but of a herd of at least half a dozen, including, however, one, if not two, bulls. After them we proceeded at a pace which seemed to me much too fast but to our guides much too slow. And they were right. It was now eight o'clock and the tracks moved upwards and the bamboo clumps grew closer together and were now in places twenty feet or more in height. Now and again we had to crawl, and once the muffled cracking of a twig earned for me an angry scowl. I had almost reconciled myself to another long day of bamboo crawling. Suddenly the leader froze in his stride and distinctly we heard a crackle not more than 300 yards away. Care was redoubled now and every step brought an agony of apprehension. Luckily noise was all we had to fear; not a breath of wind stirred in the forest.

About 100 yards we advanced, hearing now and again the tell-tale crackle ever louder. Then the elder Dorobo went down on hands and knees and touched my rifle, and leaving the other two we crawled forward, 10, 20, 50 yards to where a fallen tree-trunk lay. After a cautious peep he silently pointed, and there, dimly among some sparse bamboos, I made out the form of a large beast which from its dark colour I took to be a bull. Now the distance was, I estimated, about 120 yards, the light was bad, and another fallen tree some thirty yards nearer and perhaps ten feet below me interfered with my view. I refused the shot, most reluctantly, and halting the Dorobo, crawled round my log and down towards the next.

The distance seemed quite interminable, but I got there without a sound, and now I could see my quarry plainly. Somehow it seemed a richer red and I had less confidence about its sex, though its horns looked good as it cropped the herbage. Anyhow I had no choice, so squeezed the trigger and down it went. I looked back at Kiriboto and the others, expecting to see them rushing forward, but instead I saw them pointing below me. I was squatting on my haunches and though I peered in the direction saw nothing, though I heard crashes all around me. At that moment the beast I had shot struggled to its feet and I had to give the second barrel of my .360. Then up came Kiriboto and explained that a huge bull, of course the biggest ever, had at the shot crossed my front at quite close range. Sure enough there were the tracks, huge in the soft earth, in a cutting of ground dead to me, but plainly visible from my first halt. It was, and *is*, for no time can soothe this, maddening to think that had I taken the first chance, I must, even if I had missed it, have got this splendid bull, passing a bare fifty yards from me, with my second barrel.

My beast, as will be guessed, was a very ancient cow with two-foot horns. It took the Dorobos, working with most inadequate tools, but a few minutes to remove the head and body skin. The carcase they then dismembered, eating greedily the while raw, warm delicacies from the entrails. They then bound the varied sections with creepers, and moving like monkeys, attached them to boughs forty feet up, and safe from even the most agile leopard. We were back at camp by two o'clock, and so ended the shortest, most successful and most disappointing of my bongo hunts.

Kenya Chronicles Lord Cranworth.

The rhythm of Africa.

We would often go out hunting porcupine. After supper we would collect a number of boys, let out the dogs, and with spears in our hands make our way towards the potato patch. Porcupine used to do an astounding amount of damage to these vegetables. They would work right through the rows, unburying the roots. They came from great distances for the satisfaction of doing this. We sometimes hunted them back to holes in a rocky hill-side several miles away. They had a kind of small rattle of quills on the ends of their tails, and when once we had started one of them out of the potatoes it would make a most infernal jingling with this instrument as it trundled along over the veld. Hunting porcupine requires no little skill. They have a trick of dashing off at top speed and then, at the most exciting moment of the hunt, stopping dead still and rushing backwards, reversing gear, so to speak, to the utter confusion of their pursuers, who, unless very alert, find themselves in collision with a curious battering-ram of sharp spikes.

Most of the dogs, from bitter experience, gave chase to these animals in a very wary and diffident way, keeping always at a safe distance. Micky we never took with us on these occasions, because we knew that nothing would keep him back when once his blood was up. The rest of the pack knew just what to do. They would run the porcupine until it was out of breath and then bay it up till we and the boys appeared. We used to have some exciting moments even then. The light shed by our lantern was never sufficient, and the fretful animal would charge backwards and forwards in all directions, its tail keeping up a continuous jangling like a bunch of keys at an old woman's apron. I have known the leg of a boy to be speared right through by a porcupine. When the animal was dead we used to pull out the best quills, and my brother would send them home, wrapped up in *The East African Standard*, to be used as pen-holders. The carcass we would leave where it was, that extraordinary carcass, with its strong legs and black rabbit-like face. If we happened to pass by the place during the next few days the air to windward would be villainously tainted, but this would not last long; very soon the carrion birds, the hyenas, the jackals, the rats, the ants, would clear it all up, so that, except for a little heap of black-and-white quills, nothing would remain of the odd bulky animal which possessed so keen a relish for the imported American root and knew how to find its way about over the veld on the darkest night. Kill! Kill! Kill! that was what one had to do to keep in tune with the African rhythm, with that inexorable rhythm, the sublimest cadence of which is only to be heard when backbones are being snapped and throats cut.

After all, men must live; and when an army of black ants streamed into the house to devour a shoulder of mutton, what else was one to do but pour boiling water on their crowded roadway, that roadway which stretched up the stone wall and over the window sill. In Africa not only is Nature indifferent to the fate of the manifold forms of life she has created, she is malignant also. In all directions a crafty and merciless war is being waged. It was not nice for the porcupine to be stabbed to death nor for the ants to be boiled alive, but neither was it nice for "Ugonjwa's" newly born puppies to have their blind eyes eaten out of their heads by these same insects.

Black Laughter Llewelyn Powys.

The birth of blood lust.

When I got back to headquarters I was allotted the extremely distasteful task of eliminating game on the TOL* farms along the Samburu border – principally zebra and oryx. The decision to take this drastic step was due to incessant complaints from the farmers that at a time when it was necessary to increase production to help the war effort the game was seriously competing with livestock for grazing. Perhaps the decision was a right one, but to add to the tragedy thousands of the animals I was obliged to kill were wasted. Neither meat nor hide were taken and the carcases were allowed to rot where they fell. (A thousand oryx and zebra represented over a hundred and fifty tons of perfectly wholesome meat). . . .

Daily I went out in my car over the plains and would return in the evening weary and sick at heart having killed anything up to a hundred animals. A dreadful aspect of the slaughter was that while engaged in the actual shooting I observed that I unconsciously developed a ruthless blood lust. This gave me pause for thought and some inkling into the mentality which perpetrates massacres.

Bwana Game George Adamson.

*Temporary Occupation Licence.

"The way of a serpent upon a rock."
Holy Bible

Few headmasters can have had a more unexpected reply when questioning a pupil than that delivered by the young Ionides to the principal of Rugby School. "Have you anything in your study that is not allowed?" was the question "A sawn-off shot-gun, two pistols, ammunition, six rabbit nets, a cosh, a knuckle-duster, a tobacco pouch and a pipe" the answer. Ionides became in turn a soldier, an ivory poacher, a white hunter, a game ranger and, finally, a snake collector.

I remember three black mambas we located in a hole under a dead tree on a disused ant heap, quite a favourite kind of hide-out for the black mamba as it is for the black and white cobra and the Egyptian cobra, particularly during the seasonal burning of the dried grass which had just been completed. My forked stick worked perfectly for the first of the three mambas, the largest. It was boxed and got out of the way, and my men and I then turned our attention to the other two. . . .

One of my assistants that day was a mature man named Mahomedi Ngelelo who claimed to possess immunity from snake bite. I knew that in showing off to local people he cheerfully let himself get bitten by small puff adders and night adders, and twice I had myself seen him take bites from small spitting cobras. He would have a swollen hand all right, for a few days, but otherwise it seemed to do him no harm.

After a while he succeeded in getting a noose round one of the black mambas, so I dropped the stick with which I had been poking about and went to his assistance. I told him to pull out the snake so that I could get hold of the neck with my hand, the idea being to box it before proceeding to deal with the remaining mamba. Mahomedi managed to extract about two feet of the snake and I grabbed the neck, removing the noose which then had to be worked under the hand finger by finger. We then found that the snake had wound its prehensile tail round a root and could not be budged.

In the middle of the tug-o-war the head of the other mamba appeared at the second entrance of the hole before which I was squatting with my feet against the tree on either side of it. Opening its mouth wide, it started shaking its head at me, which I took to be an expression of displeasure. So turning to Mahomedi I said, "Let us get this snake back in the noose where it can be held. It would be better if I caught the other one before we go any further."

The mamba at the entrance remained demonstrating, while I released my captive to Mahomedi's noose, but the moment I was ready the head disappeared. Rushing round to the other side I put a noose over the small hole. I saw the head emerge, hesitating, then the snake came out fast and I was able to nab it round the neck. By keeping the string tight, and reaching down the stick hand-over-hand, I got hold of the neck and successfully removed the noose.

Meanwhile Mahomedi had been busy on his side. He had given his stick with the noosed mamba to a porter to hold and, putting his hand into the hole, had unhooked the tail from the root to which it still clung. The snake was then eased out, but it seems that in returning the head to Mahomedi, the porter let the string get a little slack, and the black mamba, twisting its head round, cut at Mahomedi's hand with one fang and drew blood.

"Bwana," he called to me, "I've been bitten."

"Well," I replied, "what do you expect me to do about it? My hands are full of mamba."

I was, in fact, engaged in a Laocoönic struggle in which the body had coiled round both forearms and I was having to exert all my strength to prevent my left hand being drawn towards the head which was straining forward to give it a nip.

"There is only one thing to do," I said. "If you feel any faintness, or that you are losing control of the snake, you must kill it because I cannot help you."

That was not necessary however as our camp was very near. We boxed the snakes without further incident. I then asked the man how he was feeling. It was one thing to flirt with death with juveniles of less poisonous species, but this time it was an adult black mamba, the most deadly snake in Africa.

"Oh, perfectly all right. Nothing wrong," was his reply. . . .

Next morning with my coffee I asked after Mahomedi and was told he was out taking a walk round looking for more snakes.

Apparently at nine pm the night before he had suddenly begun to get rigors and my watch party were debating whether or not to call me when the shivering wore off. As the patient had shown no further untoward symptoms they had not disturbed me. And that, I am happy to relate, is the end of the story. Beyond a handsomely swollen hand which subdued after two days, Mahomedi suffered no other ill effects.

In looking at his case the factors to be considered are: first, that all he got was a glancing cut with one fang, not a full bite which is in fact a proper double injection of two fairly long fangs; and secondly, that the snake had expended a good deal of its poison in attacking the forked sticks. On the other hand to kill a man a black mamba only needs to inject two minims of its deadly venom, against which serums, good for cobras, puff adders and the other snakes that had bitten Mahomedi, are of minimal value. To me his continued good health was nothing short of remarkable.

A Hunter's Life G. J. P. Ionides.

Duck shooting on Lake Naivasha.

Imagine if you can, sitting in a punt, gun across your knees, in one of the many lagoons that fingers its way from the open water of the main lake between massed banks of tall papyrus to the shore. The time is five o'clock and the pre-dawn temperature at six thousand feet has a chill that penetrates. You are awaiting the first light of day which will herald the dawn flight of the wild duck and geese that you know are all about you. Somewhere fairly close a hippo grunts with loud, paunchous solemnity, and is answered in similar tone by other hippos. There is the splashity-splash-splash of a coot skimming water followed by his call of "coot, coot." A gallinule hoots and little grebes trill their awakening to a new day. "Kraak," cries a heron as he wings his way to work.

Stars still flicker in a sky that is fast becoming lighter. The outlines of the nearest papyrus thickets can be seen; in the east the silhouettes of Longonot and the Aberdares appear darkly against a paler background.

Now all around on the water flappings can be heard as water-fowl flex their wings in preparation for dawn flight. There is much quacking.

A rapid flurry of wing-beats passes overhead, another, and another. Unmistakable ducks. Too dark yet to see, but any minute now you'll be in business.

Boom-Boom. The first shots are followed instantaneously by the roar of wings as a thousand ducks take to the skies. Gun shots come from all round the thirty-odd miles of lake shore whilst birds fly from one lagoon to another in search of safe water. This bombardment lasts perhaps a quarter of an hour and then comes a lull. The ducks have climbed high out of range and made for the safety of open water.

In the excitement the dawn, that at first crept stealthily, has come unnoticed in all its glory. The Mau Escarpment which forms the western wall of the Rift Valley is already bathed in sunlight, so also is Eburru, another extinct volcano which rises from the western shore of the lake.

Sitting in your punt among the blue flowering water lilies you will see a purple gallinule stalking, head bobbing, on the verge of the papyrus and there! a bronze jacana, aptly named the lily trotter, hopping daintily from one lily pad to another on its long thin stilts with their enormously elongated toes which enable the bird to spread its weight over the whole surface of each lily-pad. There are dabchicks and coots diving unceasingly for their weedy meals. Spoonbills and egrets, herons and cormorants pass overhead. And now the duck begin to return from open water to their lagoon feeding grounds. Have a look at your watch: seven thirty already, and only half a dozen birds to hand. At eight o'clock, by law, all shooting must cease, and is only permitted again from four o'clock until sundown in the evening.

With luck you should bag another half dozen or so, for there are duck coming in steadily in small parties. Yellow-bill, teal, shoveller, pochard, hottentot and white-face. The water reflects the blue of the wide African sky and there is the deeper blue of the water lilies, the luxuriant green of the papyrus, the occasional "plop" of a feeding bass. Soon you will be wolfing a plate of eggs and bacon cooked on the tail board of the truck there under the fever trees. . . .

In past times the lake was a duck shooter's mecca providing some of the finest duck shooting in the world in peerless surroundings. The varied bird-life to be seen on the lake, in the lagoons and papyrus thickets has attracted world wide attention and today Naivasha is a bird sanctuary of international repute.

Wide Horizons Venn Fey.

Hunting big fish off the Kenyan coast is a sport of growing popularity. Lorenzo Ricciardi entered a fishing competition with three friends.

At noon, with one hour to go, we turned for home. We were about a mile from shore and the only boat in sight was two miles to the north. Suddenly I saw a splash. My muscles tightened as if hit by an electric shock. The mullet I trawled disappeared in a twirl of foam, the reel screamed. One hundred yards of line went out, then two hundred, and three. A black marlin rose out of the water and leaped once in a perfect semi-circle. No words were uttered as Madeka adjusted his course a little. I felt cool, calm and collected, although I knew my eighty-pound test-line was worn, frayed and barby.

Suddenly the reel screamed again and at once my fish was on his tail running on the surface like a tightrope walker. He shook his massive head, then plunged back into the water and sounded. I played the line with my thumb – it was all I could do now. I willed the fish to stay on. I told him how important it was for me and my family. He was deep down now, rolling and twisting; I could feel the line stretching out. I knew how easily it could snap. Then I thought of sharks, for mutilation would disqualify the fish. I glanced at Madeka, who looked down at me with his big flashy smile. Ben, my fisherman friend, and Barry Allen were behind me and I turned to them and said, "Now. Have the gaff ready."

"*Hapana*," said Ben. ("No.")

"You sure, Ben? It's big."

"*Hapana* – no gaff," repeated Ben in Swahili. "I'm sure. I'll take him with my hands. I'm stronger than he is."

I turned, placing my feet on the transom, and started reeling in, pumping the fish up. Madeka kept the boat in line with the tip of the rod. Ben saw the fish first and moved to the transom; it came up easily, doing what I asked. He was tired. I reeled it in smoothly and firmly; it was now almost under the boat, a foot maybe from the surface. Ben looked at me. I nodded. Barry held the *rungu* (club), Madeka kept the engine in gear – forward, slow. The fish followed, waving its tail in the churning wake. Ben bent down slowly and stretched out his powerful arms until he had the fish by its bill. The muscles in his chest expanded; he moved steadily and powerfully. He knew that the fish was doomed. When the head appeared well out of the water, Barry struck with the club while Ben eased the fish over the transom into the boat.

Madeka came down from the flying bridge to touch the fish and I shook his hand, still not believing our success. "Let's get home quickly," I said. The boat near us had been circling all the time out of the way and was now heading back. I kept thinking there could be a bigger bill-fish, or maybe two smaller ones caught by one of those sixty-five boats. I hoisted the blue flag to signal I had a marlin on board and noticed a similar flag on another boat. I prayed it would not be bigger. It wasn't. Mine was just under two hundred pounds, the other just over a hundred.

The Voyage of the Mir-el-Lal Lorenzo Ricciardi.

A familiar figure between the wars was the chief game warden, conspicuous, when in Nairobi, in his vintage yellow Rolls Royce with a rhino horn mascot on the bonnet.

Archie Ritchie was a big man in every way. With his mane of white hair, his bristling white moustache, and his massive, powerful frame, he had always reminded me of a cross between an old and regal lion and a majestic bull elephant. . . .

Archibald Thomas Ayres Ritchie had been born near Dublin in the year 1890. Blessed with a fine physique, a brilliant brain, and with a silver spoon planted firmly in his mouth, it was not long before he revealed that he also had a strong character and a likeable personality; and over the years he made good use of the generous physical and material talents with which he had been endowed.

At Harrow, he became head of the school and captain of the shooting eight, as well as excelling on the rugby field. At Magdalen College, Oxford, he became President of the Junior Common Room and, shortly before the start of the First World War, he left the University with an honours degree in zoology.

When War broke out Archie enlisted in the famous French Foreign Legion, with whom he fought in France until, in 1915, "Caporal Ritchie" was commissioned in the equally famous Grenadier Guards of the British Army. That year he was wounded at Loos, and again on the Somme in 1916, and yet again near Ypres in 1917. For his exploits he was mentioned in despatches, awarded the Military Cross, and made a Chevalier of the Légion d'Honneur. . . .

Archie had a silver tongue when he wanted to use it and he always kept an old bongo-skin bag by the side of his desk. He referred to it as his "medicine bag". It contained two glasses and what he called "Dr Ritchie's miracle cure for dissatisfied customers" – a large bottle of gin! The combination worked wonders.

The Shamba Raiders Bruce Kinlock.

Poachers have been at work in game reserves and national parks ever since those sanctuaries were started, but in the 1980s they stepped up and modernized their techniques. Well-organized gangs of professional poachers, often composed of well-armed Somalis linked to the international trade in horn and ivory, penetrated parks and reserves: profit became the aim rather than meat. This incident, typical of many, took place in the Amboseli National Park.

The elephants were spread out, feeding among the low bushes. Far in the distance they heard the sound of a car engine, a Land Rover, not a tourist minibus. It came slowly from the south, stopping from time to time, then starting up and moving again, gradually coming closer. The elephants became more alert and wary when the Land Rover was about a mile and a half away, but then it stopped and they did not hear it start again. It was now to the west of them and downwind. Teresia and a few of the other wise old females raised their trunks and smelled in the direction that the sound of the engine had come from, but they could not catch any troublesome scent on the wind.

Nearly an hour passed and the elephants fed peacefully. It was midday and they began to get sleepy. A few small resting subgroups had already formed in the shade of some of the larger trees. The Ts* were still feeding on the western edge of the aggregation. Torn Ear and her three-year-old son were at the front of the movement. Torn Ear was just reaching for a small succulent herb that was nestled in amongst the grass when a quick movement to her left caught her eye. She whirled toward the movement and there were two men only thirty yards away. Without hesitation she put her head down and charged toward them. She did not even hear the explosion before the bullet ripped through the light airy bone of her forehead and penetrated deep into her brain. She was dead by the time she fell forward onto her head and tusks and skidded along the ground for several feet from the momentum of her charge. Her son was hit next, first in the shoulder, which made him scream with pain and rage and then through his side into his heart.

The instant Torn Ear had seen the men, even before the shot rang out, the rest of the herd knew there was extreme danger because Torn Ear had uttered an alarm call just as she charged. All the others heard it and knew who made it and acted accordingly. Most of the elephants immediately began to run away from the source of the danger, but Torn Ear's bond group instantly came to her aid. They ran toward her and even when they heard the shots and saw her fall they kept coming. The men turned and began to run but let off one volley of shots, missing most of the elephants but catching Tina in the chest with a shot that went into her right lung. These shots turned the Ts and they too began to run away from the danger. In the meantime, the rest of the herd ran to the north, which is what the poachers had hoped for, and two more men were waiting there. The WA family was in the front, led by their matriarch, Wendy, closely followed by the next oldest female, Willa. Wendy ran straight into the guns, but these men were not as experienced as the others, and it took seven shots in her head and neck and shoulders before Wendy fell and died. Willa behind her veered off and caught a bullet through her tail, severing it in half except for one bit of skin that kept the lower portion from falling off.

The whole aggregation was now tightly bunched and running at full speed. The mothers were literally pushing their babies forward to keep their pace up. They ran to the north and then to the east, skirting around the wet slippery lake bed. The Ts, having been farthest west and delayed by trying to aid Torn Ear, were at the rear and Tina was the very last. Her family knew she was hurt; they could smell the foamy pink blood dripping from her mouth. She managed to keep up until she got to the ridge, but the incline slowed her down and she groaned with the pain. Her mother, Teresia, kept dropping back to run beside her, reaching over and touching her with her trunk, but finally Tina had to slow to a walk.

Teresia took them to the far side of Meshanani, a small hill upon the ridge

---

*Scientists studying these elephants identified each family by a letter of the alphabet.

above the lake. There was some protection here, and Tina could go no farther. The blood pouring from her mouth was bright red and her sides were heaving for breath. The other elephants crowded around, reaching for her. Her knees started to buckle and she began to go down, but Teresia got on one side of her and Trista on the other and they both leaned in and held her up. Soon, however, she had no strength and she slipped beneath them and fell onto her side. More blood gushed from her mouth and with a shudder she died.

Teresia and Trista became frantic and knelt down and tried to lift her up. They worked their tusks under her back and under her head. At one point they succeeded in lifting her into a sitting position but her body flopped back down. Her family tried everything to rouse her, kicking and tusking her, and Tallulah even went off and collected a trunkful of grass and tried to stuff it into her mouth. Finally Teresia got around behind her again, knelt down, and worked her tusks in under her shoulder and then, straining with all her strength, she began to lift her. When she got to a standing position with the full weight of Tina's head and front quarters on her tusks, there was a sharp cracking sound and Teresia dropped the carcass as her right tusk fell to the ground. She had broken it a few inches from the lip well into the nerve cavity, and a jagged bit of ivory and the bloody pulp was all that remained.

They gave up then but did not leave. They stood around Tina's carcass, touching it gently with their trunks and feet. Because it was rocky and the ground was wet there was no loose dirt; but they tried to dig into it with their feet and trunks and when they managed to get a little earth up they sprinkled it over the body. Trista, Tia, and some of the others went off and broke branches from the surrounding low bushes and brought them back and placed them on the carcass. They remained very alert to the sounds around them and kept smelling to the west, but they would not leave Tina. By nightfall they had nearly buried her with branches and earth. Then they stood vigil over her for most of the night and only as dawn was approaching did they reluctantly begin to walk away.

Elephant Memories Cynthia Moss.

Cynthia Moss spent over fourteen years studying elephants in the Amboseli Park. In 1989 the Kenya Government launched a campaign, headed by Dr Richard Leakey, to quell the poachers.

Two Points of View

Manhood I am, therefore I me delyght
To hunt and hawke, to nourish up and fede
The greyhounds to the course, the hawk to th'flyght
And to bestride a good and lusty stede:
These thynges become a very man in dede.

Sir Thomas More

I hold in all seriousness what seems to most Englishmen the fantastic opinion that it is wrong to kill any animal – whether an elephant or a partridge – for pleasure. The temper which makes a man who sees a beautiful antelope walking in its pride across the plain long to bring his rifle up to his shoulder and convert it into a bleeding mass of lifeless flesh seems to me devilish.

The East Africa Protectorate Sir Charles Eliot.

Now, much as I might desire to shoot an elephant in self-defence, I have never had any desire to kill them for sport. They are such wise animals, and might be so useful to humanity. Domesticated elephants are delightful characters, and to kill them for the fun of killing, or for the monetary gain of the value of their ivory, is to my mind immoral. It is a pity that an intelligent creature like the elephant should be shot in order that creatures not much more intelligent may play billiards with balls made from its teeth.

Kenya Diary 1902–1906 Richard Meinertzhagen.

PART VIII

Lifestyles

There are some forty tribes, or ethnic groups as they are today more often called, in the Republic of Kenya, as well as people drawn from many other races, nations and faiths. Animists and Christians, Muslim and Hindu, Bantu cultivators, Hamitic pastoralists, Cushitic nomads, Dorobo hunters, Nairobi politicians, Bajun fishermen, British entrepreneurs (and a few surviving farmers), witch-doctors and consultant surgeons, peasant women bartering in open-air markets and bankers' wives dancing in discos, all co-exist within the country's borders in relative, if not absolute, amity and peace. Each tribe, each community, each national group has its distinctive lifestyle, its own way of living, dying, being born, marrying, toiling, worshipping its god. An encyclopedia would be needed to reflect them all. This is a random selection drawn from past and present, from experiences as diverse as those of the Maasai moran to the colonial DC, and from environments as contrasting as the nomad's encampment to the palace of the Sultan of Zanzibar.

Childhood

Ripeness is all.

One day, Ibrahim brought a small deputation of elderly notables to the house (at Marsabit). We sat round in a circle, drinking tea out of saucers – they seemed to prefer it that way and I followed suit. Conversation lagged at first. The very oldest was going on the Haj, the pilgrimage to Mecca, and he mumbled something which Ibrahim interpreted.

"He say he pray for you on this Haj," he explained.

I bowed and murmured my thanks, and we all sucked appreciatively at our tea. After a pause there was more mumbling.

"He say he pray for very long life for you and the Bwana."

I nodded brightly and replied that it was very good of him. There were more murmurings into his meagre grey beard.

"He pray for many children for you," translated Ibrahim impressively. At that everybody wagged their heads.

"Many, many children!" they chorused. It seemed ungracious to say that just a few would do.

Perhaps Ibrahim doubted that the old man's piety by itself would prove effective, for soon after that he waited on me, cradling a strange shape cocooned in a yellow silk cloth in his arms. I felt like a child about to open a birthday present. What could it be? I adored surprises. Slowly and importantly Ibrahim unwrapped the shining silk and revealed the offering. I moistened my lips and felt remarkably short of words.

"Fertility emblem, Mumma," he murmured delicately, lowering his gaze as he handed it over.

"Yes . . ." I said, swallowing hard, "I guessed that."

For indeed, there was no understatement here. The huge, mellowed ostrich egg, festooned with suggestive sea-shells, shrieked its significance. It was the ugliest thing I had ever seen, and it took a little getting used to. Reverently Ibrahim took it back from my trance-like clutch. He walked to my bed and hung it on a nail at the head.

"There!" he said with satisfaction, stepping back to admire it.

After this, I would wake in the night to see it looming over me like a featureless face wreathed with little snakes. I hated it. But I knew it would break Ibrahim's heart if I took it down from the wall before it had fulfilled its mission.

Fulfil its mission it did: the District Commissioner's wife was soon able to announce her pregnancy. She also injured her thumb.

Soon after this Ibrahim asked if the "ladies of the town", as he called the wives of the leading merchants of the small community, could pay their respects. We arranged a time. Gerald was away again on safari, and I did not have his support, but with the help of a Swahili dictionary and the Police Officer, I prepared a speech of welcome which I hoped they would understand. . . .

As soon as I appeared Ibrahim gave a signal and they all let out a fearful warbling yell such as one associated with old-world cannibals sighting a new missionary. They stood on the lawn, some forty or fifty of them with their daughters, hullabalooing with zest and clapping their faces to ululate the better. I was unprepared for such a greeting and found it unnerving, but Ibrahim, as master of the ceremonies, beamed approval and said in a reassuring way: "Somali welcome, Mumma."

The leading matrons in their gorgeous silks advanced towards me as gracefully as swans sailing before the wind, their hands outstretched. The bandage on my thumb was enormous; I could not imagine how anyone could fail to notice it and hoped they would let me off lightly, but the first stout lady grasped my hand with both hers, and then in Somali style seized my thumb tightly and shook it separately. This took me completely by surprise and the effort to keep quiet about the pain she innocently caused left me speechless. The bandage came off. The lady looked at it in considerable embarrassment and threw it deftly behind the nearest bush. After that there was nothing to warn the others and now that the ice was broken, they advanced on me eagerly with the loveliest smiles – Somali women are almost always beautiful – and tortured me with their enthusiastic thumb-grips. The pain was excruciating, and my face felt frozen with the effort I was making to keep a grin, however stricken, on it. As for my speech, it was now quite beyond my power to make it.

The emblem worked but only partially: the first-born was a girl.

When things had calmed down and returned to normal I realized that nobody of any importance had come to call on me. After the interest they had shown beforehand I had rather expected a visit from the "ladies of the town". One or two unmarried girls had come out of curiosity to examine the baby's clothes and bath things and toys, but no one else. Ibrahim sighed when I drew his attention to it.

"They would have come if it had been a son, Mumma," he said gently, as one who tried to share the burden and help me over a bad patch in my career as an NFD wife. "It is not the custom for a daughter."

"In our country we like daughters," I said indignantly.

Ibrahim smiled tolerantly but shook his head. It was clear that he still felt responsible and it weighed on his mind that his emblem had been second-hand.

It was, however, no surprise to me when he brought it back.

"Allah will do better for you next time," he said piously, with one of his reproachful looks. . . .

Ibrahim's emblem was finally vindicated and we achieved our first son in 1945. It was something of a relief in the cicumstances. I could return with him from Nairobi, where the baby had been born, with my head high, and prepare to receive a formal visitation from the charming "ladies of the town". There would be no more condolences and sorrowful head-wagging. Everyone would be beaming with congratulation and would remind me that they had been long praying for just this. That much I expected, but I was totally unprepared for what actually happened.

The day after we got back presents began to pour in from all over the mountain. The local Boran headman presented our son with the prettiest black and white bullock we had ever seen. My dear old friend Harub, the Arab butcher, brought a fine ram, and so did several other old local residents. Sergeant-Major Gabbra Mikhail loaded up two donkeys with sacks of oats for Andrew's pony. Nor was it only the well-to-do folk who brought presents: some of our humbler friends brought chickens or a stem of bananas or a few eggs with their genuine good wishes, and perhaps their smaller gifts were even more touching than the splendid bullocks and rams. Before our son was two months old he seemed to have acquired considerable property, and I myself felt fully reinstated with the local people. *To My Wife – Fifty Camels* Alys Reece.

A different view of the birth of daughters was held by the Kikuyu.

From the moment of her birth a girl baby is even more welcome than a boy; her work at home is valuable, and when she is marriageable she will fetch thirty goats. The Kikuyu baby makes its first acquaintance with the world from the point of view of its mother's back, where, secure in her cape in the form of a hood, it becomes inured to sun and flies, and takes part, generally head downwards, in the work of the day. The elder children, as all the world over, act as nursemaids to their little brothers and sisters, and endeavour in quaint fashion to carry them after the manner of their elders. The children of both sexes are singularly quiet and well behaved; they are never to be seen playing games, and they seem to need no occupation. I have counted as many as twenty-two children together at one time, under the age of some fourteen years, all sitting quietly, and none of them engaged in any way, with the exception of some of the little girls who were making bags. This quiet apathy of childhood is in singular contrast with the energy put forth in movement and dances in later years. When a girl is from ten or twelve to fifteen years, comes the great day of her initiation into the tribe. No man would marry a girl who has not gone through these rites; but they do not marry very young, not apparently before sixteen or seventeen years, and possibly later.

These young years are very cheerful ones to the Kikuyu maiden. She of course assists her mother in the household and fields, but she has an amount of gaiety which many an English girl would envy. Almost every moonlight night she can go to a dance, where she chooses her own partner. The young men come in properly adorned and turned out, for if they did not, as they inform us, "none of the girls would dance with them."

With a Prehistoric People W. S. and K. Routledge

Muslim custom forbade Swahili girls the freedom and indulgence enjoyed by peoples of the interior.

A girl is called *kigori* when she is seven years old. At fifteen she is called *mwari*. It is usual for such children to remain at home. First the ears are pierced with a thorn, and the day of piercing them is celebrated like a wedding. The child is taught how to behave in the house, to wash pots, plates, and basins. Then she is given the beginning of plaiting, and her daily occupation is to plait mats and to learn to cook.

She may never go out except at night to visit near relations, but not alone. She is escorted by a slave girl or an old lady. If she strays all over the place, her elders beat her, and she finds it hard to get a good husband. People call her a gadabout who is familiar with every place.

In addition, if she is in the house and a stranger comes to the door, whether man or woman, but they do not know, she must hide in another room and not talk to the stranger. If her elders hear her they reprimand her severely, saying, "If you hear a call do you poke your face in so that anybody can see you?" When people hear that she does not hide her face, they say, "So-and-so's face is sunburned; she has no shame; she is not a girl to marry." She may get a husband, but not quickly. When a girl reaches the age of ten, a woman comes who is her *kungwi* and puts around her loins her *utunda*. This is her most intimate friend, and the *utunda* means love, to attract a man to want her as his wife. If a woman has no *utunda* it is said her loins are paralysed.

The Customs of the Swahili People Mtoro bin Mwinyi Bakari.

African childhood ended, as it often ends today, in circumcision, perhaps the most important event in the life of every boy and girl. Everything depended on unflinching courage. A Kikuyu writer describes his own experience.

As far as I was concerned my ceremony was to be very simple. Yet, on the night of 20 August 1940, I did not sleep at all. I lay there wondering how a circumciser's knife would feel upon my delicate flesh. One of Karanja's brothers was to be my aide. He went out at 5 am to get a circumciser named Macharia wa Muriu to come and circumcise me. At about 6 am I saw my aide and Macharia coming across Kayahwe River. I felt like a soldier just before he is given his orders and is ready to go to the front to face the enemy!

After they had arrived at Karanja's home I was asked to go and wash myself in the Itare River on the western side of Karanja's home about half a mile away. It is usual for candidates to wash their bodies, and especially the penis that there may be no offensive dirt thereon. It is also considered a bad thing if one should engage in sexual relations before the day of circumcision. So Muchaba, my aide, followed me to the river. Along with him were fifteen or twenty women and girls. I did not want to be followed by a large number of people like that who might later on see me naked! However, I could not help it. I was very embarrassed.

After I had washed myself Muchaba advised me not to wear anything again. So we walked back near Karanja's home where I was to be circumcised. I was naked and followed by a large number of women who were happy – singing, dancing, and shrilling. I felt even more embarrassed.

These songs were consolation, advice, and encouragement to dispel any fear that I might have had. They told me that "We of the Ethaga clan have never cried, do not cry, and shall never cry when we are initiated, or show any sign of fear. Those who may do so are only the children whose mothers were not wedded when they had them, but were wedded afterwards.

"Be firm, our Mugo, be firm and brave, so that you may encourage the young ones who will be circumcised after you. Be firm."

As we approached Karanja's home I saw Karanja with a crowd of people forming a circle and waiting for me.

The circumciser was in the crowd. As soon as I arrived I was told to go to the centre of the crowd. Muchaba, my aide, was very close beside me. My heart was pumping fast! I sat down in the centre of the crowd. But now I was completely fearless. Muchaba was about nine feet from me holding a white sheet which was to be put on me after circumcision. Beside him was Karanja holding a fried chicken and a kettle of chicken soup to be given to me after circumcision.

The crowd was very silent, waiting perhaps to detect whether I would show a sense or feeling of fear. I was aware of them and their expectations. After I had sat down I folded my two fists like a boxer and put them on the right side of my neck. I then turned my face towards the Aberdare Mountain on the western side of the Kikuyu Country. I was now ready for the knife!

In a few seconds I heard the circumciser approaching me from the right side. I was not supposed to look at him so I kept on looking on the left side. He held my penis, pulled the foreskin back and cut it off. It was very, very painful! But I did not show any feeling of fear or even act as if I were being cut. No medical aid was applied first or later, and this made it extremely painful.

The cutting was over. I was now a grown-up Christian Kikuyu. I was a man. . . .

Muchaba, my aide, came to me and put a sheet around me. I was now allowed to look down at the handiwork of the circumciser and see what had been done to me. Blood was streaming from me like water from a pipe. Thank God I did not faint for I would have been disgraced! The crowd was glad because I had shown courage. They dispersed singing and happy that another Kikuyu child had been brave and had become a man. They sang out: "He is brave." (Arikuma!) Muchaba showed me how to hold the sheet around me so that it would not become soiled with blood, and he proceeded to guide me home.

Child of Two Worlds Mugo Gatheru.

Forty years on little had changed, although most of the candidates were schoolboys. This Maasai ceremony was observed in 1983 not far from Nairobi.

The day after Christmas, Sekento [a Maasai school-teacher] and I went to Empaash for Noah and Penina's circumcision ceremony, arriving at the *boma* with a contingent of newly circumcised girls and boys in dark-charcoal *shukas* [a toga-like cloth]. The boys wore head-dresses like Noah's with stuffed birds and spiral brass earrings tied around their heads. The metal chains of the girls' headpieces draped across their high foreheads. The group had come to lend support and encouragement to Noah and Penina. . . .

Penina, her head shaved and wearing a beaded leather cape, was whispering with her girlfriends behind one of the huts. Noah wore a turquoise *shuka*, like a woman's, another fertility symbol, and the elders were outlining his feet with a knife on a piece of hide, cutting special sandals for him. His head was shaved, and he looked very solemn, his thoughts perhaps on the next morning, when the circumcisions would take place. I waved, but it did not seem fitting to interrupt or talk to him. Sekento and I, who stood out in our Western clothes, kept to the edges and observed. . . .

Semoi asked if we would like to meet the man who would circumcise Noah. He was a Dorobo, a member of a small hunting tribe that had a long association with the Maasai. In the past, the Dorobo, who were beekeepers, provided the Maasai with honey, and with smelted metal to make their spears and swords, a task too demeaning for the Maasai themselves. They also specialized in circumcisions.

This circumciser's name was Kesi. He was a short man with bright, feverish eyes; he was wearing a black-and-maroon-striped blanket, metal bracelets, two strings of beads around his neck, and metal earrings. We found him sitting on a rock, guarding his knife, which was wrapped in cloth. "So, you have come very far – perhaps from London – to talk with me?" he inquired. "Ask me whatever you like, because I am expert at this job." Semoi told us that Kesi's father had circumcised him. Kesi said he hoped his own son, though he was a schoolboy, would carry on the family tradition. He said he had performed more than a hundred circumcisions. "All of the boys were brave; none of them ran away." Sekento asked him how he was paid. "When I started, I was paid only in animals," Kesi said. "But nowadays it is more convenient to be paid in shillings." . . .

These days, he said, there was growing competition in the circumcision business. "Some Maasai take their sons to clinics to be circumcised," he said. "It's cheaper, but I think it is very wrong to go against our traditional culture. At the clinic a nurse will wrap a boy's penis in a dressing after the circumcision, and who can be sure the thing was done properly? But with me you can see everything; you can be sure you are not cheated."

Kesi unwrapped his knife and used the cloth to polish the blade. "I have used this knife for twenty years," he said proudly. "It is very good for the job – hard and sharp."

Semoi handled the instrument, a seven-inch knife with a curved end, running his index finger along the blade, turning it over, examining the handle. "When I was circumcised, I told Kesi's father to make the blade of his knife dull – to crush it on stones – because I was ready and brave and could stand the pain," he said.

Kesi said he was very sure that Noah would not cry out. "Once I look a boy in the eye, I can tell immediately if he is brave or a coward," he said. "This boy is clean and brave."

The women stayed inside while the men blessed their cattle sticks with cow's urine. No women would be allowed to watch the circumcision, but Musei joked that since I had long hair – like a moran – I could not be counted as female. The boys who had sung the night before formed a reception line on the rocks, watching for Noah. Kesi began his preparations, painting his face with white chalk. Semoi stood stiffly, not speaking to anyone. As the sky grew lighter, the boys and younger men rattled their cattle sticks and performed a frenzied storklike dance, some yelling out with emotion. The elders began pacing, predicting disaster. It would be a sad day, they said, as Noah would surely let down his family and the tribe. This was tradition, Sekento explained. Everyone prepared for the worst.

With a huge orange sun rising behind him, Noah appeared, first walking, then running toward the *boma*. The young men around me began to tremble, waving their cattle sticks and screaming. Noah ran past us, threw down his *shuka* and grabbed the goat hide on which he would be circumcised. Several men pinned him to the ground. An elder squatted behind him and supported his back. Kesi splashed his face with milk, then knelt down and held out the knife for everyone to see. The men drew in closer. Noah looked as if he were in a trance, his eyes closed, his arms limp. Kesi rang a small bell and began the cutting. Sekento flinched and turned away. Noah remained perfectly still. As blood poured from the wound, there was more frenzy. One boy began to jerk violently and cried out that if Noah was a coward he would take his place. The boy began hyperventilating and fell to the ground unconscious. Other boys followed, dropping one after another, overcome with emotion. The older men stood in a tight circle watching Noah's face for any trace of reaction, but his expression was placid. The cutting, following the Maasai practice by which the foreskin was loosened but not entirely removed, took several minutes, and when Kesi stood back to let the elders examine his work he looked satisfied. Semoi, who had stood by silently, his lips pursed, splashed milk on the wound and hugged Mr Sha, Naisiawua and Musei. Then the men carried Noah, who remained motionless, to one of his mother's huts.

"Noah is a free man now," Sekento said. "The father can no longer dictate to him."

The circumcision of girls – in this case also Maasai – is not for the squeamish.

Naseyo, the female circumciser, was painting her face with white chalk in preparation for Penina's surgery, which was next. She had taken off her floral-print dress and now wore traditional *shuka* and a knit cap. The circumcision was to take place inside Agnes's other hut, as Agnes had planned it would, in the small, dark compartment where lambs and kids were normally kept. The night before, pans of water had been left outside on the roof to chill. The cold water, which was thought to act as a mild anesthetic, would be splashed on Penina. Two little girls got up on the roof and dug out a small whole to let in some light. Agnes told me to follow her inside the hut when Penina was taken in. "You have asked us so many questions about this thing, and now you can see for yourself," she said. There was none of the public drama surrounding Noah's circumcision. Most of the men were squeamish about female circumcision, and some had already drifted across the street to Mr Sha's bar.

Unceremoniously, Kipeno and Nanta grabbed Penina and took her inside. Agnes motioned me to follow. The women handled Penina roughly, which seemed to frighten her. They removed her *shuka* and laid her on the dirt floor. The hole in the roof let in only a small stream of dusty light. There were flies everywhere. The women held Penina by her shoulders, and pulled back her knees. Naseyo bent down, splashed her with cold water, and, using a curved razor, began the cutting. Penina screamed, "You are killing me! You are killing me!" The pain must have been stupendous. "Stop! Save me!" Her clitoris was sliced away, as were the outer lips of her vagina. Blood ran down her legs. I steadied myself against the wall and looked away. Penina continued to scream while the women shrieked with laughter. Finally, the cutting was over, though Penina continued to whimper, and her face was streaked with tears. Naseyo splashed the wound with milk, and then Penina was carried to a sleeping platform. "Are you all right?" I asked her. She could not speak. Outside, people were singing and dancing. The younger boys were serenading Noah, praising his courage. A second olive sapling was planted outside the hut, and guests stood naming their gifts to Penina – cows, sheep, goats. Naseyo, the circumciser, kissed me on the cheek. "Would you like to be next?" she asked. Then she winked and opened a bottle of beer with a can opener hung around her neck. A second ox was shot with an arrow, and the blood was collected for Penina. Agnes said she would also be given sheep fat to drink, as this would make her vomit and prevent infection. Two men smothered and slaughtered the sheep in the compartment where Penina's surgery had taken place. I stepped away quickly.

"Are you okay?" Sekento asked when I met him outside. "Your face is green."

Maasai Days Cheryl Bentsen.

Warriors

One of the last observers to see Maasai moran in action, before their battle array dwindled to small, illicit cattle-raiding parties, recorded these impressions.

Nothing more romantic can be pictured than the return of a raiding party. Far away behind some undulation of the ground is heard the first faint refrain of the Blood Song. Everybody rushes out wild with excitement. The captured cattle gradually come into view, with here and there a guard tending them. Then the warriors appear in a compact body of regular formation, moving very slowly with measured tread. The rhythm of the song is marked by slightly throwing the spear vertically up into the air, making it spin, and catching it again. As the spears are bright as silver, and the blades four feet long, they throw back the sun's rays like so many revolving mirrors. The warriors in their song recount what they have done, and will do, and every now and again an individual under its influence works himself up to such a pitch of frenzy that he loses all self-control, especially if he has failed to kill a man, and has to be disarmed and held down till the fit passes off, or he would certainly kill somebody. For this reason an old man always heads the procession as it approaches the crowd, in order to give the word to disarm any too excited warrior. Lean, gaunt, tall, and taciturn, they move at the walk or the run, with the long, easy, tireless stride of the bird of their own plains – the ostrich. Distance they hardly seem to consider. To cover it seems to cost them no effort. With sufficient incentive they perform extraordinary feats of endurance. Given that meat is available when fighting, they seem capable of eating an indefinite quantity: nothing is left, however large the original amount.

When on the warpath sleep seems absolutely to be laid aside: they march and fight all day, and eat and sing round the fire all night; no sentries are posted or watch kept. They sit in small circles round a number of fires, each man's shield being placed on edge behind him and maintained by his spear driven into the ground butt-end downwards. Clothes they have none, but look exceedingly smart and well groomed, and a picture of manly strength and beauty, rubbed down with mutton fat and red ochre, their hair elaborately dressed in a short pigtail, and their arms and ornaments brightly burnished. . . .

Essentially men of the plains, in the open they are splendid fighters, but become absolutely useless if confronted by an enemy in cover. Nor will they cross a river: the smallest stream that is unwadeable will turn an army. No Masai can swim, nor will he learn to swim, though its military advantage is obvious to him, and all adjoining nations are expert swimmers. This point is quite characteristic of the unadaptable character of these people. The Masai is certainly by nature a brave man: fighting, or, more accurately speaking, the taking of life in war, he loves for its own sake, and he is quite willing to stake his own life for the fun of the thing and the chance of distinction and plunder.

A few years ago the rinderpest broke out and almost exterminated the herds. Famine and disease followed to the herdsmen. Starving, they fell on one another, the eastern clans against those of the west, for the possession of the surviving cattle. One day more than a thousand dead lay on the Arthi plain, the result of a pitched battle: in other words, the result of a thousand simultaneous duels – shield and spear against shield and spear – for such is Masai battle. Time and place is specified and no quarter given. Similarly, when fighting with other nations, no quarter is given. Old men, women, and children, the sick and the wounded, all alike are speared, for no other motive than the satisfaction of taking life.

With a Prehistoric People W. S. and K. Routledge.

A brave and ferocious warrior caste was not unique to the Maasai. An officer of the King's African Rifles posted to north-western Kenya records a conversation with a Turkana chieftain.

"Chaggi, you have the scars for women victims as well as men victims; have you killed many?"

"Effendi, I have killed a great many. I have few scars; there would not be room for them all if I put one for every one of our enemies, the Suk, that I have killed!"

"Tell me, Chaggi, when you raid the Suk, do you lead out a large army of spearmen?"

"Effendi, I often raid alone! I go over the border with no one else at all; I reach a manyatta as day is about to dawn; I kill everyone there and then I go home with the cattle. It is the custom of our tribe to raid for cattle and that has been the custom *always!*"

"What glory is there, Chaggi, in killing women?"

"It isn't glory, it's sense!"

"So you deliberately kill women, Chaggi?"

"And children too!"

"Have you no use for women as wives?"

"Effendi, I am a Turkana. The Turkana like Turkana girls as wives. I do not want Suk women; I do not want a wife who is grieving over the husband whom I have killed."

"Why don't you just let the women go, Chaggi?"

"Do you know anything about women, Effendi?"

"Not much; I am hoping you will tell me."

"Effendi, women are the ones to make trouble! If I raid for cattle and kill all the men and let all the women go, the women run off screaming until they find some more men, and then they so disturb the hearts of those men that those men set out on a raid to get all the cattle back again. That is why I run after the women and push a spear into them. It is just a matter of sense; no Turkana thinks it a glory to kill a woman."

"And then about the very small children – do you even spear them?"

"Effendi, what do you expect? Little children need mothers and milk to keep them alive. When the stock have gone with me taking the milk with them, and when the mothers are lying dead, what is there for the little children to look forward to when the sun goes down except a Fisi (hyena)?"

"So then, Chaggi, once you pick on a Suk manyatta, you kill everyone in it, even to the babes that can neither speak nor walk?"

"Certainly! Kluch!" (Sound of spear penetrating!)

"You have been punished for doing these things, Chaggi."

"I have been punished!"

"If the white authority were to leave the country, what would you do?"

"Effendi, if the white authority were to leave the country and you were to pack up and leave this afternoon, before light came into the morning sky I should be over those hills and into the country of the Suk!"

"But if I remain, Chaggi, and if I ask the authority to make you once more chief of your own people, can I count upon you to refrain from raiding the Suk ever again?"

"Is there a maggot in my brain, Effendi?" Chaggi's fore-finger was placed against his temple in an expressive manner!

I asked the son of Aijigwa whether he had any desire to return to the raiding habits as of old. "Certainly not!" said this young chief.

"Then why is Chaggi so keen on it?"

"Effendi, you will with difficulty understand the Turkana. Chaggi has become a chief whilst retaining the heart of a young warrior. It is the young women, the girls of our tribe, who incite the young men to deeds of bravery and the blooding of their spears! That is the thing you should seek to change, Effendi; find something else for the girls and the young Moran to do. But Chaggi has never grown up; he is the bravest of the brave, but his heart remains the heart of a young warrior in the breast of a chief."

I reinstated Chaggi with the most reluctant consent of my own superiors.

The Desert and the Green Earl of Lytton.

Dickson, a Maasai schoolboy living near Nairobi in the mid 1980s, tried to combine lion hunts and cattle raids with schooling and cities.

The Keekonyokie moran numbered more than a thousand and ranged in age from about fifteen to twenty-five. The older moran lived in the *manyattas*, which their mothers built. There were elders around to give instruction on the social order, and mothers to act as chaperons for the uncircumcised girls who stayed with the boys. The moran competed at wrestling and club throwing and practised with spears, swords and shields; at night they danced and sang with the girls. Hairdressing was another preoccupation; the upkeep of a moran's hairdo required long hours of tedious work. Bits of wool had to be twisted into the hair to lengthen it for styling into the moran's distinctive plaits. Dickson's friend Runges, a senior moran, wore a tight plait that hung to his shoulder blades.

Dickson once wrote out for me a list of rules for moran, most of which were designed to instill discipline and group spirit. Moran were not allowed to eat or drink alone, or to drink milk at their family *bomas*. I asked him about the rule that forbids moran to have sex with circumcised women – or to eat meat that the women have seen or handled – and he acknowledged that the sex prohibition was not strictly followed. The moran referred to their secret affairs as "night traveling".

The traditional duties of the moran were to defend the tribe and restock the herds through cattle raids. But since there were no more wars to fight, except an occasional border skirmish, he said the moran mostly roamed about in small competitive bands, stealing cattle, hunting lions and building up reputations.

Dickson had been on lion hunts, the most recent a "fantastic adventure" in which twenty-eight moran took part. With bells strapped to their thighs, they had hiked to a remote area and made camp. Throughout the night they heard roaring; nobody slept. At dawn, they scattered across the countryside. When one group spotted a male lion, they shouted for the others. A senior moran ordered some to hold back, in case the first group's spears missed their mark. But the back-up regiments – including Dickson's – objected: everyone wanted a chance to throw the first spear and claim the lion's mane, or to snare the tail as a prize. Ignoring the command, the moran charged forward. Dickson threw his spear quickly, but the lion jumped out of the way. A second moran hit the lion's chest, and a shower of other spears followed. The lion sprang, and within seconds two moran were on the ground bleeding and groaning. The wounded lion lay beside them, writhing and near death. All eyes were on the unclaimed tail. Several scrambled to hack it off. When it was certain the lion was dead, the scalp and mane, which rightfully belonged to one of the wounded boys, were sawed off. The moran then loaded their injured friends onto their backs, taking turns carrying them, and hiked to a road where they flagged down a passing truck to take them to the district hospital. The wounded boys were soon back in action, proudly showing off their scars.

Dickson said the highlight of moran life was *olpul*, the meat-feasting camps at which the moran gorged on meat to build up strength before a lion hunt or a cattle raid. To bolster their courage, the moran also drank a special "soup" made from herbs, roots and bark that acted as a narcotic to rouse their aggression. High on this soup, they were ready to face lions.

Once, at Saikeri, I happened to see several moran who had taken the brew. They behaved as if they were having seizures, flew into fits of hysteria, made strange choking sounds and foamed at the mouth; two of them fell on the ground rigid. At first I assumed it was mere acting, since all the moran have a theatrical air about them. But Joseph, Noah and Dickson assured me the soup was powerful, and the frenzy was "real". In severe cases, often at ceremonies, little girls were made to sit across the fallen moran's legs, an act that generally restored them to consciousness.

"Once you start shaking, you can't stop," Dickson said, and added that drinking the soup also brought on sweating and headaches, and sometimes a hangover.

After his circumcision, Dickson was invited for the first time to attend an *olpul* in the forest with his older brother and his friends. Neighbouring *bomas* donated eight bulls for the feast, and the moran had slaughtered and eaten two of them when he arrived from school. Dickson did not drink the soup but watched the others. "First, they started shaking and bragging about how great they were," he said. "Then they decided to go on a cattle raid." He stayed behind to tend the camp. Later that night, the moran returned with seventeen stolen cows. The cows belonged to a high-ranking Kenya Army officer who later sent helicopters to search the bush for them. When the cattle were not located, the officer made a radio plea for the return of four of the cows that had recently calved. Some Maasai elders heard the news in Ngong and relayed the message to the moran, who, for the sake of the calves, complied, leaving the four where they were easily found. They kept the rest.

There came a time when the warrior had to lay aside his spear, renounce love-making with the maidens and settle down to marriage and the raising of a family. The Eunoto ceremony marked the graduation of the warrior to the status of a junior elder. This event, which took place near Ngong in the mid 1980s, may have been the last Eunoto ever to be held.

The ceremony began in late October, on a full moon. A strong, hot wind was blowing across the plains. The air was heavy with dust. The Keekonyokie moran were to arrive in regiments – in stately single-file processions of twenty or thirty at a time – from Euaso, Saikeri, Narok, Nairragie-Enkare and the Kaputei plains. Hundreds of celebrants had gathered at the *manyatta* to await them. At first, you could not see them. There was only the distant trumpeting of kudu horns and the clang of bells strapped to the warriors' thighs. A deep chanting grew louder as they finally appeared on the plains, still far in the distance. They approached the *manyatta* with a slow, rhythmic step, their footfalls resounding with bells, and paraded into the *manyatta*, some in head-dresses made of black ostrich feathers or lions' manes. They wore red cloths tied around their hips, some ornamented with spangles; many had ritual scars, like welts, in patterns across their chests. Their ornate hairdos were caked with grease and red ochre; the same paint had been applied to their legs in swirling patterns. With each step they thrust forward chins, the movement coinciding with a deep bass grunt – *Hhooohn! Hhooohn! Hhooohn!* – a warlike sound, which in the old days was fair warning to all who heard it.

Letangwua, dressed in a full-length cape of dark hyrax fur, stood with commanding dignity, reviewing the troops as they circled inside the *manyatta*. The moran looked straight ahead, with expressions of grave and sullen pride that seemed remarkable, even for the Maasai. The women and girls backed away a respectful distance. . . .

By late afternoon, all of the moran had arrived. It was the first time the entire group had come together since the ceremony preceding their circumcisions. There were predictable skirmishes between rival groups – pushing, shoving, wrestling – and some warriors restrained their comrades from inflicting injuries on each other or themselves. No emotions were held in reserve. Some moran trembled and writhed on the ground, high on the potent herbal brews concocted in the bush.

No one was seriously hurt, but the women fled the *manyatta*. Joseph broke up fights and told his friends to "act sensibly". When the moran were worn out, they assembled outside the *manyatta* where the elders gave final instructions. The old men waved their clubs and fly whisks and sternly warned that ancient differences were to be put aside in the interests of peace and community. The moran half listened and worked on each other's hair plaits. Some held hands or draped their arms around each other's shoulders. Many were quite young, their military service cut short by the early graduation. Some were schoolboys who had joined up at the last minute. But Dickson's friends, including Runges, were men in their early twenties who had spent years in the bush. With long pigtails and flinty eyes, they seemed of another era, and their swagger and belligerence intimidated the younger moran. . . .

That evening, as the wind died down, I set up a tent outside the *manyatta*, made a fire and watched the full moon rise. In the darkness, the valley seemed to draw in on itself, and the flanking mountains stood like a wall barring the outside world. The sky thickened with stars; I was sorry Noah had not come with me.

Most of the moran left the *manyatta* for the night to drink more of their powerful herbal soup and sleep in bush camps. The older men were singing drunkenly in their huts. A few children ran around in the dark, too excited to sleep, and several boys tried to calm a moran who cried out for others to join in a lion hunt. Around nine o'clock I noticed a reddish-brown stain spreading across the face of the moon.

A string had been tied around the perimeter of the *manyatta* as a symbolic protection against bad luck, and I climbed under it and went inside. The Maasai were watching the moon with surprise, some with fear; it seemed the eclipse was unexpected, and troubling. A full white moon is auspicious for the holding of major ceremonies, but when the moon disappears – "dies" – the Maasai become circumspect. The moon's dark phase is symbolic of death, and significant activities are curtailed at that time to avoid the possibility of bad luck.

The shadow on the moon – the color of ochre – continued to creep. I stood with Joseph, his mother and some of his school friends from Saikeri, all of us looking up at this strange sight. The Maasai were silent, then some of the women cried out. "The moon has died!" Others began singing a song which tells the legend that links the moon with death.

An elder scorned the women's concern. "This is nothing new; I have seen such a thing before."

"It is blood from the war in Uganda spoiling the moon!" another man yelled.

The moran began trembling. "It is a curse," one of them said bitterly. Others shouted, "Enemies have cursed our ceremony!" Some proposed going on a cattle raid, before it was too late.

An old woman sobbed. "These moran are right – the world is ending! We will all die!"

An elder shouted her down. "It might be a good thing," he said. "It is a message from Engai that the Maasai should not be ending moranship."

A schoolboy who was with Joseph said, "It is only an eclipse, a natural thing."

Letangwua seemed to agree. "Calm down, go back to your huts!" he ordered. I returned to my campfire. At midnight the moon was completely dark, and the air was still.

Maasai Days Cheryl Bentsen.

The ceremony lasted for four or five days and involved much dancing, singing, consumption of mead and emotional fits intensified by the broth of herbs favoured by the moran. Bulls were sacrificed, the morans' locks shorn, their bodies decorated, and a ceremonial pilgrimage took place to the summit of Mount Suswa. Finally the participants were blessed by the elders and received a collective name – Ilmirisho, Those Who Will Not Be Defeated. A week or so later Joseph, one of the participants, lunched at a Nairobi restaurant with Cheryl Bentsen to celebrate his election as youth-wing chairman of the local branch of the ruling political party. He was employed as a salesman of veterinary medicines and was writing a book.

Courtship and Marriage

A Meru girl from north of Mount Kenya is fattened up for marriage (circa 1965).

We bumped across forbidding country for as far as even a Land Rover could go and then continued on foot, accompanied by the local headman. He guided us to a tiny hut which seemed deserted, for nobody answered our calls. While we were waiting for someone to turn up, the headman told us that here in Tigania a girl lives in seclusion for two years with an older woman who instructs her in her future duties and all that married life will entail. During this period the girl has to behave in a helpless manner, is only allowed to speak in a whisper, and has to keep her eyes downcast under a fringe of metal chains; she is made as fat as possible and, when she leaves the hut, has to be led by her "mother's" hand and walk extremely slowly.

All this seemed to me to indicate a symbol of rebirth, the fringe across the eyes intimating that she has not yet learned to see, the whisper that she does not know how to speak, nor can she walk alone. During these two years she sometimes occupies herself by looking after a small child or making string-bags or ornamenting calabashes.

If her bridegroom wants to visit her during her seclusion, he has to bring costly presents, not only to her but also to her family; in consequence he cannot afford to see her often. At the end of the period he marries her within a week. . . .

I hardly could believe what I now saw. When I entered the tiny hut I almost banged into a partition facing the entrance. After my eyes had become accustomed to the darkness inside, I realized that this was one of the walls of the girl's sleeping room which was only just large enough for her to crouch in. On one side of the cubicle, between it and the outer wall of the round hut, was a small storage place for her belongings. The inside walls of the hut were plastered with mud on which representations of ornaments such as a man's armlet made of buffalo horn or a design of women's skirt-embroideries were painted.

Most intriguing were little mud receptacles, plastered like swallows' nests on the wall and painted white. Each contained three different seeds, probably charms. I was told that these were taken away by the bridegroom when he finally came to get the girl. From the roof hung pieces of wood which, when burnt and allowed to smoulder, gave off a pleasant scent.

The girl herself was very plump and covered in a long, charcoal-blackened skin, decorated with cowries and blue seeds. Her head was shaven except for the top where the hair was shaped into a crown. From the back of her neck across her skull and hair ran a broad white mark painted with a strong-smelling substance, which was also painted on her nose. Her "mother" showed a similar line across her shaven head. In the girl's hand I noticed a piece of string with many knots and was told these had to be unravelled by her bridegroom or his supporters before the marriage could be consummated.

The Peoples of Kenya Joy Adamson.

Polygamy is the norm in most parts of Africa. The women have often been the first to defend it.

Polygamy is of course an integral part of the tribal system. It is not merely a question of domestic arrangement, but of social organization. The poverty stricken condition of the "rich" white man in respect of wives aroused unfailing interest. My husband's attempted explanation, "that a white woman preferred to have her husband to herself," fell extremely flat. "Exactly an opposite view," Mungé assured us as we sat round the camp fire, "obtained among the best people in Kikuyu. The first wife would soon say, 'Why have I to do all the work; why do you not buy another wife?'"

"If," she said, "there is much food or drink to get ready, it is very hard work for one, it is very easy for many." The first wife also retains her pre-eminence, and her child is in any case regarded as the eldest, if it even should have been actually born after that of a later wife. She is usually about the same age as her husband; the man's later wives are considerably younger than he is, and the older he grows the more difference there is in age between himself and his latest acquisition. Sentiment and prestige are thus on the side of being an early comer in the matrimonial establishment; on the other hand, some girls of a practical turn of mind prefer to marry older and richer men.

It is quite usual to come across a man with only one wife; many such exist, but this is by force of circumstance, and is a sign of poverty. Two or three wives is a fairly ordinary allowance, while the rich man has six or seven. The chief Karuri is said to have as many as sixty, who perform a useful office in looking after his interests in various parts of the country.

It is impossible to suppose that there are no heartburnings and jealousies in a homestead, but I have never heard of such, and the fact that each wife has her own hut, shamba, and independent establishment, places the whole on the footing of a village under one headman.

With a Prehistoric People W. S. and K. Routledge

A Swahili writer expresses a different point of view.

A man with two wives is in a difficulty. He has to foreswear himself every day to keep the peace between them, for between co-wives there is incessant jealousy. If he buys anything, he cannot come into the house to divide it. He must do so outside and then send each her portion. If he divides it indoors, there will be trouble. And food, too, he cannot eat a full meal at one house, because when he goes to the other and does not eat, there will be trouble. And sleep, he must share it equally, three nights here and three nights there, and whichever house he sleeps in, his wife must sleep with him. If he sleeps with one wife only, in the morning there is trouble. The other will complain to her parents that he does not sleep with her.

If he wants to marry a third wife, he must have the consent of the first two and must give them a present called "Reconciliation".

If he buys a concubine, he may not give her the same share of his sleep as his wives, but three nights with his wife and one with his concubine. If he buys clothes to give them, he must not give the concubine the same quality as the wives, or they will be vexed. But despite such fair dealing, there is no end to the troubles of a man with two wives. One wants this and the other that, and if they share a house, they disagree, particularly at night, if he goes to a wife when it is not her turn. The other will hear them talking and laughing, and in the morning there will be trouble.

When they quarrel it is most unpleasant. They bite each other and hit each other with sticks. Two wives should not be kept in one house. Some get along well, but not really. The customary treatment of two wives should be taught to a man thoroughly, or he should read about it in books. If he does not know it, there will be perpetual trouble.

The Customs of the Swahili People Mtoro bin Mwinyi Bakari.

An Arab wedding.

In Faza we met an Arab whom we knew from our previous visits to the coast. He was a wealthy merchant, temporarily here to marry a young local girl, an addition to his older wives. As he was an old friend of ours he invited us to his wedding, a great privilege. I had a long talk with the bride's mother, a dignified and still very attractive Arab woman. From her I learned that, though the bridegroom is not supposed to see his bride before their marriage, it can sometimes be arranged for him to have a glance at her from a distance.

For three days before the wedding her daughter had been kept at home to be beautified for the great occasion. She was massaged with fragrant oils, carefully groomed, and the palms of her hands were painted with a network-pattern. During this time she had to keep silent while all her women friends, who were helping and chattering around her, were given refreshments and generally had a good time.

On the evening preceding the wedding we heard a low singing, now and then broken by piercing shrieks. Following the sound, we saw a procession of veiled women wearing *buibuis*, swaying step by step through the village while clapping their hands and using rattles and drums to accompany their chanting. As far as I could see in the dim light, their rattles were made out of a segment of a buffalo horn. Others beat ox-horns with little sticks or shook tambourines. But the most arresting was the haunting tune of the *zomari* flute which was played by the men. The women went on chanting and swaying, and long after we had gone to bed I could hear the sombre tune of the *zomari*. The party only came to an end at dawn.

The wedding had been fixed for 10pm the next day, for at this hour, according to the astrologers, there was the most favourable conjunction of stars for the bridegroom. He spent all day with his future male relations, while the women put the last touches to the bride's attire. I was allowed to be present, but kept in the background. The girl was very young and exceptionally beautiful. Her delicate, pale features were enhanced by a thick coat of mascara round her eyes. Two golden coins adorned her cheeks; I was told that they were kept in position by some kind of mastic. Jasmine blossoms covered her black hair and part of her dress, and their scent mixed with the heavy perfume with which the women constantly sprayed her. While the bustle went on she sat motionless, aloof and silent in the middle of a large bed. . . .

During the day the bride received a present from her betrothed; this was not part of the brideprice which he had already given to her parents. If she accepted the gift, he knew that she was still willing to marry him and the wedding could then be performed without the bride being present.

With male relations as witnesses, the bridegroom was then seated on a chair that was slightly higher than the one opposite on which the *mullah* sat. He held the Koran in his hands while the wedding was being sealed. Immediately afterwards the men went to the house in which the bride was waiting and, firing shots to announce the arrival of the bridegroom, danced the sword dance.

While all this went on outside the house, the women who were with the bride grew more and more excited. The door was still kept shut but there was much whispering behind it. Suddenly there were three knocks and immediately a curtain was drawn across the bed to hide the bride, and after this the door was opened to let the men in. They spent only a short time in the bridal room and then retired, leaving the bridegroom behind. The women, who were now very quiet, brought refreshments to the bridegroom who seated himself opposite the curtain which concealed his bride. Women oiled his head and arms, and he washed his feet. Then everyone left, except for one woman who kept discreetly behind the curtain of the bed to chaperone the bride. There was silence. At that moment the bride stretched her hand from behind the curtain and the bridegroom placed another gift in it while talking to her softly.

Then the woman in the corner gave me a signal and we left the pair alone. For the next seven days they would remain together in the house.

The Peoples of Kenya Joy Adamson.

Three views on the position of women in traditional society: first, the Swahili.

When a man lives with his wife, she is allowed to do nothing whatever without her husband's consent. If he forbids something that he does not like, that is the end of it, and if the woman does it she is called recalcitrant, because she does not obey her husband. A free woman may not go out by day without excuse, except for natural calls. She must be veiled if she wants to go for a talk at a friend's house, and she must go at night between seven and nine, and she must be accompanied by a slave girl. If a woman disobeys her husband, it is for him to correct her; but for serious offences he takes her to the magistrate for correction.

The Customs of the Swahili People Mtoro bin Mwinyi Bakari.

Among the Pokot (Suk).

PASTORAL SUK

Women have no liberty, they must do as they are told.

AGRICULTURAL SUK

"Woman is a property, and must do as she is told and all the work." – Elders of Kerūt.

ENDO

"Women are just like slaves and do all the work." – Lōseron.

TURKANA

"Women do all the work, bring water and firewood, build huts, milk the cows, and cultivate the land. If they refuse we beat them." – Aijigwa.

EN-JEMUSI

Women's work is to grind corn, cultivate the fields, milk the cows, etc. If she likes her husband she will do all these things. If she does not like him she will probably run away to some one else." – Launjali.

The Suk Mervyn Beech.

Among the Somali round Wajir.

Here women are normally regarded as no better than slaves. Their work is hard in a hard country. They face a never-ending string of pregnancies, of malnutrition, of fighting for their children's survival. Perhaps the most burdensome of their circumstances is their degrading position in the community. There are even extremists who hold that women have no souls, and sometimes a Somali girl at marriage is kicked and beaten by her husband, to ensure submission in the future. Infibulation (sewing up of the vulva) is still practised. A young girl will be infibulated until her marriage, and when a man goes away he first infibulates his wife to make sure that she is faithful to him in his absence. This is also common practice in parts of Ethiopia, Somalia and the Sudan.

It does not require much imagination to understand the degradation, pain, and even sepsis that must be endured by these women, and finally the extra pain and difficulty endured at childbirth. The idea of the primitive races giving birth with ease is a total myth. Both circumcision and infibulation cause distortions and deformities, adhesions and scar tissue which add greatly to the difficulties of childbirth. Into this environment Annalena* has set a community run by women for the benefit of those who, in the battle for survival, have not been considered worth saving. A sort of wonder seems to cling to the girls' faces as they begin to take part in a world of which they could not have dreamt.

Different Drums Michael Wood.

Major Njombo, 1983.

One of the people I had hoped to see, and did see, was Major Esther Wambui Njombo. She arrived in time for tea in her civilian clothes, small and trim and

---

*An Italian nun who founded a rehabilitation centre at Wajir in northern Kenya for rejected and sick Somali women.

neat, driven by a formidable lady twice her size in army uniform. Major Njombo had been born on my parents' farm at Njoro and was the daughter of our headman Njombo, and a much younger wife. Njombo had died in 1952 when she was about three.

She went on to a secondary school and then became a teacher. One day in 1973 she heard that women were being recruited for the army. This was a revolutionary measure introduced by M'zee Kenyatta, and only ten girls were initially accepted. Esther Wambui got in on the ground floor, and in less than ten years rose to her present rank. After a spell at Sandhurst, she was given command of the women's section of the Kenyan army. When a detachment went to Britain to take part in the Royal Tournament at Earl's Court, she was its commander. Now, at thirty-five, the army provides her with a house, a car and driver, generous pay, and a pension in a few years' time.

Did she ever go back to Njoro? "Oh, yes, I go back sometimes. I have a shamba there – not on your mother's old farm but close to it, on Major Adams'." She has two other properties: four valuable acres at Langata, Nairobi's fashionable suburb, and two hundred acres north of Mount Kenya where she grows wheat on contract. She has a son of ten. Wambui, her mother, shares her house in Nairobi.

It is almost as if a new species has appeared on earth, the young Kenyan woman who has put tribal ways behind her. Self-assured, well-mannered, elegantly clad and with a neat Afro hair-do, these independent young ladies cope competently with word-processors and computers; they staff banks, manage shops, work as stylists in hair-dressing salons, as flower-arrangers, as secretaries and drivers. How much initiative and ability must have gone to waste for all those centuries, how much talent lain buried! I know that women had, and have, a respected place in tribal society, that their rights were no less well defined than their duties, and to think that they had been regarded as mere beasts of burden was a superficial view. Nevertheless their place in tribal society was subservient; child bearing and rearing their purpose, and the scope for any form of self-expression small. On any road leading from the capital, within a mile of the Kenyatta Centre, you can see, today, women looking older than their years, toiling along under their loads. The smoke-blackened hut, three cooking stones, the gathering of firewood are far from obsolete. That was Major Esther's background. The image of a butterfly emerging from a chrysalis is compelling.

Out in the Midday Sun Elspeth Huxley.

A contemporary Kikuyu describes his own marriage.

There are certain things that we do in our country to increase the bonds between the two families involved in any marriage. People who do not know talk about "bride-price" and "buying" wives; these words confuse the purpose and effect of what happens, which is the transfer of cattle and other property from the family of the bridegroom to that of the bride. If the couple do not agree together it is not then so easy for them to divorce each other without good reason. The father of the bride will not lightly gather together all the property he received because of some minor domestic tantrum or lovers' tiff. Great family pressure will be brought on the bride to continue with her marriage as long as it is reasonable for her to do so. It was necessary for me to hand over nine cattle to my father-in-law. One cow equals ten goats, and one goat equals twenty shillings, so each cow was worth two hundred shillings. I had these cattle because when my sisters married we were brought many by the families of their husbands. . . .

It is also a tradition for the bridegroom to give certain gifts to the mother and father of the bride (*muhiki*) to replace those that the bride's father gave to the bride's mother's parents. These gifts would differ from family to family but normally include a *mukwa* (head strap), *kiondo* (basket) and *nguo ya maribe* (women's skin dress embroidered with beads) for the mother and a *ruhiu* (small sword), *itimu ria nduthu* (special spear) and *githii gia ikami* (a man's skin cloak) for the father. Sometimes the father or mother would say that they preferred something else instead of one of these things. If this was the case it would be agreed upon and handed down the generations. For example, I gave Gordon a mackintosh and I shall now expect that when my daughter is married my son-in-law will give me one as well. My lover's parents said that it would be best to commute all the other articles into a sum of money and we agreed on one thousand shillings. They allowed me to pay this in instalments since I had been so prompt with the cattle, and I am still giving it to them.

For an educated man getting married in our country is a very expensive business as we have to comply with both the old and the new customs. Fortunately I still had with me some of the money which had accompanied me to the Three Dry Hills. Having done so much political work it was now going to finance a more social occasion. My family and nearest relatives, together with some of my close political friends, provided the rest. Money was needed for fitting out the three best men with new suits, buying the three bridesmaids new outfits, a reception at Doris's home and my home, a dance at the Ruringu Social Club, photographs, transport and church expenses. The total cost was three thousand shillings. Although my faith had often weakened I was still a Christian, so was Doris, and we decided to get married in the Presbyterian Church at Nyeri. Doris's dress was white flecked with gold, and it looked really wonderful to me. . . .

On 10 September 1960 I woke up before the cocks began crowing, very excited at what was going to happen. As the sun stole up out of the ground Wangui called me and soon my three friends came to take me with them amidst much joking and laughter. In the peace of the church I led Doris before the altar and we stood in front of the old man together, answering the questions he asked us. Then I placed the ring (*gicuhi*) on Doris's finger and I quietly told her that we had now created a new person, Mrs Josiah Mwangi.

The first party, the bride's reception, was held at Riamukurwe School, organized largely by the headmaster. The school-children had been excitedly preparing for it for days and there was a huge banner over the entrance saying "WELCOME" and hung with flowers from the school garden. One of our customs is that the women of a village make a pretence of preventing the bride leaving her home: their sorrow at losing her is usually only consoled by a large "bribe". Sure enough as we neared the school I saw hundreds of women barring the way and dancing the "*mikondi*". They had with them a *gitaruru*, a large basket they used for keeping food in. Our people also throw the grain up in the air from it and blow the chaff away as it comes down. Until this was filled they would not let me through. My assistants had foreseen this, however, and we had with us in the car a bucket filled with a hundred shillings' worth of ten- and five-cent pieces, which we showered into the basket. The dancing ranks opened and we progressed a few yards until the singers closed in on us again. This time we poured in a hundred shillings' worth of fifty cent and shilling pieces and we went jerkily on to the entrance, where we had to pay a final tax of two hundred shilling notes. Our women are stubborn on these occasions. Usually this money is given back to the bridegroom's mother, but this time it went to Doris's parents.

We had a superb two-tier cake, made by Mrs Diment, the wife of the Community Development Officer in Nyeri, and many of my friends from all races came to eat it with me, including the District Commissioner who had released my mother. This was the time when the Nyeri students were going on the airlift to America and Josef Mathenge took some of the cake with him that evening to Nairobi to eat it with them as they waited for their aeroplane. There was another reception at my own home in Kariko which the whole village joined in and then the dance at the Ruringu Social Club. The next day we went to Mombasa for our honeymoon. We had invited many people to our wedding and the last guests were still coming along in April 1961, seven months afterwards.

Mau Mau Detainee Josiah Mwangi Kariuki.

The Common Task

The trivial round, the common task
Would furnish all we need to ask.
John Keble

The common task indeed furnished all that any African woman would need to ask in the way of toil. This sketch of daily life among the Elgeyo people would fit almost any of the cultivating tribes in the period to which it relates, the 1920s, and after.

The Elgeyo do not have many distractions to upset the daily routine. The women, in particular, lead a very cut-and-dried existence, which would not appeal to a European. They do all the work of the home and most of the cultivating. Their day starts at 5am, and does not finish until they retire with the rest of the household about 10pm. Their first job on rising is to cleanse the gourds ready for the morning milking. They use a little water and a brush made of the stem of the *Doum* palm leaf, frayed by chewing the thicker end. The gourds are left in the sun until dry, when a smouldering brand of olive wood is rubbed round the inside. Finally, a stick is used to extinguish the embers left. This method of cleansing is not very thorough, as large quantities of ash are left in the gourd, and discolour the new milk put into it.

While the gourds are drying, the women grind the Eleusine grain (*wimbi*) for the morning meal. They use two stones – a large smooth one is put on the floor, and on it is placed some grain which is then ground with a smaller stone held in the hands.

At 6am the milking is done by the women and young girls. . . . The milker takes up her position on the right side of the cow. She milks with one hand, and holds her gourd in position with the other. At the same time, she holds the head of the calf under the arm nearest the cow. It is firmly believed in most parts of Kenya that a native cow will not give her milk unless her calf is near. This belief is shared by some European stockowners, who skin calves that die, and stuff the hides with grass, so that the dummies can be placed alongside the mothers at milking-time. The cows are never tied up during milking unless vicious.

By 7am the milking is finished, and then the family feeds. Their menu is monotonous. The food may be either a stiff porridge made of *wimbi*, or of millet meal, or a thin broth which is really porridge diluted with water. Variety is lent to the menu by the addition of meat, milk and blood, green vegetable, or maize cobs when available. The meat (beef or mutton or goat's flesh) is either dried over the fire on sticks, or boiled in water. In the latter case, the meat is removed when cooked, and the liquid, thickened with grain flour, is served as a broth. The vegetable, when boiled, resembles spinach. Maize cobs are roasted whole in embers – the Elgeyo have no means of grinding the grains to a fine meal. They do their cooking in earthenware pots, the food being stirred by a stick rubbed between the palms of the hands. Liquid foods are put in small crudely-shaped wooden basins, one for each person. Stiff porridge is served on plates made of ox-hide, whitened with flour. The plates vary in size, according to the ages of the different members of the family. The woman serves out the food, first to the husband, then to the children in order of seniority. She keeps only a small portion for herself, and supplements her share with such food as is handed back to her by the children. In times of famine, she keeps no portion for herself, and is dependent for her meal on these contributions from her children. . . .

After the morning meal, the man, if his hut is on the highlands, opens the cattle *boma*, and takes his herd to pasture – or, more usually, deputes a small boy to look after it. It is no uncommon sight to see a diminutive lad in sole charge of stock worth hundreds of pounds. The now empty kraal is cleaned out by a boy, who sometimes has also to keep an eye on the cattle while he works. In the Ndo valley, when the goats are let out to feed, the boy in charge of them is sometimes accompanied by another lad, whose job it is to climb an acacia tree, and walk along its horizontal branches, knocking down seed pods, to be eaten by the goats which are driven under the tree by the herd boy. If the pods were not thus removed when green, monkeys would strip the trees, and the goats would miss an important part of their meagre food-supplies.

The girls meantime sweep out the hut with a broom, made roughly of green twigs tied together, which lasts about a week. The women go off for water, which is carried in two or three large gourds placed in a carrier made of very strong laced twigs, and strapped to the women's backs. These tasks completed, the women-folk go off to work in the fields, taking with them their naked babies, which are laid on skins on the ground and then covered over with other skins. They toil steadily till about 3pm, gathering any edible weeds they come across. Then they go off in small parties to collect firewood. Burdening themselves with as much as they can carry, they make their long journey back to their homes chatting and laughing happily. Observing the size of these burdens and contrasting them with the small loads which my "warrior" porters found difficulty in managing, I asked one day if the men were not ashamed of their inferiority to the women in this respect. The question surprised the man, and he replied as if amused, "But why? The women are our transport." Then they busy themselves grinding the grain for the evening meal, and fetching such water as may be needed. At 7pm the family reassembles for the meal. Visitors feed with them, but must themselves arrange for sleeping accommodation with members of their own age-clan. An hour later, the young children go to bed. About 10pm, the elders retire for the night.

The Cliff Dwellers of Kenya J. A. Massam.

Nomads take their primitive shelters with them and their daily round is one of plodding over sun-baked plain and desert.

During the afternoon we came across an immense caravan, slowly winding ahead, like a trail of ants. They were Samburu moving towards their dry season grazing grounds in the Losai Hills. The tribesmen were accompanied by more cattle, sheep and goats than I had ever seen before. A few camels jogged along but they were not of a kind I should have cared to hire, even to supplement our own; they were scrawny beasts, emaciated by the loss of blood which is drawn from them once a week and drunk mixed with milk. Each family walked beside its own donkeys to which they had lashed everything lashable. As we drew near I peered inside the panniers on the donkeys' backs. The uprights were distinctive objects, made of wood and thongs, not unlike two snowshoes, one on each side of the animal's flanks and joined at a point above its back, in such a way that it gave the impression of a big tent.

Inside these contraptions babies howled, goats bleated and puppies yapped. All the inmates were trussed like chickens, immovable except for their wobbling heads. When I tried to take a photograph of living cargo mixed up with mats and cooking pots, the indignant father dragged the donkey along so fast that I feared for the safety of the child's wildly wobbling head. One blind old woman stumbled along with head bowed, her hand on her daughter's shoulder; another dragged a foot that was severed at the ankle; it left an almost circular impression in the red earth. I had the feeling that if either of them had stopped they would have been left alone, probably to die. The caravan swept on with a disturbing sense of urgency. "Over endless plains, stumbling in cracked earth. Ringed by the flat horizons only."

The Samburu are a curious people. Closely related to the Masai in almost everything including hypertrophy of the ego, they are exceptionally good-looking, arrogant and lazy. Condemned to a life of incessant wandering they take their leisure seriously, existing for days on the principle of least effort. When I met the Samburu alone I sometimes had the impression that they were staring at me but their eyes showed that they were staring forward and I happened to be in the way. Like the Masai, the tribal braves or *morans* of the Samburu crop their hair except for a top-knot on the crown which is usually decorated with a bobbing feather. They also plaster themselves with brick-red pigments and stand with one leg curled around the other, leaning on their spears.

Journey to the Jade Sea John Hillaby.

Maasai life is centred on their cattle.

The huts were invisible behind the zareba and small wonder for they are not as high as your shoulder and are made of dung and clay, grey and caked into cracks by the sun. We went in. On top of nearly every hut a woman was standing plastering the roof with fresh green cattle-dung, using her hands. They were half naked and round the neck wore rings of wire, rather like a big watch-spring, which stuck out like a huge ruff. It is said to assist them in the defence of their chastity but must be as uncomfortable for the wearer as for the would-be seducer.

The moment of sunset was approaching and from every direction, like spokes to a hub, cattle and goats were streaming into the kraal. The barriers were opened at half-a-dozen points and the animals came tumbling into the space of caked mud and dung between the huts. Soon the kraal was a mob: nothing but a tangle of backs and horns: there was much lowing and bleating and rising of dust in the air. Yet, considering the numbers and the congestion, there was very little noise or confusion. I became completely engulfed in cattle, including big bulls, and had to use all my strength to push through them. But the gentle beasts showed neither fear nor resentment at my handling of them. Even the bulls, with their alarming up-curling horns did not so much as shake their heads at me. They were terribly scrawled over by the brandings they had been given. I noted that some of their throats bore the marks of small wounds. So the owners demonstrated for me their economical method of getting sustenance from their beasts. They chose a young bullock and tied two thongs tightly round its neck. They then shot a small arrow into the artery at the bulge of the neck between the thongs and caught the blood in a calabash. The arrow carried a crosspiece to prevent too deep a penetration. Having drawn the proper amount of blood they removed the ropes and the beast shook his head and walked away apparently little, if any, the worse. Blood and milk, with very occasional meat, are the main food for the Masai.

I went down on hands and knees and crawled into one of the huts. It was dark, and darker still with the clouds of wood-smoke that hung in it. I crawled on and on, trying to feel the shape of the hut and the furnishing. Of the latter there seemed to be none. I could see only the red eye of a burnt-out fire but now and then I touched soft living creatures which struggled out of my grasp, kids and calves, women and children, and from the shadows came nervous twittering and giggling. Then I half saw that the hut was roughly cut up with a framework of branches, which held the little animals and perhaps the children, away from the fire. I was suddenly overwhelmed by the accumulated smells of smoke, human-beings, animals and manure and, fearing attack from the living offsprings of dirt, I crawled backwards into the throng outside.

East African Journey Margery Perham.

A modern man.

Just a mile or two from Mathare Valley, in the heart of downtown Nairobi, Francis Thuo can look out of his window in the International House at the sprawling city below and can see, far off in the distance, the African plains where giraffes and zebras and antelope still roam in great numbers. Thuo, a prosperous business-man in his mid-forties who is chairman of the Nairobi Stock Exchange, wears a three-piece business suit with a Lions Club emblem in the lapel. He sends his five children to private schools and his office is tastefully and expensively decorated, with wall-to-wall carpeting and mahogany furniture.

A long time ago, shortly after he had dropped out of school, Thuo remembers walking across a bridge in Nairobi with his father, a meatcutter who could not afford the fees to educate his eight children. They stopped to watch a dozen men, bare-chested and sweating, labour with pick and shovel along the roadside.

"Look at them," his father said. "If you do not take your studies seriously, you will end up like them. There will be nothing for you to do in life but dig ditches."

Thuo never forgot the advice. He went to work in a gas station, then for an accounting firm. He taught himself to read and write. He studied economics at night and took correspondence courses in history, and in 1964, the year after independence, opened the first African brokerage house in East Africa. He is proud that he bucked the odds and won, particularly when he recalls that in his youth the colonialists gave the Africans virtually no opportunity "to prove our worth" except as common labourers.

"What concerns me these days is that our children are having it much too easy," he mused. "Unless we push, they just don't seem to be pulling their own weight. They want life handed to them on a silver platter."

His anxieties aren't much different than those you might hear in Middle America. That's not surprising, for Africans like Thuo – members of a new, emerging middle class – have dreams and goals and values with a distinctly

Western flavour. They are educated, economically ambitious and dedicated to making their children's lives better than their own. They sacrifice for their children, complain about inflation, worry about the unruly behaviour of today's youth and are greatly concerned with increasing their own wealth and security.

Thuo escaped from his past through sheer hard work and tenacity. Others moved up in class more through circumstance than design, being the beneficiaries rather than the creators of a system inherited from the colonialists. They simply stepped into the void left by the departing colonialists and expatriates, and as often as not, stayed there more because of tribal nepotism than merit.

"Capitalism has been part of the African life since time immemorial," Thuo says. "Measuring your wealth in cattle or the size of your family was a sort of capitalism. This is a new world we live in now and what we're dealing with is just another form of capitalism – money instead of cows."

The Africans David Lamb.

Politicians also have their daily tasks, more rewarding as a rule than those of peasants.

"*Uhuru* [independence] is a sweet commodity," he declared, "because it has enabled me to own several sleek cars, a twelve-room house, twelve wives and sixty-seven children. What else do we want?" Oloitipitip's* fleet included a Citroën DS20, a Mercedes-Benz 350SLC and a Range Rover. At his homestead, near the border with Tanzania, he built a school to accommodate all his children.

Maasai Days Cheryl Bentsen.

The old lady and the baboon.

I came on an old Malakote woman planting out rice seedlings in a mudflat at the side of the river. Her back was towards me and I stopped to watch. The sight of elderly peasants working against desperate odds for the merest pittance is always moving, an act of faith in a setting of eternity. I wondered whether she would ever see any reward for her labours. The Tana is an unpredictable river and is often in flood after heavy rainfall miles away. When the floods subside it is sometimes found that the river has changed its course, and the river bed continually changes its contours. One cloudburst out of sight might mean the old lady lost her rice crop and went hungry for a season.

While I stood there watching I had that curious sixth sense of not being alone. I looked round and at first could see nobody though the chill down my spine increased. There, almost invisible against the dark trunk of a palm in the shadows, only a yard or two away, was one of the biggest male baboons I have ever seen. He was absolutely motionless, and he too was watching the old lady out in the brilliant sunlight. It was an intriguing situation and, though he was remark-

*Stanley Ole Oloitipitip, Maasai Member of Parliament for Kajiado South and Minister of Culture and Social Services until 1982.

ably unlovely and I could have wished he were not so close, I stayed to watch. He must have known I was there, but he was too absorbed in the old woman's activities to take any notice of me. We watched for some time. The old woman set the last rice plant in the last hole and straightened up, her hands at her aching back. Then she lifted her dibber and empty container and plodded wearily away across the mud. The baboon chuckled evilly to himself, forgetting me, and with a hideous dancing gait came down from his perch and went to the newly planted rice. With studied malevolence he began to pull out each carefully planted seedling, one by one, and threw it away. It was the most wanton piece of mischief one could imagine, but he had forgotten me. I raised the alarm and soon, gibbering and cursing, he was routed by a few stray people armed with sticks and stones. The old lady came back, her impassive face the epitome of patience, and the last glimpse I had of her she was again bending down, replanting the rice.

To My Wife – Fifty Camels Alys Reece.

Good behaviour.

To spit upon a person or thing is an expression of goodwill. The blacksmith spits upon the sword he has forged before handing it over to the owner: so, too, courtesy demands that a man should spit in his hand before offering it to a friend, and the female visitors spit on the newly-arrived youngster as a sign of welcome.

I once saw an amusing instance of this spitting in accordance with politeness. An unarmed old man was going across the hollow camp square when a large boarhound puppy sprang on its legs and galloped after him for a frolic. The old fellow suddenly saw it coming, and never having seen such a creature, for the Akikúyu have no dogs, was very frightened, and turned to fly. Then it dawned on him that it was the strange beast of the white man, so he stopped, knelt down, spat into the palm of his hand and extended it to the pup so as to express amity in the same way as he would have done to its master. Now the dog had been taught to "shake hands," so, of course, when it reached him, it sat up and extended its paw, and the friendliest relations were established between them.

With a Prehistoric People W. S. and K. Routledge.

The broad sun
Is sinking down in its tranquillity:
The gentleness of heaven is on the sea
Wordsworth

Every evening over the next week, as the sun lowered in the western sky, the Turkana and Merille fishermen hauled in their nets, rippling the surface of the dark water with crescents of phosphorescence as the nets bellied, dragged at both ends by willing hands. As they reached the shallows, the men brought the ends of the beach seines together and hauled them, dripping, hand over hand up on to the beach; the fine mesh bristling with tiny fishes which glistened whitely in the fading light and flapped jerkily about, caught by their gills. Coal-black children scampered about the narrow shoreline like wide-eyed leprechauns, their feet and ankles shiny with pearly fishscales, running naked through the flotsam of the tidemark and stopping now and then to help free the fishes from the beached nets.

On one such evening, as I walked along the foreshore, scuffing the damp tangles of lake-weed and savouring the moist shoreline smells of old rope, wet dogs and stale sardines, a huddle of young girls hooked fingers and looked at me with traces of smiles playing about their lips, their dark unsophisticated eyes sprung with what seemed like awe and dreaming Heaven knows what.

Some way out on the still, black water, fishermen poled their dug-outs to shore, the dull-red sun slipping quickly and cleanly beneath the horizon and painting a long, reflecting brushstroke of gold across the surface of the lake. As the dug-outs neared the shore I could hear the paddles plopping softly into the water at each stroke, the silhouetted bodies of the naked fishermen like ebony cut-outs, blacker than the night. The hushed sea fell slack, its polished surface mirroring the sky, and the wavelets slumped languidly on the shore in muffled rhythm, like the gentle breathing of a sleeping lover. All else was still, as the velvet darkness closed in on us.

It was a scene as old as time, and was surely the closest one could hope to get to the *anima mundi*; the serene, uncorrupted soul of the world.

Black Moon, Jade Sea Ian Meredith Hughes.

In recent times, foreign aid has focussed on the people from whom Lake Turkana derives its modern name.

The Scandinavians are good donors. They owe little to the developing world but give more per capita than anyone else. Like others, they make serious mistakes; no one has long experience in development. But unlike most, they study their mistakes and admit them. The Turkana disaster is described in excruciating, anguished detail in an evaluation report ordered by the Norwegian aid agency.

The Turkana are cattle herders, numbering 220,000, who are especially susceptible to drought on their bare hills of northern Kenya. What they needed, the Norwegians decided, was a fishery. The first step was a handsome cold-storage plant, at a cost of $2 million, and a $20 million road to connect it to the nearest highway. All things being equal, the Turkana Fisherman's Cooperative Society would sell Nile perch and tilapia to cities down south.

But freezing the fish, from Turkana room temperature (about 100 degrees), took more electricity than the region could provide. After a few days, operators cut the power and created, as the *Washington Post*'s Blaine Harden put it, "Africa's most handsome dried-fish warehouse."

Then, part of the lake vanished, the part where eighty per cent of the fish were caught. Norwegian planners had been thrown off by a temporary boom. "When we see a lake, we think in fairly static terms," remarked an official from Norad, the Norwegian aid agency. "We see a lake, we assume it will be there for 100 million years." In fact, the lake dried every few decades, whenever the Omo River from Ethiopia ran low because of the drought against which the fishery was supposed to protect the Turkana.

But officials had already herded 20,000 Turkanas to the shores of the lake, where they were given nets, boats, and fishing lessons. They had lost their livestock – victim of overcrowding and disease along the inhospitable lake banks – and they were destitute. Like so many Africans in so many other such failed schemes, they turned to food aid.

As a symbolic white elephant, the Norwegian research vessel *Iji* sits in the mud and, according to the donors' report, "appears to be damaged beyond the possibility of repair."

Squandering Eden Mort Rosenblum and Doug Williamson.

Dance, Diet and Adornment

The dance was perhaps the supreme art form of the East African. Every important event had its appropriate dance: war, marriage, harvest and just enjoyment. This account is of a war dance held in 1907 by the Kikuyu.

The performance began at 2.30pm. At that hour a lad suddenly burst, shrieking, through the crowd, and tore down the length of ground, crying out that a Masai raiding party were on them, and were sweeping off the cattle, etc. He then disappeared for good. After due pause, to allow this appalling news to go home, a young warrior appeared in a lather of sweat and in an exhausted state, who reported to the audience what he had seen when scouting. As he finished speaking, far down in the valley below was faintly heard the war song, which rapidly gained in volume of sound as the warriors mounted the winding path. They soon appeared from amongst the trees as a long single file, faultlessly accoutred and moving in a conventionally stealthy way. Each man kept perfect distance and step, and made exactly the same complicated gestures as his fellow. . . .

Finally the General Officer Commanding left the arena unobserved and took up a position behind the spectators at one end of the ground, in fact just behind us. Suddenly, at his shout, the wall of spectators broke and separated on his either hand, and down the slope he came like a whirlwind, a magnificent specimen of savage manhood, with his shield half raised and his spear poised, each of which he slightly raised still more as he sprang with a yell into the air at intervals of about thirty yards, by means of the peculiar trick previously mentioned of jumping vertically upwards from one apparently stiffened leg. Numbers of the warriors thus independently burst into the arena, and were received by the women with rounds of applause, which varied considerably in degree according to the

popularity of the individual. Applause was given by the women throwing one leg
forward and then inclining from the waist, whilst at the same time they feigned as
it were to throw their handkerchiefs, in the form of a bouquet of leaves, to the
favoured individual. As this action is done rhythmically by all, whilst at the same
time they utter a compliment, the effect, as one looks down the encompassing
wall of spectators, is most pleasing. When a woman has made her complimentary
remarks anent the individual, she joins her fellows in uttering the peculiar cry of
lu-lu-lu-lu-lu-lu, rendered as a descending scale, which has a liquid sound like
water gurgling from a calabash. It much resembles the note of one of the native
birds that greets the traveller in all directions in the freshness of the dawn in this
part of Africa. Thus the dance ended, having lasted about an hour and a half.

With a Prehistoric People W. S. and K. Routledge.

*Broadly speaking, diet had, and has, two separate bases: milk and blood, the
staple of cattle/camel owning nomads, and cereals and pulses, the staple of the
cultivators. Meat, as a rule, was common to both groups but for the most part
eaten only on ceremonial occasions; cattle, being currency, were too valuable to
be killed just for a meal. As regards wild animals, customs varied. The Dorobo
(more correctly Okiek) lived mainly on their flesh. Many peoples prized
especially the flesh of elephants, falling avidly upon it and eating it raw. The
Maasai shunned the meat of almost all wild animals. Some African delicacies
did not appeal to European tastes.*

At the next village I went ashore for some food. A native had killed a crocodile the
day before, and it was now being cooked. The man who killed it was the hero of
the village; he looked very happy, for the feat conferred on him the rights of
manhood, and he could now be married. I made the usual sign of hunger, and the
kind-hearted natives pressed on me the best they could offer. Crocodile intestine
cut open and baked in the ashes of a wood fire is esteemed the greatest delicacy in
the Pokomo bill of fare, and a supply of this was at once offered me. I pointed to
some old Indian corn cobs beside the fire, and signed to them that I should prefer
some of these. The natives appeared a little hurt at my low tastes, and pressed the
crocodile's guts so warmly upon me that I felt bound to accept them, and grin with
gratitude, if not with pleasure.

The Great Rift Valley J. W. Gregory.

That night I drank my first bowl of blood. It had been brought over from the next
manyatta and was slightly congealed, but Orip, a daughter of the house, had kept
it for me. She mixed in a little milk and offered it to me with a grin. I sealed off my
sensibilities and shut my eyes. It slid down my throat in a rush and I was wiping my
beard, smiling and saying how good it was. I did not mind it at all really, but I did
find the soup Orip had made pretty nauseating. Pieces of offal were cut and
boiled together with the goat's chopped but unwashed stomach. The result was a

hot green morass with oily blobs floating in the steam. Stomachless soup was fine for me but like chips without vinegar for the Shangalla. I stuck to tea and milk.

Another Land, Another Sea Stephen Pern.

The supposed dietary habits of Europeans could be no less disconcerting to Africans.

It is a curious fact that most Nandi women think that Europeans eat Nandi girls. I think the idea started when, some years ago, Dr Mann of Kisumu, under whose care a Nandi girl died, held a post-mortem examination in the mortuary and took some anatomical specimens home with him for diagnosis at his leisure. This was observed by some of the dead girl's friends, who at once jumped to the conclusion that the mortuary was Mann's private larder and that a particularly delicate morsel was being taken home for the evening meal.

Eating people isn't wrong.

I have a corporal in my company who is a Manyema, and this tribe practise cannibalism insofar as they eat their enemies, thereby gaining the enemy's strength. When this man returned from patrol yesterday he shouldered arms with his left hand level with his belt and to my amazement I saw five other black hands stuck in his belt. I asked him the reason and he said they were for his supper, explaining that the fingers are the tenderest part of a man. I made him bury the hands and told him I would talk to him today. He obviously did not think he had done anything wrong. I searched the Army Act in vain for any offence of that nature. This moring I had him up and told him that he must not in future mutilate his enemies. I then asked him about cannibalism; he tells me that the fingers are the most succulent, adding: "But the best of all is the buttocks of a young girl."

Kenya Diary 1902–1906 Richard Meinterzhagen.

Dinner with the Sultan of Zanzibar.

The Palace itself was built in a style I came to call tea-planter's manorial. As we were foreigners, we ate in the European manner, with cutlery, rather than our right hands. European appearances, however, were only knife-deep. First of all the banquet was an all-male affair. The servants who brought in the food were pitch-black and later in the day I was to pick up the insistent whisper that they were still slaves in all but name, and eunuchs to boot. The only hints of feminine presence were odd glimpses I caught of saffron-coloured faces with large black eyes made larger and darker by a liberal use of mascara, peering curiously and furtively at our table, then vanishing as they caught my eye. The food too was far from European and of a kind that I had never encountered before. As might have been expected in the Sultan's palace, it was the best the island could produce.

The main foundation of the meal was rice. It was accompanied by fish, mutton and, above all, a supremely roasted chicken. The fish and the mutton as far as I remember were not exceptional but the chicken course deserves a paragraph to itself. First of all, however, there was the rice. The savour of it is still with me. I was from a country where rice is eaten as a matter of course at all main meals. Moreover, I had just come from the greatest rice countries of the world, Japan, China, the Straits of Malacca, India and Ceylon – yet I had never eaten rice like it. The first experience of anything in life, just by virtue of being first, has a unique impact. I was to eat similar rice in Mombasa, in the ancient Arab port of Lamu and in Dar-es-Salaam but it never compared to that first experience in Zanzibar. . . .

The person mainly responsible was a young German chef in Nairobi who had not only been to Zanzibar but cooked in Persia as well. He mentioned five elements that were of fundamental importance to the success of the dish: patience, time – from start to finish in his estimation you could not do the dish in less than twelve hours – rice consisting only of unblemished grain, water with a considerable content of chalk and a wood fire. The royal household of Zanzibar was so full of servants, to say nothing of a harem full of idle women, that time and patience could not have been lacking, and this would explain why the rice served there was so good. I can understand that the modern cook's impatient imagination might boggle at the preparation and the labour involved, just as I am convinced that once a gourmet tried such rice he would insist on having it again and again. For the truth is that in cooking as in all other problems of living, short cuts are retrogressive, leading only to increasingly barbaric solutions. In the kitchen, the longest way round is still the shortest way to the perfect dish.

I learned how this young chef would get his assistants to select each grain of rice specially some twelve hours before cooking the dish. Any grain that was in the least bit damaged or mis-formed was rejected and when the collection was complete the rice was washed thoroughly twice. I reminded him of an Italian kitchen proverb: "Wash your face, wash your hands, wash your feet but never wash rice because rice is not proud." He dismissed this with scorn as another example of how the Mediterraneans undercook everything from beef and lamb to rice and pasta. He went on to explain that the twice-washed rice was placed in a flat dish, just covered with water and layers of white clean linen pressed into the dish to protect it from dust. On top of the linen some rock salt was put, both to keep the linen pressed down firmly on the rice and also to impart its own savour, through the damp cloth, to the grains. So dedicated a cook was he that he preferred one form of rock salt to all others – it was gathered in an Asiatic desert and it gave the dish, he claimed, something no other salt could. Two hours before cooking, the rice was extracted from the dish and washed again, parboiled until it whitened and then drained. The rice was then put, in layers, in a large iron pot – in Persia the pot is of copper – and each layer covered with small lumps of butter or ghee, until the pot was about three-quarters full. It was then covered again with several folds of dry cloth, in order to absorb and seal in the steam. It was most important, he said, that the lid of the pot should be made to fit so that no steam could escape.

The rice was then cooked over a wooden fire, not only from underneath the pot but also by charcoal placed on the lid. The great secret was to ensure that the rice was cooked at a constant temperature. He said that a dedicated cook in Persia would not allow even an earthquake to distract him from attending in person to this phase of the operation. Patiently, squatting by his fire, he would watch the flame, one minute encouraging the heat by fanning the coals with a palm leaf, the next damping it down with a dash of water and constantly renewing the live coals on the lid. All this lasted about an hour and when the lid was finally removed one would see that the rice had risen to the brim, white and light as snow in the middle and at the sides just faintly bronzed, with each grain of rice doubled in size. It was then ready to be served, steaming and fragrant. And that, precisely, is how the Sultan offered it to us in Zanzibar.   *First Catch Your Eland* Laurens van der Post.

Adornment of the body was a major African art. Angela Fisher spent seven years recording the ingenious forms of ornament devised by different peoples.

Samburu girls like to wear many strands of loose beads rather than the flat collars favoured by their neighbours the Maasai. The beads are gifts from admirers, and by the age of fifteen or sixteen the girls should have collected enough to invite a proposal of marriage. It is held by Samburu men that women do not have enough beads until their chin is supported by their necklaces.

To show that they have given birth to their first son, Rendile women of the northern desert wear their hair in a cockscomb made from mud, animal fat and ochre. This permanent fixture is constantly repaired, and will be worn until the boy is circumcised or until a close male relative dies, when the head will be shaved. Highly prized necklaces of *doum* palm fibres bound together with strips of ochred cloth are received at marriage. When elephants were numerous these necklaces were made of hairs from an elephant's tail.

Before imported glass beads were readily available in any quantity jewellery was made sometimes of iron and clay but mainly of bone, horn, hair, wood, roots and seeds. Ostrich eggshells were chipped and rounded into beads, a process used in Kenya since at least 7,000 BC.

Turkana men say of a lovely woman: "It is the things she wears that make her beautiful." When a young girl is ready for marriage she covers her body with ochre and fat, and wears an elaborate bead pendant necklace and an ostrich feather in her hair. An ostrich eggshell belt holds up her long beaded skirt.

Clay is traditionally used by Turkana men to fashion their elaborate hairstyles. The hair is twisted into small plaits which are covered with clay and shaped into a bun on top of the head. Status is shown by inserting ostrich feathers into holders of cow gut or macramé, which are placed in the hair while the clay is still wet. The hairstyle may take up to three days to perfect, and is meticulously re-made every three months.

Africa Adorned Angela Fisher.

One of the aims of the early Christian missionaries was to persuade the local people to substitute European forms of clothing for their own. Sometimes there were setbacks.

One day an old woman came to see me, with whom I had a lengthened conversation, leading up to the one thing needful. I deeply sympathized with the old creature, for her tiny apron was almost worn out, and I thought of how she might appreciate a garment to cover her nakedness. I measured her for a loose gown, and asked her to wait while I made something for her. The scissors were soon plied on a piece of calico and the garment cut out. Having a little hand sewing machine I was not long in running it together. Seeing that she was getting impatient I tried to interest her in the machine while the cloth was being fed to the needle as quickly as possible. To make her garment more pleasing and acceptable, I trimmed it with a band of red turkey muslin. A button-hole was worked at the neck, and a showy brass button of good size was attached, and the garment was then ready to be worn.

I enshrouded the old dame with the surplice, and as soon as it was buttoned on her she ran off at full speed, never stopping until she vanished from my sight among the bushes. There, as the sequel proved, she divested herself of the garment, threw it to the winds, and went home in the happy nude state to which she had been accustomed all her days.

In the Heart of Savagedom Rachel Stuart Watt.

Illness and Death

The prevalence of spirits.

The seasons, and all major events in life, are controlled by spirits. At the coast before the great rains, cattle will sometimes be taken down to the water's edge and sacrificed at dawn to the rising sun. As their blood mingles with the white surf, prayers are said for the blessing of rain. All along the coast there exist caves in which prayers are still said to numerous malign or benevolent spirits. The priest or spirit healer stands in a shaft of light under a hole in the roof of the cave; lifting his arms in prayer he is bathed in soft light, and benefactions from the spirit world flow through him, bringing ordinary men and women hope.

The sorcerers, the real witchdoctors, are the last category of medicine men and they deal in spells and magic. Africa has long been held in thrall by them. A disgruntled neighbour, a jealous relative, in fact anyone with a grudge or envious of another man's wife, riches or good luck, can call upon the witchdoctor to cast a spell and no modern medicine can avail against such a disease. It can only be exorcized by a more potent witchdoctor or perhaps by religious faith. It is well known in Africa for a man to be perfectly healthy, then one day to start to ail, becoming no more than a shadow of himself, until he turns his face to the wall and dies as if he himself had willed it. Nothing can deflect the course of this condition for the patient is embroiled by a growing sense of guilt, fear and evil, often cultivated by sorcerers with weird spells and rituals. Ritual murders to provide the materials for these spells still take place in secret.

Different Drums Michael Wood.

The power of spells.

It is very curious that in spite of their enviable physical qualities, many Africans lack resistance to psychic suggestion, and easily succumb to witchcraft. Only recently we had lost one of George's best Game Scouts as a result of a spell. He was an intelligent, middle-aged Akamba who had previously served for many years with the Kenya Police. His wife had run away with a lover who, wishing to get rid of the husband, had arranged for a spell to be cast on the poor scout; he was to die within a certain time limit. We visited him and found him in a state of advanced emaciation. We tried our best to talk him out of his conviction that he must die, and we took him to the hospital where the doctor assured him that there was nothing physically the matter with him. Nevertheless, he died on the day forecast by the spellbinder.

The Peoples of Kenya Joy Adamson.

In cases of illness the task of the medicine-man or witchdoctor was to identify the spirit that was causing the trouble and then propitiate or expel it. The Swahili called this process "reduction".

If a woman has a three-day fever, she attributes to herself a spirit in need of reduction, especially if there is something wrong with her husband. Her sickness becomes worse daily, and she does not leave her bed. When the parents see that their child is sick, they say, "Your wife has inherited her grandmother's spirit, and that is what is making her ill. When she was small we raised to her head the spirit of her grandmother, saying, 'Take care of this child until she grows up, and then we will give you your platter.' Now her grandmother is dead, and her spirit demands its platter and has possessed its grandchild." If the husband does not attend to the words of his parents-in-law, people are offended with him and say that he is mean. They call him the one who has swallowed iron. But if he agrees with them that his wife has a *pepo* and that there must be a reduction, her parents are pleased and say that their daughter has a loving husband, and the woman agrees that he is a loving husband. He calls in a doctor to consult the omens, asking what is causing his wife's illness.

"There is nothing more than a spirit."

"Will you treat her?"

"First we must uncover the pot for her to see what is her condition."

There are two sorts of "pot" – stones and steam.

For the pot of stones, "queen bread" is dug up. This is the fungus grown in white-ant hills. Seven lumps are dug out and set on fire, for this stuff is inflammable. A matting hut is built, and the sick person comes and sits on a stool. A hole is dug, and a pot of water is brought. Her face is covered, and the lumps are quenched in the water in the hole. She inhales the steam and breaks into a sweat. That is the stone pot.

The steam pot is made by plucking leaves that will steam and putting them to cook in a pot. The patient leans over the steam and breaks into a sweat, and with more of the steaming water she bathes her whole body. That is the steam pot.

Every day for seven days the pot is made ready from late afternoon to sunset, and she sits over it for an hour. She is glad when it is over, because she knows that she will soon be reduced. When the pot treatment is finished, they make ready for the reduction, saying to the doctor, "She is your patient; tell your other patients that we are going to hold a dance." The husband goes to the shop to buy the spirit clothes, red cloth, black calico, and white muslin. Trousers are made of the white and the red, and a hut is built either in the town or outside. It is called a *kilinge*.

At sunset the woman is taken to the *kilinge*, and there a platter is made ready. In it are placed bananas, sugar, cane, raw eggs, bread, and all sorts of good food. At the time of evening prayer the possessed person has her face painted with black, white, and red spots, and then they start the sound to entice the spirit up to her head. They dance and sing the song of enticement:

I pray thee, O Lord,
Thou, O Lord,
Undo my fetters,
Thou, O Lord.

The people respond, singing for something like an hour. As the spirit rises, it shakes all her limbs. Then the doctor interrogates, that is, talks with the spirit; but what he says no one knows but the doctor and his patient. The doctor orders the drum to be beaten hard, and the spirit rises to dance. The initiates dance, and the sound of the drum carries them away. Some of them fall down in the *kilinge*, and when they reach home they are themselves in need of reduction. . . .

This dance goes on day and night for seven days. If the spirit is a good dancer, it is given presents by the people; but these presents belong not to it but to the doctor, the drummers, and the piper, for everyone who attends to watch the dance brings some money. This is not compulsory but voluntary. Every time the drum is beaten, the spirit dances and the people put money on its head.

The sixth day is the day for the spirit to be named. This is the day of revelation on which it is disclosed whether it is or is not a spirit. It gives a demonic name that no one knows, and when it does so all are much pleased.

The seventh day is the day of release. A goat is slaughtered on the shore, and all the spirits come together to drink the goat's blood. If anyone does not drink the blood, he is not possessed. When they see the others drinking the blood, the spirits rise into the heads of those into whose heads they have not yet risen. After drinking the blood, the spirit is carried home cured.

The Customs of the Swahili People Mtoro bin Winyi Bakari.

This treatment for colic was witnessed by von Höhnel during his and Count Teleki's expedition to Lake Rudolf in 1892–3.

A man died during the march, and we had to doctor another for violent colic. The general mode amongst the people of caravans of treating colic is to lay the sufferer on the ground with outstretched legs, then to fasten the feet together above the ankles with a strip of stuff, pass a stick through the stuff and turn it round and round till the patient gives vent to terrible screams of agony. When he leaves off crying out the Prophet's name, to which he volubly adds some half dozen of his most familiar attributes, he is released from the rack, by which time he is always quite cured, as we ourselves witnessed in more than a hundred cases.

The Discovery of Lakes Rudolf and Stefanie Ludwig von Höhnel.

Kikuyu surgery.

The edges of the wound are drawn together, and held in that position with the fingers of the left hand, while with the right a bull-dog ant is picked up and held so that the jaws grip one on each side of the wound; the body of the ant is then twisted off, while the head still remains, tenaciously holding on to the flesh. From this habit of holding on they have acquired the name of bull-dog. The Kikuyu did not make any such use of these ants, though their method of sewing up wounds was scarcely less primitive. In their case the edges of the wound were drawn together and a long thorn run through both. A fine thread, made of fibre from the bark of certain trees, is then wound over both ends of the thorn, in the same way that sailors wind the spare ends of ropes round the cleats. The thorn is left in place till the wound heals, and then drawn out in the same way that a surgeon removes the stitches after more civilized operations.

John Boyes, King of the Wa-kikuyu, ed. C. W. L. Bulpett.

To be barren was a woman's worst affliction, leading to rejection, shame and often to the status of a beggar.

It will be recalled that my aunt, The Beautiful One, had been barren for a long time until she met Karanja. Her first husband had consulted many Kikuyu medicine-men in an attempt to find out why she did not have children, but had found no remedy. In all this time my aunt was very unhappy indeed. Her husband became ashamed and began to ill-treat her. He would shout angrily:

"What's wrong with you, you skinny barren woman? I wasted the dowry which I paid to your parents."

Later, my aunt married Karanja and explained her difficulties to him. Karanja was sympathetic, loving, and would have done anything to help her. He was certain that the famous medicine-men of Fort Hall could find a cure.

In a village opposite Karanja's home and across the River Kayahwe there was a famous and powerful medicine-man called Kimani. His fees were higher than those of other medicine-men, but Karanja decided to consult him. His elder brother was a friend of Kimani and so they went together.

Kimani insisted that the whole family history must be known to him before he treated his patient. A close relative, Nyutu, was summoned.

When he came, Nyutu told my aunt's story, even mentioning the woman who had cooked the ram at my aunt's circumcision ceremony. Kimani stopped him at that point and pointed his long gourd towards Mount Kenya to the north, Mount Nyandarwa to the west, Kilima-Mbogo to the south-east, and then poured down some *mbugu* (seeds). He asked Karanja, his brother, and Nyutu to count them. There were four.

"The woman was related to your wife's family but she was angry while she was cooking the meat."

"What did she do?" asked Karanja.

"While she was cooking the meat she took a small piece of meat and tied it secretly in her leather skirt. Later, she buried the meat at the foot of a tree near the village, pretending that she was burying your wife's future children and this is why your wife is barren."

"What can be done?" asked Karanja eagerly.

"We must re-enact your wife's circumcision ceremony. First, you must get a spotless fat ram which my helpers and I will strangle in your yard. We shall then roast some of the meat. The rest will be cooked by a man of your wife's clan who will bury a piece under a fig tree. She will do this alone, secretly, but we shall later ask her to take us where the meat is hidden. The woman will dig up the meat which represents your wife's children and give it to us. We shall then return to your home where I shall bless the meat and throw it under your wife's bed. This ceremony is very important and it should be done after your wife's menstruation is over," Kimani explained.

A day was fixed for the ceremony and Karanja, his brother, and Nyutu returned home, satisfied by Kimani's interpretation. On the way, Nyutu told Karanja that the woman responsible for my aunt's misfortune had always been ill-treated by her husband and had eventually committed suicide.

Now the whole story was clear and Karanja and my aunt were ready for the "purification" which is called "Kuhakwo ng'ondu". Kimani and his two aides arrived and performed the ceremony as planned, smearing oil from the fat tail of the strangled ram on the legs, hips, hands, face, and neck of my aunt. After only a few weeks my aunt conceived! It was exciting, incredible, and thrilling. I did not myself attend the ceremony but I know they believed completely in Kimani's diagnosis and that he was responsible for the cure.

Death and its sequel.

The fact that the Kikuyu did not bury their dead does not mean that they did not revere them. On the contrary, the Kikuyu believed in the continued existence of the spirits or "ngoma" of the dead. The body might be destroyed by fire or eaten by wild dogs, but the spirit did not perish. Only the spirit of a man was important after his death, and in fact if a body was not eaten up by the animals it was assumed that the dead man had not been a good-natured person. It was therefore said that sorcerers would not be eaten by the hyenas who are them-selves scavengers and the lowest of animals, as even they would recognize the evil in these men and reject their bodies although their spirits had left them.

It was also believed that whenever a sorcerer had killed a man by his witchcraft he would follow the relatives of the dead person into the bush, taking infinite care that they did not discover his presence. After the relatives had left, the sorcerer would go immediately to the body, before the animals had time to discover it, and would cut a piece of flesh from the dead one. He would then burn the flesh and mix the ashes with his poison to add more "power" to his poison. . . .

One day a boy of one of our friends in Stoton died suddenly in the evening hours. Mwando and Kimani were called at once. They suggested that the boy's body should not be sent into the bush right away, but that it should be kept at a distance of about one mile from the village. The plan was that a group of young men armed with pangas should accompany Mwando, Kimani, and the boy's relatives to the spot where the dead boy's body was so that they could sit there under the bush and see whether they could catch the sorcerer. They also hoped that they would bring the dead boy home alive! This sounds pretty fantastic, but the rumour had it that before a sorcerer cuts a piece of flesh from his victim he first of all has to bring the dead person to life again, ask him or her several questions such as: "Who brought you here?" "Would you like to curse your people?" and then order: "Do not look at me." The sorcerer would then re-poison the person, cut some flesh, and go away.

They thought that they would wait until the sorcerer brought the boy back to life and when questioning started, capture him instantly. Mwando, Kimani, and the rest of the young men sat down silently as if they were soldiers near the enemy line. Unfortunately, no sorcerer appeared. They sat there for hours, and at about three in the morning they went home leaving the dead body behind. At about eleven in the morning some young men went there to see the boy's body. On their arrival at the place they found the dead boy's body had been cut! This accelerated the fear among people tremendously. Many people decided to leave Stoton for some neighbouring farms.

Child of Two Worlds Mugo Gatheru.

Among the Maasai.

On the death of a child, or a warrior, or a woman amongst the Masai, the body is thrown away, and the person's name is buried, i.e. it is never again mentioned by the family. Should there be anything which is called by that name, it is given another name which is not like that of the deceased.

For instance, if an unimportant person called Ol-onana (he who is soft, or weak, or gentle) were to die, gentleness would not be called en-nanai in that kraal, as it is the name of a corpse, but it would be called by another name, such as epolpol (it is smooth). And if anybody of that kraal were to ask for news of the great medicine-man Ol-onana, he would call him Ol-opolpol.

If an elder dies leaving children, his name is not buried, for his descendants are named after him.

When old men or women die, they are not wept for, nor are they thrown away like others who die young. New sandals are made, a sheep is slaughtered, the fat is roasted, and the body anointed. After this the corpse is carried to a shady place, where a bullock is slaughtered, and all the meat is eaten on the spot. The bones of the bullock are left with the body so that the hyenas may smell it, and come and carry it away, and devour it.

On the death of a Masai medicine-man or rich person the corpse is not thrown away. An ox or a sheep is slaughtered, and the fat is taken and rubbed on the body, after which it is put in an ox-hide and carried to a shady spot. A small hole is then dug resembling a trench, into which the body is laid and covered with stones. This is called a grave.

The Masai: Their Language and Folklore A. C. Hollis.

Religion and Magic

During a visit to Mount Elgon in 1925, Dr Carl Jung questioned elders of the Elgonyi people about their religion.

At the end of that palaver an old man had suddenly exclaimed, "In the morning, when the sun comes, we go out of the huts, spit into our hands, and hold them up to the sun." I had him show me the ceremony and describe it exactly. They held their hands in front of their mouths, spat or blew vigorously, then turned the palms upwards towards the sun. I asked what this meant, why they blew or spat into their hands. My questioning was in vain. "We've always done it," they said. It was impossible to obtain any explanation, and I realized that they actually knew only that they did it, not what they were doing. They themselves saw no meaning in this action. But we, too, perform ceremonies without realizing what we are doing – such as lighting Christmas tree candles, hiding Easter eggs, etc.

The old man said that this was the true religion of all peoples, that all Kevirondos, all Buganda, all tribes for as far as the eye could see from the mountain and endlessly farther, worshipped *adhista* – that is, the sun at the moment of rising. Only then was the sun *mungu*, God. The first delicate golden crescent of the new moon in the purple of the western sky was also God. But only at that time; otherwise not.

Evidently, the meaning of the Elgonyi ceremony was that an offering was being made to the sun divinity at the moment of its rising. If the gift was spittle, it was the substance which in the view of primitives contains the personal mana, the power of healing, magic, and life. If it was breath, then it was *roho* – Arabic, *ruch*, Hebrew, *ruach*, Greek, *pneuma* – wind and spirit. The act was therefore saying: I offer to God my living soul. It was a wordless, acted-out prayer which might equally well be rendered: "Lord, into thy hands I commend my spirit."

Besides *adhista* the Elgonyi – we were further informed – also venerate *ayik*, the spirit who dwells in the earth and is a *sheitan* (devil). He is the creator of fear, a cold wind who lies in wait for the nocturnal traveller. The old man whistled a kind of Loki motif to convey vividly how the *ayik* creeps through the tall, mysterious grass of the bush.

Memories, Dreams, Reflections C. G. Jung.

The religious ideas of the Pokot (Suk).

Nothing could be more delightfully vague than the religious ideas of the Suk: indeed it is difficult to find two men having ideas on this subject exactly coincident. All, however, agree as to the existence of a Supreme Being, who is to most men *Torôrut*, the Sky, and to a few *Ilat*, the Rain. Preferably I give here the version of Tiamolok, one of the oldest of Suk now living (1911), and one renowned for his knowledge of folklore.

"Torôrut is the Supreme God. He made the earth and causes the birth of mankind and animals. No man living has seen him, though old men, long since dead, have. They say he is like a man in form, but has wings – huge wings – the flash of which causes the lightning, and the whirring thereof is the thunder.

"He lives above, and has much land, stock, ivory, and every good thing.

"He knows all secrets; he is the universal father; all cattle diseases and calamities are sent by him as punishment to men for their sins.

"His wife is *Seta* (the Pleiades), and his first-born son is *Arawa* (the Moon). *Ilat* (the Rain) is another son, as are *Kokel* (the Stars) his other children.

"*Topogh* (the Evening Star) is his first-born daughter.

"*Asis* (the Sun) is his younger brother, who is angry in the dry season.

"All these are gods, and all are benevolently disposed towards mankind."

But others say, "The only god we know is *Ilat*," who is supreme and lord of life and death. Others, again, say *Ilat* is the servant of Torôrut, whose duty it is to carry water, "and when he spills it it rains." Karôle, the chief of the Suk, says that *Kokel* are the children of *Ilat*, who is the lord of death.

"There are" he says, "such things as spirits, but we don't understand much about them. All we know is that death is the uttermost evil – there can be nothing worse. When a good man dies, and his body is thrown away, we occasionally go to where his head lies and bring a little food and tobacco, to make, if possible, his deadness more endurable; but if a bad man dies we give nothing. 'Let him die still more,' we say. Torôrut has nothing to do with men after death. They get nothing further from him either good or bad."

Nevertheless, it seems to be generally believed that a man's spirit passes into a snake at death. If a snake enters a house, the spirit of the dead man is believed to be very hungry. Milk is poured on to its tracks, and a little meat and tobacco placed on the ground for it to eat. It is believed that if no food is given to the snake one or all of the members of the household will die. It, however, may none the less be killed if encountered outside the house, and if at the time of its death it is inhabited by the spirit of a dead man, "that spirit dies also." If the snake be met with on the road, and it is coiled up with head invisible, "pluck a handful of grass and place upon it and pass on." If, however, it darts up its head it may be killed with impunity. Death being a non-enviable existence, to exterminate the spirit of one's ancestor need not be a culpable, and may even be a beneficial act.

The Suk Mervyn Beech.

Belief in the equal worth of rich and poor in the next world, if not in this, formed no part of Nandi philosophy.

The *Oiik*, i.e. the spirits of departed ancestors and adult relations, are held to be responsible for sickness and death, and they are appealed to and propitiated with milk, beer, and food whenever necessary. The human soul is embodied in a person's shadow, and it is firmly believed that after death the shadows of both good and bad people go underground and live there. People who have great possessions on earth are equally blessed when they die, whilst the spirits of poor people have as bad a time after death as they had during life. Years ago a man is said to have gone to the land in which the spirits live. He fell into a river one day and lost consciousness (or died). When he came to himself again he was in a strange country, where there were hills, rivers, plantations, and oxen, just as on earth. The spirits came to him and said: "Young man, your time has not yet come when you should join us. Go back to the earth." With that they struck the ground and the man lost consciousness again to wake up near the place where he had fallen into the river.

There is also a devil called *Chemosit*, who is supposed to live on the earth and to prowl round searching to devour people, especially children. He is said to be half man, half bird, to have only one leg but nine buttocks, and his mouth, which is red, is supposed to shine at night like a lamp. He propels himself by means of a stick which resembles a spear and which he uses as a crutch. His method of catching children is to sing a song at night-time near where they are living, and the children seeing the light and hearing the music think that a dance is being held, and are lured on to their destruction.

The Nandi A. C. Hollis.

> *Eye of newt and toe of frog,*
> *Wool of bat and tongue of dog. . . .*
> William Shakespeare

The most hated and unpopular magic among the Gikuyu is *orogi*. The possessor of such magic is looked upon as a dangerous and destructive individual. *Orogi* is used exclusively for nefarious purposes and, as such, its practice is against the ethical and moral laws of the community. . . .

The substance of *orogi* consists of burnt ashes, or ground powder from poisonous herbs and roots. This toxin and the ritual ingredients go together, because into the toxin a powder ground from human, animal, and reptile flesh is mixed. In this form the mixture is ready to fulfil its deadly purposes. The chief parts of the human or animal body required for the manufacture of *orogi* are the following: genital organs of both male and female, breasts, tongues, ears, hands and feet, blood, eyes, and noses. These articles are extracted from human bodies, the victims of the magician's work. They keep watch over the persons whom they have poisoned, to find out when they die and where their bodies are laid; then they go stealthily at dead of night and extract the required parts. But from animals and reptiles the list is enlarged by adding the internal organs such as heart, kidneys, part of the stomach and intestines, liver, testicles, and fat. The materials collected in this way are dried and are then preserved for immediate or future use.

Facing Mount Kenya Jomo Kenyatta.

A suspected sorcerer was frequently submitted to an ordeal, of which there were many kinds. This is a Swahili version.

The Ordeal of the Billhook or Axe

If a man has stolen something and not been seen but people suspect him, or a magician has been caught or someone is suspected of being a magician, the suspects ask for an ordeal. A doctor is called in, and he is given the ordeal of the billhook. This is of iron, and a verse of the Qur'an is written on it. Then it is made red-hot on a fire of ebony. Or an axe is taken and made red-hot. It is then given to the person undergoing the ordeal to lick, in the morning before he has had any food. The person who licks says, "I have been accused of sorcery; I know nothing of it, white or black, and now I take the ordeal. If I go out at night to cast spells, or if I prepare food for a neighbour's child to cause its death, may the truth of the ordeal fall upon me. No, neither I nor my father or mother know anything of this art. I am being slandered, and may the ordeal clear me." Then he licks the billhook with his tongue, and after this the doctor tells him to open his mouth, and he shows him. If his tongue is not blistered, the ordeal has cleared him; if it is, he is convicted. If the ordeal has convicted him, everybody speaks openly of him as a criminal who brings evil to the neighbourhood. They say, "Now we will put you on oath to abandon these practices," and he consents to be sworn.

The Customs of the Swahili People Mtoro bin Mwinyi Bakari.

If found guilty, the sorcerer was generally condemned to death. This was the Kikuyu procedure.

On reaching the place appointed the *kiama* [council of elders] formed a ring. Immediately the *morogi* [sorcerer] was brought in under the escort of the *njama ya ita* [warriors]. He was made to stand inside the ring while preparations for his execution were being made. First, a small he-goat from the *morogi*'s flock was brought and handed to him. He was asked to kill it, to symbolize his own death. At the same time he was asked to declare that he had not, and would not, at the time of his death, utter, silently or loudly, curses on anyone; and that he was willing to die silently for his wickedness. After the *morogi* had completed this, he was given the heart of the goat to eat and thus brighten his own heart before he was put to death. Then a short concluding ceremony was performed. It consisted of mixing the blood of the goat with cow's milk. This mixture was poured on the *morogi*'s head, and thence on his whole body. During this act the assembly stood in dead silence. After a few moments a few verses of a ritual song were sung, the officiating elder leading the ceremony. . . .

While the elders and the warriors were singing this song they went round and round, circling the wizard. Everyone present put a dry banana leaf on the condemned man. At the end of the ritual song the leading elder called upon one or two of the *morogi*'s close relatives. They were asked to tie the banana leaves on their kinsman. By performing this act they signified that the *morogi* was disowned by them and by their clan; they handed him over completely to the authorities and, for example, could never afterwards bring a claim for blood money or any compensation on account of losing one of their clansmen. After the relatives had taken the initial steps and had shown their willingness to get rid of the *morogi*, they were helped by others, and the banana leaves were tied on the *morogi* from head to foot. On the top of the banana leaves dry grass and other inflammable substances were added.

In the meantime ceremonial elders were busy drilling fire from sacred fire-sticks. Immediately the fire was ready the *morogi* was asked to make his will, and at the same time to confess the names of the men he had killed by poisoning. After his confession, one of his relatives was given a brand from the sacred fire and requested to set fire to the *morogi*. As soon as the fire was lit the assembly rose and stood at a little distance with their backs turned to the scene, leaving the guard who acted as executioner to keep the fire burning.

This was one way of getting rid of a *morogi* and of discouraging others from indulging in the nefarious profession. Another way was to crucify a *morogi* at the junction of main roads, but this method was less used.

When the business was over a ceremonial horn was blown and the elders formed a procession towards a sacred grove. Here a ceremony of purification was performed to provide a ritual cleansing to the assembled public before they returned home.

Facing Mount Kenya Jomo Kenyatta.

A were-hyena.

On my way down to Wamba I heard a strange story of a plague of the animals on the edge of the Turkana escarpment. It was told to me by the game warden at Moroto in Karamoja. He said that among the Karamajong there is a belief that at night the *Imuron*, the tribal witchdoctors, can either turn themselves into hyenas or travel from one place to another on the backs of the animals. *Imuron* are not among the most popular members of the tribe.

During the great drought in East Africa the cattle began to die in thousands and hyenas became a menace. With an abundance of carrion they increased in numbers and, instead of scavenging in twos and threes, a pack of thirty or forty animals would gang up together and attack living animals. The warden killed them by pouring a tin of cattle dip into the stomach of a dead cow and leaving the poisoned carcass in the bush. In this way he sometimes collected twenty or thirty dead hyenas in one night.

After one successful onslaught his chief scout told him with evident satisfaction that he had killed an *Imuron*. Among the dead hyenas they found one animal decorated with the sacred ear-rings of the soothsayers. They could not have been put on after death. The bone rings were embedded in the pierced ears and the flesh had grown around them. The animal was also wearing a sacred necklace and its chest was painted with the characteristic stripes of the medicine men. The warden could offer no explanation for the decorated animal but the tribe considered he had done them a good turn.

Journey to the Jade Sea John Hillaby.

"The Jews of Africa"

In the colonial period Asians prospered in trade, banking and the professions. Their dukas – equivalents of the British village shop – were to be found in every outpost from the Ethiopian to the Tanzanian borders, and their emporiums in every town and mart. Uneasiness followed the abrupt expulsion, after independence, of Uganda's Asians. But confidence returned.

The last few years (late 1980s) have seen a significant mellowing in the African's hostile attitude toward the Asians. Though he is still discriminated against, far more than whites or any other minority in black Africa, the Asian today seems to have earned a permanent and fairly secure role in the future of the continent. His presence has quietly ceased to be an issue.

"I'm convinced there couldn't be another repeat of what happened in Uganda, although I wouldn't have told you that a couple of years ago," an Asian friend, Abdul Hamid, told me over lunch one day in Nairobi's Red Bull restaurant, where the hundred or so predominantly male customers were about evenly divided between Africans, Asians and Europeans. Hamid, who was forty and ran one of the biggest printing companies in East Africa, was a Sunni Moslem, one of the 200,000 members of Kenya's Asian community, the largest and most economically and politically influential in black Africa.

"I mean, my kids' generation can't identify with India anymore. They don't even care about learning the language. All our ties are to Kenya, not India. My family's been here over a hundred years. The Asian is a tribe of Africa now."

Hamid was raised in Mombasa in a house with sixty relatives. The men, women and children ate in shifts. His marriage was arranged. His grandfather was an uneducated dhow repairman. But like almost all Asians in Africa, Hamid escaped the mire of poverty, insufficient education and tradition that his ancestors had known. Economically and socially, he outdistanced his African counterpart.

"When I moved to Nairobi from Mombasa eight years ago," Hamid said, "I came with nothing. Absolutely nothing. I lived on bananas and a pint of milk a day for two years, putting every shilling into my business. An African wouldn't do that. But I wasn't afraid to work and I wanted to make money for my children. I will admit the Asians collect money almost as a hobby. We are the Jews of Africa."

The Africans David Lamb.

Today there is a top layer of affluent and successful Asians.

One, who kindly invited me to cakes and coffee at his home, is a High Court judge. Other morning coffee guests included a consultant dermatologist and a Sikh business tycoon, the latter an elderly gentleman clad all in white and with a fine white beard. He laughed as he said: "I have lost seventy-three million shillings in Uganda and six million shillings in Tanzania. And I am still a happy man."

He had started his career as a station-master; done a bit of buying and selling, invested in a posho mill and in a cotton ginnery in Uganda, and gradually built up an empire, mainly in the shape of mills. One day, driving down from Eldoret, he stopped at a saw-mill whose European owner did not shake hands or ask him into the house. The Sikh drove back to Eldoret, arranged matters with the bank, returned and said to its owner: "I have come to buy your saw-mill. I will pay you £20,000." This time he *was* invited into the house. "It was a good investment," said the Sikh.

Are Asians, I asked, better or worse off now than in colonial times? The High

Court judge shrugged his shoulders. "The upper millstone has become the nether millstone. It does not make much difference to those in between." He recalled regulations that had formerly prevented him and his kind from buying land in the white highlands, and the exclusion of Asians from the higher ranks of the civil service. "We had little choice but to become duka-wallahs." Nevertheless, I suggested, he seemed to have done pretty well. "I was lucky. The gods watched over me. I used to tell the Europeans with whom I worked that my loyalty was suspect because I was not white, although Kenya did not have a more loyal subject. Still equally loyal, I am not black. I do not know. What I do know is, I do not want any other home than Kenya." In the past, whites made Asians feel inferior; now, blacks make them feel insecure.

Out in the Midday Sun Elspeth Huxley.

Law and Order

In up-country Kenya, until colonial times there were no prisons and no money. There was also little crime. Tribal law was backed by supernatural sanctions: if theft was likely to be followed by disasters such as sickness, your wife's miscarriage or the death of your best bull, you left your neighbour's mealies and his goats alone. Sometimes, however, temptation proved too strong; then penalties could be so severe as to act as a powerful deterrent.

If a man is caught stealing, or if a theft is brought home to him, he is beaten and fined four times the value of the stolen property. The fine has to be paid by the relations if the man is himself too poor. Should a thief be caught a second time, or even suspected, he is tortured. A thong or bow-string is tied tightly round his head just above his eyebrows and ears, and the ends after being twisted are fixed to stakes in the ground. They are then beaten with sticks which makes the thong cut deeply into the flesh. Twigs are also thrust in underneath the thong, and water is poured over the man's head to make the wound smart. After a couple of hours of this torture, during which time the wretched man has seen his houses and granaries burnt, his crops destroyed, and half his goats and cattle confiscated, he is released; but he bears the mark of the thong and is branded as a thief to his dying day.

On the occasion of a third theft the thief is killed and his goats and cattle slaughtered. The animals are not killed in the ordinary way, but are thrown on their sides and cut or hacked in half. The mode of execution adopted is partial strangulation, after which the person is clubbed to death. Two thongs are tied tightly round the neck and pulled in opposite directions by about twenty people; other people then rush in and use their clubs.

If a woman steals, she is severely beaten the first time, and on the second occasion she is tied up and thrashed with stinging nettles, her face and body being in a terrible state before she is released. The same treatment is meted out to children; and if goats enter the plantations they are also tortured with stinging nettles, which are thrust up their nostrils, into their mouths, and wherever they are most vulnerable.

The Nandi A. C. Hollis.

Honesty carried to extremes among the Wakamba.

Another characteristic which was lovable and almost unbelievable was their inability to steal any inanimate thing. Theft of livestock was an honourable pastime; but things, at this period of their history, were sacred. To possess something to which they had no right was unthinkable. Such things had to be restored to their rightful owner. So thought a Mukamba tribesman who had been arrested and tried on a charge of cattle thieving, found guilty and sentenced to a long term of imprisonment which entailed his transfer to the central prison in Nairobi. On the way there, handcuffed and escorted, he bolted one night back to his own country, and took good care not to be caught again. Within a week a messenger brought in the handcuffs to me with an apology from the thief. He had had difficulty in sliding them off or he would have returned them sooner. To suppose that this was a gesture of defiance or bravado would argue a complete misunderstanding of their moral code.

Lion in the Morning Henry Seaton.

In colonial times enforcement of law and order became the function of the British. To the District Commissioner fell the delicate task of blending the old with the new.

Outside the township boundaries, the Chiefs and Headmen administered their own tribes with the backing of the District Commissioner, who nevertheless interfered as little as possible. It was his job to see that the people ruled themselves and dealt out summary justice according to their own customs, which varied with their religion and history. For example, if a man killed another in a fight and there was insufficient evidence to bring a case of murder, it would usually be settled with a payment of "dia" or bloodmoney by the family of the survivor to the family of the deceased. The amount was fixed by custom, and the matter would be dealt with at a baraza or big open meeting called by the Chief. In such cases the Chief knew he had the backing of the District Commissioner, and if the people concerned refused to abide by the Chief's edicts, he could appeal to the District Commissioner to intervene. Equally, any aggrieved person also had the right to appeal to the District Commissioner if he felt he had been unfairly treated, though this rarely happened. For a straight case of murder, the matter was reported to the Police or the District Commissioner, and the District Commissioner conducted the preliminary inquiries, writing down all the evidence in longhand. Among the tribespeople in the desert there was remarkably little petty crime. One man would not steal from another of the same tribe. His small daughter would be perfectly safe herding the family goats out of his sight – unless some raiding party from over the border came her way. Rape was rare except in border incidents. Straight killings were not so rare.

Within the township boundary it was a very different state of affairs. The population of the township at Marsabit was small, but the people were mixed. Outwardly it looked prim and neat, each plot carefully swept and cared for, each with its own clump of bananas and pomegranates and limes. But with many different people living cheek by jowl there was bound to be friction. There were the Goan and Indian traders, many of them with local wives, the half-castes who fitted in nowhere, the alien Somalis, the Pakistani carpenter and all his relatives, the Hindu tailor, the keeper of the little "hoteli" who hailed from Uganda, and old government servants who had been given permission to settle there. There were also those who by reason of some infirmity were unable to live the nomadic life in the bush and had been cast away in youth. This small but pathetic class had nothing and lived from day to day. It was small wonder that there were numbers of petty crimes as well as breaches of the peace and some bizarre litigation. Every District Commissioner had magisterial powers, and the cases that came before his court ranged from murder and manslaughter, being in the area without a pass, illegal possession of firearms, to cases such as one when he was called upon to lay down just what the client could expect from the local "Magdalene" in return for the shilling fee she had charged. He would have to listen to family wrangles, complaints about wild animals damaging crops, accusations that the Kikuyu dresser at the small dispensary withheld the magic of his sindano (hypodermic syringe) unless handsomely bribed; claims that the interpreter had accepted a bribe and given no value in return; or simply that the wells were running dry.

To My Wife – Fifty Camels Alys Reece.

The District Commissioner was almost everything to almost everyone.

The DC was a man of many parts. Thrashed in his youth for daring to read *Stalky & Co.* in preference to *Eric or Little by Little*, admonished by no less than three Anglican bishops for his many small sins, while still young he left England to complete an education in Tasmania, but spent most of his time in and about his father's stables. He became an exceptionally fine horseman. There hung on a wall of his house in Kitui a silver-mounted riding-whip engraved with the words "To one of my straightest riders"; it had been presented to him by the Master of the Kangaroo Hunt. In the closing stages of the Boer War he arrived in South Africa too late to see active service, so he declined any medals, and later joined the Constabulary where, for a time, he took charge of the audit department. With the retrenchment of English staff which soon followed the peace, he left that job, came up the East Coast to Mombasa and enrolled as a stock-inspector. Helped by an uncle, who was then Commissioner for Lands, he transferred to the administration with a background very different from that of the little Oxford boys with their logic. He was a top-class native administrator, and we were ready enough to tread in his footsteps.

The routine was cast-iron. Up at dawn. If we were all three in the station at the same time, we took separate paths, each of us supervising a different activity: police parade, prison labour, new building, sanitary services. We went to the office or the courtroom from 9 am till 1 pm, and again from 2 pm till 4 pm. In the evening we went for a walk, each in a different direction, and when the sun went down we all met for drinks in one house or the other. The drinks never varied – five minims of liquid quinine followed by whisky and soda. On Saturday nights we dined together in some state, with immaculate table linen, glass and china. We sat long over a five-course meal with wine, coffee and liqueurs, talked of everything under the sun, went late to bed and lazed as long as we liked on the Sunday morning.

On safari under canvas we all maintained the same high standard – no tin plates or iron mugs. If china got broken, what did it matter? In actual fact I do not remember so much as one broken tumbler. To avoid the intense heat, all marching was done from the night into the day. Regardless of the length of the march, we had to be in camp and under canvas by 10 am. This sometimes meant striking camp at two o'clock in the morning. . . .

Every one of the twenty-four locations into which the Reserve was divided had to be visited once a quarter. The distances were considerable – a hundred miles to the north and eighty miles to the south, with a varying width of up to fifty miles. The transport was all done by porters, and we had a mule each which we could take into the fly-free areas. With a staff of three it was a fairly strenuous life, but when it fell to two, it was tough.

Lion in the Morning Henry Seaton.

When he came on a visit, a safari was a grimmer business. A scrap of paper left on a camp site, a slipping camel-load, a dull belt or an unshaven head among the *Dubas* [tribal policemen] would earn a searing rebuke. Turnbull strode along on seven-league boots, four and a half or five miles an hour, counting thirty miles a very modest day's march, flinging over his shoulder scraps of NFD lore.

"That tree over there – *Lebbi* in Somali – they make camel bells from it. . . . Never turn aside for a few twigs of thorn: bash straight through. It's quicker in the end." Suiting action to word, he ducked down and, with a noise of ripping cloth, forced his way through a dense thicket of wait-a-bit thorn. Half an hour later he suddenly bent down, picked up a pellet of dry goat-dung and, with the air of a connoisseur, bit it in two. "H'm – Aulihan, Rer Afab, I should think – 1949, and a hard *Jilaal* [dry season]."

Hanging from his mouth was a handkerchief, the well-chewed corner of which he sucked to keep his mouth moist. Neither he nor any member of his safari might drink water during the march, though milk at *manyattas* was permitted.

I said, "You know, I find myself liking these Somalis."

"Oh, you do, do you? Then I must keep an eye on you. And if ever I find them liking *you*, you're out."

"Anyway, I'm learning their language."

"Certainly: no harm in that. In fact, so you should. Start by learning a few civilities: they always make a good impression. Common phrases like 'Good day to you, madam' . . . 'If you please, my dear fellow' . . . 'Thank you very much' and 'I'm so sorry, I didn't know it was loaded'."

It was important to anticipate, and to be well briefed upon the particular subject which engaged his interest. One month it would be cattle sales. "Why haven't the Rer Musa section of the Abd Wak filled their quota? That headman needs chasing. . . . The Rer Farah Jibrail sold a lot last month: find out if it was their own stock, or came from Somalia."

Another month, he might be interested in the hide and skins trade, for the NFD produces the best goat-skins in the world, needed for the manufacture of kid gloves. Then at every small trading centre he would inspect the hides store, drying-racks, grading, washing and cleaning arrangements, stock books and receipts.

"This bloody fellow . . . Haji Abdulla – just *look* at his grading! Call that a second-grade skin? Cancel his licence!"

Off he strode, fuming, through the bush. Twenty minutes later he suddenly remarked, "There's nothing like an occasional, resounding injustice: does all the good in the world!" And, after another twenty minutes silence, "That poor beggar, Haji Abdulla. . . . Not his fault at all, really. You can give him back his licence in a couple of months, but don't tell him you'll do it."

But he amply compensated for all the trials of a safari by his company in camp in the evening. Stretched out in a canvas chair, a whisky and water beside him, witty, erudite and scandalous, he discussed anything in the world, from Stravinsky to mountaineering, from camel-breeding to Shakespeare.

It was gratifying to discover that he had his weaknesses. Bumping along in the front seat of a lorry, he saw a flock of guinea-fowl beside the road, and commanded the driver to halt. It was not enough that the lorry should be stationary and the guinea-fowl walking: or that the lorry should be slowly moving and the guinea-fowl stationary. Both had to be standing still before he would venture a shot. Resting a battered 12-bore on the lorry door, he took careful aim and discharged both barrels. Away flew the birds, with an indignant squawk and a feather or two fluttering down.

It was the one subject on which Turnbull had no sense of humour. "A bit high, I think, sir," I said.

"Yes," he replied, "I must take a finer sight next time."

"Paid to persuade people to do what they didn't want to do."

Samburu's problems were typical of the over-grazed, over-crowded pastoral areas of Africa. In the past, disease and tribal war had kept the cattle-population down to the carrying capacity of the land. We were doing our best to abolish both: with the result that the grass was eaten and trampled away, and the rain, instead of restoring it, washed away the top-soil.

So legions of experts – experts on grass and experts on water, experts on soil and on animal husbandry, experts on tsetse-fly and experts on ticks – were called in to adjust the balance of nature, rather as a horse-coper adjusts a lame horse's trot by giving the sound leg a knock. Back they went to their offices to write recondite memoranda on how to do it; but they could agree on only one thing, that nothing useful could be done until the Samburu got rid of their surplus livestock. So along came the experts in marketing and slaughtering, experts in converting cows into blood-meal and bone-meal, hides and glue and meat-powder and biltong, to tell us how most efficiently we could kill off all the cattle their veterinary colleagues were diligently keeping alive. Holding an uneasy balance between experts was the DC, expert in nothing in particular, but paid to persuade people to do what they didn't want to do.

What they didn't want to do with most conviction was to cull their cattle.

Hear the Turkana Chief Mfupi Kone on the subject.

"We can't have grazing-schemes here," he declared, his ostrich plumes nodding defiantly as he emphasized each point. "We have no grass. Can cattle eat stones? Perhaps English cattle can." (Loud cheers and laughter.) "Ours can't. And if we had grass," he concluded with triumphant logic, "then we wouldn't need grazing control."

Uncomfortable words came, too, from the Samburu Lepara-chao. "We have no farms, no crops like other tribes. We have no salaries, like you people. All we have are our goats and our cattle. We live on goat mutton and cow's milk, and sell a few steers to pay fines and taxes. If you take away our goats, what shall we eat? If you take away our cows, where shall we find milk? If you take away our steers, how can you expect us to help the Government? We love to collect cattle as white men love to collect money. Why don't you get rid of all your surplus money? You like to keep it in the bank: our cattle *is* our bank. If you want to double our taxes, don't beat about the bush, but say so. Perhaps we shall agree. But don't tell us we'd be better off without our cattle."

"Old man," said Robert Chambers, exasperated, "wouldn't you rather have a hundred good cattle than two hundred living skeletons?"

"I'd rather have a thousand, starving till God gives us grass. If a man has a lot of cattle and some die, he still has plenty left. But if a man has few cattle and some die, how will he and his family live? How will he buy wives for his sons or pay their fines when they steal cattle? You are young." (This, with a benign and patronizing glance at Robert.) "How many cattle have you got in England? We hear you never have droughts there: just wait till you see one here, when all the calves die, the cows dry up and there is only goat's meat to keep us alive."

"Old man, if you get rid of all your useless stock, which do nothing but consume grass and water, the remainder will have enough grass and water even in a drought."

"That may be true in England," said a squeaky voice from the back row, "but things are different here. We like to play safe and have a lot of cattle, so that some are still alive at the end of the dry weather. . . . And what's all this about grazing-fees? Are we to pay for our own grass?"

The Desert's Dusty Face Charles Chenevix Trench.

Plus ça change . . .

A shika kamba was the small boy who walked ahead of a team of oxen to guide them. This shika kamba (of the Nandi tribe) grew up to start a small primary school, and his son Paul won a bursary to the University of Arizona to study range management. On his return with his degree he was posted to the North, with the task of persuading the nomadic tribes to take part in range management schemes. He found that this was by no means as easy as it was in the United States. "Our trouble here is people," he said. "Instead of co-operating, they quarrel all the time among themselves, especially the Somalis. They will not follow instructions given them for their own good." It all sounded very familiar. If one closed one's eyes it might have been Glenday, Reece or Turnbull speaking. Same problem, same response.

Out in the Midday Sun Elspeth Huxley.

Eight Pokot elders who had condemned a sorceress to death by stoning – tribal law – were sent by the District Commissioner to be tried for murder – British law – in the High Court. The judge acquitted them on the grounds that they had acted in self-defence. The DC reports the sequel.

Presently a distant chant arose and, as it grew louder, I could hear the ringing of a thousand ankle-bells. Across the plain, in a wide arc, they came, singing and prancing, three steps forward, one step backward. Shields waving, spears aloft, their bodies, limbs and faces smeared with white clay – they looked like a cohort of ghosts dancing in the daylight.

They closed round me in a circle and, with one great shout, grounded their spears and sank on their haunches. Chief Akanichum, topped now with ostrich plumes, came forward with a host of elders and welcomed me. He brought a gift of an ox for my porters to kill and eat, and many gourds of milk. Everything in life was splendid – peace reigned and cattle prospered. There was but one trouble.

"What is this trouble?" I asked.

The gaiety died suddenly away. A grave note, sounding in the voice of Akanichum, drew a murmur from the warriors at the back of the circle and from the elders in the foreground.

"It is a matter concerning the case of Mama Malungwa, the witch." He spoke as though he were utterly perplexed and paused while he took a pinch of snuff from the horn in his head-dress. "The case was judged," he resumed, "and judged rightly. No other judgement was possible. And yet, when my people returned home from the trial in Nakuru, it became clear to us that the judge was displeased." Akanichum shook his head in the stress of his perplexity.

"What is the trouble?" I asked again. The chief took a deep breath, as though great force were necessary to expel his words.

"Bwana," he said, "it is like this; Lawola is bewitched. He declares that the judge has cast a spell upon him, and we are persuaded it must be so. From the time that the trial ended Lawola has been wellnigh stone-deaf. The judge has deprived him of the use of his ears. Lawola has proof. He is here now, and though he has little power of hearing yet, with his own lips let him tell you and I will interpret his words."

It has been truly said that the make-up of a District Commissioner must be that he have the constitution of an ox, a fund of common sense and, above all, the patience of a saint. It seemed to me that this was a right occasion to exercise to the full the last of these three attributes.

Lawola stepped forward with the air of one deeply injured, as indeed he was. In primitive surroundings a sense of hearing is of the utmost importance. As he spoke he stared me in the face, watching my reactions as the chief interpreted. He was utterly convinced that the judge had the power and the will to bewitch him. "For the judge," he said, "wore the hair of his ancestors upon his head. In his hand he held a feather and I could see him dip it in a pot and when he wrote upon the paper, it was the mark of blood." He looked at me intently. Would I understand? Of course – feathers and blood! Prime symbols of witchcraft!

What use to tell him that the wig was made of silk, that goose-quills are time-honoured pens and that the use of red ink on a court record was the jealous prerogative of a judge of the supreme court?

I did my best, with the aid of the chief bellowing in his ear. But Lawola shook his head, worried his ears, spat on the ground and, with his foot, rolled the spittle in the dust.

Then he turned to Akanichum and spoke softly at great speed, snapping his fingers in emphasis and, when he had done, dropped on to his heels and spread out his hands in supplication while the chief translated.

"He asks that you will write to the judge and pray that he will remove the curse and restore his hearing. If it is a matter of money, he will pay well. He knows not what money he possesses, but it is a great deal and readily available."

"Tell Lawola," I said, "that he is altogether mistaken; and he should know that justice is a thing that cannot be bought."

Lawola's reply denoted dismay tinged with boredom.

"I'm not asking for justice," he said shortly. "What I want is the use of my ears."

His implication was that I was being stupid; and it struck me, suddenly, that he was right.

In the dramatic opening of the conference, the panoply, the war dance and the singing, and this all-pervading obsession with witchcraft, my wits had been distracted. It dawned on me that Lawola's sudden affliction could only be what I had experienced when I left Jubaland for Nairobi – an excess of wax on his ear-drums, induced, naturally enough, by the violent difference between the great heat of the Suk plains and the cold heights of Nakuru where he had stood trial. It was a happy thought. Witchcraft, indeed!

I suppose my manner changed – a sudden lightheartedness perhaps. Lawola sensed the change. His dark eyes shifted furtively from side to side as though I were now an enemy devoid, not only of understanding, but of sympathy and patience. His confidence in me was lost.

I knew I must do something to restore it, and I should never do that by casting doubt on his belief that he was bewitched. Akanichum, also, was eyeing me with doubt. There was a nervous twitch in the lines about his mouth. So I stood up.

"Tell Lawola," I said, "my sympathy is with him, and if he will stay behind when all of you have gone, I will restore to him the use of his ears."

This was greeted with acclamation. The warriors leapt up and stamped their feet. Ankle-bells were ringing, spears and shields were raised aloft, a rhythmic movement started on the perimeter. The elders raised their arms in salute and then moved off in the wake of the dancing warriors.

The sun was low in the sky. The shadows of the rocks and the scattered trees were lengthening as the song faded away. Akanichum and Lawola alone remained.

The chief looked up at the sky. Marabou storks were circling overhead, watchful of the ox-bones which needed picking.

"You can do this thing?" he asked.

"Oh, yes," I said, "if Lawola is willing."

"Then I will leave him with you, and I shall come again and see you when the sun has set."

In my chop-box there was olive oil and in my medicine chest a syringe. Lawola submitted himself to treatment like a trusting child. It was completely successful. He left my camp chanting a triumphal hymn of praise for all the world to hear!

Darkness had fallen and the camp-fire was burning brightly. A camp-table with drinks and a deck-chair were set out within the circle of light cast by the flames. At this hour Africa was at her best. The purple covering of night and a gentle wind made blissful atonement for the savage heat of the day. On the far side of the fire a sentry was on duty, passing the time by singeing the hair off his shins in the flickering tongues of flame – smoothing them with his free hand.

Presently Akanichum came out of the shadows with his stool and squatted beside me. For a time we sat in silence. I was thinking of the power for evil that witchcraft exerts in every corner of Africa – in every breast.

"Akanichum," I said, at length, "it was wrong of Lawola and, indeed, of all of you, to ascribe powers of witchcraft to a judge of the supreme court."

"Yes, Bwana. It was wrong in him and in us."

"The judge was concerned only with justice within the law, and it is the same law for one and all."

"Yes, Bwana."

"You must make that known to your people."

"I will do so."

"And they will believe you?"

He leaned towards me. His eyes, glinting in the light of the camp-fire, looked deep into mine with that respect which is always given to the witch-doctor.

"I shall have no difficulty whatever," he confided. "Be assured, Bwana, I can persuade my people it was not the judge who cast the spell."

Lion in the Morning Henry Seaton.

PART IX

Legend and Poetry

Traditionally, stories were told to children by their mothers of an evening beside the cooking fire. As with European fairy tales, the supernatural was a major theme, though ogres and monsters were more in evidence than the courtiers of Oberon and Titania; witches and wizards were common to both genres. Spirits, talking animals and sometimes cannibals were often in the cast. Among the animals, the elephant was generally regarded as king, the lion the most feared, and the hare the trickster, though sometimes the hyena appeared in this role. Similar but different versions of certain myths and legends are to be found among the various Bantu-speaking peoples throughout much of the African continent. With the spread of Western education, most of them are dying out.

The Creation according to the Maasai.

THE BEGINNING OF THE EARTH

We were told by the elders that when God came to prepare the world he found three things in the land, a Dorobo, an elephant and a serpent, all of whom lived together. After a time the Dorobo obtained a cow.

One day the Dorobo said to the serpent: "Friend, why does my body always itch so that I have to scratch whenever you blow on me?"

The serpent replied: "Oh, my father, I do not blow my bad breath on you on purpose."

At this the Dorobo remained silent, but that same evening he picked up his club, and struck the serpent on the head, and killed it.

On the morrow the elephant asked the Dorobo where the thin one was. The Dorobo replied that he did not know, but the elephant was aware that he had killed it and that he refused to admit his guilt.

During the night it rained heavily, and the Dorobo was able to take his cow to graze, and he watered it at the puddles of rain. They remained there many days, and at length the elephant gave birth to a young one. After a time all the puddles became dry except in one place.

Now the elephant used to go and eat grass, and when she had had enough to eat, she would return to drink at the puddle, lying down in the water and stirring it up so that when the Dorobo drove his cow to water he found it muddy.

One day the Dorobo made an arrow, and shot the elephant, and killed it.

The young elephant then went to another country. "The Dorobo is bad," it said, "I will not stop with him any longer. He first of all killed the snake and now he has killed mother. I will go away and not live with him again."

On its arrival at another country the young elephant met a Masai, who asked it where it came from. The young elephant replied: "I come from the Dorobo's kraal. He is living in yonder forest and he has killed the serpent and my mother."

The Masai inquired: "Is it true that there is a Dorobo there who has killed your mother and the serpent?" When he had received a reply in the affirmative, he said: "Let us go there. I should like to see him."

They went and found the Dorobo's hut, which God had turned upside down, and the door of which looked towards the sky.

God then called the Dorobo and said to him: "I wish you to come to-morrow morning for I have something to tell you."

The Masai heard this, and in the morning he went and said to God: "I have come." God told him to take an axe, and to build a big kraal in three days. When it was ready, he was to go and search for a thin calf, which he would find in the forest. This he was to bring to the kraal and slaughter. The meat was to be tied up in the hide and not to be eaten. The hide was to be fastened outside the door of the hut, firewood was to be fetched, and a big fire lit, into which the meat was to be thrown. He was then to hide himself in the hut, and not to be startled when he heard a great noise outside resembling thunder.

The Masai did as he was bid. He searched for a calf, which he found, and when he had slaughtered it he tied up the flesh in the hide. He fetched some firewood, lit a big fire, threw in the meat, and entered the hut, leaving the fire burning outside.

God then caused a strip of hide to descend from heaven, which was suspended over the calf-skin. Cattle at once commenced to descend one by one by the strip of hide until the whole of the kraal was filled, when the animals began to press against one another, and to break down the hut where the Masai was.

The Masai was startled, and uttered an exclamation of astonishment. He then went outside the hut, and found that the strip of hide had been cut, after which no more cattle came down from heaven.

God asked him whether the cattle that were there were sufficient, "for," He said, "you will receive no more owing to your being surprised."

The Masai then went away, and attended to the animals which had been given him.

The Dorobo lost the cattle, and has had to shoot game for his food ever since.

Nowadays, if cattle are seen in the possession of Bantu tribes, it is presumed that they have been stolen or found, and the Masai say: "These are our animals, let us go and take them, for God in olden days gave us all the cattle upon the earth."

The Masai: Their Language and Folklore A. C. Hollis.

THE STORY OF THE DOGS

In olden times dogs were just like men; they lived in kraals, they kept cattle, and they married like men and women.

On one occasion they engaged in war with their enemy man, and were beaten. Their cattle were taken from them and driven to a far-off country. They at once made an attempt to re-capture their cattle and pursued their enemies, but when the latter heard the dogs approaching they took some sand and climbed up into some high trees. The dogs being unable to follow them stood at the bottom of the trees looking up, and their enemies threw the sand down into their eyes. They were thus defeated and retired to their kraals; but as soon as they had collected their forces together again, they returned to the attack. The men pursued the same tactics as before and took a lot of sand with them into some high trees. When the dogs approached them, they poured the sand down into their eyes, and so effectually prevented them from seeing that the dogs lost themselves and have never since been able to find their kraals. Thus the dog became the slave of man.

The Nandi A. C. Hollis.

THE LIONESS AND THE OSTRICH

Once upon a time there lived on the same plain, that is to say on the same flat earth with yellow grass, an ostrich and a lioness. It happened that at the same time, both had children. The ostrich had six beautiful chicks and the lioness six rather moth-eaten cubs. The reason why they looked moth-eaten was that they had mange and scratched a lot. The lioness, convinced that only the best was good enough for her, one day exchanged her scraggy brood for the six very beautiful chicks. The mother, returning to her earth nest, found her chicks replaced by cubs, and was furiously angry.

A great meeting was held on the plain, which every animal in the world attended, to hear the ostrich's complaint against the lioness. When all had gathered together – some animals had to wait, for others came from a great distance – the ostrich put her case to the meeting. "Do these moth-eaten cubs belong to me? Do those little feathered perfections belong to the lioness?" But almost all the animals in the world feared the lioness: she was the Queen. So they told the mother ostrich to keep the cubs as they were hers, and to leave the lioness with the chicks. It seemed to be decided, but as the animals started to go home a ground squirrel called Susue said that he had not cast his vote, as being so small he had gone unnoticed. He demanded that they find a tall termite-hill for him to stand on, so that his height would be equal to the other animals. Then he sat on top of it, with his tail hanging down the termite-hill's chimney, and addressed the animals.

"Tell me, animals, do you know what chickens and what cats are?" They all agreed that they did. "Then tell me, animals, have you ever known a cat give birth to an egg?" "No" was the immediate reply. "And have you ever known a chicken give birth to a kitten?" That clinched matters; but before the animals had reached the obvious conclusion, Susue had jumped down into the termite-hill's chimney.

The lioness, enraged that anyone had dared to doubt her word, ordered the elephant to put his trunk down the hole and pull out the squirrel. The elephant thrust his trunk down the hole and caught the squirrel by the leg. "Oh, how comic," the squirrel shouted up to the elephant. "You've caught hold of a root and you think it's my leg! Mind you don't get ants up your nose." The elephant let go of the squirrel very quickly and went on trying to catch it with his trunk, until he caught hold of a root. "Oh! Oh! the elephant has caught me and now I shall be brought before the enraged lioness!" "Pull that squirrel up and bring it to me" the enraged lioness growled. So the obedient elephant pulled up the root and got ants in his nose.

Told by Ngatini Leboyare and transcribed by Simon Hook, Maralal, 1979.

A Maasai legend of the sun and the moon.

We have been told that the sun once married the moon.

One day they fought, and the moon struck the sun on the head; the sun, too, damaged the moon.

When they had done fighting, the sun was ashamed that human beings should see that his face had been battered, so he became dazzlingly bright, and people are unable to regard him without first half closing their eyes.

The moon however is not ashamed, and human beings can look at her face, and see that her mouth is cut and that one of her eyes is missing.

Now the sun and the moon travel in the same direction for many days, the moon leading. After a time the moon gets tired, and the sun catches her up and carries her. She is carried thus for two days, and on the third day she is left at the sun's setting place. At the expiration of these three days, i.e. on the fourth day, the donkeys see the moon reappear, and bray at her. But it is not until the fifth day that men and cattle see her again.

When a Masai sees the new moon, he throws a twig or stone at it with his left hand, and says, "Give me long life," or "Give me strength"; and when a pregnant woman sees the new moon, she milks some milk into a small gourd which she covers with green grass, and then pours away in the direction of the moon. At the same time she says: "Moon, give me my child safely."

Now cattle feed on grass, and the Masai love grass on this account. Whenever there is a drought, the women fasten grass on to their clothes, and go and offer up prayers to God.

If a warrior beats a boy on the grazing ground, the boy tears up some grass, and when the warrior sees that the child has grass in his hand, he stops beating him.

Again, if the Masai fight with an enemy, and wish to make peace, they hold out some grass as a sign.

Whenever warriors return from a raid, and it is desired to praise those who have killed some of the enemy, a girl takes a small gourd of milk, and having covered it with green grass, sprinkles it over them.

Then, if people move from one kraal to another, they tie grass on to the gourds.

Should one man ask forgiveness of another with grass in his hand and his request be not attended to, it is said that the man who refuses to listen to his prayer is a Dorobo, and that he does not know about cattle.

Again, if a man who is proceeding on a journey sees a tree which has fallen on the road, he pulls up some grass, and throws it on the tree; otherwise he fears that his journey will not be successful.

The Masai love grass very much, for they say: "God gave us cattle and grass, we do not separate the things which God has given us."

Whenever Masai women milk their cows, they take some milk from the gourd and pour it away, for they say: "God likes this."

The Masai: Their Language and Folklore A. C. Hollis.

MOTHER-LOVE

An old woman, who had only a son left to her, was so poor that she had no cattle for him to marry with. One day she told him to go and shoot a bushbuck. When the skin had been stretched and dried, the old woman made it into a cloak. After she had told her son to go and warn the neighbours that buck were eating their crops, she put on the cloak and went to a nearby field, where she crouched in the scrub on the border of the cultivation. She moved about slowly in a stooping position as if searching for vegetables. Presently one of the neighbours saw what he thought was a bushbuck feeding, shot it with an arrow and then found the old woman lying dead in the bush. He had to pay the compensation cattle, and so the dead woman's son was able to marry.

The Kipsigis I. Q. Orchardson.

HARE AND SUN

This is a short story about why Hare leads a solitary life under bushes. One day when Sun came up he called down to the animals below: "Please let me come and join you, for life up here is very lonely." The animals heard the Sun, and that night voted for him to come to join them on earth. That is, all the animals were in favour except Hare, who explained that if Sun came down to join them, they would all be burnt up. Next morning when Sun came back the animals said they were sorry, but he couldn't come to join them on earth because Hare had said that he would burn them all up. This angered Sun, who put a curse on Hare, that Hare would have as many companions as Sun had throughout his life.

Told by Ngatini Leboyare and transcribed by Simon Hook, Maralal, 1979.

A GREEDY HYENA

Once upon a time, during a severe shortage of meat, a pack of hyenas roamed the plains. In their search for food a hyena called Pilli-Pilli came across a dead elephant. Not wishing to share his find with the rest of the pack, Pilli-Pilli led them away from it to spend the rest of the day roaming the plains. In the evening, when they had all gathered in some caves for the night, he told them that he knew of a place where the members of the pack could gorge themselves forever, such was the never-ending supply. Of course, they all wanted to know where this heavenly larder was. Pilli-Pilli said that a witch-doctor had told him of it, and that next morning, very early, he would lead them to it.

And so, very early, they set off with Pilli-Pilli in the lead in the direction of the rising sun. They ran and ran as the blood-red sun began to show itself over the horizon. Then Pilli-Pilli sat down and said to them: "You see that mound of glowing red in the distance: that is all meat, and as the witch-doctor said, meat for everyone. I'm tired, but you go on and I'll catch you up later." So the rest of the pack sped on towards the prize and Pilli-Pilli returned to the elephant and had it all to himself.

He ate and ate, and left off eating to try out his strength. He made a jump and tried to clear the elephant, but there was so much meat inside him that he couldn't leave the ground. Pilli-Pilli was one of those who believed that meat gives strength, so when he found that he could not jump off the ground, he thought that more meat was needed. He went back to eating and ate and ate, then tried his strength again and found that there was no improvement. So back he went to eating until he ate so much that he burst. And that was the end of Pilli-Pilli.

Meanwhile his friends had run for miles and miles and, seeing their prize float up into the sky, began to climb on top of one another in an attempt to reach it. As soon as the weight got too much, the hyenas at the bottom collapsed and so they all came crashing down. And that is why hyenas are still limping to this day.

Told by Ngatini Leboryare and transcribed by Simon Hook, Maralal, 1979.

A COMPASSIONATE HYENA

The old people used to tell us long ago of the old widow who was the mother of eight sons. War broke out and one of the sons was killed; again they made war and another was killed and so on until only the youngest was left. He in his time went to war and when the warriors returned, the old woman asked them where her son was. They replied: "He is coming but is behind", as they did not like to tell her that he had been killed. When she asked again and received the same reply, she knew they were not telling her the truth. So she went in search of her son and took a rope with her, saying: "If he is dead, I will hang myself so that he will not die alone." She searched everywhere and passed many bodies until at last she found that of her son. She sat down and clasped his body to her.

It was late at night and the hyenas began to arrive and to ask one another:

"Where is Kopchebanyin?" for so they called this man as all his brothers were dead. When they found his body they called their elder, Kokomondoe, and said "Taste him for us."

If there is an elder in a house at meal times, it is customary for him to taste the food first before the younger people eat, even though he does not himself partake of the meal. But when Kokomondoe arrived the mother said to him: "You shall not taste this one this time. Why have you finished all my sons? If only you had left me just one." She threw the rope she had brought round Kokomondoe's neck.

He said: "Don't tie me and I will raise your son for you. But if I raise him you will go and tell people I made your dead son live."

"No," replied the woman, "I will say nothing."

He told her to move out of the way and came and sat down and closed all the wounds. Then he smacked the body and asked the mother what his name was. When she told him, he raised the head so that the man sat up and held him so that he should not fall, for he was as if drunk. Kokomondoe then asked him who he was and he replied: "I am so and so."

"Who is this?" asked Kokomondoe.

"My mother," he replied.

"Where are you?" asked Kokomondoe.

"I don't know," was the reply for the man was still confused.

The mother ran and embraced her son and said: "Thank God for my only child."

"Who brought you to life?" then asked Kokomondoe.

"How should I know," was the reply.

"I did," said the hyena, "but when you reach home do not say so."

"I will not tell," he replied.

"That is not true. You will."

After the warrior had sworn he would not tell, the hyena told him not to boast of it because if he did he would die.

Then the mother said: "If I find he is really alive, he shall not go to war again."

"Let him go to war," replied the hyena, "no one will be able to kill him." The hyenas went with the mother and her son to their home and then left them.

The son went to war continually but no one could kill him. He always came back with cattle for his mother and he married four wives who bore him many children. At last he became an old man and could no longer go to war. When he was very old, his grandchildren and their children used to lead him about as he could no longer go alone. One day he was drinking beer with his sons, when the guests became noisy as they vied with each other in boasting of their exploits and in telling stories of the cattle they had captured.

At last the old man said: "Be quiet while I also speak. If the hyena had not raised me from the dead, where should I be now?" At once the old wounds burst open, the blood flowed and his bowels gushed out so that he died where he sat.

The Kipsigis I. Q. Orchardson.

Throughout much of Africa the chameleon, most harmless of reptiles, is dreaded and abhorred. There are many versions of the reason why. This is one.

Almost the only other four-limbed creature I saw was a chameleon. Most natives of East Africa dislike and kill this creature, probably on account of his forbidding appearance, but various curious stories are current as to the origin of their dislike. One which I once heard in Zanzibar imputes to the beast the introduction of natural death into the world. A long time ago, when things went better than they do now, people used to die for some sufficient reason – when they were killed by their enemies or eaten by their friends, for instance – but they did not grow old and decay in the deplorable modern fashion. The consequence was that there were too many people, and not enough rice and bananas for them to eat. The kings and political economists of the period became alarmed, held a conference, and decided to send an embassy to the powers of the other world and ask for the introduction of natural death, at the end of a certain term of life. They selected the lizard as their messenger.

The populace, hearing of their deliberations, determined to anticipate this petition by one of their own, and to beg that the request of the kings might be refused. Their choice fell on the chameleon as messenger on account of his great family connections, for he is nearly related to the powers of the other world, as you will clearly see if you look at him. Observe the contemptuous deliberation of his movements because he knows no other animal dare touch him, and the cold, incurious stare in his diabolical eyes, which he turns superciliously round without moving his body. The chameleon admitted that he had influence with his relations, and undertook the task, but, instead of going straight and quickly, sauntered off in his usual listless way. On the road he saw a pleasant shrub, and, forgetting what he had promised, sat upon it for three days catching flies with his long, sticky tongue. At last he arrived at his destination, and found his near relatives, the powers of the other world, sitting in their dim, mysterious hut by a swampy river. They received him with great deference and cordiality, and he sat there twelve hours being entertained and exchanging greetings. Then at last he mentioned the object of his visit. His relations exclaimed at once that if they had only known that he took the faintest interest in such things they would have been most happy to meet his wishes, but the lizard, they said, had been there a few hours before he arrived and had taken natural death with him. The chameleon was annoyed, but said nothing for another twelve hours, when he suddenly observed, "I have an idea." "What is it, dear cousin?" inquired his relatives with interest and anxiety. "We might send after the lizard and stop him." "To hear is to obey," they said. "We have a messenger who is as quick as thought; we will send him after the lizard." The messenger went, but returned almost immediately and reported that the lizard had just arrived and had handed the fatal invention to the kings. So natural death entered the world all through the laziness and apathy of the chameleon.

The East Africa Protectorate Sir Charles Eliot.

Cannibals appear in many tribal tales throughout East Africa. This is a Samburu version.

THE MORAN AND THE MAN-EATER

Once upon a time the moran of a manyatta went far into the forest to feast on a bull which they drove before them. When they had reached a suitable glade they slaughtered and cut up the bull, and gave one of their number the stomach to fill with water at a nearby pool. While he was filling the stomach with water a voice from behind him demanded: "Who are you, and why are you taking my water?"

Looking about him, the moran saw N'gambit, a man-eating monster with nine heads and one large leg on which he hopped about. The moran nervously replied that he was only a moran collecting water to drink. Then he dropped the bull's stomach and ran back to tell his friends that he had seen N'gambit, and they had better leave before it ate them up. Not believing him, another moran went to collect firewood in the same place, but he was quickly back saying that he had seen N'gambit and that they must leave at once, as N'gambit was getting angry at being disturbed.

With the moran was a pretty girl called Sikinan and her impetuous lover. Seeking to impress her with his bravery, the impetuous moran went down to the stream and filled the bull's stomach with water. Then he picked up a pile of fallen firewood and began to make his way back to the glade. He had almost reached the glade when a voice from the forest demanded to know who he was and what he was doing. "I am a warrior lover of a beautiful girl called Sikinan and I am collecting water and firewood in preparation for a feast. What's it to you?" N'gambit then emerged from the forest and terrified the moran with his bellowing from all his nine heads.

Fearing for their lives, the moran threw the back leg of the bull to N'gambit who caught it with one of his nine heads, while the remaining eight heads shouted back that the leg was unfit for N'gambit because urine had been spilt on it. Then they threw the bull's thigh to N'gambit. Again, one head gobbled it up while the other eight shouted that the thigh should be eaten only by elders and he feared the curses of his father. Then they threw the back; that, too, was eaten by one head while the others shouted that this was fit only for girls and he feared the anger of his sisters. This continued until the whole of the bull had been thrown to N'gambit who was still hungry for more. The only thing now was to run for it which they did at great speed.

The moran were fast enough to make good their escape but Sikinan was not so fast a runner and was soon left behind to the mercy of N'gambit. Not knowing what else to do when faced by a nine-headed one-legged monster that had every intention of eating her, Sikinan sang a song praising N'gambit's courage and strength. This pleased the monster, who soon began to fall asleep to the sweet sound of Sikinan's voice. When he began to snore, Sikinan crept away and, once far enough away to be out of hearing, ran to join the moran who were waiting for her on the bank of a swift river. They had felled a tree from bank to bank at a narrow place and all had crossed over. They saw N'gambit, who had woken up, chase Sikinan towards the bridge. When Sikinan had crossed it and N'gambit was half-way over they rolled the tree trunk over and sent the one-legged monster into the fast river, and as each of the nine heads came up for air they were chopped off by the morans' long knives.

Told by Ngatini Leboyare and transcribed by Simon Hook, Maralal, 1979.

THE MAGIC BIRD

A man cultivated his fields, and then planted rice, but soon the rice birds arrived in swarms and began to devour it. The man decided to catch the birds, and he set many snares. One day he caught a beautiful golden bird. It opened its mouth and said to him: "Do not kill me, son of Adam, I will reward you!" So he let it go. The next day he found many dozens of birds caught in his snares. He took them to the market and sold them. This went on for a long time, so that he became a rich man.

One day he caught the talking bird again, but this time he did not take any notice of what it said, however much it pleaded for its life. He killed it, and put it in his pan to fry. The dead bird began to sing:

Fry me well, fry me well,
you will see great wonders.

The man took no notice; he put the bird on his plate and cut it into pieces. Each of the pieces began to sing:

Finish me off, eat me completely,
you will see great wonders.

When the man had eaten up all the pieces of the bird, they reassembled in his stomach and became one bird again. The bird came back to life, it stood up, stretched, and the man's stomach split open so that he died in great pain. The bird stepped out and flew away, back to the rice fields, where it went on eating rice.

Myths and Legends of the Swahili Jan Knappert.

An African Prometheus.

A long time ago a man borrowed a spear, *katimu*, from a neighbour to kill a porcupine which was destroying his crops. He lay in wait in the field and eventually speared one, but it was only wounded and ran off with the spear in its body and disappeared down a burrow. He went to the owner and told him that the spear was lost, but the owner insisted on having it back. Whereupon, the man bought a new spear and offered it to the owner in place of the lost weapon, but the owner refused it and again insisted on the return of the original spear. The man then proceeded to crawl down the porcupine burrow, and having crawled a long way found himself eventually, to his surprise, in a place where many people were sitting about cooking food by a fire. They asked him what he wanted and he told them of his errand. They then invited him to stay and eat with them; he was afraid and said he could not stay as he must go back with the spear which he saw lying there. They made no effort to keep him, but told him to climb up the roots of a *mugumu* tree, which penetrated down into the cavern, and said that he would soon come out into the upper world. They gave him some fire to take back with him. So he took the spear and the fire and climbed out as he was told.

This is said to be the way fire came to man; before that people ate their food raw.

When the man reached his friends he returned the spear and said to the owner, "You have caused me a great deal of trouble to recover your spear, and if you want some of this fire which you see going away into smoke, you will have to climb up the smoke and get it back for me." The owner of the spear tried and tried to climb the smoke but could not do it, and the elders then came and intervened and said, "We will make the following arrangement: fire shall be for the use of all, and because you have brought it you shall be our chief."

Bantu Beliefs and Magic C. W. Hobley.

Several East African peoples share a legend about the origin of elephants. This version was related to Llewelyn Powys by a Kikuyu acquaintance.

"Long ago," he began, "in the days when the mountains spat fire, elephants were men. And these men were very rich. They had *ngombi, kondo, mbuzi, kuku* (cattle, sheep, goats, and chickens) in numbers like the grass on the plains. They were, indeed, so wealthy that they had no need of work. They simply looked about all day, covering themselves with oil and red earth and making love together in the noonday heat. They had so much milk that they did not know what to do with it. Then one day one of them washed in milk, and when the others saw him they did the same thing, so that in time it became a practice with them every morning and every evening to toss this white water over their polished bodies. Well, it came to pass on a certain evening that Muúngu (God) came through the forest to see if all was in order with the animals he had created – with the rhinoceroses, with the hyenas and with the lions, and with all the others. And all was in order. On his way back he suddenly caught the sound of man's laughter and turned aside to see if they also were well. Now it chanced that it was the time of their evening washing, and when God saw the good milk splash over their bodies he fell into a great passion. 'I created cows to give them the white water of life and they now throw it away or do worse with it.' And he called the men to him as he stood there in the shadow of the forest. And the men, when they heard God's voice louder than the roaring of a lion when its belly is full, trembled and came creeping to him on hands and knees like so many baboons. And God cried with a loud voice: 'In so much as you have proved yourselves to be unworthy to receive my gifts and have been guilty of this great waste, you shall become Nyama (wild animals), a new kind of Nyama, bearing on your heads milk-white teeth, so that you shall be constantly reminded of your guilt.' So God transformed them all into elephants, and they moved off into the forest, huge grey forms with gleaming tusks set in their bowed heads for ever and ever."

Black Laughter Llewelyn Powys.

The greatest of the Maasai medicine-men was Mbatian, after whom the summit of Mount Kenya is named. He died in about 1890, at the time when an outbreak of rinderpest swept through East Africa.

When on the point of death, he called the elders of Matapato, the sub-district in which he lived, and said to them: "Do not move from your country for I am about to die, and I will send you cattle from heaven. If you move, you will die of smallpox, your cattle will all perish, you will have to fight with a powerful enemy, and you will be beaten. I wish my successor to be the son to whom I give the medicine-man's insignia. Obey him."

The elders said: "Very well," and left.

When they had gone, Mbatian called his eldest son Sendeyo, and said to him: "Come to-morrow morning for I wish to give you the medicine-man's insignia."

Sendeyo replied: "Very well," and went to lie down.

While this was taking place, Lenana, who had hidden himself in the calf-shed, overheard the conversation. He arose early in the morning and went to his father's hut. On his arrival he said: "Father I have come."

Now Mbatian was very aged and he had only one eye. He therefore did not see which of his sons was before him and gave to Lenana the insignia of the medicine-man (the iron club and the medicine horn, the gourd, the stones, and the bag), at the same time saying: "Thou shalt be great amongst thy brothers and amongst all the people."

Lenana took the medicine-man's insignia and went away.

Sendeyo then went to his father, but was told that his brother had already been there and been given the medicine-man's insignia. When he heard this, he was very angry and said: "I will not be subject to my brother; I will fight with him till I kill him."

Mbatian died and was buried near Donyo Erok.

When he was dead, some of the people proclaimed Lenana principal medicine-man, "For," they said, "Mbatian told us that he would give the insignia of his office to whichever of his sons he wished should succeed him." They therefore remained with Lenana.

But others said: "We will not acknowledge this man for he is a cheat," and they threw in their lot with Sendeyo.

Now disease broke out amongst Sendeyo's people, many of whom died, their cattle all perished, and they were defeated by the Germans; whilst those people who remained with Lenana did not fall ill, and they obtained cattle, as Mbatian had predicted.

The two rivals waged war for many years, and eventually Sendeyo was beaten. He came in 1902 to beg his brother to allow him to live with him, and peace was concluded between the two parties.

The Masai: Their Language and Folklore A. C. Hollis.

A story from colonial times.

THE LITTLE *DUKA*

There is a place in the Maranga district, a little green lawn of thick, close-growing grass on the edge of a miniature plateau above the river, where two roads cross. The roads are only native roads of red earth, and they, too, are grass-grown in patches. There is a hanging wood along the hillside, beside the valley. The trees have tall white trunks that tower the height of two huts and a half, then burst into a froth of dark evergreen. It is a pleasant spot, with its torrent of cold water falling through thickets of tree-fern, and there once a Government surveyor camped, equipped with very large pieces of paper and strange iron implements on sticks. He stuck in the pegs for two *dukas* [small shops], which he said would come, and then he went away, and there was nothing but the white pegs sticking half a foot out of his red heelmarks in the trampled mud and the grey, wet ashes of two fires to show that he had been there, or make any alteration in the rich greens and flashing silver, the white tree-stems like slim ghosts against the grove's dark foliage, the brawling note of the river, the silence of the woods, an occasional spiral of blue woodsmoke, the chatter of a group of barefooted natives drifting along, a few birds stirring among the croziers of the bracken, the sound of a far axe or of a drumming hyrax.

But his magic must have stayed, for the next morning in the blue haze there was something there: to some people a denser patch of morning mist, to some very clear, and they said it was a shop. Sometimes the shop would move away to the hill across the valley, and sometimes to the far horizon, and sometimes it would vanish altogether, till the scorners would begin to say that the white man had taken all his magic with him, and that the belief he had left any was an imagination and a pretence. And then, again, it would be there in full daylight, dazzling white in its new corrugated iron, and full of red and yellow and blue and glittering objects on the open side where the goods were displayed. Women as well as men could see it, and some of the elders as well as any. The children persuaded those who saw it most clearly to come and describe to them all the things they just could nearly distinguish but weren't quite sure about. But the old men told the children not to touch anything there nor to approach it nearer than ten paces, and, when the children asked them why, they answered that it was not good to do so. So the children went back and played that they could not see the shop, though some of them sat down before it first for a good quiet stare. . . .

There was this difficulty about the little shop, that two people did not always see the same things in it at the same time. Can goods come from Nairobi and fill a shop in a moment? Yet Chegi wa Kimutwa saw it full of red blankets at the same time as, to Mbaria wa Kinyanjui, it was a shimmering curtain of blue and white beads. The missionary's little daughter saw only doll's parasols, caps, and underclothing, and a motor car for Frank, and she got into trouble even for that – the child was growing so imaginative. That was the little shop's mistake, showing itself to the missionaries, who are a nice people, friendly and kind, and speak ki-Kikuyu, and know all about the people, and give medicine for nothing, but are very talkative and ought not to be shown everything. To show everything to a missionary only offends him, and is bad for the tribe. The missionary wrote to the Boma about this new belief, to the District Commissioner, who read the *Golden Bough* daily and was a keen collector of Kikuyu myths.

When the District Commissioner came, the old men were doubtful. They knew some claimed to see the vanishing shop, they reported, but perhaps it was not true. One or two of them said they themselves had *thought* they had seen the shop on such-and-such a day, but no doubt they were mistaken. They could not say at what time they had seen the little *duka*. Yes, sometimes perhaps it was in the evening. Yes, they did drink beer at night occasionally. They needed alcohol in the evening because it kept them warm of nights; they weren't hardy like the Athungu.

In spite of the charming position of his camp, the District Commissioner had not had a restful safari, and came rather irritated to the conference. He had had to speak to his servants and interpreter for leaving the camp at night and going off to dance and sing – "Make an infernal row, at any rate" – on the level ground of the surveyed site. This they flatly denied, but fell silent when he said that he had seen the lamp they had with them. Then, too, the trails of Scotch mist which hung about the camp half the day, though it muffled all sounds into strange undertones, must make the place unhealthily damp. So he was not sorry to give his decision. He said that he had spent the best part of two days of his leave at the camp solely to find out about the vanishing shop, and he had heard and seen nothing, simply because there was nothing there. They knew how keen he was on collecting their ancient stories, and they had told him some very good ones about former days – ones which he knew were all true. (A stir of relief passed down their shrivelled limbs as he said that). But this one about a modern *duka*, an ugly, dirty, tin trader's station, was ridiculous. They must be aware that in any fog you can see queer shapes like the one they had pointed out to him last night, which they knew was not really there, for whenever they walked towards it it receded. Let him hear no more of it.

Since then no European has ever seen the shop. As a matter of fact, hardly any have had the chance. The missionary grew fanciful, and was transferred by his bishop from the district. No surveyor has been there since, and a European trader who arrived one day, and wrote from the camp, enthusiastically applying for the leasehold of a plot, cancelled his application the next morning on his way back to Nairobi. And the Kikuyu? Well, could the Kikuyu go on seeing it after the District

Commissioner forbade? His Assistant District Commissioner has had to speak to them before about their silly superstitions. So the vanishing shop is never seen by anyone? Come! Come! Don't be childish! If there's any doubt, ask the Kikuyu. They are a simple race. If you can get them to understand what you mean, they will tell you they do not. They would never hide anything from a Muthungu.

Kenya Sketches J. G. Le Breton.

Swahili Poetry

The poetic tradition of the Swahili people spans four centuries and embraces many forms. Most poems were intended to be sung. They were written down by copyists, generally from memory, in Arabic script, therefore different copies of the same poem often vary. Poetic technique was formal, subtle and allusive – therefore often hard for Europeans to construe. Here is an example. At a dance preceding the installation of a jembe *(magistrate) the people might sing:*

> *What is hidden, let it be hidden.*
> *Take a cloth to catch a shrimp.*
> *A man and his mother-in-law.*

The people are giving advice to the judge. First: keep secrets well. Second: exercise patience and perseverance as the shrimp fisher must. Third: use caution and diplomacy, as when dealing with a mother-in-law. The most serious verse form was the epic, the utendi, *plural* tendi. *These were generally long, schematic, and permeated with the doctrines and traditions of Islam. One such is the* Utendi of Mwana Kupona, *wife of the Sheikh of Siu in the Lamu archipelago, composed some two years before her death in or about 1860. In this* utendi *she instructs her daughter in correct behaviour towards God and his Prophet, her parents, persons of rank and towards her husband above all.*

Let your husband be content (with you), all the days that you live together – do not worry him with requests, let it be he who recognizes you.
And as you go on do you (still) thenceforward seek to please him; and that is how you will find the way.
And in the day of resurrection, the decision is with your husband; he will ask (of God) what he wants, and what he wishes will be done.
If he wishes you to go to Paradise, you will forthwith be brought thither: if he says you are to go to the fire, there is no escape, you will be placed there.
Live with him befittingly, do not provoke him to anger: if he speaks (angrily), do not answer him, endeavour to be silent.
Keep faith with him always; that which he wishes do not withhold; let not you and him quarrel: the quarreller gets hurt.

If he goes first, take leave of him; when he returns, salute him: then prepare a place for him (to sit down) together with you.

If he lies down, do not disturb him; come near him that you may massage him, and (as to) fresh air, let him not want a person to fan him.

If he sleeps do not awaken him: neither speak in a loud voice; sit there and do not rise, that he may not have to look for you when he wakes.

When he wakes, delay not in preparing his meal, and look after his body, rubbing him and bathing him.

Shave him, both backwards and forwards, and trim his beard for him; pour water over him and fumigate him morning and evening.

Look after him just like a child who knows not how to speak – look well after everything that goes out and comes in!

Make him comfortable that he may be at ease, do not refuse (to obey) his commands; if he treats you badly God will rebuke him for it.

My child do not be slovenly, do as you think best; but sweeping and washing out the bathroom, do not neglect it even once;

Nor washing and scenting yourself, and plaiting your hair, not stringing jessamine blossoms and putting them on the coverlet.

And do you adorn yourself with garments like a bride – put anklets on your legs and bracelets on your arms.

Nor take off from your neck the necklace and clasp, nor cease perfuming your body with rose water and dalia.

Do not take the rings off your fingers or cease dyeing your nails with henna; do not remove the antimony from your eyes nor (refrain from) putting it on your eyebrows.

Let your house be clean; honour your husband – when people meet together you will bring him praise.

(You ought to) know what he likes and follow that; a matter which he hates, do not enter into it.

When you want to go out, you must ask leave; if you see that he is annoyed return and stay (in the house).

Follow his directions, and you will be truly at peace; (if you go out) do not stay on the road till the fourth hour has arrived.

And do not talk by the way, neither open your eyes to evil, look down on the ground with a modest countenance.

Return home quickly and sit with your master, and get ready the bedding that he may lie down at his ease.

Take every opportunity of exalting your lord, spread about his praises, and do not require of him more than he is able to perform.

What he gives you, receive (thankfully) and let your heart rejoice; what he does not do of his own accord, you have no need to tell him.

When you see him, uncover your teeth in a smile; what he says, attend to it, unless it should be something impious.

My child, do not sharpen your tongue; be like your mother; (look at me) I was
married ten years and we did not quarrel once.

I married your father with joy and laughter, there was no want of mutual respect
all the days that we lived together.

Not one day did we quarrel; he met with no ill from me; neither did I from him, till
the day of his election.

When death comes, if he tells me he is content with me, I shall praise God and
follow His commands; (but at that time) my heart, was astounded.

*There follow entreaties to God to cherish her children and her brothers and
sisters, to protect her from evil and succour her in misfortune, and to watch over
her daughter.*

I wish to warn her – see that you pay attention and follow God; return together
with the women:

Read this all ye women, so that ye may understand, and may bear no blame before
the blessed Lord.

Read: (these words are like) wheat springing up; obey your husbands, that ye may
meet with no loss in this world and the next.

She who obeys her husband, power and prosperity are hers; whatever place she
goes to she becomes known, and (her fame) is spread abroad.

She who wrote this poem is lonely and acquainted with grief: and if she was ever
uplifted in spirit (she trusts) the Lord will pardon it.

Let me give you the number (of verses); it is a hundred and one; and two in
addition: they are what I have added.

Completed by the help of God.

The Advice of Mwana Kupona Upon the Wifely Duty trans. Alice Werner.

The following Utendi, *like others, begins with a number of verses extolling the
limitless power and glory of God and of His Prophet. The Prophet is discoursing
to his companions in the mosque about the path of righteousness and the horrors
of hell. He hears a feeble voice greeting him and singing his praises.*

THE UTENDI OF THE CAMEL AND THE GAZELLE

When the beloved, the Lord of Arabia, heard the voice calling his praises, he
lifted his head. The eyes of the trusted Prophet scanned the mosque to see who
was calling. He cast his eyes around inside the mosque; but he saw no one calling.

The Prophet said to Sheikh Ali, Go and find out whose voice is calling. When
you have found out whose is the greeting, do not delay, but come back at once.

Haidar went at once and when he arrived, he found a camel. When he came to
the entrance of the mosque, there he saw a camel standing and weeping. Her

flesh was wasted and her bones stuck out from long stress and weariness. Her body was shrunken and her two eyes poured a flood of tears in a spate.

Ali spoke and asked the beast, "Was it you calling to Muhammad the chosen? Was it you who used human speech and gave the Prophet the greeting that he has received?"

The camel said, "Yes, son of Hashim. It is I that was greeting Muhammad of the Qureish."

Then Ali said to the camel, "Tell me your need and what is your purpose. What is it that you want? Tell me, and when I understand, I will inform the trusted one, who can remove trouble."

The camel said, "My need is the Hashemite, the prince of the coast, the great one of the land beyond. I want him to appear, the receiver of secrets, Muhammad the purified, who shines like a lamp. I want the chosen one, the famous, the renowned, who knows and can make clear."

Ali went quickly to his wife's father and told him what had been said and the message, saying, "Sir, this greeting comes to you from a camel; do not imagine that it is from a man. She wants to come before you from where she is and to meet you face to face. I must also tell you that this camel is worn out; her flesh is wasted and she is very thin. Her muscles stand out, her skin is wrinkled, only her bones are left and she can hardly walk. From her two eyes flow tears like the water of the sea or of the rains. Her tears flow so that it is sad to look on her."

When Sheikh Ali had spoken and the Prophet had heard him, they went immediately to the place where the camel was. The Prophet asked and said to the camel, "Will you not tell me your trouble and why you are here? Tell me what ails you and why you come to me. Do not be afraid, nor fear to tell me what you want."

The camel spoke in clear language – this extraordinary animal. She said first, "O Intercessor of the people, intercede for me today. I, Muhammad, am a camel belonging to Abu Masud, an infidel. My master, I tell you, is a rebel against God, an unbeliever, who does not believe in the Almighty nor take refuge with the Lord God. He has made use of me for a long time and up to my arrival here I am still in his service.

Then, when I came here, he loaded me grievously; there is no mercy in him nor consideration for me. He loaded me, Sir, with an unreasonable burden, a load of such weight that I was not strong enough for it. Young as I was and in my condition, I found it too heavy; I was charged with the burden of two camels. With this great load I ran fast, and in the contest of the camels I was not the last. Among a thousand camels I was the fastest; I came out ahead of them and was their leader. I would not appear to be smaller than the other camels and even now I cannot bear to be among the last.

But yesterday he put upon me an impossible load that I could not carry. I was so tired and worn out that I could go no further, and I fell under it with him watching. Ten times, Sir, no less, my face met the sand. The tenth time, Sir, I could not get up again, and, as I knelt, the infidel beat me. He went on beating me like a stubborn ox until he nearly broke my heart. I struggled on and O my Lord, how brutally he treated me. I went sadly on until I reached home and he off-loaded me and tied me up. He tied me, Sir, wickedly tight; he intended to tie me without mercy. He and his brothers, Sir, went on to jeer at me and to say harsh things in my hearing. Before his brothers he said, "My friends, this camel has annoyed me. She is thin, she has no fat, nor flesh nor strength, and she cannot carry a heavy load. Tomorrow morning I will slaughter her and sell the meat and buy a better camel that is of some use."

I pray you, my Lord, Prince Ahmad, blessed of the Loving and receiver of His grace, Blessings be on you, child of Mecca, grant me, I beg you, my desire. I am a creature, your slave under the power of the Lord, who has given it to you to intercede."

When the Prophet heard what the camel said his heart could not bear it; he fell down and wept. The tears of the Prophet, the Lord of Arabia, flowed like rain, pouring down his beard, and his heart was torn with compassion for the camel. The Companions too wept bitterly, when they saw how the Meccan was weeping. The Companions wept in all the corners of the mosque and their hearts were filled with sorrow.

Then the Prophet, the chosen, said to the beast, "Be patient for a while and I will speak further with you. Give praise and thanks to the One, the Living God for the great glory of deliverance that will come to you. Go and wait for me in the plain of the bani Hajar. I, the foreteller, am coming; do not doubt that I shall come."

So the camel went quickly to the plain and there she stopped to wait for him. And he, the beloved, the covered, went with the Companions to the entrance of the tent of the Arab.

The cruel Arab defied and abused the Prophet, who expressed the wish to buy the exhausted camel. The infidel refused, and added, "It is true that I shut up the camel. But how did you find out?"

"In fact your camel came to us and told us all about you."

The man said, "This is even more of a marvel than the first. A camel is a brute beast; how can it speak in human language for people to understand? A camel is an animal; how can it use its tongue to speak intelligibly?"

"You shall find out for certain what is going on. Let you and me go where the camel is. Let us go together and you shall see for yourself and hear what she says."

So the Beloved and the Companions and this person went together.

On their way, all going together, they saw more wonderful and surprising things. They looked up and they saw a pen with a gazelle shut in it, tied fast to the gate with an iron collar.

When the gazelle saw the Foreteller, she bowed down and made obeisance to him. Then she spoke in clear speech and all who were there heard her. She said, "Greetings to you, Hashemite, first of the great ones, and to all the Companions; greetings to you, the Dedicated, the Perfection of Light, the equal of the moon, the rival of the sun; greetings to you, Prophet, Apostle of the Almighty, the first created, the seal of the prophets."

When the gazelle had ended, she said to the Prophet, "I have a boon that I ask you to grant me."

Muhammad asked her to tell him her need, leaving nothing out nor fearing to tell all.

Then the gazelle said to the trusted one, "I was in the forest with the babies that I had borne; but then trouble came upon me and it is now four days since I left my children and they are still in the forest. It is now four days since I bore them and was parted from them. They have no food and have not found my udder. When I was delivered of them, I went straight to the forest to feed them and to find the best pasture, and there I was captured. I was in the pasture when I fell into the trap of a terrible enemy, a worshipper of false gods. When this cruel man took me, he robbed me of everything, and now, O Prophet, it is four days since this disaster overtook me. I am very unhappy; I have babies, you understand, and for four whole days they have been crying in the forest. I have been in great distress, I have had a terrible struggle and my heart cries for death. Morning and evening I am cut to the heart and I can see no way out at all. I would rather my master took my life to end my sorrow and dry my tears. I weep for my babies, because I cannot see them; do not imagine, Sir, that I weep for myself. My capture, man of Mecca, made me miserable, and putting me here fills me with sorrow. It were better to cut my throat and still my heart and end my longing for my babies.

"See, Prophet, how I am overcome with worry and distress and to what a state I am reduced. As I have told you, I have no skin or flesh and I stagger as I walk."

So distressed was the Prophet by her story that he fell on his face and wept floods of tears. The gazelle's owner greeted him with contempt and refused to sell the gazelle.

The wicked fellow answered Muhammad, "Your request is impossible and cannot be considered. If I had at my house all the buck in the world, I would not give you a single one, if you asked for it. I will not sell this perfect gazelle. I want to have nothing to do with the Prophet and to do nothing for you."

When she heard this, the gazelle said, "Muhammad, try harder to recover my rights. Tell this unbeliever to loose my bonds and to let me find my babies and give them suck. Tell him to let me go free, my Lord, and I will go and come back. For you, Prophet, if I go, I will return."

The Prophet asked the man, "Are you not touched by your gazelle's own words?"

The false enemy of God replied, "Go and do your magic in your own house of tricks." Then he said to Muhammad, "Release the gazelle; but the Prophet is her surety."

Muhammad said, "I am surety for her." Then he went and released her, and he said to the gazelle, "Go, and return with the speed of an arrow. Just as an arrow leaves the bow, so come back to me here where I am."

The gazelle returned to her fawns in the forest, who entreated her to return without delay to the Prophet in order to redeem his pledge. This she did. Seeing this miracle, her owner acknowledged the Prophet as the Chosen One and released the gazelle. The Prophet and the wicked Arab went on to find the ill-treated camel, who repeated her complaint.

When the man heard what the camel had to say, he answered, saying to Muhammad, "Now I admit, and myself am witness that God is One, and that you are his Prophet. You are the true Prophet and what you say is true, and I too will bear witness to this. The word of the Lord that he has caused to be written, I will place in my heart and speak with my tongue. Listen while I testify that God is One and at the same time that Muhammad is his Prophet. *The Word of the Lord: I certify that there is no God but God, and I certify that Muhammad is the Prophet of God.*" Then he said to the Prophet, "The camel's complaint leaves it free. Hear, O Prophet, as for this beast, I give it its freedom to go where it will."

So the Arab became a Muslim and released the camel and his wife and his children accompanied him. They became followers of God in virtue and piety and lived holy lives. They diligently recited the prayers; they died well and Paradise received them.

And the camel – the Prophet favoured her and gave her the grazing grounds of the Bani Hajjar to dwell in. The camel lived in this grazing ground until old age overtook her. Every Friday she would go to the Hashemite, the Prophet, to visit him. She went gladly to Muhammad the generous and gave him her greetings, and Muhammad received them. She never missed, but went every Friday, until the time came for the Prophet to leave the world. Then the days were confused and Friday was delayed. The camel started to visit the Prophet; but when she came to the mosque, she found all in confusion. She looked at the mosque and did not see the trusted one, but only Hasan's father and all the Companions. All the Companions were at the mosque weeping bitterly together. They wept with cries and groans, believing that the last day had come.

When the camel came and understood about the death, she too wept and was full of sorrow. She continued to weep and to show sincerely how much she was distressed by the death of the Prophet. She came to the tomb; she betook herself to the grave and knelt on the stones. She rubbed herself on the tomb and the Companions and the Faithful watched her. She remained at the grave, mourning for the trusted one. Then her spirit found peace and the camel died.

On the death of the camel the Companions were grieved and each one arose to go to her. On her death, when the breath left her body, the Companions came and buried the camel. The Companions thought about her and repeated the story of her good deeds, making mention of the Prophet and repeating "God is Great."

Tendi J. W. T. Allen.

The bush-strangled ruins of once magnificient courts and mansions on Pate Island in the Lamu archipelago inspired the sombre Al-Inkishafi *of Sayyid Abdulla bin Ali bin Nasir. The poem was written between 1810 and 1820; the translation from which these extracts have been taken is by James de Vere Allen.*

How many wealthy men have we not seen
Who in their splendour shone like the sun itself,
Strong in their great hoards of ivory,
Powerful in stocks of silver and of gold?
To them the whole world bowed down in homage,
For them the Road of Life was broad and straight.
They went their ways in arrogance, unafraid,
Heads high in air, their eyes screwed up in scorn.
They swung their arms and tossed their haughty heads,
Retainers went behind them and before.
Wherever they went they took the seat of honour
And many bodyguards surrounded them.

Their lighted mansions glowed with lamps of brass
And crystal, till night seemed like very day;
And in their halls dwelt Beauty everywhere
And Veneration stalked them all their days.
Their homes were set with Chinese porcelain
And every cup and goblet was engraved
While, placed amidst the glittering ornaments,
Great crystal pitchers gleamed all luminous.
The rails from which they hung the rich brocade
Were made – I swear by God, Source of all Wealth –
Of teak and ebony, row upon row of them,
Rank upon rank with fabrics hung displayed.

The men's halls hummed with chatter, while within
The women's quarters laughter echoed loud.
The noise of talk and merriment of slaves
Rang out, and cheerful shouts of workmen rose.
And when they went to rest, they had massage
And fans and gay-robed women for their ease
And music-makers, playing and singing songs
Ceaselessly till they slept. And when they slept
It was on exquisite beds of finest timber
Carefully chosen, with soft mattresses
With pillows of green cloth at head and foot.
Embroidered with silver thread and fine-spun gold.

Fabric was draped on canopies above
To shelter them. Their limbs were sprinkled over
With rosewater, and their bodies anointed
With attar and sandalwood and incense-smoke.

And yet, for all their wealth and proud grandeur
They took, with Death's great Caravan, their leave
And journeyed to the mansions of the grave
And crumbled like blowing sand, and came to dust.
So sleep they now, in a city of a finger's span.
No curtains there, no cushions nor silk couch.
Their bodies are broken, mutilated all
And crushed by the merciless constraint of tombs.
Their cheekbones have caved in and decomposed,
And pus and blood ooze through their parted lips;
Maggots infest their nostrils and their throats
And the beauty of their countenances is transformed.
They have become food for insects and for worms,
Termites and ants devour and bore them through.
Their bodies are eroded. Venomous snakes
And scorpions coil in the cavities.

Their lighted mansions echo emptily;
High in the painted rafters flutter bats.
There are no murmurings, no happy shouts,
And on carved bedsteads spiders spin their webs.
Where once in wall-niches the porcelain stood
Are now the ragged nests of wild birds.
Owls hoot in the solitude of the ruined halls
And quail and gamebirds scuttle and cry below.
On painted curtain-rails now vultures perch,
And young doves pout and coo between themselves
Or start, and flap their wings, and whirr away.
Swallows build their nests, and wood-pigeons.

Cockroaches rustle in the empty courts.
Where once men gathered, now the crickets shrill.
The chatter in the ante-rooms has ceased
And there remains only dirt and foul decay.
The courtyards now are choked with weeds and thorns,
Bushes are canopied over with wild vines.
Men fear today to pass these yawning doors
For inside Silence and Darkness reign supreme.
If you believe me not, and say I lie,

Then go yourself and peer about those halls.
Call out. Your echo will come back, naught else,
For human voices can be heard no more.

* * *

My soul, all mortal men are thus: for all
The Pen of God has signed an equal Writ;
And it is certain you will be as they
Unless you have and hold to your true faith.
O soul, beware, be not a firebrand,
Abandon false pride, hold to truth and right.
Your friends are saved – make sure to save yourself
Or else the Fires of Hell will eat you up.

Know you, the day will come when over all
The World there will be change: the Seven Heavens
Will be moved from their place. The Sun and Moon
Will tumble from the sky. And for us men
There will be fire and heat, both without cease.
Where will you turn on that last day, when flames
Rage within your spleen, and from your scalp
The skin is singed – where will you flee for help?
Tell me your refuge, for I would share it too.

Never forget that Day, when multitudes
Will assemble for every deed to be revealed;
That Day when the oppressed will kneel before
Their God and cry, "Decide between him and me!
Judge us, O Lord God! See how I was wronged
By this man – judge us in Thy rectitude!"
And God, by Whom all things shall be disposed,
Shall judge, repaying each his wrongs as due.
Nor can the injured ever be paid back
With golden nuggets, nor with coin of gold.
Money, even were it offered as recompense.
Is not accepted. Compensation must
Be rendered in good deeds performed in life.
And he whose record shows neither good deeds
Nor wrongs incurred from others – he, like a horse,
Is bridled, with bit pressed to his mouth,
And forced to bear the sins of those he wronged –
Ordered to carry their burden and begone.

Al-Inkishafi: Catechism of a Soul Sayyid Abdulla bin Ali bin Nasir

Swahili love poems range from the utendi *to the lyric, of which these literal translations are examples.*

BIRD OF THE NIGHTS

O you bird of the nights,
receive my greetings,
I do not eat at all
you have penetrated me, proud one,
like an anchor into a rock.
I, your slave, am conquered.

Accept my letter,
read its contents,
so that it may be clear to you,
and enter your mind entirely,
forgive me many things again,
while reading my greetings.

I came to you, my friend,
it was your friendship I needed,
you embraced me round the waist,
love has enveloped me
like a fish by the ocean,
and has covered me all over.

Nor do I see any change,
in this getting entangled in one another,
I grazed everywhere in the fruit,
and I have seen no other one
except you; in the belly,
my lover, you embraced me.

In the belly you embraced me,
you hurt me, my lover,
you held me with great strength,
it shone like ivory.
Come, come, my girl,
let your lips enfold me.

THE SCALES

I am looking for a pair of scales,
to weigh my love for you;
let us put it on the weighing scale,
let us compare it, precious one,
your love is invisible,
mine can be clearly seen.

O pair of scales, judge the truth,
you are the umpire,
do not be biased,
clearly show the truth.
Weigh, O scales of truth,
without withholding.

I have shown you my love,
I do not see yours, precious one,
I am giving you my secret,
act discreetly with it.
I love alone,
and you know it, beloved.

Give me your love
let it equal mine;
permit me to come to you,
or come to me,
lest you remain alone,
lest I love alone.

A Choice of Flowers Jan Knappert.

THE GRAPE

I passed along a fruit garden,
where there were many flowers,
and Paradisiac fruits,
the finest one could wish to choose from.
Grapes and pomegranates,
all neglectful of themselves.

O my heart, calm down,
you do not know the grape yet,
we do not know who owns it,
or how we shall carry it away.
The best thing is to exclaim: "Go away,
    Satan!"
Taking it would be equal to adultery.

My heart is full of zeal
to choose the grape,
even if the owner is Satan,
I will lure it away
so as to take it home with me,
to enjoy it and press it out.

The grape is already in my hands,
then the owner discovers me,
and at once it is in my mouth,
but I have not yet enjoyed it
    completely.
He put me in jail,
and took the grape away.

Refrain
The grape is in the heart
to eat it gives me trouble.

A Choice of Flowers Jan Knappert.

The grape and the pomegranate are erotic symbols in Islamic literature.

TO HIS FIRST WIFE
MUYAKA BIN HAIJI

I would rather have the small boat,*
My first little vessel,
Although it was unsteady and shaky
The waves never rose above her head,
But she drowned near Ngoaoa
On a dark night.
That is what I am thinking about today.
It makes me confused and numb.

* The boat is a symbol for the first wife.

My little boat, my seaworthy boat:
When I first made it float on the water
It was full of playfulness
And I was pleased and charmed by it.
In it I crossed over to the other shore
And the waves did not rise above it.
That is why I am thinking of her
And feel confused and numb.

Four Centuries of Swahili Verse
Jan Knappert.

Under Islamic law, a man may divorce his wife by abjuring her three times before a magistrate; the children of the marriage then belong to him. This is the song of a woman of Mombasa.

Should a mother be prevented from seeing her child?

Forgive me gentlemen, from the Coast and from up-country too,
To withhold a child from her mother, is it custom or law?
Give me a meaningful answer, so that the mind can retain it:
To withhold a child from her mother, is that custom or law?

My husband and I were married, and God granted us,
That we had a child, a gift in this world.
In features we looked alike, her name was Rukia.
To withhold a child from her mother, is that custom or law?

In the end we quarrelled, as discord entered (our house),
And we were divorced, my husband wrote a divorce note for me,
I no longer live with him now, I have gone back to my parents' home.
To withhold a child from her mother, is that custom or law?

My husband took the child away, and lectured me as well:
"She is no longer your child, you are now divorced, I tell you,
Even when you are ill, she may not go to see you."
To withhold a child from her mother, is that custom or law?

So I was without (help from) the law, as my husband had told me,
While we were divorced, and he kept the child away from me.
Yet, even though the child is her father's, he did not get it alone.
To withhold a child from her mother, is that custom or law?

I felt so much pain, when I was with child,
At night and in daytime, I had no rest on earth.
And now I have no child, and this is then the law.
To withhold a child from her mother, is that custom or law?

From "Songs of the Swahili Women", *Afrika und Übersee* Jan Knappert.

A Swahili sailor's song.

Praise be to God
let us thank the Giver,
Oh victorious Giver,
What sort of thing is the world?

Those who once owned palaces
are now sleeping under the sky
Those who once owned dhows
are now collecting firewood;
Those who once owned palm trees
are now craving for palm wine!

The world is treacherous
it deceives like the winds
suddenly they blow from below,
but the ones from above are the most
dangerous,
stripping off the sails
nothing lasts here.

Travel by the seasons,
the sea is king!
He that does not know the world,
let him watch the coastal waters:
at ebb it goes out,
at rising tide it goes in.
If the winds do not blow,
we make no progress at sea.
Be careful, fellow men!
do not fall down the cliffs
Life will not last.
That which floats is a dry leaf.

From "Swahili Sailors' Songs", *Africa and Übersee*
Jan Knappert.

A modern Swahili poet is Ahmad Nassir of Malindi, who wrote this poem in or about 1960.

THE FIRE

The forest has caught fire.
The great forest is blazing;
Shut your eyes
You will still see it burning.
It burns, friends, it burns.
Be careful with fire!

The shrubs are already consumed.
Tall trees are on fire.
Tiny gazelles flee.
Elephants are confused,
They walk without seeing their way
For the fire surrounds them.
It burns, friends, it burns.
Be careful with fire!

Fire has scorched all the grass
And young shoots are on fire,
And big lions, all of them
Have moved out of the bushes:
They are running – catch him! catch him!
But they know no place to hold on to.
It burns, friends, it burns.
Be careful with fire!

The fire has put even buffaloes to flight
Who are praised for their valour;
Rhinoceroses are caught in the middle,
Fire has surrounded them too.
Birds up in the trees
Have flown from their nests.
It burns, friends, it burns.
Be careful with fire!

Four Centuries of Swahili Verse Jan Knappert.

"Guests and fish stink after three days" – Chinese proverb.

The guest on the first day,
Give him rice and coconut heart
Served in the shell,
To welcome the guest.

The guest on the second day,
Give him milk and butter.
As affection grows,
Show more to the guest.

The guest on the third day,
There is nothing in the house
But three kibaba,
Cook them and eat with the guest.

The guest on the fourth day,
Give him a hoe to use,
On his return, take leave of him,
And let him go home.

The guest on the fifth day
Pricks like a needle.
The house is full of whispering,
All against the guest.

The guest on the sixth day –
Go into the corners
To hide when you eat,
From that guest.

The guest on the seventh day
Is no guest but a pest.
If the thatch catches fire
Blame it on the guest.

The guest on the eighth day –
"Come in, let us part."
When he goes outside –
"Goodbye, go along, guest."

The guest on the ninth day –
"Go, man, go,
Do not come back,
Do not return, guest."

The guest on the tenth day –
With blows and kicks,
Get rid of no one
So long as you are rid of the guest.

The Customs of the Swahili People Mtoro bin Mwinyi Bakari.

Modern Poetry

With the spread of Western education, poems written in English replaced traditional songs chanted in tribal languages. Preeminent among the new poets was Okot p'Bitek (1931–1982) whose Song of Lawino *dramatically juxta-posed the tribal customs of the past and the pseudo-European ways of many of the rising Westernized generation. It is a very long poem and only extracts can be given here.*

I

MY HUSBAND'S TONGUE IS BITTER

Husband, now you despise me
Now you treat me with spite
And say I have inherited the stupidity of my aunt;
Son of the Chief,
Now you compare me
With the rubbish in the rubbish pit,
You say you no longer want me
Because I am like the things left behind
In the deserted homestead.
You insult me
You laugh at me
You say I do not know the letter A
Because I have not been to school
And I have not been baptized

You compare me with a little dog,
A puppy.

My friend, age-mate of my brother,
Take care,
Take care of your tongue,
Be careful what your lips say.

First take a deep look, brother,
You are now a man
You are not a dead fruit!
To behave like a child does not befit you!

Listen Ocol, you are the son of a Chief,
Leave foolish behaviour to little children,
It is not right that you should be laughed at in a song!
Songs about you should be songs of praise!
Stop despising people
As if you were a little foolish man,
Stop treating me like salt-less ash;
Become barren of insults and stupidity;

Who has ever uprooted the Pumpkin?*

*

My husband treats me roughly.
The insults!
Words cut more painfully than sticks!
He says my mother is a witch,
That my clansmen are fools
Because they eat rats,
He says we are all Kaffirs.
We do not know the ways of God,
We sit in deep darkness
And do not know the Gospel,
He says my mother hides her charms
In her necklace
And that we are all sorcerers.
My husband's tongue
Is bitter like the roots of *lyonno* lily,
It is hot like the penis of the bee,
Like the sting of the *kalang*!

---

*Pumpkins, which grow wild throughout Acoliland, are highly esteemed, and to uproot one
would be an act of wanton destruction.

Ocol's tongue is fierce like the arrow of the scorpion,
Deadly like the spear of the buffalo-hornet.
It is ferocious
Like the poison of a barren woman
And corrosive like the juice of the gourd.

*

My husband pours scorn
On Black People,
He behaves like a hen
That eats its own eggs
A hen that should be imprisoned under a basket.
His eyes grow large
Deep black eyes
Ocol's eyes resemble those of the Nile perch!
He becomes fierce
Like a lioness with cubs,
He begins to behave like a mad hyena.

He says Black People are primitive
And their ways are utterly harmful,
Their dances are mortal sins
They are ignorant, poor and diseased!

Ocol says he is a modern man,
A progressive and civilized man.

2

THE WOMAN WITH WHOM
I SHARE MY HUSBAND

Ocol rejects the old type.
He is in love with a modern woman,
He is in love with a beautiful girl
Who speaks English.

But only recently
We would sit close together, touching each other!

Only recently I would play
On my bow-harp
Singing praises to my beloved.
Only recently he promised
That he trusted me completely.
I used to admire him speaking in English.

Ocol is no longer in love with the old type;
He is in love with a modern girl.
The name of the beautiful one
Is Clementine.

Brother, when you see Clementine!
The beautiful one aspires
To look like a white woman;

Her lips are red-hot
Like glowing charcoal,
She resembles the wild cat
That has dipped its mouth in blood,
Her mouth is like raw yaws
It looks like an open ulcer,
Like the mouth of a field!
Tina dusts powder on her face
And it looks so pale;
She resembles the wizard
Getting ready for the midnight dance.

She dusts the ash-dirt all over her face
And when little sweat
Begins to appear on her body
She looks like the guinea fowl!

The smell of carbolic soap
Makes me sick,
And the smell of powder
Provokes the ghosts in my head;
It is then necessary to fetch a goat
From my mother's brother.
The sacrifice over
The ghost-dance drum must sound
The ghost be laid
And my peace restored.

I do not like dusting myself with powder:
The thing is good on pink skin
Because it is already pale,
But when a black woman has used it
She looks as if she has dysentery;
Tina looks sickly
And she is slow moving,
She is a piteous sight.

Some medicine has eaten up Tina's face;
The skin on her face is gone
And it is all raw and red,
The face of the beautiful one
Is tender like the skin of a newly born baby!

And she believes
That this is beautiful
Because it resembles the face of a white woman!
Her body resembles
The ugly coat of the hyena;
Her neck and arms
Have real human skins!

*

I am not unfair to my husband,
I do not complain
Because he wants another woman
Whether she is young or aged!
Who has ever prevented men
From wanting women?

Who has discovered the medicine for thirst?
The medicines for hunger
And anger and enmity
Who has discovered them?

*

When the beautiful one
With whom I share my husband
Returns from cooking her hair
She resembles
A chicken
That has fallen into a pond;
Her hair looks
Like the python's discarded skin.

They cook their hair
With hot iron
And pull it hard
So that it may grow long.
Then they rope the hair
On wooden pens
Like a billy goat
Brought for the sacrifice
Struggling to free itself.

They fry their hair
In boiling oil
As if it were locusts,
And the hair sizzles
It cries aloud in sharp pain

As it is pulled and stretched.
And the vigorous and healthy hair
Curly, springy and thick
That glistens in the sunshine
Is left listless and dead
Like the elephant grass
Scorched brown by the fierce
February sun.
It lies lifeless
Like the sad and dying banana leaves
On a hot and windless afternoon.

*

All I ask
Is that you give me one chance,
Let me praise you
Son of the chief!
Tie ankle bells on my legs
Bring *lacucuku* rattles
And tie them on my legs,
Call the *nanga* players
And let them play
And let them sing,

Let me dance before you,
My love,
Let me show you
The wealth in your house,
Ocol my husband,
Son of the Bull,
Let no one uproot the Pumpkin.

Song of Lawino Okot p'Bitek.

Okot p'Bitek was a Ugandan, but his work was influential throughout East Africa, and from 1968 onwards until shortly before his death he was attached to the University of Nairobi. He followed Song of Lawino *with* Song of Ocol, *in which Lawino's husband answered back.*

The coming of independence in 1963 generated a mood of hope and confidence among young African writers. When a new Jerusalem did not arise in Kenya's brown and pleasant land, disillusionment set in. Many modern poems reflect this attitude.

THEIR CITY

Lennard Okola

City in the sun
without any warmth
except for *wanaotosheka**
and the tourists escaping
from civilized boredom

---

wanaotosheka – Swahili word for those who are satisfied – symbolically, those who are privileged.

Sit under the Tree
any Saturday morning
and watch the new Africans,
the anxious faces
behind the steering wheels
in hire purchase cars,
see them looking important
in a tiny corner
behind the chauffeur

We have seen them
in a nightmare,
the thickset directors
of several companies;
we have seen them
struggling under the weight
of a heavy lunch
on a Monday afternoon
cutting a tape

to open a building,
we have seen them
looking over their
gold-rimmed glasses
to read a speech
And in the small hours
between one day and the next
we have strolled through
the deserted streets
and seen strange figures
under bougainvillaea bushes

in traffic islands,
figures hardly human
snoring away into
the cold winds of the night;
desperately dying to live.

An Anthology of East African Poetry, ed. A. D. Amateshe.

I SPEAK FOR THE BUSH

Everett Standa

When my friend sees me
He swells and pants like a frog
Because I talk the wisdom of the bush!
He says we from the bush
Do not understand civilized ways
For we tell our women
To keep the hem of their dresses
Below the knee.
We from the bush, my friend insists,
Do not know how to "enjoy":
When we come to the civilized city,
Like nuns, we stay away from nightclubs
Where women belong to no men
And men belong to no women
And these civilized people
Quarrel and fight like hungry lions!

But, my friend, why do men
With crippled legs, lifeless eyes,
Wooden legs, empty stomachs
Wander about the streets
Of this civilized world?

Teach me, my friend, the trick,
So that my eyes may not
See those whose houses have no walls
But emptiness all around;
Show me the wax you use
To seal your ears
To stop hearing the cry of the hungry;
Teach me the new wisdom
Which tells men
To talk about money and not love,
When they meet women;

Tell your God to convert
Me to the faith of the indifferent,
The faith of those
Who will never listen until
They are shaken with blows.

I speak for the bush:
You speak for the civilized –
Will you hear me?

Poems from East Africa, eds. David Cook and David Rubadiri.

A PREGNANT SCHOOL GIRL

Everett Standa

He paid for her seat in the matatu*
And walked away;
As he disappeared in the city crowd
All her dreams vanished;

One more passenger squeezed in
And lit a cigarette,
She opened the window
And spat cold saliva out,
As the cigarette smoke intensified
She wanted to vomit:

She remembered the warm nights
When she was her man's pet,
She remembered the promises
The gifts, the parties, the dances –

She remembered her classmates at school
Who envied her expensive shoes,
Lipstick, wrist-watch, handbag
Which she brought to school
After a weekend with him

The future stood against her
Dark like a night without the moon,
And silent like the end of the world;

As the matatu sped away from the city
She began to tremble with fear
Wondering what her parents would say;

* Small ramshackle bus.

With all hope gone
She felt like a corpse
going home to be buried.

An Anthology of East African Poetry, ed. A. D. Amateshe.

BETROTHED

Obyero Odhiambo

The bride, they said
had gone through school
primary secondary university upwards:
Three thousand shillings is not enough.

For having fed her
    schooled her
    employed her
Three thousand shillings is not enough –

For having borne her
    cared her
    doctored her
And "she is pure"
Three thousand shillings is not enough.

Look at her silky black hair
Darker and finer than that
Flywhisk there
Look at her forehead, a
Nice wide trace between
hairline and eyes:
"She is immensely intelligent."

Look at her eyes. Yes, look again
Two diviners' cowries spread out
symbolically on the divination mat
deep profound intelligent;
Look at those lips "ndugu" . . .
Three thousand shillings is not enough
even to shake her by the hand.

"Fathers, this is what we walked with!
Three thousand shillings
As a token of our
Love
for your daughter and you
our intended kin
It was just a token
The size of the token does not reflect
The size of the heart that bringeth it
My heart is full to the brim with
Love
for your daughter
Mine is just a token of my
Love
for her and you my intended kin."

But, young man, you say, you love
and you possibly expect love
But, young man, don't you
Don't you really feel
Three thousand shillings is not enough
even to get love?
Three thousand shillings is not enough!

An Anthology of East African Poetry, ed. A. D. Amateshe.

TIME AND THOUGHT

J. Angira

Perhaps we should have stayed
Little longer at the harbour
Before risking the moat
Between happiness and despair

Perhaps we should have delayed
Little longer at the tower
To gauge the moods of the sea
Before letting go the anchor

Perhaps we should have waited
Little longer at the hangar
To watch the clouds in the sky
Before risking the flight

Perhaps we should have waited
Little longer in umbilical safety
Before venturing into this Kingdom of Dreams
Where Life and Death play military games.

Boundless Voices: Poems from Kenya, ed. Arthur Luvai.

RHYTHM OF THE PESTLE

Richard Ntiru

Listen – listen –
listen to the palpable rhythm
of the periodic pestle,
plunging in proud perfection
into the cardial cavity
of maternal mortar
like the panting heart
of the virgin bride
with the silver hymen,
or the approaching stamp
of late athleting cows
hurrying home to their bleating calves.

At each succeeding stroke
the grain darts, glad to be scattered
by the hard glint
of the pestle's passion.

During the aerial suspension
of the pendent pestle
the twice-asked, twice-disappointed girl
thinks of the suitor that didn't come,
of her who dragged her name through ashes
uncleansed by the goat-sacrifice,
of her bridal bed
that vanished with the ephemeral dream,
of her twin firstlings
that will never be born,
and her weltering hands
grip, grip, rivet hard
and downright down
comes the vengeance pestle.

I have seen the hearth
and the triplets,
but no trace of ash. . . .

Now the grain jumps, reluctantly,
each time lower and lower,
smiling the half-white smile
of the teething baby,
glad to be crushed,
glad to be sublimated
to the quintessential powder
after the consummation.

In the bananas
the girls dance, singing of one
who saw her father in sleepy drunkenness
and confided in the birds of the sky.

Still the perennial pestle
pounds the tribulations of a battered soul
and the caked countenance of an orphaned age
to the intensity and fineness
of a powder.

An Anthology of East African Poetry, ed. A. D. Amateshe.

THE TROUBLED WARRIOR

Alexander Muigai

I'll put aside my hoe:
Let them call me lazy.
I'll lay aside my stick:
Let my cattle rove alone.
I'll bid farewell my girl
And my laughing sister
Despite their sweet tears.
I'll pat my younger brother.
Then I'll go and kneel down
Before the two heaps of stones
Where my parents lie;
I'll plead with them to call
The blessing of their gods
On me, a troubled youth,
Before I go in the pursuit.

Then I'll gird my loin-cloth.
Sling my bow and the sword
Of my clan. Spear in hand
I'll go to face the foe.
The dewy grass shall be
My couch; on the cold rock
My head shall rest;
The damp night air shall blanket me;
And to the wild beast
I'll be a guest.
I'll drink from the wandering streams;
Suck on wild fruits.
Till I have faced my foe
I'll be ashamed to face my home.
Courage; hate and my enemy's fate
Drive me on. Mighty he stands
But curse be on me if
I show him my naked heels:
No! Never, never!
Come death before surrender
But I'll slay him – this I know.

Then I'll dry my bleeding
Sword on my thirsty tongue;
And proclaim victory –
The will of my fathers.
Thus, all having been done,
And my poor heart settled,
I'll venture to go home.
I'll take up my hoe and dig;
I'll pick up my stick and herd;
I'll court my girl and wed.
Having done my duty,
I'll sit by the fire
And grow old.

Poems from East Africa, eds. David Cook and David Rubadiri.

A LEOPARD LIVES IN A MUU TREE

Jonathan Kariara

A leopard lives in a Muu tree
Watching my home
My lambs are born speckled
My wives tie their skirts tight
And turn away –
Fearing mottled offspring.
They bathe when the moon is high
Soft and fecund
Splash cold mountain stream water on their nipples
Drop their skin skirts and call obscenities.
I'm besieged
I shall have to cut down the muu tree
I'm besieged
I walk about stiff
Stroking my loins
A leopard lives outside my homestead
Watching my women
I have called him elder, the one-from-the-same-womb
He peers at me with slit eyes
His head held high
My sword has rusted in the scabbard.
My wives purse their lips
When owls call for mating
I'm besieged
They fetch cold mountain water
They crush the sugar cane
But refuse to touch my beer horn.
My fences are broken
My medicine bags torn
The hair on my loins is singed
The upright post at the gate has fallen
My women are frisky
The leopard arches over my homestead
Eats my lambs
Resuscitating himself.

Poems from East Africa, eds. David Cook and David Rubadiri.

GRASS WILL GROW

Jonathan Kariara

If you should take my child Lord
Give my hands strength to dig his grave
Cover him with earth
Lord send a little rain
For grass will grow

If my house should burn down
So that the ashes sting the nostrils
Making the eyes weep
Then Lord send a little rain
For grass will grow

But Lord do not send me
Madness
I ask for tears
Do not send me moon hard madness
To lodge snug in my skull
I would you sent me hordes of horses
Galloping
Crushing
But do not break
The yolk of the moon on me.

Introduction to East African Poetry Jonathan Kariara and J. Kitonga.

THE DEATH OF MY FATHER

H. Indangasi

His sunken cheeks, his inward-looking eyes,
The sarcastic, scornful smile on his lips,
The unkempt, matted, grey hair,
The hard, coarse sandpaper hands,
Spoke eloquently of the life he had lived.
But I did not mourn for him.

The hammer, the saw and the plane,
These were his tools and his damnation,
His sweat was his ointment and his perfume.
He fashioned dining tables, chairs, wardrobes,
And all the wooden loves of colonial life.
No, I did not mourn for him.

He built colonial mansions,
Huge, unwieldy, arrogant constructions;
But he squatted in a sickly mud-house,
With his children huddled stuntedly
Under the bed-bug bed he shared with Mother.
I could not mourn for him.

I had already inherited
His premature old-age look,
I had imbibed his frustration;
But his dreams of freedom and happiness
Had become my song, my love.
So, I could not mourn for him.

No, I did not shed any tears;
My father's dead life still lives in me,
He lives in my son, my father,
I am my father and my son.
I will awaken his sleepy hopes and yearnings,
But I will not mourn for him,
I will not mourn for me.

Boundless Voices: Poems from Kenya, ed. Arthur Luvai.

STANLEY MEETS MUTESA

David Rubadiri

Such a time of it they had;
The heat of the day
The chill of the night
And the mosquitoes that followed.
Such was the time and
They bound for a kingdom.

The thin weary line of carriers
With tattered dirty rags to cover their backs;
The battered bulky chests
That kept on falling off their shaven heads.
Their tempers high and hot
The sun fierce and scorching
With it rose their spirits
With its fall their hopes

As each day sweated their bodies dry and
Flies clung in clumps on their sweat-scented backs.
Such was the march
And the hot season just breaking.

Each day a weary pony dropped,
Left for the vultures on the plains;
Each afternoon a human skeleton collapsed,
Left for the Masai on the plains;
But the march trudged on
Its Khaki leader in front
He the spirit that inspired.
He the light of hope.

Then came the afternoon of a hungry march,
A hot and hungry march it was;
The Nile and the Nyanza
Lay like two twins
Azure across the green countryside.
The march leapt on chaunting
Like young gazelles to a water hole.
Hearts beat faster
Loads felt lighter
As the cool water lapt their sore soft feet.
No more the dread of hungry hyenas
But only tales of valour when
At Mutesa's court fires are lit.
No more the burning heat of the day
But song, laughter and dance.

The village looks on behind banana groves,
Children peer behind reed fences.
Such was the welcome
No singing women to chaunt a welcome
Or drums to greet the white ambassador;
Only a few silent nods from aged faces
And one rumbling drum roll
To summon Mutesa's court to parley
For the country was not sure.

The gate of reeds is flung open,
There is silence
But only a moment's silence –
A silence of assessment.

The tall black king steps forward,
He towers over the thin bearded white man
Then grabbing his lean white hand
Manages to whisper
"Mtu Mweupe karibu"
White man you are welcome.
The gate of polished reed closes behind them
And the west is let in.

Introduction to East African Poetry Jonathan Kariara and J. Kitonga.

POEM IN FOUR PARTS

William Kamera

I

The leaves are withered
Roses fold and shrink.
Dog, the panting athlete, shows his tongue.
A dwarfed shadow flees –
Hides under my legs
Nuts wrinkle and crack.

II

The sun is old
The west glows like a worm
Shadows are long
There are cool whispers in the trees
The weavers make for their homes
Old Kibo in his "kanga" appears.

III

Like honey you covered the lawn
    Fleeting beauty –
In the cool of the morning air
Peace-placid and pleasant.

The moist crystals of yesternight
    Where are you gone?
I would have you for my own.
Surrendered at the approach of dawn.

IV

Sun from his eastern cradle
Like a chameleon measures his steps
Stretches his tender arms
Over the silent hills.
The trees exchange greetings
In the gentle whispers of dawn.
The lazy night is over.

The weaverbird disturbs my rest.
Day hatching from the eastern shell
Uncovers ice-shouldered Kibo.
Life blooms with the rose
In the cool of the morning air
The lazy night is over.

Poems from East Africa, eds. David Cook and David Rubadiri.

THE DEAD

Francis Nnaggenda

The dead are not under the earth
They are in the tree that rustles
They are in the woods that groan
They are in the water that runs
They are in the water that sleeps
They are in the hut, they are in the crowd
The dead are not dead.
Those who are dead are never gone
They are in the breast of a woman
They are in the child that is wailing and in the fire that flames.
    The dead are not under the earth
They are in the fire that is dying
They are in the grass that is weeping
They are in the whimpering rocks
They are in the forest, they are in the house
They are not dead.

When my ancestors talk about the Creator they say:
He is with us . . . We sleep with him. We hunt with him.
We dance with him.

From *Queen of Shaba* Joy Adamson.

THE SINGING NAMES OF AFRICA

Isiola and Naivasha, Timboroa, Kiambu.
   Names like prayers to heaven stealing
   Full of lovely sound and feeling
      Falling on the heart like dew.

Kilindini, Londiani, Rumuruti, Menengai.
   On the mind and spirit laying
   Benisons of music playing
      Softly, sweetly as a sigh.

Embakasi, Karatina, Naro Moru, Kericho.
   Like the note of trumpets calling,
   With a perfect cadence falling
      Rhythmic melodies that flow.

Serengeti, Amboseli, Kiminini, Eldoret.
   From the realms of fancy bringing
   Sound of bells a-swinging, ringing
      Singing in my memory yet.

Poems of Kenya Phyllis Haynes.

ACKNOWLEDGEMENTS

My grateful thanks are due to many who have helped me with suggestions and advice in compiling this anthology. In particular I should like to thank Sir Michael Blundell, whose knowledge of the literature is all-embracing; Adrian House, whose editorial counsel was constructive and valuable; Dr John Lonsdale for his advice on aspects of history; Mr James de Vere Allen and Dr Jan Knappert on Swahili verse; and many others.

The author and publisher are grateful to the copyright holders for permission to reprint the following copyright material: George Adamson: *Bwana Game* and *My Pride and Joy*, William Collins, London; Joy Adamson: *Born Free, Queen of Shaba* and *The Searching Spirit*, William Collins, London; Joy Adamson: *Peoples of Kenya*, William Collins, London, and the Estate of Joy Adamson; J. W. T. Allen: *Tendi*, William Heinemann Ltd, London; Lord Altrincham: *Kenya's Opportunity*, Faber and Faber, London; Mtoro bin Mwinyi Bakari: *The Customs of the Swahili People*, translated and edited by J. W. T. Allen, University of California Press, Berkeley, Copyright © 1981 The Regents of the University of California; Donald Barnett and Karari Njama: *Mau Mau from Within*, William Collins, London, and Monthly Review Press, New York, Copyright © 1966 by Donald R. Barnett, Reprinted by permission of Monthly Review Foundation; Mervyn Beech: *The Suk: Their Language and Folklore*, Oxford University Press, Oxford; W. D. M. Bell: *The Wanderings of an Elephant Hunter*, The C. W. Daniel Company, Saffron Walden; Cheryl Bentsen: *Maasai Days*, William Collins, London, and Summit Books, New York, Copyright © 1989 by Cheryl Bentsen; Felice Benuzzi: *No Picnic on Mount Kenya*, William Collins, London; Karen Blixen: *Out of Africa*, The Bodley Head, London, Random House, New York, and the Estate of Karen Blixen, Los Angeles, Copyright 1937 by Random House, Inc. and renewed 1965 by Rungstedlundfonden; Leslie Brown: *The Mystery of the Flamingos*, Octopus Publishing Group, London; Angus Buchanan: *Three Years of War in East Africa*, John Murray (Publishers) Ltd, London; C. W. L. Bulpett (ed.) *John Boyes, King of the Wa-kikuyu*, Methuen, London; Aline Buxton: *Kenya Days*, Edward Arnold, Sevenoaks; Luis da Camoens: *The Lusiads*, trans. Richard Fanshawe, Cambridge University Press, Cambridge; Guy Campbell: *The Charging Buffalo: A History of the Kenya Regiment*, Leo Cooper/Secker & Warburg, London; V. M. Carnegie: *A Kenyan Farm Diary*, Pillans and Wilson Ltd, Edinburgh; Winston Churchill: *My African Journey*, Curtis Brown Ltd, London, and the Estate of Sir Winston Churchill; Lady Evelyn Cobbold: *Kenya: The Land of Illusion*, John Murray (Publishers) Ltd, London; Cyril Connolly: *The Evening Colonnade*, Rogers, Coleridge & White Ltd, London; Hugh B. Cott: *Looking at Animals*, William Collins, London; Mervyn Cowie: *Fly Vulture*, Harrap, London; W. E. Crosskill: *The Two Thousand Mile War*, Robert Hale, London; Basil Davidson: *The African Past*, Curtis Brown Ltd, London, Copyright © Basil Davidson, 1964; Iain and Oria Douglas-Hamilton: *Among the Elephants*, William Collins, London; Kenneth Gandar Dower: *The Spotted Lion*, William Heinemann Ltd, London; E. A. T. Dutton: *Kenya Mountain*, Jonathan Cape Ltd and the Estate of E. A. T. Dutton; J. J. L. Duyvendak: *China's Discovery of Africa*, Arthur Probsthain, London; Venn Fey: *Wide Horizons*, the Estate of Venn Fey; Angela Fisher: *Africa Adorned*, William Collins, London; G. S. P. Freeman-Grenville: *The East Africa Coast: Select Documents*, Dr G. S. P. Freeman-Grenville; Mugo Gatheru: *Child of Two Worlds*, Routledge & Kegan Paul, London; Sir John Gray: *The British in Mombasa 1824–1826*, Macmillan Ltd, London; Gerald Hanley: *Warriors and Strangers*, Hamish Hamilton Ltd, London; Ronald Hardy: *The Iron Snake*, William Collins, London; Lyndon Harries:

Swahili Poetry, Oxford University Press, Oxford; Phyllis Haynes: *Poems of Kenya*, Mrs Phyllis Haynes; Ernest Hemingway: *Green Hills of Africa*, Mayor, Brown and Platt (Chicago) on behalf of the Estate of Ernest Hemingway; John Heminway: *The Imminent Rains*, Mr John Heminway; John Hillaby: *Journey to the Jade Sea*, Constable Publishers, London; C. W. Hobley: *Bantu Beliefs and Magic*, Frank Cass & Co. Ltd, London; *Kenya: From Chartered Company to Crown Colony*, H. F. & G. Witherby, London; Geoffrey Hodges: *The Carrier Corps: Military Labor in the East Africa Campaign 1914–1918*, Greenwood Press, Westport, Copyright © 1986 by Geoffrey Hodges; A. C. Hollis: *The Masai: Their Language and Folklore* and *The Nandi*, Oxford University Press, Oxford; Simon Hook: *Samburu Legends*, unpublished collection of oral tales, Mr Simon Hook; Ian Meredith Hughes: *Black Moon, Jade Sea*, First Frost Ltd, London; G. W. B. Huntingford (ed): *The Periplus of the Erythraean Sea*, Hakluyt Society, London; Elspeth Huxley: *Out in the Midday Sun, The Sorcerer's Apprentice, White Man's Country*, Chatto & Windus, London; *Nellie: Letters From Africa*, Elspeth Huxley; Elspeth Huxley and Arnold Curtis: *Pioneers' Scrapbook: Reminiscences of Kenya 1890–1968*, Evans Brothers Ltd, London; Elspeth Huxley and Hugo van Lawick: *Last Days in Eden*, William Collins, London; Juliette Huxley: *Wild Lives of Africa*, William Collins, London; G. J. P. Ionides: *A Hunter's Life*, W. H. Allen, London; C. G. Jung: *Memories, Dreams, Reflections*, William Collins, London; Josiah Mwangi Kariuki: *Mau Mau Detainee*, Oxford University Press, Nairobi; Jomo Kenyatta; *Facing Mount Kenya*, Martin Secker & Warburg, London, and Random House Inc., New York, all rights reserved under International and Pan-American copyright conventions; Valerie Kibera (ed): *An Anthology of East African Short Stories*, Longman, Harlow; Bruce Kinlock: *The Shamba Raiders: Memoirs of a Game Warden*, Ashford Press, Southampton; James Kirkman: *Men and Monuments of the East African Coast*, Lutterworth Press, Cambridge; Frank Kitson: *Gangs and Counter-Gangs*, Barrie & Jenkins, London; G. F. V. Kleen (ed): *Bror von Blixen: The Africa Letters*, St Martin's Press Inc., New York, Copyright © 1988 by G. F. V. Kleen; Jan Knappert: *A Choice of Flowers, Four Centuries of Swahili Verse, Myths and Legends of the Swahili*, "Songs of the Swahili Women" and "Swahili Sailors' Songs", Mr Jan Knappert; David Lamb: *The Africans*, The Bodley Head, London and Random House, Inc., New York, Copyright © 1983 by David Lamb; Hugo and Jane van Lawick-Goodall: *Innocent Killers*, William Collins, London; Mary Leakey: *Disclosing the Past*, Weidenfeld & Nicolson, London; *Olduvai Gorge: My Search for Early Man*, William Collins, London, and the Curtis Brown Group Ltd, London, on behalf of the author, Copyright Mary Leakey 1979; Richard Leakey: *The Making of Mankind*, Michael Joseph Ltd, London; Richard Leakey and Roger Lewin: *People of the Lake*, William Collins, London; David Lockwood and Alan Binks: *A Cry From the Wild*, Kenway Publications, Nairobi; Arthur Luvai (ed): *Boundless Voices: Poems From Kenya*, Heinemann Kenya Ltd, Nairobi; Earl of Lytton: *The Desert and the Green*, Macdonald, London; Beryl Markham: *West with the Night*, Laurence Pollinger, London, on behalf of the Estate of Beryl Markham and North Point Press, Copyright 1983 by Beryl Markham; Esmond and Chryssee Bradley Martin: *Cargoes of the East*, Hamish Hamilton Ltd, London, and Esmond and Chryssee Bradley Martin; J. A. Massam: *The Cliff Dwellers of Kenya*, Frank Cass & Company Ltd; Richard Meinertzhagen: *Army Diary 1899–1926*, Longman, Harlow, and *Kenya Diary 1902–1906*, Eland Books, London; Cynthia Moss: *Elephant Memories*, Hamish Hamilton Ltd, London, and William Morrow & Company Inc., New York, Copyright © 1988 by Cynthia Moss; Shiva Naipaul: *North of South*, André Deutsch Ltd, London, and Aitken & Stone Ltd, London; Obyero Odhiambo: "Betrothed" in A. D. Amateshe (ed), *An Anthology of East African Poetry*, Longman, Harlow; I.Q. Orchardson: *The Kipsigis*, Kenya Literature Bureau, Nairobi; A. B. Percival: *A Game Ranger on Safari* and *A Game Ranger's Note Book*, the Estate of A. B. Percival; Margery Perham: *East African Journey*, Faber & Faber Ltd, London; Stephen Pern: *Another Land, Another Sea*, Mr Stephen Pern; Earl of Portsmouth: *A Knot of Roots*, Garnstone Press, London; Laurens van der Post: *First Catch Your Eland*, Chatto & Windus, London; John Reader and Harvey Croze: *Pyramids of Life*, Peters, Fraser & Dunlop

Group Ltd, London; Alys Reece: *To My Wife–Fifty Camels*, William Collins, London; Lorenzo Ricciardi: *The Voyage of the Mir-el-Lal*, William Collins, London; Mirella Ricciardi: *African Saga*, William Collins, London; Mort Rosenblum and Doug Williamson: *Squandering Eden: Africa at the Edge*, The Bodley Head, London, and the Carol Mann Agency, New York, Copyright © 1987 by Mort Rosenblum and Doug Williamson; George Schaller: *Golden Shadows, Flying Hooves*, William Collins, London, and Alfred A. Knopf Inc., New York, Copyright © 1973 by George B. Schaller; John Schmid: *The Kenya Magic*, Breachwood Publications, Hitchin; Henry Seaton: *Lion in the Morning*, John Murray (Publishers) Ltd, London; Philip Snow: *The Star Raft*, Weidenfeld & Nicolson, London; Everett Standa: "A Pregnant School Girl" in A. D. Amateshe (ed), *An Anthology of East African Poetry*, Longman, Harlow; C. H. Stigand: *The Land of Zinj*, Constable Publishers, London; Harry Thuku: *An Autobiography*, Oxford University Press, Nairobi; Charles Chenevix Trench: *The Desert's Dusty Face*, Pillans & Wilson Ltd, Edinburgh; Errol Trzebinski: *Kenya Pioneers* and *Silence Will Speak*, William Heinemann Ltd, London; Vivienne de Watteville: *Speak to the Earth*, Methuen, London; Evelyn Waugh: *Remote People*, Peters, Fraser & Dunlop Group Ltd, London; Colin Willock: *Africa's Rift Valley*, Time-Life Books, London, © 1976 Time-Life Books; Michael Wood: *Different Drums*, Curtis Brown Group Ltd, London, Copyright © Michael Wood 1987; Francis Brett Young: *Marching on Tanga*, David Higham Associates Ltd, London.

Bibliography

Adamson, George, *Bwana Game* Collins Harvill, London, 1968.
Adamson, George, *My Pride and Joy* Collins Harvill, London, 1986.
Adamson, Joy, *Born Free* Fontana/Collins, London, 1960.
Adamson, Joy, *Peoples of Kenya* Collins Harvill, London, 1967.
Adamson, Joy, *Queen of Shaba* Collins Harvill, London, 1980.
Adamson, Joy, *The Searching Spirit* Collins Harvill, London, 1978.
"Advice of Mwana Kupona Upon the Wifely Duty", trans. Alice Werner, Azania Press, 1932.
Allen, J. de Vere, *Al-Inkishafi: Cathecism of a Soul* East African Literature Bureau, Nairobi, 1977.
Allen, J. W. T., *Tendi* Heinemann, London, 1971.
Altrincham, Lord, *Kenya's Opportunity* Faber, London, 1955.
Amateshe, A. D., ed., *An Anthology of East African Poetry* Longman, Harlow, 1988.

Bache, Eva, *The Youngest Lion* Hutchinson, London, 1934.
Bakari, Mtoro bin Mwinyi, *The Customs of the Swahili People*, ed. & trans. J. W. T. Allen, University of California Press, Berkeley, 1981.
Barnett, Donald and Njama, Karari, *Mau Mau From Within* MacGibbon & Kee, London, 1966.
Beech, Mervyn, *The Suk: Their Language and Folklore* Oxford University Press, Oxford, 1911.
Bell, W. D. M., *The Wanderings of an Elephant Hunter* Neville Spearman, London, 1923.
Bentsen, Cheryl, *Maasai Days* Collins, London, 1990.
Benuzzi, Felice, *No Picnic on Mount Kenya* William Kimber, London, 1952.
Blixen, Bror von, *African Hunter* Cassell, London, 1937.
Blixen, Karen, *Out of Africa* Putnam, London, 1937.
Blundell, Michael, *So Rough a Wind* Weidenfeld & Nicolson, London, 1964.
Breton, J. G. le, *Kenya Sketches* George Allen & Unwin, London, 1935.
Brown, Leslie, *The Mystery of the Flamingos* Country Life Books, London, 1959.
Buchanan, Angus, *Three Years of War in East Africa* John Murray, London, 1920.
Bulpett, C. W. L., ed., *John Boyes, King of the Wa-kikuyu* Methuen, London, 1911.
Buxton, Aline, *Kenya Days* Edward Arnold, London, 1927.

Camoens, Luis de, *Lusiads*, trans. Richard Fanshawe, Cambridge University Press, Cambridge, 1940.
Campbell, Guy, *The Charging Buffalo: A History of the Kenyan Regiment* Leo Cooper/Secker & Warburg, London, 1986.
Campbell, Roy, *Adamastor* Faber, London, 1920.
Carnegie, V. M., *A Kenyan Farm Diary* William Blackwood & Sons, Edinburgh, 1930.
Chanler, W. A., *Through Jungle and Desert* Macmillan, London, 1896.
Churchill, Winston, *My African Journey* The Holland Press/Neville Spearman, London, 1962.

Cobbold, Lady Evelyn, *Kenya: The Land of Illusion* John Murray, London, 1935.
Connolly, Cyril, *The Evening Colonnade* David Bruce & Watson, London, 1973.
Cook, David and Rubadiri, David, eds., *Poems From East Africa* Heinemann, London, 1971.
Cott, Hugh B., *Looking at Animals* Collins, London, 1975.
Cowie, Mervyn, *Fly, Vulture*, Harrap, London, 1961.
Cranworth, Lord, *A Colony in the Making* Macmillan, London, 1912.
Cranworth, Lord, *Kenya Chronicles* Macmillan, London, 1939.
Crosskill, W. E., *The Two Thousand Mile War* Robert Hale, London, 1980.

Davidson, Basil, *The African Past* Penguin, London, 1966.
Douglas-Hamilton, Iain & Oria, *Among the Elephants* Collins Harvill, London, 1975.
Dower, Kenneth Gandar, *Abyssinian Patchwork* Frederick Muller, London, 1949.
Dower, Kenneth Gandar, *The Spotted Lion* Heinemann, London, 1937.
Dutton, E. A. T., *Kenya Mountain* Jonathan Cape, London, 1930.
Duyvendak, J. J. L., *China's Discovery of Africa* Arthur Probsthain, London 1949.
Dyer, Anthony, *Classic African Animals: The Big Five* Winchester Press, New York, 1973.

Eliot, Sir Charles, *The East Africa Protectorate* Edward Arnold, London, 1905.

Fey, Venn, *Wide Horizons* Vantage Press, New York, 1982.
Fisher, Angela, *Africa Adorned* Collins, London, 1984.
Fisher, Suzanne, *We Lived on the Verandah* New Horizon, 1980.
Freeman-Grenville, G. S. P., *The East African Coast: Select Documents* Oxford University Press, Oxford, 1962.

Gatheru, Mugo, *Child of Two Worlds* Routledge & Kegan Paul, London, 1964.
Gray, Sir John, *The British in Mombasa 1824–1826* Macmillan for the Kenya History Society, London, 1957.
Gregory, J. W., *The Great Rift Valley* John Murray, London, 1896.
Gregory, J. R., *Under the Sun* The English Press, Nairobi, 1951.

Hanley, Gerald, *Warriors and Strangers* Hamish Hamilton, London, 1987.
Hardy, Ronald, *The Iron Snake* Collins, London, 1965.
Haynes, Phyllis, *Poems of Kenya* Published privately, Nairobi, n.d.
Hemingway, Ernest, *Green Hills of Africa* Jonathan Cape, London, 1936.
Heminway, John, *The Imminent Rains* Little Brown & Co, Boston, 1968.
Henderson, Ian and Goodhart, Philip, *The Hunt for Kimathi* Hamish Hamilton, London 1958.
Hillaby, John, *Journey to the Jade Sea* Constable, London, 1964.
Hobley, C. W., *Bantu Beliefs and Magic* Frank Cass, London, 1967.
Hobley, C. W., *Kenya: From Chartered Company to Crown Colony* H. F. & G. Witherby, London, 1929.
Hodges, Geoffrey, *The Carrier Corps* Greenwood Press, Westport, 1986.
Höhnel, Ludwig von, *Discovery of Lakes Rudolf and Stefanie* (2 vols) Longmans Green, London, 1894.
Hollis, A. C., *The Masai: Their Language and Folklore* Oxford University Press, Oxford, 1905.
Hollis, A. C., *The Nandi* Oxford University Press, Oxford, 1909.

Hughes, Ian Meredith, *Black Moon, Jade Sea* Clifford Frost, London, 1988.
Huntingford, G. W. B. ed., *The Periplus of the Erythraean Sea*, Hakluyt Society, London, 1980.
Huxley, Elspeth, *Forks and Hope* Chatto & Windus, London, 1964.
Huxley, Elspeth, ed., *Nellie: Letters From Africa* Weidenfeld & Nicolson, London, 1980.
Huxley, Elspeth, *No Easy Way* East African Standard, Nairobi, 1957.
Huxley, Elspeth, *Out in the Midday Sun* Chatto & Windus, London, 1985.
Huxley, Elspeth, *The Sorcerer's Apprentice* Chatto & Windus, London, 1948.
Huxley, Elspeth, *White Man's Country* (2 vols) Chatto & Windus, London, 1935.
Huxley, Elspeth and Curtis, Arnold, *Pioneers' Scrapbook: Reminiscences of Kenya 1890–1968* Evans Brothers, London, 1980.
Huxley, Elspeth and Lawick, Hugo van, *Last Days in Eden* Collins Harvill, London, 1984.
Huxley, Juliette, *Wild Lives of Africa* Collins, London, 1963.

Ionides, G. J. P., *A Hunter's Life* W. H. Allen, London, 1965.

Jackson, Frederick, *Early Days in East Africa* Edward Arnold, London, 1930.
Johnston, Sir Harry, *The Uganda Protectorate*, Vol. 1, Hutchinson, London, 1902.
Jung, C. G., *Memories, Dreams, Reflections* Collins, London 1983.

Kariara, Jonathan and Kitonga, J., *Introduction to East African Poetry* Heinemann Kenya, Nairobi, n.d.
Kariuki, Josiah Mwangi, *Mau Mau Detainee* Oxford University Press, Oxford, 1963.
Kenyatta, Jomo, *Facing Mount Kenya* Secker & Warburg, London, 1937.
Kibera, Valerie, ed., *An Anthology of East African Short Stories* Longman, Harlow, 1988.
Kinlock, Bruce, *The Shamba Raiders: Memoirs of a Game Warden* Ashford Press, Southampton, 1988.
Kirkman, James, *Men and Monuments of the East African Coast* Lutterworth Press, Cambridge, 1964.
Kitson, Frank, *Gangs and Counter-Gangs* Barrie & Rockliff, London, 1960.
Kleen, G. F. V., ed., *Bror von Blixen: The Africa Letters* St Martin's Press, New York, 1988.
Knappert, Jan, *A Choice of Flowers* Heinemann, London, 1972.
Knappert, Jan, ed., *Four Centuries of Swahili Verse* Heinemann, London, 1979.
Knappert, Jan, *Myths and Legends of the Swahili* Heinemann Kenya, Nairobi, 1970.
Knappert, Jan, "Songs of the Swahili Women" *Afrika und Übersee*, Vol. 69, Hamburg, 1986.
Knappert, Jan, "Swahili Sailors' Songs" *Afrika und Ubersee*, Vol. 68, Hamburg, 1985.
Krapf, Johann Ludwig, *Travels, Researches and Missionary Labours* Frank Cass, London, 1968.

Lamb, David, *The Africans* The Bodley Head, London, 1982.
Lawick-Goodall, Hugo and Jane van, *Innocent Killers* Collins, London, 1970.
Leakey, Mary, *Disclosing the Past* Weidenfeld & Nicolson, London, 1984.
Leakey, Mary, *Olduvai Gorge: My Search for Early Man* Collins, London, 1979.
Leakey, Richard, *The Making of Mankind* Michael Joseph, London, 1981.
Leakey, Richard and Lewin, Roger, *People of the Lake* Collins, London, 1979.
Lettow-Vorbeck, General von, *My Reminiscences of East Africa* Hurst & Blackett, 1920.

Lipscomb, J. F., *We Built a Country* Faber, London, 1961.
Lloyd-Jones, W., *Havash!* Arrowsmith, 1925.
Lockwood, David and Binks, Alan, *A Cry From the Wild* Kenway Publications, Nairobi, 1989.
Lugard, F. D., *The Rise of Our East African Empire* Frank Cass, London, 1968.
Luvai, Arthur, ed., *Boundless Voices: Poems From Kenya* Heinemann Kenya, Nairobi, 1988.
Lytton, Earl of, *The Desert and the Green* Macdonald, London, 1957.

Macdonald, J. R. L., *Soldiering and Surveying in British East Africa 1891–1894* Edward Arnold, London, 1897.
Mackinder, Halford, "A Journey to the Summit of Mount Kenya, British East Africa" *Geographical Journal*, Vol. XV, no. 5, London, 1900.
Mackintosh, Brian, *The Scottish Mission in Kenya 1891–1923* University College, Nairobi, 1968.
Markham, Beryl, *West with the Night* Houghton Mifflin, Boston, 1942.
Marsh, Zoë, *East Africa Through Contemporary Records* Cambridge University Press, Cambridge, 1961.
Martin, Esmond and Bradley, Chryssee, *Cargoes of the East* Hamish Hamilton, London, 1978.
Massam, J. A., *The Cliff Dwellers of Kenya* Frank Cass, London, 1968.
Matson, A. T., *Nandi Resistance to British Rule* East African Publishing House, Nairobi, 1972.
Meinertzhagen, Richard, *Army Diary 1899–1926* Oliver & Boyd, Edinburgh, 1960.
Meinertzhagen, Richard, *Kenya Diary 1902–1906* Eland Books, London, 1983.
Miller, Charles, *The Battle for the Bundu* Macdonald & Jane's, London, 1974.
Miller, Charles, *The Lunatic Express* Macdonald, London, 1971.
Moss, Cynthia, *Elephant Memories* Hamish Hamilton, London, 1988.

Naipaul, Shiva, *North of South* Andre Deutsch, London, 1978.
Neumann, Arthur H., *Elephant Hunting in East Equatorial Africa* Rowland Ward, 1898.

Orchardson, I. Q., *The Kipsigis*, ed. A. T. Matson, East African Literature Bureau, Nairobi, 1961.

Patterson, J. H., *The Man-Eaters of Tsavo* Macmillan, London, 1914.
p'Bitek, Okot, *Song of Lawino and Song of Ocol* Heinemann, London, 1984.
Pease, Sir Alfred, *The Land of the Lion* John Murray, London, 1913.
Percival, A. B., *A Game Ranger's Note Book* Nisbit & Co., 1924.
Percival, A. B., *A Game Ranger on Safari* Nisbit & Co., 1928.
Perham, Margery, *East African Journey* Faber, London, 1976.
Pern, Stephen, *Another Land, Another Sea* Gollancz, London, 1979.
Portsmouth, Earl of, *A Knot of Roots* Geoffrey Bles, London, 1965.
Post, Laurens van der, *First Catch Your Eland* Chatto & Windus, London, 1977.
Powys, Llewelyn, *Black Laughter* Jonathan Cape, London, 1929.
Preston, R. O., *The Genesis of Kenya Colony* Colonial Printing Works, Nairobi, n.d.

Rainsford, W. S., *The Land of the Lion* Doubleday, Page & Co., New York, 1909.
Ravenstein, E. G., trans., *A Journal of the First Voyage of Vasco da Gama* Hakluyt Society, London, 1898.

Reader, John and Croze, Harvey, *Pyramids of Life* Collins, London, 1977.
Reece, Alys, *To My Wife – Fifty Camels* Collins Harvill, London, 1963.
Ricciardi, Lorenzo, *The Voyage of the Mir-el-Lal* Collins, London, 1980.
Ricciardi, Mirella, *African Saga* Collins, London, 1981.
Roosevelt, Theodore, *African Game Trails* John Murray, London, 1910.
Rosenblum, Mort and Williamson, Doug, *Squandering Eden: Africa at the Edge* The Bodley Head, London 1988.
Routledge, W. S. and K., *With a Prehistoric People*, London, 1910.

Schaller, George, *Golden Shadows, Flying Hooves* Collins, London, 1973.
Schmid, John, *The Kenya Magic* Breachwood Publications, Hitchin, 1983.
Seaton, Henry, *Lion in the Morning* John Murray, London, 1963.
Sheldrick, Daphne, *The Tsavo Story* Collins Harvill, London, 1973.
Snow, Philip, *The Star Raft* Weidenfeld & Nicolson, London, 1988.
Stapleton, James, *The Gate Hangs Well* Hammond, Hammond & Co., London, 1956.
Stigand, C. H., *The Land of Zinj* Constable, London, 1913.
Strandes, Justus, *The Portuguese Period in East Africa* East African Literature Bureau, Nairobi, 1961.

Thomson, Joseph, *Through Masai Land* Sampson Low, 1885.
Thuku, Harry, *An Autobiography* Oxford University Press, Nairobi, 1970.
Trench, Charles Chenevix, *The Desert's Dusty Face* William Blackwood & Sons, Edinburgh, 1964.
Trzebinski, Errol, *Kenya Pioneers* Heinemann, London, 1985.
Trzebinski, Errol, *Silence Will Speak* Heinemann, London, 1977.

Watt, Rachel Stuart, *In the Heart of Savagedom* Pickering & Inglis/Frank Cass, London, 1968.
Watteville, Vivienne de, *Speak to the Earth* Methuen, London, 1935.
Waugh, Evelyn, *Remote People* Duckworth, London, 1931.
Whittall, Errol, *Dimbilil: The Story of an African Farm* Arthur Barker, London, 1956.
Willock, Colin, *Africa's Rift Valley* Time-Life Books, London, 1974.
Wilson, C. J., *The Story of the East African Mounted Rifles* East African Standard, Nairobi, 1938.
Wood, Michael, *Different Drums* Century Hutchinson, London, 1987.

Young, Francis Brett, *Marching on Tanga* Alan Sutton, Gloucester, 1984.

Index

Boise, Charles, 2; Fund, 2
boma, 29, 48, 72, 73, 86, 88, 110, 293,
320, 321, 326, 338
Boran (tribe), 234, 293, 317
boriti, 218
Boyes, John, 51–4; *King of the Wa-kikuyu*,
53
Bradley, Martin, Esmond and Chryssee,
Cargoes of the East, 220
Brehm, A. E., 258
British, colonization by, xxiii, 9, 205; rule,
132–40; East Africa, xxiv, 70, 71, 140;
enforcement of law and order, 364–72;
Imperial East Africa Company, 9, 45;
Government, 45, 69, 77, 95, 119, 140;
Protectorate, xxiv, 9, 23, 45, 46, 53, 56,
69, 73, 76, 86, 94, 95, 140, 141, 145,
152
Brocherel, Joseph, 38
Brown, Leslie, *The Mystery of the
Flamingoes*, 185, 255
Brown, Monty, 275
Bubissa, battle of, 160
Buchanan, Captain Angus, 146, 151;
Three Years of War in East Africa, 147,
151
Buganda, kingdom of, 39, 45, 357
buibuis, 219, 220, 332
Bulpett, C. W. L., ed., John Boyes, *King
of the Wa-kikuyu*, 53
bundu, 60
Bura, 25
Burkitt, Dr Roland, 89–91
Burma, 162
Burnt Forest, 86, 99
Buxton, Aline, *Kenya Days*, 204
Buzurg ibn Shahriyar of Ramhormutz,
Kitab al-Ajaib al-Hind, 16
Bwana, 42

Cairo, 11, 15, 63, 64, 109
castration, 30
Cambay, 128
Cameroon, xxv
Camoens, Luis de, 19, 20; *Lusiads*, 20
cannibalism, 12, 13, 128–30, 347; in
legend, 383–4
Cape, 63, 146
Cape Town, 63
Carnegie, V. M., *A Kenyan Farm Diary*,
60, 109, 117
Casuarina Point, 222
Chagga (tribe), 23

Chamberlain, Joseph, 76
Chania river, 170
Chanler, William Astor, 34; *Through
Jungle and Desert*, 35
Chartered Co., 23
Chemosit, 358
Cherangani hills, 30
Cholmondely, Hugh, 72; *see* Delamere,
Lord
Christian, 18, 21, 114, 130, 139, 169,
181, 182, 315, 336; Kikuyu, 320;
missionaries, 9, 23–6, 350
Churchill, Winston, 295; *My African
Journey*, 80
Church Missionary Society, 23
circumcision, 319–23, 334, 349; of girls,
322–3; re-enactment of ceremony in
cure for infertility, 354–5; value placed
on courage during, 319–20
climate, 76, 79, 117–18, 185; drought,
188–9, 190–1, 198, 207, 344–5, 368;
dust devils, 191, 211; monsoon, 216,
217, 230, 232
Cobbold, Lady Evelyn, *Kenya: The Land
of Illusion*, 111
Cobham-Blackburn Company, 63
Colito, battle of, 159, 160
colonialism, xxv, 70
Columbus, Christopher, 16–17
Colvile, Gilbert (Nyasore), 81
Congo, 63, 192
Connolly, Cyril, *The Evening Colonnade*,
248
Cook, David and David Rubadiri, eds.,
Poems from East Africa, 415, 420, 421,
426
Cooley, W. D., 25; *Inner Africa Laid
Open*, 24
coolies, 47, 48, 51
Cott, Hugh B., *Looking at Animals*, 258
courtship and marriage, 219–20, 325,
326, 327, 329–37, 345, 402; *see also*
polygamy
Cowie, Mervyn, 269, 292; *Fly, Vulture*,
293
Cranworth, Lord, *A Colony in the Making*,
286; *Kenya Chronicles*, 85, 141, 302
Crosskill, Captain W. E., 157; *The Two
Thousand Mile War*, 157, 162

da Gama, Vasco, 18–19, 20–2, 127, 219;
"Vasco da Gama Pillar", 22; *see also*
Ravenstein, E. G.

448   NINE FACES OF KENYA

travel – *cont.*
62, 71, 77, 78, 137, 148, 150, 152,
192, 193, 194, 235, 273, 282, 366;
characteristics of, 40–42; deprivations
suffered during First World War, 148;
and musical instruments and singing,
279–80; return from an expedition and
payment, 274–5; safari, 40–2, 59–60,
63, 71, 93, 192, 209, 260, 274,
279–80, 298, 366–7, and the
honey-guide, 256; (safari) chronicler,
278–9; Denys Finch Hatton's tips for
comfort on safari, 282–3; sedan chair,
77, 78; "sewn boats", 9, 10; *see also*
Uganda Railway
Trench, Charles Chenevix, *The Desert's
Dusty Face*, 369
tribes, 315; animal sacrifice, 350, 353;
belief in spirits, 350–3, 355, 357,
358–9; blood-brotherhood, 54; blood
money, 360, 364; black magic, 166;
body and face painting, 51, 77, 321,
322, 328, 349, 352, 369; cannibalism,
12, 13, 128–30, 347; cattle-raiding,
323–7; costume and ornamentation,
49, 51, 77, 115, 173, 202, 221, 287,
320–8, *passim*, 340, 349–50, 369;
dance, 77, 115, 288, 321, 345–6; diet,
287, 338, 339, 340–1, 346–7; fishing,
343–4; games, 72; inter-tribal conflicts,
52–3, 70, 78, 127, 135, 213, 272, 366;
law, 363; mythology, 328–9, 356–9;
375–6, 378–9 (*see also* Gikuyu and
Mumbi); Native Reserves, 94–5, 110;
nomadism, xxiii, 69, 78, 225, 270, 272,
339–40, 346, 369; oath-taking, 164–7;
ordeal and punishment of sorcerers,
359–61; poisoned arrows, 51, 135, 271,
308; manufacture of poison for, 272–3;
polygamy, 330–2; resistance to white
settlement, 132–40; ritual scars, 328;
spitting as token of good behaviour,
343; susceptibility to psychic
suggestion, 351; taking of life (attitude
to), 324–5; thumb-pulling, 299–300,
316–17; witch doctors, 166, 315,
350–1; 355–6, 359–61, 369–72; *see
also laibon*; Mau Mau; *moran; and
individual tribes*
Trzebinski, Errol, *The Kenya Pioneers*, 72,
76, 89; *Silence Will Speak*, 283
Tsavo, 47, 48, 189; East National Park,
188, 246, 269

Turkana, 103, 185, 190, 349; (tribe), 200,
240, 343, 344–5, 368; conversation
with a chieftain, 324–5; disaster,
344–5; escarpment, 361; Fisherman's
Cooperative Society, 344; Lake, 2, 4,
34, 198–9, 273, 344
Twist, Captain, T. K., 63

Uasin Gishua plateau, 76, 85, 87, 98,
112, 229, 287
Uganda, 41, 42, 46, 133, 137, 141,
185, 196, 258, 276, 329, 361, 362,
365
Uganda Railway, 45–7, 49–51, 53, 83,
99; defended against Germans, 141–3;
as social institution, 56–8; thefts by
Nandi tribesmen, 49–50; travelling tips
and conducted tour, 55–6
uhuru, 120, 342
Ukambani, 26, 28
utendi, 389, 391, 399
utunda, 319

van der Post, Laurens, *First Catch Your
Eland*, 349
vegetation, acacias, 186, 187, 189, 190,
198, 199, 214, 248, (*elatior*) 187; pods
as food for goats, 338–9; *adenia*, 220;
Akokanthera tree, 272; bamboo, 192,
194; banana, 196; baobabs, 187, 188,
214, 217; bauhinea, 196; "bayonet
grass", 281; beard-moss, 193;
bignonias, 208; blue gums, 211;
Bougainvillea, 203, 207, 208;
combretum, 189; convolvulus, 186;
datura (moonflower), 242; dhum palm,
34, 338, 349; elephant grass, 56;
eucalyptus, 201; euphorbia, 196;
everlasting plants, 192; fever trees, 306;
flamboyant, 221; giant senecios, 192;
gladioli, 196; gum tree, 158; henna,
242; hibiscuses, 207, 208; jacarandas,
207, 208; jogoo jogoo tree, 245;
juniper, 73; kei-apple thorn, 166;
Kikuyu grass, 117; Kirago, 263;
leleshwa, 59, 78, 108; mango tree, 58,
214; mangrove, 218, 219; mimosa, 277;
mswaki, 198, 199; mushrooms, 196;
Muthaiti, 262; olive, 192, 244, (Elgon),
192; orange trees, 203; orchids, 196;
papyrus, 197, 201, 204, 305, 306;
passion flowers, 202; podo trees, 111,
192; *Podocarpus gracilior*, 192;